HOW CONSTITUTIONS C

This set of essays explores how constitutions ch. number of countries, and how the 'constitution' of the EU changes and is changed. For a range of reasons, including internal and external pressures, the constitutional arrangements in many countries are changing. Constitutional change may be formal, involving amendments to the texts of Constitutions or the passage of legislation of a clearly constitutional kind, or informal and organic, as where court decisions affect the operation of the system of government, or where new administrative and other arrangements (for example, agencification) affect or articulate or alter the operation of the constitution of the country, without the need to resort to formal change.

The countries in this study include, from the EU, a common law country, a Nordic one, a former communist state, several civil law systems, parliamentary systems and a hybrid one (France). Chapters on non EU countries include two on developing countries (India and the Republic of South Africa), two on common law countries without entrenched written constitutions (Israel and New Zealand), a presidential system (the USA) and three federal ones (Switzerland, the USA and Canada). In the last two chapters the editors conduct a detailed comparative analysis of the jurisdiction-based chapters and explore the question whether any overarching theory or theories about constitutional change in liberal democracies emerge from the study.

How Constitutions Change

A Comparative Study

Edited by

Dawn Oliver

and

Carlo Fusaro

·HART·
PUBLISHING

OXFORD AND PORTLAND, OREGON
2013

Published in the United Kingdom by Hart Publishing Ltd
16C Worcester Place, Oxford, OX1 2JW
Telephone: +44 (0)1865 517530
Fax: +44 (0)1865 510710
E-mail: mail@hartpub.co.uk
Website: http://www.hartpub.co.uk

Published in North America (US and Canada) by
Hart Publishing
c/o International Specialized Book Services
920 NE 58th Avenue, Suite 300
Portland, OR 97213–3786
USA
Tel: +1 503 287 3093 or toll-free: (1) 800 944 6190
Fax: +1 503 280 8832
E-mail: orders@isbs.com
Website: http://www.isbs.com

First published in 2011. Reprinted in paperback in 2013.

British Library Cataloguing in Publication Data

Data Available

ISBN: 978-1-84946-094-1 (hardback)
ISBN: 978-1-84946-498-7 (paperback)

Typeset by Columns Design XML Ltd, Reading
Printed and bound by CPI Group (UK) Ltd, Croydon, CR0 4YY

Contents

Contents

List of Contributors

Giovanni Biaggini Professor of Constitutional, Administrative and European Law, Faculty of Law, University of Zurich

Sophie Boyron Senior Lecturer in Law, University of Birmingham

Hugh Corder Professor of Public Law, University of Cape Town

Renaud Dehousse Jean Monnet Professor of European Law and Politics and Director of the Centre d'études européennes, Sciences Po, Paris

Ascensión Elvira Professor of Constitutional Law, Universidad Carlos III de Madrid

Carlo Fusaro Professor of Public Comparative Law, Faculty of Political Sciences 'C Alfieri', University of Florence

Stephen M Griffin Rutledge C Clement, Jr Professor in Constitutional Law, Tulane University School of Law

Tsvi Kahana Associate Professor, Faculty of Law Queen's University, Kingston, Ontario

Suzie Navot Professor of Constitutional Law, Law School, COMAS (College of Management Academic Studies) Rishon Lezion

Dawn Oliver Emeritus Professor of Constitutional Law, University College London

Paul Rishworth Professor of Law, University of Auckland

Mahendra Pal Singh Vice-Chancellor, National University of Juridical Sciences, Kolkata. Formerly, Professor of Law, University of Delhi

Markku Suksi Professor of Public Law, Åbo Akademi University

Maxim Tomoszek Senior Lecturer in Constitutional Law, Faculty of Law, Palacky University in Olomouc

Jens Woelk Associate Professor of Comparative Constitutional Law, University of Trento

Part I

1

Changing Constitutions

CARLO FUSARO AND DAWN OLIVER

INTRODUCTION

THIS BOOK IS about how constitutions change in 15 different jurisdictions, 14 states (all liberal democracies) and the European Union. We shall seek to draw some lessons about the workings of constitutions, their amendment, and organic or evolutionary change within constitutional systems.

We need to explain what we mean by 'constitution' and by 'change'. The word 'constitution' can refer to the fundamental document that sets out the rules regulating the government of a state and which has a specially protected legal status: all states except Israel, New Zealand and the United Kingdom have such documents. Most such documents also contain a Bill or Charter of Rights. It is convenient to refer to such instruments as 'Constitutions' with a capital C. Most of the countries which are members of the United Nations have such a document, and most are 'entrenched' in some way. But 'constitution' can cover something wider, 'constitutional law', and can thus embrace not only the rules set out in a country's fundamental document but also other rules, whether found in laws passed by the legislator or in decisions of the courts. In most countries there are many such laws, it being considered impossible or inappropriate to include all of the laws about the system of government in a single foundational document. Thirdly, 'constitution' can refer to the de facto system of government in a country. This will include the Constitution if there is one. Constitution in this 'system of government' sense includes case law and legislation of a 'constitutional' nature, and what in the United Kingdom are known as 'constitutional conventions', codes, guidance, concordats and memorandums of understanding which set out how certain aspects of government are or should be conducted. Not all of these documents or rules are 'laws' in the sense of being enforceable in the courts. Of course it is possible that these rules do not actually represent the de facto system of government in a country. All they do is set out the rules. They do not tell us whether those rules are in fact obeyed or enforced. If they are not obeyed then the de facto constitution is what happens rather than what the rules require.

The rules regulating how a country—or the EU—is governed and the ways in which they operate or are applied or interpreted change from time to time. Constitutions are commonly characterised by continuous structural development and in this respect they resemble living organisms—they are organic or evolutionary. They are a product of society; they reflect or respond to changes in society. Thus constitutions both change continuously, and may be changed continuously.

Constitutional change takes place in a variety of different ways. Change takes place, for instance, when the courts decide on a new interpretation of the Constitution or of other foundational or constitutional documents. The case of *Marbury v Madison* (1813) where the US Supreme Court decided that it had a judicial review jurisdiction over the acts of Congress is the classic example of such constitutional change. The European Court of Justice (ECJ) jurisprudence on the primacy of European law and its direct effect provides another more recent example of organic change, both in a body once thought to be international but, by virtue of that jurisprudence, in reality supranational, and in the constitutions of member states which have subsequently accepted the doctrines of primacy and direct effect as developed by the ECJ and altered their constitutional arrangements and the theories underlying them (for example sovereignty) as a result.

Much constitutional change, however, is *formal* in the sense that it is produced by amendments to the text of the entrenched written Constitution, often by a special procedure which may include qualified majorities in the legislature or a referendum, or of other Acts which can be regarded as of fundamental nature: the addition of the Bill of Rights to the US Constitution by the adoption of its first 10 Amendments was one of the first examples (1791), followed by countless others. Formal changes to constitutional arrangements may also be effected by the passing of laws of a constitutional nature rather than by changes to an entrenched Constitution: this is the case with the Basic Laws of Israel and the unentrenched Constitution Act 1986 of New Zealand. The possibility of Acts of Exception in Finland provides another exception of formal constitutional change.

Even in countries which, unlike Israel and New Zealand, do have an entrenched Constitution, changes of a constitutional nature may be effected by ordinary Acts of Parliament: that is to say by Acts which are not strictly 'constitutional' in their legal nature according to the hierarchy of the sources of law developed by Hans Kelsen but which nevertheless change the operation of the system of government.

Many Constitutions lay down formal requirements as to participation in the process of constitutional change. The involvement of the electorate via a referendum as in Switzerland is an example. But apart from such formal requirements there may be political or public traditions or expectations in a country to the effect, for instance, that amendment should only be by consensus between political parties, or that reform should be non-partisan—neutral between parties—or that there should be wide consultation before reforms are introduced, or that the Cabinet should, or should not, participate in reform proposals, or that reform should follow on from recommendations by a body of non-political experts.

The subject of constitutional change is topical, since the constitutions and systems of government of many democracies are responding to a range of pressures, internal and external, and in the process their de facto operation is changing, or they are undergoing processes of formal constitutional amendment or reform. The pressures for change include: the internationalisation and Europeanisation of countries' obligations; the international and supranational economy and politics (globalisation); the terrorist threat; religious fundamentalism; migration; and citizen demands, whether for enhanced protection of human rights of various kinds, or for greater transparency, or for a more responsive governmental arrangement. Such demands may crystallise in pressures for devolution, federalisation or even secession or independence, and in many instances for a more efficient and open system of government and for better representative democratic institutions.

Our project, then, is to identify (a) the factors which influence changes to constitutions, and (b) the processes and procedures by which change takes place, and to obtain insights into these issues by making comparisons between a range of differing countries and constitutional arrangements. These matters will be influenced by factors such as the existence or absence of an entrenched Constitution, the legitimating constitutional justifications that are current in a particular country, the question whether constitutional laws are directly or indirectly effective and the role of 'soft law' in the system.

THE ANALYTICAL FRAMEWORK

The chapters in the next Part of this book will cover a range of democratic countries and the EU. We have deliberately selected countries whose arrangements seem to us to reflect the basic requirements of modern constitutionalism from which comparative analysis is possible.

Each of the chapters in this collection will stand on its own as an account of the jurisdiction and how it changes and is changed. Each author has been asked to deal with a number of issues:

— the basic features of the constitutional arrangements in their jurisdiction;
— a brief summary of the changes in those arrangements since a Constitution first came into effect or, if no such document exists, changes of significance over, say, the last 100 years;
— what is embraced in the category of 'constitutional' rules and what is not;
— what is included in a country's current 'Constitution' and what is not, and why;

5

— how constitutional provisions are implemented—whether they have 'direct effect' or are self-executing or whether they require implementing legislation to be passed;
— the formal and de facto procedures for constitutional amendment or change—to what extent the Cabinet, Parliament, other bodies and the electorate participate in the process;
— the influence on a system of government of changing social norms and culture, demographic influences, economic pressures, political culture or electoral behaviour, internationalisation and Europeanisation;
— formal and informal or evolutionary changes that have taken place or are under consideration;
— the extent to which conventions, cultural expectations and traditions affect the working of formal constitutional laws and are recognised; and
— what, if any, legitimating constitutional values, theories or ideologies underlie Constitutions and the de facto system of government.

The authors of the country-based chapters and the EU chapter will focus on the issues in this framework that are most relevant to their own jurisdiction, and adopt the concepts as understood in their own country (or the EU) and explain them.

This approach will enable us to conduct a joint comparative analysis and to try to develop a theory of constitutional change in the final chapters.

Part II

2

Canada

TSVI KAHANA*

INTRODUCTION

T HE CONSTITUTION OF Canada is a hybrid: it is partly written and
partly unwritten, partly colonial and partly organic, it allows for judicial
review of the constitutionality of legislation but it also includes a mechanism for a legislature to displace rights. Until 1982, the Constitution of Canada
was primarily made up of a set of British legal instruments and traditions. The
1982 'patriation' of the Constitution, included securing formal legal independence from Britain, creating an amendment procedure for the Constitution, and
entrenching the *Canadian Charter of Rights and Freedoms*.[1] Although this chapter
makes reference to the British tradition and the way in which pre-patriation
developments have shaped the Canadian constitutional environment, emphasis
has been placed on post-1982 change since this is when Canada became constitutionally independent.

This chapter demonstrates that the text of Canada's constitution has undergone little change. Most constitutional changes have happened in other ways, not
through amendment by the institutions endowed with constituent powers but
instead by state organs whose mandate does not include the amendment of the
Constitution. These are the Supreme Court of Canada and the Parliament of
Canada. The Supreme Court of Canada created unwritten yet justiciable constitutional principles, and by using these principles effectively wrote into the
Constitution a provision that disallows the unilateral secession of a province.
Parliament, for its part, created something of a constitutional change by creating

---

* I would like to thank Jonathan Shanks for commenting on a first draft of this chapter, as well as
Kristen Allen and Samantha Crumb for exceptional research assistance.
[1] See R Romanow, J Whyte and H Leeson, *Canada Notwithstanding* (Toronto: Carswell/
Methuen, 1984). The term 'patriation' was coined specifically for the Canadian experience to
highlight the legal validity of the UK-made Canadian constitutional documents, while acknowledging
the transfer of constitutional power from the UK to Canada. It is thus the opposite of repatriation, as
it recognises that constitutional control did not originally reside within Canada and thus could not be
reclaimed. See James Ross Hurley, *Amending Canada's Constitution* (Ottawa: Canada Communication
Group Publishing, 1996) at 26.

legislation that effectively gives four provinces a veto power over some future constitutional amendments. Some scholars also argue that Parliament's adoption of the North American Free Trade Agreement (NAFTA) similarly effected constitutional change in Canada.

Because Canada's Constitution is composed of a variety of sources, the discussion must begin with those fundamental aspects that might be more obvious in other jurisdictions. Accordingly, the next part of this chapter presents a typology of Canadian constitutionalism. It presents three types of constitutional norm—written principles, unwritten principles, and conventions. The written and unwritten principles are the formal part of the Constitution; the conventions are the informal part. Once the typology and terminology is defined, the third part outlines the substantive principles of Canadian constitutionalism, and the way they are divided among the various types of sources. The fourth part then introduces the numerous ways to modify the Constitution of Canada. Unlike other constitutions, the amending provisions of the written Constitution provide for seven different formulae, depending on the subject matter and the affected parties. In addition, the unwritten constitutional principles and constitutional conventions may also be changed in their own ways.

The fifth part discusses how constitutional changes have taken place without constitutional amendment in Canada. It opens with a discussion of the scholarship which considers NAFTA to be tantamount to a constitutional change. It then asks whether, and under what conditions, judicial decisions may be regarded as having changed the Constitution, concluding that this may be the case only when the court engages in the *creation* of constitutional rules, rather than in their interpretation.

The analysis that follows demonstrates that this is precisely what the Supreme Court of Canada has done. After many years during which unwritten constitutional principles were used for the interpretation of the written Constitution, in the late 1990s the Court upgraded these principles and gave them independent constitutional status, using a debatable textual anchor, namely the Preamble of the Constitution Act, 1867. Unwritten constitutional principles, the Court said, underlie the entire structure of constitutionalism, and therefore it is legitimate for the Court to use them to fill gaps in the Constitution. Thus, government activities that seem permissible under the written Constitution may be ruled unconstitutional by a court if they are inconsistent with the unwritten principles.

In the famous decision of the *Secession Reference*,[2] the Court used these principles to create a constitutional mechanism available to Quebec and then Canada if the former wished to secede. Part of the very reason Quebecers considered doing so was their lack of acceptance of the patriation package. One of the elements of the package they objected to was the amending formula of the Constitution, which they believed did not give Quebec a sufficient say. By reading

---

[2] *Re Secession of Quebec*, [1998] 2 SCR 217 at para 50 [*Secession Reference*].

a secession provision into the Constitution of Canada, the Court essentially offered Quebec an alternate amending formula. Using that formula would not amend the Constitution, but it would allow Quebec to act as if the Constitution was amended, and secede. I end the chapter by pointing to a possible connection between the role the Court sought to play in the *Secession Reference* and the role it has sought to play in other contexts.

THE TYPOLOGY OF CANADIAN CONSTITUTIONALISM

In Canada, there is no single constitutional document that is definitively referred to as 'the Constitution'. Instead, the constitutional text is dispersed among various sources. In addition to the variety of textual sources, the Canadian Constitution is also made up of two additional *types* of constitutional sources: unwritten constitutional principles (that are said to be embedded within the written principles) and constitutional conventions. The written text and unwritten constitutional principles can be said to constitute the formal Constitution because they are justiciable; the conventions constitute what may be called the informal part of the Constitution, because they are not. Some scholars argue that in addition to the constitutional conventions, there are other elements of the Canadian legal apparatus that have constitutional status. For now, we will discuss Canadian constitutionalism in reference to the three sources mentioned above; in the final section of this chapter, these other potential sources of constitutional norms will be explored.

Statutes and Case Law: The Formal Constitution

The formal Constitution of Canada includes both written and unwritten principles. The written part of the Constitution is composed of 31 statutes and orders, the two most important of which are the Constitution Act, 1867[3] and the Constitution Act, 1982.[4] The Constitution Act, 1867, originally named the British North America Act, 1867, is a British statute that marked the confederation of Canada in 1867.[5] As such, it contains provisions concerning the federal-provincial division of power, the various political institutions of the country and the judiciary. The Constitution Act, 1982 includes the Canadian Charter of Rights and Freedoms,[6] and provisions relating to aboriginal rights and constitutional amendment.

---

[3] Constitution Act, 1867 (UK), 30 and 31 Vict, c 3, reprinted in RSC 1985, App II, No 5 [Constitution Act, 1867].

[4] Constitution Act, 1982, being Schedule B to the Canada Act 1982 (UK), 1982, c 11 [Constitution Act, 1982].

[5] The British North America Act is now officially cited as the Constitution Act, 1867, above note 2.

[6] Canadian Charter of Rights and Freedoms, Part I of the Constitution Act, 1982, being Schedule B to the Canada Act 1982 (UK), 1982, c 11.

Section 52(2) of the Constitution Act, 1982, provides a basis for this, stating that the Constitution of Canada 'includes' both the 1867 and 1982 Constitution Acts, the Canada Act, 1982, and the 29 additional statutes and orders in the Schedule, which supplement the Constitution Act, 1867, in terms of the creation and maintenance of Canada's legal apparatus.[7] Section 52(1) establishes the supremacy of the Constitution; it states that: 'The Constitution of Canada is the supreme law of Canada, and any law that is inconsistent with the provisions of the Constitution is, to the extent of the inconsistency, of no force or effect.'

The formal Constitution of Canada also includes unwritten constitutional principles. Although unwritten, they enjoy the same constitutional supremacy as the written text, since they are 'implicit in the very nature' of the Constitution.[8] Thus, a court could strike down legislation that is inconsistent with an unwritten principle. Unwritten constitutional principles in Canada may be classified as one of two types: incorporated British principles or implicit Canadian principles.

Incorporated British principles, such as parliamentary privilege,[9] have been anchored by the judiciary in the text of the Constitution. The judiciary has used the Preamble of the Constitution Act, 1867 to legitimise this entrenchment. The Preamble notes that the founding provinces have 'expressed their Desire to be federally united ... under the Crown of the United Kingdom of Great Britain and Ireland, with *a Constitution similar in Principle to that of the United Kingdom*'.[10] These words were interpreted by the courts to mean that the principles of British constitutionalism that were not explicitly or implicitly negated by the Canadian Constitution were implicitly adopted by it. While an alternate reading of the Preamble could provide that these incorporated British principles have only *interpretive force* in reading the written text, the Supreme Court has deemed them to have independent *operative force* instead, and, as we shall see, has struck down legislation solely on the basis of an inconsistency with some of these principles.

The other type of unwritten—yet formal and supreme—constitutional principles are unrelated to the United Kingdom. These principles are embedded in the written Constitution and, thus, are implicitly binding by virtue of its supremacy. They have been declared by the courts to be embedded in the actual text of the Constitution. The most famous of such principles are the ones enunciated in the *Secession Reference*.[11] In that case, the Supreme Court prescribed a legally binding

---

[7] Section 52(2) states: 'The Constitution of Canada includes (*a*) the Canada Act, 1982, including this Act; (*b*) the Acts and orders referred to in the Schedule; and (*c*) any amendment to any Act or order referred to in paragraph (*a*) or (*b*).'

[8] *Secession Reference*, above note 2.

[9] See *New Brunswick Broadcasting Co v Nova Scotia (Speaker of the House of Assembly)*, [1993] 1 SCR 319. In this case, the Court held that the Preamble of the Constitution Act, 1867 had established 'a Constitution similar in principle to that of the United Kingdom', and as such, the Charter of Fundamental Rights could not displace parliamentary privilege.

[10] Constitution Act, 1867, above note 2 at Preamble [emphasis added].

[11] *Secession Reference*, above note 2.

formula for the secession of a province, based on four principles: federalism, democracy, constitutionalism and the rule of law, and the protection of minorities. While the court did connect these principles to the UK, section 52 and the Preamble, the court also made it clear that even without these connections, it would be willing to acknowledge such principles merely because they inform, create, or support the written text.[12] Indeed, one of these principles, federalism, is entirely foreign to British constitutionalism.

Conventions: The Informal Constitution

The Constitution of Canada also includes informal principles. These are constitutional conventions that inform the way in which the formal constitutional powers are to be exercised. A well established institution in the UK, conventions guide most government behaviour and detail the aspects of governance that the written Constitution does not address.[13] They are not legally binding and hence, by definition, cannot form part of the formal Constitution. That said, they enjoy de facto constitutional supremacy because the political culture in Canada has rendered them binding. Moreover, while a court will not enforce conventions, it also will not shy away from considering them in interpreting formal principles.[14] Finally, the court may transform a convention into a common law rule.[15]

It is difficult to account for the creation of constitutional conventions. Indeed, by virtue of their informality, they require no set procedure to be followed prior to their recognition. Generally, conventions come into existence in two different ways: through practice over time or through an explicit agreement between all the relevant actors.[16] For conventions that come about through practice, there is no established period of time that must pass before the practice obtains 'convention' status. Some scholars have argued that a reliable indicator of convention status is the moral obligation that attaches itself to the practice over time. For example, the fact that members of Parliament feel bound to follow the practice because they believe it is a principle of higher law, is evidence that the practice has in fact obtained that higher law status.[17]

---

[12] Ibid, at para 48.
[13] See Andrew David Heard, *Canadian Constitutional Conventions* (Toronto: Oxford University Press, 1991) at 1 (stating that: 'As many areas of the constitution are structured by archaic or incomplete laws, the political arena has given birth to binding conventions and customary usages that not only direct political actors in these matters, but ultimately determine the full substance and character of the Canadian constitution'); Eugene A Forsey, 'The Courts and the Conventions of the Constitution', (1984) 33 *University of New Brunswick Law Journal* 11 (defining conventions as 'the acknowledged, binding, extra-legal customs, usages, practices and understandings by which our system of government operates').
[14] Peter W Hogg, *Constitutional Law of Canada*, looseleaf (Toronto: Carswell, 2009), s 1.22(b).
[15] Ibid, at s 1.10(e).
[16] Heard, above note 13 at 10.
[17] Colin Turpin and Adam Tomkins, *British Government and the Constitution*, 6th edn (New York: Cambridge University Press, 2007) at 157.

Ultimately conventions take shape in a multitude of ways. Although each pattern or practice may be scrutinised for its moral importance and its significance to the constitutional setting, there will always be some degree of ambiguity in defining constitutional conventions. This is not unexpected, given that they are an informal—rather than formal—source of law.

Now that the various types of constitutional norms have been introduced, the following part will outline their content.

The Hierarchy of Constitutional Norms

All sources of constitutional norms in Canada are supreme in the sense that legislatures may not enact measures which are inconsistent with them—formally so, in the case of written and unwritten constitutional principles, and informally so, in the case of constitutional conventions. Still, an internal hierarchy exists between these types of supreme sources. Not surprisingly, this hierarchy has both formal and informal dimensions as well.

Formally, the text is the ultimate source of constitutional law. A constitutional convention or unwritten principle that is inconsistent with the text cannot stand.[18] Unwritten principles are second in the hierarchy. That is, they are inferior to written constitutional principles and superior to constitutional conventions. They are inferior to written principles because they are inferred from the text and may never contradict an explicit written principle. They are superior to conventions because they are inferred from the text and are justiciable, and hence may overrule a convention. Therefore, if a court was to rule that a certain unwritten constitutional principle was inconsistent with a convention, the unwritten principle would prevail.

Informally, however, constitutional conventions can enjoy supremacy over the formal constitution for the same reason they are supreme over legislation. This is illustrated by the history of section 56 of the Constitution Act, 1867. Known as the 'disallowance' power, this section provides that the federal Parliament has the power to 'disallow' or veto any provincial legislation.[19] This power was frequently exercised by the dominant federal government in the early years of Confederation to thwart provincial activism.[20] However, over time, the political actors of

---

[18] In the *Secession Reference*, above note 2 at para 49, the Court also suggested that no single constitutional principle can be interpreted to trump or exclude the operation of another. However, Jean Leclair argues that the Supreme Court's subsequent interpretation of judicial independence contradicts this by treating judicial independence as an absolute concept. Jean Leclair, 'Canada's Unfathomable Unwritten Constitutional Principles' (2002) 27 *Queen's Law Journal* 389 at 417.

[19] *Constitution Act, 1867*, ss 55–57. One cannot avoid the obvious comparison with the Virginia suggestion, at the Philadelphia Constitutional Convention of 1787, to give this power to the US Congress. This suggestion was obviously not adopted by the Convention. See Thornton Anderson, *Creating the Constitution: The Convention of 1787 and the First Congress* (Pennsylvania: Pennsylvania State University, 1993) at 50ff.

[20] Hogg, above note 14, s 3.1.

the day began to question its political legitimacy.[21] By the 1930s, a political consensus emerged that it was an illegitimate power, although no formal amendment was undertaken to remove it from the constitutional text.[22] Today, its use would not be considered by even the most nationalist of federal governments. As the Supreme Court articulated in 1943, 'disallowance of provincial legislation, although in law still open, [has,] to all intents and purposes, fallen into disuse'.[23] The disallowance example demonstrates that, at least informally, a convention can circumscribe the text of the Constitution and give rise to what appears to be a constitutional amendment.

On a formal level, this does not present a doctrinal inconsistency nor does it render conventions superior to the formal constitution. Doctrinally speaking, constitutional conventions refer not to the very *existence* of a constitutional power, but to *the way* in which a power is to be exercised. Moreover, if the Constitution was afterwards amended to override the convention explicitly, then the convention's constitutional authority would yield to the written text. Informally, however, the difference between the very creation of the power and the questions of who may exercise it, and how it may be exercised, are not easily sustainable. In practice, a formal constitutional amendment has never been made in response to a convention, even when such a convention had the effect of changing the constitutional text.

This is similarly the case for a possible conflict between a constitutional convention and a formal unwritten constitutional principle. Formally, the Supreme Court may interpret the Constitution: since the unwritten principles form part of the Constitution, they are subject to the Supreme Court's interpretation as well. Informally, however, the Supreme Court of Canada is not likely to interpret an unwritten principle in a way that would be inconsistent with a constitutional convention. Indeed, many of the unwritten principles that the Supreme Court has acknowledged actually had their origins as constitutional conventions.[24]

SUBSTANTIVE CONSTITUTIONAL PRINCIPLES

The chart below provides an overview of some of the important constitutional principles in Canada. Although not exhaustive, it provides a necessary context for the discussion of constitutional change that will follow in the final sections of this chapter.

---

[21] Ibid.
[22] The disallowance power was formally discussed at the Imperial Conference of 1930 and it was agreed that it would no longer be exercised by the UK government.
[23] *Re Resolution to Amend the Constitution*, [1981] 1 SCR 753 at 802.
[24] See Heard, above note 13 at 118.

Content of Constitutional Principles		Type of Constitutional Principle		
		Formal Principles		Informal Principles
Separation of Powers		Written principles	Unwritten Principles	Conventions
	The Executive	Section 9 and ss 55–58 of Constitution Act, 1867, respectively, grant the Governor General authority to assent to or signify disallowance of any law, as well as the power to appoint Lieutenant Governors. Section 90 extends the same authority over laws to the Lieutenant Governor of each province.	Democracy, constitutionalism the rule of law and federalism have all been recognised as unwritten constitutional principles.[25]	It is the democratically elected Prime Minister who actually has powers of appointment and law-making. The Prime Minister is to resign if he cannot maintain the confidence of the House of Commons.
	The Legislature	The Senate and the House of Commons have theoretically equal law-making powers. (The exception is money bills which are constitutionally required by s 53 to originate in the House.)		Law-making power rests predominately with the House of Commons—the Senate operates as a process of 'sober second-thought'.

25 *Secession Reference*, above note 2.

Content of Constitutional Principles			
Separation of Powers	The Judiciary	Sections 96–100 of the Constitution Act, 1867 set out the composition of the judicature. Section 11(d) of the *Charter* guarantees the right to a fair hearing by an 'independent and impartial tribunal'.	Judicial independence of all courts—involving security of tenure, financial security and administrative independence—recognised as an unwritten constitutional principle.[26]
Division of Powers	Federal	Section 91 of the Constitution Act, 1867 sets out the legislative jurisdiction of the federal government, including the residual power to make laws for the 'Peace, Order and Good Government' of Canada. Sections 55–57 of the Constitution Act, 1867 grant disallowance and reservation of federal laws to the Governor General, who, by convention acted on the advice of the British Government.	In 1930, it was agreed between the governments in the UK and Canada that this power would not be used.

26 *Reference Re Remuneration of Judges of the Provincial Court (PEI)*, [1997] 3 SCR 3 [*Provincial Judges Reference*].

Content of Constitutional Principles	Division of Powers	Provincial	Section 92 of the Constitution Act, 1867 sets out the legislative jurisdiction of the provinces. Section 90 extends disallowance and reservation of provincial laws to the Lieutenant Governor of a province. According to convention, the Lieutenant Governor acts on this matter under the advice of the federal government.	This power has not been exercised since 1961 and a convention prevents it current use.
	Rights	Charter of Rights	Entrenched after the patriation of the Constitution by the Constitution Act, 1982.	Respect for minority rights recognised as an unwritten principle.[27]
		Notwith-standing Clause	Entrenched after the patriation of the Constitution by the Constitution Act, 1982.	

18

[27] *Secession Reference*, above note 7.

Content of Constitutional Principles	Aboriginal Peoples of Canada	Aboriginal rights, treaty rights, and aboriginal titles are entrenched in s 35 of the Constitution Act, 1982. Those rights are not subject to the notwithstanding mechanism.[28] Legislation concerning aboriginal peoples is within the power of the federal government.[29]		

[28] See text to note accompanying note 36 below.
[29] Constitution Act, 1867, above note 3, s 91.

Written Principles

As mentioned above, Canada's written constitutional principles can be found in several documents that were created throughout the last two centuries. The most notable of these documents was the Constitution Act, 1867, which united the then separate provinces together as the 'Dominion of Canada' and set out the basic framework for Canada's federalist system.[30]

As a federalist state, the power to govern is divided between a central authority (the federal government) and several different regional authorities (the provinces and territories). Like many other federations, the division of powers in Canada is not hierarchical but rather is 'coordinate' in the sense that the provinces are constitutionally guaranteed law-making autonomy in certain important areas of public policy.[31] The division of powers between the two levels of government is set out in sections 91 and 92 of the Constitution Act, 1867. Briefly, and not exhaustively, the federal government has the exclusive power to regulate trade and commerce, banking, marriage and divorce, penitentiaries, national defence, postal services, navigation and shipping, and matters relating to aboriginal peoples.[32] The provinces have the power to legislate exclusively within the area of property and other private law matters, health care, the administration of justice, education, and matters of a local and private nature.[33]

Although the Constitution Act, 1867 marked Canada's first step in the direction of political independence, it was noticeably silent on a number of important aspects of Canadian constitutionalism. The Constitution Act, 1982 entrenched the Canadian Charter of Rights and Freedoms into Canada's constitutional system, elevating civil rights in Canada to higher law status. Consequently, after 1982, the judiciary could strike down laws that were found to conflict with the rights contained in the Charter as unconstitutional. That is, any law could be challenged in the courts and ultimately declared void by the judiciary if it infringed the enumerated rights. As a result, it is generally understood that the enactment of the *Charter* transformed Canada from a parliamentary democracy into a constitutional democracy.[34] However, it must be noted that section 33 of the *Charter*—the 'notwithstanding' mechanism—allows a legislature to enact a law 'notwithstanding' certain *Charter* rights.[35] This returns some elements of

---

[30] Constitution Act, 1867, above note 2.
[31] Hogg, above note 14, s 5.3.
[32] Ibid, s 91.
[33] Ibid, s 92. Some matters that are formally within provincial control are deeply affected by federal policy because adherence to these policies is a condition for the receipt of federal funds. The most prominent example is health care. See *British Columbia (Attorney General) v Auton (Guardian ad litem of)*, 2004 SCC 78 (Appendix A).
[34] See eg Lorraine E Weinrib, (2001–2002) 'Canada's Charter of Rights: Paradigm Lost' 6 *Review of Constitutional Studies* 119.
[35] Section 33 prescribes that in order to use the notwithstanding mechanism, a legislature must expressly declare that it is doing so. Notwithstanding declarations are valid for five years, but can be renewed. Not all Charter rights are subject to the mechanism. Section 33 can be applied to

legislative supremacy constitutionalism to Canada. In practice, the political disincentive to the use of the notwithstanding clause has rendered Canadian constitutionalism closer in status to judicial supremacy constitutionalism than to parliamentary sovereignty constitutionalism.[36] Against this background, Canada's constitutionalism is most aptly described as what Mark Tushnet calls a system of 'weak form' judicial review.[37]

To acknowledge the importance of Aboriginal peoples to Canadian law, constitutionalism, and culture, the Constitution Act, 1982 entrenches their rights outside of the Charter. Aboriginal rights, treaty rights, and aboriginal title are thus not subject to the notwithstanding mechanism, or to the section 1 limitation clause.[38]

Unwritten Principles

In this section, I provide an overview of the concepts as a framework for the later, more critical, discussion in the final part. Robin Elliot usefully provided a list of 11 unwritten constitutional principles.[39] In most cases, unwritten principles have been not been used to strike down legislation; instead, they are used to assist in

fundamental freedoms (s 2), which include freedom of religion and conscience, freedom of expression and assembly, and freedom of association; legal rights (ss 7–14); and equality rights (s 15). In contrast, s 33 cannot be invoked with respect to democratic rights (ss 3–5), mobility rights (s 6), rights regarding the official languages of Canada (ss 16–22) and minority language education rights (s 23). For various ways to understand the notwithstanding mechanism, see Tsvi Kahana, 'What Makes For a Good Use of the Notwithstanding Mechanism?' (2004) 23 *Supreme Court Law Review* 191.

[36] See Tsvi Kahana, 'The Notwithstanding Mechanism and Public Discussion: Lessons from the Ignored Practice of Section 33 of the Charter' (2001) 44 *Canadian Public Administration* 255.

[37] See Mark Tushnet, *Weak Courts, Strong Rights: Judicial Review and Social Welfare Rights in Comparative Constitutional Law* (Princeton: Princeton University Press, 2008) at 24. Tushnet uses this term to describe models in which the legislature has the final say regarding constitutional questions. Stephen Gardbaum use the term 'commonwealth constitutionalism'. See 'Reassessing the New Commonwealth Model of Constitutionalism' (2010) 8 *International Journal of Constitutional Law* 167.

[38] Nevertheless, the court read into s 35 a limitation clause, similar to that found in s 1 of the Charter. See *R v Sparrow*, [1990] 1 SCR 1075.

[39] Robin Elliott, 'References, Structural Argumentation and the Organizing Principles of Canada's Constitution' (2001) 80 *Canadian Bar Review* 67 at 99ff. The constitutional conventions he includes are: Federalism, Democracy, The Rule of Law, Protection of Minorities, Judicial Independence, the Role of Provincial Superior Courts, Individual Rights and Freedoms, Interprovincial Comity, Separation of Powers, Economic Union, the Integrity of the Nation State, and the Integrity of the Constitution. Mark Walters believes that that aboriginal rights of self-government are also part of Canada's unwritten constitution. See Mark D Walters, 'The Common Law Constitution in Canada: Return of Lex Non Scripta as Fundamental Law' (2001) 51 *University of Toronto Law Journal* 91 at 136.

the interpretation of the written text[40] or in determining the legitimate scope of administrative power.[41] In one case, an unwritten principle was used to uphold, rather than strike down, legislation.[42] Although important, because these cases not do not involve the striking down of legislation, they do not strike at the heart of constitutional discourse. In contrast, the five unwritten principles I focus on have been relied on by the Court to strike down existing legislation or to make clear that certain types of future legislation will be unconstitutional.

The first unwritten principle recognised by the courts, and the only one that has served as the basis for striking down of legislation is the principle of judicial independence. In the *Remuneration Reference*,[43] the Court relied on this principle to prevent a government from reducing the salaries of provincially appointed judges. Although there is a textual constitutional basis for acknowledging judicial independence in superior courts or inferior courts of criminal jurisdiction,[44] the Supreme Court chose to transform judicial independence into an unwritten principle that applies to all courts regardless of jurisdiction. The Supreme Court strengthened judicial independence further by interpreting it to require that 'independent, effective and objective' commissions recommend the level of remuneration for the judiciary.[45] The four additional unwritten constitutional principles were announced in the *Secession Reference*.[46] The Supreme Court relied on the principles of federalism, democracy, constitutionalism and the rule of law, and respect for minority rights to impose a constitutional obligation on all other governments to negotiate with a province that votes to secede.

Conventions

Constitutional conventions are responsible for dictating the legislative process in Canada. Some of the most important constitutional conventions address: (1) the

---

[40] See eg *R v Demers*, [2004] 2 SCR 489. In this case, the Court argues that our current conception of human rights must inform the interpretation of ss 91 and 92 of the Constitution Act, 1867. The Court stated that, while the rights and freedoms expressed in the Charter do not *formally* modify the scope of the powers in ss 91 and 92 of the Constitution Act, 1867, they do 'provide a new lens through which those powers should be viewed. In choosing one among several possible interpretations of powers that implicate human rights, the interpretation that best accords with the imperatives of the Charter should be adopted' at para 85.

[41] See eg *Lalonde v Ontario* (2002), 56 OR (3d) 505 (CA) (the Court uses the unwritten principle of respect for minority rights to prevent the government from reducing the functions of a French-language community hospital).

[42] In the *Manitoba Language Reference*, [1985] 1 SCR 721, the court held that the Manitoba legislature must abide by the Constitution and enact all legislation in English and French. However, the rule of law required that at any given time, a set of positive laws must be in place. Consequently, the court used the unwritten principle of the rule of law to allow the existing unconstitutional body of laws to remain in place until they could be translated and re-enacted in both languages.

[43] *Provincial Judges Reference*, above note 26.

[44] Constitution Act, 1867, above note 3, ss 99–100; Charter, above note 6, s 11(d).

[45] *Provincial Judges Reference*, above note 26 at para 169.

[46] *Secession Reference*, above note 2, at paras 55–82.

powers of the Governor General and Prime Minister; (2) the functioning of legislatures; and (3) the role of the Senate.

The Role of the Governor General

Perhaps the most significant role that constitutional conventions play in Canada is to define the offices of federal Governor General and provincial Lieutenant Governors. Though the Governors are the official representatives of the King or Queen (the head of state),[47] convention dictates that the executive in fact possesses most of their legal powers and duties.[48] Convention has transformed these positions from ones of great power into symbolic roles that hold nominal power alone.[49] For example, although Canadians are constitutionally entitled to elect their Members of Parliament (or provincial representatives), on paper it is the Governors who choose who will form the working government. Convention, however, dictates that the Governors must appoint the leader of the party most able to form a stable government (which is almost always the party with the most seats).[50] The Governors then appoint the members of the cabinet in consultation with the newly appointed Prime Minister (or Premier), according to their wishes.[51] The removal of such broad power from the Governors is not surprising, given that they are unelected.[52] Conventions thus allow the written Constitution, which creates and dictates the role of the Governors, to exist harmoniously with the more democratic inclinations of modern Canada.

---

[47] Though Canada has been constitutionally independent since 1982, the Queen is still the official head of state of Canada. David Estep, 'Losing Jewels from the Crown: Considering the Future of the Monarchy in Australia and Canada' (1993) 7 *Temple International and Comparative Law Journal* 217.

[48] AV Dicey, *Law of the Constitution* (London: MacMillan and Co, 1885) at 428–29.

[49] While rarely, it has happened that this nominal power has had tremendous effects on Canadian politics, and decisions by the Governor General have had a practical, real life implication for the survival of government. This was exemplified most recently by the prorogation controversy of 2008, in which the Governor General acceded to a request by the Canadian Prime Minister to prorogue Parliament in the face of a no-confidence motion in the House. Arguably, this decision undermined the duty to foster 'responsible government', a corollary of which is to ensure parliamentary support for the government of the day. For a detailed account of the political climate leading up to the prorogation of Parliament, and an analysis and critique of the Governor General's decision, see Peter H Russell and Lorne Sossin, (eds) *Parliamentary Democracy in Crisis* (Toronto: University of Toronto Press, 2009).

[50] Dicey, above note 48 at 417.

[51] This is not to say that the Governor is entirely without power in deciding who will form the government, and many scholars would argue strongly that 'a governor also has a right and duty to protect other important principles of the constitution, especially in situations where the reserve power of the Crown provides the only effective defence for those principles' (such as when there is no clear party capable of governing in a minority situation). However, for the most part, power over the formation of the government rests with the Prime Minister or Premier. Dicey, above note 48 at 417.

[52] Interestingly, some scholars have suggested that the Governor's role is actually preserved by the very same conventions that limit it. For example, Heard goes as far as to suggest 'it is only because of these conventional restraints that the broad legal powers of this monarchical office are tolerated within Canada's democratic constitution'. Heard, above note 13 at 26.

Legislative Structure and Process

The written Constitution is largely silent on legislative structure and process. As noted above, the jurisdiction of the various legislatures was set out in the Constitution Act, 1867, but how the legislatures were to go about creating and implementing law was left largely undefined.[53] Conventions, often called the 'law and customs of Parliament', dictate the functioning of the legislative bodies.[54]

Of the procedural rules that make up the 'law and customs of Parliament', the government-dominated agenda is one of the most important legislative conventions. The ability to control which bills are discussed in the legislature and to corral backbench votes for government-sponsored bills is arguably 'the most basic characteristic of Canadian political systems'.[55] Here the conventions of Cabinet confidence, confidentiality and solidarity, play a key role in solidifying the power of the executive branch. Confidence, otherwise known as responsible government, requires the Cabinet to maintain the support of the House of Commons in order to remain in office. It is largely the product of an electoral system that tends to generate majority governments. Cabinet confidentiality and solidarity, on the other hand, are commonly described as tools of political discipline. Confidentiality allows the cabinet to operate behind closed doors, while solidarity requires that all members of the governing party publicly support cabinet decisions.[56] If a Cabinet minister publicly disagrees with government policy, they will likely be dismissed by the Prime Minister or expected to resign.[57]

The Senate

Convention also defines the relationship between the Senate and the House of Commons. Although section 17 of the Constitution Act, 1867, provides that the two chambers have equal law-making authority, convention dictates that legitimate law-making power ultimately rests with the House of Commons. The unelected Senate is primarily a venue for 'sober second-thoughts' and the fine-tuning of government bills. It is no longer considered appropriate for the Senate to reject a bill that has already passed through the House of Commons; however, the Senate has been known to overstep convention on occasion and stall the enactment of government bills.

---

[53] Ibid, at 76.
[54] Dicey, above note 48 at 423.
[55] Heard, above note 13 at 7.
[56] Nicola White, 'Deconstructing Cabinet Collective Responsibility' (2005) 1:4 *Policy Quarterly* 4 at 6.
[57] Hogg, above note 14, s 9.3.

CHANGING THE CONSTITUTION

Changes to the Written Constitution

The Constitution Act, 1867, vested ultimate constitutional power in the Parliament of the United Kingdom.[58] Constitutional interpretation remained within the province of the Judicial Committee of the Privy Council. Though the provinces had the power to amend their own constitutions, the Canadian Parliament did not have the corresponding power to amend the federal Constitution. Thus the UK Parliament was frequently required to introduce amendments.[59] In 1949, the UK Parliament passed a statute that gave the Canadian Parliament the power to amend its own Constitution, with the exceptions of matters pertaining to provincial powers, denominational school rights, language rights and parliamentary session requirements and limitations.[60] Generally speaking, the UK Parliament preferred the federal interest over provincial interests, but did not entirely dismiss the interests of the latter.[61]

Against this background, the task for the political leaders who brought about the 1982 patriation, was to create an amendment formula reflecting a more balanced relationship between the federal government and the provinces. Indeed, amending formulae aspire to reflect a consensus, at the time of the creation of the constitution, concerning the relative weight that constituencies, institutions, and ideas should have on the decision to alter the foundations of the state's organisation. Accordingly, Canada chose to have seven different formulae, depending on the subject matter. At one end of the spectrum is a formula requiring consent of all the provinces in matters at the heart of the federation, and on the other end are formulae that allow unilateral procedures by the federal Parliament or a provincial legislature.[62] The general (and default) formula outlined in section 38 of the Constitution Act, 1982, is the 7/50 formula. To pass an amendment, seven provinces comprised of at least 50 per cent of the country's population must pass the amendment in their legislatures. The amendment must also be passed in the Senate and House of Commons. Given the way in which the population of Canada is divided, such an amendment requires the consent of Ontario or Quebec, plus six other provinces. Significantly, this formula does not

---

[58] Constitution Act, 1867, above note 3.
[59] See Hurley, above note 1 at 12.
[60] Ibid.
[61] Ibid. Ross notes the Empire followed several principles in its approach to constitutional changes for the Canadian dominion: (1) no act of the UK Parliament affecting Canada would be passed unless requested and accepted by Canada; (2) the UK Parliament would enact every amendment requested by Canada; (3) amendments were to be requested by Canada through a joint address of the House of Commons and Senate of Canada to the Crown (starting in 1895); (4) the UK Parliament would not enact a provincial request for an amendment unless the federal government also requested it; and (5) the federal government would not request an amendment that directly affected federal–provincial relationships without consultation and agreement with the provinces.
[62] Constitution Act, 1982, above note 4, Part V.

endow any one province with a veto power. This basic formula includes two sub-formulae allowing a province to opt out of an amendment, with or without compensation. First, when an amendment derogates from the powers of the provinces, a province may opt out of the amendment, in which case the amendment does not have an effect in that province.[63] This does not affect the validity of the amendment outside that provincial jurisdiction. When an amendment transfers powers relating to education or other cultural matters from a province to Canada and the province chooses to opt out of that amendment, the province is entitled to reasonable compensation from the federal government.[64]

The general formula and its two sub-formulae lie at the centre of the stringency spectrum; at the most stringent end is a unanimous consent formula. This is obviously the most difficult to employ as it requires the consent of all the provinces. It applies in relation to five matters which are understood to be the most central to Canadian constitutionalism, significantly including amendment to the amending formulas.[65] At the least stringent end, are three formulae, one bilateral and two unilateral. The bilateral formula is employed when an amendment only applies to a specific province (or provinces), and it requires the consent of Parliament and the legislature of the relevant province (or provinces). The federal unilateral formula allows Parliament to amend the Constitution in matters relating to the federal executive, to the Senate, or to the House of Commons. And, finally, if an amendment affects only 'the Constitution of a Province' it may be passed by that province alone.[66]

The most substantial change to Canada's written Constitution occurred upon the adoption of the Constitution Act, 1982, which was the result of a half-century long process of negotiation that culminated in patriation.[67] Notably, this change itself did not comply with the amending formula because it is that change that enacted the formula. Instead, this change was done by way of British legislation.[68]

Since 1982, the Constitution of Canada has been amended 10 times, mostly via the bilateral formula in matters relating to one province. Seven amendments of this nature allowed Quebec to restructure its school boards along linguistic lines;[69] relieved Parliament of its obligations to provide a ferry service to Prince

---

[63] Ibid, s 38(3).

[64] Ibid, s 40.

[65] The other matters are: the office of the Queen, the Governor General and the Lieutenant Governor of a province; the right of a province to a minimum number of members in the House of Commons by the number of senators it is entitled to; the use of the English or French language; and the Composition of the Supreme Court (interestingly, a Supreme Court is not mandated by the Constitution and is created by the Supreme Court Act, RSC 1985, c S-26. For possible consequences of this, see Hogg, above note 14 at s 4.27.

[66] Constitution Act, 1867, above note 3, s 45.

[67] See Hurley, above note 59.

[68] Canada Act 1982 (UK), c 11.

[69] Constitutional Amendment Proclamation, 1997 (Quebec), Can Stat Instruments, SI 97–141.

Edward Island;[70] guaranteed equal rights and privileges to the English and French linguistic communities in New Brunswick;[71] and changed the name of New-foundland and Labrador;[72] it was used three times to amend the school boards of Newfoundland.[73]

The other amending formulae have been used more rarely. Parliament alone has only amended the Constitution according to the section 44 formula twice: once to authorise the national legislature to readjust provincial representation,[74] and a second time to provide Nunavut with representation in the Senate and the House of Commons.[75] The only multilateral amendment under the 7/50 formula happened almost immediately after the patriation of the Constitution.[76] This amendment redefined aboriginal rights regarding land claims and guaranteed aboriginal peoples the right to political negotiations with the government to re-establish their constitutional rights. It also added a provision to the Constitu-tion Act, 1982, that provided for equality between the sexes.[77] Finally, neither the opt-out option (with or without compensation) nor the provincial unilateral formulas has ever been used.

The matter of the amending formula is closely related to the matter of the Canada–Quebec relationship. The patriation package was created in Canada and approved by the UK without the consent of Quebec. Therefore, Quebec has argued that the Constitution Act, 1982 does not bind it. In the late 1980s and early 1990s negotiations took place between Quebec and the rest of Canada but eventually failed. As part of the efforts to bring Quebec in, in 1996 the Federal Parliament enacted the act commonly referred to as the 'Regional Veto Statute.'[78] The act effectively prevents the federal government from consenting to any constitutional amendment under the 7/50 formula, without the consent of Ontario, Quebec, British-Columbia, at least two of the four Atlantic provinces whose population is at least 50 per cent of the population of the regional area,

[70] Constitutional Amendment Proclamation, 1993 (Prince Edward Island), Can Stat Instruments, SI 94–50.
[71] Constitutional Amendment Proclamation, 1993 (New Brunswick Act), Can Stat Instruments, SI 93–54.
[72] Constitutional Amendment Proclamation, 2001 (Newfoundland Act).
[73] Constitutional Amendment Proclamation, 1987 (Newfoundland Act), Can Stat Instruments, S1 88–11; Constitution Amendment Proclamation, 1997 (Newfoundland Act), Can Stat Instruments, SI 97–55; Constitutional Amendment Proclamation, 1998 (Newfoundland Act), Can Stat Instruments, SI 98–25.
[74] Constitution Act, 1985 (Representation), Appendix II of RSC 1985, No 47.
[75] Constitution Act, 1999 (Nunavut), SC 1998, c 16, Pt II.
[76] Constitutional Amendment Proclamation, 1983, Appendix II of RSC 1985, No 46.
[77] Ibid. Quebec was the only province that did not pass these two amendments through its legislature. However this is most likely not because of its substantive disagreement with the content of the amendments but based on a political protest against the adoption of the patriation package without its consent.
[78] An Act Respecting Constitutional Amendments, SC 1996, c 1 [assented to February 1, 1996]

and two of the three Prairie provinces whose population is at least 50 per cent of the population of the Prairie region. The latter stipulation provides Alberta with a veto right as well.[79]

While this is a statutory scheme it may be legitimately viewed as part of Canada's constitutional apparatus. First, it addresses the amending process in the most direct way possible. Secondly, while it can be repealed by Parliament, the political repercussion of such an act would likely make it too costly. Therefore, it can probably be said that the 7/50 amending formula now includes an element of regional veto.

Changes to Unwritten Constitutional Principles and Conventions

When the Supreme Court of Canada acknowledged that the Constitution contained unwritten principles it did not prescribe how they were to be changed. Clearly, a constitutional amendment to the written text may change the unwritten principles since, as we saw above, the written text is superior. However, is that the only method by which these principles may be amended? To answer this question, we must distinguish between incorporated British principles and implicit Canadian principles embedded in the constitutional text.

British principles are incorporated into the Canadian Constitution through the Preamble to the Constitution Act, 1867. The Preamble makes reference to 'a Constitution similar in Principle to that of the United Kingdom'. The court charged with interpreting the Constitution including the Preamble may determine the meaning of these principles but may not alter them. In terms of clarifying their meaning, the court has left some general questions unanswered. First, it is unclear if the Preamble merely imported the principles as they were in 1867, or whether they can be developed within the Canadian state. Secondly, it is unclear whether specific principles are imported, or whether the language of the Preamble imports only the type of principles that a system similar to the British system would adopt. If one believes that the principles are imported at a very high level of abstraction, then courts can easily adjust the principles for new situations without a need for a constitutional amendment. However, if one believes that specific principles are imported, then there is a limit to the possibility of their development: the court must inquire into the nature of the

---

[79] I say that the act 'effectively prevents' amendment without regional consensus, since formally the technique that the act uses prohibits a Minister of the Crown from proposing a resolution authorizing an amendment to the Constitution of Canada unless it follows the act's stipulations. This has two implications. First, a Member of Parliament who is not a Minister of the Crown may introduce a resolution consenting to a constitutional amendment even without regional consent. Second, if a Minister were to ignore the terms of the statute, there is no doubt that the resulting constitutional amendment would be legally valid. That said, given the slim likelihood of either of these scenarios, and the even slimmer likelihood of a successful constitutional amendment resulting from them, I believe that it is safe to say that the act effectively provides for regional vetos.

principles in the UK, either in 1867 (if one believes that principles are not permitted to develop) or at the time of the court's decision (if the principles are permitted to develop).

With regard to implicit Canadian principles, it is commonsense that these principles may be changed only to the extent that the constitutional text upon which they are established changes. That said, because the interpretation of the constitutional text is done by the judiciary, they may also implicitly adjust and amend unwritten constitutional principles.

Conventions may change in the same way they are created—through practice over time or through an explicit agreement between all the relevant actors. Conventions, too, are imported to Canada through the 1867 Preamble, and as a result, the discussion about changes to the British principles is also applicable here.

REFORM WITHOUT CONSTITUTIONAL AMENDMENT

Thus far, I have explored the various components of the Constitution and explained how they can be amended. It is clear that a change to the Constitution by amendment is a constitutional change. Discussing 'external' constitutional changes is also important for several reasons. First, one of the hallmarks of constitutionalism is that constitutions are relatively difficult to change. If it is found that societal and political processes provide an alternative to internal constitutional changes, then the entire project of constitutionalism may need re-assessment. Moreover, many constitutional systems expend significant deliberative energy, time and resources on constitutional deliberations. If much constitutional change takes place outside of the Constitution, such energy and resources may need to be reallocated.

Another way to look at this question is through an institutional lens. Constitutions are ordinarily changed by constituent assemblies. Often these do not literally exist, and instead constituent power is exercised by several institutions acting together. This is the case in Canada. As we saw, in order to change the formal Constitution of Canada, an amendment generally has to be passed by both Parliament and one or more provincial legislatures. However, at times changes to the Constitution may happen without engaging the literal or constructive constituent power.

This part of the chapter addresses changes to the Constitution of Canada by institutions that do not have constituent power: economic globalisation gives rise to international trade agreements, signed by the federal government and implemented by Parliament; the Supreme Court has developed unwritten principles; and, lastly, the story of the *Quebec Secession Reference* and its fallout demonstrate the Supreme Court's leadership on constitutional change, heeded by the Parliament and the Quebec National Assembly

Economic Globalisation: The New Constitutionalism?

I wrote above that the *Regional Veto Statute* may be considered part of the Constitution of Canada; I arrived at this conclusion based on the fact that that Act implicated the Constitution directly and was extremely difficult to change. Is this the only type of legislation that may be viewed as externally affecting the Constitution and changing it? Some scholars think not, arguing that legislation implementing international trade agreements may be viewed as bringing about constitutional change.

International trade agreements often have a more profound effect than simply altering a country's economic relations with other countries. Their very purpose is often to create legal conditions conducive to economic globalisation. Thus, arrangements such as the NAFTA, 'rather than bypassing the state ... amount to a drastic reorganization of the State'.[80] By effectively limiting the legislative authority of legislatures, some Canadian scholars have argued that this departure marks the emergence of a new form of constitutionalism.[81]

The North Atlantic Free Trade Agreement

David Schneiderman's work has shown that globally speaking and across various legal systems, investment rules demonstrate or have created a new form of constitutionalism. Applying his general theory to NAFTA, he convincingly shows that this agreement has altered the operational framework of Canadian constitutionalism so that previous legislative sovereignty in the domain of property regulation has been eroded. Chapter 11 of NAFTA regulates 'takings' with respect to investment interests. Such takings are prohibited unless they comport with, among other things[82] 'due process of law', language drawn directly from the US Constitution.[83] This is a significant divergence from the Canadian jurisprudence and the decision to leave property rights out of the Charter. Few economic rights are expressly recognised in the Charter and, although businesses have attempted

---

[80] See eg Harry Arthurs, 'Constitutional Courage', (2004) 49 *McGill Law Journal* 1 at 5; Harry Arthurs, 'Governing the Canadian State: The Constitution in an Era of Globalization, Neo-Liberalism, Populism, Decentralization and Judicial Activism', (2003) 13:1 *Constitutional Forum* 60 [Arthurs, 'Governing the Canadian State']. See also David Schneiderman, *Constitutionalizing Economic Globalization: Investment Rules and Democracy's Promise* (Cambridge: Cambridge University Press, 2008) [Schneiderman, *Constitutionalizing Economic Globalization*]; Stephen Clarkson, *Uncle Sam and Us: globalization, neoconservatism, and the Canadian state* (Toronto: University of Toronto Press, 2002); David Schneiderman, 'NAFTA's Takings Rule: American Constitutionalism Comes to Canada' (1996) 46 *UTLJ* 499 [Schneiderman, 'NAFTA's Takings Rule'].

[81] L Pantich, 'Rethinking the Role of the State' in James H Mittelman (ed), *Globalization: Critical Reflections* (Boulder, Colorado: Lynne Reiner Publishers, 1996).

[82] Under Chapter 11, takings must be (a) for a public purpose; (b) on a non-discriminatory basis; (c) in accordance with due process of law and Article 1105(1); and (d) on payment of compensation.

[83] Schneiderman observes that the NAFTA provision incorporates both the Fifth Amendment law of takings and the Fourteenth Amendment law of due process. Schneiderman, *Constitutionalizing Economic Globalization*, above note 80 at 80.

to invoke other Charter guarantees to frustrate economic regulation, the government's ability to regulate property and economic activity has been affirmed.[84] NAFTA entitles investors, whose interests have been directly or indirectly 'taken', to sue before a private arbitrator, whose awards are enforceable within the Canadian courts.

Harry Arthurs' account of contemporary Canadian constitutionalism represents a bolder trend in current constitutional thought. Not only does globalisation affect the constitutional order, but constitutions, writes Arthurs, count for 'not that much'.[85] Instead, what really matters are societal processes. He highlights five such processes in Canada—globalisation, neoliberalism, populism, decentralisation, and judicial activism—and argues that, together, they significantly weaken the Canadian state, and make for a new constitutional order.

It is clear that economic policies—be they neoliberal or other—affect a polity just as much, if not more, than its Constitution. But economic policies are made and changed by a complex set of state instruments, the most important of which, for my purposes, is legislation. Sometimes economic policies are extremely difficult to change regardless of their constitutional status. What makes NAFTA, for example, unique? In what way is it more 'constitutional' than, for example, the Canada Health Act?

The first answer is that it is a matter of degree. Every policy affects our lives, but economic globalisation 'fundamentally shape[s] the way we think about things as lawyers and citizens'.[86] Moreover, international agreements 'bind across generations',[87] and attempting to change legislation creating this new constitutional order is 'as difficult to change as any provision of the Constitution Act itself'.[88] Put differently: even if other types of policies may be important and may be difficult to change, the effect of international trade agreements on the economy, on politics, and on the polity are so all-encompassing, that changing them would be unthinkable, and hence, they bind future generations.

The idea of legislation having constitutional importance is not unique to Canada. In the US, John Ferejohn and William Eskridge have shown that contemporary American constitutionalism is made of and affected by 'super statutes' as much as it is affected by judicial decisions interpreting the US Constitution.[89] However, the fact remains that the difference between ordinary legislation and quasi-constitutional legislation is a matter of degree. What makes

---

[84] Schneiderman, 'NAFTA's Takings Rule', above note 80 at 505.

[85] Arthurs, 'Governing the Canadian State' above note 80 at 16.

[86] Ibid, at 22.

[87] Schneiderman, *Constitutionalizing Economic Globalization*, above note 80 at 38; Clarkson, above note 80 at 64–66.

[88] Arthurs, 'Governing the Canadian State' above note 80 at 22.

[89] William N Eskridge, Jr and John Ferejohn, 'Super-Statutes: The New American Constitutionalism' in Richard W Bauman and Tsvi Kahana (eds), *The Least Examined Branch: The Role of Legislatures in the Constitutional State* (Cambridge: Cambridge University Press, 2006).

legislation implementing international trade agreements in Canada, and 'super statutes' in the US, quasi-constitutional, is the all-encompassing and omnipotent subject matter.

The other reason for considering international trade agreements to be constitutional is not a matter of substance but a matter of institutions. Schneiderman and Clarkson note that these agreements provide for judicial review of legislation. This constitutes a qualitative, rather than a quantitative difference between legislation implementing international trade agreements and other important legislation. The Canada Health Act[90] for example, is considered by many to be more important to Canada's identity than the Charter. If Parliament were to enact a statute that is inconsistent with the Canada Health Act, the new act would prevail. The matter, of course, is not merely technical. The new piece of legislation would be viewed as the more recent, and hence overriding, will of the polity—not a small matter for a democracy. This is not the case when a piece of legislation is inconsistent with NAFTA. Investors or corporations may complain to an arbitral tribunal, and while the impugned piece of legislation is legally valid in Canada, and indeed may well express the will of Canadians, remedies in the international arena such as compensation, would be the cost to Canada for exercising its legislative power. The ability of a non-state entity to complain against a piece of legislation that violates some form of higher law, is the hallmark of constitutions. Again it goes without saying that this dynamic does not present a formal constitutional conflict, as domestically speaking Parliament may repeal the legislation implementing an international trade agreement. However, given that the government is not likely to do so, and as long as it does not do so, we may comfortably observe that something constitutional has happened.

The most important lesson I wish to draw from the literature on constitutional change via economic globalisation goes back to the question of deliberative resources mentioned in the previous section. Polities and scholars should pay attention to processes that affect their constitution indirectly equally as much as the processes which affect their constitution directly. This notion is not relevant only for the left leaning, even if in our current political culture the erosion of the Constitution seems to be coming from the right.

The Judiciary and the Constitution: The Canadian Debate

International trade agreements are created by the federal government and are implemented by the legislative branch. What about indirect changes to the constitution via the judiciary? There has been no discussion in Canada concerning the question of whether judicial decisions should be viewed as part of the

---

[90] RSC 1985, c C-6.

Constitution. However, the notion of unwritten constitutional principles invites such an inquiry. The starting point for this discussion is the two opposing outlooks on the relationship between constitutional change and judicial interpretation. At one end of a spectrum of views it is held that that the very legitimacy of constitutional interpretation requires a separation between the interpreted (the text) and the interpreter (the judge). Under this notion, the role of the judge is to interpret the Constitution; interpretation is possible, constitutional interpretation is different from unconstrained law-making by judges. Judges act legitimately when they interpret the Constitution and act illegitimately when they rewrite it. At the other end of the spectrum is the view that it is difficult to distinguish between text and interpretation (especially when the text is ambiguous), that constitutions require development and growth, and bringing about this development and growth is appropriately the role of the judiciary.

If one subscribes to the latter view, namely that constitutional interpretations are to be thought of as part of the Constitution, one must suggest criteria for distinguishing constitution-interpreting decisions from constitution-changing decisions. For example, one could classify important judicial decisions on some central matters to Canadian constitutionalism, such as official languages, the future of Quebec, or health care as matters of interpretation rather than change. This would render the exercise of identifying constitutional changes extremely subjective. The challenge here is very similar to the challenge of distinguishing constitutional legislation from ordinary legislation addressed in the previous section. However, it is a more important task with regard to the judiciary. Legislators do not directly engage with the constitution on a regular basis and not every piece of legislation implicates the constitution in an obvious way. Judges, on the other hand, deal with the Constitution in every constitutional case. Unless there is a good way to distinguish constitution-making decisions from constitution-interpreting decisions, it is not far-fetched to say that *every* judicial decision on constitutional interpretation changes the constitution. This would trivialise the Constitution and could render judicial review on the constitutionality of legislation illegitimate altogether.

The distinction I would like to make, in the Canadian context, is based not on the content of certain judicial decisions, but on a structural distinction between the interpretation of rules and the creation of rules. When a court interprets the text of the constitution, even on an extremely important matter, it does not bring about constitutional change. However, when a court gives an unwritten constitutional principle constitutional status by declaring it superior to legislation, it changes the constitution. In order to support this distinction, and the idea that an unwritten constitutional principle should be viewed as a change to the constitution, we must examine the way in which the court announces these principles.

If the principles are created without a textual anchor,[91] then the distinction is watertight. It is a distinction between judicial pronouncement of what the constitution *is* (interpretation), and what the constitution *implies* (creation). Before the judicial pronouncement of what the Constitution implies, that which is implied does not form part of the Constitution and could therefore not be employed in the same way that the Constitution is—to strike down legislation. Once the court announces the implied, unwritten principle, it brings that principle into the Constitution itself.[92]

But the distinction between interpreting principles and creating them is still valid if the creation of unwritten principles is based on a textual anchor.[93] In that case, the distinction is between a judicial pronouncement of what the Constitution is (interpretation), and a judicial importation of principles from an external source (creation).

It is important to stress that here that I say nothing about the legitimacy of the exercise. That would require a theory about the limits of legitimate judicial creativity. All I am saying is that even if the Court's announcement of unwritten constitutional principles is legitimate, creating unwritten principles is conceptually different from traditional judicial constitutional interpretation and is akin to reforming the Constitution. Whether or not the announcement of unwritten constitutional principles is based on textual anchoring, it is possible to distinguish between interpreting the Constitution and adding to the Constitution, either based on judicial reasoning (if there is no textual anchoring) or based on textual authorisation (if there is textual anchoring).[94]

[91] As I mentioned above, it is not entirely clear from the *Provincial Judges Reference* or the *Secession Reference* to what extent the creation of unwritten principles depends upon the Preamble of the Constitution Act, 1867, and whether the court would have recognized unwritten constitutional principles without the Preamble, based solely on the idea that the principles are implicit in the Constitution.

[92] Framing the processes of creating unwritten principles demonstrates how risky the process is in terms of interpretive legitimacy. That process of course can continue infinitely until all the court is left with is abstract concepts such as democracy or rights. For a view that renders this result acceptable and to naturally flow from the idea of the common law, see Mark Walters, 'Written Constitutions and Unwritten Constitutionalism' in Grant Huscroft, (ed) *Expounding the Constitution: Essays in Constitutional Theory* (Cambridge: Cambridge University Press, 2008) 245.

[93] One may notice that I call the distinction between interpreting the constitutional text and announcing unwritten principles 'water-tight' if there is no textual anchoring for the unwritten principles, whereas I call this distinction merely 'valid', if there is such anchoring. This is because the distinction between a textual authorisation for the court to create principles (in the Preamble) and the general expectation that the court interprets the text of the Constitution (in the rest of the Constitution) is not as strong as a distinction between interpretation and creation.

[94] Most scholarly work has focused on the legitimacy of the Supreme Court of Canada's creation of these unwritten constitutional principles. Hogg, above note 14 at s 15.9(g), suggests that it is an illegitimate exercise altogether since it bypasses and undermines the amending formula. Similarly, Jean LeClair believes that unwritten principles could be used for interpretive purposes and in order to uphold legislation but not in order to strike down legislation. Leclair, above note 18 In contrast, Mark Walters writes that unwritten constitutional principles and the courts legitimate role in developing them are consistent with Canada's constitutional histories and customs. Walters, above note 92.

We may say, then, that in addition to the 10 amendments of the text of the Constitution of Canada, the Constitution has been amended whenever the Supreme Court has declared that an unwritten constitutional principle enjoys supremacy over legislation. As mentioned above, this has happened in only two contexts. The first was in the context of judicial independence when the court struck down provincial legislation that regulated the salaries and other working conditions of provincial court judges. The second context was in relation to the *Quebec Secession Reference.*

The Provincial Judges Reference

At issue in the *Provincial Judges Reference* was the claim that provincial govern-ments' control over provincial judges' salaries violated judicial independence and hence was unconstitutional.[95] The parties argued the case with reference to the guarantee of judicial independence protected by section 11(d) of the Charter and as a result, the decision refers mainly to this section.[96] However, the court also held that, in addition to this Charter protection, judicial independence is an unwritten constitutional principle recognised and affirmed by the Preamble of the Constitution Act, 1867. Further, provincial courts, despite being created by statute, must also have a certain level of institutional independence. The consti-tutional parameters for the power to change or freeze superior court judges' salaries under section 100 of the Constitution Act, 1867 are equally applicable to the guarantee of financial security provided by section 11(d) to provincial court judges.

The majority of the court held that for the judiciary to be institutionally independent three requirements must be satisfied. First, judicial salaries could be adjusted as part of an overall economic measure affecting all or some public sector employees, or as part of a measure directed at provincial court judges as a class. However, the provinces are constitutionally obligated to first refer the matter to an independent commission to avoid the possibility, or appearance, of economic manipulation. The commission would issue a report on the salaries and benefits of judges to the executive and the legislature, thereby depoliticising the process. The report would be non-binding, but the legislature would have to justify its decision to ignore or vary the commission's report on the basis of a 'simple rationality test'.[97] Secondly, under no circumstances could the judiciary negotiate remuneration with the executive or the legislature, although this would not prevent chief justices or judges, or bodies representing judges, to express their

---

[95] The issue of provincial governments' power over judicial remuneration arises only in the case of provincial judges since 'superior' court judges in the provinces are federally appointed and paid according to s 96 of the Constitution Act, 1867.

[96] Charter, above note 5, s 11(d). Section 11(d) reads: 'Any person charged with an offence has the right to be presumed innocent until proven guilty according to law in a fair and public hearing by *an independent and impartial tribunal*' (emphasis added).

[97] *Provincial Judges Reference*, above note 26 at para 183.

concerns on remuneration to the government.[98] Finally, any reduction to judicial remuneration could not take judicial salaries below a basic minimum level. This was to ensure that the public confidence in the judiciary's ability to resist political or economic manipulation would not be undermined.[99] All three pieces of provincial legislation that were before the court failed to meet the requirements of this new test for judicial independence. The test for reviewing a government's decision to reject a commission's recommendation was later loosened, but the principle remains intact.[100]

The *Provincial Judges Reference* was the subject of harsh academic criticism. It was argued that: the Court's bias should have prevented it from ruling on this issue; the Charter already provides for judicial independence in criminal proceedings and extending it to civil proceedings is tantamount to rewriting the constitution; the jurisprudence is unclear and confused; and the elaborate commission process is properly a matter of legislation, not judicial decree.[101] That said, beyond a toll on the public purse and perhaps some damage to the judiciary's reputation, I believe that this matter has had little effect on the Canadian state. It was certainly a constitutional change, but an arguably unimportant one. The same cannot be said about the *Quebec Secession Reference*, the subject of the next section.

The Quebec Secession Reference

The *Quebec Secession Reference* may be the most discussed decision in the history of Canadian jurisprudence. It is also part of a larger story, the Canada–Quebec relationship, that may be the most studied topic in Canadian history. It is therefore impossible to offer a robust account of this decision and its full context, in this chapter, and so I merely offer some general and relatively uncontested history of the case. In accordance with my view that the creation of unwritten constitutional principles is a form of constitutional change, I focus on the way in which the *Secession Reference* changed Canada's Constitution.[102]

---

[98]   Ibid, at para 134.

[99]   Ibid, at para 135.

[100]   The test was modified in *Provincial Court Judges' Assn of New Brunswick v New Brunswick (Minister of Justice)*, 2005 SCC 44. In addition to this case and the *Provincial Judges Reference*, legislation was also struck down for violating the unwritten principle of judicial independence in *Newfoundland Assn of Provincial Court Judges v Newfoundland*, [2000] NJ No 258; *Alberta Provincial Judges' Assn v Alberta*, [1999] AJ No 47; *Newfoundland Assn of Provincial Court Judges v Newfoundland*, [1998] NJ No 120; *Mackin v New Brunswick (Minister of Finance)*, 2002 SCC 13; *Manitoba Provincial Judges Assn v Manitoba (Minister of Justice)*, [2001] MJ No 339.

[101]   See eg Hogg, above note 14 at s 15.9(g); Leclair, above note 18. This writer also criticized the decision at Tsvi Kahana, 'The Constitution as a Collective Agreement: Remuneration of Provincial Court Judges in Canada' (2004) 29 *Queen's LJ* 445.

[102]   While not directly on the matter of constitutional amendment, the literature on the *Secession Reference* is voluminous. For a good typology of the literature see Sujit Choudhry and Robert Howse, 'Constitutional Theory and the Quebec Secession Reference' (2000) *Canadian Journal of Law and*

Quebec was the only province that did not consent to the 1982 patriation, and many Quebecois believed that the Constitution Act, 1982, including the Charter and the amending formula, was illegitimate. Part of Quebec's objection to the act was that the amending formula did not acknowledge Quebec's importance in the federation and that the Charter did not acknowledge the importance of preserving the French culture. Constitutional negotiation during the late 1980s and and early 1990s failed and in the mid-nineties the growth of the separatist movement in Quebec sparked a referendum in which the vote against secession was very close.[103] Canada feared that Quebec would decide to secede unilaterally. The federal government therefore asked the Supreme Court three questions, the most important of which for our purposes is the first one: does Quebec have a right under the Constitution of Canada to secede from Canada unilaterally?[104]

The Court's answer was neither a yes nor a no. Instead, it ruled that if a 'clear majority of the population of Quebec' responding to a 'clear question' wishes 'to pursue secession', Canada must enter constitutional negotiations with Quebec.[105] The Court arrived at this formula after considering the four unwritten constitutional principles discussed above—federalism, democracy, constitutionalism and the rule of law, and respect for minorities.[106] The interconnectedness of the four principles, the fact that they are defined with reference to each other, and the fact that one cannot trump any of the others, led the Court to conclude that there could be no legal right to unilateral secession under the Constitution. However, the same principles support the conclusion that a 'clear expression of democratic will'[107] in favour of secession in a provincial referendum would give rise to an obligation on the part of all parties to Confederation to negotiate a resolution that responded to that political will.[108] The negotiation process would be governed by the same constitutional principles that gave rise to the very duty to negotiate.[109] Finally, both the 'clear majority on a clear question' and the positions of the parties in the negotiations were to be subject to evaluation by the political process alone and not to scrutiny by the courts.[110] In effect, the Supreme Court thus added a secession provision to the Constitution.

It is rather obvious that the subject matter of this addition to the Constitution is tremendously important. The Court disabled the strong threat of unilateral secession wielded by Quebec separatists; however, it still implied that at the end

---

Jurisprudence 143 at 144 (of course more has been written since, but the typology provides a useful classification of the various approaches and arguments).

[103] 50.58% voted against secession. Directeur général des élections du Québec, *Référendum du 31 octobre 1995*, online: http://www.electionsquebec.qc.ca/francais/tableaux/referendum-1995-8481.php.

[104] *Secession Reference*, above note 2 at para 2.

[105] Ibid, at para 92.

[106] Ibid, at para 32.

[107] Ibid, at para 86.

[108] Ibid, at para 88.

[109] Ibid, at para 90.

[110] Ibid, at para 100.

of the day Quebec could secede. This issue goes to the heart of the survival of a federation. But beyond substance, both the normative character of, and the institutional structure assumed in, the decision makes it more akin to a constitutional amendment than a judicial decision. In terms of normative character, judicial decisions are themselves justiciable: they may be executed, applied or distinguished by subsequent judicial decisions. In contrast, the Court announced in the *Secession Reference* that the test it creates—the requirements of 'clear question' and 'clear majority'—is itself not justiciable and is to be evaluated by the political branches. Unlike judicial decisions, constitutional provisions are in some instances non-justiciable.

The institutional structure the decision envisages is also more similar to that of a constitutional amendment than that of a judicial decision. Ordinarily, a constitution—representing the will of the people—sets out idea, formulas and terms, and the courts—having interpretive expertise—interpret those terms, or, if the provisions are not justiciable, declares them to be so. However, in the case of the *Secession Reference*, the opposite occurs. The Supreme Court sets out the general terms, and the legislatures—representing the people—are left to interpret them. The court is at once a constituent assembly (creating the rule) and a court (declaring that the rule is non-justiciable).[111]

Indeed, what followed the *Secession Reference* was an exercise of legislative constitutional interpretation about those new terms—'clear question' and 'clear majority'. First was the response of the federal government, known as the Clarity Act.[112] Underlying the Act appears to be the federal suspicion that the Quebec government might not properly represent the polity. The federal interpretation was that for a question to be clear, it must be a question about secession, rather than about negotiation, and it must be only be about secession, rather than about an alternative.[113] This means that Quebec politicians could not proceed gradually or present secession on a continuum of possibilities for the type of arrangement between Canada and Quebec. As for the clear majority, the federal government stated that it would consider the size of the majority, the voter turnout, and any other consideration it deemed relevant.[114] Finally, the Act states that the federal government may consider formal statements made in Quebec institutions or by political parties, in addition to the referendum, hinting at the possibility that the

---

[111] Hogg, above note 14 at s 15.9(g), implies the *Secession Reference* is tantamount to a constitutional amendment in a much more obvious, and hence troubling, sense. For him it is obvious from the text of the Constitution that a province may not secede without a constitutional amendment providing for the secession. Therefore there was no gap in the Constitution, and not only did the Court add an amendment to the Constitution, it actually replaced the existing text of the Constitution with an amendment based on unwritten principles.

[112] An Act to give effect to the requirement for clarity as set out in the opinion of the Supreme Court of Canada in the Quebec Secession Reference, SC 2000, c 26 [Clarity Act].

[113] Ibid, s 1.

[114] Ibid, s 2.

referendum might disregard minority votes. This presumably seeks to protect minority groups in Quebec that oppose secession but are disregarded by the majority.

In response to this Act, Quebec passed its own Act,[115] which reads more like a separatist manifesto, declaring that the Quebec National Assembly 'has never adhered to the Constitution Act of 1982, which was enacted despite its opposition', and referring throughout the act to the 'Quebec State' and the 'Quebec People'.[116] On the matter of clear majority and clear question the act merely states that the winning option would be 'the option that obtains a majority of the valid votes cast, namely 50% of the valid votes cast plus one'.[117]

This exchange between Parliament and the National Assembly of Quebec was the last meaningful shot fired in the battle over the Canadian Constitution. After some public debate in the early 2000s, Canadians 'have shifted gears and fallen back on older, quieter, less conflictual, and more piecemeal ways of adjusting and adapting their constitutional system'.[118] It is not clear to what extent the *Secession Reference* contributed to this blessed fatigue, but it is clear that the Court's decision—the amendment to the Constitution it created—was one of the factors.

ALL ROADS LEAD TO THE SUPREME COURT?

The written Constitution of Canada is at a standstill. Russell is right to observe that Canadians have tired of attempting to work on their Constitution and it seems they have decided to live with what they have. There is a gap then, not only with regards to judicial independence and to secession, but with regards to the very existence of a Constitution. The Constitution Act, 1867 is accepted by all parties, but the 1982 Constitution is not. Canadians have given up, for now, in trying to change this. And the Supreme Court has decided to step in to fill that gap. Significantly, it did not impose a solution on the parties. Rather, it required that whatever they do shall be the result of a robust democracy (clear question and clear majority) and of deliberation (negotiations). At least on the surface, there can be nothing wrong with a Court declaring that bilateral processes are preferable to unilateral processes.

The risks in such a bold—and perhaps, courageous if you think it was the right thing to do, brazen if you think it was not—approach are obvious. The immediate one, which thus far has not seemed to occur, is that the Court will be viewed as a political institution and will lose its credibility. But the more subtle one is what Mark Tushnet calls 'democratic debilitation'. This happens when the polity

---

[115] *An Act Respecting the Exercise of the Fundamental Rights and Prerogatives of the Quebec People and the Quebec State*, RSQ, c E-20.2.

[116] Ibid, Preamble.

[117] Ibid, s 4.

[118] Peter H Russell, *Constitutional Odyssey: Can Canadians Become a Sovereign People?* (3rd edn), (Toronto: University of Toronto Press, 2004) at 272.

substitutes the Supreme Court for the Constitution, and substitutes its delibera-tions and judgments for constitutional pronouncements. This fear is not unsub-stantiated, and can be exemplified in two examples, relating to two Canadian constitutional mechanisms—the reference mechanism, and the Charter's not-withstanding clause. The reference process has been a part of the Canadian constitutional apparatus since 1867. It gives the Supreme Court the power to issue advisory opinions on constitutional issues. Indeed, both the *Provincial Judges Reference* and the *Secession Reference* were delivered according to this mechanism. In practice, while the opinions are not technically binding, they are in fact treated as binding precedents.[119] Similarly, the notwithstanding mecha-nism allows for a legislature to override judicial decisions, and presumably one of the reasons for doing so would be when the legislative branch heard what the court had to offer but chose not to follow it. In practice however, this mechanism is almost never used, and has been used only once in response to a Supreme Court decision.[120]

Even in the context of the *Secession Reference* itself, it looks as if this happened to some extent. In the Quebec statute responding to the federal Clarity Act, while declaring the illegitimacy of the Constitution Act, 1982, it stated that it recog-nised the 'political importance' of the *Secession Reference*.[121]

It may very well be that the polity looks up to the Supreme Court of Canada and is interested in the Court making decisions on its behalf. It might be that at least for the time being, the Supreme Court enjoys just as much legitimacy as—if not more than—the Constitution itself. However, the Supreme Court should be cautious when assuming this role, and its recent reluctance to resort to the idea of unwritten constitutional principles is commendable. The real accomplishment of a Constitution is that it constitutes the polity, not that it authorises (or does not authorise) the Supreme Court to do the constituting job itself.

[119] L Huffman and M Saathoff, 'Advisory Opinions and Canadian Constitutional Development: The Supreme Court's Reference Jurisdiction' (1990) 74 *Minnesota Law Review* 1251.
[120] See Kahana, 'The Notwithstanding Mechanism and Public Discussion', above note 36.
[121] Above note 113 at Preamble.

3

The Czech Republic

MAXIM TOMOSZEK

INTRODUCTION

THE INDEPENDENT CZECH Republic started its existence on 1 January 1993 as a successor of the Czech and Slovak Federal Republic. Its constitutional system is based on the Constitution of the Czech Republic (Constitutional Act No 1/1993 Coll, hereinafter referred to as the Czech Constitution) as amended by later legislation, which was adopted by the Czech National Council on 16 December 1992.

Although the Constitution of the Czech Republic was constructed as a 'rigid' or inflexible constitution, constitutional changes and the adoption of Constitutional Acts are rather common. In the 18 years of its independent existence, 105 constitutional bills have been proposed, 14 of which were adopted. Out of the adopted Constitutional Acts, six were direct amendments of the text of the Czech Constitution. These numbers cannot be interpreted as a deficiency in the constitution or as mistakes of the legislator. The reason for frequent constitutional changes is primarily to be found in the political culture, or lack thereof, and low respect for the Constitution, both of which are part of the unfortunate constitutional heritage resulting from the period of more than 50 years of undemocratic regimes on the territory of the Czech Republic.

The analysis of constitutional changes in this chapter will focus on the Constitution of the independent Czech Republic. However, some of the present constitutional arrangements derive from particular historical circumstances, including changes in past Czechoslovak Constitutions. Recent constitutional history also contains examples of interesting constitutional changes. After the next section on the general characteristics of the Czech constitutional system and its basic principles, there follows a brief overview of the constitutional evolution of Czechoslovakia, starting with the year 1918 and highlighting the most important events. Subsequent parts will deal with the rules regulating the formal amendment of the Czech Constitution, and with particular formal and informal changes of the Czech Constitution. The chapter ends with some generalisations and conclusions.

GENERAL CHARACTERISTICS AND BASIC PRINCIPLES OF THE CZECH
CONSTITUTIONAL SYSTEM

The Czech legal system belongs to the civil law family, more specifically to the Germanic tradition and even more specifically to its Austrian part. This reflects the long-lasting integration of Bohemia, Moravia and Silesia, which were traditional components of the Czech Kingdom, into the Austrian Empire. The main source of inspiration of the current Czech Constitution was the Czechoslovak Constitution of 1920, which was, according to its drafters, mainly inspired by French, Belgian and United States Constitutions.[1]

All generally binding laws[2] together with other important legal acts and decisions[3] are promulgated in the official publication of the Czech Republic called *Sbírka zákonů* (Sb). In this chapter, this term will be translated as the Collection of Laws and abbreviated as Coll. As from 1 January 2000, all international treaties binding on the Czech Republic are published in a special Collection of International Treaties.[4]

The Czech legal system is hierarchically structured according to the status of legal acts in three basic levels—constitutional, statutory and sub-statutory (that is implementing laws and regulations). Legal acts must always be in accordance with higher level legal acts. As a member state of the European Union, the Czech Republic must respect all obligations deriving from European law, which is considered to be part of the Czech legal system and has supremacy over all three of the above-mentioned categories of domestic legislation. The only exception to this model is represented by unamendable constitutional provisions, which will be analysed in more detail later. International treaties approved by the Parliament are considered to be part of the Czech legal system as well, but their supremacy only applies to statutory law and subordinate legislation.[5]

A Poly-textual Constitution

Probably the most important part of the Austrian constitutional heritage is the idea of a poly-textual constitution, that is a constitution consisting of several separate documents, which all possess constitutional force and content. The

---

[1] V Pavlíček, and M Kindlová, 'The Czech Republic' in C Kortmann, J Fleuren and W Voermans, (eds) *Constitutional Law of 10 EU Member States. The 2004 Enlargement* (Deventer: Kluwer, 2006) II-8.

[2] Constitutional Acts, acts, ordinances of the government and regulations issued by ministries or other administrative authorities.

[3] Decisions of the Constitutional Court and Supreme Court, if promulgation is required by law; decisions of the President of the Czech Republic; important resolutions of chambers of the Parliament or of the government; or announcements of central administrative authorities, if required by law.

[4] Sbírka mezinárodních smluv.

[5] See commentary to Art 10 of the Czech Constitution, K Klíma et al *Komentář k Ústavě a Listině*, 2nd edn Part 1. (Plzeň: Aleš Čeněk, 2009) 120ff, V Sládeček, V Mikule and J Syllová *Ústava České republiky. Komentář*. (Praha: CH Beck, 2007) 75 ff.

reflection of this principle may be found in Article 112 of the Czech Constitution, which defines 'the constitutional order', that is the set of legal norms with the highest legal status within the Czech legal system.[6]

The constitutional order consists of:

1. the Constitution of the Czech Republic;[7]
2. the Charter of Fundamental Rights and Freedoms (hereinafter referred to as the Charter);[8]
3. Constitutional Acts dealing with certain arrangements connected to the dissolution of the Czech and Slovak Federal Republic;[9]
4. separate Constitutional Acts dealing with specific issues—the Constitutional Act on the Security of the Czech Republic,[10] the Constitutional Act on the Establishment of Higher Territorial Self-governing Units, the Constitutional Act on the Referendum on Accession of the Czech Republic to the European Union;[11]
5. Constitutional Acts defining the borders of the Czech Republic; and
6. the Constitutional Act on the shortening of the term of office of the Chamber of Deputies of the Parliament of the Czech Republic.

Although Constitutional Acts are supposed to be consistent with the Constitution, there are two possible situations of inconsistency:

1. Constitutional Acts can provide for a different rule from one that is already in the Constitution (amendment) or they can introduce a new constitutional regulation (addition)—this is a standard procedure for constitutional change and is relatively obvious.
2. However, Constitutional Acts can also be inconsistent with the Constitution in the sense of being contrary to the unamendable provisions of the Constitution, which means they may be repealed or set aside by the Constitutional Court. This is something the Constitution did not anticipate and it derives from the case law of the Constitutional Court (the case of the

---

[6] See commentary to Art 112 of the Czech Constitution—Klíma et al ibid, Part 1, 846 ff, Sládeček, Mikule and Syllová ibid, 898 ff.

[7] Constitutional Act No 1/1993 Coll, the Constitution of the Czech Republic, as amended; the full text of the Constitution in English is available at http://www.psp.cz/cgi-bin/eng/docs/laws/1993/1.html.

[8] The Charter of Fundamental Rights and Freedoms, promulgated under No 2/1993 Coll, as amended; the full text of the Charter in English is available at http://www.psp.cz/cgi-bin/eng/docs/laws/1993/2.html.

[9] Constitutional Act No 4/1993 Coll, on certain arrangements connected to dissolution of the Czech and Slovak Federal Republic, and constitutional law No 29/1993 Coll, on certain further arrangements connected to the dissolution of the Czech and Slovak Federal Republic; the full text of Act No 4/1993 Coll in English is available at http://www.psp.cz/cgi-bin/eng/docs/laws/1993/4.html.

[10] Constitutional Act No 110/1998 Coll, on the Security of the Czech Republic; the full text of this act in English is available at http://www.psp.cz/cgi-bin/eng/docs/laws/1998/110.html.

[11] Constitutional Act No 515/2002 Coll, on The Referendum on Accession of the Czech Republic to the European Union; the full text of this Act in English is available at http://www.psp.cz/cgi-bin/eng/docs/laws/2002/515.html.

Constitutional Law on shortening of the term of the Chamber of Deputies, which is analysed later in the chapter).

According to a decision of the Constitutional Court,[12] international treaties on human rights must also be regarded as part of 'the constitutional order'. The text of the Constitution defines the constitutional order precisely and does not include international treaties in it, so this decision is an example of an informal change of the Czech Constitution and will be dealt with in more detail later.

The principle of poly-textuality is one of the reasons for the Czech Constitution being among the shortest in Europe, consisting of 113 Articles and 5,426 words. Although it is constantly criticised by most Czech politicians, who call for a more meticulously detailed text, its brevity must be one of the most positive features of the Czech Constitution. In this respect, one must agree with Giovanni Sartori, who states that constitutions should focus on the basic principles of the organisation of the state, not on detailed rules, which should be contained in ordinary statutes or even in subordinate legislation.[13]

Many important constitutional provisions are contained in the Charter and other Constitutional Acts and sometimes even in ordinary acts. Poly-textuality is recognised by several constitutional provisions, which define, for example, the status of the Charter (Article 3) and the constitutional order (Article 112), and require Constitutional Acts to be adopted to regulate some issues (Articles 2 and 10a regarding the referendum, Article 11 dealing with state borders, Article 100 paragraph 3 dealing with higher territorial self-governing units), or enable the Parliament to pass Constitutional Acts (Articles 9 and 39).

To avoid ambiguity, the term Czech Constitution will be used to address the Constitutional Act No 1/1993 Coll, the Constitution of the Czech Republic, while terms such as constitution, constitutional system or constitutional order will be used to address the constitution in a wider sense, that is the sum of all Constitutional Acts in the Czech Republic.

The Structure of the Czech Constitution and other Constitutional Acts

The Czech Constitution consists of a Preamble and eight chapters. The first chapter (Articles 1–14) establishes the basic principles of the state, the relationship between the state and the individual, the political system, international relations and the status of international law, the state territory and borders and state symbols. The second chapter (Articles 15–53) deals with legislative power, which is exercised by the bicameral Parliament. The third chapter (Articles 54–80) regulates three executive bodies—the President, the government and the public prosecution office. The fourth chapter (Articles 81–96) is dedicated to the

---

[12] Pl ÚS 36/01; this decision will be analysed in detail below.
[13] G Sartori, *Srovnávací ústavní inženýrství*, 2nd edn (Praha: SLON, 2001) 198–99.

judiciary including the Constitutional Court. The fifth (Article 97) and sixth (Article 98) chapters, dealing with the Supreme Control Office and the Czech National Bank, are very short. They both contain only one article and the detailed regulation of these independent constitutional bodies is provided for by ordinary acts. Chapter seven (Articles 99–105) deals with territorial self-government (the regions). The eighth and final chapter (Articles 106–113) contains transitional and final provisions.

The Charter of Fundamental Rights and Freedoms is a self-standing catalogue of human rights, which was transferred into the Czech constitutional order from the legal system of the Czech and Slovak Federal Republic, where this document was first adopted on 9 January 1991. This solution resulted from the fact that at the time of drafting of the Czech Constitution, there was not sufficient political agreement on the extent and content of human rights guarantees that should be included in it. However, the Charter has proved to be a complete catalogue of human rights, consistent with the highest international standards. It even includes guarantees of social, cultural and economic rights, which are (unlike all other constitutional provisions) not self-executing, that is they require implementation through other legislation.

The Charter consists of 44 articles divided into six chapters. The first chapter (Articles 1–4) provides for principles such as equality, non-discrimination, legality, and basic conditions for limitations of human rights. The second chapter stipulates fundamental human rights (Articles 5–16) and political rights (Articles 17–23). The third chapter (Articles 24–25) deals with the rights of ethnic and national minorities. The fourth chapter (Articles 26–35) provides for economic, social and cultural rights, while the fifth chapter (Articles 36–40) provides rights to judicial protection and fair trial. The sixth chapter (Articles 41–44) contains general provisions for the interpretation and application of the Charter.

Most other Constitutional Acts belonging to the constitutional order are rather short and focus on particular issues.

1. Constitutional Acts dealing with arrangements connected to the dissolution of the Czech and Slovak Federal Republic focus on the continuity of the legal system and of state power during the transition from the Czechoslovak Federation to the unitary Czech Republic.
2. The Constitutional Act on the Security of the Czech Republic provides for different states of emergency and allows some special measures to be applied in those situations.
3. The Constitutional Act on the Establishment of Higher Territorial Self-governing Units defines the regions and their territory.
4. The Constitutional Act on the Referendum on the Accession of the Czech Republic to the European Union only contained provisions regarding the referendum on accession to the EU (now obsolete).

BASIC PRINCIPLES

The basic principles of the Czech constitutional system are set out in Articles 1 to 14 of the Czech Constitution. In Article 1, the Czech Constitution defines the Czech Republic as a sovereign, unitary and democratic state based on the rule of law and respecting the obligations deriving from international law.

Article 2 provides for the sovereignty of the people, who may exercise their power directly or through their elected representatives in accordance with the principle of separation of powers. In constitutional reality, the emphasis is on representative democracy. There has only been one referendum, on accession of the Czech Republic to the EU. The principle of legality established in Article 2 paras 3 and 4 requires all limitations on the freedom of the individual to be provided for by law. The basic rules for the exercise of state power should be set out in laws.

Article 3 establishes the concept of 'the constitutional order' and thus of the poly-textual constitution, both mentioned above, by referring to the Charter of Fundamental Rights and Freedoms for the regulation of human rights, which are to be protected by judiciary (Article 4).

Article 5 stipulates the fundamental principles of the political system—the free and voluntary establishment of and free competition between political parties, which must respect basic democratic principles and reject violence as a way of achieving political aims.

Article 6 provides for the principles of majority decision-making and the protection of minorities.

Article 7 contains a constitutional basis for environmental protection, while Article 8 guarantees the autonomy of the self-governing territorial units or regions.

Article 9 contains the general principles for integrating, changing and amending the constitution; it also provides that it is forbidden to 'change the essential features of the democratic state and the rule of law'. This article is undoubtedly extremely important for the analysis of constitutional changes and will be analysed in detail below.

Article 10 defines the relationship of domestic law and international law as based on monism and implemented through a general incorporation clause providing for the supremacy of international law. Articles 10a and 10b were added through the so-called Euro-amendment adopted in 2001. Article 10a allows the transfer of competences to an international organisation and Article 10b regulates the relations between the Parliament and the government regarding issues of membership of such international organisations.

Articles 11 to 14 provide the basis for further legislation on the basic attributes of the Czech Republic—its territory and borders, citizenship, capital and state symbols.

The relationships between supreme constitutional bodies conform to the principles of a parliamentary form of government: the Parliament is the only directly elected body and its status in relation to other branches is superior. The position of the President is a little stronger and less dependent on other constitutional bodies than in other parliamentary republics, which is mainly due to the fact that the Czech Constitution was drafted to suit the impartial and apolitical personality of Václav Havel.[14]

THE HISTORICAL DEVELOPMENT OF THE CZECH CONSTITUTION

The Path to Independence

The independence of the Czech State since 1993 draws on the strong historical traditions of the Czech Kingdom. During the years 1526 to 1918 it was ruled by the Habsburg dynasty and was therefore merged with Austria and later became part of the Austrian and Austro-Hungarian Empire. This connection (together with the influence of legal theorists Hans Kelsen and František Weyr) is the reason for the many concepts shared by Czech and Austrian constitutional traditions, especially the poly-textual constitution and the specialised constitutional court.

The connections between the Czech and Slovak nations were not particularly strong until the second half of the nineteenth century, when they started a political cooperation stimulated by the desire for autonomy. Therefore it may seem surprising that in 1918, in the aftermath of World War I, a single state of Czechs and Slovaks, actually of the Czechoslovak nation, was established.

There were several reasons for this solution. Most importantly, it was perceived as impossible to establish an autonomous state of Slovaks while there was a strong demand for the separation of Slovakia from Hungary. A strong Slavic country in central Europe, as a counter-balance to Austria and Hungary, which were significantly weakened in consequence of World War I, was also favoured by the victorious powers. However, the problem of a very large German minority within the intended Czechoslovakia, even larger than the Slovak population, remained. It was fear of their influence within Czechoslovakia that produced the rather abstract concept of a Czechoslovak nation.[15]

The weakness of this concept was clear from further developments in relations between Czechs and Slovaks, who never really merged into a single nation. Finally in 1992 Czechoslovakia broke up into two autonomous republics.[16]

---

[14] E Wagnerová *Ústavní soudnictví*, (Praha: Linde, 1996) 36.
[15] J Zimek, *Ústavnost a český ústavní vývoj*, (Brno: MU, 2006) 56–57, V Pavlíček et al *Ústavní právo a státověda*, Vol II, Part 1, 2nd edn (Praha: Linde, 2008) 37–41.
[16] The longing of Slovaks for independence manifested itself constitutionally on several occasions during the 20th century—in 1938, after the Munich Pact, it led to the de facto federalisation of the remnants of the Czechoslovak Republic, and in 1939 it led to the creation of an autonomous Slovak

The independence of the Czechoslovak Republic was proclaimed at the international level by the Washington Declaration on 18 October 1918. After its international acceptance, the struggle for the independent state of Czechoslovaks was completed by the revolutionary actions of the Czechoslovak nation, such as the creation of Czech representative and governing bodies, acquisition of de facto power in the administrative centres of Czechoslovakia, declaration of independence, and so on. In some places there were even fights between revolutionary crowds and Austrian armed forces. These actions led to the declaration of the independence of the Czechoslovak Republic on 28 October 1918.

The First Republic

From the constitutional point of view, there were three steps in constitutional evolution after the declaration of independence of the Czechoslovak Republic. The first step was carried out on the day that independence was declared, that is on 28 October 1918. It was the Act No 11/1918 Coll LR,[17] on the establishment of the autonomous Czechoslovak state, which provided for a transitional basic legal system until the interim constitution was adopted. This Act also contained a so-called 'reception norm', that is a provision accepting all valid Austro-Hungarian law into the legal system of the newly established Czechoslovak state. This provision is a source of the strong influence of Austrian-Hungarian law on Czechoslovak law.

The Interim Constitution of the Czechoslovak Republic was adopted very soon after, on 13 November 1918, under Act No 37/1918 Coll LR The Interim Constitution established a democratic republic with a very strong Parliament (National Assembly), which was the central and most powerful institution.

The transitional period ended on 29 February 1920 with the adoption of the Constitutional Charter of the Czechoslovak Republic.[18] This constitution was strongly admired throughout the world for its extraordinary democratic features and was considered one of the best in the interwar period.[19] Its status within the Czechoslovak Republic was no less positive, which resulted in its exceptional stability and the strong respect in which that Constitution was held. The Constitutional Charter of 1920 was also the primary source of inspiration for the Czechoslovak Constitution of 1948 and the Czech Constitution of 1992.

In the 28 years of its existence (1920–1948) the Constitutional Charter was never directly amended. Of the few indirect changes, only one was carried out

State; in 1968, the Czechoslovak Republic was transformed to a federation of the Czech Republic and the Slovak Republic; and finally, in 1992, the federation broke up, and the independent Czech Republic and Slovak Republic were created.

[17] Collection of Laws and Regulations.
[18] Act of 29 February 1920, No 121/1920 Coll LR, introducing the Constitutional Charter of the Czechoslovak Republic.
[19] Pavlíček, note 15 above, 53.

during the time of the First Republic (1918–1938). The majority of indirect changes were carried out through presidential decrees during and after World War II.[20]

The Constitutional Charter established a classical parliamentary form of government with the President having a weak constitutional position. However, the respect for the personality of TG Masaryk, who held the office of President in the years 1918 to 1935, made the real significance of the presidential office much stronger. A special feature, which was unique at the time of the adoption of the Constitutional Charter, was the specialised Constitutional Court.[21] The Czechoslovak and Austrian Constitutions, both adopted in 1920, were the first to introduce and successfully employ this special and important role for judicial power, based on Kelsen's normative theory,[22] and served as examples for later constitutions in this respect.

Another important feature of the Constitutional Charter was the strong protection of minorities. This was partly a consequence of the Versailles Peace Treaty, but also a response to memories of the weak position of minorities in the Austro-Hungarian Empire. Paradoxically, it was the German minority which significantly contributed to the end of the First Republic, encouraged by the Munich Pact of 1938.[23]

From Munich to Communism

The Munich Pact represented an external impediment to the sovereignty of the Czechoslovak Republic, which meant that its legitimate authorities could no longer freely exercise their power. Therefore, beginning from 30 September 1938, the period of non-freedom started.[24] There were two sets of constitutional authorities existing and acting simultaneously, but only one of them was legitimate. All acts of the non-legitimate authorities were retrospectively held to be null and void.[25] This dichotomy ended only at the end of World War II, when the Czechoslovak Republic re-acquired its sovereignty and the Constitutional Charter re-entered into force.

The Constitutional Charter of the Czechoslovak Republic did not and could not foresee such a situation, but it was nevertheless suited to deal with it. The

---

[20] Sovinský, 'Úvahy nad reformou Ústavy ČR', *Acta Iuridica Olomucensis*, Vol 3 (IX), 2008, No 5, 259.

[21] However, its real potential was not discovered during the First Republic. The Constitutional Court was established only for its first term of office (1921–31). Its activity was considered insignificant (due to weak competences) and therefore it was established for its second term only in 1938. During WWII it did not operate and after it was not re-established.

[22] J Blahož *Soudní kontrola ústavnosti*, Srovnávací pohled. (Praha: ASPI, 2001) 55.

[23] Sovinský, note 20 above, 259.

[24] Presidential decree No 11/1944, published under No 30/1945 Coll.

[25] At first those were authorities of the so-called Second Republic, and later of the Protectorate of Bohemia and Moravia.

Czechoslovak President, Edvard Beneš, who had been forced to resign on 5 October 1938, resumed his office abroad, in exile, and repealed the legislative measures of the non-legitimate authorities by issuing presidential decrees. The Czechoslovak parliament approved all presidential decrees by Constitutional Act No 57/1946 Coll, and thus they remain part of Czech legal system. They are an example of a constitutional reaction to destruction of a constitutional system by external influence and of a constitutional change carried out in complicated circumstances.

After World War II, the primary goal was to reconstruct the Czechoslovak constitutional system based on the Constitutional Charter of 1920. However, due to rivalry between foreign Czech representative bodies established in London and Moscow (representing democratic and communist ideas), it was not possible to achieve this goal. Instead, there was a widely accepted agreement on adopting a new constitution, which started to be prepared in 1946.

Unfortunately, the new constitution was adopted only after the Communist Party seized power in February of 1948, leading Czechoslovakia 'down the Soviet path using Soviet methods'.[26] It must be noted that this was not a typical illegal coup, as the Communist Party had to some extent used parliamentary and constitutional means to gain power. This was made possible by the result of 1946 election, in which the Communist Party achieved 43 per cent of votes in Bohemia and 34.5 per cent in Moravia, winning 93[27] out of a total of 300 seats in the National Assembly.[28] Even more importantly, its leader, Klement Gottwald, became the prime minister. In February 1948, a constitutional crisis arose. Twelve of the 26 members of the government resigned, as a reaction to one of the communist ministers not obeying the decision of the whole government—a breach of collective responsibility. This led to the reconstruction of the government, which was in the result controlled by the Communist Party.

Aside from this procedure, which strictly followed constitutional rules, a number of non-democratic actions were initiated by the Communist Party to put pressure on President Edvard Beneš, such as strikes, the creation of a People's Militia (Lidové Milice), an armed force of labour union members and the persecution of political opponents.[29] Under this pressure, combined with the fact that all of his decisions required the countersignature of a member of the government, the President was not able to oppose the communists, who eventually acquired the de facto power they were striving for.

[26] Pavlíček and Kindlová note 1 above II-12.
[27] It also had the support of the Communist Party of Slovakia, represented by another 21 mandates (deputies).
[28] Pavlíček, note 15 above, 180.
[29] Zimek, note 15 above, 141.

Communist Constitutionalism

The 1948 Constitution[30] was prepared after 1946 by several expert commissions. It was mostly based on the 1920 Constitutional Charter, but the influence of the Communist Party during the final phase of drafting diverted it significantly from democratic principles towards so-called 'people's democracy'. The most important change compared to the 1920 Constitution was the fact that the 1948 Constitution did not re-establish the Constitutional Court. That allowed the Communist Party to repeal constitutional provisions through ordinary acts and thus to create 'legalised repression'. For example, the 1948 Constitution contained a relatively wide catalogue of human rights. However, most of the fundamental rights were effectively denied by later ordinary acts or even subordinate legislation, which were obviously unconstitutional, but—in the absence of a Constitutional Court—there was no authority to set them aside. On the other hand, social, cultural and economic rights were guaranteed very broadly both in the Constitution and in reality, which corresponded with the aim of establishing socialism.

The basic features of the 1948 Constitution were rejection of the principle of separation of powers, a centrally controlled economy, stipulation of several types of ownership with different levels of protection, and recognition of the autonomy of the Slovak nation.[31] Even more important was the vast gap between constitutional reality and the constitutional text. Evasion and direct breaches of the Constitution by state authorities were the basic means used by the Communist Party to preserve and strengthen its power.

Several changes to the 1948 Constitution were made during the 1950s. Their aim was to remove some of the remaining democratic features in order to strengthen the dominance of the Communist Party. In this way, the government gained direct control of local governments, the independence of judges was abridged by provisions for them to be elected, and the general election was changed from a proportional to a majority system.[32]

In 1960, reflecting the shift in Soviet ideology, the Communist Party proclaimed that Czechoslovakia had already advanced to the stage of socialism, and therefore needed a new Constitution. After a rather quick drafting process, the 1960 Constitution was approved by the Central Committee of the Communist Party and only four days later, on 11 July 1960, the National Assembly unanimously adopted it as Constitutional Act No 100/1960 Coll, the Constitution of the Czechoslovak Socialist Republic, which immediately entered into force.

Paradoxically, the 1960 Constitution corresponded with constitutional reality much better than the 1948 Constitution. It resulted from application of Soviet

[30] Constitutional Act of 9 May 1945 No 150/1948 Coll, the Constitution of the Czechoslovak Republic.

[31] Zimek, note 15 above, 150.

[32] Pavlíček, note 15 above, 205–07.

constitutional theory and terminology, which, however, meant that the real legal value of the Constitution was negligible. It contained plenty of empty proclamations and was more an ideological than a legal document, which allowed for arbitrary and targeted application and interpretation.

The 1960 Constitution openly proclaimed the dominance of the working class and stipulated the leading role of the Communist Party in state and in society (Article 4 of the 1960 Constitution). The structure of state bodies was determined by the principle of the unity of state power, with the economy operating on the basis of socialist planning. Deputies were subject to mandate by the party, elections were manipulated. The autonomy of Slovaks and the competences of their representative bodies were significantly reduced.[33] This led to a growing demand for federalisation, which was finally realised through the Constitutional Act of 27 October 1968 No 143/1968 Coll, on the Czechoslovak Federation, even after the invasion of the occupational forces of the Warsaw Treaty. The trend towards democratisation, the so-called 'Prague Spring', was unfortunately stopped by the invasion, which brought so-called 'normalisation' instead.[34] The only remnants of democratic trends were provisions establishing the Constitutional Court which were included in the Constitutional Act on Czechoslovak Federation. However, they were not brought into effect until 1992.

Further amendments to the 1960 Constitution were adopted in 1970 and 1971 to centralise state power and to reduce the autonomy derived from federalisation. After that, constitutional development came to a standstill, which was in reality reflected by the gradual destabilisation of the communist regime. One of the important impulses was the ratification of the International Covenant on Civil and Political Rights by the communist regime in 1975, despite the systematic denial and abridging of these rights. The demand to respect these rights and fulfill them in reality was the basis for the Charta 77 movement.

In conclusion, it must be stressed that communist constitutionalism was clearly only another means of sustaining the totalitarian regime, while building an illusion of its legality and legitimacy. The discrepancy between the constitution and reality was replaced by the constitutional embodiment of the totalitarian regime. This approach is best illustrated by the statement of Klement Gottwald that the Constitution was an old skin, which had to be filled with fresh wine. All this devalued Czech constitutionalism and destroyed all confidence in the constitution, which had to be completely re-established after 1989.

---

[33] The autonomy of Slovaks was represented by the Slovak National Council, which was 'national authority of state power and government in Slovakia'. It could adopt laws binding for Slovak part of Czechoslovakia and had other competences, but they were not of much significance due to totalitarian nature of communist regime.

[34] Pavlíček, note 15 above, 226–27.

The Transition to Democracy

The fall of the communist regime on 17 November 1989 had to be reflected in constitutional changes. The first step was the abolition of the leading role of the Communist Party in Article 4 of the 1960 Constitution.[35] This was followed by changing the mandating of deputies by the Communist Party to a representative role and vesting sovereignty in the people, not the working class.[36]

Changes to the economic system were also needed. They were carried out by deleting the introductory proclamations on socialism in the Constitution; changing the general provisions of the 1960 Constitution; re-defining ownership; and introducing a free market economy.[37] Further changes were related to the abolition of the local authorities of central government (National Committees) and establishment of local self-government (municipal councils);[38] the re-establishment of political pluralism;[39] enacting a Charter of human rights;[40] establishing the Constitutional Court[41] and introducing provisions for a general referendum.[42]

Altogether, over 50 Constitutional Acts were adopted between November 1989 and December 1992, and this resulted in the destabilisation of the constitutional system overall. The focus of constitutional changes gradually shifted from transitional measures towards disputes regarding the division of competences between the federation and its members, resulting from the growing desire for independence of the Slovak Nation.[43] After the 1992 election, the federal concept was abandoned. On 1 September 1992, the Slovak Constitution was adopted, which meant the de facto secession of Slovakia from the federation and consequently the break-up of the federation. Unlike in other socialist federations (for example, Yugoslavia), this process was peaceful, carried out legally[44] and based on negotiations between the political representatives of the two nations.

---

[35] Constitutional Act No 135/1989 Coll, on change of the Constitution.

[36] Constitutional Act No 46/1990 Coll, on change of the Constitution and Constitutional Act No 143/1968 Coll.

[37] Constitutional Act No 100/1990 Coll, on change of the Constitution and Constitutional Act No 143/1968 Coll.

[38] Constitutional Act No 294/1990 Coll, on change of the Constitution and Constitutional Act No 143/1968 Coll.

[39] Constitutional Act No 376/1990 Coll, on change of the Constitution.

[40] Constitutional Act No 23/1991 Coll, the Charter of Fundamental Rights and Freedoms.

[41] Constitutional Act No 91/1991 Coll, on the Constitutional Court of the Czech and Slovak Federal Republic.

[42] Constitutional Act No 327/1991 Coll, on referenda; unfortunately, this federal law was not transferred to the Czech legal system.

[43] Pavlíček and Kindlová, note 1 above, II-16.

[44] Constitutional Act No 542/1992 Coll, on dissolution of the Czech and Slovak Federal Republic, and Constitutional Act No 541/1992 Coll, on the division of the property of the Czech and Slovak Federal Republic between the Czech Republic and the Slovak Republic and its transfer to the Czech Republic and the Slovak Republic.

Maxim Tomoszek

RULES FOR CHANGING THE CONSTITUTION

Any part of the Czech constitutional order can be changed *formally* through an act of the legislature or in an *informal* way, usually through the exercise of judicial power or through practice. Formal changes can be either by *direct* amendments of the respective act or *indirectly* by the adoption of a new Constitutional Act, but without changing the text of the existing act, on the basis of the rule *lex posterior derogat priori*.[45] Formal change can thus create a new constitutional law in the form of a separate Constitutional Act, for example, the Constitutional Act on Security of the Czech Republic.

Formal changes to the Czech constitutional order, that is the adoption of Constitutional Acts, are subject to a more complicated procedure than adoption of an ordinary act, which means that the Czech constitution is a *rigid* or inflexible one, at least from the formal point of view. However, in reality the Czech Constitution is changed relatively often (in the 18 years of its existence it has been directly amended six times).

Some scholars in the area of constitutional law criticise the low level of de facto rigidity or inflexibility of the Czech Constitution[46] when compared to other constitutions which require a referendums or dissolution of the Parliament and approval of the newly elected one before a formal constitutional change can take place.[47] An example of insufficient rigidity was the change of the Czech Constitution which took place on 11 September 2009.[48] A constitutional bill introduced by the Senate in 2006, having rested forgotten in the unfinished legislative procedure within the Chamber of Deputies, was suddenly resurrected, changed through amendment by one of the deputies and approved by both Chamber of Deputies and Senate on the same day. It was adopted as a direct reaction of the Parliament to the decision of the Constitutional Court, which set aside the Constitutional Act No 195/2009 Coll, on shortening the term of office of the Chamber of Deputies. This 'reaction' Constitutional Act was a direct textual change of the Czech Constitution in its Article 35. It added a new procedure leading to dissolution of the Chamber of Deputies as a result of its own resolution adopted by qualified majority of Deputies.

The main differences between adopting an ordinary act and a Constitutional Act are as follows:

---

[45] 'More recent law prevails over earlier law'. Klíma et al, note 5 above, 849.
[46] J Syllová, 'Souvislosti a následky nedostatečné rigidity Ústavy ČR', in B Dančák and V Šimíček (eds) *Aktuálnost změn Ústavy ČR*, (Brno: MU, MPÚ, 1999) 37 (32–37).
[47] J Matulík, 'Stabilita ústavy a legitimita její změny, aneb co postrádáme v textu návrhu ústavních změn', in B Dančák and V Šimíček (eds) *Aktuálnost změn Ústavy ČR*, (Brno: MU, MPÚ, 1999) 39–41 (38–43).
[48] Constitutional Act No 319/2009 Coll, which amends Constitutional Act No 1/1993 Coll, the Constitution of the Czech Republic, as amended.

1. Both chambers of the Parliament must express their approval of the Constitutional Act, while in the case of ordinary acts the Chamber of Deputies may override the disapproval of the Senate.
2. The approval must be expressed by qualified majority, that is three-fifths of all deputies and three-fifths of senators present at the session.[49]
3. In the case of ordinary acts, the bill is passed even if the Senate does not report on it, which results in adoption of the bill by the Chamber of Deputies alone;[50] this is not possible in the case of constitutional bills: the Senate has the obligation to report on such bills.
4. The 30 days period, in which the Senate must decide on whether to report on ordinary bills, does not apply to constitutional bills.
5. The President cannot apply his veto to Constitutional Acts.

Otherwise, the procedure for constitutional bills is similar to standard legislative procedure, going through three readings in the Chamber of Deputies. The procedure in the Senate is not divided into readings, but still there is place for discussion in committees and for proposing amendments.

A constitutional bill may be proposed by a Deputy or a group of Deputies, the Senate, the government or a representative assembly of a region. This further emphasises the stronger position of the Chamber of Deputies in the legislative process, because a single member of the Senate cannot introduce a bill, in contrast to the single Deputy, who has the competence to do so.

The legislative procedure for constitutional bills starts in the Chamber of Deputies, which may alter the bill through amendments; only after its approval is the constitutional bill forwarded to the Senate. The Senate may either approve it (in which case it is adopted) or disapprove it (in which case it is rejected) or it may propose amendments to the bill. In that case the bill returns to the Chamber of Deputies, which has the final say. It may either approve the constitutional bill, including the Senate's amendments (in which case it is adopted) or disapprove it (in which case the bill is rejected).

In 2008, there was a proposal for an act to regulate relations between the Chamber of Deputies and Senate, which contained a 'navette' system, allowing the bill to go back and forth between the chambers and to be changed in the process. It was criticised for further decreasing the rigidity of the constitution.[51] It also contained also other controversial issues, which led to its rejection.

---

[49] A qualified majority is also required for parliamentary assent to ratification of international treaties which transfer competences of Czech authorities to international organisations.

[50] In this case, the approval of the Senate is implied. The Senate must approve or disapprove ordinary bills approved by the Chamber of Deputies in 30 days; if it does not, the bill is considered to be approved by the Senate. The Senate can also pass a resolution that it will not deal with the bill, which has the same effect, except that the 30 days period does not have to pass, so that the bill goes immediately to the president.

[51] J Syllová, 'Malý letní útok na rigiditu Ústavy', *Právní zpravodaj*, Vol 2008, No 8, 13.

It is also remarkable that the Senate, which is overall the weaker chamber, acquires a much more significant role in relation to the adoption of Constitutional Acts. It even allows the Senate to trade-off its support for constitutional bills which have been approved by the Chamber of Deputies for the expansion of the Senate's competences. This was the case with the Constitutional Act on Security of the Czech Republic, which had to be adopted due to the proposed accession of the Czech Republic to NATO. By this act, the Senate gained wider competences in security issues and also in situations in which the Chamber of Deputies could be dissolved.[52]

However, the key stage of debates about constitutional change takes place in the Chamber of Deputies. In total, in the period since 1993, the Chamber of Deputies has approved 20 constitutional bills and sent them to the Senate. Of these, the Senate has approved 13, rejected four, and sent three back to the Chamber of Deputies with amendments. Of these three, only one was approved by the Chamber of Deputies; the other two were rejected.[53] Only two of the adopted Constitutional Acts were proposed by the Senate. This means that, once a constitutional bill is approved by the Chamber of Deputies, its chances of becoming a binding Constitutional Act are around 70 per cent.

Apart from procedural rules, there are also rules dealing with the content of Constitutional Acts. The basic rules are stipulated in Article 9 of the Czech Constitution. Its first paragraph states that the 'Constitution may be supplemented or amended only by Constitutional Acts'. This means that any changes to the Czech Constitution itself must be adopted in the form of a Constitutional Act. The word *supplemented*, that is widening the scope of constitutional laws, means that virtually anything can be regulated by the Constitutional Act, but this is not without limits.

According to the text of Article 9 paragraph 1 of the Czech Constitution, this applies to the Constitution meaning the Constitutional Act No 1/1993 Coll. However, from the logic of the constitutional order it is clear that these rules apply in the same way to all Constitutional Acts. Newly adopted Constitutional Acts may contain provisions which are inconsistent with provisions of existing Constitutional Acts (that is one of the purposes of adopting Constitutional Acts—to amend existing Constitutional Acts). The only provisions they must not change, that is they must be consistent with, are the provisions mentioned in Article 9 paragraph 2 of the Czech Constitution. It states: 'Change of the essential requisites of the democratic legal state is inadmissible',[54] which brings into the

---

[52] J Syllová, P Kolář, J Kysela, et al *Parlament České republiky*, 2nd edn (Praha: Linde, 2008) 256.

[53] R Suchánek and V Jirásková, Ústava České republiky v praxi. 15 let platnosti základního zákona, (Praha: Leges, 2009) 144.

[54] The phrase *democratic legal state* is a literal translation of the Czech phrase 'demokratický právní stát'. The words legal state (právní stát) should be understood as similarly to the German concept of Rechtstaat, which is in its principles very similar to the concept of rule of law. However, these concepts are not completely equivalent; therefore the literal translation 'legal state' is used to emphasise the difference when appropriate.

Czech constitutional system an eternity clause similar to the *Ewigkeitsklausel* in Article 79 paragraph 3 of the German Basic Law.

There was lengthy debate as to the practical meaning of this provision. As no enforcement mechanism was attached to it, it seemed to be a purely declaratory provision. It could however be regarded as an instruction to the Senate, which is supposed to be the 'correcting agent' with responsibility for revising legislation passed by the Chamber of Deputies. However, the Senate failed to perform this role, as is illustrated by the case of Constitutional Act No 195/2009 Coll, which provided for shortening the term of office of the Chamber of Deputies. This uncertainty as to the status of Article 9 was resolved by the decision of the Constitutional Court Pl ÚS 27/09,[55] by which the Constitutional Court set aside Constitutional Act No 195/2009 Coll and thus assumed for itself the role of protector of Article 9 paragraph 2 of the Czech Constitution.

The Czech Constitution requires some issues to be regulated by Constitutional Acts—the state borders, the establishment or abolition of higher territorial self-governing (regional) units and referenda at national level. It may therefore seem strange that there are two ordinary acts regulating the referendum at the level of municipality and region. This is explained by the fact that these referenda can only deal with matters of self-government, whose legitimacy and source are different from those of state level power. The Czech Constitution in Article 2 paragraph 2 requires the use of Constitutional Acts only when the people directly exercise *state power* (for example, the referendum on accession to the EU). Proposals for the general regulation of referenda at national level have been the commonest subject of constitutional bills, but no Constitutional Act on referenda has yet been adopted.

The normal rule is that Acts must be general, that is they should apply to an indeterminate number of future situations; they must have normative (regulatory) content; they have to be clear and definite; and they must conform to requirements of legal certainty and legitimate expectations. Each Act should also be monothematic, dealing with a single issue. These general rules, which are not stipulated by any formal legislation, but rather derive from the nature of legal rules themselves, were formulated in legal theory and further interpreted and applied by the Constitutional Court.[56] The single issue requirement was often not observed, as the Parliament had developed the bad habit of adopting acts

---

[55] Pl ÚS stands for the decision adopted in the Plenary session of the Constitutional Court; for more detailed analysis of this decision, see below in the following section.

[56] For an overview of the theoretical basis see eg J Filip, 'Legislativní technika a judikatura Ústavního soudu', *Časopis pro právní vědu a praxi*, Vol 13 (2005), No 3, 242–245, P Mlsna, 'Vláda jako materiální zákonodárce a bezmocný hybatel proměn právního řádu' in R Šínová (ed) *Olomoucké právnické dny 2008. Sborník příspěvků z konference*, (Olomouc: Iuridicum Olomoucense, 2008) 78; the fundamental cases of the Czech Constitutional Court in this area are Pl ÚS 36/05, Pl ÚS 77/06, Pl ÚS 2/08, Pl ÚS 24/08 and Pl ÚS 27/09.

containing so-called *legislative riders*, that is provisions added through amendments during the legislative process, and introduced although completely uncon-
nected to the bill at hand.[57] Fortunately, this problem does not affect
Constitutional Acts. The problem of legislative riders grew to such extent that the
Constitutional Court had to step in and repeal a couple of Acts breaching this
requirement.[58] Since then, the problem has diminished as the single issue
requirement is much more rigorously observed by the Parliament.

Informal changes of the constitutional order also take place which do not
follow any strict procedure and are not the product of a legislative process. They
do result from the practical application of the constitution. The basic two types
of informal change are constitutional conventions and the case law of the Czech
Constitutional Court.

Constitutional conventions developed by practice usually fill in the gaps in the
constitution. For example, the Czech Constitution does not explicitly determine
who should be appointed by the President as a prime minister after the election
of the Chamber of Deputies. Until now, the President has always respected the
unwritten rule that he should appoint the leader of the party which acquired
most seats in the election. However, in the 2010 election the social democrats
won the most seats, but were not in a position to form a government, so after
consultation with their leader (Bohuslav Sobotka) confirming their inability to
create a government, the President asked the leader of the Civic Democratic Party
(Petr Nečas) to start negotiations to form a government.

Informal changes of the constitution deriving from the case law of the Czech
Constitutional Court[59] are made through constitutional interpretation. They
usually provide a way out of a very complicated situation created by the
imperfect constitutional legislation. Particular cases will be analysed below.

FORMAL CHANGES TO THE CONSTITUTION

Due to the principle of discontinuity of the legislative process, all bills (including
constitutional bills) must be adopted within a single term of office of the
Chamber of Deputies.[60] Terms of office of the Chamber of Deputies[61] also show

---

[57] See R Suchánek and V Jirásková, note 53 above, 139–41.
[58] The leading case in this respect is Pl ÚS 77/06.
[59] The most important decisions of the Czech Constitutional Court have been translated into
English and may be accessed at the website of the Czech Constitutional Court http://www.usoud.cz/
view/726.
[60] This cannot apply to the Senate, as election is always only partial—every two years, one third of
senators is elected. Moreover, the Senate cannot be dissolved.
[61] The terms of office of the Chamber of Deputies are divided by elections and went as follows:
First Term: 1 January 1993–31 May 1996; Second Term: 1 June 1996–19 June 1998; Third Term: 20
June 1998–14 June 2002; Fourth Term: 15 June 2002–2 June 2006; Fifth Term: 3 June 2006–28 May
2010; Sixth Term: started on 29 May 2010.

different common themes regarding constitutional changes and therefore are a good basis for analysis.

As has already been mentioned above, there have been a total of 105 proposals for the adoption of Constitutional Acts since 1993, 14 of which were successful.[62]

This number is more or less evenly divided into particular terms of office of the Chamber of Deputies and is usually around 20, with the only exception of the third term, when 29 constitutional bills were proposed. It is also worth noticing that in the second term, which lasted only two years, the number of constitutional bills was in the same range as in other terms, and the number of adopted Constitutional Acts was actually highest of all terms.

Almost 70 per cent of constitutional bills were introduced by deputies, but only 6 per cent of them were successful. The government and the Senate, although not being as active as deputies, are much more successful. Twenty-two per cent of the constitutional bills proposed by the Senate and 38 per cent of constitutional bills introduced by the government were adopted. The legislative initiative vested in representative assemblies of regions has proven marginal, at least in the area of Constitutional Acts. The lack of constitutional bills introduced by the Senate and Regions in years 1993 to 1998 results from the fact, that the Senate was established in 1996 and the regions in 2000.When analysing the timeline, it is interesting that there was no constitutional change during the first four years after the Czech Constitution was adopted. The time for drafting the Czech Constitution was rather short as a result of the dissolution of the Czechoslovak federation. Moreover, the final outcomes were determined by a number of political trade-offs.[63] Not only did this result in the Czech Constitution being short, but there were also numerous problems concerning interpretation, legislative lacunae or clear mistakes made during the drafting or legislative process. Another consequence was the huge pressure put on the legislators, which resulted in the impossibility of achieving consensus on certain questions, which should have been part of the constitution, but were not included in the constitution at that time (referendum, human rights, territorial self-government, and provisional Senate). The human rights problem was solved by including the

---

[62] Of these, there were the six direct amendments of the Czech Constitution (No 347/1997 Coll, No 300/2000 Coll, 395/2001 Coll, 448/2001 Coll, 515/2002 Coll, 319/2009 Coll) and one direct amendment of the Charter (No 162/1998 Coll). Further there were the Constitutional Act No 74/1997 Coll, on the change of state borders with the Slovak Republic; Constitutional Act No 347/1997 Coll, on the Establishment of Higher Territorial Self-governing Units (amended by Constitutional Act No 176/2001 Coll); Constitutional act No 69/1998 Coll, on shortening of the term of office of the Chamber of Deputies; Constitutional act No 110/1998 Coll, on the Security of the Czech Republic; Constitutional Act No 515/2002 Coll, on a Referendum on Accession of the Czech Republic to the European Union; Constitutional Act No 76/2004 Coll, on the change of the state borders with the Austrian Republic; Constitutional Act No 633/2004 Coll, on the change of the state borders with the Federal Republic of Germany; Constitutional Act No 195/2009 Coll, on shortening of the term of office of the Chamber of Deputies; this Constitutional Act was set aside by the decision of the Constitutional Court of 10 September 2009, Pl ÚS 27/09.

[63] J Jirásek, 'Okolnosti vypracování a přijetí Ústavy České republiky' in R Šínová (ed) *Olomoucké právnické dny 2008. Sborník příspěvků z konference,* (Olomouc: Iuridicum Olomoucense, 2008) 52–53.

Charter in the constitutional order (see earlier discussion), but all other issues were left for later regulation by Constitutional Acts.

In this situation, it may seem surprising that none of the 16 proposed constitutional bills were finally adopted, especially because during the first term of the Chamber of Deputies, the Senate was not established and therefore the whole legislative procedure took place in one chamber. However, it must be stressed that the Chamber of Deputies in its first term was not newly elected, but was drawn from members of the Czech National Council, that is the legislative body of the Czech Republic within the Czechoslovak Federation. The Czech National Council was the body which adopted the Czech Constitution. This gives the clear explanation of the unwillingness to change the constitution—the Chamber of Deputies was protecting the outcome of its own work.[64] The subject matter of constitutional bills introduced in the first term of the Chamber of Deputies shows that they were proposed with the intention to implement provisions of the Czech Constitution (referendum, self-government, interim Senate) or to reverse unpopular constitutional provisions (abolition of the Senate). As none of the constitutional bills proposed in the first term were successful, the Constitutional Act establishing higher territorial self-governing units called Regions was adopted only in 1997 and entered into force on 1 January 2000. The general regulation of referenda at the national level has still not been adopted, despite the fact that 25 constitutional bills (24 per cent of total) have been dedicated to this issue.

The lack of success in the first term was compensated for in the second term, which lasted only two years, but was the most productive up to the present day, with five Constitutional Acts adopted. Two of them fulfilled constitutional requirements—one established regions and the other defined the border between the Czech Republic and Slovakia. The Constitutional Act on Security was required by accession to NATO and also corrected some inaccuracies in the Constitution. The Constitutional Act on Shortening the Term of Office of the Chamber of Deputies was an ad hoc solution to a complicated political situation in Parliament. Moreover, as the decision of the Constitutional Court Pl ÚS 27/09 shows, that act was unconstitutional. An amendment of the Charter was also adopted, extending the time of detention without charge from 24 to 48 hours. The main argument for this change was to make the work of police easier, but surprisingly it did not arouse any serious discussion.

The third term brought the most extensive change of the Czech Constitution, the so-called Euro-amendment, which prepared the Czech Republic for accession to the EU. It also significantly changed the position of international law from a dualistic to a monistic approach with a general incorporation clause and acceptance of the supremacy of international law. The other three Constitutional Acts were also amendments of the existing Constitutional Acts, although much less

---

[64] J Syllová, P Kolář, J Kysela et al note 52 above, 255.

extensive. They concerned dispatching and accepting military forces to and from abroad, changing the goal of the Czech National Bank from stability of currency to stability of prices[65] and changes in the names of regions.

In the fourth term, the Constitutional Act on a Referendum on Accession of the Czech Republic to the EU was adopted and also implemented. The other two Constitutional Acts concerned the change of state borders with Austria and Germany. The fifth term could be called a disgrace as far as constitutional change was concerned. Although there were several very promising constitutional bills, in the end a second Constitutional Act shortening the term of the Chamber of Deputies was adopted, and then set aside by the Constitutional Court. Parliament reacted to that by adopting the quickest ever constitutional change, introducing a new way to dissolve the Chamber of Deputies.

Analysis of subject areas of constitutional bills shows that they fall into two groups: in the words of the vice-president of the Czech Constitutional Court Professor Pavel Holländer, in his lecture held in Olomouc on 13 May 2010—the evergreens and neuroses. The evergreens are the four most common subject areas of constitutional bills (together 62 per cent of all proposed constitutional bills), that is referenda (general regulation on national level or referenda on a specific problem) with 25 bills, self-government with 16 bills,[66] President with 11 bills[67] (direct election or change of competences), and immunity of deputies, senators and sometimes constitutional judges with 13 bills. These constitutional bills are introduced in almost every term in many variants, but (with the exception of regional self-government) these issues remain unsolved. The first five constitutional bills proposed after the 2010 election aim to regulate exactly these four areas. Their fate is however unpredictable, as these bills are mostly unsuccessful—only three of 65 constitutional bills on these three subject areas were adopted during years 1993 to 2010.

The neuroses are current, pressing problems, which politicians are unable to solve in any other way than by proposing a constitutional bill. A good example would be Constitutional Acts on shortening the term of office of the Chamber of Deputies or the constitutional amendment introducing a new way to dissolve the Chamber of Deputies, noted above.

This overview clearly shows that most of the successful constitutional changes have been forced or required by some external influence and that discussion about them has concerned mostly how or what to change, not whether the change should be carried out at all. These are changes of state borders, which had already been agreed upon in an international treaty, or accession to the EU or NATO.

[65] This change resulted from binding the Czech Crown to the Euro.
[66] The issue of self-government was evergreen only until approximately 2000. At that time most important questions had been solved and there was no need to re-open them.
[67] The Presidency started to be an evergreen topic of constitutional change in 2002 when Václav Klaus was elected and did not continue in the 'constitutional manners' of Václav Havel.

So far, most adopted constitutional changes appear of limited relevance. The content of some of the constitutional bills which have not been adopted seems more important, which might be precisely the reason why they have not been adopted. Probably the most pressing need for change of the Czech Constitution is perceived in connection with the role of the President. This perception results from complications which arise at every election, the expansive interpretation of presidential competences by Václav Klaus and the unaccountability of the President. Dealing with all of these issues requires very extensive changes to the Czech Constitution, essentially even re-considering the overall balance between constitutional institutions and maybe even changing the form of government to semi-presidential. Dealing with the unaccountability of the President would probably also require change to the immunities of Deputies and Senators, maybe even of judges in order to preserve the balance and proportionality of legitimacy, competences and immunities.[68]

INFORMAL CHANGES TO THE CONSTITUTION THROUGH THE CASE LAW OF THE CONSTITUTIONAL COURT

Euro-amendment and International Treaties on Human Rights

The so-called Euro-amendment of the Czech Constitution, which was adopted to prepare the Czech Republic for accession to the EU, has been the most extensive and most important constitutional amendment in the Czech Republic. A number of very good and rational solutions were implemented by this Constitutional Act. However, it also incidentally induced a serious problem, which was soon identified and dealt with by the Czech Constitutional Court.

The Euro-amendment incorporated all ratified international treaties into the legal system of the Czech Republic and stipulated their superiority over domestic acts. In case of conflict between an international treaty and a domestic act, the international treaty is to be directly applied. This is a very effective legal device for the proper domestic application of international law.

The Czech Constitutional Court spotted a potential problem regarding international treaties on human rights. The above-mentioned law would give every court jurisdiction to resolve conflicts between an international treaty and a domestic act. However, this would have several problematic consequences.

1. There would not be a single binding ruling concerning a domestic act violating internationally protected human rights, so the outcome could be different in every case depending on the opinion of the deciding court.
2. The domestic act in conflict with an international treaty on human rights could not be struck down by the Constitutional Court, so it would remain

---

[68] D Havránek, 'Přímo volený prezident republiky—nad návrhem novely Ústavy', *Právní zpravodaj*, Vol 2 (2008) 16.

part of the legal system ready for future use; the only way of setting it aside would be through the legislative process in the Parliament.

3. This approach would in fact mean reducing the level of protection of human rights compared to the situation before the Euro-amendment, when the Constitutional Court could strike down a domestic act in case of conflict with an international treaty on human rights.

The whole situation was made even more complicated by the fact that human rights are not only protected in international agreements, but in the Charter as well. There would be an unjustified difference in the protection of human rights stipulated by the Charter and by international treaties.

The Czech Constitutional Court found an elegant solution to this problem. If international treaties on human rights were perceived as part of the constitutional order, all the above-mentioned problems would be eliminated. In case of conflict between a domestic act and an international treaty, all courts would have to bring the case to the Constitutional Court, which could give a binding and final ruling on the question and strike down the domestic act if necessary. Moreover, international treaties on human rights would then be on the same level, as the Charter.

However, in order to implement this solution the Czech Constitutional Court had to interpret the Czech Constitution contrary to the explicit wording of its Article 112, which defines the constitutional order as the sum of all Constitutional Acts. According to the Constitutional Court, international treaties on human rights must be perceived as a part of the constitutional order. In this way the Czech Constitutional Court, which is (consistently with continental legal tradition) described as a negative legislator, achieved a change in the Czech Constitution, which would otherwise be possible only through a Constitutional Act.

This decision of the Constitutional Court was seriously criticised and it took a long time before it was accepted by constitutional experts. According to critics,[69] the Constitutional Court misused its power and unacceptably interfered with the power of the legislature, not to mention the fact that this interpretation was expressed in obiter dictum, which means that the issue was not the object of the proceedings. Today, this decision of the Constitutional Court and its consequences are still not universally accepted.[70]

---

[69] J Filip, Nález č. 403/2002 Sb. jako rukavice hozená zákonodárci Ústavním soudem, *Právní zpravodaj*, No 11, Vol 2002, 12–15, Z Kühn, J Kysela, Je Ústavou vždy to, co Ústavní soud řekne, že Ústava je? *Časopis pro právní vědu a praxi*, No 3, Vol 2002, 199–214 and others.

[70] It was accepted eg by Klíma et al, note 5 above, 122–23, and it is still criticised by Sládeček, Mikule and Syllová, note 5 above, 83.

Shortening the Term of Office of the Chamber of Deputies

An even more controversial decision of the Constitutional Court came in September 2009, declaring a Constitutional Act contrary to the constitution order and setting it aside on that basis. The story started on 28 May 2009, when the Czech Parliament adopted Constitutional Act No 195/2009 Coll, on shortening the term of office of the Chamber of Deputies. This Constitutional Act suspended several provisions of the Czech Constitution and electoral law to solve a political crisis through an early, pre-term election.

A similar Constitutional Act adopted in 1998[71] started a lively discussion and was heavily criticised,[72] but since it was not challenged before the Constitutional Court, it was fully carried out and it is still part of the Czech legal system (and constitutional order). However, in 2005 the vice-president of the Czech Constitutional Court, Pavel Holländer, published an article in the prominent Czech legal journal, *Právník*, in which he clearly demonstrated that this act was contrary to Article 9 paragraph 2 of the Czech Constitution and that any similar act adopted in future would have to be set aside, if it were challenged before the Constitutional Court.[73]

And indeed, this particular scenario actually took place in September 2009, producing the most important decision of the Czech Constitutional Court in the whole time of its existence.

One of the deputies, whose term of office was to be shortened by Constitutional Act No 195/2009 Coll, Miloš Melčák, filed a constitutional complaint asking for the setting aside of this law and thus preventing the pre-term election. He objected that the act interfered with his right to exercise elected public office, that it was retroactive and that it violated Article 9 paragraph 2 of the Czech Constitution.

The first serious problem that the Constitutional Court had to solve was whether it had jurisdiction to decide the case. The constitution does not empower the Constitutional Court to decide on Constitutional Acts; on the contrary, the Czech Constitution explicitly states that the justices of the Constitutional Court are bound by Constitutional Acts. However, without an effective mean of protection Article 9 paragraph 2 of the Czech Constitution would be meaningless, therefore the Constitutional Court decided to take the case on. Its arguments for doing so were quite weak, making it one of the weakest points of the decision.[74]

[71] Constitutional Act No 69/1998 Coll, on shortening of the term of office of the Chamber of Deputies.
[72] J Filip 'Zkrácení volebního období ad hoc?' *Parlamentní zpravodaj*, Vol 1997, No 12, 132–34, J Filip, 'Rozpuštění Poslanecké sněmovny', *Časopis pro právní vědu a praxi*, Vol 1998, No 1, 48–57.
[73] P Holländer, 'Materiální ohnisko ústavy a diskrece ústavodárce', *Právník*, Vol 144 (2005), No 4, 313–36.
[74] J Kudrna, Počátek nového pojetí 'ochrany ústavnosti' v České republice. *Acta Iuridica Olomucensis*, Vol 2009, No 7, 344–45.

Regarding the substantive controversy contained in the case at hand, the Constitutional Court stated three requirements, which must be cumulatively fulfilled for a Constitutional Act to be valid—procedural, material and the existence of competence. According to the Constitutional Court, the legislative procedure had been duly carried out and there was no problem of competence. In this particular case, it held, the material requirement was not fulfilled.

The Constitutional Court identified several reasons which rendered the challenged Constitutional Act unconstitutional. First, it was individual in its nature, not general, as a piece of legislation should be. It did not introduce any new law, but just suspended certain existing provisions of the Czech Constitution and other laws. This resulted in breach of Article 9 paragraph 1 of the Czech Constitution, which allows for Constitutional Acts to amend or supplement the constitution, but not to suspend it. Secondly, the act in question was held to be retroactive, because it altered rules for the termination of the performance of an elected function only after the representatives had been elected. Thirdly, the challenged act circumvented the existing constitutional regulation of the dissolution of the Chamber of Deputies, which again is in breach of Article 9 paragraphs 1 and 2 of the Czech Constitution.

This decision was severely criticised by politicians, who were already in the middle of the electoral campaign for the pre-term election, and also by constitutionalists due to weaknesses in the argumentation of the Constitutional Court, its activist approach and inadmissible interference with competence of the Parliament.[75] However, it is hard to imagine that the Constitutional Court would have decided in any other way, taking into account the rigorous argumentation given by Holländer[76] and also the risk of legitimising a negative precedent allowing Parliament to adopt a Constitutional Act violating some of the most fundamental principles of Czech constitutional system.

The issue of legitimacy which was raised poses a serious problem, because in case of conflict between Parliament and the Constitutional Court, the Czech Constitution strongly prioritises the directly elected Parliament. The Constitutional Court is aware of this problem and it perceives its decision as an exceptional, though necessary action which it was forced to carry out in order to protect the constitution and to draw boundaries against the growing disrespect in Parliament for fundamental legal and constitutional principles.

In this case, we may also see a strong parallel with the German Federal Constitutional Court, which, in the so-called Article 10 case, declared its readiness to declare any constitutional amendment contrary to the eternity clause to

---

[75] J Kudrna, Počátek nového pojetí 'ochrany ústavnosti' v České republice. *Acta Iuridica Olomucensis*, Vol 2009, No 7, 339–52.

[76] P Holländer, Materiální ohnisko ústavy a diskrece ústavodárce. *Právník*, Vol 144 (2005), No 4, 313–36.

be unconstitutional.[77] This position is quite understandable in the light of decreasing trust in the law-makers, based on a number of disconcerting misuses of their power during the twentieth century, especially regarding human rights.[78]

CONCLUSIONS

To conclude, the most discussed, probably most needed and certainly most complex changes of the Czech Constitution are still to be made. It is a part of the Czech political tradition to try to force some trade-offs when adopting Constitutional Acts, which results from the qualified majority requirement being especially hard to achieve considering the almost equal representation of left-wing and right-wing parties on the Czech political scene. In fact, even the most recent election did not produce a majority commanding enough votes to amend the constitution (which can be regarded as fortunate or unfortunate according to one's opinion on the merits). Therefore there is not much chance of success for the constitutional bills which have so far been introduced.

The Czech Constitution has still not undergone significant and complex changes, not even those which appear necessary for several reasons—to correct some inaccuracies which were in the Czech Constitution from the beginning, to introduce direct election of the President and re-define his constitutional position, and to reduce the immunities of constitutional officers and others. There are also some debts still to be paid to the 'fathers' of the Czech Constitution (and also to the international obligations of the Czech Republic), such as the constitutional regulation of national referenda. These seem the most likely candidates for future changes or additions to the constitutional order of the Czech Republic.

The activist approach of the Constitutional Court is also striking. The Court has not hesitated to adopt very expansive interpretations of laws, or even to interfere with the legislative power of the Parliament, in order to protect the Constitution. Its decision repealing the Constitutional Act on shortening the term of the Chamber of Deputies was strongly criticised by politicians from across the political scene. Czech President Václav Klaus has even asked the Parliament to limit the competences of the Constitutional Court, to prevent it from becoming all-powerful. The Constitutional Court can resist these attempts by setting aside acts that would limit its competences, but this may in the end lead politicians to limit the Constitutional Court in the only way it cannot resist—by carefully choosing its members in such a way that they will exercise the office according to wishes of the politicians. If the Constitutional Court could be manipulated by politicians, then its strong competences, based on precedents described in this chapter, would be a real threat allowing the Constitutional

---

[77] DP Kommers, 'Germany: Balancing Rights and Duties', in J Goldsworthy (ed) *Interpreting Constitutions. A Comparative Study*, (Oxford: Oxford University Press, 2006) 172.

[78] T Koopmans *Courts and Political Institutions. A Comparative View*, (Cambridge: Cambridge University Press, 2003) 33.

Court to seriously disrupt the balance of the whole constitutional system. This means that the Constitutional Court should to some degree defer to Parliament, and at the same time fully respect the Constitution and try to avoid or limit excessive confrontations with Parliament.

Overall, the Czech Constitution has proven itself to be a concise document that is general enough in its terms to allow a solution to be found to almost any difficult situation. This also results in increasing consensus and respect for the Czech Constitution and cherishing of its stability as a value, thus rehabilitating Czech constitutionalism after 40 years of communism. It is to be hoped that future changes will be well considered and will further contribute to the quality of the Czech Constitution.

4

The European Union

RENAUD DEHOUSSE

INTRODUCTION

EVEN TODAY, REFERENCES to a constitution, or even to constitutionalism, in relation to the European Union are a matter of dispute. Some stress that not being a state, the EU cannot possibly have a constitution; others that it is not even desirable that it be given one. The ambiguity of the 'Draft Treaty establishing a European Constitution' was used by its detractors to depict a drift towards a European superstate, which contributed to convincing French and Dutch voters to reject the project in the referenda organised in their respective countries. This notwithstanding, looking at the construction of Europe using constitutional lenses is quite useful to make sense of such a complex process. First, the idea of a European Constitution has been a constant reference point in this process—an objective for some, a project to oppose for others. It therefore provides us with a good marker to study the stops and starts of the integration process. Moreover, a key feature of the European brand of regional integration has been the subjection of state sovereignty to a degree of supranational control, which, no matter how one wants to qualify it, comes close to a kind of 'supranational constitutionalism'. Secondly, even though the rules governing Treaty change are quite conservative, unanimity being required for any amendment, the EU system has been characterised by a remarkable dynamism, particularly in the last 25 years. Understanding the dynamics of change also enables us to understand the peculiar nature of a process in which states, while formally remaining the masters of the treaty, have been forced to accept a steady erosion of their autonomy.

Renaud Dehousse

EUROPEAN INTEGRATION AND CONSTITUTION-MAKING

Unlike other compound political systems,[1] the EU was not born of a dramatic and sudden revolution. The long period that began after the Second World War is marked by a fitful succession of advances and setbacks. There were frequent clashes between the advocates of a federal (r)evolution, those of a more gradual approach, and supporters of a more traditional Europe, in which states would retain the upper hand. Compromise after compromise, an unprecedented form of international governance gradually emerged. The idea of a constitution appeared in the very early stages. Yet it only met with short-lived success. Surprisingly, the most striking innovations came from the legal sphere and it is to these that we owe the original brand of 'constitutionalism without a constitution'[2] that characterises the European project in its present state.

A Succession of Constitutional Setbacks

From the outset, the idea of a constitutional path towards unity has held a central place in discussions on European integration. At the Hague Congress in May 1948, organised by the International Committee of the movements for European Unity, there were many who spoke in favour of the idea that a European constituent assembly should be convened to define the basic rules of cooperation between the European states. The American model was a constant source of inspiration for these federalists, who insisted that Europe should have its own 'Philadelphia Convention'. In the months that followed, however, disagreement between the pro-federalist governments and those that envisaged the future of Europe along more traditional lines of intergovernmental cooperation showed that the time was not yet ripe. Ten governments finally agreed to sign the treaty establishing the Council of Europe in May 1949. But the basis of the consensus that gave birth to what was then called 'Greater Europe' was so narrow that it seemed doomed to stagnation.

The Schuman declaration of 9 May 1950, whereby France launched the idea of a 'coal and steel pool', marked a change in strategy. Here we read how: 'Europe will not be made all at once, or according to a single plan. It will be built through concrete achievements which first create a de facto solidarity.' From thereon, the States most interested in European construction committed themselves to a functionalist approach: by developing projects involving transnational cooperation, they intended to advance step by step towards an ambitious political union.

---

[1] I deliberately avoid the word 'federal', always a source of confusion. For an analysis of the EU as a would-be federal system, see Sergio Fabbrini, *Compound Democracies. Why the United States and Europe Are Becoming Similar*, (Oxford: Oxford University Press, 2007).

[2] Renaud Dehousse, 'Naissance d' un constitutionnalisme transnational', *Pouvoirs*, n 96, 2001, 19–30.

For them, the only difference between federalism and functionalism was a tactical one; their long-term objectives were the same.

In the months following the signature of the Treaty of Paris, the dynamics of integration did indeed appear to gain momentum. With the intensification of the Cold War at the forefront of the international scene, the six members of the European Coal and Steel Community[3] (ECSC) envisaged (again on France's initiative) extending their cooperation to areas of military concern. To this purpose a treaty was negotiated that was to establish a 'European Defence Community' (EDC). Since the European army envisaged for this project had to be subjected to some form of political authority, the governments of the six member states convened a 'constitutional assembly' (in fact an extended version of the ECSC Assembly, cautiously referred to as an 'ad-hoc assembly' in official texts) to define a single institutional framework that would encompass the different forms of cooperation between the European States. In March 1953 the assembly adopted a draft constitution for a 'European Political Community', clearly inspired by federalists.[4] This constitutional phase did not last long, however: one year later, after an exceptionally heated public debate, the French national assembly rejected the EDC and the project of a political community foundered with it.

The collapse of the EDC prompted a renewal of interest in the functionalist approach. The 'relaunch' of European integration initiated by the Messina conference in 1955 led to the Treaties of Rome (1957) and the creation of the Common Market and the European Atomic Energy Community (Euratom). The (numerous) amendments that ensued were made within this framework or outside the treaties. The road to a constitution seemed to be well and truly closed. Although the 'Draft Treaty Establishing the European Union', brainchild of the unflagging militant Altiero Spinelli and adopted in 1984 by the first elected European Parliament, was of clear federalist inspiration, it carefully avoided any explicit reference to a constitution. This did not prevent it from failing. All major institutional reforms that followed were presented as amendments to the existing treaties. The main ones among them, the Single European Act (1986) and the Maastricht Treaty (1992), fit into the functionalist mould. The Single European Act was presented as the institutional consequence of the 'Single Market' project the Delors Commission had launched and the Maastricht Treaty went down in history (though not without struggle!) as the text that gave birth to the single currency.

Two key ideas seem to run through the turbulent course of European integration. From the outset, the federalist ideal has been a benchmark and, for some, an objective. Yet the main advances can be attributed to the functionalist approach. The history of European integration can be seen as a series of concrete,

---

[3] France, Germany, Italy and the Benelux countries (Belgium, the Netherlands, Luxembourg).
[4] Richard Griffith, *The First European Constitution*, (London: IB. Tauris, 2001).

though far-reaching, projects, from the coal and steel community to the Delors Commission's Single Market to the single currency. In contrast, all attempts to give the European venture a constitutional basis, from the political Community of the early 1950s to the draft Treaty Establishing a Constitution for Europe, solemnly signed in Rome in 2004, have ended in failure. Seen in this light, the rejection of that treaty after unsuccessful referendums in France and the Netherlands, can hardly be viewed as a surprise. The historical continuity is so great as to suggest that its causes are due to structural factors. The dominance of the functionalist approach largely stems from the role of the national governments in the reform procedure of the treaties. Since unanimity is required for any amendment, the member states have a central role in negotiating transfers of power to the European level. And given the wide diversity in their political traditions and in their immediate interests, it was easier for them to agree on relatively concrete projects whose benefits can be evaluated with a certain amount of precision, rather than on an abstract vision of what is right and proper. As to the reasons behind the rejection of the 'constitutional treaty', they are to be looked for in the growing disarray of many a European citizen in the face of an arrangement that does not seem to respond to his/her immediate concerns.[5]

Constitutionalism without a Constitution

If the traditional constitutional option, whereby the representatives of a polity determine the way in which they want to be governed, has proved out of reach until now, several aspects of the institutional construction of Europe of the last 60 years are nevertheless indirectly in keeping with a constitutional system.

In the aftermath of two world wars that had bled Europe dry and left a trail of destruction and bloodshed, the pioneers of the European cause clearly felt the need to move beyond the old order created by the Peace of Westphalia, built on the principle of unlimited state sovereignty and where interstate relations were above all based on a struggle for power. The idea of a new European order, in which the states would be subjected to a set of regulatory principles seemed to be the only alternative to the 'natural state' of war in which the nations of Europe had co-existed up until then.

Human rights were the starting point of this attempt to establish a new order, even before Jean Monnet and Robert Schuman came up with the idea of 'de facto solidarity' and set off a virtuous circle of collaboration. There was a broad consensus on the need to create safeguards against the atrocities that had marked the Second World War. The European Convention on Human Rights, signed in

[5] Renaud Dehousse, *La fin de l'Europe*, (Paris: Flammarion, 2005); Nicolas Sauger, Sylvain Brouard, Emiliano Grossman, *Les Français contre l'Europe ? Les sens du référendum du 29 mai 2005*, (Paris: Presses de Sciences Po, 2007).

Rome on 4 November 1950 was the first formal expression of a political will to subject the action of the states to the control of what was not yet called the international community. To this end, the convention had to move beyond the purely declaratory principles of the Universal Declaration of Human Rights, adopted by the General Assembly of the United Nations in December 1948, and bind the states in a network of international commitments that could be enforced in case democracy and fundamental rights were disregarded.[6]

Internationalising the protection of fundamental rights pursued the same goal as granting them constitutional status: in both cases, they were set up as a higher rule of law to protect them from infringement. Although 'internationalisation' primarily concerns relations between states rather than between ruler and ruled, it has here the same ambitions as constitutionalism: to combat absolutism and arbitrariness by subjecting the acts of the rulers to the rule of law.

At first sight, the treaties establishing the European Communities did not have the same 'constitutionalising' ambition. Yet, driven by the ambition to make war 'not merely unthinkable but also materially impossible', in the words of the Schuman declaration, they established a revolutionary institutional structure, centred on transfers of sovereignty to supranational bodies. In their original version, however, in line with functionalist thinking, the treaties looked at first glance like a long list of provisions of an essentially technical nature. All the same, the proponents of a German school of thought—*ordoliberalism*—saw in the Treaty of Rome a recognition of the market economy, raised to the status of a metalegal principle that could be called upon to inform treaty interpretation and Community case law—and indirectly, therefore, the behaviour of the member states.[7] Although this vision of the Community 'economic constitution' never won unanimous support, it is symptomatic of a willingness to use the Treaty of Rome in a constitutional fashion.

Moreover, from the early 1960s on, the European Court of Justice has been the main agent of a gradual 'constitutionalisation' of the treaties. Without going into detail on a subject that is amply dealt with in many law books, it might be useful here to summarise some of the key elements of this process. First, as early as 1962, the Court gave an extremely broad interpretation of several provisions contained in the EEC treaty. It saw these as a source of rights that plaintiffs could invoke in national courts, even when the wording of these provisions made it clear that they were mainly directed at the member states[8]. By interpreting the treaty as a long list of individual rights, it provided private plaintiffs with an array of arguments that could be used whenever they felt their national authorities had

---

[6] On the origins of the convention, see Emmanuel Decaux, 'Les Etats parties et leurs engage-ments', in L-E Petiti, E Decaux and P-H Imbert (dir), *la Convention européenne des droits de l'homme*, (Paris : Economica, 1995), 3–25.

[7] On ordoliberalism and its influence on EU law, See Christian Joerges 'What is Left of the European Economic Constitution? EUI Working Paper 2004/13.

[8] Case 26/62, *Van Gend & Loos*, ECR 1963, 3.

violated their rights. Disregarding the fact that the treaties made no mention of the question, the Court then went on to declare that in case of conflict with national constitutional laws, Community law should always prevail.[9] Finally, responding to concerns expressed by some national courts, which feared that the primacy of Community law might jeopardise their own constitutional provisions for the protection of fundamental rights, the Court of Justice gradually came to accept that it must ensure that Community legislation and related national legislation should be compatible with the 'fundamental rights established and guaranteed by the [national] constitutions' as well as with the 'international treaties for the protection of human rights, on which the Member States have collaborated or of which they are signatories'.[10]

Ruling by ruling, the Community judges thus laid the foundations of a legislative structure that was to be imposed on the member states. To this purpose, they used methods of interpretation much closer to those of constitutional courts than international courts. Far from taking account of the real or supposed intentions of the contracting parties—an obligatory point of reference in the interpretation of international agreements—they drew inspiration from the ultimate objectives of integration, formulated in general terms in the preamble to the Treaty of Rome, which earned them a lasting reputation of judicial activism and occasional critiques.[11]

This judicial construction has been described as a 'constitutionalisation' of the treaties[12] since, by proclaiming the primacy of Community law over national legislation, it tended towards an implicit transfer of sovereignty. This planted the seeds of a conflict with constitutional courts, which were often reluctant to accept the principle of the primacy of Community law as developed by the ECJ. Generally, while accepting the principle and its consequences—the need to set aside a piece of national legislation that is in contravention of Community law—they stressed that it corresponded to the will of the member states who had agreed to entrust certain tasks to Europe, whereas the Court of Justice has always identified the specific nature of integration as the source of primacy. The difference may seem slight but it is significant. If we accept the thesis of the constitutional courts, we must also accept that the states could take back what they have given. By officially endorsing the rule of primacy of Community law, the draft constitution of 2004[13] clearly intended to go beyond a mere codification of existing law, since it made expressly obligatory what was before accepted freely,

---

[9] Case 6/64, *Costa v ENEL*, ECR 1964,1141.

[10] Case 4/73, *Nold v Commission*, ECR 1974, 491.

[11] See eg Hjalte Rasmussen, *On Law and Justice in the European Court of Justice. A Comparative Study in Judicial Policymaking*, (Dordrecht: Nijhoff, 1986).

[12] Eric Stein, 'Lawyers, Judges, and the Making of a Transnational Constitution', *American Journal of International Law*, 1981, 1–27; G Federico Mancini, 'The Making of a Constitution for Europe', *Common Market Law Review*, 1989, 595–614; Joseph HH Weiler, 'The Transformation of Europe', *Yale Law Journal*, 1991, 2405–83.

[13] Arts 1–6.

and not without qualifications. But its failure leaves the Union as it was: with a Treaty that is recognised to be supreme, albeit within limited fields, and, as the German *BundesVerfassungsGericht* recalled in its ruling on the Lisbon Treaty, without real *Kompetenz-kompetenz*.[14]

Constitutionalisation and Judicialisation

The constitutionalisation of the EU treaties was accompanied by a parallel development of judicial authority. To ensure that the higher principles defined in the basic treaties are applied, international courts were set up. The novelty of the process was all the more remarkable, as the States had long been hostile to any form of 'judicialisation' of international relations as it could undermine their autonomy. However, the wind of constitutionalism that had blown across post-war Europe had grown into a search for an effective counterweight to totalitarianism. The weakness shown by the European parliamentary systems in the face of the rise of Nazism and fascism made it impossible for the national parliaments to put themselves forward as guarantors of fundamental freedoms. It was therefore only natural to turn to specialised bodies. Here too, the logic was similar to that which had led to the development of constitutional justice at the national level in the immediate post-war period: in both cases, a specialised court appeared to provide better guarantees that the foundational rules of the new system would be duly obeyed.

It would be exaggerating to portray this move towards forms of international control by judicial bodies as a triumphal march from the shadows to the light. On the contrary, what is striking about the debates surrounding the birth of the European Convention on Human Rights, for instance, are the objections raised by the many people imbued with the traditional spirit of international law to what rightly appeared to them to be a threat to the omnipotence of the states. The court system established by the Convention provided multiple safeguards and sought a synthesis between legal and diplomatic action. In contrast, when the ECSC was created, the decision to set up a Court of Justice did not cause so much alarm, as this new body was mainly supposed to control the High Authority rather than the member states. As the ECSC had been granted considerable administrative powers, it seemed only natural to provide for the possibility of some form of judicial control over its decisions. The Treaty of Paris thus included an array of provisions for legal recourse inspired by French administrative litigation procedure. At the same time the member states of the European communities accepted the authority of the Court, which has compulsory jurisdiction. The EEC treaty also gave an autonomous body, the European

---

[14] 30 June 2009. See Katrin Auel and Julio Baquero Cruz, *Karlsruhe's Europe*, Notre Europe Studies & Research, No 78, 2010, http://www.notre-europe.eu/uploads/tx_publication/Etud78-Karlsruhe_sEurope-en_01.pdf.

Commission, a vital role in preventing breaches of Community law: as guardian of the treaties, the Commission can refer a matter to the Court when it considers that a state has failed to fulfill its obligations (Article 258 of the Treaty on the functioning of the European Union). This centralised model of judicial control stands in sharp contrast to the international law principle whereby states are free to choose the means of dispute settlement.

However, the setting up of courts did not necessarily guarantee that the law would be obeyed. In the name of the nation's higher interests, governments could choose to close their eyes to transgressions, rather than get involved in what they discreetly call their partners' 'domestic affairs'. The situation would, of course, be significantly different if all the people who could somehow claim a right from the new treaties were given a chance to go to court to protect them. The European Court of Justice took radical steps in this direction in its first years of activity, through far-reaching interpretations of the concept of 'direct effect', of which the Treaty said very little, and by agreeing to hear cases where private parties alleged that their individual rights had been disregarded by national authorities, which was not dealt with in the treaties. This was a considerable qualitative leap in the constitutional logic behind European integration: it brought individuals onto the international scene, traditionally the preserve of states. It is therefore no surprise that it met with determined opposition.[15] Time was to overcome much of this resistance, however. Nowadays, it is mainly on the initiative of private plaintiffs that the conduct of member states is subjected to the judgment of the European Court of Justice.

By seeking the support of private litigants to enforce the basic principles contained in the Treaty and in subsequent legislation, European institutions have indirectly encouraged a form of 'adversarial legalism' that is actually closer to the American model than to the traditions of European countries.[16] Yet this evolution has not been without limits. Going through the Luxembourg courts is still a long and arduous process and their doors are closed to outsiders who do not have the necessary expertise or the means to pay for it. Even today, there are only limited possibilities for private persons to directly challenge EU decisions. Be that as it may, through these bold rulings, which are now to be considered as part of the constitutional *acquis*, individuals have been given an active role in the process of integration. As we shall see, this has not been without consequence on the dynamics of integration.

---

[15] See Renaud Dehousse, 'Un nouveau constitutionnalisme ?', in R Dehousse (dir), *Une constitution pour l'Europe ?*, (Paris: Presses de Sciences Po, 2002), 19–38, where these aspects are dealt with in more detail.

[16] R Daniel Kelemen, 'The Americanisation of European Law? Adversarial Legalism *à la* (sic) *européenne*', *European Political Science*, vol 7 (2008), 32–41.

HOW RIGID IS THE EUROPEAN CONSTITUTION?

The mechanism for reforming EU treaties is remarkably conservative. First, the revision procedure is typically very rigid: amendments must be adopted by common accord by the member states' government representatives in a diplomatic conference, and can only enter into force after being ratified by all of the States in accordance with their respective constitutional procedures (Article 48, Treaty of the European Union). Secondly, despite the many amendments that have been made in the post-1986 period, this procedure has remained essentially unchanged since the construction of Europe was initiated, whereas the number of member states has quadrupled and public demands for democratic control have increased dramatically. This conservatism is easily explained. By retaining control over the revision process, governments made sure that European integration does not take a direction incompatible with their wishes. At the same time, however, the procedure's conservative nature does not necessarily imply a paralysis of the political system. Since the Single European Act, the treaties have undergone five reforms which have significantly transformed the European project, with the launch of major initiatives such as the completion of the internal market and the adoption of a single currency. This tension between rigidity and movement illustrates the basic indeterminacy about the ultimate objective of the integration process, which some would like to see evolving towards a clearer federal model, while others insist that it should retain its intergovernmental character.

As the difficulties surrounding the ratification of the draft constitution and on the Lisbon Treaty have shown, the current procedure has many shortcomings. Its diplomatic nature does not make it a model of transparency, despite the leaks which occasionally come from one or other of the participants. Its decentralised nature—with each member state allowed to present its own proposals—can sometimes lead to disjointed negotiations, particularly in the final phases of the conference. The lack of strong leadership is often sensed, especially since the number of participants has continued to rise.[17] Generally, the thorniest problems tend to be referred up to meetings between foreign affairs ministers, or even Heads of State and Government, which can create bottlenecks. As early on as the signing of the Treaty of Amsterdam in 1997 several voices were raised in criticism of the erratic nature of intergovernmental negotiations, in which crucial decisions are often made at the last minute by Heads of State and Government rushing to reach a conclusion.[18] This often results in what has been described as a 'joint decision trap': self-interested bargaining yielding sub-optimal results, with

---

[17] Colette Mazzucelli and Derek Beach (eds), *Leadership in EU Constitutional Negotiations,* (London: Palgrave, 2006); BPG Smith, *Constitution-building in the European Union: The Process of Treaty Reforms,* (The Hague/London: Kluwer Law International, 2002).

[18] Philippe de Schoutheete, *The Case for Europe: Unity, Diversity and Democracy in the EU,* (Boulder: Lynnne Rienner, 2000).

each state striving to maximise its own advantage, regardless of the general interest.[19] During the last Intergovernmental Conferences (IGCs), it has become increasingly challenging to organise debates efficiently—inducing UK Prime Minister Tony Blair to exclaim in Nice (2001): 'We cannot go on working like this!'

The problem is exacerbated by the double unanimity required to conclude an IGC. Each delegation thus has the right to veto the final outcome and, the latter taking the form of an amendment to the existing treaties, it must still be ratified by each member country according to its own constitutional procedures. In a multi-level co-decision system bringing together 27 countries today, and possibly 30-plus tomorrow, possibilities of deadlock are manifold. The number of bodies having veto power is actually much higher than the number of member countries: a parliamentary assembly can refuse to ratify a treaty signed by 'its' government, as the French National Assembly did at the time of the European Defence Community Treaty, just as constitutional courts may raise objections against a draft treaty, as the German *BundesverfassungsGericht* has done in relation to the Lisbon Treaty.[20] Moreover, dividing the process into two phases— preparation and negotiations on the one hand and ratification on the other— creates a harmful break between debates held at the European level and those held at the national level. This break was cruelly felt in the referenda campaigns of the spring of 2005, largely dominated by domestic concerns and the unpopularity of the French and Dutch governments of the time. Moreover, this segmentation into two phases unavoidably confers a binary character on the national debates: no modification of the draft treaty being allowed at the ratification stage, only a Yes/No answer is possible, which leaves little room for a true deliberative process, irrespective of the ratification mode chosen (parliamentary or by referendum).

The repeated difficulties that have been met in the ratification phase, first by the draft constitutional treaty, then by the Treaty of Lisbon, have amply shown how excruciating the process can be in a Union of 27 members. Over the past few years, a consensus has therefore emerged over the need for a 'reform of the reform process'. The half-failures recorded in Amsterdam, and later on in Nice, on questions of institutional reform, stressed the need for more open procedures. The successful convention that had formulated the EU Charter of Fundamental Rights served as a blueprint for a new model. The establishment of the Convention on the Future of Europe at the Laeken European Council (2001) brought about several significant changes to the amendment procedure set out by the Treaty of Rome. It allowed a greater variety of actors to participate in the reform process, as it included members of national parliaments and of the European Parliament, and greater transparency in the debates. This led to a partial change

---

[19] Fritz Scharpf, 'The joint decision trap', *Public Administration*, 66 (1988), 239.
[20] See above note 14.

in the rules of the game, since a deliberation-oriented approach was, on occasion, substituted for one based on negotiation in the IGCs.[21] This enabled the Convention to reach a compromise on certain issues that had stymied the discussions in Nice, such as the dismantling of the 'pillars' structure, the simplification of the Treaties, and the Union's legal personality.

However, it would be wrong to conclude that this innovation made a decisive difference to the balance of power within the content of the revision procedure. The requirement of a 'double unanimity' (at the IGC and in the ratification phase) was retained, which made quantum leaps near impossible. It was known that the Convention would be followed by an IGC in which the Member States could voice any strong objections they had to the draft text in order to gain additional concessions. The most delicate phases of the debate were thus over-shadowed by the threat of the final compromise being called into question, which often led the delegates to moderate their demands.[22] In other words, the States remained largely in control of the final compromise. From this perspective, the cautious approach taken by the draft Constitution with regard to revision is not surprising: governments could scarcely be expected to relinquish their powers willingly.[23] It was foreseeable that they would insist on retaining unanimity for both the signing and ratification of any amendment of the new EU Charter of Fundamental Rights. Such a status quo revealed much about the nature of the text: using the word 'Constitution' to refer to a document of which the real masters remained the states had all the appearances of a sleight of hand.[24]

The Lisbon Treaty essentially leaves the balance of power unchanged. True, the summoning of a convention is now foreseen for the most important treaty revisions, and provisions have been made for simplified revision in some (narrowly circumscribed) cases. It nonetheless remains the case that the member states have refused to relinquish the control power which they derive from the double unanimity system. Calls for further reforms have been made, advocating for instance more transparency in the treaty revision process[25] stressing the necessity to do away with unanimity,[26] but so far they have fallen on deaf ears. In

---

[21] Paul Magnette, 'La convention européenne: argumenter et négocier dans une assemblée constituante', *Reveu française de Science Politique*, 2004, vol 54, 5.

[22] Renaud Dehousse and Florence Deloche-Gaudez, 'The Making of a Transnational Constitution', *Cahiers européens de Sciences Po*, 02/2005, http://www.cee.sciences-po.fr/fr/publications/les-cahiers-europeens/2005.html.

[23] Article IV-447 of the Constitution, now 48 of the European Union Treaty.

[24] Renaud Dehousse, *La fin de l'Europe*, (Paris: Flammarion, 1995).

[25] Gaëtane Ricard-Nihoul et al, 'The Revision of the European Treaties: the Convention Moment. Six arguments for its Continuation, six Proposals', Notre Europe, Policy paper No 31, 2007. for its reform. http://www.notre-europe.eu/uploads/tx_publication/Policypaper31-GRN-Convention-en.pdf.

[26] Hervé Bribosia et al, 'Revising the European Treaties: A plea in favour of abolishing the veto', Notre Europe, Policy paper No 39, 2009. http://www.notre-europe.eu/uploads/tx_publication/Policy-Paper37-en-Hbribosia-Revising_European_treaties.pdf.

such conditions, prospects of large-scale reform of the Treaties remain limited. More targeted reforms, possibly confined to a limited number of countries, would certainly be easier to carry out.[27]

EPPURE SI MUOVE … THE DYNAMICS OF INSTITUTIONAL CHANGE

Given all these constraints, one could have expected the European institutional structure to remain fairly stable. Yet actually the opposite is true: the careful balance designed by the Founding Fathers has been radically altered by a series of changes. Some have been of a formal nature, and took the form of changes to the treaties establishing the Communities first, then the Union. Others have been of a more informal kind, linked to changes in the practice followed by the institutions.

Formal Changes

Despite the complex procedure foreseen for treaty amendment, the Treaty of Rome, after a period of stability of nearly 30 years (1957–86) entered into a regime of repeated modifications from the Single European Act (1986) onwards. Reforms have occurred on average every five years. Although one of the rationales for the convening of the convention was to give the Union a stable institutional framework, it is far from certain that this has been achieved. The ink of the Lisbon treaty was not even dry when an instant IGC had to be summoned to change the number of members of parliament to solve a conflict between different legal provisions. More importantly, the sovereign debt crisis of early 2010 has led the most powerful member country, Germany, to call for more substantial changes in order to ensure fiscal discipline within the EU and to consolidate the financial solidarity mechanism hastily put together at the height of the crisis.

This is not the place to discuss the various phases of this evolution. It is however worth noting that notwithstanding the tight control exerted by national governments, they have willy nilly come to accept a fair degree of 'Europeanisation' of a large number of policies, to a point that very few had foreseen. Who would have thought that by the end of the twentieth century, Europe would have its single currency (even though the latter has not been adopted by all countries) or joint battle groups deployed in remote parts of the world?

From the late 1950s on, so-called 'integration theories' have tried to offer an explanation the magnitude and the pace of change highlighting the important part played in this evolution by national governments, supranational institutions or business interests, the respective roles of ideas, institutions and interests. The

---

[27] Philippe de Schoutheete, 'Scenarios for escaping the Constitutional impasse', *Europe's World*, Summer 2006, 74–79.

fact is that none of these accounts, on its own, can do justice to the complexity of the process. Security concerns (first the Cold War, then the collapse of the Soviet Union) and economic constraints (the emerging of strong competitors such as Japan in the 1970s, China, India or Brazil today; the gradual shift towards a service economy in a number of European countries) all contributed to convince the governments of the member countries to revisit frequently the initial blueprint. And the process was far from mechanical: it has required the talent of gifted policy entrepreneurs to take Europe where it is today.[28]

Informal Changes

The steady evolution of the balance of powers in the Union is also explained by the fact that it did not always require formal treaty amendments. In between, the power play between the institutions also contributed greatly to the transformation of the decision-making process. The study of European institutional history would therefore not be complete without a discussion of the dynamics of informal change.[29]

As said above, one of the original features of the European brand of regional integration was the setting up of supranational institutions which could take a number of decisions without having to seek the support of the member states. Unsurprisingly, the members of these bodies were often imbued with 'a certain idea of Europe', to use the words of one distinguished member of the European Court of Justice, Judge Pierre Pescatore,[30] an idea which, more often than not, led them to favour the consolidation of the central power.

Thus, the Court of Justice, being called upon to interpret the Treaty and ensure that the law is obeyed, according to Article 164 of the Treaty of Rome, was able to take a number of decisions that clearly altered the course of integration. Its early rulings on direct effect and supremacy have already been mentioned; suffice it therefore to mention that it is often in cases brought by private litigants, and against the will of a number of member states, that key rules of Community law have been made: the alliance between the Court of Justice and private individuals has shaped the course of European integration more than once. Moreover, without those rulings, the European Community would have been deprived of a substantial part of its authority, since it would have been considerably easier for states to evade their obligations under European law. The fact that the control of fiscal discipline has been kept out of the European Court's hands when economic

---

[28] See Renaud Dehousse and Paul Magnette, Institutional Change in the European Union', in J Peterson and M Shackleton (eds), *Institutions of the European Union*, 2nd edn, (Oxford: Oxford University Press, 2006), 17–34 for a discussion.

[29] Adrienne Héritier, *Explaining Institutional Change in Europe*, (Oxford: Oxford University Press, 2007).

[30] Pierre Pescatore, 'La carence du législateur communautaire et le devoir du juge', in *Rechtsvergleichung, Europarecht, Staatsintegration. Gedächtnisschrift für L-J Constantinesco*, (Cologne: Heymanns, 1983), 559–80.

and monetary union was established by the Maastricht Treaty is emblematic of states' long established aversion to anything that comes close to judicial (let alone supranational) control of the policies they pursue. But the gradual erosion of the Stability pact that followed is a useful reminder of the fact that without independent monitoring, 'peers' control' is unlikely to suffice to make governments abide by burdensome international rules.

Be that as it may, the 'constitutional role' of the European Court of Justice did not stop there. In its capacity as the ultimate umpire of institutional disputes it has often been in the position to shape decisively the contours of the Union's institutional order. At the request of the Commission, for instance, it has ruled that trade policy was an exclusive competence of the European Community[31] and that member states could not conclude international agreements under their own name in areas where the competence to do so was vested in the Community.[32] In so doing, it has of course greatly enhanced the international profile of the Union. The Court has also ended up supporting the European Parliament's claim for *locus standi* consonant with it legislative powers, accepting—against the letter of the Treaty—that it was to be recognised as having the right to initiate annulment proceedings against decisions taken by other institutions, in case those decisions threaten its own prerogatives[33]—a decision subsequently ratified by the Treaty of Maastricht (1992). In response to pressure from national constitutional courts, it has gradually recognised the legal status of human rights in the EU legal order, which has also inspired further treaty amendments. In other words, its case law has considerably altered the institutional structure of the Union, as is the case with most constitutional courts.

The European Parliament has also been a regular source of informal change. This was particularly true after direct elections were organised in 1979. A majority of members were convinced that as it enjoyed an elective legitimacy of which other European institutions were deprived, it had to fight in order to secure a better role for itself. The Parliament was quite successful in convincing large sections of the population that there was in Europe a democratic deficit that needed to be redressed. This has led to a steady expansion of its legislative and budgetary powers on the occasion of each treaty reform.[34] But in between two reforms, the assembly has also been quite effective in using every inch of power it was given in order to maximise its influence. Whereas in the past, being deprived of effective policy-making influence, it had acquired the reputation of a somewhat unruly forum in which publicity-seeking politicians sought to attract media attention by organising debates on issues which were often remote from the heart of the European agenda, it started disciplining itself from the moment it was

---

[31] Opinion 1/75, *Re the Draft understanding on a Local Cost Standard*, [1975] ECR 1355.
[32] Case 22/70, *Commission v Council (ERTA)* [1971] ECR 263.
[33] Case C-70/88, *European Parliament v Council (Chernobyl)*, [1990] ECR, I, 2072.
[34] Stefan Goetze and Berthold Rittberger, 'A Matter of Habit? The Sociological Foundations of Empowering the European Parliament', *Comparative European Politics*, 2010, 8, Issue 1, 37–54.

given a legislative role, with the establishment of the so-called cooperation procedure by the Single European Act. Rules of procedures were a key instrument in this process: they limited the right of individual members to table amendments so as to concentrate the debate with the Council and the Commission on a few strategic points. Similarly, when the co-decision procedure was set up (Maastricht Treaty, 1992), the Parliament chose to delegate to a limited number of members the right to participate in conciliation meetings between the two branches of the legislature, which allowed for a learning process that contributed to improving their impact on EU policy-making.

It was also able to avail itself of the weakness of the Commission in the 1990s to extract major political concessions. Whereas the Maastricht Treaty foresaw only a 'vote of approval' on the college as a whole each time a new Commission was to take office, the Parliament obtained two major concessions: first, the organisation of a vote on the President of the Commission prior to the designation of the commissioners and second, the organisation of 'hearings' inspired by the American model, in which would-be commissioners appear before the relevant parliamentary committees, which pass judgment on their suitability for the job they aspire to. Experience has shown that this was more than a formal exercise: it has enabled the Parliament to impinge on the distribution of portfolios in the Commission or even to force incoming president Jose Manuel Barroso to seek the replacement of some candidates who had failed the test.

Even though the first of these two changes rapidly found its way into the Treaty on the occasion of the Amsterdam Treaty, this is not necessarily the case for all changes in the 'customary constitution' of the Union. The evolution of the rules governing the functioning of the Council of ministers offers an interesting counter-example. As is known, majority voting is one of the hallmarks of the 'Community method' and has featured in the treaties from the outset. Yet it has been used with great caution: the 'empty chair' crisis triggered by General de Gaulle in 1965 showed that governments would not lightly accept being outvoted.[35] Indeed, the 'Luxembourg compromise' which put an end to the crisis, although lacking clear legal status, de facto ended up ruling out votes whenever states considered that their 'vital interests' were at stake. This shows that informal changes may occasionally 'trump' formal rules. When, some 20 years later, in a radically transformed context, a majority of states accepted the prospect of a greater use of majority voting, they had to face the problem: what was the point of changing the treaty rules, since they were not really applied? A change in the Council's rule of procedures, making it possible for the Commission or one government to demand that a vote be organised, was therefore agreed, but even that would have been of little avail if the members of the Council had not

---

[35] See Jean-Marie Palayret, Helen Wallace and Pascaline Winand (eds), *Visions, Votes and Vetoes. Reassessing the Empty Chair Crisis and the Luxembourg Compromise 40 Years On*, (Bruxelles, Bern, Berlin, Frankfurt/M, New York, Oxford, Wien : Presses interuniversitaires européennes/Peter Lang, 2006).

accepted that voting was no longer a departure from a major (yet unwritten) rule. Here again, the main change was informal.

CONCLUSION: PARADOXES OF EUROPEAN CONSTITUTIONALISM

Considering the evolution that has taken place since the launching of the Coal and Steel Community in 1950, one cannot but be struck by the magnitude of the change that has taken place. True, formally speaking, one remains in the ambit of interstate cooperation. Even after Lisbon, the 'supreme law' of Europe remains enshrined in a treaty which, like any international agreement, is supposed to be in the hands of the states that have ratified it. The ambiguous solution adopted by the European convention—a 'treaty establishing a constitution'—having being unambiguously rejected in some countries, one might think that things are destined to stay so in the foreseeable future.

Yet this reading of the situation needs to be qualified. If one adopts a dynamic approach to the situation, the picture becomes rather different. The treaty in question has been largely interpreted in the same fashion as constitutional documents, more attention being paid to the integration *telos* than to the 'original intent' of the signatories. In its quest for effectiveness, the European Court of Justice has construed EU law as superior to any divergent rule, be it of a constitutional character, and it keeps refusing invitations to regard state competences as 'islands of sovereignty' that should stay immune from European interference. The reference to a constitution is therefore unavoidable, no matter how one wishes to qualify the current status of the EU Treaty.

On paper, the supreme charter of the Union stays firmly under state control, since it can only be amended with the unanimous consent of the member states. This formal rigidity notwithstanding, it keeps changing, and it does so in ways that do not appear to be responding primarily to state concerns. Nearly 20 years ago in Maastricht, national governments signalled their uneasiness vis-à-vis what some have described as a seemingly endless process of erosion of state powers by introducing the subsidiarity principle in the Treaty. In several countries, the constitutional courts have stressed that there were to be limits to this erosion process. Yet in the two decades that followed, three major treaty changes have taken place, new areas have been opened to EU intervention, we have witnessed the emergence of the European Parliament—and there is no indication that the process is over, since, at the time of writing, yet another reform is contemplated in the wake of the financial crisis. Moreover, informal changes have also considerably altered the balance of power on the horizontal plane (between the institutions) as well as on the vertical plane (between the EU and the member states). All of this, let it be said, does not respond to popular demand, citizens being at most willing to accept an evolution which they perceive as necessary, but on which they are convinced they have little influence.[36]

European constitutionalism therefore appears as a source of paradoxes. If one accepts that 'the touchstone of constitutionalism is the concept of limited government under a higher law',[37] then the elements of constitutionalism are manifold in the EU legal order, though the very idea of a constitution remains largely 'opposed by many. Likewise, whereas on paper the states that have given birth to the Union remain in theory the masters of its destiny, and whereas they retain a central role in European policy-making, when it comes to 'constitutional' issues, their grip on decision-making has not been as strong as one might have expected.

Why it has been so is a complex question. Clearly, part of the answer lies in the question itself. The rigidity of the 'constitutional charter' is one of the main causes of the fundamental ambiguity of most reforms. Unanimity being required for any change, reforms must appeal both to supranationalists and supporters of states' rights. Hence the piecemeal character of most reforms: Maastricht gave us both a federal central bank and the famous 'pillar system', aimed at Europeanising traditional state prerogatives (foreign policy and security) without conceding too much power to the supranational institutions. Similarly, Lisbon has considerably expanded the prerogatives of the European Parliament and the scope of majority voting—two typical supranational features of the EU political system— while at the same time consolidating the role of the European Council, now recognised as an institution and endowed with a stable president, whose influence is strongly felt. The fundamental ambiguity of these reforms in turn explains their rhythm: not only does the distribution of power between actors evolve, but external factors may call into question carefully constructed compromises. There is little doubt that a majority of states were satisfied with the loosely coordinated macroeconomic governance agreed in Maastricht; yet by questioning its credibility, the markets may end up forcing governments to accept a greater degree of centralisation.

Obviously, the 'why' question cannot be answered by lawyers alone. One must make sense of the logic underlying complex international negotiations, of the changes in the international environment that may affect the perceptions of European countries, or of the possibility for agents like the Court of the Justice to evade the preferences of their principals, on some occasions at least. One must also analyse the socialisation mechanisms under way in transnational professional networks, be they composed of governmental experts, of diplomats, or of judges. In other words, one must mobilise the toolkit of many social sciences. The

---

[36] See Sophie Duchesne et al, 'Europe between integration and globalization. Social differences and national frames in the analysis of focus groups conducted in France, Francophone Belgium and the UK 'Politique Européenne*, 30, hiver 2010, 67–106.

[37] David Feldman, 'Constitutionalism' in Philip P Wiener(ed), *Dictionary of the History of Ideas: Studies of Selected Pivotal Ideas*, (New York: Charles Scribner's Sons, 1968), vol 1, 485–92 at 485.

task is challenging. Despite its intrinsic difficulty, it is definitely worth undertaking it if one wants to make sense of the EU brand of constitutionalism.

5

Finland

MARKKU SUKSI

INTRODUCTION

IN THE GENERAL debates about two main forms of constitution-making, the *pouvoir constituant* or the exercise of the constituent powers, on the one hand, and the *pouvoir constitué* or the exercise of the amending powers, on the other, Finnish constitutional development can relatively easily be placed in the latter.[1] Constitutional development in Finland during the past 200 years has thus normally been achieved in accordance with the amendment formula of the constitutional text that exists at the time of each amendment.[2] A new constitutional text or an amendment has been legitimised by reference to the then existing amendment formula.

In Finland, formal constitutional change has not come about as a result of dramatic moments of constitutional upheaval or the collapse of constitutional continuity.[3] Instead, it has followed established formulae for constitutional amendment. Recent constitutional experience in Finland has identified a number

---

[1] See M Suksi *Making a Constitution—the Outline of an Argument*, 1995; M Suksi 'On mechanisms of decision-making in the creation (and re-creation) of states' (1997) *Tidsskrift for Rettsvitenskap* 426. However, as explained below, the moment of independence in 1917 could also be viewed from the perspective of *pouvoir constituant*. On this, see A Jyränki *Lakien laki*, 1989, 472–80.

[2] Very conveniently for the purposes of the writing of this article, Government Bill 60/2010, in which the Government is proposing amendments to the Constitution of Finland, is at the moment being dealt with by Parliament. Also, Government Bill 1/1998 that led to the enactment of the current Constitution of Finland is used as a source for constitutional principles. The principles of constitutional development and evolution can therefore to a great extent be found in the preparatory materials of the current amendment procedure but also in more recent ones, such as those leading up to the enactment of the Constitution of Finland during the latter part of the 1990s and those leading up to the reform of the chapter on constitutional rights in mid-1990s. Therefore, emphasis in the sources to this article is on the official documentation, which is relatively fresh and covers the last two decades. The different Governmental Bills as well as the Opinions and Reports of the Constitutional Committee are available in the Finnish and the Swedish languages at the website of the Finnish Parliament. See http://www.eduskunta.fi or http://www.riksdagen.fi.

[3] This conclusion makes an exception for the revolutionary moment of 1917 in Russia, which placed the *pouvoir constituant* in Russia and forced a reaction in the Finnish jurisdiction—or gave a convenient opportunity to the political forces in Finland—to transfer the powers of the Russian

of strategies for amendments and expressed them in, for instance, the *travaux preparatoires*, but there also exist features that stem from earlier phases of constitutional development and are worthy of consideration in this context.

In terms of the Constitution, Finland embarked on the twenty-first century in quite a new situation compared with most of the twentieth century: the Constitution of Finland (731/1999), in force since 1 March 2000, is now a single coherent text that is consistent and modern. The Constitution of Finland is intended to strengthen the parliamentary features in the Finnish constitutional and political system and, at the same time, to decrease the powers of the President, which were considerable until the 1990s. Since the entering into force of the new Constitution in 2000, it is probably no longer possible to characterise the constitutional structure of Finland as semi-presidential. Thus Finland is not now comparable to France, but is moving towards more streamlined parliamentary accountability.

FINLAND'S CONSTITUTIONAL PRE-HISTORY IN THE KINGDOM OF SWEDEN

The 'evolutionary' method of Finnish constitutional development was preceded by a formal breach of constitutional continuity in 1808–1809 in the Great Nordic War, in which the Russian Empire separated Finland from the Kingdom of Sweden and established Finland as an autonomous Grand Duchy. Normally, such separation would have meant that the new territories would have been made a regular province of Russia. However, for various reasons the Russian Czar decided that Finland would not be a province, but instead a separate jurisdiction in which the former Swedish legislation would continue to be in force, including constitutional and fundamental laws such as the 1772 Form of Government (Constitution) Act and the 1789 Union and Security (Constitution) Act. Finland's present constitutional continuity can, at least in theory, be traced back to this imperial decision, which in the Russian constitutional setting meant that the Czar, an autocratic emperor without any constraints of a written constitution (at least until 1906[4]) in other parts of Russia, was a constitutional monarch in the Finnish jurisdiction.[5]

Czar/Grand Duke of Finland to Finnish organs in the Fall of 1917. That transfer and the independence of Finland thus created was clad in the costume of the *pouvoir constitué* in the Form of Government (Constitution) Act of 1919: the revolution was in Russia, not in Finland. Strategies in the area of the *pouvoir constituant* as methods of constitutional amendment are relevant, eg, in Thailand, where more than 20 entirely new constitutions have been adopted during the past 50 years by way of not observing the amendment formula in the previous constitution.

[4] See M Szeftel *The Russian Constitution of April 23, 1906*, 1976.
[5] Art 2 of the 1906 Constitution of Russia: 'The Grand Duchy of Finland, while it constitutes an indivisible part of the Russian State, is governed in its domestic affairs by special institutions on the basis of special legislation.' As quoted in Szeftel above note 4, 84.

The roots of the Finnish legal and constitutional system are thus shared with those of Sweden,[6] and Finland is therefore firmly placed not only in the Nordic family of legal orders, but also in a constitutional tradition which is similar to that of today's Sweden and which, both in theory and in principle, dates back to the medieval kings' codes of 1347 and 1442.[7] This relationship is obvious, inter alia, because of the absence of judicial review of the constitutionality of legislation adopted by Parliament through a Constitutional or Supreme Court. (However, both the Finnish and the Swedish constitutions recognise the possibility that ordinary courts could exercise some limited measure of judicial review in concrete cases, that is, in a decentralised form when laws are applied: see below.)

The principle of parliamentary sovereignty in the context of constitution-making is also important from the point of view of the organ that makes the amendment decision: the constitution-maker is the same body as the law-maker—Parliament—except that constitutional amendments require a qualified majority and, if the normal procedure for constitutional reform is being applied, that two identical decisions are made by two consecutive parliaments, separated by an election (see below). These two features of constitution-making are attributable to the Swedish roots of the Finnish constitutional system: the requirements are that if a proposal for constitutional amendment is presented and approved at one session of the parliament, the final decision is made by the next parliament, and that at the final stage of decision-making, there must be a qualified majority in favour of the constitutional amendments.[8]

The understanding that there is a normative difference between ordinary legislation and constitutional legislation started to develop in Sweden during the eighteenth century.[9] The first time that this understanding manifested itself was in the Freedom of the Press Law of 1766, which in section 14 declared itself to be of a constitutional nature. Although that piece of law was revoked after the *coup d'état* that the king performed in 1772, the subsequent Form of Government (Constitution) Act also declared itself to be a Constitution in the Preamble, and the king referred in his confirmation of the Act to the concept of fundamental law. At this point, the 1772 Form of Government (Constitution) Act was

---

[6] However, Sweden departed from the 1772 Form of Government (Constitution) Act and the 1789 Union and Guaranty (Constitution) Act as early as 1809, after King Gustav IV Adolf had been deposed, at which point a new governmental order was created on the basis of the 1809 Form of Government (Constitution) Act.

[7] Jyränki, note 1 above, 52–57.

[8] The current Swedish constitution does not require any qualified majority, but produces amendments on the basis of two identical decisions in two consecutive parliaments, albeit with the possibility of a constitutional referendum.

[9] See Jyränki, note 1 above, 69–72. Section 39 of the 1772 Form of Government (Constitution) Act revoked all those Acts since 1680 that were regarded as constitutional. It deserves to be mentioned that the 1766 Freedom of the Press Law was a pet project of a member of the priestly estate of the Diet of Sweden, Mr Anders Chydenius, who was born and worked in areas that now constitute parts of Finland. See P Virrankoski *Anders Chydenius—demokratisk politiker i upplysningens tid*, 1995, 179–96.

approved by all four estates of the Swedish Diet in one session.[10] This was in breach of the newly established amendment formula. Ordinary legislation was adopted by the majority of three estates. Hence in the beginning, the distinction between the adoption of a Constitution or amendments thereto, on the one hand, and ordinary legislation, on the other, was less clear than now, and not particularly refined.[11] It was only later that it became generally followed.

EMERGING DOCTRINE AND RIPENING CONSTITUTION

After separation from Sweden, political life in Finland stalled for half a century. The winds of liberalism, however, made it necessary to pass new legislation and a new Diet (Constitution) Act was passed in 1869. According to section 71 of this Act a proposal for constitutional amendment would be laid down by the Emperor and Grand Duke, to be adopted unanimously by all the four estates at the Diet or, upon the request of two estates, postponed to the next Diet.[12] During the latter half of the nineteenth century, a practice started to evolve according to which a bill which was in at least some conflict with the Constitution could be adopted by the Diet as an ordinary law, provided that the bill was adopted in the procedure prescribed for the enactment of Constitution. This legislative method, which did not result in formal amendments to the Constitution but entailed the making of substantive exceptions to the prevailing Constitution, is similar to the German concept of *Verfassungsdurchbrechung* that existed in, for example, Prussia during the nineteenth century and also in the Weimar Republic between 1919 and 1933.[13] In due course it developed into the doctrine of Acts of Exception (see below). At that time, the Legislation Committee of the Diet started to perform abstract *ex ante* scrutiny of the constitutionality of bills.

By the turn of the nineteenth century and into the twentieth, conflict between Finland and Russia and attempts to 'Russify' Finland resulted in the strong reliance in Finland on legality as a defence against Russian influence. The defeat of Russian forces in the Russo-Japanese war led in 1906 to political pressure which caused the Czar of Russia to agree not only to the enactment of the 1906 Constitution of Russia but also to constitutional reforms in Finland. As a consequence of the enactment of the 1906 Parliament (Constitution) Act, the old-fashioned Diet was transformed into a modern unicameral parliament based

---

[10] The enactment took place more or less under gunpoint. The representatives of the different estates were assembled in the house of the Diet, which was surrounded by the royal guard and sealed off until the decision was made. The current Constitution of Sweden does not require qualified majority for the second decision concerning amendment.

[11] Jyränki, note 1 above, 82, 423f.

[12] The Diet (Constitution) Act of 1869 was itself adopted pursuant to this amendment formula, and in the Preamble of the Act, the Diet Act of 1617 was declared revoked.

[13] Jyränki, note 1 above, 244–50, 348–53, 433–38.

on universal, direct and proportional suffrage. Section 80 of the Act revoked the Diet (Constitution) Act of 1869 and identified itself as a Constitutional Act.

The 1906 Parliament (Constitution) Act created by section 35 a Constitutional Committee in the Parliament which was tasked in section 40 with reporting on issues referred to it concerning the enactment, amendment, explanation or revocation of constitutional Acts. Hence since 1907 the Constitutional Committee has performed an *ex ante* abstract review of the constitutionality of bills (see below). The amendment formula was established in the form that has applied since, namely approval of the bill by a simple majority and re-approval at the new Parliament after elections by a qualified majority of two-thirds of those present and voting ('1/2 + elections + 2/3'). At this point, a fast track for constitutional amendments was also established, under which an amendment can be passed by one Parliament without leaving the proposal in abeyance until the next one after the elections, provided that five-sixths of those present and voting first declare the amendment to be urgent in a separate procedural decision, after which the amendment may be approved by the qualified majority of two-thirds of those present and voting ('5/6 + 2/3').

The strategic intention in the normal procedure of constitutional amendments was that the election between the two Parliaments at which decisions would be made, would function as a forum for discussion: the constitutional issues subject to on-going amendment would be referred back to the voters, so that voters could exercise a measure of consideration during the election campaign. While this intention was probably never fulfilled, the '1/2 + elections + 2/3'—formula was effective in the sense that it required the decision to be based on a broad consensus, not only during the last stage of the two-thirds requirement, but actually even in the Parliament where the amendment proposal was first presented. The fast-track formula required even greater consensus in support of the procedural issue of whether or not to amend the Constitution without awaiting for elections.[14]

By Finnish independence in 1917, at least four Acts of a constitutional kind were in force: (i) the 1772 Form of Government (Constitution) Act, which was of Swedish origin and had remained in force when Finland was separated from Sweden in 1809 and made an autonomous Grand-Duchy within the Russian Empire; (ii) the 1906 Parliament (Constitution) Act, which introduced universal and equal suffrage and proportional elections in Finland; (iii) the 1906 (Constitution) Act on Freedom of Speech, Assembly and Association, which introduced these freedoms as civil liberties the exercise of which could be limited only by an Act, not by lower statutory or administrative measures; and (iv) the 1789 Union and Security (Constitution) Act, which defined the prerogatives of the four Estates.

[14] At each election, the voters should, in theory, be aware of the (very remote) possibility that the MPs to be elected could, by using the fast track formula, entirely transform the Constitution without waiting for the next elections.

Although a case can be made for a breach of constitutional continuity at this juncture,[15] the 1919 Form of Government (Constitution) Act (94/1919) was formally enacted with reference to the amendment formula in the 1906 Parliament (Constitution) Act. The 1919 Form of Government (Constitution) Act repealed constitutional Acts of Swedish origin.[16] Later on, the multi-documentary formal Constitution of Finland was broadened by the 1922 Ministerial Responsibility (Constitution) Act (274/1922) and the 1922 Court of the Realm (Constitution) Act (273/1922). Finally, the 1906 Parliamentary (Constitution) Act was repealed by the 1928 Parliament (Constitution) Act (7/1928).

While all this was happening between 1906 and 1928, the evolution of the multi-documentary constitution of Finland may be understood as being based on certain very foundational elements that could be identified as 'the social contract in Finland' (although constitutional life in Finland is not normally described in terms of a social contract). In fact, it is highly unusual to use the concept of the social contract in Finland, but by using the concept in this context, some light can be shed on why constitutions change, or, more importantly, why they do not change, at least not very much, and, if they do change, why some changes are more difficult than others to make. The first element of the social contract would have emerged in 1906 and contains direct and proportional elections to the legislature on the basis of universal suffrage. The second one would have occurred in 1917 and would underline the self-determination, independence and (external and, in particular, internal) sovereignty of Finland. In 1918, the third element emerged and would identify Finland as a republic with a strong presidency.[17] Finally, in 1919, these elements were restated at the same time as Finland was not defined in the Form of Government (Constitution) Act as a pure nation state based on the idea of 'one people, one state, one language',[18] but instead as a language-liberal state based on the idea of 'one people, one state, two languages'.[19] Below, a number of elements are touched upon through more

---

[15] See Jyränki, note 1 above, 472–76.

[16] However, in relation to the amendment involving constitutional rights in 1995, it was noticed that some prerogatives of the estates from 1723 and 1789 had remained in force, and at that point they were finally formally repealed. At the same time, the 1906 (Constitution) Act on the Freedom of Speech, Assembly and Association was repealed.

[17] The civil war that was fought between the Reds and the Whites in January—April 1918 would probably have challenged, at least in the long run, the independence of the country and also the multi-party system of the country, but it certainly did pose an immediate challenge to the market economy based on private ownership, and therefore, because almost half of the population wished to create a Socialist system and was ultimately defeated, it could be argued that market economy and private ownership are not foundational elements embedded in the social contract in Finland.

[18] After the First World War, all new states created, except Finland, were organised as pure nation-states.

[19] This feature would place Finland in the same group of countries as Switzerland and Canada, and it can also be said that the European Union, with its numerous official languages, has adopted a language-liberal position.

concrete examples, namely the Åland Islands issue, the permissibility of referendums and the impact of Finnish membership in the European Union on the office of the President of Finland (see below).[20]

The text of the Finnish Constitution, as laid down in the four above-mentioned Acts, remained largely unamended until the mid-1980s, with the exception of some minor adjustments.[21] Does this mean that there was no constitutional development in Finland between 1919 and 1985? No. Instead there were different methods by which the Finnish Constitution was affected, such as Acts of Exception, constitutional interpretation, and—probably to be viewed a part of the latter—also some organic development. After that period, a series of piecemeal constitutional amendments took place, the most important one being the reform of constitutional rights in 1995. These amendments and the enactment of the new Constitution of Finland were made using the amendment formula in section 67 of the 1928 Parliament (Constitution) Act, requiring the '1/2 + elections + 2/3' model, now replicated as the main method of amendment in section 73 of the current Constitution.[22] Within that amendment formula, a certain development of principles for constitutional amendments has taken place: but what are they, where do they stem from and how are they implemented?

[20] The more recent discussion concerning the system with two national languages and the possible challenges that this system is undergoing will not be discussed in this context. However, see M Suksi 'Finland: four different regimes of linguistic minority rights' (2008) *Percorsi costituzionali* 223, at 224–30, M Suksi 'Finland: Reform of Regional State Administration and Universities' (2010) 16 *European Public Law* 357, at 360–64.

[21] It deserves to be pointed out that the Constitution of Finland continued to be in force also through the Second World War and that Parliament remained in session and operative during that difficult time. After the war, a so-called war liability trial was instituted against such members of Government who held the most central governmental positions during the war and who could be viewed—in particular by the Soviet Union—as politically responsible for Finnish involvement in wars against the Soviet Union as a co-belligerent (but not a formal ally) of Germany. The legislation, which created retroactive criminal law against the prevailing constitutional principles and a temporary court for issues of war responsibility, was enacted by Parliament pursuant to the doctrine of the Act of Exception. See Act on the Punishment of Those who Caused the War (890/1945). There have been several attempts to declare void the sentences passed in the illegitimate process, with the aim of restoring the honour of those sentenced, but the Supreme Court declared in the case KKO 2008:94 that this cannot be done, because there exists no legal basis for such a decision. Thus the Supreme Court felt that it was not competent to try an application to revoke the sentence of one of those condemned. In the case, the Supreme Court made the point that the enactment of the Act as an Act of Exception shows that a notable majority of Parliament viewed the treatment of the war responsibility issue as so important for the implementation of the so-called interim peace treaty that it just had to be done under the circumstances, although the Act at the same time violated several core principles of the legal order.

[22] Some amendments were effectuated by means of the fast track formula of '5/6 + 2/3', without intervening elections. In a case dealt with under the new Constitution, the Constitutional Committee stopped the fast track procedure in its Report 10/2006. The Committee was of the opinion that the constitutional amendment proposed by the Government was necessary, but concluded that the fast track procedure should be available only in situations where there is a de facto compelling need for the use of the fast track procedure. The general rule is that constitutional amendments are made by using the normal amendment formula, and the amendment Bill was eventually dealt with in the normal order of amendment of '1/2 + elections + 2/3'.

PIECEMEAL AMENDMENTS RESULTING IN A NEW CONSTITUTION

There was an attempt to carry out a total reform of the Finnish Constitution in the 1970s. However, at that point it was difficult to reach political agreement between the Left and the Right on a number of issues of substance, and as a consequence work towards a total reform of the Constitution collapsed.[23] Thereafter a revised strategy for constitutional reform emerged, involving piecemeal and step-by-step amendment which became operative in the mid-1980s and included such issues as the introduction of the advisory referendum in the text of the Constitution, the alteration of the method of election of the President of the Republic from an indirect to a direct one, specification of the mechanism of parliamentary accountability, replacement of the absolute veto of the President concerning Acts of Parliament by a suspensive veto, and abolition of the right of the minority in the Parliament to vote to leave an Act of Parliament pending to the next Parliament, to mention just a few.[24] The accession of Finland to the EU was implemented in the Constitution by way of amendments of some relevant parts of the Constitution.[25] A major change in the text of the Constitution was effectuated by the reform of the constitutional or basic rights of the individuals that entered into force on 1 August 1995, at which point an entire chapter of the 1919 Form of Government (Constitution) Act was renewed.

The piecemeal amendments made during independence to the Finnish Constitution, that is, to the four constitutional documents mentioned earlier, had caused the Finnish Constitution to look like a patchwork of provisions.[26] The text of the Constitution had lost its consistency (if there ever was much) and it was difficult for an ordinary citizen to extract from the four separate documents of the Constitution the different procedures regulated therein. In particular, it may have been difficult to make connections between the Form of Government (Constitution) Act and the Parliament (Constitution) Act, for instance, when tracing the decision-making path concerning a particular issue. Moreover, the

---

[23] See *Valtiosääntökomitean välimietintö 1974* (the interim report of a governmental committee tasked to draft a new constitution), 1974, in which report the chairperson of the committee brought out the political divisions by subjecting different constitutional issues to internal votes in the committee and by recording those votes in the committee report. The consequence of this method was that the lack of such broad consensus that would have been needed for a total reform of the constitution was effectively demonstrated. Concerning the Socialist influences in constitutional thinking, see, eg, H Karapuu, ed, *Harvojen tasavalta—perustuslain epädemokraattisuus*, 1970, which even contained a (hopefully not seriously meant) proposal for a constitution influenced by Socialist thoughts. Concerning the work of the committee and the ideas approved by the committee as a whole, by its majority and by its minority as well as the extent to which they have been realised in the Constitution 25 years later, see A Jyränki 'Vuosien 1970–1974 valtiosääntökomitea: mitkä tavoitteet ovat toteutuneet' (1999) 97 *Lakimies* 856.

[24] For a complete review of amendments to the Finnish Constitution between 1919 and 1999, see Government Bill 1/1998, 8–11.

[25] See A Rosas, 'Finland's Accession to the European Union: Constitutional Aspects' (1995) 1 *European Public Law* 166.

[26] See, eg, J Salminen 'Om revideringen av grundlagen—beredningen av nödvändiga ändringar i Finlands grundlag' (2010) *Förvaltningsrättslig tidskrift* 161, at 164.

almost 900 Acts of Exception adopted between 1919 and 2000, some of them temporary, some of them more permanent, contributed some confusion to the actual substantive contents of the Constitution (see below).

A reform project started by the mid-1990s, after an initiative by the Constitutional Committee,[27] resulted on 12 February 1999 (on the basis of Government Bill 1/1998 concerning the enactment of a Form of Government (Constitution) Act) in the adoption by the Parliament of a new consolidated and modernised text of the whole Constitution.[28] This consolidated text was re-adopted by a majority of two thirds by the new Parliament after the parliamentary elections in March 1999.[29] At the entering into force on 1 March 2000 of the new Constitution, the four constitutional Acts that had, during independence, formed the written constitution of Finland, were repealed and replaced by one single document, the Constitution of Finland.[30] The Constitution was enacted on the basis of the Government Bill with only minor substantive adjustments made in the Parliament. The most visible one was the change of the traditional name of the main constitutional document into 'the Constitution of Finland'. The new Constitution of Finland starts with a very short procedural Preamble in which reference is made to section 67 of the 1928 Parliament (Constitution) Act on constitutional amendment and which means that the amendment procedure involving a qualified majority was used in the Parliament when the new Constitution was adopted. The reference also establishes the formal link of the new Constitution with the previous constitutional documents and underlines formal constitutional continuity. In section 130, the text declares itself a Constitution.

The numerous partial amendments to the Constitution in the 1980s and 1990s created a platform for the idea that the development of the Constitution was based on continuity.[31] The Constitution of the year 2000 did not aim at changing the fundamentals of the Finnish Constitution, but was based on the solutions that had ripened and that had been adopted during previous decades, the main objective being the consolidation and modernisation of the Constitution.[32] Hence although an entirely new constitutional text was produced that marked a formal constitutional change, the material contents of the Constitution did not

---

[27] Report of the Constitutional Committee 16/1994. See also *Perustuslaki 2000—Grundlag 2000. Komiteanmietintö—Kommittébetänkande* 1997:13, 1997; Government Bill 1/1998, 5; Report of the Constitutional Committee 10/1998.
[28] The text was approved the first time under the requirement of a simple majority of those voting in the third reading on 12 February 1999 by 170 votes to four in favour of the new Constitution.
[29] The final approval took place after the intervening regular elections on 4 June 1999 by 175 votes to two in favour of the new Constitution.
[30] President Tarja Halonen, elected in January—February 2000, assumed her office under the new Constitution on 1 March 2000. A separate Act on the Measures Required for the Implementation of the Constitution (732/1999) was passed, too, in order to regulate the practical modalities of the coming into force of the new Constitution.
[31] For instance, during the parliamentary period of 1991–95, 28 amendments received final approval. See *Selvitys perustuslakiuudistuksen toimeenpanosta* 2002, 19; Government Bill 1/1998, 5.
[32] Government Bill 1/1998, 30 f.

change very much from what had been achieved during the 1980s and 1990s through the partial amendments. The new Constitution is mainly a codification of existing practice and a re-writing of certain provisions. There was no intention to make far-reaching changes to the actual contents of the Constitution, but to polish the text and make it more current. One of the guiding principles of the enactment of the new Constitution was the principle of relative permanency of the Constitution. At the same time there was a wish to avoid legislating at the constitutional level on concrete visions about future details and temporal procedures of a technical nature.[33]

The reform was to a large extent based on the contents of the then existing constitutional Acts, and the aim was to rewrite constitutional norms so that the resulting coherent document would form a well-functioning whole and a fairly permanent set of provisions for the start of the new millennium. The new Constitution was not intended to be too susceptible to the short-sighted demands of everyday politics, but instead flexible and adaptable. Hence the reform was not only about the rewriting of the written constitution against the background of the existing constitutional documents, but it also took into account developments that had taken place in constitutional practice and in the material constitution. It was, however, recognised in the preparatory works that the reshuffling of the constitutional provisions and principles in one single document could in itself lead to changes in the interpretation of the constitutional mechanisms and provisions and hence influence the substance of the Constitution. Indeed, the Constitution, as adopted, contains a number of clear amendments of substance, but the primary aim was not to carry out extensive amendments that would affect the fundamental principles of the previous constitutional set-up.[34] Instead, a fairly low-key refurbishing of the text was carried out, partly with the aim of avoiding political confrontations in the face of an amendment formula which requires a great deal of consensus.

The number of sections in the new Constitution is low, only 131, in comparison with the four 'old' constitutional Acts, that altogether contained well over 200 sections.[35] Combined with the logic and consistency of the new Constitution as well as with the more modern and to-the-point language, the document is considerably more user-friendly than the previous constitutional Acts. However, in relation to the individual, the Constitution is not self-executing to any great

---

[33] Government Bill 1/1998, 31.

[34] The following fundamental principles are mentioned in Government Bill 1/1998, 32: the republican form of government, the sovereignty of the state, inviolability of human dignity, the freedoms and rights of the individual, promotion of justice in society, the democratic character of the Constitution, the principle that state power belongs to the people, the principle of representative democracy, the separation of powers, the independence of judiciary, the principle of parliamentary accountability, and the principle of the rule of law.

[35] Concerning a description of the contents of the Constitution, see M Suksi 'Finland: the Constitution 2000' (1999) 5 *European Public Law* 338. For an unofficial translation into English, see http://www.finlex.fi/fi/laki/kaannokset/1999/en19990731.pdf.

extent, although it is more so than its predecessor. In relation to the individual, the Constitution operates very much under the assumption that the Parliament has to adopt implementing legislation in order to give effect to the provisions of the Constitution. Therefore, the immediate source of law concerning the rights and obligations of the individual is not the Constitution as such, but the ordinary legislation adopted by the Parliament.

One crucial novelty, a limited form of decentralised judicial review *post legem*, was recorded in section 106 of the Constitution. This form of judicial review does not allow for parliamentary legislation to be declared unconstitutional *per se*, and at the same time, the possibility to review constitutional problems between state organs is excluded. Instead, in Finland, the main form of constitutional interpretation is still the scrutiny or review *ante legem* of an abstract kind of the constitutionality of bills, performed primarily by the Constitutional Committee of the Parliament.[36] The emphasis that the Finnish constitutional system places on the principle of parliamentary sovereignty is visible also in the role that the Opinions of the Constitutional Committee are given in the concrete review of constitutionality of application of Acts under section 106 of the Constitution: if the Constitutional Committee has dealt with the Act when it was passed and concluded that the dimension of an Act, the constitutionality of which is allegedly in doubt in a court proceeding, does not prevent the bill from being passed in the ordinary legislative procedure by simple majority, then the court cannot—as a rule—find an evident unconstitutionality in the concrete application of the Act.[37] Hence the institution of judicial review was not introduced in the extensive and centralised way known from many of the fairly fresh constitutions of Central and Eastern Europe, but is implemented in a highly conditional manner that is likely to leave the practical value of the institution at a relatively low level.

The new Constitution had, by 2010, already been amended twice. The first amendment dealt with the concentration of parliamentary oversight over accounting procedures in a new standing committee of the Parliament. The second amendment made it possible under an ordinary act enacted by the Parliament to transfer a citizen against his or her will to another country for

---

[36] The Constitutional Committee is a standing committee of the Finnish Parliament, composed of a minimum of 17 MPs. It is assisted by three legal councillors and it normally hears professors and other experts on constitutional issues before issuing its reports to the plenary of Parliament or opinions to other committees of Parliament. It is tasked in section 74 of the Constitution to 'issue statements on the constitutionality of legislative proposals and other matters brought for its consideration, as well as on their relation to international human rights treaties'. The issues determined by the Constitutional Committee are regarded as authoritative interpretations of the Constitution of Finland, normally followed by the plenary and the other organs of Parliament.

[37] This interpretation of the term 'evident conflict' is provided in the *travaux preparatoires* to section 106 and it means that the normative status of an Opinion of the Constitutional Committee concerning an ordinary act suspected of evident conflict with the Constitution is elevated to a determining one in a manner which is probably not the most transparent one and which might affect the independence of the judiciary.

certain purposes, mainly necessitated by EU law.[38] At the same time it was made possible to appoint a stand-in for the Vice-Ombudsman of the Parliament. In the spring of 2010, the Government presented amendment bills to the Parliament which, if adopted, affect 15 provisions of the Constitution. By April 2011, the amendment bills had been adopted by the (previous) Parliament, and are awaiting final approval after the elections by the new Parliament (see next section).

REFORM WITH ACTIVE FOLLOW-UP

The stated aim of constitutional reform in the year 2000 was to maintain the relative stability and permanence of the Constitution.[39] The general idea was that it would not be necessary to amend the Constitution, at least in the immediate future.[40] Hence the approach to constitutional amendments would be restrictive, but at the same time the aim was that the Constitution should paint the correct picture about the system of exercise of state power and about the basic elements of the legal position of the individual as well as about those fundamental decisions that are implemented through ordinary legislation.[41]

Therefore, the new Constitution that entered into force in the year 2000 did not mark the end point of a 25-year-long reform period. Instead, the implementation and application of the Constitution has been actively followed up since the entering into force of the new text.[42] In the spring of 2001, the first follow-up report concerning the implementation of the constitutional reform was published.[43] In November 2002, a report by the constitutional follow-up group was published,[44] after which the Government gave to the Parliament a Notification from the Prime Minister on the issue,[45] followed by a discussion in plenary in January 2003.[46] The governmental programme of the second government of Prime Minister Vanhanen of 19 April 2007 stated that the functioning of the Constitution would be reviewed and that a parliamentary steering group would be established. In October 2008, a working group on the Constitution prepared a report concerning amendment needs,[47] and in October 2008, the Government

---

[38] The expulsion of a citizen was categorically forbidden in section 9 of the Constitution, but possibilities to do so had been opened up in some Acts, all of which had been enacted as Acts of Exception. The amendment thus brought the text of the Constitution into line with the factual situation. See also Salminen 2010, above note 26, 165, 170 f.

[39] Government Bill 60/2010, 12.

[40] Government Bill 1/1998, 31.

[41] Government Bill 60/2010, 4.

[42] Government Bill 60/2010, 4, 31.

[43] See *Uuden perustuslain seurantaraportti I. Katsaus perustuslakiuudistuksen toimeenpanoajalta* 1 March 2000–28 February 2001.

[44] *Selvitys perustuslakiuudistuksen voimaanpanosta.* Perustuslain seurantatyöryhmän mietintö. Oikeusministeriö, työryhmämietintö 2002:7.

[45] PI 4/2002.

[46] PTK 173/2002.

[47] *Perustuslaki 2008 –työryhmä.* Oikeusministeriö, työryhmämietintö 2008:8.

established a committee for the adjustment of the Constitution in order to prepare the necessary amendments to the Constitution.[48] The work of this broad-based governmental committee led to the handing over to the Parliament of Government Bill 60/2010 with the proposal for amendments to the Constitution of Finland. There was a broad hearing procedure amongst the various interest groups on the basis of the work of the committee.[49] However, this follow-up from the point of view of the executive power was not only necessitated by the wish of the executive power to ascertain the functioning of the Constitution during its first years of existence. Impulses in that direction came also from the Constitutional Committee of the Parliament, at least as concerns certain issues, such as the delegation of law-making powers during states of emergency and modernisation of the concept of state of emergency and its scope[50] as well as mention of the membership of Finland in the EU and a provision concerning transfer of national powers to the EU.[51] Although the evaluation projects concerning the Constitution have contributed to the identification of those constitutional issues which were creating needs for amendment or adjustment,[52] this conscious work has also been influenced by the evolution of the EU and the effects of that development at the national level.

When the first amendment to the new Constitution was being prepared in Parliament in 2005, the Constitutional Committee published a number of amendment principles.[53] First, there should be a restrictive attitude towards amendments to the Constitution. The reason for this is that everyday politics should not determine the need for constitutional amendments, and amendment proposals should not weaken the stability of the basic constitutional mechanisms or the position of the Constitution as the foundation of the state order and the constitutional order. Secondly, and to some extent in opposition to the restrictive principle, consideration should be given to the fact that the Constitution should give an accurate picture of the system for the exercise of state power and the basis of the legal position of the individual.[54] Thirdly, if amendment needs emerge, they have to be carefully evaluated and the amendments found necessary have to be made on the basis of thorough preparation, surrounded by a broad discussion and consensus. Evidently, consensus is mandated by the qualified majority of

---

[48] *Perustuslain tarkistamiskomitean mietintö.* Oikeusministeriön mietintöjä 9/2010.
[49] Government Bill 60/2010, 32.
[50] Opinion of the Constitutional Committee 6/2009.
[51] Opinion of the Constitutional Committee 13/2008 and Opinion of the Constitutional Committee 36/2006.
[52] Government Bill 60/2010, 4.
[53] Report of the Constitutional Committee No 5/2005, 2.
[54] In the Government Bill 60/2010, 27, the Government follows the Report of the Constitutional Committee by specifying the correctness principle further. According to the Government, the Constitution should give such a picture about the exercise of public powers in Finland, about the relationship of the public powers and the individual and about the fundamental elements concerning public powers and the individual that has sufficient clarity and coverage at the same time as the picture is informative and current.

two-thirds required for the final amendment decision, which in the Finnish political setting means that at least the three largest parties (at that point the Conservatives, the Social Democrats, and the Centre Party) should forge a common understanding about the amendments. These three principles can be identified as the restrictive principle, the correctness principle, and the consensus principle. In addition, it is possible to identify some drafting principles that were in operation when the Constitution was adopted at the end of the 1990s. The first one is the principle of transparency of constitutional legislation.[55] The second one is the aim to follow the principle of completeness, originally identified by the Constitutional Committee in 1994.[56]

Although the new Constitution has been amended twice since it entered into force in the year 2000, none of those amendments has actually resulted from the follow-up work, but are the consequence of other needs. The two amendments are relatively limited in the totality of the Constitution and are of a detailed nature. Moreover, they were not the reason for a general consideration of the need to amend the Constitution a decade after its enactment. Instead, the Government Bill 60/2010 on the amendment of the Constitution of Finland, given to the Parliament in 2010, was based on a broad and systematic evaluation of the totality of the Constitution, based on experiences and information from the ten-year period, which was considered a sufficient time-frame for overhaul.[57] Although the Government Bill has not been adopted yet (in April 2011) by two parliaments, the five principles of constitutional amendment (restrictiveness, correctness, consensus, transparency and completeness) are forward-looking and mean that most probably the Constitution of Finland will undergo amendments in the future, even if the current amendment proposal does not eventually receive the required level of support.

Almost parallel to the general process of updating the new Constitution on the basis of a more general review, there is a particular process of amending the electoral system so as to correct it in a direction that ensures a more complete overall proportionality. No such amendment was made in the new Constitution in 2000, although the issue had been raised several times during the past decades. The Government Bill 7/2010 was preceded by three governmental committees during the first decade of the 21st century, but after the discussion in the Parliament, it is still somewhat unclear if the proposal, adopted by the Parliament for abeyance over the elections of 2011, will achieve sufficient consensus to meet

---

[55] Government Bill 60/2010, 27. See also Government Bill 1/1998, 6.

[56] Report of the Constitutional Committee 14/1994. See also Government Bill 1/1998, 6, Government Bill 60/2010, 27.

[57] Government Bill 60/2010, 4, 12. On 16 February 2011, the Parliament approved the amendment bill by 144 votes to 26.

the requirement of qualified majority in the new Parliament.[57a] The amendment
proposal aims at remedying the current variance between 3 and 14 percent in the
so-called hidden support threshold between different multi-member constituencies by distributing the seats amongst the regional constituency seats in a way
that uses the entire state as an electoral district and by establishing a national
support threshold of 3 percent for access to the Parliament. The seats would be
distributed following a combination of the current d'Hondt method and the
Hare-Niemeyer method, but the system is already criticised for lack of
transparency. This means that one of the drafting principles from the end of the
1990s may become sidelined.

ACTS OF EXCEPTION—AND AVOIDING THEM

It has been noted above that during the latter half of the nineteenth century the
practice of using so-called Acts of Exception started to form within the Legislation Committee of the Diet, and that the Constitutional Committee of Parliament continued with the practice after 1906. The practice was based on the
understanding that in the legislative life of a nation, there may, for political
reasons, exist moments when a piece of law needs to be adopted which is against
the formal letter of the Constitution. In such situations, so the doctrine establishes, the parliament may, by using the same formulas as prescribed for constitutional amendments, pass an 'ordinary' Act of Parliament which is, from a
substantive point of view, in breach of the Constitution. Such an Act of Exception
introduces limitations or conditions, embedded in an ordinary Act of Parliament,
that open up 'holes in the wall' which the formal Constitution creates. The
possibility of such exceptions was indicated in section 95 of the 1919 Form of
Government (Constitution) Act and section 94 of the 1928 Parliament (Constitution) Act, which referred to the possibility to enact, amend, explain or make
exceptions to these documents in the order prescribed for constitutional amendment, where the term 'exceptions', in particular, could be used as a legal basis for
Acts of Exception.[58]

[57a] The Report of the Constitutional Committee (11/2010) to the plenary of the Parliament
contained several dissenting opinions in spite of the fact that the Committee recommended that the
threshold be lowered to 2 percent. The Parliament decided to set the threshold at 3 percent, as
proposed by the Government, and adopted the amendment on 15 March 2011 for abeyance over the
elections by 134 votes to 50.

[58] Jyränki, note 1 above, 492–500.

An Act of Exception can be defined as an 'ordinary' Act of Parliament through which it has been possible to accept a violation of the core meaning of a constitutional provision. When a bill contains an infringement of the formal Constitution in a manner that affects the core meaning of the constitutional provision in question, such an enactment can, nevertheless, be approved by Parliament as a so-called Act of Exception, provided that the decision is made in the manner prescribed for the adoption of constitutional amendments. The Constitution of the year 2000 made the mechanism somewhat more explicit than the previous constitutional Acts by the provision in section 73, according to which a proposal on the enactment, amendment or repeal of the Constitution *or on the enactment of a limited derogation of the Constitution* shall in the second reading be left in abeyance, by a majority of the votes cast, until the first parliamentary session following parliamentary elections (author's emphasis).

Under the current Constitution, the determination of the constitutionality of the bill is still the responsibility of the Constitutional Committee of the Parliament: under section 74 of the current Constitution of Finland, the Constitutional Committee is the authoritative organ to perform the *ex ante* scrutiny of the constitutionality of bills. This control is focused on a choice between the ordinary procedure of enactment and the use of an Act of Exception, and the choice is made by the Constitutional Committee in a manner which is customarily binding for the Parliament. However, not all bills dealt with in the Finnish Parliament are checked by the Constitutional Committee, but only around 50 bills per year (of which most can be enacted as ordinary Acts of Parliament, either as proposed or after amendments proposed by the Constitutional Committee).[59] Therefore, the control of constitutionality is not systematic and all-encompassing, but dependent on whether potential constitutional issues are identified by the Government in its original bill, by the plenary of the Parliament at the reference reading of the Bill or by the relevant standing committee charged with reporting on the matter in Parliament. It is the relevant standing committee that normally requests an opinion of the Constitutional Committee concerning constitutional issues.

The deliberations of the Constitutional Committee result in a statement on whether a bill could be enacted as an ordinary Act of Parliament or whether the enactment of the bill into law is possible only pursuant to the amendment formula of the Constitution. In order to make possible the enactment of a law under the ordinary procedure of simple majority, the Constitutional Committee may make recommendations on how the bill should be amended by the standing committee in charge of reviewing the bill. However, at the same time, the Committee is of course itself a standing committee of Parliament that consists of

---

[59] Sometimes, the opinions of the Constitutional Committee may cause the Government to withdraw its proposal. This happened in relation to Government Bill 110/2005 concerning military crisis management, because the Opinion 54/2005 of the Constitutional Committee raised a number of fundamental problems, in particular in relation to the position of the President in the context.

Members of Parliament, not an independent court, although the Constitutional Committee has developed a praxis of interpretation of a legal nature in which it tends to refer back to its earlier opinions and statements in reports. The political character of the Committee has, at least in the past, caused it to provide, inter alia, a battleground for the political right and the political left, in particular during the 1970s within the substantive area of the protection of property. In this context, the representatives of the right have had the option of pressing for a qualified majority, which in turn requires a very broad political consensus in law-making that has, in effect, led to the watering down of proposals which may have seemed progressive at the time but which would probably not be welcomed today. The mechanism of Acts of Exception, with the requirement of a qualified majority, has also offered a platform for political deals, where political support towards a qualified majority may have been pledged in exchange for support for other pieces of law that otherwise might not have stood the chance of adoption.

There are two particular features attached to Acts of Exception. First, an Act of Exception does not become a constitutional law, but remains at the level of an ordinary law. An Act of Exception does not define itself as a constitutional Act although it is enacted in a manner prescribed for constitutional amendments. Secondly, because it remains at the level of ordinary law in spite of its purpose to punch a hole in the wall of the formal constitution, the repeal or amendment of an Act of Exception in a way that decreases the hole in the constitutional wall, that is, that abolishes or decreases the material scope of the exception to the constitution, only requires a simple majority of those voting, that is, the ordinary procedure for law-making. This method of producing material exceptions to the formal constitution has added a good deal of flexibility to what is, in principle, a fairly rigid constitution lacking the full-blown mechanism of judicial review through a Constitutional Court or a similar court. At the same time, a consequence of such substantive exceptions to the Constitution has been that it has not always been easy to sort out what the content of the Constitution is at a given moment. Also, a piece of law may have been deemed unconstitutional only in respect of one provision, but the consequence has, nevertheless, been that the entire Act has been enacted pursuant to the constitutional amending formula. Although the Finnish system of abstract constitutional review of bills *ante legem* can be criticised, it has, as a home-grown mechanism fitted by evolution into the constitutional fabric, functioned surprisingly well as the motor of constitutional development, in particular as concerns the material contents of the constitution.[60]

---

[60] It is, from a comparative point of view, worth noting that a somewhat similar procedure for exceptions has been explicitly established in Art 84 of the 1978 Constitution of Sri Lanka concerning bills inconsistent with the Constitution: '(1) A Bill which is not for the amendment of any provision of the Constitution or for the repeal and replacement of the Constitution, but which is inconsistent with any provision of the Constitution may be placed on the Order Paper of Parliament without complying with the requirements of paragraph (1) or paragraph (2) of Article 82. (2) Where the Cabinet of Ministers has certified that a Bill is intended to be passed by the special majority required by this Article or where the Supreme Court has determined that a Bill requires to be passed by such

In spite of the difficulty of enacting an Act of Exception, almost 900 Acts of Exception have been passed since 1919.[61] Not all of them have been in force simultaneously or permanently,[62] but in most instances their application has been limited in some way, such as temporally or materially. However, in 2002, there were up to 114 such Acts of Exception in force that had been enacted during the period 1919–2000. As explained above, before the year 2000, the possibility of enacting Acts of Exception was not very explicitly laid out in the constitutional document. It was argued during the drafting of the new Constitution that this possibility should be abolished altogether, but it was instead granted a somewhat more visible place in the constitutional text and included in section 73. The preparatory documents to the provision nevertheless establish a number of limitations to the use of Acts of Exception. First, the *travaux preparatoires* recommend the interpretation that Acts of Exception would not be used in relation to the most fundamental elements, such as the comprehensive system of constitutional rights and the position of Parliament as the highest state organ. Secondly, although section 73 of the Constitution makes explicit provision for the possibility of exceptions to the Constitution, the *travaux preparatoires* recommend an interpretation of the provision that restricts the use of Acts of Exception.[63] As a consequence, only one Act of Exception has so far been enacted

---

special majority, such Bill shall become law only if the number of votes cast in favour thereof amounts to not less than two-thirds of the whole number of Members (including those not present) and a certificate by the President or the Speaker, as the case may be, is endorsed thereon in accordance with the provisions of Article 80 or 79. (3) Such a Bill when enacted into law shall not, and shall not be deemed to, amend, repeal or replace the Constitution or any provision thereof, and shall not be so interpreted or construed, and may thereafter be repealed by a majority of the votes of the Members present and voting.' In Sri Lanka, the Supreme Court has assumed the position of the arbiter of when a Bill is inconsistent with the Constitution, and there is no requirement of a period of waiting over elections.

[61] N Kasurinen 'Ennen 1.3.2000 säädettyjen poikkeuslakien suhde uuteen perustuslakiin' in *Perustuslakiuudistukseen liittyviä selvityksiä*. Oikeusministeriön työryhmämietintö 2002:8, 2002, 134. See also Kasurinen 2002, 131, who reports following numbers of Acts of Exception over several decades: 1920s: 49 Acts of Exception; 1930s: 82; 1940s: 293; 1950s: 116; 1960s: 99; 1970s: 121; 1980s: 55; 1990s: 59. During the first decade of the current century, there was only one Act of Exception.

[62] One of the more controversial ones—of a temporary nature—was the Act by which the term of office of the incumbent President of Finland, Mr Kekkonen, was prolonged by Parliament for an exceptional four-year period without subjecting the presidency to an election in spite of the fact that the president should, at that point, have been elected by an electoral college for a six-year period. The Act on the Prolongation of the On-Going Term of Office of the President of the Republic (232/1973) was enacted pursuant to the fast track procedure. Finland had signed the UN Covenant on Civil and Political Rights on 16 December 1966, so therefore, arguably, Finland should have tried to avoid undertaking measures that are in conflict with Art 25 of the CCPR by preventing participation through elections. However, Finland ratified the CCPR only on 23 March 1975, and the Covenant entered into force internationally on 23 March 1976, so formally, the prolongation of the term of office of the President by an Act of Exception was not in violation of international law. By one of the piecemeal amendments to the 1919 Form of Government Act, the method of election of the president was changed to direct election in two phases, with the possibility of a run-off election between the two candidates who received most votes in the first round, if none of them gained more than 50% of the votes in the first round.

[63] Government Bill 1/1998, 125.

since the year 2000,[64] which is a dramatic reduction in the number of such Acts in comparison with the situation during the twentieth century.

Today, there are actually three principles that limit the use of Acts of Exception. The first one is that Acts of Exception should be avoided as far as is possible. For the Constitutional Committee of Parliament this means that it tries to explore avenues that permit the enactment of the bill by simple majority as an ordinary Act, in which context the Committee may propose substantive changes to the bill so as to make it conform to the provisions of the Constitution. The second limitation principle is that Acts of Exception should not be adopted in the area of the most fundamental constitutional principles, mentioned above. The third limitation principle is that where it is necessary to enact an Act of Exception, material and, where possible, also temporal limitations should be used. Against this background, an Act of Exception should only introduce an exception to the Constitution which is as circumscribed as possible, that is, that the exception is as little as possible, and that an Act of Exception should be in force for as short a period of time as possible, that is, it should not be in force permanently.[65]

There is, however, an exception to these limitation principles: as concerns international obligations, it is not necessary (and indeed in most cases not even possible) to impose substantive or temporal limitations.[66] Instead, international treaties which stand in conflict with the Constitution in one way or the other are accepted by the qualified majority of two-thirds in a simplified procedure without the constraints of the limitation doctrine.[67] However, the *travaux preparatoires* also make the point that Finland should not conclude treaties that are contrary to the fundamental democratic elements of the Finnish Constitution.[68] As concerns this principle, it could be said that it perhaps indicates the existence of an 'unamendable' core of the Finnish Constitution,[69] although such a conclusion is by no means an established interpretation. Although the provisions in the Constitution concerning the self-government of the Åland Island are not protected against amendments, it may be said that the particular legislation outlining the modalities of the autonomy arrangement of the Åland Islands is entrenched in a manner that approaches the position of an unamendable core (see below).

---

[64] In the Act on Military Crisis Management (211/2006), a permanent exception is made to Section 93(2) of the Constitution, because the President of Finland is given the authority to decide on participation in EU-initiated crisis management missions, although the Council of State is in charge of decision-making in such matters. See also Opinion of the Constitutional Committee 6/2006.

[65] Government Bill 1/1998, 125. See also Government Bill 60/2010, 46.

[66] See also Government Bill 60/2010, 28, where the Government proposes an addition to the Constitution concerning the transfer of national powers to international bodies such as the European Union that would diminish the need to use Acts of Exception in conjunction with the national implementation of international obligations.

[67] Government Bill 1/1998, 125. The *travaux preparatoires* refer, however, to the requirement of a limited exception also in relation to the international treaties.

[68] See also Government Bill 60/2010, 44.

[69] Salminen 2010, above n 26, 169, who makes a reference to Germany in this regard.

DEVELOPMENT IN RELATION TO SOME FUNDAMENTAL ELEMENTS

There is little space for British-styled constitutional conventions in Finland. Instead, the emphasis is on positive legislation as a basis for different measures. This does not, however, mean that the Finnish Constitution does not include or has not, in the past, included unwritten or customary mechanisms or praxis.[70] Different areas of the constitutional life may have experienced some organic development that has not, at least originally, been a part of the written constitution, and it is possible to account for some features that might be interesting in this context, such as the autonomy of the Åland Islands, the advisory referendum and representation in the European Council. As the exploration of these examples indicates, there may exist a preference for eventually recording established institutions or organic practices in the written Constitution. Some other substantive areas could also be analysed from this perspective.

Excursus concerning the Autonomy of the Åland Islands as a Super-Constitutional Feature

Immediately after the entering into force of the 1919 Form of Government (Constitution) Act, the formula of 'one state' as well as the newly gained sovereignty of Finland was challenged. The Swedish-speaking Åland Islands presented claims for unification with Sweden, and the Åland Islands issue evolved into an international conflict between the two states. As an alternative to secession and union with Sweden, the Parliament of Finland enacted in 1920 the Self-Government Act for the Åland Islands (124/1920) that granted extensive law-making powers to the Åland Islands. The Self-Government Act was enacted on the basis of the constitutional amendment formula and thus actually became an Act of Exception. The inhabitants of the Åland Islands refused to become involved in the self-government institutions, and the conflict continued until the matter was subsequently brought to the League of Nations. In 1921, the Council of the League of Nations decided—after negotiations between representatives of Finland and Sweden—that the Åland Islands would belong under the sovereignty of Finland, but under certain conditions established in the so-called Åland Islands Settlement, which is not a formal treaty under public international law. One of the conditions was that the Self-Government Act of 1920 would be complemented by substantive rights and measures pursuant to the same legislative order in which the Self-Government Act had been adopted, thus including the requirement of a corresponding decision by the Legislative Assembly of the

---

[70] One example is the practice of the so-called Evening School, an informal preparatory meeting of the Council of State one day before the general meeting of the Council and, as a consequence, two days before the joint sitting of the President in the Council of State. That practice commenced in the latter part of the 1930s, but has recently faded away.

Åland Islands. Consequently, the Parliament of Finland adopted a direct translation of the Settlement in the form of the so-called Guaranty Act (189/1922),
which thereby got the same status as the Self-Government Act. The implementation of the provisions in the Settlement concerning the right to possess real
property were, however, delayed until the 1930s.[71]

In 1951, the second Self-Government Act (670/1951) was enacted by the
Parliament of Finland and, in the same form, by the Legislative Assembly of the
Åland Islands, following requirements of qualified majority. Finally, the current
Self-Government Act (1144/1991) was enacted in the same manner, and when
doing so Parliament decided explicitly not to qualify the Self-Government Act as
a constitutional Act,[72] because it contained very detailed provisions of a special
kind which were not deemed to be suitable for introduction in a constitutional
Act. Instead, it can be viewed as a particular Act somewhat akin to an Act of
Exception that distributes legislative powers between mainland Finland and the
Åland Islands, creating a special entrenchment of some sort for the
arrangement.[73]

The current Self-Government Act is still an implementing Act in relation to the
1921 Åland Islands Settlement, which is recognised by Finland as an effective
international obligation, thereby creating international entrenchment of the
self-government arrangement of the Åland Islands. So, too, is the Property
Acquisition Act (3/1975) for the Åland Islands, enacted by the Finnish Parliament
by a two-thirds qualified majority pursuant to the constitutional amendment
formula, but without declaring itself a constitutional Act. In respect of property
and the right to carry out business operations in the Åland Islands, there is
something close to an unamendable core of the Constitution: section 28 of the
Self-Government Act lays down that the amendment of the Constitution or
another Act shall not enter into force in Åland without the consent of the
Legislative Assembly of the Åland Islands insofar as it relates to the principles
governing the right of a private person to own real property or business property
in the Åland Islands. This means that the Parliament of Finland cannot, by
amendments to the Constitution, try to diminish the particular Ålandic property
rights if the Legislative Assembly of the Åland Islands is opposed to such a
measure. This particular material entrenchment is an extra safeguard, but it has
never been needed.[74]

---

[71] Concerning the Åland Islands, see M Suksi, *Ålands konstitution*, 2005. While mainland Finland
is a bilingual territory, the Åland Islands, with currently around 28000 inhabitants, is unilingually
Swedish-speaking.

[72] See Suksi ibid, 463.

[73] For a comparison of different autonomy arrangements and the various entrenchment types, see
M Suksi 'On the Entrenchment of Autonomy' in M Suksi, ed, *Autonomy: Applications and Implications*, 1998, 151–71. Concerning the elevation of the permanency of the Åland Islands legislation, see,
in particular, 156 f. See also M Suksi, *Sub-State Governance through Territorial Autonomy* (forthcoming, 2011).

[74] See also Suksi note 71 above, 170, 462 f, 500 f. It could be mentioned in addition that Finland
achieved, in the negotiations concerning EU membership, a particular arrangement at the level of

Only in 1994, the Form of Government (Constitution) Act was amended so as to make explicit the position of the Åland Islands in the constitutional setting by means of a so-called general entrenchment. Hence during more than 70 years, it was not possible to discern from the formal constitutional texts that there existed, in Finland, a distribution of legislative powers between the Parliament of Finland and the Legislative Assembly of the Åland Islands. The constitutional definition of the Åland Islands was carried over to sections 75 and 120 of the Constitution of Finland. The position of the Åland Islands cannot be opened up for a broader discussion in this context, but the Self-Government Act is peculiar in the sense that it can only be repealed or amended by Parliament in the procedure prescribed for constitutional amendments, provided that the Åland Legislative Assembly makes a similar decision by a qualified majority of two-thirds, recognised in general terms by the constitutional provisions.

In addition, there is a normative level of constitutional law in the internal legal order of the Åland Islands. Concerning local government elections in the Åland Islands, the Self-Government Act makes it possible for the Legislative Assembly to enlarge the scope of the eligibility requirements, provided that the decision is made by a two-thirds qualified majority (albeit without the requirement of an intervening election). A similar requirement of qualified majority of two-thirds exists in the Act on the Acquisition of Real Property for the adoption by the Legislative Assembly of an additional Ålandic Act that further specifies the methods of transfer of property. Finally, the Legislative Assembly has itself decided to adopt legislation under the requirement of a qualified majority of two-thirds, and the Supreme Court of Finland has, as the oversight body concerning the use of legislative competence in the Åland Islands (but not in mainland Finland), recognised that the Legislative Assembly of the Åland Islands is within its competence if it decides to create Ålandic Acts under the requirement of a two-thirds qualified majority.[75] Hence it is clear that even within the Ålandic jurisdiction, there can be a hierarchy of Ålandic norms which recognises a separation between ordinary Ålandic acts and Ålandic acts of a constitutional nature.

Excursus concerning Interpretation Leading to Codification I: the Advisory Referendum

The substantive Constitution is not only affected by Acts of Exception dealt with above. Just months after the formal Declaration of Independence on 6 December

primary law, the Protocol 2 on the Åland Islands, attached to the Finnish accession treaty. Protocol 2 makes exceptions in EU law for the Ålandic property regime and the right to carry out business operations in the Åland Islands. See Suksi note 71 above, 260–63.

[75] See Opinion of the Supreme Court of 20 November 1971, in which the creation of a requirement of a qualified majority for the amendment of Ålandic acts was deemed to be in harmony with the legislation concerning self-government. See also Suksi note 71 above, 473–79.

1917, there was a domestic challenge to the legitimate government by way of an insurgence of the so-called Reds, who aimed at a revolution and were opposed by the so-called Whites, who were identified as the possessors of the legitimate governmental powers. The Reds were clearly interested in creating a breach in the constitutional continuity of Finland and to replace the then constitutional legislation with a new Constitution, the draft of which was drawn up with far-reaching direct democratic features and provisionally approved by the legislative assembly of the Reds. Against the background of the civil war of 1918 and the Red draft constitution loaded with provisions concerning the referendum and other forms of direct participation, it is not surprising that the White side, which was victorious in the civil war, drafted the 1919 Form of Government Act entirely along representative lines.

Already in 1922, a proposal was made by an MP that an ad hoc referendum be held on the Prohibition Act that limited the production, sale and consumption of alcoholic beverages. The Constitutional Committee of the Parliament held that such a direct recourse to the voters was possible only in the advisory form and *ante legem*, because the referendum should not become an organic outgrowth of the Constitution.[76] The Prohibition Act, however, led to increasing social problems and, in particular, smuggling and other illegal activities in a way that started to threaten the established social order. In the elections of 1928, none of the parties pledged to abolish the Prohibition Act, but the problems with the Act grew to the extent that by 1931 the Government was forced to do something to resolve the situation. A comparative look at Iceland, Norway, Sweden and some states in the United States justified in part the conclusion that in Finland, also, the matter could be resolved by a referendum.[77] In that way, a direct recourse to the people on a single issue that cut across the supporters of all parties was found reasonable. Therefore, the Government proposed to Parliament that a referendum on prohibition should be held.

The Government bill was dealt with by the Constitutional Committee of Parliament, which reversed its earlier opinion in the matter. The Committee concluded in its Opinion that it is possible to organise advisory referendums *post legem* in Finland on the basis of ordinary legislation (that is, an Act of Exception was not needed), but under two conditions: (1) that the issue belongs to the sphere of knowledge and experience of the voters; and (2) that there exist compelling and exceptional reasons for such an advisory referendum. From the point of view of the theory of holes in the constitutional wall, the deviation from the formal constitution was not so great as to necessitate the enactment of the Act concerning the Organization of a Consultative Referendum for the Purpose of Clarifying the Grounds for Legislation on Intoxicating Liquors (340/1931) as an Act of Exception, so the deviation could be handled by means of an ordinary Act

---

[76] See M Suksi, *Bringing in the People—a Comparison of Constitutional Forms and Practices of the Referendum*, 1993, 221.
[77] Suksi, above note 76, 222.

adopted by simple majority. Parliament enacted a unique Act including provisions concerning the advisory referendum on the prohibition issue, and in the subsequent referendum with three alternatives (continued Prohibition, allowing wine, abolishing Prohibition), more than 70 per cent of the voters supported the abolition of the Prohibition Act. In an exceptional parliamentary session, called together immediately after the referendum between two regular Parliaments, the Parliament decided to revoke the Prohibition Act and to establish new legislation concerning the sale of alcoholic beverages based on a state monopoly.

The two principles for the organisation of advisory referendums formulated by the Constitutional Committee were used later on in the 1930s to fend off proposals concerning other referendums on single issues, but there were other proposals, for instance, in the 1960s to amend the Constitution so as to make possible decisive, binding referendums for constitutional amendments. In the abortive overhaul of the Constitution in mid-1970s, the advisory referendum gained some support. When the constitutional 'pressures' that were built up over time caused a series of amendments to be made, the first one was the introduction of the advisory referendum in section 22a of the Form of Government (Constitution) Act. In many ways, it is possible to conclude that the provision was, after a half-century low period in terms of application, a codification of earlier practice permitting advisory referendums, but without the specific conditions that the Constitutional Committee had developed in 1931. This provision was used in 1994 as the legal basis for the advisory referendum on accession to the EU, which was deemed to involve such a measure of transfer of sovereign powers to the EU that the people had to be consulted before the final decision was made by Parliament. Although the principles developed in the 1930s for the organisation of advisory referendums do not apply any longer, it could be argued that the EU referendum fulfilled very well at least the second condition, the existence of compelling and exceptional reasons, while it could also be argued that the EU matter did not, at that point of time, belong to the sphere of knowledge and experience of the voters.

It was never the intention of the drafting work towards the new Constitution to alter the fundamental features of the Constitution and of national decision-making in Finland. It is therefore very natural that, for instance, the institution of the referendum was carried over from the Form of Government (Constitution) Act to the new constitutional text without any real changes, although there was some discussion about the possibility of creating a decisive referendum, for instance, for the final approval of constitutional amendments. Section 53 of the new Constitution is, nevertheless, considerably shorter than the old provision.[78] However, the meaning of the provision, if read together with section 14, subsections 1 and 3 on electoral and participatory rights, is the same as that of

---

[78] Section 53 Referendums: (1) The decision to organise an advisory referendum shall be made by an Act that contains provisions on the time of the referendum and on the alternatives to be put to the voters. (2) Provisions concerning the procedure at referendums shall be laid down by an Act.

the old provision: the determination of the right to vote and the duty of the state to inform have been moved to section 14, although in a somewhat less explicit form than what was included in Article 22a of the Form of Government (Constitution) Act.

Although the Constitution reiterates the contents of the institution of the referendum without any substantial changes in comparison with the previous Form of Government (Constitution) Act, it is, however, possible to claim that the attitude of the Finnish Constitution even towards the theoretical possibility of creating a decisive, binding referendum by means of a so-called Act of Exception, which has never taken place in respect of the referendum, has grown more hostile.[79] The preparatory works for the Constitution recommend the interpretation that Acts of Exception would not be used in relation to the most fundamental elements of the Constitution, such as the position of the Parliament as the highest state organ.[80] Therefore, a decisive referendum could not be created by using an Act of Exception.

Excursus concerning Interpretation Leading to Codification II: Representation in the European Council

Issues of foreign policy have traditionally been the prerogative of the President, who can be understood as the hallmark of the republic and whose position has been sustained by the switch to direct election in the 1990s, although simultaneously, the formal powers of the President in other areas were diminishing. However, with the Finnish accession to the EU, the situation concerning foreign policy changed dramatically: the different competencies and functions of the Union do not necessarily assume the traditional format of foreign policy with one focal point in the State, but lead to a structure in which the various sectors of the Union are referred, according to the subject matter, directly to the relevant national administrations, and many of the Union matters have little to do with traditional foreign policy. The Finnish Presidency was not well equipped to deal with the situation after the accession, although constitutional amendments were made to that effect: in spite of section 33 in the Form of Government (Constitution) Act providing in principle for the competence of Finland to participate in the meetings of the European Council in the Council of State (that is, the meeting of the Ministers accountable to Parliament), the then President, Mr Ahtisaari, formulated a *dictum* to the minutes of the meeting of the Council of State when the amendments to the Form of Government (Constitution) Act were ratified that indicated that the President would decide which matters belong to

---

[79] It should be mentioned that Government Bill 60/2010 with proposals to amend the Constitution also contains a draft provision for a so-called agenda initiative by which a certain number of voters could initiate a piece of draft law with Parliament and compel Parliament to deal with it.

[80] Government Bill 1/1998, 125.

the competence of the President. As a consequence, the praxis developed during that Presidency that the President made an announcement of his participation in the meetings of the European Council,[81] that is, in the top level summit of the EU that met twice a year, and that announcement was brought to the minutes of the meeting of the Council of State. Hence the President wished to be represented at the top level, with the consequence that a constitutional problem emerged between the President and the Constitutional Committee in Parliament due to their different interpretations of the situation. The consistent position of the Constitutional Committee has been that Finland would be represented through the Government that is accountable to Parliament, not through the President. In practice, this problem, commonly referred to as the problem of two plates, has been visible in the double representation of Finland at the EU summits, when both the President and the Prime Minister have participated in meetings.

From the year 2000 onwards, section 93 of the Constitution provided for the parliamentary Government to participate much more than before in decision-making concerning foreign policy. According to the provision, the foreign policy of Finland shall be directed by the President of the Republic in co-operation with the Council of State, but the Council of State is responsible for the national preparation of the decisions to be made in the EU and shall decide on the concomitant Finnish measures, unless the decision requires the adoption of the Parliament. According to the interpretation of the Constitutional Committee, it would clearly be the Council of State that should decide on the representation of Finland in the European Council, and the Council of State should also be in charge of the preparation of all Union matters, including matters relating to joint foreign and security policy.[82] The President, Mrs Halonen, did not give in on this point, and the double representation of Finland in the EU summits continued until the end of 2009, when Articles 10(2) and 15(2) of the new Treaty of the European Union entered into force as a consequence of the entering into force of the Lisbon Treaty on 1 December 2009. According to those provisions, each member state would be represented either by the head of state or the head of government, but not by both.

In its report to Parliament pursuant to the changes necessitated by the entering into force of the Lisbon Treaty and affecting Finland at the meetings of the European Council, the Government of Finland concluded in December 2009 that

---

[81] See T Tiilikainen 'Suomen ulkopoliittinen johtamisjärjestelmä uuden perustuslain mukaan' in *Perustuslakiuudistukseen liittyviä selvityksiä*, (Oikeusministeriö, työryhmämietintö, 2002)8, 11. See also Salminen, above note 26, 172–77.

[82] Report of the Constitutional Committee 10/1998, 26. See also Opinion 13/2008. Practice during the past decade has been such that the President has made an announcement to the Government about her wish to participate in the meetings of the European Council. The Government has, however, always decided that Finland shall be represented by the Prime Minister and perhaps assisted by other ministers. In addition, the Government has decided that the President participates in the summit when the meeting deals with matters that belong to the competence of the President. Nonetheless, when participating in the summit, the President has been present when all or at least most of the matters have been dealt with. See Government Bill 60/2010, 18.

the representative of Finland in the European Council should be the Prime Minister.[83] This reinforced position of the Council of State has not yet been properly tested, but the practice relating to the dispute between the President and the Council of State is now developing under the EU Treaty rule of one representative in the European Council. The likely consequence is that the position of the Council of State will prevail and that the President will be sidelined in the meetings of the European Council. However, in order to create a clear rule for such situations, the Government proposed in its Bill 60/2010 to amend the Constitution so that a provision be added to section 66 of the Constitution on the functions of the Prime Minister, making the point that the Prime Minister represents Finland in the meetings of the European Council and in other activities of the EU that require the representation of the highest leadership of the state.[84]

CONCLUDING REMARKS

The constitutional legislation of Finland has, to a great extent, evolved by the use of the *pouvoir constitué* or the regular amending powers pursuant to the amendment formula in force. As a general rule, constitutional development by means of piecemeal amendments has emphasised constitutional continuity, and this was also the explicit point of departure when the current Constitution was drafted and adopted in the late 1990s. In addition, it seems that the main way of introducing new provisions in constitutional legislation is by codification of practice that has evolved during a longer or a shorter time before an actual constitutional amendment is made. Few amendments have been introduced without previous practice and experience about how a projected amendment would be likely to function. The preferred amendment formula is the normal one, that is '1/2 + elections + 2/3', while the fast track formula of '5/6 + 2/3' is reserved for situations where a quick amendment is absolutely necessary. Both amendment formulas require a great measure of consensus amongst the political forces in Parliament.

One very particular feature of constitutional law of Finland is the possibility of making substantive exceptions to the formal Constitution. The political system is not yet ripe for a repeal of the mechanism that makes it possible to enact Acts of Exception, although the mechanism is to a great extent circumscribed in the new Constitution. However, the avoidance of the use of Acts of Exception in respect of the core features of the constitution (which, consequently, could only be affected

---

[83] E 162/2009. At this point, the Constitutional Committee obviously supported the position of the Government in the matter because the Government was in line with the earlier opinions of the Committee. See Opinion of the Constitutional Committee 2/2010. See also Government Bill 60/2010, 19.
[84] Government Bill 60/2010, 54.

by formal amendments to the constitution) and the substantive and temporal limitations to the use of Acts of Exception introduce a new rigidity into the Finnish constitutional set-up.

At the same time, the rigidity created by the principle of avoiding Acts of Exception may be balanced by the open attitude towards formal constitutional amendments on the basis of active follow-up where the need for amendments is recognised in line with certain principles for constitutional amendments. Because the law-maker and the constitution-maker are the same body, the Parliament of Finland, and because the Constitutional Committee of Parliament is constantly involved in the interpretation of the Constitution in relation to bills that may or may not have to be enacted as Acts of Exception, it is only natural that the political scene is relatively actively engaged in constitutional issues and produces pressures for constitutional renewal.

The constitutional life of the EU is likely to create amendments to the Finnish Constitution, in particular if the basic treaties are amended. In light of amendments during the past 15 years, it seems that the Finnish Constitution is relatively open to pressures from the EU and would tend to incorporate at least some basic features and consequences of EU membership in the Constitution. Such incorporation of EU features resulting from future amendments to the treaties is a likely area for the use of the fast track amendment formula of '5/6 + 2/3'. An amendment need could also arise from other legal acts of the EU so as to qualify them as so significant that they would justify the fast track formula. Of course, EU treaties not in harmony with the Constitution would be ratified in the simplified constitutional procedure with a 2/3 qualified majority in one Parliament, but potentially, such treaties might also include features that the correctness, transparency and completeness principles would justify for inclusion in the formal Constitution by way of amendments. The Åland Islands issue may be viewed as a more permanent feature in the constitutional fabric of Finland than the Constitution itself and will probably continue to be so because of the various entrenchment forms that the autonomy arrangement is blessed with. However, the framework provisions in the formal Constitution of Finland concerning the Åland Islands are unlikely to undergo amendments, because adjustments in the autonomy arrangement can be inserted in the relatively detailed Self-Government Act.

The introduction of a provision on the primacy of the Constitution is a new mechanism not based on much previous experience. It can be expected that this mechanism may further enhance the position of the individual in the legal order of Finland. In spite of the fact that the provision on the primacy of the Constitution has produced more cases than envisaged when the Constitution was enacted at the end of the 1990s (although, at this point, there is only a handful of cases), none of the cases concerning constitutional primacy has been linked to the two amendment bills proposed by the Government in 2010. Evidently, the Finnish Constitution is characterised by relative permanency, which does not support the production of amendments lightly but which at the same time is open for necessary amendments that are carried by a sufficient majority.

6

France

SOPHIE BOYRON

INTRODUCTION

THE REGULATION OF constitutional change is at the heart of the doctrine of constitutionalism. Indeed, in most constitutional systems, the processes by which constitutional norms change will determine fundamental questions for the regime such as its survival, efficiency and legitimacy. Furthermore, a close analysis of the manner in which a constitutional system evolves often reveals the deep nature and specific characteristics of that system.[1]

However, to write about constitutional change in France may appear fool-hardy: for a long time, constitutional change was not really framed by the formal procedures of constitutional amendment. Constitutions came and went and were entirely at the mercy of political actors and events. Constitutional documents survived for as long as was politically expedient, but no longer. This was certainly not the enlightened expression of classical constitutionalism expected from a country which brought down the absolute monarchy in 1789.

The 1958 constitution introduced a new constitutional reality: the urge for revolutions and coups had finally been controlled. Although the 1958 constitution has evolved, it has done so 'quietly'. For the first time in French history, a constitution has been allowed to adjust itself successfully, and to a large extent constitutional change has been framed by the constitutional amendment procedure. Moreover, the number and extent of constitutional revisions and amendments demonstrate that there is no constitutional impediment to change in the regime of the fifth Republic. Indeed, the French constitution has evolved dramatically since its inception in 1958. It has been altered in so many ways and at so many levels that one would be well justified in considering the present French constitutional system to be a permanent and living experiment in constitutional change. This is all the more remarkable since historically France has had some difficult constitutional baggage.

---

[1] For more information on the French constitution, see Sophie Boyron *The Constitution of France: A Contextual Analysis*, (Hart Publishing, forthcoming, 2011).

Sophie Boyron

FRENCH HISTORY: THE ART OF CONSTITUTIONAL INSTABILITY

In France, the revolution of 1789 which put an end to absolute monarchy represents an unprecedented paradigm shift in constitutional change: a total break from the past. For this reason, French modern constitutional history is often regarded as having begun at that time. This representation emphasises the ideological, societal, cultural and legal break that took place in 1789; it captures the ideals of the new political elite: with revolutionary zeal, the old legal system in its quasi-entirety—institutions, legislation, rules and all—had been quickly abolished. The constitutional slate was wiped clean. However, a survey of French constitutional history since then highlights the difficulties in adapting classical constitutionalism in France. The next 200 years witnessed the succession of 17 different regimes, four coups, three revolutions and the adoption of 11 codified constitutions.[2] Clearly, France did not become a stable liberal democracy soon after 1789. For this reason, France can be regarded a real constitutional laboratory: it has tried almost every possible regime and has acquired a prodigious experience in constitutional drafting. Also, this search for a stable constitutional system has led to the emergence of strong traditions with regard to constitutional change—traditions that can still be felt to this day. Finally, behind this apparently chaotic constitutional evolution, some continuity can be identified: not everything changed all the time. An analysis of these aspects will help understand the provisions and practices of the present constitution with regard to change.

A Laboratory of Constitutional Change

French constitutional history is replete with instances of constitutional documents either ignored or wilfully misinterpreted. This partly explains the short life of some constitutions and the rapid succession of regime change. It is fair to say that over the last 200 years, the French have tried most known systems of government and have even invented many constitutional mechanisms of their own.

When the revolution took place in 1789, revolutionaries were not ready to adopt a republican system of government; instead, they opted for a constitutional monarchy and chose to maintain Louis XVI as the head of the Executive. Soon, however, the behaviour and decisions of the king compromised the fragile political equilibrium and by the summer of 1792 this constitutional experiment had ended. Interestingly, the French turned to the monarchy again later. In an

---

² See the following list of the regimes and constitutions to date:

3/14 September 1791: first codified Constitution (constitutional monarchy); 24 June 1793: first Republic; 22 August 1795: *Directoire*; 13 December 1799: Consulate and first Empire; 4 June 1814: Restoration—interrupted by the episode of the 'Cents jours' (return of Napoléon)—first constitutional Charter; 14 August 1830: July monarchy—second constitutional Charter; 4 November 1848: second Republic; 14 January 1852: second Empire; 4 September 1870: third Republic; 27 October 1946: fourth Republic; 4 October 1958: fifth Republic.

attempt to adapt a system of constitutional monarchy, a restoration allowed three kings to sit on the French throne in succession: Louis XVIII (1814–24), Charles X (1824–30) and Louis-Philippe (1830–48). The constitutional charters established a parliamentary system by borrowing many of their provisions from the British constitution.[3]. However, both Charles X and Louis-Philippe were forced into exile by revolutions in 1830 and 1848 respectively. While a restoration was envisaged at the beginning of the third Republic, the unrealistic demands of the heir to the throne, the Duke of Chambord, made this impossible. Constitutional monarchy is consigned to the past.

After the fall of the monarchy in 1792, the first Republic was proclaimed and a constitution was adopted on 24 June 1793. However, the revolution had come under threat from the war waged by a coalition of European powers and from a strong counter-revolutionary uprising in the west of the country. As a result of this national emergency, a dictatorship was soon decreed and the constitution of 1793 was never implemented. The notable failure of the first Republic may explain why it took 53 years before another Republic was contemplated. After the final failure of the restoration in 1848, politicians decided to establish a presidential regime and a second Republic. Again, this Republic was short-lived as Louis-Napoléon Bonaparte was the first President of the Republic to be elected: soon a coup led to the second Empire. After the disastrous defeat of 1870,[4] France finally succeeded in establishing a Republican tradition: the constitutions of the third, fourth and finally fifth Republic were adopted in 1875, 1946 and 1958 respectively. Both the third and fourth Republics were parliamentary regimes, while the fifth Republic has established a 'mongrel' regime.

In between the bouts of republican and monarchical regimes, the French also experienced two empires: the first empire was headed by Napoléon Bonaparte (1804–15) and the second by Louis-Napoléon Bonaparte (1848–70). Although both regimes were largely autocratic, uncle and nephew arrived to power by different means: while Napoléon Bonaparte triggered a coup which brought the *Directoire* down, Louis-Napoléon Bonaparte was elected President of the Republic by direct universal suffrage and only resorted to a coup after two years of continued opposition by Parliament.[5] Still, both Empires were important for the development of the country: while Napoléon I engaged in a vast programme of legal and institutional reforms, Napoléon III's policies facilitated the emergence of the industrial revolution.

[3] In the 1814 charter, Parliament was composed of two houses (the house of peers and the house of deputies). Ministers were accountable and could be members of either chamber of Parliament. The accountability of ministers was strengthened with the 1830 charter.

[4] This was the Franco-Prussian war which resulted in France losing a large part of its territory. This territory was regained following the defeat of Germany in 1918.

[5] The single chamber which was also elected by direct universal suffrage had a royalist majority and opposed Louis-Napoléon Bonaparte every step of the way.

The Emergence of Constitutional Traditions

Although constitutional change in France appears random and chaotic, it has given birth to strong constitutional traditions which in turn have inspired the process of change.

Early on, a general understanding emerged that a failed constitution was irremediably tainted by its past and that it could not be improved by amendment. Little value was attached to the continuity of constitutional regimes and few were given the chance to adapt. On the contrary, successive constitutions followed the revolutionary example of 1789 and founded their legitimacy on clean breaks from the past. This created a chronic inability of regimes to evolve. Even though some constitutions experienced dysfunctions that could have been addressed, the frenzy of constitutional drafting continued. Indeed, the French people chose to terminate the third Republic, the longest surviving regime, rather than attempt to curb its more glaring dysfunctions by amending it. Constitutional longevity was neither a recognised value nor a legitimating factor in constitutional change in France. Instead, there seemed to exist an unspoken belief that there was a regime and constitution out there which would match the requirements of the French polity; it was simply a case of finding it. Constitutional change was strongly guided by this search for constitutional perfection: regimes, once declared unfit for purpose, were discarded to make place for a new experiment.

In the same vein, new constitutional instruments were often drafted in opposition to previous texts and regimes. Constitutional practices and experiences of one regime tended to inform the drafting of the next constitutional document. For example, in the constitution of 22 August 1795 drafted soon after the fall of Robespierre, two innovations were introduced: Parliament was comprised of two chambers and the executive was headed by three *directeurs*. This institutional structure was clearly adopted to prevent a dictatorship of either branch of government: while the legislative chambers would keep each other in check, the collegiate nature of the executive would make it difficult for a dictator to rise to power.[6] In fact, new mechanisms were crafted and new institutions often created in an attempt to quell past behaviours and undesirable practices. This may have forced constitutional lawyers to experiment and be creative, but evolution has not been smooth: regimes tended to lurch violently from one solution to its opposite.

Finally, some constitutional experiences were so painful that they resulted in constitutional taboos: today, it would be difficult (if not impossible) to convince the French people that a single chamber parliament is a viable option. There is a diffuse belief that the single chamber parliament of both the Convention and the second Republic resulted in those regimes becoming dictatorships. This popular belief seems to be deeply rooted: during the twentieth century a single chamber

---

[6] However, the drafters may not have realised at the time that this complex institutional structure multiplied potential conflicts.

was twice proposed and twice rejected. Many commentators attribute the failure of the first draft constitution in 1946[7] in part to its single-chamber parliament and explain, similarly, the rejection by referendum of de Gaulle's proposal in 1969 to limit the second chamber to consultative powers only.[8] A single-chamber parliament may have become a constitutional taboo in France.

Behind Change, Continuity

On the surface, French constitutional history has had so many stops and starts that continuity is not easily identifiable. However, beyond the constitutional instability, a clear thread of continuity exists.[9] Indeed an analysis of the elements of this continuity tends to put the constitutional instability into perspective. In any event, the permanence of administrative law and structures combined with a certain vision of society allowed the country to survive crises and upheavals and to maintain a certain coherence throughout.[10]

Public administration provided a strong element of continuity throughout French history: many new administrative structures were put in place soon after the revolution or by Napoléon Bonaparte. Once in place, they continued in existence whatever the regime. For instance, the division of the French territory into *départements* is a lasting legacy of the 1789 revolution. Similarly, the *Conseil d'Etat*, once the creation of Napoléon Bonaparte, has evolved slowly to become the institution that it is today. The continuity of these administrative structures is further strengthened by the development of administrative law: in contrast with constitutional law, administrative law has enjoyed a relative stability and peaceful evolution. Administrative law developed independently of and largely unhindered by constitutional change. Not only did administrative structures last, but the law underlying them was mostly constant. In fact, administrative law also engineered a certain stability of constitutional law: by integrating a number of constitutional principles gradually into its case law, the *Conseil d'Etat* did more to give effect to key constitutional concepts than the succession of constitutions ever did.

An element of continuity is also found in the adoption and conservation of the basic societal choices and principles established by the revolution and enshrined

---

[7] The first draft constitution was rejected by referendum on 5 May 1946.

[8] See the referendum of 27 April 1969; arguably there were other political factors which may also have explained this rejection.

[9] See AFDC, PUAM, *La continuité constitutionnelle en France de 1789 à 1989*, (Economica, 1990).

[10] Also, many changes of regimes may have been brutal and may have followed a revolution or coup. A surprising number of politicians managed not only to survive the changes but to lead successful political careers spanning multiple regimes. Even during the volatile revolutionary period, of the 400 deputies of the Convention, 189 had been members of the previous Legislative Assembly and 96 had been members of the Constituting Assembly.

in the Declaration of 1789.[11] Beyond the rights and freedoms that the revolutionary movement wanted to proclaim, the *Déclaration* encapsulated a certain vision
of society and the necessary values for its establishment. This new organisation of
society remained unchallenged by successive regimes, even after the restoration.
Similarly, the political status of citizens may have been unequally protected
throughout French constitutional history but the Declaration of 1789 contains
clear goals in this regard; these often served as references and reminders. This
created a commonality of ideals which remained constant whatever the degree or
extent of constitutional change.[12] Indeed, the Declaration of 1789 has become
such a point of symbolic reference that it received a mention in both the
constitutions of the fourth and fifth Republics.

Behind the Chaos, a Pattern?

On the surface, French constitutional history has a rather confused and chaotic
story line. Although lawyers have tried to give meaning to this evolution, the
search for a pattern behind the rapid changes of regimes is a challenge.

  Still, some constitutional lawyers have come to believe that the evolution of
French constitutional law could be explained as a succession of alternating
cycles.[13] Each cycle creates a dialectical dynamic as it encompasses three distinct
periods: the first period recognises the primacy of Parliament; the second
reactionary period gives primacy to the Executive and finally; the third and
longer period synthesises these experiences and establishes a period of cooperation of all branches of government. This last era creates a period of comparative
stability until another cycle starts again. According to this representation, since
1789, France has already completed two full cycles: while the first cycle started in
1789 and ended in 1848, the second began in 1848 and ended in 1940.[14] This
representation of French constitutional history has the merit of unearthing a
deeper pattern and of bringing order to an otherwise confusing constitutional
history. Surprisingly, it also highlights an underlying trend of constitutional
stability: over the 151 year period covered by the two constitutional cycles
(1789–1940), the two periods of synthesis, stability and cooperation of power
add up to a total of 99 years. France's constitutional past may not be as troubled
as it seems.

---

  [11] The Declaration of the Rights of Man and the Citizen was adopted in 1789 soon after the
revolution. It proclaims many first generation rights.
  [12] See J Bell, *French Constitutional law* (Oxford University Press, 1992) 2.
  [13] See E Gicquel and JE Gicquel, *Droit constitutionnel et institutions politiques* (Coll Domat,
Montchrestien, 2000), 421.
  [14] Within these cycles, the Legislature was a dominant power 1789–95 and again in 1848–51. In
reaction, the Executive had clear primacy in the second periods 1795–1814 and 1851–70. Finally, the
two eras of synthesis, stability and cooperation of power spanned the long period of the restoration
(1814–48) and the third Republic (1875–1940).

This brief constitutional history reveals that all major constitutional regimes had been experimented with in France in any number of combinations but largely unsuccessfully. When the fifth Republic was proclaimed, France was still searching high and low for the perfect regime and the ideal constitution. It was difficult to see how the unprepossessing 1958 constitution would fare any better.

THE DISCOVERY OF THE IDEAL REGIME?

The 1958 constitution was drafted quickly against the background of the Algerian war, a threat of a military coup, and a deep political crisis. The return to power of General de Gaulle, the hero of World War II, may have saved the country from chaos but the atmosphere was not conducive to the drafting of the perfect constitution. In fact, the new constitution was far from groundbreaking: it seemed to be establishing another parliamentary system, albeit an odd one. Also, there was neither time nor political momentum to adopt a Declaration of Rights. The 1958 constitution did not stand out from all the previous constitutions which had been adopted over the last 200 years.

However, a curious and haphazard combination of constitutional practice and constitutional and political change came together to engineer a presidential reading of the constitution. It resulted in an untypical and tailor-made system that has survived all political challenges that have been thrown at it so far.

The Original Constitutional System

On paper, the Constitution of 1958 did not strive for originality. The drafters of the new constitution were constrained by political reality and by the constitutional statute of 3 June 1958. This statute was passed in the last days of the fourth Republic to guide the drafting of the new constitution: it settled the procedure for its adoption and listed the principles that were to be found therein (for example, ministerial responsibility, separation of legislative and executive powers, independence of the judiciary and universal suffrage). Furthermore, de Gaulle may have favoured a system with a strong executive,[15] but the consultative committee in charge of the initial draft was composed in large part of members of the Parliament of the fourth Republic.[16] These politicians were unlikely to support the demise of the legislative branch. A compromise was therefore necessary and the original 1958 constitution was clearly the result of these competing demands. The original document was rather ambiguous but tended to reproduce a parliamentary system; to this effect, Parliament has two chambers and the Government

---

[15] See the speech made by de Gaulle in Bayeux on 16 June 1946, where he presented his constitutional ideas and argued for a strong Executive, http://www.charles-de-gaulle.org/pages/espace-pedagogique/le-point-sur/les-textes-a-connaitre/discours-de-bayeux-16-juin-1946.php.

[16] Professional politicians did not trust de Gaulle and made sure that they played a key role in the establishment of the new regime. This could also explain the apparently traditional result.

is responsible to Parliament. The second chamber, the *Sénat* has a weaker legitimacy and less power[17]. Although the Executive power was (and is) divided between President of the Republic and Prime Minister,[18] the Prime Minister, as head of Government, appeared to be in the driving seat. As in previous constitutions, the President of the Republic, as Head of State, seemed destined to a symbolic and formal role. As the President was elected indirectly by an electoral college of local and national elected representatives, he did not have the necessary electoral legitimacy to intervene in policy and decision-making. A strong presidential leadership would not easily be based on such shaky foundations.

However, there are some important innovations in the 1958 constitution. As is often the case in France, the new constitution engaged in lesson learning, and tried to 'cure' the dysfunctions that caused the fourth and third Republics to fail, namely the uncontrolled power and behaviour of Parliament. First, the requirement imposed by the statute of 3 June 1958 that executive and legislative powers be separate, led to the adoption of a 'deviant' parliamentary system: members of the Government are prohibited from being Members of Parliament.[19] If a Member of Parliament is given a ministerial portfolio, he/she must vacate their parliamentary seat.[20] This strict divide was meant to help tackle the chronic governmental instability of the previous regimes. Despite this, the constitution organises a full accountability of the Government to Parliament.[21] According to the constitution, members of Government have access and can address both chambers whenever they wish.[22] They also answer questions in the house, participate in debates in plenary, are heard by parliamentary committees and so on. Should confidence be withdrawn in the *Assemblée Nationale*, the Prime Minister tends the resignation of the Government to the President of the Republic.

Moreover, Parliament was reined in in a number of ways; in fact, some of the new mechanisms marked a real departure from long-accepted constitutional

[17] The *Sénat* is elected by indirect electoral suffrage. Elected representative of local and devolved governments are convened in an electoral college for each senatorial election. In turn, the electoral college elects the *sénateurs*.

[18] In this respect, the 1958 constitution plagiarised the arrangements of both the third and fourth Republics.

[19] See article 23: 'Membership of the Government shall be incompatible with the holding of any Parliamentary office, any position of professional representation at national level, any public employment or any professional activity.

An Institutional Act shall determine the manner in which the holders of such offices, positions or employment shall be replaced.

The replacement of Members of Parliament shall take place in accordance with the provisions of article 25'.

[20] The loss of the parliamentary seat is only temporary. The reform of July 2008 constitutionalised a practice which allowed former ministers to return to their seat on leaving the Government.

[21] See article 20: '[The Government] shall be accountable to Parliament in accordance with the terms and procedures set out in articles 49 and 50.'

[22] See article 31: 'Members of the Government shall have access to the two assemblies. They shall address either assembly whenever they so request'.

practices and beliefs. For instance, the French Parliament is no longer free to pass legislation on any topic; it can only legislate on matters listed in article 34 of the constitution. Similarly, a new institution was introduced: the *Conseil constitution-nel* was to keep Parliament in check and protect the Executive from any usurpation of power. Although the traits of the original 1958 constitution were reminiscent of the previous regime, the innovations mentioned above are typical of the evolution of constitutions in France. These provisions led to a deep and lasting transformation of the fifth Republic, beyond anything the drafters could have imagined.

A Presidential Reading of the 1958 Constitution

As demonstrated above, the 1958 constitution was meant to put in place a parliamentary regime, albeit a 'rationalised' one. However, from the start the interpretation of many constitutional provisions favoured a presidential reading of the constitution.

In 1958, de Gaulle was elected President of the Republic. He had agreed to return to power to resolve the Algerian crisis and to oversee the adoption of a new constitution. When this was endorsed by referendum in September 1958 by a majority of 82.6 per cent, he had fulfilled half his brief. The Algerian crisis still needed to be solved. One might have guessed, however, that the appointment of such a political figure to the presidency would lead to a strong interpretation of this office. Furthermore, indirect election of the President was unlikely to create much difficulty for de Gaulle as he had a strong personal or 'historical' legitimacy. The head of the French government in exile during World War II did not need electoral legitimacy. He was already regarded as the country's saviour and for many he was on a second rescue mission. Furthermore, his personality was well known and he would find it difficult to reproduce the passive behaviour and low profile that was expected of a President of the third or fourth Republics. In fact, one might safely argue that de Gaulle would never have been elected President of the Republic in either regime: he was not the political type. His election in 1958 was made possible by the urgency of the situation. Politicians accepted this 'presidential novelty' because of necessity.

From the very beginning, de Gaulle imprinted his own interpretation on the 1958 Constitution. First, he added to the principle of ministerial responsibility by requiring that the Prime Minister be also directly responsible to the President of the Republic. Although the Constitution does give the President the power to appoint the Prime Minister, de Gaulle read this literally, that is as implying a freedom of choice in the matter. Furthermore, de Gaulle demanded that all important decisions be reported to him and indicated that the Prime Minister held the appointment at the pleasure of the President.[23] Therefore, from the beginning, the principle of ministerial responsibility, the core principle of any parliamentary system, was totally transformed and some may even say perverted.

Although de Gaulle had an important historical and personal legitimacy, he was always careful to seek popular support too. To do so, de Gaulle resorted to referendums at regular intervals. Article 11[24] of the 1958 Constitution allows for a referendum to be organised when major institutional questions are in issue. De Gaulle used these to conduct a dialogue directly with the French people and to provide his presidency with popular legitimacy. Between 1958 and 1969, four referendums were organised.[25] De Gaulle clearly indicated that he linked his own future to each referendum: a rejection would trigger his resignation. In fact, when the referendum of 1969 was rejected, de Gaulle stepped down immediately.

Also, the use of the referendum of Article 11 granted some welcome power to the President of the Republic. According to the constitution, the President of the Republic and Head of State had few powers and no day-to-day governmental role. The first referendum that de Gaulle organised was concerned with Algeria: the French people were asked whether they would agree in principle to its independence. The referendum gave the President of the Republic the necessary powers to conduct the negotiations. Not only were new powers granted to the President of the Republic but they created a presidential figure responsible for

---

[23] To this effect, de Gaulle instituted the practice that Prime Ministers would sign a resignation letter but leave the date blank, so that the President would fill in the date when he felt the time had come to change his Prime Minister.

[24] 'The President of the Republic may, on a recommendation from the Government when Parliament is in session, or on a joint motion of the two Houses, published in the *Journal Officiel*, submit to a referendum any Government Bill which deals with the organization of the public authorities, or with reforms relating to the economic, social or environmental policy of the Nation, and to the public services contributing thereto, or which provides for authority to ratify a treaty which, although not contrary to the Constitution, would affect the functioning of the institutions.

Where the referendum is held on the recommendation of the Government, the latter shall make a statement before each House and the same shall be followed by a debate.

A referendum concerning a subject mentioned in the first paragraph may be held upon the initiative of one fifth of the Members of Parliament, supported by one tenth of the voters enrolled on the electoral register. This initiative shall take the form of a Private Member's Bill and shall not be applied to the repeal of a statutory provision promulgated less than one year earlier.

The conditions by which it is introduced and those according to which the Constitutional Council monitors respect for the provisions of the previous paragraph, are set down by an Institutional Act.

If the Private Member's Bill has not been considered by the two Houses within a period set by the Institutional Act, the President of the Republic shall submit it to a referendum.

Where the decision of the French people in the referendum is not favourable to the Private Member's Bill, no new referendum proposal on the same subject may be submitted before the end of a period of two years following the date of the vote.

Where the outcome of the referendum is favourable to the Government Bill or to the Private Member's Bill, the President of the Republic shall promulgate the resulting statute within fifteen days following the proclamation of the results of the vote'.

[25] De Gaulle organised four referendums over his two presidential mandates: two concerned the independence of Algeria (8 January 1961 and 8 April 1962), the third changed the electoral system for the President of the Republic and the last one planned to create regions and to transform the second chamber of Parliament.

major policy decisions. To this end, de Gaulle also resorted to the exceptional powers of Article 16[26] when a coup was attempted in April 1961. Although the coup was ended quickly and the perpetrators arrested, the exceptional powers of Article 16 were still in use five months later. De Gaulle hijacked many constitutional powers to give effect to his presidential interpretation. As these interpretations conflicted with the apparent parliamentary logic of the 1958 constitution, commentators doubted at the time that this practice would survive the departure of de Gaulle. In fact, many politicians expected that, the architect of this interpretation gone, they would return to the parliamentary practices of old. De Gaulle was aware of the frailty of his reading and understood that only a strong electoral legitimacy would secure its future. Consequently, de Gaulle contrived in 1962 to have the electoral system of the President of the Republic amended. In turn, this constitutional amendment triggered a sequence of political events which led to the birth of the present semi-presidential regime.

The Emergence of the Semi-presidential System

Many believed that few (if any) future presidents would have enough personal legitimacy to compete with the directly elected first chamber, the *Assemblée Nationale*. To avoid a return of the Presidents of the previous republics, a reform of the presidential electoral system was therefore required.

On 2 October 1962, de Gaulle announced his intention to begin the process for amending articles 6 and 7 of the Constitution and have the President of the Republic elected by direct universal suffrage.[27] However, de Gaulle knew that most members of Parliament would not support the revision: it altered too dramatically the nature of the regime. The majority of politicians hoped that, the Algerian crisis over, de Gaulle would leave and that they would revert to a parliamentary regime. Consequently, de Gaulle was once more creative with his

[26] These powers give all constitutional powers to the President of the Republic in national emergencies.

Article 16: 'Parliament shall sit as of right.

The National Assembly shall not be dissolved during the exercise of such emergency powers.

After thirty days of the exercise of such emergency powers, the matter may be referred to the Constitutional Council by the President of the National Assembly, the President of the Senate, sixty Members of the National Assembly or sixty Senators, so as to decide if the conditions laid down in paragraph one still apply. The Council shall make its decision publicly as soon as possible. It shall, as of right, carry out such an examination and shall make its decision in the same manner after sixty days of the exercise of emergency powers or at any moment thereafter'.

[27] Although de Gaulle was elected for seven years and was not due to face an election for another three years, the question of 'succession' became a hot topic with the attempt on de Gaulle's life in August 1962. In fact, Antoine Pinay who had been Prime Minister during the fourth Republic was tipped to be a possible successor; it would undeniably have signaled a return to past practices.

interpretation of the constitution. Article 89[28] which contains the formal amendment procedure, requires the approval of the reform by both legislative chambers. Instead, de Gaulle decided to bypass Parliament by organising a referendum on the basis of article 11.[29] In this way, the constitutional amendment would be decided directly by the people: once successful, it would be difficult for anyone to contest the direct expression of the will of the nation. In fact, de Gaulle's plans worked beyond his dreams.

Following the announcement, the *Assemblée Nationale* passed a motion of no confidence on 5 October 1962 to condemn the policy pursued by the President of the Republic.[30] The President reacted swiftly and dissolved the *Assemblée Nationale* on 9 October.[31] The subsequent elections triggered political events which marked the foundation of the present regime.

First, on 28 October, the French people, undeterred by the use of article 11, approved the referendum by 62 per cent of the votes. Clearly, the sovereign decision of the people settled beyond doubt the procedural 'constitutionality' of the reform.[32] However, the key political change was still to come: the elections to the *Assemblée Nationale* brought a clear Gaullist majority which served to support the President of the Republic and maintain the Government in office. The majoritarian phenomenon, which is indispensable to a presidential reading of the constitution, was born. From then on, with the exception of the cohabitation periods,[33] all Presidents of the Republic would be supported by a majority in the *Assemblée Nationale*. At last, the unstable coalition governments of the third

---

[28] 'The President of the Republic, on the recommendation of the Prime Minister, and Members of Parliament alike shall have the right to initiate amendments to the Constitution.
A Government or a Private Member's Bill to amend the Constitution must be considered within the time limits set down in the third paragraph of article 42 and be passed by the two Houses in identical terms. The amendment shall take effect after approval by referendum.
However, a Government Bill to amend the Constitution shall not be submitted to referendum where the President of the Republic decides to submit it to Parliament convened in Congress; the Government Bill to amend the Constitution shall then be approved only if it is passed by a three-fifths majority of the votes cast. The Bureau of the Congress shall be that of the National Assembly.
No amendment procedure shall be commenced or continued where the integrity of national territory is placed in jeopardy.
The republican form of government shall not be the object of any amendment'.
[29] Even though electoral reform could arguably be regarded as a major institutional reform, article 11 was to be used for reforms other than constitutional amendments.
[30] The second chamber, the *Sénat* was also strongly opposed to the constitutional reform but had fewer constitutional tools to express it.
[31] As is the French tradition, the Government stayed on to deal with current matters until the appointment of a new one.
[32] This was clearly understood by the *Conseil constitutionnel*. It declared that it did not have jurisdiction to check a statute adopted on the basis of a referendum as it is the direct expression of national sovereignty: see decision 62–20 of 6 November 1962.
[33] Three times during the life of the fifth Republic, the President of the Republic lost his parliamentary majority with elections to the first chamber granting the former opposition, a majority in Parliament. In the circumstances, the President of the Republic is left with little choice: he has to appoint a Prime Minister from the new majority. Also, the interpretation of the constitution reverts to a parliamentary reading with a Prime Minister in charge. However, the constitutional reform of 2000 has made the reoccurrence of this political phenomenon virtually impossible.

and fourth Republics were firmly relegated to the past. From a complex dynamic of political change, constitutional interpretation and constitutional reform emerged the semi-presidential regime of the fifth Republic. France had found its constitutional Elysium.

Amending the Constitution: Article 89 and the Place of the People

Although the very first revision was arguably a breach of the constitution, the 1958 constitution was first amended only four years after its introduction. In fact, the fifth Republic has taken to changing the constitution by formal amendments like a duck to water. After centuries of failing to proceed in this way, this is puzzling to say the least. Furthermore, constitutional amendments have engendered deep political changes and finally triggered the emergence of a virtuous synergy between law and politics in France. This is all the more unexpected since nothing in article 89 seems to warrant this outcome and explain this transformation of French constitutionalism. A further analysis of the provision is therefore necessary.

The Constitutional Limitations

First, article 89 paragraph 4 places some temporary limitations on the amendment procedure: it is not possible to amend the constitution when the integrity of French territory is compromised (for example, in time of war). Constitutional change needs serenity and peace; otherwise the urgency of the situation may result in the adoption of a rash, undesirable, and possibly undemocratic amendment. This limitation sprang from the adverse experience of the constitutional revision of 10 July 1940: while the German army advanced rapidly through French territory, the French Parliament amended the constitution and handed all powers of the (third) Republic to General Pétain. This led to the Vichy regime and in effect ended the third Republic. Both the 1946 and 1958 constitutions learned from this and prohibited any constitutional amendment in such circumstances.[34] In addition, other provisions of the constitution limit the timing of a constitutional amendment: according to article 7 paragraph 6,[35] it not possible to amend the constitution when the President of the Republic has resigned, died or been impeached. The *Conseil constitutionnel* has also declared that no amendment of the constitution can proceed as long as the President of

---

[34] It is interesting to note that this provision was obviously breached in 1958, when the constitution was adopted: the Algerian war undoubtedly compromised the integrity of French territory.

[35] Neither articles 49 and 50 nor article 89 of the Constitution shall be implemented during the vacancy of the Presidency of the Republic or during the period between the declaration of the permanent incapacity of the President of the Republic and the election of his successor.

the Republic is using the emergency powers of article 16.[36] Still, these temporary limitations recognise that the revision process is intrinsically risky and needs to be shielded from adverse circumstances.

Article 89 paragraph 5 also imposes a permanent and substantive limitation on the amendment procedure: the Republican nature of the Government cannot be altered. At first glance, this provision seems clear: the constitution must ensure that France stays a Republic, presumably as opposed to a monarchy or empire. However, it is possible to adopt a wider interpretation of this prohibition: the Republican nature of the regime is dependant on a number of rights (for example, equality) and principles (for example, territorial unity): any change of these would consequently compromise the nature of the regime and the existence of the Republic. The *Conseil constitutionnel* was in fact called to rule on this question in 2003. Senators had referred the constitutional bill introducing the principle of decentralisation of local Government in article 1 of the constitution to the Conseil: they claimed that this revision undermined the unitary and therefore Republican nature of the regime. The *Conseil,* however, rejected this interpretation.[37]

If a proposed amendment does not fall within one (or more) of these limitations, the procedure of article 89 can be triggered.

The Amendment Procedure

The procedure reproduced in article 89 of the 1958 constitution contains three stages and specifies two possible routes.

(i) The Right of Initiative

All amendment procedures start in the same way: according to article 89, the right of initiative belongs equally to Members of Parliament and to the President of the Republic on a request from the Prime Minister. In reality, the right of initiative belongs largely to the President of the Republic. Although Members of Parliament have drafted and introduced constitutional bills to amend the constitution, none has ever succeeded. In fact, political reality makes it difficult for Members of Parliament to use their right of initiative fully: either they are members of the presidential majority and the Executive is better placed, both politically and constitutionally to propose a constitutional amendment,[38] or they are members of the opposition and their proposals can only fail. Although the three periods of 'cohabitation' provided an opportunity for Members of Parliament of the majority to propose constitutional amendments, none did so; they

---

[36] See C. cons. n. 92–312 DC 2 September 1992, European Union Treaty, rec. 76.

[37] See C. cons n. 2003–469 DC 26 March 2003, decentralization, rec. 293.

[38] Article 5 of the constitution describes the role of the President of the Republic: not only does he ensure the respect of the constitution but he guarantees the proper functioning of the institutions.

did not want to be responsible for the inevitable political tensions that would ensue between the parliamentary majority and the President of the Republic.

Similarly, the request of the Prime Minister for a constitutional amendment is mostly superfluous: for a large number of amendments, the initiative has come solely from the President. Only in 'cohabitation' periods, has the role of the Prime Minister being pivotal: although Jacques Chirac was not convinced that the presidential mandate should be shortened to five years in an attempt to avoid the reoccurrence of 'cohabitation', he was forced by the socialist Prime Minister, Lionel Jospin, to trigger a revision in 2000.

(ii)   The Pre-legislative Stage

Once it has been decided that the constitution is to be amended, the Executive engage in a wide consultation exercise to determine the exact content of the reform. On three occasions, the President of the Republic first convened an expert committee to advice on this content. Prior to making their proposals, the committees have all engaged in wide consultation. Although only a small number of constitutional reforms have resorted to expert committees, all three were key reforms, either because of their subject matter or their ambit.[39]

Once the Executive has negotiated the content of the reform with a wide cross section of the political community, a bill is drafted. Then, as with the ordinary legislative procedure, the *Conseil d'Etat* is consulted on the constitutional bill prior to its adoption by the Government in the Council of ministers. Although the opinion of the *Conseil d'Etat* is only communicated to the Government, the annual reports of the *Conseil d'Etat* often contain information with regard to the control exercised. Generally, the *Conseil d'Etat* is less likely to proffer advice on the policy choices of any reform, be it constitutional. Instead, the *Conseil* concentrates on the means chosen to fulfil the policy objectives, their efficiency and coherence. Still, this careful advice may have the consequence of undermining the bill itself as exemplified by the opinion given on the constitutional bill on decentralisation in 2002.[40]

(iii)   Adoption by Parliament

Once drafted, the bill is introduced in Parliament (in either chamber). Article 89 requires that both chambers approve the text in identical terms. The extent to which the ordinary legislative procedure can be used to vote on a constitutional

---

[39]   Expert committees were convened to make proposals prior to the two attempts at wide-ranging reform in August 1995 and July 2008. Furthermore, the reform of February 2007 clarified the criminal liability of the President of the Republic on the recommendations of another expert committee.

[40]   In its opinion, the Conseil d'Etat queried the need and merit of inscribing the principle of decentralisation in article 1 of the constitution. It also questioned the normative status of the principle of subsidiarity. See *Rapport du Conseil D'Etat—2003*, 55 http://www.conseil-etat.fr/cde/media/document//rapportpublic2003.pdf.

amendment has been the subject of debates. In France, the Government has any number of weapons to ensure that ordinary legislation is adopted by Parliament. However, commentators have argued against the use of these when debating and voting on a constitutional bill. This may be for political reasons—the Government needs to cultivate the support of members of Parliament and negotiate a compromise—or legal arguments—there is uncertainty among commentators as to which weapon can be legally used. In reality, while threats have been made,[41] there seems to be a general reluctance to curtail the legislative process. In fact, the Government will often have tried to build strong support in favour of the proposal prior to its introduction.

(iv)   The Final Approval: Two Routes

At this point, the procedure of article 89 allows two options: the constitutional bill needs to receive parliamentary or popular approval. The President has discretion over the route that the constitutional bill takes. The first option requires that both chambers convene together in a single chamber, called Congress. The constitutional amendment is carried if it receives at least 60 per cent of the votes. The second option requires approval of the electorate by referendum.

Article 11: Popular Sovereignty and the Revision of the Constitution

Although article 89 makes the fifth Republic a rigid constitution, it achieves a good balance between flexibility and protection of the constitution and is definitely simpler than the amendment procedures of many previous constitutions. Consequently, the 1958 constitution has been revised successfully on numerous occasions since its inception. This is definitely an achievement and a break from the past. After all, the revision process during the fourth Republic was so drawn-out that when the 1946 Constitution ended, there were still two amendments pending.

The present amendment procedure may be straightforward, but the involvement of the French people in the successive revisions has been controversial. First, in 1962, when the electoral system for the election of the President of the Republic was amended, de Gaulle bypassed Parliament and relied on article 11 and the people instead. He reasoned that the legitimacy granted by direct democracy would be enough to quell any challenge. Indeed, the referendum was successful and made it difficult for anyone to contest the direct expression of the will of the nation. Even the *Conseil constitutionnel* when asked to review the constitutionality of the referendum, declined to do so: its decision made it clear

---

[41]   For instance, the Government threatened to use the 'blocked vote' during the constitutional amendment which was required to ratify the Maastricht treaty.

that it could not review directly the will of the sovereign people.[42] It would have been untenable for any constitutional court, however legitimate, to contest such a decisive declaration of popular sovereignty. Nevertheless, a continued use of article 11 to amend the constitution may have created problems in the long run: for instance, commentators began to wonder whether a new constitutional practice was fast emerging when article 11 was used a second time to amend the constitution in 1969. The failure of the 1969 referendum and the subsequent resignation of de Gaulle marked the end of this unorthodox interpretation the constitution. Article 11 has been used sparingly since and never to amend the constitution: politicians have quickly learnt to be wary of the people's verdict.

In fact, since the departure of de Gaulle, there has been a tendency to exclude the sovereign people from decisions on constitutional amendments: all revisions since the 1962 reform have opted for the parliamentary route, with one exception. In 2000, the sovereign people were asked to approve the reduction of the presidential mandate from seven to five years: this was seen as a way to avoid the return to the period of cohabitations which had plagued the regime. All other 23 revisions of the constitution were decided upon exclusively by Parliament. This may be justifiable for small and technical amendments, but the parliamentary route was even preferred for the most recent revision of the constitution. On 23 July 2008, the deepest and widest revision of the constitution yet was adopted: over half of the articles of the constitution were amended (48 articles in total) and many of the changes made, can be labelled as fundamental (for example, the reform of the *Conseil constitutionnel*). Again, the sovereign people were not asked to underwrite this major constitutional revision. Considering the number and impact of the constitutional amendments in the last two decades, one may rightly question what role is left to the sovereign people in this regard. While de Gaulle strove to strengthen the foundations of the political system with universal direct suffrage, politicians nowadays tend to eschew the mechanisms of direct democracy when amending the constitution: the sovereign is left speechless. This is all the more surprising since the general trend at the moment is to promote the use of mechanisms of direct democracy: increasingly, referendums be they national or local, and popular initiatives are included in legislation and constitutions. The place of the French people in constitutional reform may have changed dramatically since the beginnings of the 1958 constitution, but it still triggers strong debate and controversy. Indeed, for some the quasi-systematic use of the parliamentary route when revising the constitution, has resulted in the emergence of a constitutional convention.

---

[42] See C. cons n. 62–20 DC 6 November 1962, Referendum, rec. 27.

ANALYSIS OF FORMAL CONSTITUTIONAL AMENDMENTS

The 1958 constitution has been amended 24 times since coming into force. If it were impossible to amend any French constitution in the past, nowadays it is proving difficult to refrain from amending the constitution every year. Further-more, the pace of constitutional reform is quickening: while the constitution was revised five times in the first three decades, it has been amended 19 times in the last 20 years. A study of the reasons, the type, the extent and the impact of the amendments will reveal much with regard to the evolution of the French constitution and the catalysts of constitutional change.

Confirming the More Creative Interpretations of the Constitution

As we mentioned above, a number of constitutional amendments have aimed at confirming existing interpretations, especially when those are remote from the original intention of the drafters of the constitution.

First, the presidential reading of the regime was granted the constitutional seal of approval in 1962; this choice was reaffirmed in 2000. In 1962, the institutional practices adopted by de Gaulle were continued thanks to a change of the presidential electoral system. The direct universal suffrage system gave the electoral legitimacy necessary to perpetuate a strong presidency. However, this reading was undermined by the three cohabitation periods: three times, a President of the Republic lost his supporting majority in the *Assemblée Nationale* during his mandate. This was possible because of a discrepancy between the presidential and the parliamentary mandates (seven and five years respectively). The experience of cohabitation imposed a parliamentary interpretation of the constitution. Although this may have been the intended interpretation of the constitution, there was a wide consensus among politicians and electors that the presidential reading should be protected. In 2000, the mandate of the President of the Republic was shortened from seven years to five years, so that the mandate of the first chamber and the President would coincide. Since then, the semi-presidential regime has not been threatened by a return to cohabitation.

Secondly, the *Conseil constitutionnel* has altered its role considerably from being a guardian of the Executive to a guarantor of rights and freedoms. Interestingly, far from encountering strong resistance, the 1974 amendment of the constitution strengthened considerably the role of the *Conseil constitutionnel*. Valery Giscard d'Estaing, then President of the Republic, sponsored a constitu-tional amendment extending the right to refer a bill for review to the *Conseil constitutionnel* to 60 *députés*[43] or 60 *sénateurs*.[44] Thus, members of the opposi-tion were given the right to refer any legislation which they felt was unconstitutional. Again the constitutional change was confirmed and even

---

[43] *Députés* are members of the first chamber, the *Assemblée Nationale*.
[44] *Sénateurs* are members of the second chamber, the *Sénat*.

amplified by amendment of the constitution. Similarly, the amendment of the constitution of July 2008 strengthened further the role of the *Conseil constitutionnel*. Since March 2010, the ordinary courts can refer an act of Parliament relevant to an action before them to the *Conseil* for constitutionality review. Although its name has not changed, the *Conseil* now fulfils a role akin to that of a constitutional court. It has taken 40 years and two constitutional amendments to finally reach this stage. And in all likelihood, the *Conseil constitutionnel* will be reformed further. Although the legitimacy of the appointment procedure has been strengthened by the amendment of July 2008, its strong political flavour is still open to criticism. In addition, the automatic membership of past Presidents of the Republic and the absence of professional requirements (for example, legal qualifications, judicial experience and so on) to become a member of the *Conseil*, may undermine the legitimacy of some appointments and come to endanger the institution. Further amendments may be needed in the future.

Strengthening Parliamentary Democracy

The presidential reading of the constitution has had a negative effect on French democracy. Originally, the constitution was aimed at 'rationalising' the powers of the Parliament to ensure that a return to the practices and instability of the fourth Republic would not take place. However, the majoritarian phenomenon which emerged with the 1962 parliamentary elections has led in the main to the French Parliament being controlled by the Government. With so many limitations dictated by the constitution itself, Parliament is no longer able to provide a check on the formidable Executive. Arguably, this situation was triggered by changes in the political circumstances highlighted above; the resulting accountability deficit ought to have been addressed in the 1970s or 1980s. However, in reality, it has taken all this time to try to redress the balance. There were two major constitutional revisions in this regard: one was completed in 1995 and the second in 2008. Both tried to find ways to strengthen Parliament and counterbalance the extraordinary power of the Executive.[45] To this end, the amendments created a single, annual parliamentary session, increased the number of permanent parliamentary committees, created a status for opposition parties, bestowed on each chamber greater control over their agenda, and limited some of the Government's legislative weapons. Parliament has undeniably gained from these reforms.

Interestingly, the 1995 revision was originally triggered by Parliament's rebellion during the amendment of the constitution which was necessary to ratify the Maastricht treaty in 1992. Parliament felt that it lacked the necessary power to

---

[45] In the 1958 constitution, the President of the Republic, the Prime Minister and the Government all participate to the Executive branch.

protect French sovereignty. Arguably, years of 'parliamentary frustration' were also taking their toll. To meet the demands of Parliament and avoid a lengthy revision process, the President of the Republic, François Mitterrand, vowed to organise a revision of the constitution soon after. In 1993, a committee of experts chaired by Professor Vedel produced a report and made a number of recommendations. However, parliamentary elections and a change of majority intervened before the process was completed. The revision was scaled down with a number of proposals abandoned. The resulting amendments were a far cry from what was really needed to redress the institutional balance and soon demands for another revision were heard. This movement culminated in the reform of July 2008.

Holding the Executive to Account

Many politicians and commentators have lamented that that the presidential interpretation of the constitution has created an imbalance to the detriment of the French Parliament. Also, many have argued that the new political configuration, while consolidating the role of the Executive as a whole, compromises the standard mechanisms for their political accountability, namely ministerial responsibility. This accountability gap was so strongly felt that it led to the passing of two constitutional amendments strengthening the judicial accountability of the Executive. Originally, a specialist court, the High Court of Justice was given jurisdiction over the criminal activity of members of Government while in office and to decide on the possible impeachment of the President of the Republic. However, it soon became clear that these provisions gave rise to more questions than they answered. When the actions of the Government in the contaminated blood affair required further investigation,[46] the failings of the High Court of Justice made it necessary to overhaul the criminal liability of members of the Government. Consequently, in a reform of July 1993, a new court the Court of Justice of the Republic, and a new criminal liability were created to judge the actions of members of Government as a result of their appointment.

Furthermore, in July 2007, articles 67 and 68 which regulated the criminal liability of the President of the Republic were amended to clarify their ambit. The original principle of presidential irresponsibility is limited to actions and decisions resulting from the presidential mandate. The irresponsibility for all other actions and decisions is only temporary: it is lifted one month after the end of the mandate. While in office, the President of the Republic cannot take part in any judicial proceedings (not even as a witness). Article 68 which softens the prohibition of article 67, organises a procedure for the impeachment of the President of the Republic. Prior to July 2007, the President could be impeached

---

[46] Three ministers were accused of having acted negligently with regard to contaminated blood: they were too slow in taking appropriate action to avoid the use of contaminated blood products.

for high treason, but the constitutional reform changed this to allow an impeachment in the event that the President fail to fulfil his duties in a way manifestly incompatible with the exercise of his/her mandate. Not only have these processes of accountability aimed to address the accountability gap mentioned above, but they also reflect a deep change of attitude in society with regard to morality in political life.

Allowing the Ratification of International Treaties

According to article 54, international treaties and agreements can be referred to the *Conseil constitutionnel* for review prior to their ratification. If the *Conseil constitutionnel* finds that the treaty or agreement contravenes the French constitution, the constitution must be amended first.

No revision of the constitution was declared to be necessary prior to 1992. However, the new Treaty on the European Union was found to contain provisions which compromised French national sovereignty: amendment of the constitution was therefore necessary. The 1958 constitution was duly amended and a new title of the European Union was incorporated in the constitution. Not only were the necessary transfers of sovereignty authorised therein, but parliamentary control over European affairs was strengthened. Furthermore as Members of Parliament wished to keep European integration and future transfers of sovereignty under review, the constitutional provisions do not contain a blanket approval for the European Union: future transfers will need to be authorised individually whenever the *Conseil constitutionnel* identifies them. In fact, Title XV has already being amended three times: for the ratification of the Amsterdam treaty,[47] the constitutional treaty[48] and the Lisbon treaty.[49]

Other international treaties have also required amendment of the constitution: for instance, provisions of the treaty creating the International Criminal Court were found to interfere with the constitutional regime determining the liability of members of the Executive.[50]

Amendments Reflecting the Development of Constitutionalism

Finally, a number of constitutional amendments have tended to reflect new trends in constitutional thought and ideals. Interestingly, many of these changes have been witnessed in other constitutional systems around the world.

[47] See C. cons. n. 97–394 DC 31 December 1997, Amsterdam treaty, rec. 344.
[48] See C. cons. n. 2004–505 DC 19 November 2004, European Constitution, rec. 173. Although the constitution was amended prior to the referendum on the European Constitution, the revision of the constitution never came into effect as the treaty was subsequently rejected by referendum.
[49] See C. cons n. 2007- DC, 20 December 2007, Lisbon Treaty, rec. 459.
[50] See C. cons 98–408 DC 22 January 1999, International Criminal Court, rec. 29.

Sophie Boyron

(i) The Demands for Territorial Autonomy

Local Government and overseas territories have made increasing demands for freedom during the later part of the twentieth century. Indeed, some commentators have presented this movement as a reaction to globalisation and regional integration. In France, the quest by local and regional governments for more autonomy and by overseas territories for independence, found its translation in a number of constitutional amendments. For instance, in March 2003, Title XII on local government was entirely re-drafted and new constitutional foundations were established to regulate central-local relations. A recognition of the principle of decentralisation was also incorporated in article 1 of the constitution.[51]

In addition, new constitutional provisions were introduced to address the pressing demands of some overseas territories for more independence. The constitution was amended in July 1998 and again in February 2007 and a new Title XIII on New Caledonia was included; the territory was granted a new institutional structure which recognises and facilitates the transition towards independence.

(ii) New Rights and Freedoms

New trends and evolution can also explain other amendments made to the 1958 constitution. Since 1971, the *Conseil constitutionnel* has succeeded in incorporating a large number of rights and freedoms in the French constitution. These are discussed in the next section. However, this judicial incorporation has limits and a few formal amendment have been necessary to complete rights protection.

For a long while, politicians had wished to promote women in politics. However, the *Conseil constitutionnel* opposed any attempt at positive discrimination in this domain. In July 1999, the constitution was amended to introduce a principle of parity of the sexes in political life. In July 2008, the requirement of parity was extended and imposed to private companies, public corporations, charities and other social organisations when appointing to key positions in their organisation.

In March 2005, a new Charter for the environment was drafted and incorporated in the 1958 constitution. It is noticeable that while the *Conseil* has granted constitutional status to many first and second generation rights, it has been slow to do the same for those of the third generation. Consequently, the Charter reflects the present concerns with regard to the environment and seeks to

---

[51] 'France shall be an indivisible, secular, democratic and social Republic. It shall ensure the equality of all citizens before the law, without distinction of origin, race or religion. It shall respect all beliefs. It shall be organised on a decentralised basis.

Statutes shall promote equal access by women and men to elective offices and posts as well as to positions of professional and social responsibility'.

establish a constitutional framework of environmental rights and duties. These aim to ensure an effective and constitutional protection for all citizens in this domain.

THE CONSEIL CONSTITUTIONNEL AND THE RISE OF LEGAL
CONSTITUTIONALISM: A COMPLEX DYNAMIC OF CONSTITUTIONAL CHANGE

The Conseil constitutionnel has completely altered its role and position in the regime of the fifth Republic. This change has been the result of a combination of constitutional practices and constitutional amendments forming a strong dynamic of change which culminated with the recent revision of July 2008.

Not only has the *Conseil constitutionnel* redefined its role but it has totally transformed the content of the 1958 constitution and triggered an unprecedented evolution in the understanding of French constitutionalism.

The Extension of the Constitution

When the constitution was drafted over the summer of 1958, it was not felt desirable to include a declaration or charter of rights. Moreover, the 1958 constitution asserts very few fundamental rights and freedoms in the text itself. Only the Preamble[52] proclaimed France's respect of the principles found in the Declaration of the Rights of Man of 1789[53] and the Preamble to the 1946 Constitution.[54] Moreover, not only was the legal status of the preamble of the 1958 ambiguous, but the drafters of the constitution had expressly rejected the possibility of the *Conseil constitutionnel* applying and enforcing it. In the early years, the regime of the fifth Republic did not have an effective system of rights protection. This continued until 1971 when the *Conseil constitutionnel* orchestrated a quiet constitutional revolution: as a result of an audacious interpretation of the 1958 constitution, it became a guardian of rights and freedoms and started to review the constitutionality of legislation against them. In 1971, a controversial piece of legislation was referred to the *Conseil* for review: it amended legislation of 1901 and markedly curtailed freedom of association.[55] In 1901, freedom of association was recognised for the first time and the new legislation stated that all associations would have legal personality after notice of their creation was given to the local town hall. Instead, the new legislation specified that associations would only acquire legal personality after a check by the State. Little freedom of

[52] The Preamble was amended in March 2005 to include a reference to the Charter for the Environment.
[53] The Declaration of 1789 contains a list of classical liberal principles on freedom of the individual, property and equality.
[54] The 1946 Preamble guarantees social and economic rights, such as the right to health, education, social welfare, work etc.
[55] For an in-depth analysis of this decision, see Favoreu and Philip, *Les grandes décisions du Conseil constitutionnel*, 15th edn, (Dalloz, 2009) 180.

association would be left. Still, as much as the *Conseil constitutionnel* may have wished to pronounce the new bill unconstitutional, many obstacles stood in its way.

At the time, the *Conseil constitutionnel* only reviewed the constitutionality of bills prior to their publication. However, with no declaration of rights to rely upon, the *Conseil's* power was limited. First, it had to engineer the incorporation of rights and freedoms into the 1958 constitution; it turned to the preamble of the 1958 constitution and the texts cited therein—the Declaration of the Rights of Man of 1789 and the Preamble of the 1946 constitution. In one interpretative stroke, the *Conseil constitutionnel* incorporated these into the 1958 constitution. However, this fell short of what was required as freedom of association is not listed in either text. Another audacious interpretation of the provisions of the 1946 preamble was required before freedom of association could be granted constitutional status. In its opening paragraph, the 1946 Preamble reasserts solemnly the rights and freedoms contained in the Declaration of 1789 and in the 'general principles recognised in the legislation of the Republic'. The *Conseil constitutionnel* concluded that there were constitutional principles other than those listed in the 1789 Declaration and in the 1946 Preamble. Furthermore, the *Conseil* decided that these constitutional rights were found in legislation of past Republican regimes. As freedom of association was recognised in 1901 by the Parliament of the third Republic, the *Conseil constitutionnel* found it easy to construe the freedom as a 'general principle recognised in the legislation of the Republic'. Once this was done, the *Conseil* declared the new bill to be in breach of freedom of association. The attempt to amend the old legislation was dropped forthwith.

As a result of this decision, the constitution of 1958 is no longer an exhaustive statement of all constitutional principles. Since then, commentators have regarded the French constitution as a composite and used the expression 'block of constitutionality' to designate all constitutional rules and principles.[56] The original constitution is only one component of this whole: the Declaration of the Rights of Man of 1789, the Preamble of the Constitution of 1946, the General Principles Recognised in the Legislation of the Republic, and since 2004 the Charter for the Environment, all combine to establish this French constitution—new style. In one decision, the *Conseil constitutionnel* had increased dramatically the standards against which an Act of Parliament could be reviewed. This also fundamentally altered the position of the *Conseil* in the political system.

---

[56] However, the *Conseil constitutionnel* refers to 'principles with constitutional status' or *principes à valeur constitutionnelle.*

The Transformation of the Conseil Constitutionnel into a Constitutional Court

The *Conseil constitutionnel* has never had to fulfil the role of guardianship of the Executive for which it was created. The Parliament did not have the weapons necessary to cause much constitutional mischief and in any event the Executive was soon so powerful that it did not need much protection. It is not surprising therefore that the *Conseil constitutionnel* adopted a new role for itself, a role which would also greatly benefit the constitutional arrangements of the rapidly changing fifth Republic. As a result of the audacious interpretation of the 1958 constitution presented above, the *Conseil* became a guardian of constitutional rights and freedoms instead. It reviewed the constitutionality of legislation against fundamental rights and slowly the institution started to assume the mantle of a constitutional court. This evolution was soon endorsed by amendment of the constitution. Originally, bills could be referred to the *Conseil constitutionnel* by four persons only: the President of the Republic, the Prime Minister and the presidents of both chambers of Parliament. In 1974, the President of the Republic proposed to extend this right to 60 *députés* or 60 *sénateurs*. This constitutional amendment confirmed the previous interpretation and legitimised a clear departure from the intentions of the drafters of the constitution. Furthermore, this revision of the constitution unlocked the potential of the institution: had the right to refer a bill not been extended in this way, the case law would not have grown in the same proportion. Nowadays, a reference to the *Conseil* is regarded as the last obstacle that the opposition can put across the path of a bill. The *Conseil* has had ample opportunity to recognise a growing number of constitutional principles, to build up its case law and sharpen the tools of its control.

Finally, the transformation of the *Conseil* into a body resembling a constitutional court was largely completed by the reform of July 2008: a new article 61–1[57] has given citizens the right to trigger a review of constitutionality of legislative provisions already in force. Commentators had been arguing that with a number of bills escaping it, the original review power was not sufficient. In view of the institution's evolution, it was opportune to ensure full respect for the constitution. Called 'preliminary ruling on an issue of constitutionality', the new review was also conceived as a mean to strengthen the constitutional position of French citizens. Since April 2010, the *Conseil* can be called upon by the parties to invalidate an unconstitutional statute which is incidental to an ordinary court action.

---

[57] 'If, during proceedings in progress before a court of law, it is claimed that a statutory provision infringes the rights and freedoms guaranteed by the Constitution, the matter may be referred by the Conseil d'État or by the Cour de Cassation to the Constitutional Council, within a determined period.

An Institutional Act shall determine the conditions for the application of this article'.

Sophie Boyron

The Evolution of French Constitutionalism

The evolution in the role of the *Conseil constitutionnel* has had another unexpected effect. As explained above, the effectiveness of many past constitutions was compromised. Prior to the fifth Republic, constitutions may have been legal documents but they were not easily enforceable: for instance, neither the *Conseil d'Etat*[58] nor the *Cour de Cassation*[59] accepted jurisdiction to review the constitutionality of statutes. Consequently, political behaviour took place outside and sometimes in breach of the constitutional document. By ensuring that the constitution is finally guaranteed through law, the *Conseil constitutionnel* has encouraged the rise of legal constitutionalism.

In fact, the creativity of the *Conseil* has had far greater impact than may at first appear. As the number of principles grows, so does the influence of constitutional law. Nowadays, few topics are impermeable to constitutional law: labour law, contract law, medical law, criminal procedure, administrative law, property law to name but a few, all have strong constitutional elements. Indeed, some commentators have argued that this was a long-awaited 'revenge' of constitutional law: the reach of constitutional law is now so great that many areas have an incontrovertible constitutional core. From being peripheral, constitutional law has moved and settled at the centre of the legal system, thereby displacing more traditional subjects. In doing so, both constitutional law and constitutionalism have leaped forward.

THE REFORM OF JULY 2008: ENSURING THE SURVIVAL OF THE 1958 CONSTITUTION[60]

On 23 July 2008, the French Parliament adopted the most comprehensive revision of the 1958 constitution yet. This 'modernisation' of the constitution will certainly allow the fifth Republic to survive well into the twenty-first century. This reform needs to be explained as it has silenced the previous voices calling for the adoption of a new and sixth Republic. Only now is it possible to assert without doubt that the French constitution has finally broken from the past.

Many have commented that the reform had been long overdue: the presidential reading of the constitution had led to a marked predominance of the Executive and created a permanent institutional imbalance; the reduction in 2000 of the presidential mandate to five years emphasised this situation further. In any event, during the presidential electoral campaign of spring 2007, both candidates

---

[58] See CE Sect. November 1936 Arrighi, rec. 966. With regard to the *Conseil d'Etat*, the category of general principles of law was used to guarantee a number of constitutional rights and freedoms.
[59] See C. cass. 1833 Paulin.
[60] For a presentation of some aspects of the reform see Ducoulombier 'Rebalancing power between the Executive and the Parliament: The experience of French constitutional reform' (2010) *Public Law* 688.

140

promised constitutional reform. Indeed soon after taking office, Nicolas Sarkozy announced his wish to drive through major constitutional reform.[61] A committee of experts was convened and the great majority of the proposals contained in their report found their way into the constitutional bill. After a relatively smooth parliamentary process,[62] the revision was adopted on 23 July 2008 by the Congress (two chambers sitting together) with only one vote to spare. In total, 48 constitutional provisions were either amended or introduced. Since then, Parliament has been busy passing the necessary implementing legislation to give effect to the reform.

The reform has achieved three clear aims: the powers of Parliament have been markedly increased, the independence of the judiciary has been strengthened, and finally the rights and status of citizens have been bolstered. However, with regard to the Executive, the outcome of reform is a little disappointing.

With regard to the Executive, Sarkozy had wished that the respective roles and powers of President of the Republic and Prime Minister be clarified, that the President be allowed to address the Parliament directly, and that limits be imposed on some presidential powers, particularly with regard to appointments. The reform of July 2008 fulfilled two of these proposals, but failed to clarify the respective roles of the President of the Republic and of the Prime Minister.

When it comes to Parliament, the powers of both chambers have been strengthened in a number of ways: the number of permanent committees has been increased, each chamber has been granted more freedom to set their agenda, the powers of the Government over the legislative process have been limited and a distinct status has been recognised for the opposition.

For their part, the sovereign people have been granted a right of popular initiative and the possibility of requesting the *Conseil constitutionnel* to give a preliminary ruling on an issue of constitutionality. Also, reform of the *Conseil supérieur de la Magistrature* aims to guarantee further the independence of the judiciary.

The reform of July 2008 marked a complete and final break from the constitutional past. Prior to this major revision, a number of commentators had strongly criticised the chronic institutional imbalance and called for the adoption of a new constitution; they argued that both the regime and the constitution were irremediably flawed and that the institutional imbalance was a 'congenital' defect that could not be fixed; the old habit of drafting a new constitution instead of amending, was still casting a long shadow. Hopefully, the success of the 2008 revision has marked the end of this tradition. Not only will the major constitutional amendment of July 2008 help the fifth Republic to secure a future, but it

---

[61] See speech of Epinal of 12 July 2007. http://www.linternaute.com/actualite/politique/document/discours-nicolas-sarkozy-epinal/discours-institutions.shtml
[62] Although the bill ran into some difficulty before the second chamber.

has allowed new constitutional values to come to the fore: constitutional continuity and regime longevity. However flawed the fifth Republic may be, neither politicians nor electors were ready to see it go.

CONCLUSION: CONSTITUTIONAL REFORM IN FRANCE AND THE ROLE OF COMPARATIVE LAW

During the constitutional revision of July 2008, unparalleled use was made of comparative data to influence and assess the proposals for reform. On the surface, comparative lawyers should be both encouraged by, and encouraging of, such developments. However, on further analysis, the comparative methodology, comparative data and their use were such that there may be cause for concern. Instead of relying on data produced by a reliable comparative methodology, ministers, Members of Parliament and politicians in general did not seek to explore and assess the merits of a proposal but to legitimise it. Consequently, they tended to refer to 'comparative utterances' as opposed to 'comparative data'. Many of these sweeping statements sought to justify the proposed new rule or institution by pointing to their existence in 'most Western democracies' or by indicating that they are standard in the constitutional systems of 'our European partners'. Comparative analyses used in this way tend to concentrate on crude similarities. For a system which has thrived on constitutional experimentation, the use of comparative law in this way may stifle constitutional creativity. Experiments outside the experience of 'our European partners' may be discouraged. In the long term, this may affect the evolution the 1958 constitution as the ability of future drafters to be creative and 'to think out of the box' may be compromised.

7

Germany

JENS WOELK

INTRODUCTION

CONSTITUTIONAL CHANGE IN Germany reflects the evolution of the country from a process of constitutional transition in the post-war period to protected normality during the Cold War and to complete normalisation after the end of the reunification process. The need for permanent adaptation made continuous constitutional change necessary, though it has been achieved with only a few major reforms.

In fact, after the adoption of the Basic Law (*Grundgesetz*, GG)[1] in 1949 by the Parliaments of the Western German *Länder*,[2] relative tranquillity characterised (Western) Germany for the first four decades of its existence. The German 'economic miracle' after World War II was partly due to a specific form of social and economic cohesion, the 'social market economy' supported by all political powers in the country. Political stability was seen as an important precondition for economic reconstruction and thus also became an institutional objective. The country's outstanding economic success was not matched by a proportionate increase in political power. The period of tranquillity was paradoxically due to

---

[1] The German Basic Law (Grundgesetz) was adopted on 23 May 1949, and last amended on 21 July 2010 (Federal Official Gazette, *BGBl* I, 944). See for updated texts in English: Federal Parliament *Bundestag* at https://www.btg-bestellservice.de/pdf/80201000.pdf, document Status: April 2010; International Constitutional Law ICL available at http://www.servat.unibe.ch/icl/gm00000_.html, document Status: 12 November 2009; consolidated version in German by Federal Ministry of Justice available at http://www.gesetze-im-internet.de/gg/BJNR000010949.html containing the last amendments of 21 July 2010.

[2] As it is widely known, the Basic Law' was elaborated as a Constitution of a provisional character by a 'Parliamentary Council' (the expression 'Constituent Assembly' had deliberately been avoided). With the approval of the Western Allies, the Federal Republic of Germany was formed by aggregation of the ten (Western) *Länder* established in the occupation zones and now constituent States of the Federation. In order to stress the provisional character of the federal Constitution, the Basic Law was approved by the Parliaments of the ten *Länder* (with the vote of Bavaria against!) and not by referendum. As the division of the country had become evident, on 7 October 1949 the socialist German Democratic Republic was founded in the Soviet Occupied Zone.

the artificial and protected situation of Germany as a divided country at the front-line of the Cold War in which the constitutional system could unfold and develop.

This tranquil period ended with the sudden and spectacular breaching of the Berlin Wall on 9 November 1989 which opened the road to unexpected re-unification. This historical opportunity was also a necessity due to the fast erosion and implosion of the German Democratic Republic (GDR) (with the resulting need for overall reconstruction). In addition, the acceleration of the European integration process raised important questions about the future of this very process and Germany's role in it. After the inward-looking and European-centred approach of German politics and reform in the first half of the 1990s, Germany has become a 'normal' state like many others.[3] However, over recent years critical questions regarding Germany's capacity to modernise have been raised, involving its federal system, so far seen as one of the guarantees of political stability.

The main preoccupation of the constituent fathers of the Basic Law was political and economic stability as a lesson learned from the past. A repetition of the traumatic experiences leading to the gradual destruction of the Weimar Constitution had to be avoided. In the final years of the Weimar Republic, the political context had progressively transformed the Constitution's normative content into a mere political manifesto contested by radical political forces, both on the Left and on the Right. Thus, Hitler did not (need to) 'take power': instead of a *coup d'état* or a revolution, there was institutional continuity, at least in formal terms. This is why the Basic Law aims at preventing 'revolutions under the mask of legality' and provides that its normative character applies to all of its parts and that it is binding and directly applicable law (article 1 al.3 GG). As part of the new concept of a 'self-defending democracy' (*wehrhafte Demokratie*), the Basic Law itself determines its form as a Constitution contained in one document of normative character, with values to be protected. This protection of constitutional values includes the procedure for amendment and the positive identification of an essential core of constitutional principles which are not subject to any revision (article 79 GG). The Federal Constitutional Court (BVerfG) assumes the central role in guaranteeing the Constitution and its values, in particular by opening up to the individual the right to challenge alleged violations of fundamental rights by the state.[4]

---

[3] Complete sovereignty had been achieved by the Treaty on the Final Status of Germany of 12 September 1990 (*cf* art 7 s 2), Federal Official Gazette, *BGBl* II (1990), 1318.

[4] The powers of the Federal Constitutional Court are listed in art 93 GG; they include the declaration of forfeiture of fundamental rights (art 18) and the prohibition of political parties (art 21 par 2), if either is necessary for protecting the constitutional order and its values.

CONSTITUTIONAL AMENDMENTS

In 60 years of constitutional practice, there have been 58 constitutional amendments. Although for the most part these have been minor changes of detail, the frequency of amendments is an indicator of the fact that the amendment procedure is definitively not an obstacle to change.[5] Amendments are considered a special form of legislative procedure: in fact, their regulation in article 79 GG, as part of the provisions on federal legislation, is limited to the features distinguishing them from the ordinary legislative procedure (articles 76–78, 82), in particular the formal (article 79 al.1 and 2) and substantive (al.3) limits to amendment. For all other matters, the ordinary legislative procedure applies.[6]

The Positivist Element: No Amendment Without Changes to the Text

Article 79 al.1 GG excludes any kind of 'accessory/secondary Constitutions' (*Nebenverfassungen*), in particular separate constitutional laws, as constitutional amendments require laws expressly amending or supplementing the text of the Basic Law. The principle of 'no amendment without textual changes to the Basic Law' guarantees that the Constitution—in its formal sense—is always one homogenous document, complete and accessible for citizens.[7] This does not by any means exclude the existence of ordinary legislation which is 'constitutional' in terms of substance, such as the electoral law or the law on citizenship. However, the concentration of the 'formal Constitution' in one document, serving the purpose of promoting easy recognition and legal certainty, is considered an important element of the principle of the rule of law (*Rechtsstaatsprinzip*): it is a result of Germany's positivist tradition and approach—a legal norm is

---

[5] Among the numerous amendments of the Basic Law the most important ones are: the amendment of 1956 which permitted re-armament of the Federal Republic (arts 87a and 87b); the rationalisation of the state of emergency of 1968 (arts 35 al.1 and al.3, 80a and 115a ff); the reforms of the so-called 'Financial Constitution' in 1969, adopted by the Grand Coalition of Social Democrats (SPD) and Christian Democrats (CDU/CSU) (arts 104a to 115) and the introduction of the individual constitutional complaint to the BVerfG (art 93 n 4a); the changes after German re-unification (art 4 Treaty of Unification of 31 August 1990); the adjustments in 1992, necessary for progress in European integration, in particular the new version of art 23 (article Europe); the reform of 1994 including the introduction of art 20a (Protection of the natural foundations of life and animals) as well as some changes to the legislative powers (in particular of art 72, concurrent competencies); the limitation of the guarantee of political asylum through art 16a (1993) and the introduction of the *Großer Lauschangriff* ('big bugging') in art 13 al. 3–6 (1998); the privatisation of Federal Postal Service and the Federal Railways (articles 87e and 87f LF); the recent reforms of the federal system in 2006 and 2009 by the second Grand Coalition; and, finally, the amendments permitting the ratification of the Lisbon Treaty (2009).

[6] The same technique was applied by its predecessors: the Constitution of the *Reich* of 1871 (art 78 1st period) and the Constitution of Weimar of 1919 (art 76 al. 1).

[7] This corresponds to the technique of legislative drafting in general: in Germany legislative texts are published as organic and complete texts or consolidated versions.

a written provision—and is in contrast with the historical experience of constitutional 'breach' in the shape of inconsistent single laws adopted with a qualified
majority.[8]

Over time, apart from formal amendment, constitutional evolution (*Verfassungswandel*) through interpretation can be observed as the necessary adaptation
of the text due to the frequent use of open concepts (for instance human dignity
and property) and their application in changed societal contexts.

The provisions regarding the 'confidence vote' (article 68 GG) have twice been
interpreted in a sense not foreseen by the constituents who intended to privilege
stability and to avoid elections before the end of a legislature. When federal
Chancellors Helmut Kohl (in 1982, after having been elected by a 'constructive
no-confidence vote', article 67 GG) and Gerhard Schröder (in 2005, after losing
important regional elections) asked for a confidence vote, they actually had a
majority in Parliament, but aimed at the dissolution of the *Bundestag* with
consequent anticipated elections in order to gain popular approval. In both cases,
however, the BVerfG conceded the Federal Chancellor and the President a wide
margin of political discretion in judging the political perspectives of a sustainable
support for the government by a sufficiently stable majority (a concept thus not
only defined by sufficient numbers). Consequently, in legal academia, the 'true'
vote of confidence is distinguished from the 'non authentic' one, that is, aimed at
the dissolution of Parliament (*unechte Vertrauensfrage*).[9]

However, in case of a strong discrepancy between the text and the real meaning
of a given constitutional provision, the general obligation to guarantee legal
certainty, following from the rule of law principle, might require the constitutional legislator to update the text by amendment.[10]

In accordance with this logic, no so-called 'dynamic' amendments are allowed
under article 79 al.1 GG, that is, those including references to other sources of law
which might themselves be amended; this prohibition also applies to the ratification and implementation of international treaties requiring constitutional
amendments—as a matter of principle these have to be made visible by changing
the text of the Basic Law.[11] Two important exceptions, necessary for Germany's

---

[8] In fact, there was no such express obligation of amendments of the text either in the
Constitution of 1871 or in the Weimar-Constitution of 1919. In the same way, textual clarity should
protect the highest constitutional values, as fundamental rights can only be restricted—in the cases
and within the limits indicated in the Basic Law—by laws which 'must specify the fundamental right
affected and the article in which it appears' (art 19 al.1 GG).

[9] BVerfGE 62, 1, BVerfGE 114, 107 and BVerfGE 114, 121 (Bundestagsauflösung). See SJ
Podworny, *Die auflösungsgerichtete Vertrauensfrage—unter besonderer Berücksichtigung der BVerfG-
Urteile von 1983 und 2005*, (Köln, Carl Heymanns Verlag, 2008). In July 2009, also the Parliament of
Land Schleswig-Holstein was dissolved after a no-confidence vote aimed at anticipated elections
considered in conformity with the Land Constitution.

[10] A constitutional basis was seen as necessary for the right to vote for EU citizens in municipal
elections after its introduction by the Maastricht Treaty (art 28 par.1 s.2 GG); see below (notes 86 and
87).

[11] An exception for certain international treaties (peace treaties, treaties ending an occupation
regime, or for the purpose of defence) is contained in art 59 al.2 GG. According to art 79 al.1, 2nd

international and European integration through the transfer of sovereign powers (articles 23 and 24 GG), will be discussed below.

The Procedural Elements: Rigidity, Simplicity and Parity

The procedural requirements for amendment are contained in a brief provision: any law amending the text of the Basic Law 'shall be carried by two thirds of the Members of the *Bundestag* and two thirds of the votes of the *Bundesrat*' (article 79 al.1 GG). This means *rigidity*, because the Constitution cannot be amended by occasional majorities as wide consensus is needed. However, in the 'bipolar' system of political parties which characterised Germany until the 1980s this requirement in practice allowed for great flexibility, judging by the number of amendments.[12] The procedure is also *simple*, as only the Parliament (*Bundestag*) and the Federal Council (*Bundesrat*), representing the governments of the constituent states (*Länder*), participate with the same two-thirds threshold. Neither double readings nor double votes are required, nor an approval by referendum.[13] Finally, the procedure is characterised by *parity* through the equal participation of representatives of the democratic and of the federal principles: the people through the Parliament and the *Länder* through the Federal Council.[14]

Territorial Change: Each Case is a Special One

Although the Basic Law has been frequently amended through the procedure described above, a specific procedure established by article 29 GG regulates territorial change, which also results in change within the federal structures. Despite continuous debate on the size of the *Länder* and the re-organisation of

period, in these cases, a mere declaration of conformity with the Basic Law is sufficient even without respecting the requirement of textual unity. The provision was inserted in 1954 and was used only then, for the—failed—attempt to establish a European Defence Community. Opening to 'secondary constitutional law', this exception from textual unity is considered constitutional by some (as it merely splits the amendment procedure in two separate parts: constitutional amendment with declaration of conformity and ratification), see J Lücke, in M Sachs (ed), *Grundgesetz*, (München 2003), Art 79 (sub 12), while others consider it unconstitutional, eg H v Mangoldt, F Klein, C Starck (ed), *Das Bonner Grundgesetz*, Vol 3, (München, 2001), Art 79 Anm IV 1.

[12] In the three years of the first Grand Coalition between the Christian Democrats (CDU/CSU) and Social Democrats (SPD), 1966–69, both parties together had a two-thirds majority and adopted 12 constitutional amendments. It was a period of transition: after reconstruction, the welfare state had to be (re-)organised and the—controversial—constitutional provisions for the state of emergency had to be adopted. The second Grand Coalition (2005–2009) adopted two reforms of the federal system (see below).

[13] By contrast with most Constitutions of the *Länder*, for historical reasons the Basic Law practically excludes direct popular participation apart from elections.

[14] Since 1992, this procedure also applies to the transfer of sovereign powers to the EU, art 23 al.1 in combination with art 79 al.2 GG (amendment of 21 December 1992, *BGBl* I 2086).

federal territory, in particular about resolving demographic and economic dis-crepancies,[15] this general procedure for territorial redesign has never been applied in practice. All major territorial changes, so far, have been based on special provisions: the creation of the 'Southwestern State' of Baden-Württemberg in 1952 (article 118 GG), the accession of Saarland to the Federal Republic on 1 January 1957,[16] and even reunification in 1990, which took the form of accession of the five re-constituted *Länder* in Eastern Germany.[17] In the summer of 1996, however, the fusion of Berlin with surrounding Brandenburg, envisaged in the Treaty of Unification and regulated in a new provision (article 118a GG), failed as it failed to achieve the necessary popular support in the referendum. This seems to be proof of the collective and—to some extent—historical identities of the *Länder* which after decades of existence cannot be easily replaced by new entities created exclusively according to economic criteria.

THE 'ETERNITY CLAUSE', ARTICLE 79 AL.3 GG

The Basic Law, or rather its fundamental principles, is by its own definition 'eternal': In fact, the so-called 'eternity clause' (article 79 al.3 GG) declares that 'Amendments to this Basic Law affecting the division of the Federation into *Länder*, their participation on principle in the legislative process, or the principles laid down in articles 1 and 20 shall be inadmissible.' This 'eternal and reinforced' guarantee of intangible fundamental principles allows for the easy identification of a permanent essential core of the Constitution: the constitutional identity is 'positivised'; without these principles, the Federal Republic ceases to be the same.[18] Although the guarantee of this essential core implies strong protection, the BVerfG interprets 'affecting' in a restricted way in order not to limit the room for amendment too much: a too strict interpretation of the substantive limits would make the amendment procedure impractical and lead to immobility.[19]

---

[15] See, for instance, U Leonardy, 'Territorial Reform of the Länder: A Demand of the Basic Law', in A. Gunlicks (ed), *German Public Policy and Federalism. Current Debates on Political, Legal and Social Issues*, (New York and Oxford, 2003), 65–90.

[16] *BGBl* I (1956), 1011; Agreement of 27 October 1956 on the Saar territory, *BGBl* II 1587. The accession of the Saar territory and the consequent extension of the application of the Basic Law are democratically legitimated by the referendum held on 23 October 1955.

[17] According to the procedure established by art 23 GG (prior to reunification).

[18] This essential and intangible core of the Constitution corresponds to the protection of fundamental rights which are its main *raison d'etre*. Also the guarantees of individual fundamental rights cannot be affected in their essence (art 19 al.2 GG); see P Häberle, *Die Wesensgehaltsgarantie des Art 19 Abs 2 Grundgesetz—Zugleich ein Beitrag zum institutionellen Verständnis der Grundrechte und zur Lehre des Gesetzesvorbehalts*, 3rd edn, (Heidelberg 1983).

[19] See, for the position of the BVerfG, J Lücke, in M Sachs (ed), *Grundgesetz* cit. Art 79 (sub 25, fn 40–42).

Substantive and 'Eternal' Limits to Constitutional Revision

The positions in legal doctrine and in jurisprudence regarding the four 'intangible' principles forming the essential core of the Basic Law will be briefly analysed.[20]

(a) *Guarantee of the federal structure.* This principle aims at guaranteeing Germany's pluralist territorial structure thus making its transformation into a unitary State impossible. However, it does not guarantee the current federal system, the existence of the current *Länder* or their number: the design of the territorial structures can change (which is evident, as article 29 GG contains a provision for new division of the federal territory).[21] From a substantive perspective, the principle protects against amendments aiming at abolishing the nature of the *Länder* as constituent states: an intangible essential core of their own functions has to remain among their powers ('*Hausgut*').[22]

(b) *Guarantee of participation of the* Länder *as a matter of principle in the legislative process.* The guarantee of participation, on principle, in the legislative process at federal level is complementary to the guarantee of the federal structure, as the legislative powers of the *Länder* are already protected by the latter. Again, the open and general wording guarantees neither a specific form of participation, such as co-decision or the distinction between federal legislation subject to objection or to approval by the Federal Council, nor a specific institution, like the Federal Council; only a minimum of participation is absolutely protected.

(c) *Guarantee of the principles laid down in article 1 GG.* This guarantee does not protect article 1 itself, but the principles laid down in this provision as these are fundamental and essential to the whole constitutional system: the protection of human dignity (al.1),[23] the recognition of 'inviolable and inalienable human rights as the basis of every community, of peace and of justice in the world' (al. 2), and the subordination of legislative, executive and judicial powers to the respect for fundamental rights (al.3). Human dignity is not simply an abstract concept, but assumes a concrete dimension through the fundamental rights. Although fundamental rights are not guaranteed in an absolute way and may

---

[20] See K-E Hain, *Die Grundsätze des Grundgesetzes: eine Untersuchung zu Art 79 Abs 3 GG,* (Baden-Baden, 1999).
[21] However, three *Länder* are considered to be the absolute minimum necessary for a federal system.
[22] For instance, the autonomous determination of their (administrative and territorial) organisation and structures as well as a constitutional guarantee of an adequate share in the overall revenue of the federal State; see BVerfGE 34, 19 f. This includes obligations of (financial) solidarity in favour of poorer *Länder*; see BVerfGE 72, 330 (*Finanzausgleich* I).
[23] Under a strictly logical perspective, human dignity as the supreme constitutional value is already protected by art 1 al.1 GG itself, which imposes a duty to respect and protect human dignity on 'all State authority', thus including the constitutional legislator. Reference in art 79 al.3 GG is therefore made for the sake of clarity and completeness of the principles protected against amendment.

thus be restricted, they are strengthened vis-à-vis the constitutional legislator through their—differentiated—relationship with human dignity, to be applied in each individual case.[24] Due to the (quasi) absence of any articulation of the relationship between human dignity and fundamental rights, the content of some fundamental rights might be relatively easily changed, while others are more 'resistant' to constitutional amendments due to the strong bond with the personality of the right's bearer.[25]

Some cases of amendments restricting constitutional guarantees, very controversial in the political and legal debate at the time of their adoption, illustrate the connection between human dignity and fundamental rights. After a constitutional amendment the federal law on telephone-tapping of 1968 (*G-10 Gesetz*) allows restrictions to the right to privacy of correspondence, posts and telecommunications (article 10 GG) even without informing the affected person, introducing control by a Parliamentary Committee instead of judicial control.[26] A controversial amendment to the guarantee of political asylum of 1993 (*Asylnovelle*) strongly limits the practical possibilities of requesting political asylum and no longer delays the repatriation of the asylum seeker until legal remedies against the administrative decision have been sought (article 16a al. 2 and 3 GG).[27] In both cases, the amendments substantially restrict the guarantee of effective legal remedies (by article 19 al.4 GG and by both fundamental rights) leaving those affected without protection; however, despite this problematic constitutional situation and severe criticism, both amendments were upheld by the BVerfG as not being incompatible with the essential core, human dignity.[28]

In 1998, the BVerfG used similar arguments when examining a constitutional amendment of article 13 al.3 GG authorising the use of technical means for acoustical surveillance in case of suspicion of especially serious crimes having been committed.[29] Again in these cases the constitutional judges did not find any violation of the intangible essential core of the Constitution as the possible

---

[24] For H Dreier, *Grundgesetz-Kommentar*, (Tübingen, 1996), art 79 (sub. 26), at least three areas of minimum guarantees of fundamental rights exist: personal autonomy based upon the equality principle; fundamental rights essential for a democratic system; and judicial guarantees.

[25] Examples for the first group comprise arts 5 al.1, freedom of press, and 7 al.2 GG, parents' right to decide on the religious instruction of their children; more closely related to human dignity are arts 2, 3, 4, 5 al.1 1st period, 10–14, 16a, 101, 103 and 104 GG.

[26] The amendment added a 2nd period to art 10 al.2 GG concerning cases of 'self-defence of the democratic system', ie restrictions which serve to protect the free democratic basic order or the existence or security of the Federation or of a Land.

[27] The amendment has drastically reduced the number of requests by requiring that asylum-seekers arrive in Germany directly from the country in which they are persecuted on political grounds: prior passing through ‚secure' countries leads to the request being rejected as 'manifestly ill-founded', as the request could have been made earlier, in the 'secure' country (art 29a Law on Procedure for Political Asylum).

[28] BVerfGE 30, 1 (24 ff)—phone-tapping, and BVerfGE 94, 49—*Asylnovelle* (also BVerfGE 94, 115; 94, 116).

[29] *BGBl* (1998) I 610. After this reform, the code of criminal procedure was also amended to implement the new principle (known as *Großer Lauschangriff* or big bugging operation).

restriction of the right to human dignity and inviolability of the home were considered proportionate to the objective of protecting the public interest in efficient investigation; also the safeguards were regarded as sufficient.[30] However, with this judgment, the limits of the legislator's discretion in privileging security matters over individual freedom have been reached.[31]

In its case law, the BVerfG has interpreted human dignity very narrowly:[32] originally, only the behaviour of public authorities or bodies which expresses total disregard for the value of a human being as a person would count as a breach of human dignity; this approach has subsequently been changed by eliminating reference to criteria applied by the authority or body and by referring instead to the perspective of the complainant who has been subject to treatments degrading him or her to 'a mere object vis-à-vis the State'[33] or the public authority.

(d) *Guarantee of the principles laid down in article 20 GG.* This absolute limit to constitutional amendment refers to the first article of the second title of the Basic Law, concerning the 'organisation of the State': article 20 GG 'positivises' the fundamental foundations on which Germany's post-war constitutional order was based after the catastrophe of the Third Reich. Thus, the Republican, federal, social and democratic principles, as well as the principle of the rule of law, cannot be subject of constitutional amendments (al.1–3). As further guarantee, all of these principles—with the exception of the federal principle—are also binding on the constitutional orders of the *Länder*.[34]

To elaborate, the Republican principle is a permanent obstacle to any form of monarchy, while the qualification of Germany as a 'federal state' does not allow the Federation to change and amend the Basic Law in such a way as to give away

[30] BVerfGE 109, 279; however, the examination of single amendments to the code of criminal procedure necessary for implementation of the legitimate constitutional amendment might produce different results.

[31] In a series of recent judgments, the BVerfG has struck down restrictions of constitutionally guaranteed fundamental rights imposed by ordinary legislation which aimed at facilitating antiterrorism measures. The most spectacular case has been the judgment on the Air-Transport Security Act in 2005, in which the anticipated legislative authorisation of downing an aircraft hijacked by terrorists in a 09/11-situation was declared unconstitutional, for competence reasons and for violation of the human dignity of the innocent passengers and members of the crew on board of the airplane; BVerfGE 115, 118 (*Luftsicherheitsgesetz*). See, for example, O Lepsius, 'Human Dignity and the Downing of Aircraft: The German Federal Constitutional Court Strikes Down a Prominent Anti-terrorism Provision in the New Air-Transport Security Act', *German Law Journal* Vol 7 No 9, 1 September 2006. In February 2008, the BVerfG declared online bugging of computers unconstitutional and affirmed the guarantee of a fundamental right to privacy and integrity of IT systems; any secret infiltration can only occur after the measure has been approved by a judge; BVerfGE 120, 264 (*Grundrecht auf Computerschutz*). Further judgments have confirmed the tendency of safeguarding individual rights and freedoms vis-à-vis antiterrorism legislation.

[32] BVerfGE 30, 26.

[33] BVerfGE 27, 1 (6), and—as example of the new orientation—BVerfGE 69, 1 (34) and 87, 209 (228).

[34] According to art 28 al.1 1st period GG; the so-called homogeneity clause guarantees a minimum of common constitutional values in the—autonomous—organisation of the *Länder*.

its sovereignty as a state. This limit has become important vis-à-vis the European Union: by interpretation in conformity with the Constitution (and with article 79 al.3 GG in particular), the BVerfG has judged the transfer of single 'sovereign rights' to the EU legitimate, as long as the single act of transfer or the sum of the single acts over time do not lead to a complete and irreversible renunciation or loss of German statehood.[35] Also the reference to the 'social state' (that is welfare state) is to be understood as a comprehensive and general clause. It is an obligation and mandate of the state to intervene in cases of necessity and in favour of social justice, without, however, referring to single or particular guarantees.[36] From the democratic principle follows the binding obligation for the whole institutional organisation of the Federal Republic to be organised in democratic structures: the essence of the principle is popular sovereignty as well as its exercise through elections; both are guaranteed by the 'eternity clause'. In particular, elections have to respect the criteria established in article 38 al.1 GG, which have to be interpreted as guarantees of sufficiently wide powers of Parliament and as a limit against any transfer of the substance of democratic legitimacy.[37]

The prohibition against amending the principles deriving from the rule of law-principle (*Rechtsstaatsprinzip*) only refers to the principles of separation of powers and the supremacy of the Constitution: from the formulations in article 20 al.2 and 3 GG it follows that the functional separation (existence of three distinct powers with different functions) as well as the organisational separation of powers (their exercise through specific institutions) are protected;[38] in terms of substance, the separation of powers is less protected in order to allow for eventual transfers of functions from one power to the other, although an essential

---

[35] *Cf*, in this sense, the famous Maastricht judgment of 1993, BVerfGE 89, 155 (186), although in the judgment the hypothesis of the loss of statehood is based on the democratic principle; J Lücke, in M Sachs (ed), *Grundgesetz* cit. Art 79 sub 37 (no 66–67). This approach has been confirmed in the judgment on ratification of the Lisbon Treaty, 30 June 2009, BVerfGE 123, 167 (see below at n 38).

[36] An important exception is the guarantee of an existential minimum of dignity of, BVerfGE 84, 90 (121 and 126).

[37] It was exactly the risk of going beyond this limit which made the BVerfG express its famous admonition in the Maastricht judgment, justified by its preoccupation regarding powers of effective control to be exercised by the European Parliament as the institution of democratic representation at EU level; BVerfGE 89, 155 (172, 182, 186, 207–209), *cf* J Lücke, in M Sachs (ed), *Grundgesetz* cit. Art 79 sub 41 (n 72). Because of the same preoccupation, the BVerfG twice judged the effective participatory rights of the German Parliament as insufficient and declared relevant national legislation as unconstitutional: the implementation of the EU Arrest Warrant (18 July 2005, BVerfGE 113, 273) and the Act Extending and Strengthening the Rights of the *Bundestag* and the *Bundesrat* in European Union Matters as part of the ratification of the Lisbon Treaty (30 June 2009, BVerfGE 123, 267).

[38] Art 20 al.2 GG: 'All State authority is derived from the people. It shall be exercised by the people through elections and other votes and through specific legislative, executive and judicial bodies.' Art 20 al.3 GG: 'The legislature shall be bound by the constitutional order, the executive and the judiciary by law and justice.' The latter formulation highlights the distinction between positive statutory law and natural law (*'Gesetz und Recht'*); a necessary reminder after the experience of legislative and constitutional changes adopted in the Third Reich, at the beginning, as formally legitimate acts although contrary to constitutional values.

core of functions has to be guaranteed.[39] Thus, the protection through the 'eternity clause' covers the independence of the institutions, one from another (including judges, article 97 c.1 GG), but does not include every single and concrete legal principle derived from the rule of law principle, such as the prohibition of retroactive laws, the principle of proportionality, and the principle of effective and comprehensive legal protection.

Finally, the 'eternity clause' does not extend to the 'right to resistance' (*Widerstandsrecht*):[40] although contained in article 20 al.4 GG, this right does not belong to the fundamental constitutional principles identified by the constituent legislator, as it was only introduced in 1968.[41] Subsequent additions to the 'eternity clause' are now generally considered to be inadmissible, as otherwise its modification through the elimination of some original principles would also be facilitated, which would put the effective protection provided by the provision at risk.

Interpretation, (Self-)Protection and Constituent Powers

With article 79 al.3 GG, identifying an essential core of fundamental constitutional principles, the constituent power itself has established the substantive criteria for the examination of the constitutionality of actual constitutional amendments, assigning jurisdiction over issues of respect for the protected principles to the Constitutional Court. The application of the provision depends on the making of a request or application for judicial review. This may arise in disputes between institutions or of a federal nature; from abstract review of the legitimacy/legality of legislative acts made by institutions; on the application of a citizen for judicial review of legislative acts; or even a direct individual constitutional complaint in case of an alleged violation of fundamental rights.[42]

A judgment of the 'inadmissibility' of a constitutional amendment means that the Act of amendment is unconstitutional, that is, there is a declaration of its nullity by the BVerfG, as well as a prohibition order against the constitutional legislator.[43] However, any amendment respecting the listed limits is possible,

---

[39] The absolute limit is the institutions being deprived of their principal functions; in the example of the law on wire-tapping (*G 10-Gesetz*) the necessary prior constitutional amendment was seen as problematic regarding human dignity, but not because of the transfer of judicial functions to institutions established by Parliament.

[40] *Widerstandsrecht* is ambiguous as it means justified (civil) disobedience, but also action, against unconstitutional rule or against attempts to establish such a rule. It is similar to the Resistance against Nazi-rule (alas, mostly in the occupied countries).

[41] Amendment of 24 June 1968, *BGBl* I 709 ff; art 20 al. 4 GG: 'All Germans shall have the right to resist any person seeking to abolish this constitutional order, if no other remedy is available.'

[42] Where this takes the form of a direct complaint by a citizen, the BVerfG decided for example the cases of the phone-tapping act, mentioned above, the Maastricht Treaty and political asylum.

[43] This declaration is independent from the concrete form of constitutional amendment and also includes changes through arts 23 and 24 GG, ie transfer of sovereign powers to international or EU institutions.

including those concerning fundamental principles, provided that they respect the inherent logic of the system as a whole.[44]

But can the 'eternity clause' itself be changed or even be eliminated? As nothing is expressly foreseen in the provision itself, it is generally assumed that its logic makes self-protection an implicit necessary limit: if it were not of itself of superior rank, it would be impossible to guarantee the essential core of fundamental principles effectively and permanently.[45]

A different question is whether the application of the 'eternity clause' and the protection of fundamental principles might be hindered or overcome by the adoption of a new Constitution which replaced the Basic Law. This possibility is expressly foreseen by the Basic Law itself: Article 146 GG and the distinction between amendments of the Basic Law and its complete substitution can only be explained by its origins in the post-war period, in particular with the adoption of the Basic Law as a 'provisional Constitution', intended to be in force (only) until re-unification of Germany was achieved.[46]

Clearly going beyond a mere revision of the Basic Law, the adoption of a new Constitution in a 'revolutionary act' would be the expression of constituent power—by definition and nature not restricted by any formal or substantial limits. An analogous application of article 79 al.3 GG to these cases is already impossible due to its character as an exception. However, today it is generally recognised that even the constituent power would have to respect those limits that are inherent in the general objective of the State, that is, 'inviolable and inalienable human rights as the basis of every community, of peace and of justice in the world' (article 1 al.2 GG).[47]

[44] BVerfGE 30, 24 f.
[45] It would, in fact, be a complete contradiction, if the constitutional legislator is permanently bound by a provision which the same constitutional legislator could quite easily abolish. The BVerfG confirmed the prohibition of self-liberation from these limits by means of constitutional revision, BVerfGE 84, 90 (120).
[46] This is confirmed by the original formulations, ie before re-unification in 1990, of art 146 GG ('This Basic Law shall become invalid on the day when a constitution adopted in a free decision by the German people comes into force.') as well as of the preamble ('The entire German people is called upon to accomplish, by free self-determination, the unity and freedom of Germany.').
[47] Although this provision does not (and cannot) have binding character due to the very nature of constituent power, it reflects a solemn promise of the constituents to realise its creation within the guarantees and structures following art 1 al.2 GG as well as the anticipated conviction that any legitimate new Constitution will have to respect these minimum standards; see J Lücke, in M Sachs (ed), *Grundgesetz* cit. Art 79 sub 43 (n 74). This seems to be confirmed by developments after 1989 at international level and by the constitutional transition of former Communist countries, (in particular by the OSCE's Charter of Paris (1991; 'Democracy is our only form of government') as well as the concept of 'democratic security' developed by the same organisation and by the Copenhagen criteria for EU accession. In an integrated world, the idea of an absolute power seems anachronistic.

RECENT MAJOR CHANGES

Stability and constitutional continuity, inside Germany and towards its neigh-bours, were seen as necessary preconditions for achieving reunification. With the incorporation of the five Eastern *Länder* which had been (re-)constituted in the GDR,[48] on 3 October 1990, the German Basic Law became the definitive and legitimate Constitution of Germany as a whole.[49] It had been a deliberate—and much criticised—choice in the Treaty of Unification to include the new Eastern *Länder* by extending the Basic Law's sphere of application (after accession, according to Article 23 GG) rather than drafting a new Constitution as foreseen in Article 146 GG.[50] Only the well-known and generally appreciated Basic Law seemed to offer a guarantee of German reliability to its neighbours as well as a solid constitutional basis for the difficulties and time constraints of the reunifi-cation process. However, apart from these important advantages, Eastern Ger-mans saw virtually everything they had known turned upside down and transformed according to Western design, which created a psychological problem that has not yet been overcome. Moreover, old problems of the (Western) federal system, such as the negative effects of cooperative federalism, were far from being resolved and were even stressed during the process of re-unification. At the end of the 1990s high reform expectations not matched by any progress were creating the impression of total incapacity to reform, which seemed confirmed by the failure of a joint reform commission in December 2004. This situation was finally unblocked by the Grand Coalition which managed to adopt federalism reform in 2006 (and again in 2009). The impact of these two major events in terms of constitutional reform are analysed below.

Reunification of Germany

In terms of procedure, in application of article 23 GG (in the version prior to reunification) the German territories on their accession automatically became part of the Federal Republic, which had to extend the Basic Law to the territory of the acceding parts. Obviously, the act of accession had been preceded by intense

---

[48] The five Eastern *Länder* had been abolished in 1952 and replaced by 14 districts; their restoration, (as well as the introduction of a parliamentary system) backed by strong political support, was an autonomous decision of the new political elite of East Germany.

[49] Thus it had lost its provisional character: this change was particularly evident in the re-formulation of the preamble (the obligation to strive for unification was removed) as well as in Art 146 GG. On German reunification see P Zelikow and C Rice, *Germany Unified and Europe Transformed*, (Cambridge, MA, 1995); C Jeffery (ed), *Recasting German Federalism. The Legacies of Unification*, (London/New York, 1999).

[50] A new Constitution would have meant discontinuity and required a constituent assembly; this hypothesis had been judged legitimate by the BVerfG already on the occasion of its judgment on the Fundamental Agreement between Federal Republic and GDR of 31 January 1973, BVerfGE 36, 1 (28); *cf* K Hesse, *Die Verfassungsentwicklung seit 1945*, in E Benda, W Maihofer, H-J Vogel (eds), *Handbuch des Verfassungsrechts*, Vol 1 (Berlin/New York, 1995), 47.

negotiations, and three Treaties had been concluded by the two German States: the Treaty on Economic and Monetary Union, the Treaty on the first all-German Elections, and the Treaty on Unification.[51] While some constitutional amendments, adopted in the Act of Ratification of the Unification Treaty, entered into force immediately, others were only outlined in the Treaty (article 5) in order to be adopted by the re-unified Parliament.

(a)   Immediate constitutional change resulting from the Unification-Treaty

According to article 3 of the Unification-Treaty, the Basic Law enters into force in the new territories—together with the amendments listed in articles 4, 6 and 7:[52] Article 4 concerns amendments necessary for adjustments of the text to the new situation of a unified Germany, in particular by underlining the final and definitive character of the Basic Law and at the same time, in the Constitution, renouncing all territorial claims regarding German territories occupied after World War II.[53] Other amendments concern technical adjustments.[54]

As foreseen in the old version of article 23 al.2 GG, these changes were implemented following the procedure for the ratification of international treaties (article 59 al.2 GG) limiting Parliamentary participation. A complaint filed by some Members of Parliament against this procedure was rejected by the BVerfG due to the full discretion given to the constitutional institutions in carrying out their mandate and their constitutional obligation of striving for re-unification.[55]

The transitional period foreseen by amendment of article 143 GG was also problematic although it expressly required conformity with the principles of article 79 al.3 GG. However, article 143 al.3 GG included controversial 'dynamic' elements (by referring also to article 41 Unification Treaty and the rules of its implementation) which could be considered a violation of article 79 al.1 GG (respect of textual unity). In terms of substance, the problem of the 'open

[51]   The accession was foreseen in art 1 Treaty of Unification of 31 August 1990. Ratified on the same day, 20 September 1990, by *Bundestag* and *Volkskammer* (Parliament of DDR), it entered into force on 3 October 1990 (*BGBl* II, 889). At international level, the Unification Treaty had been previously approved by the four Occupation Powers with the so-called 'Four-plus-Two' Treaty, signed by the four Allied Powers and representatives of both German States on 12 September 1990, thus finally and definitively ending any limitation of Germany's sovereignty.
[52]   *Cf* M Herdegen, *Die Verfassungsänderungen im Einigungsvertrag* (Heidelberg, 1991), 6 ff, and M Kloepfer, *Verfassungsänderung statt Verfassungsreform* (Berlin, 1995).
[53]   The changes concern the preamble (list of—current—16 *Länder* and removal of the obligation to strive for re-unification) and a re-formulation of art 146 GG ('since the achievement of the unity and freedom of Germany').
[54]   Such as the inclusion of the new *Länder* in the distribution of votes in the *Bundesrat*, art 51 al.2 GG, the derogations foreseen by art 135a GG concerning obligations of the GDR and of art 143 GG related to a transitional period in which derogations from the Basic Law were declared possible.
[55]   BVerfGE 82, 316 (*Beitrittsbedingte Grundgesetzänderungen*). An International treaty can only be approved as such or rejected by the vote of Parliament: while the chosen procedure thus guaranteed the widest discretion of the government, Parliament was practically stripped off its powers to control the executive (as a vote against re-unification would not have been possible politically); also the participation of the *Länder* through the *Bundesrat* has been practically excluded.

property issues' belongs to the most complex and politically delicate questions of legal transition and economic transformation after re-unification. The general principle of 'supremacy of restitution instead of compensation' was expressly excluded for expropriations which occurred before the foundation of the GDR, in the period between 1945 and 1949. These had been carried out by the Soviet Union, and the political argument for the exclusion of any restitution for this period (article 143 al.3 GG) was that the Soviet Union had insisted on this point during the negotiations leading to re-unification. The BVerfG had to examine various individual complaints against this 'constitutional cover' and the conformity of the amendment with the criteria of article 79 GG.[56] The constitutional judges confirmed the constitutionality of the provision, underlining the special situation of re-unification which had justified the procedure of article 59 al.2 GG and therefore the limitation of Parliamentary participatory rights.[57] The amendment does not violate article 79 al.3 GG, as it cannot be considered a violation of the guaranteed sphere of private property by the constitutional legislator. The expropriations had occurred beyond the scope of application of the Basic Law and have to be considered as valid under international law. On one hand, this result did not interfere with the open question of compensation (by ordinary legislation), on the other, it justified the exception from the supremacy of the restitution principle made in fear of not being able to realise re-unification.[58]

(b) Subsequent constitutional amendments

Article 5 of the Treaty of Unification provided the legislative institutions of unified Germany with a mandate to 'resolve in terms of amendments of the Basic Law, within two years, all issues raised in the context of German unification', leaving the institutional and procedural aspects open. Despite numerous requests for reform (seen by many as a substitute for a new constitution) no major constitutional changes occurred. In 1991 a joint commission for constitutional reform was established by the *Bundestag* and *Bundesrat* (each represented by 32 members), as a compromise between a Convention and the ordinary procedure for constitutional reform. The original mandate focusing in particular on the

[56] Judgment of 23 April 1992, BVerfGE 84, 90 (119 ff, 125 ff, 131 ff).
[57] In conformity with the previous judgment, BVerfGE 82, 316.
[58] BVerfGE 84, 90 (122 ff). The judgment has been very much criticised; Mikhail Gorbachev later denied the conditional character of the issue for a successful end to the negotiations. However, the constitutional judges confirmed their decision in a second judgment, BVerfGE 94, 12 (35 ff). On 30 June 2005, the Grand Chamber of the European Court of Human Rights issued a judgment concerning the expropriation of the heirs of new farmers in the former GDR (*Jahn and others v Germany*) confirming the legitimacy of their exclusion from compensation. Ulrike Deutsch, 'Expropriation without Compensation—the European Court of Human Rights sanctions German Legislation expropriating the Heirs of 'New Farmers'', *German Law Journal* Vol 6, no 10 (2007), 1367–80.

relations between Federation and *Länder* was immediately extended with the result that despite long discussions the commission did not come up with any important proposal for changes.[59]

As a result, only minor constitutional amendments were adopted in 1994.[60] These are far from reaching the importance of those approved by the Grand Coalition in the period of 1968–69, which is astonishing considering the historical importance of re-unification, but can be explained by the desire for stability through continuity (of the Western system). Various proposals to reform the so-called financial constitution were not realised; the amendments concerned above all concurrent legislative powers (Article 72 GG). The *Länder* had used the minimal constitutional amendments of 1994 in an attempt to contain this centralising mechanism,[61] mainly by imposing different preconditions for federal legislation and by obliging the BVerfG to deal with disputes arising from the use of these powers.[62]

This amendment stands for a tendency to underline the importance of (more) competition in the future development of German federalism. It has been advocated, above all, in the field of financial relations, especially with regard to horizontal equalisation payments: in 1999, the BVerfG opened up to more competition in financial relations.[63] In the following years, limits to the exercise of concurrent and framework legislative powers by the Federation were confirmed in a series of judgments in favour of the *Länder*.[64]

---

[59] *Cf* M Kloepfer, *Verfassungsänderung statt Verfassungsreform. Zur Arbeit der Gemeinsamen Verfassungskommission*, (Berlin, 1995), 100. The final proposal of the Committee adopted as a single 'package' by a two-thirds majority in the procedure of constitutional amendment led to negotiations behind closed doors in the Mediation Committee (art 77 al.2 GG); this was in open contrast with the intention of broad, open public debate.

[60] 42nd Amendment, 27 October 1994 (*BGBl* I 3146), entered into force on 15 November 1994.

[61] The concurrent powers are exercised either by the *Länder* or by the Federation; the latter has to justify their exercise, in particular on the basis of the need for a regulation covering the whole federal territory. This was not too difficult in the past although the *Länder* participated in the legislative process via the *Bundesrat*. The BVerfG had declined its competence to judge, considering such controversies as political questions.

[62] The new formulation of art 72 al.2 GG reads: 'In this field, the Federation may legislate if and insofar as the establishment of *equivalent* living conditions in the federal territory or the preservation of legal and economic unity *necessitates*, in the interest of the state at large, a federal regulation' (italics added). Art 93 par 1 no 2a GG now expressly comprises the obligation of the BVerfG to monitor the exercise of the concurrent powers in case of claims stating the non-existence of the preconditions for federal legislation. See C Neumeyer, *Der Weg zur neuen Erforderlichkeitsklausel für die konkurrierende Gesetzgebung des Bundes (Art 72 Abs. 2 GG)*, (Berlin, 1999); C Calliess, *Die Justiziabilität des Art 72 Abs. 2 GG vor dem Hintergrund von kooperativem und kompetitivem Föderalismus*, (*DÖV*, 1997), 889 ff.

[63] As expression of the political responsibility of the respective *Länder* governments, BVerfGE 101, 158 (*Finanzausgleich* II); confirmed in 2006 by BVerfGE 116, 327 (*Berliner Haushalt*).

[64] According to the new formula in art 72 al.2 GG federal intervention has been declared unconstitutional in a number of cases: BVerfGE 106, 62 (*Altenpflege*), 24 October 2002; BVerfGE 110, 141 (*Kampfhunde*), 16 March 2004; BVerfGE, 111, 10 (*Ladenschluß*), 9 June 2004; BVerfGE 111, 226 (*Juniorprofessoren*) 27 July 2004; BVerfGE 112, 226 (*Studiengebühren*), 26 January 2005.

Reforming the Federal System

After the initial enthusiasm for unification had passed, the impression of political stagnation added to economic stagnation: different majorities in *Bundestag* and *Bundesrat* made the latter institution often seem like an instrument of the opposition used for the blocking of proposals the opposition could not stop in Parliament.[65] In the late 1990s the federal system (and the *Bundesrat* in particular) was accused of being responsible for the perceived crisis of the system and the consequent 'reform logjam' (*Reformstau*), that is, extremely slow decision-making processes with unclear political responsibilities and a general incapacity to reform.[66] However, the peculiar composition of the *Bundesrat* (its members representing the *Länder* governments) reflects the specific institutional logic of German federalism, with a preponderance of government bureaucracies and intergovernmental relationships. These features have their origins in the formative period of German federalism, especially in the Bismarck period, and are a direct result of the fact that in Germany the process of state-building was based not on the national, but on the territorial level.[67] The second important element of institutional continuity peculiar to German federalism is that the responsibility for policy implementation in most fields is and remains vested in the *Länder*, especially in the administrative sphere. The deeply rooted polycentric structure created an inherent and structural interdependence of federal and *Länder* bureaucracies and contributed to the intensive vertical and horizontal co-operation and co-ordination. The resulting '*Politikverflechtung*' (interlocking policies)[68] has proved to be nearly immune against all attempts of reform.

The reform of the federal system seemed the 'mother of all reforms' the country needed, but was not capable of adopting. However, the federal system is without alternative in Germany, as it is guaranteed by the 'eternity clause' (article 79 al.3 GG). As all reforms need the two-thirds approval of both *Bundestag* and *Bundesrat*, each agreement has to pass three possible lines of conflict: between Parliamentary majority and opposition, between the federal Government and the

---

[65] In Germany, the term 'Parliament' only refers to the *Bundestag*, the democratically elected chamber. However, the *Länder* (governments) participate in the legislative process at federal level through the *Bundesrat* without the latter being a chamber of Parliamentary nature.

[66] See in particular PM Huber, *Deutschand in der Föderalismusfalle* (Heidelberg, 2003), and U Volkmann, 'Bundesstaat in der Krise', in *DÖV* 1998, 613 ff.

[67] G Lehmbruch, 'German Federalism and the challenge of unification', in JJ Hesse and V Wright (eds), *Federalizing Europe? The Costs, Benefits, and Preconditions of Federal Political Systems*, (Oxford, 1996), 169–203, at 171 ff. The Bismarck-Empire was a federation of 25 states of which Prussia was the dominant entity. The states continued to possess considerable territorial autonomy and formed the federal council as the supreme sovereign institution corresponding to the principle that territorial interests are represented by the sovereign in negotiation with other sovereigns.

[68] See the fundamental study by FW Scharpf et al, in FW Scharpf, B Reissert, F Schnabel, *Politikverflechtung: Theorie und Empirie des kooperativen Föderalismus in der Bundesrepublik*, Vol 1, Kronberg im Taunus, 1976, and FW Scharpf, *No Exit from the Joint Decision Trap? Can German Federalism Reform Itself?* (MPIfG Working Paper 05/8, September 2005).

Länder, and between different groups of *Länder* with a veto minority in the *Bundesrat* (24 out of 69 votes). Due to the perceived crisis, pressure for reform and expectations mounted.

Finally, in October 2003, an ad hoc Joint Commission for the Modernisation of the Federal System was established to draw up a reform proposal that would be submitted to the formal amendment procedure.[69] Its composition reflected the balance between the democratic and federal principles; it also had a 'hybrid' character with inclusion of 'observers', so that it was closer to a convention rather than a normal committee.[70] The Commission worked for one year and presented comprehensive proposals for the simplification of the legislative procedure (reducing the veto powers of the *Bundesrat*), greater transparency and a clearer separation of the competencies as well as for a new system for financial relations between the different levels of government. Although they came very close to a compromise, on 17 December 2004 the two Presidents announced the end of negotiations without agreement. However, the Grand Coalition between Christian Democrats (CDU/CSU) and Social Democrats (SPD) that was formed after the federal elections held on 18 September 2005 opened a second 'window of opportunity' through the cooperation of the two major parties (thus also overcoming resistance in the Federal Council). Based on the work of the Joint Commission, the constitutional amendments were adopted in summer 2006 and entered into force on 1 September of the same year.[71] The first part of the reform, which changed more than 20 articles of the Basic Law, aimed at a disentanglement of legislative powers (for example, through the abolition of framework legislation) and at reducing the veto powers of the *Bundesrat* in the legislative process (the requirement of *Bundesrat* approval of federal legislation is estimated to have been reduced to 35–40 per cent, of measures from more than 60 per cent

---

[69] On 16 and 17 October 2003, respectively: *Kommission von Bundestag und Bundesrat zur Modernisierung der bundesstaatlichen Ordnung* (BT-Drucksache 15/1685 and BR-Drucksache 750/03). For the developments until the reform and the debate in the Commission see J Woelk, ,Farewell to the 'unitary federal State'? Transformations and tendencies of the German federal system', in S Ortino, M Žagar and V Mastny (eds), *The changing faces of federalism: Institutional reconfiguration in Europe from East to West*, (Manchester, 2004), 156–81; and the special issue 'German Federalism: Theory and Developments' of the *German Law Journal* Vol 6, no 10 (2005), in part A Gunlicks, *German Federalism and Recent Reform Efforts*, 1283–96 available at http://www.germanlawjournal.com.

[70] Besides 16 Members of the *Bundestag* and the 16 Minister-Presidents of the *Länder* (*Bundesrat*), four representatives of the federal Government participated without voting rights as well as six representatives from the *Länder* Parliaments and three from the associations of local government authorities; 12 independent experts had also been invited to participate.

[71] Act on constitutional amendment (BR 462/06) and accompanying Act on federal reform (BR 463/06) approved on 30 June 2006 by the *Bundestag*, and on 7 July 2006 by the *Bundesrat*. For a review and assessment in English, see A Gunlicks, 'German Federalism Reform: Part One', *German Law Journal* Vol 6, no 10 (2005), available at http://www.germanlawjournal.com/article.php?id=792; and C Moore, W Jacoby and A Gunlicks, 'German Federalism in Transition?' *German Politics*, Vol 17, no 4 (2008), 393–407. The latter is an introduction to a special issue of German Politics on the evaluation of the federalism reform (Issue 4, 2008: 'German Federalism in Transition'). *Cf* also S Burkhart, *Reforming Federalism in Germany: Incremental Changes instead of the Big Deal*, (Publius, 2009), 341–65.

before the reform). As a compensation for the loss of their participatory powers, the *Länder* received the right to derogate in some specific areas from federal regulation.[72]

A second part of the reform should have introduced a new system for financial relations between Federation and *Länder*, but only limited agreement was reached, mainly to give effect to a constitutional obligation to balance budgets on the part of both the Federation and the *Länder*.[73]

THE CHALLENGE OF EUROPEAN INTEGRATION

The Basic Law permits the transfer of sovereign powers to the EU (article 23 al.1) as well as to international organisations (article 24 al.1 GG) by means of a specific federal act authorising these organisations to adopt legislative, executive or judicial acts which are binding in the German legal system.[74] This has a necessary impact on the Basic Law, as German authorities, normally exclusively competent in their own fields, have to renounce some of their powers. As seen before, a German legislative act which materially changes the Constitution, the Act of Ratification (article 59 al.2 GG), is exempt from the requirement of a textual amendment (article 79 al.1 GG). Until the Maastricht Treaty, progress in the integration process was achieved by sub-constitutional legislation: the ratification act was an ordinary statute and the general clause of article 24 GG provided constitutional cover ('a window in sovereignty'). However, the incremental evolution of European integration in quantitative and qualitative terms has raised the problem of 'silent constitutional revision'.[75] This is illustrated, for instance, by the judgment of the European Court of Justice (ECJ) regarding equality between men and women in the workplace which opened the German Armed Forces to female volunteers despite an express constitutional

---

[72] This right to derogate (*Abweichungsrecht*) is seen as a symbolic turn away from a strictly symmetrical design in the exercise of the legislative powers allowing for experimentation and a certain degree of competition between the *Länder*; however, the areas are few and not very important (art 72 al. 2 GG).

[73] *Gesetz zur Änderung des Grundgesetzes* (arts 91c, 91d, 104b, 109, 109a, 115, 143d GG) Act of 29 July 2009; *BGBl* I S. 2248 (no 48), in force since 1 August 2009. According to the amendment, the Federation will have to limit its revenue from credits which, from 2016 onwards, may not exceed 0.35 % in relation to the nominal gross domestic product. For the *Länder* no revenue from credits will be admitted from 2020. In order to make the fulfilment of this obligation possible, Berlin, Bremen, Saarland, Sachsen-Anhalt and Schleswig-Holstein will receive €800 billion annual consolidation grants from 2011 until 2019, half of which will be financed by the Federation. For an overview in English, see LP Feld and T Baskaran, *Federalism Commission II: Recent Reforms of Federal-Länder Financial Relationships in Germany*, Forum of Federations (26 October 2009), available at http://www.forumfed.org/en/pubs/2009–10–26-feld.pdf.

[74] Germany follows a dualist approach in its relation with international law.

[75] 'Stille Verfassungsänderung;', H Bethge, *Deutsche Bundesstaatlichkeit und Europäische Union*, *Festschrift Friauf*, (Heidelberg, 1996), 55 ff.

prohibition.[76] However, even before this case, worries regarding the effects of such an evolution on the guarantees in the Basic Law gave rise to the famous jurisprudence of the BVerfG regarding the protection of fundamental rights, the first consideration of the constitutional limits of European integration.[77]

A Positivist Answer: The European Integration Clause

At the time of the ratification of the Maastricht Treaty a specific legal basis was created for EU integration: the new Article 23 GG, known as the 'European clause'.[78] In its first paragraph, this new article on European integration declares European unification to be an objective of the German state and explicitly permits the transfer of sovereignty rights to the EU; but it also contains a so-called 'structural guarantee' by listing the structural principles of the Basic Law which the EU has to comply with. Using a very similar formulation to the fundamental structural principles listed in articles 20, 28 and 79 par 3 GG (including the federal principle) and adding the principle of subsidiarity,[79] the drafters' intention is clear: Germany continues to participate actively in the European integration process, but—at least at this stage—cannot be merged into a fully-fledged European state. This purpose of the 'structural guarantee' clause, setting a constitutional limit, was confirmed by the much disputed BVerfG's decision on the ratification of the Maastricht Treaty.[80]

Much emphasis has been placed on the protection of the federal principle. Participation of the *Länder* is constitutionally guaranteed by paragraphs 2, 4, 5 and 6 of the 'European clause'—compensation for the loss of *Länder* competences in legislation as well as for the loss of competences of the Federal Council by strengthening their participation in the exercise of rights by the federal government at EU level.[81] The different degrees of participation, ranging from

---

[76] Case C-285/98 ECJ, 11 November 2000 ('*Tanja Kreil*'). As the constitutional prohibition— '[Women] may on no account render service involving the use of arms.' (art 12a al.4 last period)— could no longer be applied due to the supremacy of EC Law, it was cancelled by the constitutional amendment of 19 December 2000 (*BGBl* I, 1755).

[77] In part judgments '*Solange I*' of 1974 (BVerfGE 37, 271) and '*Solange II*' of 1986 (BVerfGE 73, 339).

[78] 38th amendment to the Basic Law, 21 December 1992 (*BGBl*, I, 2086). It took the place of the article on the accession of German territories considered obsolete after re-unification.

[79] The clause, addressed to the organs of the German State which participate and contribute to the EU, demands that the EU should fulfil 'democratic, social and federal requirements whilst operating under the rule of law, is governed by the principle of subsidiarity and guarantees the protection of human rights to a standard that is, in essence, equivalent to the standard of the Basic Law'.

[80] BVerfGE 55, 155 ff. In this decision the BVerfG explicitly reserved for itself the competence to decide whether Community acts were *ultra vires* or within the domain of Community competence.

[81] See for a comparative analysis J Woelk, 'A Place at the Window: Regional Ministers in the Council', in R Toniatti, F Palermo, M Dani (eds), *An Ever More Complex Union. The Regional Variable as the Missing Link in the EU Constitution?* (Baden-Baden, 2004) 117–41.

information and consultation to rights of direct representation at EU level, correspond to the domestic distribution of competences.[82]

In order to safeguard the participation of the *Länder* further, a new distinction is drawn between a simple transfer of sovereign rights and Treaty revisions: while in the former case an ordinary legislative act is sufficient, in the latter, constitutional amendments have to respect the procedural and substantive limits of amendment (article 79 al. 2 and 3GG).[83] In consequence, ratification of the Lisbon Treaty required a constitutional amendment due to the new subsidiarity complaint which national Parliaments (and thus the *Bundestag* and *Bundesrat*) can file in the ECJ.[84]

Looking for Balances: the Federal Constitutional Court's Case Law

European integration and globalisation processes pose many challenges to Germany's constitutional system. Besides the increasingly frequent participation of Germany's Armed Forces in a number of foreign missions,[85] recent legislation regarding citizenship and immigration reflects the need for measures of integration of the approximately 10 per cent of foreign residents in Germany.[86] The debate on the integration of foreign residents began in the late 1980s with

---

[82] The article does not introduce an entirely new set of procedures, but rather 'constitutionalises' the already established, so-called '*Bundesrat* procedure', putting institutional participation through the *Bundesrat* at the centre; cf D König, *Die Übertragung von Hoheitsrechten im Rahmen des europäischen Integrationsprozesses*, (Berlin, 2000). The possibility of direct representation of the Federal Republic in the Council of Ministers by a *Länder* Minister has been reduced by the federalism reform in 2006 to Council meetings regarding the subject matters of instruction, culture and media (typically directly concerning exclusive *Länder* competencies).

[83] A textual amendment is not necessary as art 79 al.1 GG is not included by art 23 al.1 GG.

[84] New paragraph 1a in art 23 GG, inserted by 53th amendment on 8 October 2009 (*BGBl* I (1926)).

[85] Since controversial re-armament in 1955, the Armed Forces have always been a delicate issue in post-war and divided Germany. Until 1989, any mandate of (Western) Germany's Armed Forces was limited to the defence of German territory. Beginning with the Airborne Warning and Control System (AWACS) missions over the Adriatic Sea including German soldiers during the Balkan wars and the participation in the UN Peace keeping operations in Somalia in 1994, this taboo has been broken, but was not undisputed. In its jurisprudence, the BVerfG has established the principle of necessary parliamentary approval to such missions (*Parlamentsheer unter exekutivem Befehl*); BVerfGE 68, 1; 77, 170; 89, 38; 90, 286, and in particular BVerfGE 121, 135 (*Luftraumüberwachung Türkei*, 07 May 2008).

[86] Already during the economic boom in the 1960s Germany badly needed skilled foreign workers: the '*Gastarbeiter*', guest-workers, came, but most often did not leave after their job had been done. A number of them did not even leave Germany for retirement and most brought their families there. Consequently, there are a lot of younger people who have grown up and live in Germany, but still do not possess German citizenship. On 1 January 2000, the new law on citizenship entered into force, providing for dual citizenship for children of foreign residents who were born in Germany according to the *ius soli* principle. The period of residence in Germany which has to pass, before foreign adults can apply for German citizenship, has been reduced. These changes provoked a controversial discussion (after all, the previous law on citizenship dated from 1913!) on the— difficult—integration of foreign workers, who are often Muslims. The citizenship act was integrated by a federal law on immigration which entered into force on 1 January 2005.

discussion of the right of foreigners to vote in elections at municipal level as a means of fostering their integration. The introduction of such a right in two *Länder* was held incompatible with the Basic Law by the BVerfG;[87] it was the first judgment in which express reference was made to the limits of constitutional amendments in article 79 al.3 GG (although with regard to the *Länder* Constitutions). However, in order to accommodate the new obligation stemming from primary Community Law to grant such a right to all EU citizens, the Basic Law was changed.[88]

As the ratification of the Maastricht Treaty occurred without a referendum, the BVerfG, on individual constitutional complaints by some citizens, had to uphold the Basic Law. In its 'Maastricht-judgment' it substantially confirmed the progress of European integration as reached in the Maastricht Treaty and also the constitutional amendment adopted 10 months before.[89] The problems identified in the judgment concern the democratic legitimacy of the European Parliament, in particular the lack of equality of votes (due to the demographic differences for single seats and to the mediation of the elections by the Member States) and its—insufficient—legislative competencies and powers of control. The constitutional judges require a perfectly parallel development of the processes of democratisation and integration. Their main preoccupation is focused on Member States maintaining control of the integration process: constitutional amendments permitting further integration require foreseeable and clear steps in the process which—despite its gradual increase—has not yet turned into the constituent power of a European State.[90] This makes German participation (still) possible.

Despite an apparently more integration-friendly position in 2000,[91] the question of constitutional 'counterlimits' to European integration is still topical. In a judgment on the EU Arrest Warrant, in 2005 the BVerfG declared the German Act of its implementation unconstitutional, mainly due to insufficient participatory rights of Parliament;[92] for similar reasons, it declared the Act accompanying

---

[87] BVerfGE 83, 37 ff (*Schleswig-Holstein*) and 60 ff (*Hamburg*), with an exception (after a relevant constitutional change) for EC nationals (obiter dictum at 59), as a right to vote for EU citizens in municipal elections to be introduced in the Maastricht Treaty had already been discussed.

[88] Article 19 par 1 Treaty Establishing a Constitution for Europe (now: art 22 Treaty of the Functioning of the European Union) and art 28 par. 1 s. 2 GG; the 38th constitutional amendment was adopted before the Maastricht Treaty was actually ratified (21 December 1992).

[89] BVerfGE 89, 155 (172, 180 ff) *Maastricht* (1992), 12 October 1993.

[90] The internationalist and dualistic conception expressed by the BVerfG (considering the EU as a mere 'association of States', '*Staatenverbund*', halfway between a Confederacy, '*Staatenbund*', and a federal State, '*Bundesstaat*', and insisting on a 'cooperation relationship with the ECJ' based on parity) has been criticised much by academia, although the latter agrees with the thesis of an absolute limit of State sovereignty ex art 79 al.3 GG. A European federal State is seen as something qualitatively different from the Federal Republic of Germany; a similar change of constitutional identity can only be realised by the exercise of constituent powers and art 146 GG; *cf* H Dreier, *Grundgesetz-Kommentar* cit. Art 79 (sub 46).

[91] Ord '*Banana Market*', 7 June 2000, BVerfGE 102, 147 (confirming the jurisdiction in 'Solange II').

[92] BVerfGE 113, 273 (*Europäischer Haftbefehl*), 19 July 2005.

the ratification of the Lisbon Treaty unconstitutional.[93] Democratic participation and legitimacy, understood as realised and guaranteed (only) through the participatory rights of the national Parliaments (*Bundestag*) in the integration process, was the main rationale in both judgments: it was disappointing in both cases that the *Bundestag* had not reserved sufficient participatory rights for itself in the first place. However, the approach is ambiguous as on the one hand the openness of the German legal system to integration is underlined, but, on the other, German sovereignty has to be defended.[94] The main instrument for this defence is the concept of 'substantive equivalence' of fundamental rights, the rule of law and democratic participation. Although this concept has, so far, been interpreted by the BVerfG as in conformity with progress in EU integration, it raises the question of who has the last say.[95] Ambiguity is certainly a way of avoiding frontal clashes with the ECJ,[96] but it seems clear that the BVerfG, although accepting '*de facto*-monism' in the relationship between German and EU legal systems, stands firm in considering the state as the ultimate defence of the rights of citizens. Thus, the question of constitutional limits to integration is not yet definitively resolved.[97]

CONCLUSIONS

The rigid revision procedure and the guarantee of an essential core of fundamental constitutional values are the expression of a balancing operation between three principles characterising the Basic Law: the democratic and the federal

[93] BVerfGE 123, 267 (*Lissabon*), 30 June 2009.

[94] With regard to the fundamental principle of the rule of law and to guarantees for the (German) citizen in the judgment on the Arrest Warrant, and with regard to the guarantee of democratic participation of (German) citizens in the judgments on ratification of the Maastricht and Lisbon Treaties.

[95] In the judgment on ratification of the Lisbon-Treaty, the BVerfG claims a 'reserve competence' vis-à-vis the ECJ, envisaging a specific instrument for the control of *ultra vires* acts by EU institutions and conformity with (German) constitutional identity, a concept developed in the EU Arrest Warrant-judgment, BVerfGE 123, 267 (sub 240 and 241).

[96] Opening up to asymmetrical solutions, the ECJ seems to take the increasing diversity between member states into account. In the *Omega* judgment, human dignity as the supreme value in the German constitutional system justified a prohibition expressed by German authorities as a legitimate exception from the fundamental freedoms of the Treaties on the grounds of public order and security; Case C-36/02 (14 December 2004).

[97] In a recent Order (6 July 2010, 2 BvR 2661/06), the BVerfG took one step back, deciding that the *Mangold* judgment of the European Court of Justice (Case C-144/04 *Mangold* [2005] ECR I-9981, 22 November 2005) does not transgress Community competence in a constitutionally objectionable manner. The constitutional judges stated that '*ultra vires* review of acts of the European bodies and institutions by the Federal Constitutional Court may only be exercised in a manner which is open towards European law. It can hence only be considered if a breach of competence on the part of European bodies and institutions is sufficiently qualified. This is contingent on the acts of the authority of the European Union being manifestly in breach of competences and the impugned act leading to a structurally significant shift to the detriment of the Member States in the structure of competences between Member States and the European Union.'

principles, represented by the necessary cooperation between *Bundestag* and *Bundesrat*, and the rule of law principle in its function as a substantive limit for the guarantee of values (through the obligations as to changes in the text and the eternity clause).

Germany's way of guaranteeing, at the same time, constitutional stability and evolution could be summarised in the formula 'positive limits and limited positivism'. It underlines the importance of the express formal and substantive limits to constitutional revision in the Basic Law as guidelines when constitutional revision is under consideration.[98] But by contrast with the positivism of the past—this is the lesson from Weimar—these limits are not neutral: The positivist approach is now limited by immutable values, in particular respect for human dignity and fundamental rights, which are considered to be the foundations or *raisons d'être* of any state organisation. The—again—positive identification of an essential core of the Constitution by the same Constitution is the paradoxical, but successful attempt to rationalise and protect the very foundation of the state. The essential core is thus a substantial counterweight to the possibility of relatively easy change. However, this rationalisation comes close to obsession when the individual right to resistance against attempts to overturn the constitutional order (article 20 al.4 GG) or the transition to a new constituent power (article 146 GG) are expressly regulated: in practice, the Basic Law 'permits' a revolution in order to protect itself. This final call to the people in defence of the essential core of fundamental principles is probably the ultimate expression of the reconciliation between natural law and positive law: the Constitution—as a legal norm—legally regulates even the most extreme act, disobedience in order to obey and respect the fundamental values. This express identification of an essential core was certainly useful during the post-war transition for anchoring these values in the population, but it has also allowed for continuous change that is necessary for the adaptation of the constitutional system. More problematic has been the achievement of major reforms: in these cases, the ordinary amendment procedure has either been applied substantively, excluding Parliament (re-unification), or integrated by prior consultation in a Joint Commission (reform of the federal system). Remarkably, even in these cases, the substantive limits of the essential core have been applied and there are only a few judgments in which the BVerfG has actually examined the legitimacy of acts of constitutional amendments; it has never found a violation of article 79 al.3 GG.[99]

---

[98] In fact, the desire for and the necessity of a normative Constitution emerge clearly from many provisions of the Basic law; the high moral aspirations after the horror of Nazism should be reconciled and combined with a traditional positivist culture of obedience: after all, historically in Germany the state was created and developed before the fundamental rights of its citizens were guaranteed.

[99] However, the combination of nearly absolute guarantees for the protected principles and their open contents makes an ample margin of interpretation by the BVerfG as the ultimate arbiter necessary.

The stability of the system is due to the general acceptance of the fundamental constitutional principles and is best illustrated by Dolf Sternberger's felicitous expression 'constitutional patriotism'.[100] However, the process of European integration challenges the principles of the essential core by opening a 'window in sovereignty',[101] which contrasts with the inward-looking character of a closed system committed to defend its own values for the sake of stability.

---

[100] As opposed to national patriotism or, worse, nationalism; D Sternberger, *Verfassungspatriotismus* (Insel, Frankfurt aM 1990).

[101] 'Window in sovereignty' expresses the open (ie non absolute) character of statehood as a member state in the EU.

8

India

MAHENDRA PAL SINGH

ABOUT THE CONSTITUTION

THE CONSTITUTION OF India adopted on 26 November 1949 and brought into force on 26 January 1950, is the longest surviving constitution in Asia next only to the Constitution of Japan. One of the reasons for its survival has been its adaptability to the changing times and situations. Such changes are much more frequent and often unexpected in developing and unstable societies than in the developed and stable societies like those of Japan or of the West. The size of the country, its phenomenal diversity and the enormity of problems associated with its political and social history, poverty, illiteracy, lack of adequate experience and expertise in constitutional governance, the disturbed region and several other factors contributed to doubts whether India could have and work with a modern constitution. Miraculously, however, not only could India produce one of the most progressive constitutions after its liberation from British rule, but the Constitution has also survived and worked reasonably well since its inception despite several ups and downs, including the consequences of partition, infiltration from and wars with neighbours, economic crises, and many other problems. The Constitution has, of course, gone through small and major amendments, and at an average rate of more than one a year, but it has retained its basic structure.[1]

The Constitution of India is famous for being the longest among the written constitutions worldwide with a reasonably long Preamble, 395 Articles augmented by more additions than deletions through amendments and 12 Schedules, some of them very long. Its length is justified for a number of reasons, foremost among them being its federal structure which apart from dealing with the relations between the general (Central or Union) as well as the regional (state) governments also includes the constitution for the latter with all the details. Except the State of Jammu and Kashmir, no other state has its own separate constitution. Later amendments have also included the third tier of

---

[1] The Constitution has been amended 95 times up to January 2010.

169

government at the village and town levels with substantial details.[2] It incorporates detailed provisions for the administration of Scheduled Tribes and Tribal
Areas; for the Scheduled Castes, socially and educationally backward classes of
people and minorities;[3] several temporary and transitional provisions for the
changeover from one system to another; a number of institutions such as the
election commission, public service commissions and services under the Union
and the States, which in other constitutions are normally left to ordinary
legislation; Fundamental Rights (FRs) along with their limitations; Directive
Principles of State Policy (DPs); and later the inclusion of Fundamental Duties
(FDs)and so on. Early commentators on the Constitution had predicted that its
length would lead to legalism and rigidity.[4] Fortunately, this did not happen and
as expected by the Constitution-makers it has proved to be quite flexible and
received some favourable comments from some foreign scholars. Wheare saw in
it wise variety[5] while Austin found the amending process as 'one of the most ably
conceived aspects of the Constitution'.[6] The number of times and the ease with
which the Constitution has been amended amply prove this point.

In the family of constitutions the Constitution of India is said to belong to the
Euro-American tradition.[7] But within that tradition, in view of the inheritance of
the common law tradition during the British period for over 150 years it is closer
to the constitutions in the common law countries such as, Australia, Canada and
the USA rather than the constitutions of the civil law countries such as France.
Although the Constitution does not have a supremacy clause, in line with the
common law countries it is considered to be the highest law of the land
enforceable by the courts. The Constitution can be changed only in accordance
with the procedure for its amendment provided in it and not otherwise. Any law
inconsistent with the Constitution is no law and can be so declared by the courts.
The constitutionality of laws can be questioned in any court but a matter
involving a substantial question of law involving the interpretation of the
Constitution must be decided initially by the High Courts and finally by the
Supreme Court.[8] Although the Constitution provides for different sets of legislative and executive machinery for the Centre and the States, it provides common
courts for both. The same courts decide matters under the Central as well as State
laws. Subject to territorial limitation the High Courts and without such a
limitation the Supreme Court, can decide all matters concerning the

[2] See, the Constitution 73rd and 7th Amendments 1992 inserting Arts 243 to 243-ZG and
Schedules 11 and 12.
[3] See, among others, Parts X and XVI and 5th and 6th Schedules.
[4] See, I Jennings, *Some Characteristics of the Indian Constitution*, (Madras: Oxford University
Press, 1953), 10; Max Beloff, *The American Federal Government*, (London: Oxford University Press,
1959), 16.
[5] KC Wheare, *Modern Constitutions*, (London: Oxford University Press, 1958 reprint), 143.
[6] G Austin, *The Indian Constitution: Cornerstone of a Nation*, (New Delhi: Oxford University
Press, 1966, 15th impression 2010), 255.
[7] Ibid, 32ff.
[8] Arts 228 and 132.

Constitution. Infringement of FRs can be challenged directly in the High Courts as well as in the Supreme Court. The right to approach the Supreme Court directly for the enforcement of FRs is one of the FRs.[9] The Supreme Court has exclusive original jurisdiction to decide legal dispute between the Centre and the States as well as between different states. Like all other common law countries, and unlike the civil law countries, the same courts decide constitutional as well as other disputes. There is no separate constitutional court deciding exclusively constitutional disputes as in the civil law countries. This is also a reflection of recognition of the unity of law in the common law system while the civil law system maintains the duality of the public and private law.

The Constitution provides for a parliamentary form of government both at the Centre as well as in the States with an indirectly elected nominal Head of State, the President of India at the Centre and Governors in the States appointed by the President of India. The real executive at the Centre is the Council of Ministers with the Prime Minister at its head and in the States the Council of Ministers headed by the Chief Minister of the State. The Council of Ministers in the Centre as well as in the States is collectively responsible to the lower house of the respective legislatures. While the Central Parliament is bicameral, many States have only unicameral legislatures directly elected by the people. Elections to the lower houses of the legislatures at both levels are held on the basis of adult franchise without any exclusion on the grounds of religion, race, caste or sex.[10] The election result is decided on the basis of first past the post.

As regards the organisation and the subject matter of the Constitution, besides the Preamble it comprises 22 parts divided into chapters on: the Union and its territory, citizenship, FRs, DPs, FDs, the structure of the Central government including the Supreme Court, the structure of the State governments including the High Courts and subordinate courts, governance of the Union Territories, structure, powers and functions of the panchayats (local government at the village level) and the municipalities, administration of tribal areas, legislative, administrative and financial relations between the Centre and the States, services under the Union and the States, administrative tribunals, elections and election commission, special provisions for certain classes including some minorities, languages of the Union and the States, emergencies including national, State and financial emergencies, amendment of the Constitution, temporary, transitional, special and miscellaneous provisions and the short title and commencement of the Constitution. It also includes 12 schedules dealing respectively with the names and territories of the States and the Union Territories, salaries and allowances of certain high dignitaries such as the President and the Vice-President of India, Governors of the States, presiding officers of the Union and State legislatures, judges of the Supreme Court and the High Courts, and the

[9] Art 32.
[10] Art 325.

comptroller and auditor general of India, forms of oath or affirmation for different constitutional dignitaries, allocation of seats in the upper house of parliament, administration of tribal and scheduled areas, administration of tribal areas in certain north-eastern States, legislative items in the Union, State and concurrent jurisdictions, languages recognised in the Constitution, list of laws that cannot be challenged on the ground of violation of fundamental rights, disqualification of legislators on ground of defection, subject matters falling within the domain of the panchayats and the municipalities respectively.

Being living and organic instruments, constitutions change and must change to keep pace with changes in society. These changes, however, occur in a systematic way, and if there is no system they are molded into a system. Among the various forms in which these changes take place in India are:

1. formal amendments,
2. legislation,
3. judicial interpretation,
4. conventions, and
5. international law.

Let me elaborate these in that order in the context of the Constitution of India.

FORMAL AMENDMENT

Constitutions are conceived and made to survive if not forever at least for the indefinite future. To ensure such a survival in a changing world they provide for their change. The Constitution of India provides for its change in the following three ways:

1. Some provisions of the Constitution can be changed by an ordinary law of Parliament without any additional requirements for or conditions of a special majority in the Parliament or participation of the States. These provisions expressly lay down that they are of this kind until Parliament provides otherwise or they are subject to a law made by parliament; examples are Articles 124 and 125 relating respectively to the number of judges in the Supreme Court and their emoluments. The Constitution has quite a few such provisions.
2. Some provisions of the Constitution may be changed by an ordinary law of Parliament with additional requirements or formalities such as a require- ment of presidential recommendation, or consultation of or request from the States; examples are Article 3 relating to alteration in the States and Article 169 relating to the creation or abolition of the upper house in the legislature of a State.
3. There is a special procedure for amendment in Article 368, which is also of two kinds: (a) amendments requiring only a special majority approval in

Parliament; and (b) amendments which as well as a special majority in Parliament also require ratification from at least half of the States.

Article 368 as amended in 1971 by the 24th Amendment reads as follows:

Power of Parliament to amend the Constitution and procedure therefore:— (1) Notwithstanding anything in this Constitution, Parliament may in exercise of its constituent power amend by way of addition, variation or repeal any provision of this Constitution in accordance with the procedure laid down in this article.

(2) An amendment of this Constitution may be initiated only by the introduction of a Bill for the purpose in either House of Parliament, and when the Bill is passed in each House by a majority of the total membership of that House and by a majority of not less than two-thirds of the members of that House present and voting, it shall be presented to the President who shall give his assent to the Bill and thereupon the Constitution shall stand amended in accordance with the terms of the Bill:

Provided that if such amendment seeks to make any change in—

(a)   Article 54, Article 55, Article 73, Article 162 or Article 241, or
(b)   Chapter IV of Part V, Chapter V of Part VI, or Chapter I of Part XI, or
(c)   any of the Lists in the Seventh Schedule, or
(d)   the representation of States in Parliament, or
(e)   the provisions of this article,

the amendment shall also require to be ratified by the legislature of not less than one-half of the States by resolutions to that effect passed by those Legislatures before the Bill making provision for such amendment is presented to the President for assent.

(3) Nothing in Article 13 shall apply to any amendment made under this article.

The following two clauses added by the Constitution 42nd Amendment 1976 to Article 368 as above were invalidated by the Supreme Court in *Minerva Mills Ltd v Union of India*:[11]

(4) No amendment of this Constitution (including the provisions of Part III) made or purporting to have been made under this article whether before or after the commencement of Section 55 of the Constitution (Forty-second Amendment) Act, 1976 shall be called in question in any court on any ground.

(5) For the removal of doubts, it is hereby declared that there shall be no limitation whatever on the constituent power of Parliament to amend by way of addition, variation, or repeal, the provisions of this Constitution under this article.

Before its amendment Article 368 was substantially what is now clause (2) above with the marginal note: 'Procedure for amendment of the Constitution'. The story of the changes in Article 368 is an interesting lesson on how constitutions change.

---

[11]   *Minerva Mills Ltd v Union of India* (1980) 3 SCC 625.

In making the above provisions the Constitution-makers were conscious that in view of the length of the Constitution and the difficulties within which it was to work they should reduce rigidity and legalism and provide for a flexible amendment procedure. Accordingly they made these provisions without facing much controversy or debate.[12] While distinguishing amendments from ordinary legislation they provided for a special majority in the two Houses of Parliament but even in respect of federal arrangements they did not provide for any special majority of the States for the approval of any amendments that affected those arrangements. Instead of one-third or three-quarters of the States approving such amendments they settled at 50 per cent of the States. Dr Ambedkar, the main architect of the Constitution, informed the Constituent Assembly that the Constitution provided for a flexible federation.[13] Experience with the amending process proves him right as some of the major amendments to the Constitution were piloted by Dr Ambedkar himself as law minister, some others were carried out during his lifetime and many more afterwards. To date the Constitution has been amended as many as 95 times.[14]

Fundamental Rights versus Directive Principles

The first amendment to the Constitution having far-reaching consequences for its nature and character came within one year of its commencement even before the Parliament came into existence and the Constituent Assembly discharged its functions as an interim measure.[15] There were several reasons for the amendment. First, some of the agrarian reform legislation enacted since Independence for which the national independence leaders had long been fighting for, were found to be inconsistent with the FRs and were declared invalid by some of the courts.[16] Secondly, the constitutional goal of social revolution expressed in the DPs could not be realised because the courts found conflict between State action in pursuance of DPs and FRs and held that in the case of such conflict the former had to give way to the latter.[17] Some of the nationalisation laws were also found inconsistent with the FRs, and the right to freedom of speech and expression could not be subjected to restrictions on the ground of incitement to commit offences.[18] All of these unexpected consequences of the Constitution led to major amendments. The political leaders in power, especially the All India Congress Party led by Nehru, saw in such an interpretation of the Constitution

---

[12] See, Austin above note 6, 255ff.
[13] Ibid, at 255 see the beginning of this chapter.
[14] As at 18 December 2010. The 95th Amendment came into effect on 25 January 2010.
[15] A detailed and authentic account of all the amendments until 1985 is given in G Austin, *Working a Democratic Constitution. The Indian Experience* (New Delhi: Oxford University Press, 1999).
[16] See, eg, *Kameshwar Singh v State*, AIR 1951 Patna 91.
[17] State of *Madras v Champakam Dorairajan*, AIR 1951 SC 226.
[18] See *Chiranjit Lal v Union of India*, AIR 1951 SC 41 and *State of Bihar v Shaialabala Devi*, AIR 1952 SC 329.

defeat of all that they had fought for during the British regime. Therefore, they embarked upon amendments of the Constitution ignoring, among others, the advice of the President of India to wait until the first elections and constitution of Parliament under the Constitution. Consequently two new articles, Article 31A and Article 31B were introduced in the chapter on FRs with retrospective effect, excluding respectively the laws for the acquisition of estates relating to agrarian reforms or taking over of management of any property or the rights of business managers from the operation of FRs, and giving immunity from challenge to the laws listed in a schedule—Ninth Schedule—introduced by the amendment. Simultaneously the right to freedom of speech in Article 19(1)(a) was subjected to laws imposing reasonable restrictions on grounds of incitement to an offence, and the right to carry on any trade, profession or business was subjected to state monopoly. Finally, the equality provisions that prohibited discrimination on the basis of religion, race, caste, sex etc in general and in admission to educational institutions in particular, were subjected to the measures taken in pursuance of DPs for the promotion of the educational and economic interests of weaker sections of the society, especially of the Scheduled Castes and Scheduled Tribes.[19] In this way all provisions of FRs that appeared to be standing in the way of social revolution or change were modified or removed.

These amendments, especially the introduction of Articles 31A and 31B, were challenged in the Supreme Court in *Shanakari Prasad Singh Deo v Union of India*[20] on the ground of violation of Article 13(2) which prohibits the making of any law abridging fundamental rights. The Supreme Court, however, unanimously dismissed the petition drawing a distinction between an ordinary law and an amendment of the Constitution in so far as the former is made in the exercise of legislative power under the Constitution while the latter is made in the exercise of the constituent power.

In spite of the drastic curtailment of property rights and its approval by the Court, these rights continued to irritate governments by getting in the way of agrarian reforms and acquisition of property either on the issue of compensation or otherwise. Similarly, challenge to nationalisation laws was perceived in the provisions of Part XII relating to freedom of trade and commerce.[21] Accordingly, once again the 4th Amendment Act, 1955 amended Articles 31 and 31A, introduced a few more Acts in the Ninth Schedule, and replaced Article 305 by a new provision protecting nationalisation laws from the freedom of trade and commerce. In between the 2nd and 3rd amendments in 1952 and 1954, were inconsequential measures making minor adjustments. The Constitution 5th Amendment Act, 1955 authorised the President to prescribe a time limit under

---

[19]   See Art 15 (4).
[20]   AIR 1951 SC 458.
[21]   See, eg, *State of W.B. v Subodh Gopal Bose*, AIR 1954 SC 92; State of *WB v Bela Banerjee*, AIR 1954 SC 170; *Saghir Ahmad v State of UP*, AIR 1954 SC 728. Part XIII of the Constitution comprising Arts 301–307 provides for freedom of trade and commerce and its regulation within India.

Article 3 within which an affected State may express its views on the decision of Parliament under that Article so as to remove the possibility of unreasonable delay in the matter on the part of that State. The Constitution 6th Amendment Act, 1956 removed some difficulties that arose in respect of tax on inter-state sales, and the Constitution 7th Amendment Act, 1956 made a major reorganisation of the States on linguistic lines which brought many consequential changes in the Constitution. All subsequent amendments up to the Constitution 15th Amendment Act 1963 related either to the adjustment of territories, or some changes in some offices which did not lead to any controversy. The Constitution 16th Amendment Act, 1963 strengthened the national unity strand of the Constitution by introducing the words 'sovereignty and integrity of India' in Article 19(2) and in the oath of candidates for election to Parliament and State legislatures.

The Constitution 17th Amendment Act 1964, which once again amended the property right exceptions in Article 31A and introduced several new Acts in the Ninth Schedule, was challenged in the Supreme Court in *Sajjan Singh v State of Rajasthan*.[22] This time besides the issues raised in *Shankari Prasad* the issue of curtailing the power of the High Courts under Article 226 in those matters in which it could be exercised before the amendment was also raised, because any change in Article 226 required reference of a proposed amendment to the States under the proviso to Article 368. Once again, following *Shanakari Prasad*, the Court rejected the challenge to the amendment of FRs and did not find much force in the argument on Article 226 because the amendment did not touch that Article. Any effect on the jurisdiction of the High Courts was seen as merely consequential on the non-existence of an FR for which the High Courts could be approached during the subsistence of that right. But unlike *Shankari Prasad* in *Sajjan Singh* the Court was divided 3 to 2. While three of the judges fully endorsed *Shankari Prasad*, two of them in their separate but concurring opinions expressed doubts whether FRs created no limitation on the power of amendment and could be amended as easily as had been the case until then.

Perhaps this split in the Court and change in its members as well as in the political scene[23] led to challenge once again in *LC Golak Nath v State of Punjab*[24] to the validity of the 1st, 4th and 17th Amendments on additional grounds that an amendment of the Constitution did not stand on the same footing as the original Constitution insofar as the Constitution was made in the exercise of constituent power while the power of amendment is a kind of legislative power. Accordingly an amendment is subject to the test of whether it is consistent with

[22] *Sajjan Singh v State of Rajasthan* AIR 1965 SC 845.
[23] Until the death of the first Prime Minister of India, Jawaharlal Nehru, in mid 1964 the All India Congress Party ruled at the Union as well as in the States. After his death, quickly followed by the death of his successor Lal Bahadur Shastri in January 1966, dissensions had emerged within the Party which led to split in the Party in several States in 1967 and later at the national level in 1969.
[24] *LC Golak Nath v State of Punjab* AIR 1967 SC 1643.

the Constitution, especially with the FRs to which the Constitution assigns a special place by expressly prohibiting the making of any law that abridges those rights and by declaring it void if made in contravention of this prohibition. Relying upon this argument a Court split by 6 to 5 held that an amendment was a law subject to the Constitution and as Article 13(2) expressly prohibited abridgement of FRs by any law and Article 13(3), which defined 'law', did not exclude an amendment from the definition of law, the challenged amendments were invalid to the extent they abridged the FRs. The Court, however, gave a prospective operation to its ruling leaving the existing amendments undisturbed but prohibiting any future amendments that abridged the FRs.

In view of some preceding and subsequent events, primarily the Chief Justice's becoming an opposition candidate for the election of the President of India after resigning from his office, but also the growing tussle between the supporters of socialism and liberalism among the political leaders and parties, the judgment acquired political dimensions.[25] By this time cracks had started emerging in the Indian National Congress that ruled throughout the country, at the Centre as well as in the States. Though the then Prime Minister Indira Gandhi retained her hold on the party at the Centre, splits had taken place in the party in the States. *Golak Nath* was the product of such a climate. Later in 1969 a vertical division took place in the party at the national level, making the position of the Prime Minister slightly precarious. After that, two of her major decisions, the nationalisation of major banks[26] and the abolition of Privy Purses (salaries paid to them),[27] were invalidated by the Supreme Court creating an apparent conflict between the Court and the then government. The Prime Minister sought a premature dissolution of the lower house of Parliament and won a massive mandate strengthening her hand for any constitutional changes. With this support from the people and representation in Parliament she moved to remove the constitutional hurdles in the path of her policy of poverty removal. Accordingly, several important amendments to the Constitution were proposed.[28] The first of them—the Constitution 24th Amendment Act, 1971—removed the limitation on the power of amendment of the Constitution laid down in *Golak Nath*. Accordingly, a clause was added in Article 13 making it clear that an amendment to the Constitution was not included within the definition of law in that Article. Article 368 was reworded as given above including the reassertion of the addition in Article 13. Equipped with this power, the 25th Amendment Act, 1971 further amended the property right in Article 31 replacing the word 'compensation' by 'amount' and adding a new Article 31-C giving priority to DPs in Article 39(b) and (c) relating to the control and distribution of the material resources of society over FRs in Articles 14, 19 and 31 and debarring the courts from making

[25] See, Austin, above note 15, 196ff.
[26] *Rustam Cavasjee Cooper v Union of India*, AIR 1970 SC 564.
[27] *Madhav Rao Jivaji Rao Scindia v Union of India*, (1971) 1 SCC 85.
[28] The Constitution 18th– 23rd amendments were merely insignificant and incidental.

any enquiry if a law included a declaration that it was made in pursuance of those DPs. By the 26th Amendment Act, 1971 references to privy purses were removed from the Constitution and a new Article 363A was inserted expressly derecognising former rulers and abolishing their purses. Further by the 29th Amendment Act, 1972 two Kerala laws and by 34th Amendment Act, 1974, many more laws from different States were inserted in the Ninth Schedule.

Fundamental Rights versus Directive Principles

The inclusion of Kerala legislation, however, led to the famous *Kesavananda Bharati v State of Kerala* case[29]: a Supreme Court divided by 7 to 6 overruled *Golak Nath*, and upheld the validity of the 24th Amendment amending Articles 13 and 368 but invalidated the portion of Article 31C which had been inserted by the 25th Amendment and which excluded judicial review of legislation made in pursuance of Article 31C. The Supreme Court so decided on the ground that although any provision of the Constitution including the FRs was subject to amendment, no amendment could change the basic structure of the Constitution; the court can examine whether an amendment changes the basic structure of the Constitution and invalidate such an amendment if it comes to the conclusion that it changes the basic structure. On the contents of the basic structure the judges in their separate opinions mentioned such features as the republican form of government, a democratic polity, the federal structure, judicial review, separation of powers, and so on.

Soon after *Kesavanada* the then Chief Justice of India retired. In his place, discarding the existing convention of appointing the next senior judge of the Supreme Court, the President appointed the judge fourth in seniority. This was taken as a step to undermine the independence of the judiciary. In the growing dissatisfaction against the government led by Mrs Gandhi, on 12 June 1975 the Allahabad High Court invalidated her election to Parliament from her constituency and also disqualified her from contesting any election for the next six years as a result of corrupt practices in her election. Having failed to get adequate relief from the Supreme Court she advised the President to impose a state of Emergency on the ground of internal disturbance while there was already a state of Emergency in force on the ground of external aggression and war. During the Emergency, while most of the leaders of opposition, including Members of Parliament, were in detention, the Constitution was amended several times in quick succession. While the 35th, 36th and 37th amendments were incidental, the 38th Amendment 1975 directly related to Mrs Gandhi's personal position insofar as it debarred judicial review of the President's satisfaction as to the grounds for imposing any kind of Emergency. More clearly, the 39th Amendment excluded from the jurisdiction of the courts election disputes including any pending

---

[29] *Kesavananda Bharati v State of Kerala* (1973) 4 SCC 225.

dispute relating to the election of the Prime Minister and the Speaker and assigned them to a special authority to be established. Much legislation including the Representation of the People Act along with its amendments after the Allahabad decision were also included in the Ninth Schedule followed by further inclusions by the 40th Amendment 1976, taking the total count to 188.

The validity of the 39th amendment, however, came into question in *Indira Nehru Gandhi v Raj Narain*[30] arising from Mrs Gandhi's appeal in the Supreme Court against the Allahabad High Court decision in her election matter. Relying upon *Kesavananda* the court invalidated the main provisions of this amendment especially the ones that provided for the abatement of the pending proceedings and upheld the election of the Prime Minister notwithstanding any decision of any court. Different judges gave different reasons for arriving at their conclusions, but *Kesavananda* was the foundation for all of them. The appeal was finally decided in favour of Mrs Gandhi in view of the retrospective changes in the election law but *Kesavananda*, which was subject of controversy until then, became entrenched. Subsequently an effort was made to get *Kesavananda* overruled by a larger bench of the Supreme Court, but in view of strong arguments against the legitimacy of such an attempt and differences of opinions among the judges, the attempt was aborted by the Chief Justice by dissolving the bench and the matter was not pursued any further.[31] With that it became clear that the basic structure doctrine would survive.

However, in view of her past experience with the courts and her inability to get rid of *Kesavananda*, Mrs Gandhi sought to review the whole Constitution and carry out such amendments as were conducive to the implementation of her policies of poverty removal through a socialist pattern of society. Accordingly a Committee chaired by Swaran Singh, a senior Congress Party leader, was set up to suggest comprehensive amendments of the Constitution. During this period the state of Emergency was in full swing; FRs were suspended and opposition leaders were in detention. Following the Swaran Singh Committee report, the 42nd Amendment Act, 1976 made about 60 significant changes in the Constitution. These included replacing the expressions 'sovereign democratic republic' by the words 'sovereign socialist secular democratic republic' and the 'unity of the Nation' by the words 'unity and integrity of the Nation' in the Preamble; giving all DPs overriding effect in Article 31C over FRs in Articles 14, 19 and 31; introducing a new Article 31D saving laws preventing anti-national activities from challenge under Articles 14, 19 or 31; introduction of Article 32A denying the Supreme Court's jurisdiction over State laws vis-à-vis FRs; addition of DPs for the welfare of children, legal aid, participation of workers in the management of industries, and protection of the environment; introduction of FDs of citizens; making the advice of the Council of Ministers binding on the President; denying

[30] *Indira Nehru Gandhi v Raj Narain* AIR 1975 SC 2299.
[31] For details see, MV Kamath, *Nani A Palkhivala: A Life* (India: Hay House, 2007), 194ff.

the High Courts jurisdiction to judge the constitutional validity of Central legislation; a requirement of a two-thirds majority of the Court for invalidation of a Central or State law; curtailment of the powers of High Courts under Articles 226 and 227; denial of their power to invalidate Central laws and special provisions for pending petitions; the deployment of Central armed forces in the States; provision for an all India judicial service; introduction of a new Part XIVA providing for administrative tribunals and excluding the jurisdiction of the courts to review their decisions except by special leave petition to the Supreme Court under Article 136; provision for declaration of a state of Emergency in any part of the country; strengthening of Centre's hold over the States during the Central rule and weakening of the position of FRs during the state of Emergency; inclusion of clauses (4) and (5) in Article 368 given above; and expansion of Central heads of legislation at the expense of the States.

Soon after the commencement of the 42nd Amendment the Emergency was revoked and fresh elections were held resulting in Mrs Gandhi's personal and party defeat in elections. Much of what she had done by the 38th, 39th and 42nd Amendments was undone by the new government and the Constitution was restored to its position as it had been by the 43rd and 44th Amendments in 1978 and 1979 respectively. A noticeable change brought by the 44th Amendment was repeal of the right to property in Articles 19(1)(f) and 31 and its introduction in brief and simple form in a new Article 300A which reads: 'No person shall be deprived of his property save by authority of law.' The 44th Amendment has also introduced several safeguards in the Emergency provisions specifically replacing words 'internal disturbance' by 'armed rebellion', and better parliamentary control and non-suspension of the FRs to life and liberty during a state of Emergency. The Supreme Court later invalidated several provisions of the 42nd Amendment, which the 43rd and 44th Amendments left unchanged.

One of the most important and earliest decisions in this regard is *Minerva Mills*[32] which entrenched the basic structure doctrine in the Constitution. Invalidating clauses (4) and (5) of Article 368 which made constitutional amendments immune from challenge in courts retrospectively was unanimously declared unconstitutional by a five judge bench of the Court on the ground that non-amendability of the basic structure of the Constitution is one of its basic features. 'Indeed,' observed the Court 'a limited amending power is one of the basic features of our Constitution and therefore, limitations on that power cannot be destroyed.'[33] Any amendment of the Constitution that makes amendments changing the basic structure of the Constitution immune from challenge in the courts is, therefore, impermissible and invalid. It also invalidated by 4 to 1 that part of Article 31C which authorised the overriding of FRs in Articles 14 and 19 in pursuance of any of the DPs and restored the original position as upheld in

---

[32] See above, note 11.
[33] AIR 1980 SC 1789 at 1798.

Kesavananda. In another decision upholding the position laid down in *Kesavananda* the Court held that while Articles 31A and 31B and the Ninth Schedule were immune from challenge, any additions to the Ninth Schedule after that decision, that is after 23 April 1973, could be challenged on the ground of violation of the basic structure.[34] However, no such law has ever been challenged even though the Court has unanimously reiterated this proposition in a larger bench decision.[35] In my view such a challenge may not be possible in view of the law laid down by the Court in *Indira Nehru Gandhi* and reiterated in subsequent cases[36] that the basic structure doctrine applies only to constitutional amendments and not to ordinary legislation enacted by a legislature in an exercise of legislative powers.[37]

Soon after *Minerva Mills* doubts were expressed about its authority as a binding precedent.[38] But ignoring these doubts in *SP Sampath Kumar v Union of India*,[39] without invalidating the exclusion of the jurisdiction of the High Courts in Article 323A introduced by the 42nd Amendment, the Supreme Court conceded that alternative judicial forums could be created by law but the law must ensure that such forum is no less effective than that of the High Courts under Article 226 and directed suitable amendments in the law to save it from unconstitutionality. Following *Sampath Kumar* in *P Sambhamurthy v State of AP*[40] the Supreme Court unanimously invalidated clause (5) of Article 371D introduced by 32nd Amendment in 1974. The clause provided that the final order of the Administrative Tribunal to be set up under clause (3) of that Article shall become effective upon its confirmation by the Government or on the expiry of three months. The proviso to clause (5) authorised the Government to modify or annul any order of the Tribunal. The Court held that the proviso was 'violative of the rule of law which is clearly a basic and essential feature of the Constitution'. As the main part of clause (5) was related to the proviso and did not have any rationale for its independent existence the entire clause was invalidated. Later in *L Chandra Kumar v Union of India*[41] a seven judge bench of the Supreme Court unanimously invalidated those clauses of Articles 323A and 323B introduced by the 42nd Amendment which excluded the jurisdiction of the Supreme Court under Article 32 and of the High Courts under Article 226. Holding that judicial review was one of the basic features of the Constitution which could not be

---

[34] *WamanRao v Union of India*, AIR 1981 SC 271.
[35] *IR Coelho v Union of India*, (2007) 2 SCC 1.
[36] See, *Kuldip Nayar v Union of India*, (2006) SCC 7 SCC 1 at 67.
[37] See, Singh, MP, 'Ashok Thakur v Union of India: A Divided Verdict on an Undivided Social Measure', 1 *NUJS Law Review* 193 at 216 and *Shukla's Constitution of India*, 1012 11th edn (Lucknow: Eastern Book Co, 2008).
[38] See, *Sanjee v Coke Mfg Co v.Bharat Coking Coal Ltd*, AIR 1983 SC 239.
[39] *SP Sampath Kumar v Union of India* AIR 1987 SC 386.
[40] *P Sambhamurthy v State of AP* AIR 1987 SC 663.
[41] *L Chandra Kumar v Union of India* AIR 1997 SC 1125.

diluted by transferring judicial power to the administrative tribunals and excluding the review of their determinations under Articles 32 or 226, the Court conceded that if the tribunals were as independent from the executive as the High Courts exclusion of High Courts' supervisory jurisdiction could be justified but not otherwise.

Prior to *L Chandra Kumar* in *Kihoto Holhan v Zachillhu*[42] the Supreme Court invalidated paragraph 7 of the Tenth Schedule to the Constitution introduced by the 52nd Amendment Act, 1985 that debarred the jurisdiction of all courts 'in respect of any matter connected with the disqualification of a member' of Parliament or State legislature on the ground that the paragraph had the effect of amending the powers of the Supreme Court and the High Courts without following the procedure required in the proviso to Article 368(2). The Court had earlier rejected the same argument in *Sajjan Singh*. If the *Sajjan Singh* situation arises today perhaps the Court will tend to follow *Kihoto Holohan*.

The Basic Structure Principle: Scheduled Castes and Scheduled Tribes

The basic structure has been an issue in several other cases too, but in all of them the Court has upheld the amendments. For example, in *Raghunathrao Ganpatrao v Union of India*[43] the Supreme Court upheld the 26th Amendment Act 1971 that derecognised the former Indian rulers and abolished their privy purses and other privileges because the amendment was consistent with the basic features of the Constitution such as republicanism, human dignity and equality. Similarly in *M Nagaraj v Union of India*[44] the Court unanimously upheld several amendments making special provisions for the Scheduled Castes (SCs) and the Scheduled Tribes (STs) in Article 16 which guarantees equality of opportunity in matters of state employment as well as in Article 335 which requires the state to give special consideration to the interests of SCs and STs in the matter of state employment. The fact that these amendments overruled decisions of the Court did not make any difference. Again, in *IR Coelho v Union of India*[45] a nine judge bench unanimously held that though the validity of the laws included in the Ninth Schedule after *Kesavananda* could be tested on the anvil of the basic structure doctrine, it declined to test the validity of any amendment that introduced these Acts into the Ninth Schedule. Once again in *Ashok Kumar v Union of India*[46] the Court upheld the validity of the 93rd Amendment of the Constitution introducing clause (5) in Article 15 under which, notwithstanding anything in Article 15 or Article 19(1)(g), a State can make any special provision for the advancement of any socially or educationally backward class or the SCs or STs in so far as such

---

[42]   *Kihoto Holhan v Zachillhu* AIR 1993 SC 412.
[43]   *Raghunathrao Ganpatrao v Union of India* AIR 1993 SC 1267.
[44]   *M Nagaraj v Union of India* (2006) 8 SCC 212.
[45]   *IR Coelho v Union of India* (2007) 2 SCC 1.
[46]   *Ashok Kumar v Union of India* (2008) 6 SCC 1.

provisions relate to their admission to educational institutions. More recently the Court has also upheld the provisions for reservation for women and SCs and STs in village panchayats and municipalities introduced in the Constitution respectively by 73rd and 74th Amendment Acts of 1992.[47]

With these precedents before us and no more attempts to change the Constitution such as were necessitated in its infancy or later for political reasons during early years of Mrs Gandhi from 1967 to 1976, it now seems on all sides that in its basic essentials the Constitution is becoming internalised among all sections and institutions of society and the body politic. The Supreme Court has also admitted that the basic structure may be damaged by its interpretation and application of the Constitution: in that case the amending body is justified in overruling the Court by amendment and restoring the basic structure of the Constitution. Such a conclusion is clearly supported by the Court's remarks in *Waman Rao* and *Nagaraj*. In *Waman Rao*, relying upon the history of the 1st Amendment, the Court drew the conclusion that Articles 31A and 31B instead of weakening strengthened the basic structure of the Constitution. Similarly in *Nagaraj* the respondents argued that 'the power under Article 368 has to keep the Constitution in repair as and when it becomes necessary and thereby protect and preserve the basic structure' while the Court admitted that the challenged amendments were 'curative by nature'.[48] Thus the Courts as well as other branches of the government representing the people must respect the basic structure of the Constitution on behalf of the people as well as for themselves.

The Basic Structure Doctrine Reviewed

In the nature of things some differences will persist as to what exactly is the basic structure of the Constitution. The judicial precedents so far have established that democracy, republicanism, independence of the judiciary, judicial review, secularism, federalism, rule of law, harmony and balance between FRs and DPs, equality and the non-amendability of the basic structure of the Constitution, are components of the basic structure of the Constitution. An enormous literature has developed around this issue in India and abroad. Legal scholars and practitioners around the world today accept that the document that emerges at 'constitutional moments' has an identity which must be preserved. This does not mean that every detail in the Constitution is to be preserved. But just as a house does not lose its identity so long as you are decorating and repairing it on the same foundations on which it was built, so a Constitution does not lose its identity if it is changed according to the requirements of changing times so long

[47] (2010) 7 SCC 202.
[48] (2006) 8 SCC 212 at 270.

as its basic foundations are maintained.[49] Following my engagement with the issue elsewhere,[50] I summarise the issue as follows.

In *Nagaraj* the Court laid down that if an amendment is challenged for violation of the basic structure of the Constitution, 'twin tests have to be satisfied, namely, the "width test" and the test of "identity"'.[51] With reference to the challenged amendments in the case the Court held: 'Applying the "width test", we do not find obliteration of any of the constitutional limitations. Applying the test of "identity", we do not find any alteration in the existing structure of the equality code.'[52] Relying upon the earlier precedents it clarified that not an amendment of a particular article but an amendment that adversely affects or destroys the wider principles of the Constitution such as democracy, secularism, equality or republicanism, or one that changes the identity of the Constitution is impermissible.[53] 'To destroy its identity is to abrogate the basic structure of the Constitution', the Court concluded.[54] Later in *Coelho* the Court varied the test in its application to FRs insofar as the Court read *Nagaraj* to have held that in respect of the amendments of the fundamental rights it is not the change in a particular article but the change in the essence of the right must be the test for the change in identity. It laid down that if the 'triangle of Article 21 read with Article 14 and Article 19 is sought to be eliminated not only the "essence of right" test but also the "rights test" has to apply.'[55] Pointing out the difference between the 'rights test' and 'essence of right' test, the Court observed that both form part of the basic structure doctrine, but:

> When in a controlled Constitution conferring limited power of amendment, an entire chapter is made inapplicable, 'the essence of right' test as applied in *M Nagaraj case* will have no applicability. In such a situation, to judge the validity of the law, it is the 'rights test' which is more appropriate.[56]

I am not quite sure of these conclusions of the Court because I could not locate the use of the expression 'essence of right' in *Nagaraj*. With reference to amendments in the Ninth Schedule, holding that each amendment must be judged on its own merits, the Court in *Coelho* concluded:

[49] For this example see, Joseph Raz, *Between Authority and Interpretation* (New York: Oxford University Press, 2009) 370: 'The point of my coda is to warn against confusing change with loss of identity and against the spurious arguments it breeds. Dispelling errors is all that a general theory of the constitution can aspire to achieve.'
[50] See references in note 37 above.
[51] (2006) 8 SCC 212 at 268.
[52] Ibid, at 269.
[53] Ibid.
[54] Ibid.
[55] (2007) 2 SCC 1 at 108.
[56] Ibid.

The actual effect and impact of the law on the rights guaranteed under Part III has to be taken into account for determining whether or not it destroys basic structure. The impact test would determine the validity of the challenge.[57]

While the Court is still struggling to find an objective test, which in the nature of the things may be difficult to lay down, the following test laid down by one of the foremost architects of the basic structure doctrine in India—Dieter Conrad—appears to be convincing:

> [F]rom the fact that the constitutional provision does not mention limitations it must be concluded that the amending power is intended to be very wide. Only clearest cases of transgression would justify judicial intervention, as a remedy of last resort. Regularly, such cases will be discernible by an element of abuse of power, of some collateral purpose appearing behind the purported scope of the amendment. In the absence of such elements a general presumption of constitutionality must operate even more than in the case of ordinary legislation.[58]

From the precedents so far it appears that the Court in India has been consciously or unconsciously following this approach towards constitutional amendments.[59]

CHANGE BY ORDINARY LEGISLATION

As the Constitution of India is not only a written one but also perhaps the one which is the longest one and most amenable to easy and frequent amendments, little scope is left to bring any changes in it through legislation or legislative practices except the ones which the Constitution expressly provides to be brought about by parliamentary legislation alluded to above. The only changes brought about by ordinary legislation are those relating to the organisation and reorganisation of the States and the consequential changes which the Constitution expressly authorises Parliament to make. The major changes in this regard were brought about by the States Reorganisation Act, 1956, which affected many provisions of the Constitution, followed by several other Acts effecting only minor consequential changes.

THE ROLE OF THE JUDICIARY

Even if in theory some doubts persist as to whether judges make the law or simply declare or apply it, it is very well recognised that they continue to develop it over time. As regards ordinary laws or legislation, dealing with specific subjects,

---

[57] Ibid, at 111.

[58] D Conrad, *Zwischen den Traditionen*, (Stuttgart: Franz Steiner Verlag, 1999), 102.

[59] For more readings on the issue see, Singh, note 37 above and a bunch of papers in 1 *NUJS Law Review*, 397–572 (2008). For a recent writing supportive of the basic structure doctrine see Sudhir Krishnaswamy, *Democracy and Constitutionalism in India* (Oxford: Oxford University Press, 2009).

they may not be capable of incorporating within them subjects that are foreign to those laws. Therefore, frequent invocation of legislative power may be required to deal with them. But a constitution which is not so specific but rather lays down broad guidelines within which laws have to be made, is capable of covering all possibilities and exigencies that may arise in the infinite life of a nation and is expected to do so. Accordingly it is said and repeated specifically in the context of the Indian Constitution that a constitution must be liberally interpreted because it is not the law on a subject but creates the mechanism for the making of laws.[60] It is an organic law which gives birth to other laws. The shorter a constitution the greater is the scope for judicial innovation. With the length of the Indian constitution the scope for such innovation gets narrowed down. Therefore, while much of the brief US Constitution is elaborated and kept up to date through judicial decisions, a long constitution like that of India leaves comparatively less scope for judicial creativity. An easy amending process as discussed above also narrows down the scope for judicial innovations. Even so, the judiciary in India has helped the Constitution to grow and change with times. The best proof of that is what has been discussed above in respect of the invention of the basic structure doctrine which remained, if not unknown, at least unrecognised until 1973.

Most of the other examples of judicial change in the Constitution are visible in the FRs. Tailoring the FR to life and liberty in Article 21 cautiously in *AK Gopalan v State of Madras*[61] soon after the commencement of the Constitution, but since *Maneka Gandhi v Union of India*[62] in 1978 the Court has vastly expanded its scope bringing within it many kinds of rights and liberties from the right to a clean environment to rights to education and health and all that is necessary for a dignified life. Since then reference to due process is often invoked though the Constitution makers had expressly eliminated it—which the Court also conceded in *Gopalan*.[63] Even though it may be argued that the Court is relying on procedural rather than substantive due process, the Court often does not draw such a distinction and expressly refers to 'substantive due process'.[64] In the initial stage the Court also found conflicts between the FRs and DPs and gave priority to the former over the latter. In the course of time it has, however, changed its stance and finally in *Minerva* it held that harmony between the two was part of the basic structure of the Constitution.

Relying upon the socialistic pattern of society advocated and pursued by the main political party as well as by the nationalist leaders, the Court from its initial impression of opposing such policies moved openly in the direction of those

---

[60] See, *Re CP Motor Spirit Act*, AIR 1939 FC 131.
[61] *AK Gopalan v State of Madras* AIR 1950 SC 27.
[62] *Maneka Gandhi v Union of India* (1978) 1 SCC 248.
[63] For details see, Singh, Shukla's Constitution of India, note 37 above at 201ff.
[64] See, eg, *Selvi v State of Karnataka*, (2010) 7 SCC 263 at 382. The reference has, however, been made in the context of Art 20(3) and not 21. For the earlier cases see, eg, *Sunil Batra v Delhi Administration*, (1978) 4 SCC 494 at 518.

policies as reflected in DPs as well as introduced in the Preamble by the insertion of word 'socialist'.[65] But when the government embarked on the new economic policy of liberalisation and privatisation in 1991 the Court upheld that too ignoring reference to 'socialist' in the Preamble.[66]

Another important innovation made by the judiciary has been in respect of its own position. After initially holding that in the matter of appointment of Supreme Court and High Court judges and the transfer of the latter from one High Court to another the executive has primacy over the judiciary,[67] it reversed this position and held that in these matters the judiciary has primacy over the executive and in respect of them the President of India, instead of acting on the aid and advice of the Council of Ministers as required by Article 74, should act on the aid and advice of the Chief Justice of India represented by a collegium of judges.[68]

THE ROLE OF THE CONVENTIONS

As noted above the Constitution of India establishes a parliamentary form of government both at the Centre as well as in the States. While some of the aspects of the operation of such a form of government have been expressed in the Constitution others have been left unexpressed. Around them conventions have developed. For example, though the Constitution vests all the executive power of the state in the Head of the State at the Centre as well as in the States, the convention has developed and the Court has held that in a parliamentary government the Head of the State is titular and must act on the aid and advice of his council of ministers except in those exceptional situations when such aid and advice is not available.[69] Even for those exceptional situations conventions have developed. For example, in the matter of appointment of the Prime Minister at the Centre or the Chief Minister in a State, the head goes by the well-established convention that the leader of the largest party represented in the directly elected house of the legislature is invited to take over as Prime Minister or Chief Minister. Similarly, though the Council of Ministers jointly as well as individually at the Centre as well as in the States hold their office during the pleasure of the President, neither the President nor any Governor has ever dismissed a Council

[65] See, eg various pronouncements of Justice Krishna Iyer in *DS Nakara v Union of India*, AIR 1983 SC 130; and *Kerala Hotel and Restaurant Assn v State of Kerala*, AIR 1990 SC 913.
[66] See, eg, *Delhi Sc Forum v Union of India*, AIR 1996 SC 1356; *BALCO Employees Union v Union of India*, (2002) 2 SCC 333. The Court has also, however, declined to consider a challenge to the inclusion of the word 'SOCIALIST' in the Preamble to the Constitution until an appropriate occasion arises: see, *Good Governance India Foundation v Union of India*, decided on 12 July 2010 at http://courtnic.nic.in/supremecourt/temp/679200731272010p.txt.
[67] *SP Gupta v Union of India*, AIR 1982 SC 149.
[68] *SC Advocates on Record Assn v Union of India*, AIR 1994 SC 268 and *Re Presidential Reference*, AIR 199 SC 1.
[69] *Ram Jawaya Kapoor v State of Punjab*, AIR 1955 SC 549 and *Shamsher Singh v State of Punjab*, AIR 1974 SC 2192.

or any of its members without the advice of the Prime Minister or the Chief Minister as the case may be. The collective responsibility of the Council of Ministers towards the directly elected house of the legislature is discharged by the practice of the Council seeking a vote of confidence in that house whenever a doubt is expressed or perceived about the support of that house in the Council. The Council also submits its resignation to the head of the state whenever the motion of confidence is defeated. Similarly, on the re-election of the lower house of the legislature the defeated Council submits its resignation or in case of winning a majority makes a claim for fresh appointment. Thus almost all the healthy conventions of the robust functioning of a parliamentary form of government have developed and are observed.

From the time of the commencement of the Constitution until 1973 a convention also developed that the most senior judge of the Supreme Court was always appointed the Chief Justice of India on the vacation of the office of the Chief Justice either on superannuation or otherwise. The convention was broken in 1973 and again in 1977 during Mrs Gandhi's tenure as Prime Minister when, superseding the then most senior judge, a junior judge was appointed as the Chief Justice of India. Since 1977 the convention has, however, again developed and has also been held as a constitutional norm by the Court.[70]

There are other conventions too that have developed or are in the process of development for the smooth function of the Constitution. For example, one of them is the practice of consulting the State government before the appointment of Governor of a State by the President of India. Similarly, in the matter of affecting the boundary of a State, which Parliament can do unilaterally, the proposal is expected from the concerned State or States. There are other areas too in the functioning of federal arrangements where efforts are being made to establish healthy conventions for their smooth functioning.

Speaking on the nature of conventions in the Indian Constitution one of the judges of the Supreme Court has observed:

> We are of the view that there is no distinction between the 'constitutional law' and an established 'constitutional convention' and both are binding in the field of their operation. Once it is established to the satisfaction of the Court that a particular convention exists and is operating then the convention becomes a part of the 'constitutional law' of the land and can be enforced in the like manner.[71]

This may not exactly be the legal position but with rare exceptions cited above the conventions have developed and are in the process of developing to keep the Constitution up to date.

---

[70] See *SC Advocates on Record Assn v Union of India*, AIR 1994 SC 268 and *In re Presidential Reference*, AIR 1999 SC 1.
[71] Kuldip Singh J in *SC Advocates on Record Assn v Union of India*, AIR 1994 SC 268 at 405.

INTERNATIONAL LAW

Unlike the constitutions of some of the civil law countries such as the Federal Republic of Germany which makes 'the general rules of public international law' an integral part of federal law to take precedence over statutes and directly create rights and duties for the inhabitants of the federal territory, the Constitution of India does not confer constitutional status on international law. Therefore international law cannot change the Constitution directly as it does in Germany. But Article 51(C) of the Constitution directs the state to 'endeavour to ... foster respect for international law and treaty obligations in the dealings of organised peoples with one another'. The Constitution also assigns treaty making and foreign affairs exclusively to the Centre[72] and authorises Parliament 'to make any law for the whole or any part of the territory of India for implementing any treaty, agreement or convention with any other country or countries or any decision made at any international conference, association or other body.'[73] In view of these provisions on the one hand the FRs have been interpreted in the light of developments in international law especially in respect of human rights[74] while on the other hand the foreign affairs and treaty making powers of the Centre have been used to curtail the powers of the States. For example, in the matter of environmental protection and WTO obligations, specially of the latter, Central legislation has been made on issues such as agriculture which fall exclusively within the domain of the States. In the era of fast-expanding economic globalisation it can very well be expected that the federal arrangements in the Indian Constitution will be quite different from what one can see in the text. Thus international law also plays a role in changing the Constitution.

SUMMING UP

To sum up, the Constitution of India has adjusted itself very well to the needs of a fast changing and diverse society ridden with poverty, illiteracy and internal and external conflicts. In view of frequent amendments in the Constitution, quite often in response to court decisions and sometimes even to curtail court powers, doubts may be expressed about the sanctity of the Constitution. But as we have noted above, being fully aware of the difficulties faced by the country at the time of the making of the Constitution and likely to arise in the future the Constitution makers had themselves provided for an easy procedure for the amendment of the Constitution hoping that it would be adjusted according to the exigencies of the situation without being destroyed or uprooted. They were convinced that only such an arrangement would ensure the unity of the nation, democracy and

---

[72] Entries 10 and 14 of List I Schedule VII.
[73] Art 254.
[74] See eg, *Vishaka v State of Rajasthan*, (1997) 6 SCC 241.

social change which Austin has perceived as the seamless web of the Indian Constitution.[75] Subject to perhaps to the temporary exception of the 1975–77 Emergency the seamless web has remained intact and un-pierced and has been safeguarded against any onslaughts in future by the basic structure doctrine. With every passing day the Constitution is also acquiring greater legitimacy with more and more people expressing their allegiance to and confidence in the Constitution. We can therefore predict that the Constitution of India will keep adjusting itself to the requirements of Indian society without losing its identity and sanctity.

[75] Austin, above note 15 at 6.

9

Israel

SUZIE NAVOT

INTRODUCTION

H ISTORICALLY, THE ISRAELI constitutional regime was based primarily on the constitutional structure of the British regime. During the
years before the establishment of the State of Israel, the Westminster
Parliament served as a model for leaders of the *Yishuv* (pre-state Jewish settlement), and even during the early years of the State reliance on the British model
continued routinely. Like its British counterpart, the Israeli government is an
outgrowth of the Knesset and the overwhelming majority of its members are
Knesset members. As in Britain, in Israel too the entrenched, founding principle
was that of parliamentary sovereignty, and only recently has this fundamental
principle undergone far-reaching changes. All the same, the British system served
and continues to serve as the historic source for many of the arrangements in
Israeli constitutional law.

In global terms, Israel is a 'young' state. Following the UN Partition Resolution
of November 1947, and after the termination of the Mandate, the State of Israel
declared its independence in May 1948.[1] Upon the establishment of the State,
Israel's Declaration of Independence determined that 'the establishment of the
elected, regular authorities of the State' would be 'in accordance with the
Constitution which shall be adopted by the Constituent Assembly'.

The Constituent Assembly, which was charged with framing a constitution for
the State of Israel, was actually elected in 1949. It changed its name to the 'First
Knesset' and, in accordance with its mandate, conducted extensive debates
regarding the constitution. Nonetheless, the actual attempt to frame a constitution triggered controversy and opposition that ultimately precluded that move at
that time. The opposition to the adoption of a constitution stemmed from a
number of considerations, inter alia the claim that the legacy of the British
tradition rendered a constitution unnecessary. Furthermore, it was claimed that
the Knesset only represented a minority of the anticipated population of Israel.

---

[1] Suzie Navot, *The Constitutional Law of Israel* (The Netherlands: Kluwer, 2007), 19–20.

Thus, it was inappropriate for the Knesset to establish a constitutional framework that would be binding upon a vastly expanded population as a result of the expected immigration. Accordingly, the framing of a constitution should wait until the initial waves of immigration subsided.

The Knesset debates on the constitution reached an impasse, and the First Knesset dispersed after it passed a compromise decision that became known as 'the Harrari Resolution',[2] according to which the constitution would be adopted 'chapter by chapter', in stages. Each chapter would bear the title of a 'basic law of its own' and the Knesset Constitution, Law, and Justice Committee was charged with the enactment of a series of Basic Laws, ultimately intending to unify all the Basic Laws into an integrated Israeli constitution. Upon its dispersal, the First Knesset passed the Second Knesset (Transition) Law 1951, in which it determined that the Second Knesset would have 'all of the powers, rights, duties, and authorities that the First Knesset and its members had', and that this provision would apply to the current Knesset and 'to any subsequent Knesset'. The Second Knesset thus began working on the adoption of the first Basic Law: The Knesset, and the enactment of Basic Laws have continued since.

The upshot of the Harrari Resolution was that the decision to adopt a complete constitution for the State of Israel was deferred. It was replaced by a process of enacting a constitution 'chapter by chapter'—a process that has led to the enactment of 11 Basic Laws, but which has yet to produce a full constitution.

THE ISRAELI CONSTITUTIONAL SYSTEM: HISTORICAL AND POLITICAL BACKGROUND

While the Israeli Parliamentary system is based primarily on the British Parliamentary system, it developed in an independent and unique manner. For example, the system of multiple parties and nationwide–proportional elections contrasts sharply with the basic tenets of the British system. The particular nature of the Israeli system has affected not only the governments' stability, but also their ability to govern. The Israeli system was characterised by a fundamental imbalance between the formal power conferred on the government as the executive authority and its lack of actual power to adopt crucial, difficult decisions, due to its dependence on the coalition partners. In Israel, no party has ever received an absolute majority in the Knesset. Some regard this as a healthy response, which actually creates a mechanism of political checks and balances in a system that

---

[2] The text of the Harrari Resolution:
The First Knesset charges the Constitution, Law, and Justice Committee with preparing a draft of the State Constitution. The Constitution will consist of separate chapters, each chapter constituting a Basic Law in its own. The chapters will be presented to the Knesset ... and all of the chapters shall be consolidated into the State Constitution.

lacks a constitution.[3] The system of purely proportional elections has actually prevented the concentration of power in the hands of a single party.

Until the 1960s, Israel was characterised by governmental stability and, despite occasional upheavals, the government was never threatened by significant opposition. Generations of Israeli governments were coalition-based and invariably included parties that opposed far reaching constitutional reforms such as the adoption of a constitution and the constitutional entrenchment of basic human rights. Nevertheless, the entire political system was thrown into turmoil in 1990 in the wake of a coalition crisis and a situation in which Members of the Knesset (MKs) were 'crossing the floor' in return for benefits. The result was a protest movement that demanded a change in the government system and in the electoral system. Against this background, a series of important changes were introduced that were intended to streamline the performance of the political system. One of these laws was an amendment to the Basic Law: The Knesset. This amendment limited an MK's ability to 'cross the floor' in return for benefits. In March 1992, both the government and the electoral systems were fundamentally altered. The new arrangement provided for the direct election of the prime minister, although the Knesset retained its power to express no-confidence in the prime minister, and the Knesset's supervisory powers were actually strengthened.[4]

The grand hopes pinned on the direct election system never materialised. The two prime ministers elected in direct elections—Benjamin Netanyahu in 1996 and Ehud Barak in 1999—had a hard time maintaining the requisite Knesset majority to support their respective governments. Though the difficulties relating to governance and the significant bargaining powers of lone MKs were the problems that precipitated the change of the system, the change itself did not solve the problems and may even have aggravated them because the new system too practically bolstered small and medium-sized parties. As a result, the majority of the Knesset decided in 2001 to return to the parliamentary system, introducing the requirement for constructive no-confidence motions, and retaining the prime minister's authority to dissolve the Knesset.

---

[3] A Rubinstein and B Medina, *The Constitutional Law of the State of Israel*, 6th edn (in Hebrew), (Israel: Schocken, 2005) 20.

[4] The political crisis in 1990 was a trigger for the change in the governmental and electoral systems but the two year struggle for reform resulted in a limited proposal which introduced only the principle of direct elections for the Prime Minister, without treating other issues. When debating the various proposals for reform, one of the possibilities considered was integrating regional election. Finally the reform did not present a comprehensive and integrated concept of governance and was confined to the executive branch. The proportional system and the process for electing candidates was left untouched and no other components of the system of government were modified. Maybe the lesson to be learned from the subsequent repeal of direct elections and the return to the parliamentary system is that changes in the system of government that have not been thoroughly studied and understood should be avoided. For further elaboration, see Navot, *Constitutional Law*, note 1 above, 24–25, 83–86.

Another important change in Israeli constitutional law of that period was the enactment of the Basic Law: Human Dignity and Liberty, and Basic Law: Freedom of Occupation. The enactment of these two Basic Laws came in the wake of the protracted failure to enact a Basic Law on human rights. By 1992, almost all of the Basic Laws dealing with government institutions in Israel had already been adopted, but the Basic Law: Human Rights (Rights of the Person and the Citizen) had yet to be passed by the Knesset. The final adoption of the Basic Law: Human Dignity and Liberty in 1992 was actually the result of the fact that Basic Law: Human Rights had been split up into a number of separate Basic Laws, which made it possible for the Knesset to agree and support the constitutional entrenchment of particular, consensual, human rights. This compromise was meant to facilitate the enactment of a Basic Law for human rights, while leaving pending the discussion of 'problematic' rights, such as freedom of religion, speech, conscience, equality and so on. This original idea enabled the Knesset to overcome the opposition of various members, paving the way for the enactment of the two Basic Laws—Basic Law: Freedom of Occupation, and Basic Law: Human Dignity and Liberty.

In 1995, following the enactment of these Basic Laws, the Israeli Supreme Court handed down a decision that became known as a 'constitutional revolution', in which it declared that Basic Laws had a 'supra-legal' constitutional status, by virtue of which they could limit the Knesset's legislative powers, and that the court was empowered to enforce these limitations by judicially reviewing Knesset legislation.[5]

The constitutional revolution was the climax of another protracted process—disengagement from the British tradition. The role model traditionally provided by the UK was replaced by reliance on the law of constitutionally governed states, primarily the USA, Germany, and Canada. The constitutional mechanism for the protection of human rights in these states is in many ways similar to the mechanism embodied in Basic Law: Human Dignity and Liberty.

In addition to constitutional changes on the legislative level, the 1990s were a period of increased judicial activism by the Supreme Court. In part, this was the result of social processes that gave rise to yet another, more intrusive and invasive policy on the part of the court, in a process that became known as judicialisation of the government.[6] The sheer volume of case law concerning the area of public law changed the face of constitutional law of Israel. The judiciary began to fill the 'legislative vacuum' that had been created by the political system: the inability of the Knesset to enact new Basic Laws and to complete the human rights chapter of

---

[5] HCJ 6821/93 *United Mizrachi Bank Ltd v Migdal Cooperative Village*, 49 (4) PD 221 (For an English translation of certain paragraphs, see *Mizrachi Bank v Migdal* (Gal Amendment)—translated extracts with commentary in (1997) 31 *Israel Law Review*, 754.

[6] See A Gal-Nor 'The Judicialization of the Public Sphere in Israel 7' (in Hebrew) (2004) *Mishpat U'Mimshal* 355; E Benvenisti; 'Judicially Sponsored Checks and Balances' (in Hebrew) (2001) 32 *Mishpatim* 797.

the Israeli constitution. The Supreme Court took on the role of pronouncing new rights that had not been expressly mentioned in the Basic Laws. Since then, the Supreme Court has been particularly active in areas that are of fundamental importance to the Israeli public.

This short survey illustrates the importance of political background for the understanding of the processes of constitutional law. As in any other state, in Israel too the political, social, and historic background exerts a profound influence on the particular character of constitutional law. One of the striking features of the Israeli system then is the contribution of the Supreme Court to the development of constitutional law.

ISRAEL—A MIXED LEGAL SYSTEM

Under the powerful influence of the English legacy, Israeli law shares many features with the common law tradition, and major fields of law still echo concepts and rules from the corresponding fields of English Law. The structure of the legal system and its legal institutions are undoubtedly influenced by common law tradition. Judicial decisions are considered a source of law, often referred to as 'the Israeli common law', and the principle of binding precedent governs the creation of judge-made law. The structure of the judiciary, its inner hierarchy, rules of evidence and procedure, and the status of judges all bear similarities to common law countries. The Israeli contribution to its own legal system, however, is rather peculiar. Great efforts were made to build and concisely codify private law, and to codify and reform public law mechanisms and the substance of public law. Each of these branches of law is influenced by different sources: The codification of public law has often relied on European legal concepts. The emerging new constitution has been heavily influenced by the reasoning and wisdom of American judges. Furthermore, the Basic Laws that deal with human rights have been heavily influenced by the Canadian model.[7] The combination of all these influences has created a mixed jurisdiction, although it is much closer to the common law family than to continental traditions.

---

[7] These Basic Laws include a 'limitation clause', which permits ordinary legislation to contradict the limitation prescribed by these laws. This limitation clause follows the Canadian Charter of Rights and Freedoms.

THE CONSTITUTIONAL REVOLUTION: BASIC LAWS AS 'THE CONSTITUTION'

Following the Harrari Resolution, which laid the foundations for a constitution comprising a series of distinct Basic Laws, and until 1992, the Knesset succeeded in enacting nine Basic Laws, most of which regulated the institutions of government.[8]

The common denominator of all the Basic Laws was the addition of the word 'Basic' to their title, and the decision to omit the year of enactment. This is evidence of the intention to place them, normatively, above regular acts of legislation. Even so, the Knesset failed to make a clear distinction between a Basic Law and a regular law. Most of the Basic Laws were adopted in accordance with the procedure for adopting regular legislation, and most of them are highly detailed, in a format similar to regular legislation, as opposed to constitutional legislation.

The Harrari Resolution did not define the normative status of the Basic Laws. Do they have the status of regular law, and will they become 'constitutional' only upon the completion of the enactment of all of the Basic Laws? Alternatively, were they 'constitutional' from the moment of legislation?

Until 1992, the classic response to this question was that the normative status of Basic Laws was equal to that of normal laws.[9] This meant that the enactment of Basic Laws did not of itself make them part of the constitution of the State of Israel. Hence, Basic Laws were of a 'declaratory' nature, attesting to the intention to include them in a future constitution. As such, the laws did not derogate from the traditional concept of parliamentary sovereignty that was absorbed from English law. In fact, apart from one exception, the Basic Laws did not contain 'entrenchment' provisions that would have prescribed the need for a special majority in order to alter or amend them.[10]

As mentioned above, two Basic Laws concerning human rights were enacted in 1992: Basic Law: Human Dignity and Liberty, and Basic Law: Freedom of

---

[8] Basic Law: The Knesset (1958); Basic Law: The Israeli Lands (1960); Basic Law: The President of the State (1964); Basic Law: The Government (1968, replaced in 1992 and in 2001); Basic Law: The State Economy (1975); Basic Law: The Army, (1976); Basic Law: Jerusalem, the Capital of Israel (1980); Basic Law: The Judiciary (1984); Basic Law: The State Comptroller (1986).

[9] HCJ 107/73 *Negev Automobile Station Service Ltd v State of Israel*, PD 28 (1) 640, 642; HCJ 148/73 *Kaniel v Minister of Justice*, 27(1) PD 794, 796 (1973); HCJ 6821/93 *United Mizrahi Bank Ltd v Migdal Cooperative Village*, 49 (4) PD 221, 272 (1995) (see English translation at http://elyon1.court.gov.il/files_eng/93/210/068/z01/93068210.z01.pdf.

[10] Certain sections of the Basic Law: The Knesset are technically entrenched in the sense that a special majority of 61 is required for any variation or violation thereof. In the Israeli system there is no 'quorum' requirement for the passage of legislation, and a law is adopted by the Knesset after three readings and after receiving a regular majority of those participating in the vote, even if only a few MKs are actually present. Section 4 of the Basic Law: The Knesset, which regulates the Israeli electoral system, is an exception to the majority rule, given that it requires an absolute majority of the Knesset members (61) in order to change it.

Section 4 of the Basic Law: the Knesset provides:

'The Knesset shall be elected by general, country-wide, direct, equal, secret, and proportional elections, in accordance with the Knesset Elections Law; this section shall not be amended, save by a

Occupation. These two laws heralded two central changes in the constitutional concept. First, they included a formal requirement for a majority of the MKs in order to amend the new Basic Law: Freedom of Occupation. This idea of structural or formal entrenchment was not new to the Israeli legal system, but it had only been used previously in order to entrench single articles and not a complete Basic Law. The innovation of Basic Law: Freedom of Occupation was the inclusion of a section that entrenched the entire law, conditioning any amendment upon mustering a majority of 61 Knesset members.

A second innovation included in both the Basic Laws was the inclusion of a clause that imposed substantive limitations on the possibility of violating rights anchored in the Basic Laws. Infringement of human rights is permitted where committed for an appropriate purpose in accordance with the rules prescribed in the Basic Law itself. In this context, in both of the Basic Laws the Israeli legislature adopted a criterion similar to the criterion prescribed by the Canadian Legislator, the 'limitation clause'.[11] Accordingly, a 'regular' law that 'violates' any one of the human rights expressly stipulated in the Basic Law is only valid if it satisfies the cumulative conditions stipulated in the limitation clause:

> The rights according to this Basic Law shall not be infringed except by a law befitting the values of the State of Israel, enacted for a proper purpose, and to an extent no greater than required.[12]

The limitation clause was an innovation in the Israeli legislature, establishing a substantive limitation on the Knesset's power to infringe on Basic Laws by incorporating the need for a proper purpose in order to infringe human rights, and the principle of 'proportionality'. This engendered a radical change in the overall structure of Israeli Constitutional Law, as well as a change in the status of all Basic Laws, and led to the recognition of the power of judicial review of laws.

In 1995 the Supreme Court gave its monumental ruling in the matter of *Bank Mizrahi* which marked the beginning of what is known as the 'constitutional revolution'.[13] In the *Bank Mizrahi* judgment, the Supreme Court ruled that the limitation clause is in fact intended to limit the Knesset's powers as a legislative

---

majority of the members of the Knesset.' This section actually protects the Israeli electoral system with an 'entrenchment' rule, meaning that there must be at lest 61 affirmative votes out of 120 in order to amend the article.

[11] See the 'Limitation Clause' appearing in section 1 of the Canadian Charter of Rights and Freedoms. The final crystallisation of the Israeli limitation clause was influenced by the wording of section 29(2) of the Universal Declaration of Human Rights. In addition, see the limitation clause appearing in section 5 of the New Zealand Bill of Rights, 1990.

[12] Section 8 of the Basic Law: Human Dignity and Liberty. A similar provision appears in the Basic Law: Freedom of Occupation.

[13] *Mizrahi Bank*, above note 9. For elaboration on this see: Navot, above note 1, 42–48.

authority.[14] This judgment not only established the constitutional guidelines for judicial review of legislation, and the principle of a limited Knesset, but also declared the supremacy of Basic Laws.

The grounds for such a 'revolution' concerning the status of the Basic Laws lie within the theory of constitutional continuity. According to this approach, the Knesset's constituent authority was based on the creation of the State on 15 May 1948. The first norm of the positive Israeli law was the legal determination that the Provisional Council of State is the supreme legislative organ of the State. The Provisional Council of State dispersed and transferred its powers to the Constituent Assembly. The Constituent Assembly enacted the Transition Law, 1949, which transferred all of the powers of the Constituent Assembly to the First Knesset. This Knesset enacted the Second Knesset (Transition) Law, 1951, which provided that the Second Knesset, the Third Knesset, and all subsequent Knessets, would have all the powers, rights and duties which the First Knesset had. From this historic development, the Supreme Court inferred the principle of constitutional continuity, which ensured the transmission of 'all the powers', including the constituent power. Therefore the Knesset has possessed constituent authority since the First Knesset, meaning that whenever the Knesset passed a 'Basic Law', it was actually exercising its constituent power.[15] This understanding views the Knesset as being vested with two 'crowns': it is both the legislative power and the constituent power. Therefore, the Basic Laws have 'constitutional' status, that is they are at the apex of the normative pyramid. The norms enacted by the Knesset in its legislative capacity are regular laws, and hence subordinate to the norms established by the constituent power. The sovereignty of the Knesset is therefore limited by norms established by the Knesset itself, in its 'constituent' capacity.

Following the enactment of the Basic Laws and the *Bank Mizrahi* ruling, the State of Israel underwent a constitutional metamorphosis: From being a state based on the English model of parliamentary sovereignty, it became a constitutional state.

The constitutional revolution has had numerous repercussions, at the political and not just the legal level. The intervening years have been characterised by increasing awareness and internalisation on the part of the politicians, of the special status that attaches to the enactment of Basic Laws. Accepting the existence of the concept of judicial review of legislation, the Knesset committed itself to ensuring the compliance of all Knesset legislation with the provisions of the Basic Laws and to examining their constitutionality in accordance therewith. Judicial review has been conducted with circumspection and restraint, but even

---

[14] *Mizrahi Bank*, ibid. This judgement is one of the most significant constitutional judgments in the history of the State of Israel. The Supreme Court addressed the question of the validity of a law enacted by the Knesset which infringed one of the fundamental rights enumerated in the Basic Law, and which—as argued—did not satisfy the requirements of the limitation clause. The Court ruled that under these circumstances, irrespective of the majority by which it was passed, an infringing law could be declared void.

[15] For further discussion see C Klein, *Théorie et pratique du pouvoir constituent* (Paris: PUF, 1996).

so the Supreme Court has consistently ruled that there is statutory judicial review in Israel, and this ruling derives from the supremacy of the Basic Laws. To date, the Supreme Court has struck down about eight laws, or sections of laws, by reason of their violation of human rights anchored in the Basic Laws, and contrary to the provisions of the limitation clause prescribed therein.[16]

On the other hand, the Constitutional Revolution has not solved all of the problems pertaining to Basic Laws. For example, the issue of identifying a Basic Law in Israel: is it in accordance with the formal test of the addition of its title—'Basic Law'—or a substantive test (contents of constitutional substance)? In the *Bank Mizrahi* case, the Supreme Court held that the totality of provisions in the Basic Laws have 'constitutional' status, and thus enjoy normative supremacy over regular legislation. However, this holding is problematic because some of the arrangements in the Basic Laws are not constitutional in nature and do not express fundamental principles. Another question relates to the procedure for adopting a Basic Law. In other words, how does the constituent authority exercise its power? Is there a difference between Basic Laws that are formally entrenched by virtue of an entrenchment clause (such as Basic Law: The Government, and Basic Law: Freedom of Occupation), and Basic Laws that do not contain formal entrenchment clauses (such as Basic Law: Human Dignity and Liberty)? Moreover, what is the status of human rights that are not included in either of the two Basic Laws concerning human rights? These are just a few of the unresolved questions.

---

[16] HCJ 6055/95 *Tzemach v Minister of Defense*, 53(5) PD 241 (1999) in which the Court declared the invalidity of a section in the Military Justice Law, 1955, which allowed the detention of a solider for up to 96 hours before bringing him before a judge (see English translation at http://elyon1.court. gov.il/files_eng/95/550/060/I15/95060550.i15.htm); HCJ 1715/97 *Investment Managers Chamber in Israel v Minister of Finance*, 51(4) PD 367 (1997), which invalidated sections of the Management of Investments Law that violated the freedom of occupation of investment managers who had been engaged in the profession before the enactment of the law; HCJ 1030/99 *Oron v Knesset Speaker*, 56(3) 640 (2002), which invalidated sections of the Telecommunications Law; HCJ 8276/05 *Adalah v Minister of Defense* (not yet reported, 12 December 2006) invalidation of section 5(c) of the Civil Wrongs Law, which totally denied rights in torts against the State for reasons of security actions by the State; (see English translation at: HCJ 2605/05) *Human Rights Division v Minister of Finance* (see English translation at http://elyon1.court.gov.il/files_eng/05/050/026/n39/05026050.n39.pdf) where the Court invalidated Amendment 28 of the Prisons Ordinance that anchored the establishment of privately managed prisons in Israel; CrA 8823/07 *Anon v State of Israel* (not yet published, 11 February 2010) which invalidated a section in the Criminal Procedure Ordinance that related to extending a detainee's detention in an *ex parte* hearing. See also three judgments in which profound constitutional claims against laws were raised, but which were dismissed and the laws were upheld: HCJ 1661/05 *Gaza Coast Regional Council v Knesset*, 59(2) PD 481 (2005), which discussed the constitutionality of the Disengagement Law; HCJ 6427/02 *Movement for Quality of Government in Israel v Knesset* HCJ 6427/02 *Movement for Quality of Government in Israel v Knesset: Movement for Quality of Government in Israel* (not yet reported, 2006), which addressed the constitutionality of the Tal Law, that regulated the exemption of Yeshiva students from military service; and HCJ 7052/03 *Adalah v Minister of the Interior* (not yet reported, 14 May 2006) that dealt with the constitutionality of the Entry Into Israel Law (The Citizenship Law), that prohibited the entry into Israel of families of Israeli Arabs who live in Arab states (see English translation at http://elyon1.court.gov.il/files_eng/03/ 520/070/a47/03070520.a47.htm)

The Knesset, which was supposed to resolve these questions, has in fact totally discontinued the task of completing the constitution. In response to the constitutional revolution, the Knesset abandoned the entire constitutional enterprise. Since 1992, the Knesset has not adopted a single Basic Law, and numerous MKs as well as Israeli academics view the *Bank Mizrahi* case as a 'judge-made constitution', especially with respect to the authority for judicial review of Knesset legislation.

Following the constitutional revolution, the feeling was that henceforth any adoption and/or amendment of Basic Laws would require broad public agreement, and that the amendment of a Basic Law could not be a routine matter. For example, soon after Ehud Barak's government was introduced in 1999, the Knesset approved an amendment to the Basic Law: The new law nullified the limitation imposed on the number of ministers that may serve in the cabinet to allow the appointment of a larger number of ministers. Another constitutional amendment was introduced to Basic Law: The Government in 2001, just before the Special Elections for the Prime Minister, so as to enable Benjamin Netanyahu, who was not a Knesset Member at the time, to present his candidacy in those elections. Rubinstein and Medina wrote:

> [T]he public criticism of these amendments, which did not pertain to the substance of the arrangements, may reflect the crystallization of a public recognition—albeit not legal-formal—of the rigidity that should characterize Basic Laws. Quite possibly, this was an experience that will militate against frequent, changes in Basic Laws.

Reality, however, tells a different story. Not only was the process of enacting Basic Laws arrested, but the Knesset's overall conception of the role of the Basic Laws has also changed. Instead of continuing the enactment of a constitution, since 1992 the Knesset has passed a growing number of amendments to Basic Laws, sometimes for very specific needs and with relative ease. For example, Basic Law: The Knesset, was enacted in 1958, and until 1992—over 34 years—was amended 15 times, whereas from 1992 onwards—over 18 years—it has been amended 24 times; Basic Law: The President of the State, enacted in 1964, and until 1992, over 28 years, was amended twice; since 1992 and until today—over 18 years—it has been appended on five additional occasions.[17]

---

[17] Similarly, the amendments to the other, newer Basic Laws were all made after 1992. Basic Law: The Judiciary, which was enacted in 1984, was amended twice. Basic Law: Jerusalem Capital of Israel, enacted in 1980, was amended once. Basic Law: The State Comptroller, enacted in 1988, was amended twice. The other Basic Laws have not been amended to date, apart from Basic Law: The Government, which was replaced twice by a totally new Basic Law. The original Basic Law was enacted in 1968, and was amended 24 times over a period of 10 years until it was replaced in 1992 by a Basic Law that regulated the direct election of the Prime Minister. It was then amended 10 times over a period of nine years, until it was replaced in 2001 by the current Basic Law: The Government, which since its enactment has not been amended at all. For an empirical survey of the amendments of Basic Laws until 1992 see A Bendor, 'Defects in the Enactment of Basic Laws', (1994) 2 *Misphat Umimshal: Law and Government in Israel*, 443, 444–45.

The constitutional revolution in Israel did succeed in inculcating the concepts of judicial review of laws and of a Knesset with limited powers. Thus the Knesset is limited in its ability to violate protected human rights other than in accordance with the conditions of the limitation clause. On the other hand, as we will presently observe, the Knesset is almost unlimited in its ability to amend Basic Laws.

THE PROCEDURE FOR AMENDING A BASIC LAW

In the formal sense, the procedure for voting on a Basic Law is identical to that of a regular law, and the process of enacting Basic Laws does not require any special procedure. All of the Basic Laws were enacted in accordance with the procedure required for enacting regular laws, and most of them do not prescribe any special proceeding for their amendment or variation. The exceptions are Basic Law: The Knesset which, as mentioned, specifically limited the MKs ability to vary particular sections thereof,[18] and Basic Law: Freedom of Occupation, which includes an 'entrenchment clause' under which that Basic Law cannot be varied other than by a Basic Law passed by a majority of 61 MKs.[19]

Addressing this issue in the *Mizrahi* case, Supreme Court President Shamgar ruled that 'there is no need for a special majority of members of Knesset in order to vary a basic law, save if this is expressly required, as a precondition, in the Basic Law being amended'[20] and that 'it is now possible to apply a standard legislative criterion according to which a basic law can only be amended by another basic law'.[21]

In a similar vein, President Barak ruled in *Bank Mizrahi* that 'A Basic Law may not be changed except by another Basic Law'.[22] Insofar as the 'rigidity' [entrenchment] of Basic Laws is expressed in only a few of the Basic Laws, 'we may conclude that in the absence of a "rigidity" provision, a Basic Law may be amended by a basic law adopted by a regular majority'.[23] However, President Barak stressed that:

---

[18] Section 46 provides that a direct change (amendment) of sections 4, 44 and 45 must be done by way of a Basic Law adopted by a majority of 61 votes in three readings. Mention should also be made of section 9A, which states that the extension of the term of the Knesset must be anchored in a law passed by a majority of 80 members, although this particular section is not entrenched (so that in principle, the Knesset can change this law by a regular majority, and that the majority required for an extension of its term is smaller). Regarding this, see *Mizrahi Bank*, above note 10, at 274–75 (President Shamgar) and 407 (President Barak), and 544–45 (Justice Cheshin).

[19] Section 7 of Basic Law: Freedom of Occupation, *SH* 5754, No 1454, at 90 (from 1994). See also *Bank Mizrahi*, ibid, at 273–74 (President Shamgar) and 547 (Justice Cheshin).

[20] Basic Law: Freedom of Occupation, ibid, 321, para 64d.

[21] Ibid. See also in particular the emphasis regarding Basic Law: Freedom of Occupation. The structure of Basic Law: Freedom of Occupation (which is the appropriate constitutional structure that should be followed in all Basic Laws) prevents the possibility of an ordinary law changing or infringing on a right that was established in Basic Law: Freedom of Occupation ibid, 273, para 26 (b).

[22] Ibid, para 60.

[23] Ibid, 408 (President Barak, para 63).

'[T]he absence of entrenchment does not lower the status of the basic law to the level of regular law. A non-rigid basic law is still a basic law. It is not a 'regular' law and cannot be amended by regular legislation.[24]

This comment is significant for it means that, for the purposes of most of the Basic Laws, a constitutional amendment can be introduced by enacting a law through regular procedure, provided that the law enacted bears the title 'Basic Law'. A Basic Law may thus be amended or changed by virtue of the vote of some few Knesset members.

The ambiguity surrounding the various forms and levels of legislation stems from the absence of legislation that explicitly regulates the legislative process in Israel. To date, Israel still lacks a Basic Law: Legislation, draft proposals for such a law already from the 1970s notwithstanding. To clarify the nature of such an arrangement, I present below part of the most recent proposal, submitted in 2000:[25]

Legislative Procedures	3.(a)	A Basic Law will be adopted in three readings in the Knesset Plenum.
		A Basic Law will be adopted in its first reading in the Knesset Plenum by a majority of the votes of Knesset members who voted and abstainees shall not be taken into account.
		A Basic Law will be adopted in the second and third readings in the Knesset Plenum by the votes of at least 70 members of Knesset.
Annulment and Change of a Basic Law	4.	A Basic Law shall not be annulled or changed other than by a Basic Law.

The proposal requires a special legislative procedure, differing both from the currently prevailing procedure regarding regular legislation, and from that of the entrenched Basic Laws.[26] The requirement for a special or weighted majority in the second and third readings is an innovation, given that the accepted concept today is that an identical majority is required at all stages of the legislation of the same legislative item.

---

[24] Ibid.
[25] Draft Proposal: Basic Law: Legislature, *HH* 2830 (1990), 339.
[26] See Weill, 'Shouldn't We Seek the People's Consent? On the Nexus Between the Procedures of Adoption and Amendment of Israel's Constitution,' *Mishpat Umimshal*, Vol 10, No 2, 2007, (in Hebrew) 449, 460, 469 (hereinafter: 'Weill, Procedures of Amendment').

THE UNBEARABLE LIGHTNESS OF AMENDING BASIC LAWS

As noted above, over the past few years, there has been a tendency in Israel towards *ad casum* amendments of Basic Laws. These amendments are usually adopted against a background of political events that demand an immediate response on the part of the Knesset. The latter then chooses the path of constitutional—not regular—legislation, which is governed by a relatively smooth legislative passage procedure. These amendments are exceptional and may be of interest to comparative constitutionalists. In what follows I will present three examples of relatively recent constitutional amendments. The first one, concerning the disqualification of political parties, was adopted. The second one relates to the introduction of a biannual budget and is currently under advanced stages of legislation, and is also the subject of a currently pending petition with the Supreme Court. The third concerns the issue of a referendum, and is currently being debated at the Knesset.

The Disqualification of Political Parties

In Basic Law: The Knesset (enacted in 1958), Israel did not include any substantive limitation on participation in the Knesset elections. Section 6 of the Basic Law: The Knesset stipulates a number of 'technical' conditions that must be satisfied by any list of Knesset candidates wishing to run in the elections. Even so, despite the absence of substantive statutory grounds for the disqualification of a candidate's list, in 1965 the Supreme Court relied on the doctrine of 'self-defending democracy' to confirm the disqualification of a list of candidates that negated the existence of the State. The list included a number of candidates who were members of what had previously been the El-Ard Movement—an association dissolved and prohibited in view of its objectives and activities that undermined the existence of the State. The Central Elections Committee had the authority to disqualify a list if it failed to comply with the formal statutory requirements. It refused to approve the list on the grounds that it was an illegal association and its members negated the integrity and the very existence of the State of Israel. Factually, the decision to disqualify the list was based on past actions by its candidates, including membership in the El-Ard Movement.[27] In 1984, on the other hand, when an attempt was made to prevent the candidacy of a racist list in the elections, again without authority for disqualification, the Supreme Court refused to confirm the disqualification. In this case, the Supreme

---

[27] Prima facie, the Committee's decision was ultra vires, given that the law contained no provision for supervising the nature of the political opinions of a list. Consequently, an appeal was filed with the Supreme Court. The Supreme Court approved the disqualification of the list, based on the concept of a 'self-defending democracy'. For further reading see: Suzie Navot, 'Fighting Terrorism in the Political Arena: the Banning of Political Parties', 14 (2008) *Party Politics* 91, 93–94.

Court ruled that if the Knesset desired to enable the disqualification of parties based on the contents of their platform, it must explicitly say so through legislation.[28]

The Knesset was not indifferent to the Supreme Court's decision, and subsequently amended the Basic Law: The Knesset in 1985, and granted the Central Elections Committee the power to disqualify a party on three substantive grounds that were stipulated in the section.[29] The new section led to the disqualification of Meir Kahane's list,[30] in the 1988 Knesset elections and to the disqualification of parties with a similar platform in 1992.[31]

In 2002 however, against the background of political events in Israel and the conduct of MK Dr Azmi Bishara, the Knesset again decided to amend section 7A, and inter alia, to add a new grounds for disqualification, relating to support of an armed struggle against the State of Israel.[32] This amendment was addressed in a Supreme Court ruling on the candidacy of MK Bishara after his disqualification by the Central Elections Committee. This time, however, despite the wording of the amendment, the Supreme Court refused to disqualify his candidacy for the elections.[33]

The Knesset's response to the Supreme Court's ruling confirming MK Bishara's participation the elections was not long in coming. In 2008, the Knesset amended section 7A of Basic Law: The Knesset. Once again, the amendment was an attempt to deal with a political phenomenon, this time in the form of Arab Knesset members who had travelled to enemy states without permission. The new amendment to the Basic Law states that:

> [A] candidate who unlawfully stayed in an enemy state during the seven years that preceded the submission of the list of candidates shall be regarded as one whose acts constitute support for armed struggle by a hostile state or a terrorist organization against the State of Israel, for as long as not proved otherwise.[34]

According to a Knesset member, visits by Knesset members amounted to support for armed struggle:

---

[28] EA 2, 3/84 *Neiman v Chairman of Central Elections Committee for Eleventh Knesset*, 39(2) PD 225 (1984) (see English translation at http://elyon1.court.gov.il/verdictssearch/englishverdictssearch. aspx.)

[29] Basic Law: The Knesset (Amendment No 9), 5745–1985, SH 5745, No 1155. The new section 7A of the Basic Law: The Knesset provides as follows: 'A list of candidates shall not participate in Knesset elections if its objectives or actions, expressly or by implication, include one of the following: (1) Negation of the state of Israel as a state of the Jewish people. (2) Negation of the democratic character of the state. (3) Incitement to racism.'

[30] The party espoused a racist platform and the adoption of tough measures against Israel's Arab population, whom he wished to deport forcibly.

[31] See EA 1/88 *Neiman v Chairman of Central Elections Committee to Twelfth Knesset*, 42(4) PD 177 (1988); EA 2858/92 *Moshkovitz v Chairman of Elections Committee*, 46 (3) PD 541 (1992).

[32] Basic Law: The Knesset (Amendment No 33) 5762–2002, *SH* 5762–2002, No 1985: 'According to the amended section, a party which supports "armed struggle by a hostile state or a terrorist organization against Israel" will not be allowed to participate in the elections.'

[33] EA 11280/02 *Chairman of Elections Committee v Tibi*, 57(4)1 (2003).

[34] Basic Law: The Knesset (Amendment No 39), 5768–2008, *SH* 5768, No 2164.

My draft proposal was the result of the much-reported visit of former Knesset Member Azmi Bishara in Syria, including his overt meetings with the heads of *Hizballah*, and the heads of state—and the only explanation of such acts is support for armed struggle. We are ready for any political struggle within the Knesset, but the rules of the game should be very clear. They should allow no person among us to negate the existence of the State of Israel as a Jewish and democratic state; no person among us may incite to racism; and no person among us may support the armed struggle of an enemy state or a terrorist organization against the State of Israel.[35]

From a certain perspective, this amendment can be regarded as a 'law for bypassing the High Court of Justice' or as the Knesset's response to the Supreme Court's refusal to disqualify MK Bishara's candidacy for the Knesset elections, despite those visits.[36] Notably, Azmi Bishara is no longer an MK.[37]

As of autumn 2010, this is the most recent amendment to Basic Law: The Knesset, and it relates to a constitutional issue of the first degree, namely the right to vote and to be elected. It is a striking example of the *ad casum* legislation of the Knesset, which is particularly problematic where it concerns an essentially constitutional amendment.

A Temporary Basic Law

A question currently pending in the Supreme Court is whether a Basic Law can be altered temporarily, and if so, whether there can be an additional extension of a temporary provision. By way of clarification: Basic Law: The State Economy was amended by way of a new Basic Law that 'amends' Basic Law: The State Economy. Our concern is with the fact that the amending law was a temporary one. The temporary provision is yet to expire but as of autumn 2010 the Knesset was attempting to make an amendment that would extend it for a second time, in two years time. Our concern here is with the idea of implementing a biannual budget in Israel.

---

[35] See comments of MK Zevulun Orlev in the session for the first reading of the draft proposal; DK, 5768, 26 May 2008, at 82.

[36] See HCJ 2934/07 Israel *Law Center v Knesset Speaker* (not yet reported); *Tibi*, above note 33; HCJ 11225/03 11225/03 *MK Azmi Bishara v AG* [2003], 60 (4) PD 287(2006). See English translation at: http://elyon1.court.gov.il/files_eng/03/250/112/v08/03112250.v08.htm

See also the comments of MK Zevulun Orlev, ibid: 'Unfortunately, even though the Central Elections Committee disqualified MK Azmi Bishara's candidacy to the Knesset *inter alia* because of his unlawful visits to enemy states, the Supreme Court decided to overturn its decision, and to allow him [to submit his candidacy]. Finally however, reality has taught us that the Supreme Court erred. We therefore request that the Knesset clarify what exactly constitutes support for an enemy state: that it is not just an article, or a speech or whatever else, but also a visit. There can be no doubt that a visit to an enemy state, generally also involves meetings with the leaders of that state as a gesture of support, and naturally would also include a visit with the terrorist organizations located there. In view of all these we seek support [for the proposal].'

[37] He resigned from the Knesset while he was abroad, apparently having absconded from Israel and being wanted for interrogation on the suspicion of offences against State security.

Suzie Navot

In 1975, Basic Law: The State Economy was enacted.[38] Section 3 of the law states that the state budget shall be prescribed 'by law'. The Basic Law further states that the Government is obliged to 'place the annual budget bill on the table of the Knesset'. The budget laws are enacted annually in Israel, providing the legal basis for the annual state budget. In 2009 however, it was decided that the 2009 budget would be a biannual one by way of exception, and it was therefore decided to found the change in a Basic Law, which would also be a temporary provision.[39]

The explanatory note to the draft proposal states:

> In view of the crisis that has beset the world economy, which also has ramifications for the Israeli market ... [and] the need to confront the consequences of the crisis ... it is proposed to determine a special arrangement, in the framework of a temporary provision, that will apply to the State Budget of 2009 and 2010. This arrangement requires basic legislation.[40]

About one year after the enactment of this Basic Law, the government decided that a biannual budget had numerous advantages, and therefore proposed 'to undertake a comprehensive examination of introducing the system of a biannual budget, in the form of an additional attempt in the years 2011–2012, by extending the Basic Law so that it also apply to the budget for these years'.[41] The amendment is unique, given that it is an extension of a temporary provision, which by definition, is supposed to be 'temporary'.

This amendment is replete with constitutional problems. Originally, the government decided to pass the legislation for a temporary budget in the form of a Basic Law, which in essence is supposed to be permanent.[42] There is nothing to indicate that this amendment will become a chapter of the constitution, and it is unclear whether Basic Laws can even be enacted in that particular manner, or whether in principle it is possible to enact a Basic Law that is not designated to be part of the constitution. Furthermore, the constitutional principle is that the government must submit its budget on an annual basis. Governmental compliance with this principle provides the Knesset with one of its central tools of

---

[38] Basic Law: The State Economy, *SH* 5735, No 777, 206.
[39] Basic Law: The State Budget for 2009 and 2010 (Special Provisions) (Temporary Provision), 5769–2009, *SH* 5769, No 2196. It should be stressed that this 'Basic Law' is also unique in that it specifies the year of its enactment. According to President Barak, an identifying feature of a constitutional norm is the appearance of the title 'Basic Law' and the omission of the year of enactment from its title (making it 'above time'). On this, see *Mizrahi*, above note 9, at 403 (President Barak, para 55). Hence, this is an additional element that indicates the 'non-conformity' of the aforementioned budgetary legislation with the overall pattern of existing Basic Laws.
[40] Draft Proposal of Basic Law: The State Budget for 2009 and 2010 (Special Provisions) (Temporary Provision), 5769–2009, Government Draft Proposals 5769, No 424, at 280–81.
[41] Draft Proposal of Basic Law: The State Budget for 2009 and 2010 (Special Provisions) (Temporary Provision), 5770–2010, Government Draft Proposals 5770 No 498, 592.
[42] As this is being written, the amendment has yet to pass three readings, and a petition has been filed against it in the HCJ, contesting its constitutionality.

scrutiny of government in a parliamentary regime. As such, the question is whether this constitutional principle can be violated in the framework of a temporary provision in a Basic Law.

As of autumn 2010 all of these questions are currently pending a Supreme Court ruling in a petition that was filed by an MK who was previously the Minister of Finance.

Referendum—A Constitutional Issue?

Israel is a representative democracy in which the people choose their representatives in parliament. Israel does not have direct democracy, making it one of the only states that have yet to anchor the referendum as one of the institutions making up its constitutional framework.

Since the establishment of the State of Israel and until the 1980s, numerous motions were tabled at the Knesset for conducting referendums on controversial issues, but they were generally rejected before even crystallising into draft bills. Over the past few years, the discourse concerning referendums has primarily related to the question of ceding the occupied territories in Judaea and Samaria, and here too a number of proposals were made, most of which were rejected outright.

The importance of this topic for purposes of this chapter is that while many of the proposals would anchor the referendum in a law related to Basic legislation, recent Knesset debates pertaining to the referendum issue have addressed it within the framework of a 'regular law' and not a Basic Law—in view of the Knesset's reticence regarding the enactment of Basic legislation.[43]

A referendum has advantages and disadvantages, but it would seem beyond dispute that its introduction into the Israeli system represents a change in our constitutional regime, and a change of that magnitude should be introduced by way of a Basic Law, and not through regular legislation. This was the Knesset's clear intention when in 1999 it enacted the Law and Administration Act (Annulment of the Application of Law, Jurisdiction and Administration), more commonly known as the 'Golan Law'. This law determines that a government decision on the ceding of territories governed by Israeli Law (such as the Golan Heights) must be confirmed both by a majority of Knesset members and by a referendum,

---

[43] The Knesset intended to enact a Basic Law for a referendum. See eg, Draft Proposal: Basic Law: Referendum, 5760–2000, *HH* 2872, 378; Draft Proposal: Basic Law: Referendum, 5766–2006, P/17/698; Draft Proposal: Basic Law: Referendum, 5764–2004 P/2348; Draft Proposal: Basic Law: Referendum, 5760–1999, P/932; Draft Proposal: Basic Law: Referendum, 5762–2002, P/377.8.

which would be regulated within the framework of a Basic Law.[44] Hence, already back in 1999 the Knesset was aware that the introduction of a referendum mechanism to the Israeli system required the enactment of a Basic Law.

The Basic Laws in Israel establish, inter alia, the principles of the regime, and regulate the powers of the branches of government. Thus it would seem indisputable that a change in the principles of the system should be done by way of Basic Laws. This is a substantive, and not a technical, matter. Indeed, the accepted norm all over the world is that the subject of referendums is regulated in the framework of a constitution, and not by way of regular legislation. It should similarly be the norm in Israel—in a Basic Law and not in a regular law.

Due to the failure to pass a Basic Law, as some political parties refuse to vote for new Basic Laws, the Knesset has enacted on the Law on referendum by way of a 'regular law', on November 2010. The question is whether it will survive High Court of Justice review, given that the Supreme Court currently regards the Basic Laws as the constitutional anchors of the State. According to this perspective, certain changes can 'only' be introduced by way of a Basic Law. Constitutional changes are not made by the 'legislative authority' but rather by the 'constituent authority'.

Like the preceding question of the biannual budget, this too is a question of Israeli constitutional law. The Knesset's decision to enact the issue of a referendum in the framework of regular legislation attests, above all, to its refusal to assimilate the principles of the constitutional revolution. The question is still pending and the position of the Supreme Court remains to be seen. Conceivably, we might see the emergence of new grounds for striking down a law: a regular law could be deemed unconstitutional purely because it ought to have been enacted specifically as a Basic Law. I dare say that the future of the entire constitutional revolution is contingent upon that kind of explicit pronouncement.

CONCLUSION

Summing up this complex matter, it may be said that Israel has a formal constitution—albeit neither complete nor perfect—but a constitution nonetheless, and its chapters—the Basic Laws—cover a large part of the substantive issues that formal constitutions cover in other democracies. This formal conclusion is

---

[44] Due to its importance I present the main components of the law: 2. A decision of the government under which the law, jurisdiction, and administration of the State of Israel shall no longer apply to a territory requires the confirmation of the Knesset in a decision adopted by a majority of its members.

3. A decision of the government, having been confirmed by the Knesset pursuant to section 2, shall also require confirmation in a national referendum, by a majority of the valid votes of the participants in the national referendum.

4. Section 3 shall go into force on the day of the commencement of a Basic Law that shall regulate the conducting of a national referendum.

partial, and even 'disabled' to a degree, but this 'constitution' provides full protection to the most important human rights and boasts excellent and effective judicial review.

Israel is distinguished from other Western democracies by the absence of a national consensus regarding certain fundamental issues, and the absence of a distinct and exclusive procedure for enacting constitutional arrangements. Political debates notwithstanding, there seems to be agreement on the need to complete the task of forming a constitution. Debates continue concerning the identity of the body authorised to interpret the constitution and to exercise judicial review of Knesset legislation. Will it be the Supreme Court, as per the current situation, or will it be a special Constitutional Court? This is an important question, but even more important is the shared awareness of all the political parties of the need for agreement regarding the rules of the game. Nevertheless, for as long as the fundamental political issues are unresolved, it will be difficult to complete the final stage of the constitutional enterprise: the completion of the Basic Laws, and their unification into a complete constitution.

10

Italy

CARLO FUSARO

INTRODUCTION

T HE 1948 CONSTITUTION OF the Republic of Italy is the first to have
been voted on by a representative, directly elected body (*Assemblea
costituente*). Previously the country, born in 1861, had inherited the 1848
Statute of Charles Albert King of Sardinia, the small Alpine kingdom nestled on
both sides of the mountains between Italy and France,[1] which unified the nation
thanks to the favourable international context and the abilities of bold and
ambitious rulers.

The Statute was a typical early nineteenth century *octroié* (conceded by the
Sovereign) constitution, granted by the Crown, pressured by the 1848 uprisings
that nearly swept away the political regimes established in Europe after Waterloo
and the Congress of Vienna. It laid down the basic rules of a constitutional
monarchy; it included a limited Bill of Rights; established a strongly centralised
administration; and it was flexible in the sense that there was no instrument to
prevent an ordinary law passed by Parliament from infringing or violating it.
However, its Preamble stated that it could not be repealed. Its provisions were
mostly not directly effective.

The absence of entrenchment is relevant for our topic. In fact, the formal
introduction after 1925 of a systematic set of provisions designed to establish a
Fascist regime was made easier by the fact that there was no need to revise or
amend the conflicting norms of the 1848 Statute, which were simply set aside.
This prompted the first studies intended to explain the conflicts between the new
Fascist institutions and the Statute, between the constitutional roles of political
parties and of the Fascist regime based upon a single-party system, and more
broadly to explain the often blurred boundary between law and politics.[2]

---

[1] In spite of its name the Kingdom included Savoy, Nice, Piedmont, Liguria and Sardinia.

[2] In the late 1930s Vezio Crisafulli and Costantino Mortati (future members of the Constitutional
Court) laid the basis of their influential theories. According to Crisafulli, in contemporary times the
separation of powers was superseded by the co-ordination and submission of them to a single

By contrast, the 1948 Constitution is the product of a representative process. It is a well-tailored example of post World War II constitutionalism. Influenced but not dictated by the Allied nations, it includes a detailed Bill of Rights; it is rigid; it provides for constitutional review of legislation; it lays down the framework for a decentralised institutional system; it establishes the strongest guarantees of the independence of the judiciary that any constitution provides for; and it ensures an original combination of representative and direct democracy, inclusive of grass-roots initiated referendums.

The establishment of a new constitutional order based upon a new written constitutional text can hardly ever result in the immediate implementation of all of its provisions: immediate and direct effect may be granted to many of them (and in the Italian case it has been), but for some it may simply be impossible, given that no constitutional text can regulate its implementation in detail.

A few examples illustrate the Italian experience on this point. The Italian Senate used to be a body nominated by the Crown. It became a directly elected body under article 57 Italian Constitution (It Const): without a new electoral law, it would have been impossible to create it (the law was passed in February 1948). The 1948 Constitution established a new Superior Council of the Judiciary (article 104 It Const), but the introduction of the rules according to which its members would be appointed or elected had to be deferred to an Act of Parliament (the law passed in 1958). The same applied to the articles laying down the constitutional framework for the Regions, subnational entities with law making power which had not previously existed: their establishment had also to be deferred to an Act of Parliament (the law was passed in 1968 only). In the case of the new Constitutional Court the text of the Constitution expressly postponed the implementation of its provisions to a subsequent Constitutional Act to be passed by Parliament in due course (this particular law was passed in 1953).[3] In other words the Constitution could not possibly be *entirely* self-executing or directly effective.

Italian scholars have since developed the concept of a 'constitutional matter', which includes all those legal provisions which are not part of the Constitution itself, and which do not have the legal status of constitutional law, but are 'constitutional in substance' insofar as they necessarily and directly implement parts of the Constitution which could not be applied in their absence. Electoral laws are the most frequently mentioned examples of such 'constitutional matters'

---

unifying goal, as pursued by the ruling party. According to Mortati, the true legal base of any constitution ought to be searched for in its societal base or rather in the social, economical and political groups which share the values which the formal arrangements are based upon (the *substantial constitution* or *costituzione in senso materiale*). See V Crisafulli, *Alcune considerazioni sulla teoria degli organi dello Stato* (Modena: Società tipografica modenese, 1938); C Mortati, *La costituzione in senso materiale* (Milano: Giuffrè, 1939).

[3] For example, see art 137.1 It Const: 'a constitutional act shall establish the conditions, forms and terms for bringing a case concerning the constitutional legitimacy of a law'. For an updated text of the Italian Constitution in English, see http://www.servat.unibe.ch/icl/it00000_.html.

(although the Constitution does not use that term or refer to them at all). The Standing Orders of each Chamber are another example (see article 64 It Const).[4]

The Italian legal system belongs to the family of civil law jurisdictions such as France and Germany: Italian sources of law are all hierarchically ordered; the (textual) Constitution of 1948 is supreme, at the top of the hierarchy; the general principle is that higher sources trump and cannot be trumped by lower sources of law. For example, regulations issued by the government (with the important exceptions of delegated legislation, article 76 It Const, and law-decrees, article 77 It Const) cannot amend a statute or contain a provision which contradicts a statute (that is an Act of Parliament or an Act of one of the Regional legislative bodies). All laws must be consistent with all of the provisions entrenched in the Constitution (which is a systematic text) and with the provisions of any other 'Constitutional Act' referred to in article 138 It Const. Constitutional Acts are statutes passed according to the special procedure laid down in article 138 It Const for amending the Constitution: their provisions do not amend the Constitution as such, but they complete it or implement provisions included in it.[5]

Italian constitutional law provisions are protected by a partially centralised system of judicial review of legislation. The body in charge of ensuring the enforcement of constitutional provisions is the Constitutional Court, which has the power to establish whether a legislative provision does or does not infringe the Constitution. If and when the Constitutional Court establishes that a provision of law infringes the Constitution, it declares it null and void from the day of publication of the Court's decision.

AMENDING THE ITALIAN CONSTITUTION: THE RULES AND THEIR INTERPRETATION (ARTICLE 138)

Article 138 establishes the procedure to be followed in order to introduce any kind of modification to the text of the 1948 Constitution or to introduce a new Constitutional Act. There is no differentiation between an 'amendment' to the Constitution and a 'revision' of the Constitution, nor even a so-called total revision (compare for example, articles 167 and 168 Constitution of Spain which provide for two different procedures for 'ordinary' and 'total' or 'comprehensive'

---

[4] The words 'materia costituzionale' had already been used in the Legislative Decree 16 March 1946, n 98 which granted temporary legislative powers to the Government, but reserved the legislative power on 'la materia costituzionale', on electoral laws and on the ratification of treaties to the Constituent Assembly to be elected on 2 June 1946. The Constitution, however, determines the features of the right to vote (freedom, secrecy, in person, direct, see art 48 It Const).

[5] For example, art 132 establishes that new Regions might be formed by Parliament passing a specific Constitutional Act; see also art 137 quoted in note 3 above.

revisions of the Constitution): unlike other jurisdictions, the Italian Constitution does not provide for different degrees of rigidity of its provisions.[6]

Article 138 establishes that in order to pass a Constitutional Act, each of the two Chambers of the Italian Parliament must vote in favour of the same text twice; the second vote cannot take place earlier than three months after the first one; a reinforced majority is required (no less than 50 per cent of members of each Chamber plus one, regardless of the number of those taking part in the vote). Within three months from the second vote, one fifth of the members of each Chamber, 500,000 voters or at least five Regional Legislative Assemblies, can request a referendum on the Constitutional Act voted by Parliament. The Act is deemed passed if a majority of those who vote approve it. However, if the Act has been approved in the second vote by a majority of two-thirds of the members of each House, no referendum can be requested, and the Constitutional Act enters into force.[7]

The main issues related to the application of article 138 concern the limits of content which may restrain constitutional amendments: article 139 provides for the only explicit limit to be found in the 1948 Constitution. It states that 'the republican form of the State may not be changed by way of constitutional amendment'. This provision was introduced as a 'natural' complement to the 2 June 1946 referendum which had abolished the monarchy (that same day, Italian voters, men and—for the first time—women, elected the Constituent Assembly). However, soon after the coming into force of the Constitution in January 1948, this provision began to be interpreted in an expansive and, it was said, 'system-atic' way (*interpretazione sistematica*), that is to say in relation to articles 1 and 2 of the Constitution. This meant that the 'republican form of the state' ought not to be taken to refer to the representative instead of hereditary selection of the head of state (the President) only, but should be taken to refer more broadly to a jurisdiction featuring the basic elements of democracy (article 1: 'sovereignty belongs to the people') and of the protection of human rights (article 2: 'the Republic recognizes and guarantees the inviolable rights of man'). The so-called *theory of implied limits* (the opposite to *express limits*) was quickly and widely accepted even by the Constitutional Court itself. Of course, this has brought about an ongoing debate concerning the extent of these implied limits, with both scholars and politicians ready to include the constitutional features of their choice.[8]

---

[6] Many recent Constitutions distinguish 'ordinary' amendments from other more extensive revisions of the Constitution: they therefore introduce a 'differentiated rigidity' within the text of the Constitution. They select articles or parts of the text which can be amended only by a more burdensome procedure. The aim is to legalise and at the same time restrain regime changes.

[7] Whether they amend, implement or complete the Constitution, all constitutional acts belong to the same category of sources of law, see A Pizzorusso, Art 138, 'Commentario della Costituzione' in *Garanzie costituzionali*, (Bologna-Roma: Zanichelli-Foro italiano, 1981) 714.

[8] Among the scholars who interpret this limit extensively, see A Pace, *La Costituzione non è una legge qualsiasi* (http://www.costituzionalismo.it, 31 March 2004); A Pizzorusso, *Postfazione* in *Leggi*

It must be added that, following a well established doctrine,[9] the Constitutional Court has asserted its competence to evaluate the constitutional legitimacy of the provisions of Constitutional Acts amending the Constitution. In one decision the Court referred to the *principi supremi della Costituzione* (the 'supreme principles of the Constitution'), as those which no Constitutional Act, however respectful of the procedures laid down by article 138, could legitimately jeopardise.[10]

A further limit to any change to the Italian Constitution can be derived from European Law: I refer to the jurisprudence of the European Court of Justice and to those provisions of the present treaties which mention the 'constitutional traditions common to the Member States'.[11] This is also more of a substantial limit (a limit of content) than a strictly formal one, because Italy could leave the Union and later change its Constitution, introducing norms contrary to those traditions: but aside from the fact that in that case it should also leave other international organisations starting with the European Convention for the Protection of Human Rights, it is clear that this is more a virtual possibility than something close to reality.

Another implied limit to the content of constitutional amendments would involve article 138 itself. According to this way of thinking, all the provisions of the Constitution could be amended except for those relating to the directly or indirectly representative head of state and the provisions regulating the adoption of Constitutional Acts, mentioned earlier. Other scholars believe that article 138 could be amended, but never to the point of abolishing the procedural distinctions between the ordinary legislative process and the constitutional legislative

---

costituzionali e di revisione costituzionale (1994–2005) (Bologna-Roma, Zanichelli-Foro italiano, 2006). Other authors stress the risks of selective rigidity, see G Volpe, *Revisioni della Costituzione e leggi costituzionali. Art 139*, 'Commentario della Costituzione' (Bologna-Roma: Zanichelli-Foro italiano, 1981) 745.

[9] Based upon the difference between the power to establish a new constitution and the power to amend an existing one, many authors share the view that the main features of the existing jurisdiction could not be legally changed, even following the procedures laid down by art 138 Const. See A Pizzorusso, Art 138, in 'Commentario della Costituzione' in *Garanzie costituzionali*, (Bologna-Roma: Zanichelli-Foro italiano, 1981) 721–24; A Pace, *Potere costituente, rigidità costituzionale, auto vincoli legislativi*, 2nd edn, (Padova: Cedam, 2002) who specifically stresses the difference between *pouvoir constituant* and *pouvoir constitué*.

[10] According to its decision 1146/1988, 'the Italian Constitution includes a set of supreme principles which cannot be subverted or modified in their essential content even by a constitutional law revising the text of the Constitution . . . Such are those principles which the Constitution itself established as absolute limits to the power of amending the Constitution, such as the republican form of the State (art 139 Const), as well as those principles which albeit not listed among those which cannot be revised, do still pertain to the very essence of the supreme values on which the Constitution is based.'

[11] See Article 6 para 2 of the Treaty on European Union (TEU): 'the Union shall respect fundamental rights, as guaranteed by the European Convention for the Protection of Human Rights and Fundamental Freedoms . . . and *as they result from the constitutional traditions common to the Member States, as general principles of Community law*'. The latest consolidate version of TEU in the *Official Journal of the European Union*, C 83, vol 53, 30 March 2010, 1.

process. In other words, Parliament could establish a different way of applying the principle of rigidity, but would not be allowed to turn the Italian Constitution into a flexible one.

The debate concerning the limits to Constitutional Acts amending the Constitution is a very political one: those scholars or politicians who do not agree with the proposals for constitutional reform show a tendency to invest their stand with the force of constitutional legitimacy by saying that some of those proposals are not just unsuitable or wholly wrong, but they would be inconsistent with the basic principles of the Constitution (as they interpret them, of course) and therefore both illegitimate and illegal.

Other scholars claim that as article 138 does not provide for a specific procedure for *total* revisions, comprehensive or broad if not total revisions of the Constitution would also be illegitimate as such (the Constitution, they assume, is rigid to the point that it would only allow for *limited* amendments *on particular points*).[12] In fact, this theory is based upon an expansion of the doctrinal assertion according to which there is a legally enforceable distinction between the power simply to change the Constitution (in the sense of amending it: *a constitutional provision amending power*) and the power to establish a new Constitution (*a constituent power* or *pouvoir constituant* in the words of those nineteenth century constitutional lawyers who emphasised this difference, starting with Abbé Sieyès[13]). According to the latter, the *constituent power* as defined above was utilised in 1947: thereafter only minor changes are to be deemed legal. Therefore it would not be legal to 'transform' the Constitution in a significant way. This way of thinking raises another issue: how can we distinguish minor from major changes, changes which respect the basic structure of the constitutional arrangements of 1948 and changes which would transform them and make out of the Italian Constitution a different constitution, *another* constitution (possibly the Constitution of a *Second Republic*)? Would it be deemed legal to abolish one of the two Chambers? Would it be legal to make Italy a truly federal jurisdiction? Would it be legal to turn Italy from a parliamentary into a presidential regime?

Another debate relates to the referendum provided for by article 138.2 It Const (when a Constitutional Act has not been passed with a two-thirds majority). Some scholars question whether Parliament is entitled to pass a single Act including a large number of amendments affecting a variety of constitutional bodies and institutions (for example, the Second Chamber and the relations between Government and Parliament, the judiciary, the Constitutional Court and State-Regions relations); they say there ought to be a specific Act for each item in

---

[12] See A Pace *L'incostituzionalità della costituzione di Berlusconi* (Roma, Astrid, http://www.astrid-online.it, 12 June 2006): this theory has been forcefully asserted to criticise the centre-right attempt to revise Part II of the Constitution in 2005.

[13] Emmanuel Joseph Sieyès, see *Oeuvres de Sieyès*, (Paris: EHIS, 1989). For a recent opinion, see Pace, note 9 above.

order to allow more referendums, one on each specific amendment or a coordinated set of amendments (they claim voters should be allowed to approve or
disapprove each one separately). This not being the case, they suggest that the
Constitutional Court should intervene and split the Constitutional Act in order
to allow more referendums. Those opposing this theory claim that there is not
one word in the Constitution providing for anything of the kind; furthermore a
Constitution cannot be conceived as a patchwork, so it is rational that one single
Act is submitted to the voters for approval once Parliament has passed it.

Others have linked together the two main parts of the Italian Constitution, on
the assumption that any major change of the second part could infringe the
implementation of the first part.[14] In fact, the 1948 Constitution includes a set of
Fundamental Principles (articles 1 to 12): Part I establishes the Rights and Duties
of Citizens (articles 13 to 54); Part II regulates the Organisation of the Republic
(articles 55 to 139). According to this point of view, values and principles
embedded in Part I (extensively interpreted) would strictly limit the possibility of
amending provisions included in Part II. For instance, the parliamentary regime
as regulated by articles 92 to 96 It Const could not be amended in a way that
would establish a different kind of regime (for instance, a presidential one) or
even a different model of parliamentary regime (with the identity of the Prime
Minister directly resulting from the general elections): the roles of political
parties, of Parliament and of the President of the Republic would be imperilled,
in violation of the principles and values affirmed by the first 54 articles of the
Constitution.

Along a similar line of thinking, the special procedure for amending the
Constitution established by article 138 is regarded as being so closely linked to
proportional representation that it does not allow for any other kind of electoral
system. In spite of the evidence that the Constituent Assembly (1946–48)
explicitly rejected all proposals for the inclusion of provisions concerning the
electoral system in the text of the Constitution, some scholars and some commentators think that proportional representation is to be assumed as *implied* by
all those provisions of the Constitution which request a higher parliamentary
majority. The conclusion is that any Constitutional Act passed by a majority of
the members of each Chamber only should be regarded as substantively unconstitutional as long as the Italian electoral system grants a majority of parliamentary seats to the party or coalition which wins (whichever percentage of votes it
obtains, possibly (and de facto often) in alteration of the proportional share of
votes).

---

[14] See G Zagrebelsky, *L'unità della Costituzione: le riforme e la revisione dell'articolo 138* (2007),
available at http://www.astrid-online.it/Dossier–r/Documenti-/ZAGREBELSKY_08_10_07.pdf.

FROM THEORY TO PRACTICE: HOW THE ITALIAN CONSTITUTION HAS BEEN FORMALLY AMENDED IN THE LAST SIXTY YEARS (1948–2007)

The 1948 Constitution has been directly amended 14 times as of 2010. Altogether, 32 out of 139 articles have been modified, some of them more than once; five have been repealed.[15]

Of the first 54 articles (*Fundamental Principles, Rights and Duties of Citizens*) only three have been amended.[16] If we set aside the three Constitutional Acts of the1960s, all amendments have been introduced since 1989. With the sole exception of the thorough revision of the Fifth Title of Part II of the Constitution in 1999 and 2001[17] (Articles 114 to 133, concerning the relations between the central government and the local and regional authorities, their powers and attributions), all amendments have been on specific points.[18]

In spite of the text of article 138 It Const, up to 1970 a constitutional amendment needed a two-thirds majority of the members of each Chamber in order to be passed: the Referendum Act implementing articles 75, 132 and 138 of the Constitution had not yet been passed (as a consequence, no referendum could be requested and article 138 was interpreted unanimously as requesting the super-majority as provided for in its paragraph 3). So one can say that, by failing to implement the referendum requirements, the constitutional text of 1948 was surreptitiously allowed to be more rigid than had been intended for over 20 years.[19]

Later, most Constitutional Acts were still passed with a very large majority. A referendum was requested only twice: in 2001, in relation to the quasi-federal reform of Title V and in 2006, in relation to a major reform passed by the centre-right majority in 2005. The first was approved by a large majority but with a very low voter turnout (consensus was almost unanimous); the latter was rejected with a relatively high turnout.[20]

---

[15] The Italian Constitution now contains 134 articles.

[16] Art 27 (to ban the death penalty even in case of war); Art 48 (to allow distance voting); Art 51 (to allow gender quotas).

[17] See Constitutional Act 22 November 1999, n 1 and Constitutional Act 18 October 2001, n 3.

[18] See the three Constitutional Acts of 1963 and 1967 (reduction of the Senate's term from six to five years; fixed number of deputies and senators; establishment of the Molise Region; reduction of the term of office of the judges of the Constitutional court, from 12 to nine years); and the other nine Acts: those which gave to ordinary Courts jurisdiction in the prosecution of crimes committed by members of the Cabinet while in office (Arts 96, 134 and 135); specified the powers of the President of the Republic during the last six months in office (Art 88); established a higher quorum for passing a law to grant a general amnesty (Art 79); abolished the authorisation by each Chamber to the judiciary as a pre-requisite to the prosecution of one of its members (Art 68); re-defined the rules of fair trial in respect of the European Convention for the Protection of Human Rights (Art 111); fixed the number of MPs to be elected by expatriate Italians (Art 56 and Art 57).

[19] The law regulating referendums is Act 25 May 1970, n 352.

[20] In 2001 the turnout had been 34% with 64.2% in favour; in 2006 the turnout had been 53% with 61.3% against.

If one looks at the context in which the 14 amendments have been passed, one can observe how they have been influenced by powerful changes in public opinion, which forced the parties in Parliament to approve some constitutional adjustment. Between 1989 and 1993, three successful amendments out of four were in answer to widespread criticism of the grip that political parties (including both majority and opposition parties) had on the political institutions. To submit the members of the Cabinet to the jurisdiction of the ordinary courts (article 96), to allow public prosecutors to proceed against a Member of Parliament without the need to obtain authorisation (article 68), to make amnesty as such nearly impossible (article 79): these were all measures passed within the frame of the trend against the overwhelming power of parties' elites, against the illegal financing of their operations and the lethal mixture of corruption, inefficiency and lack of responsiveness of the political class.[21]

Several years later when the new political arrangements (new electoral laws, new party system, new local and regional governments) had started to stabilise, a set of further amendments was passed, all but two on a consensual base. It was a set of limited reforms (see note 18). The only exception was the reform of Title Five of Part II, designed to push Italy towards a form of quasi-federalism (*riforma del titolo V*).

It should also be stressed that ever since the project of modernising the Italian Constitution became broadly accepted (although with no agreement on specific solutions), that is to say since 1983 when the first of three bicameral parliamentary commissions was established, only once was the Cabinet the initiator (in the case of the Constitutional Act passed by Parliament in 2005 but rejected by the subsequent 2006 referendum). In all other instances it was a matter of bills introduced by Members of Parliament: for decades there has been a political convention in Italy according to which constitutional matters should be regulated by bipartisan initiatives and through consensual decision making processes only.[22] A mantra of Italian politics was and in part still is: *le riforme costituzionali si fanno tutti insieme* ('constitutional reforms must be worked out and approved by all'). This approach does indeed make sense: it prevents the risk that every new majority may feel entitled to adapt the Constitution to its own manifesto. On the other hand it has recognised a de facto veto power on the part of each of the many parties which populate Italian politics. It is not surprising then, that all attempts to revise the text of the 1948 Constitution in full, or at least to revise its second part, have inexorably failed.

This is in spite of the shortcuts towards a comprehensive revision of the 1948 text which have been taken, introducing extraordinary (ad hoc) amending

---

[21] Those were the years of the so-called *Clean Hands* investigations and of popular referendums against strictly proportional electoral laws: both contributed to changing the Italian party system.

[22] In 1984 the first bicameral Parliamentary Committee on Institutional Reforms formally refused to hear what the President of the Council of Ministers of the time intended to say in relation to the project to revise the Constitution.

procedures: in 1993 and in 1997, Parliament passed two Acts for this purpose, providing for special procedures designed to make a comprehensive revision of the Constitution of 1948 finally possible. These attempts also failed and seem to have been abandoned in recent years, but it is still worth paying some attention to them as they directly deal with our main topic—how constitutional change occurs, or—in this case—could have occurred.

In 1993 and in 1997 two Constitutional Acts were approved with the required two-thirds super-majority establishing ad hoc procedures to pass a 'systematic' revision of Part II of the Constitution (with the exceptions of article 138 and article 139, and of the entire Part I of the 1948 text) (1993); and to approve a project of revision of (again) Part II only (without additional limits) (1997).[23] For our purposes the details are not relevant: what matters is that in both instances Parliament's intention was to reduce the risk of filibustering, to set a procedure designed to produce an outcome within a reasonable time span, to avoid secret voting (which secures compliance with party decisions) and to ensure that a referendum would have to be called in all instances on the whole (obviously bargained) project. These two extraordinary procedures, which technically deserve the definition of *constitutional rupture*,[24] both implicitly enhanced the role of the voters, transforming the referendum from optional to mandatory, in accordance with the shift towards a direct, citizen based majoritarian form of government.[25]

Neither of the two Constitutional Acts was implemented to the point that a text was adopted by the two Chambers and a referendum called. The attempt to revise the Constitution was abandoned, the Chambers were dissolved and an election called, thus bringing to an end the two ad hoc procedures.

Later on (2005–2006), another attempt at a systematic revision of Part II of the Constitution, this time in strict application of article 138 as it is, also failed. On this occasion, the centre-right majority by itself had approved a text amending about half of the articles of Part II with the required majority: however voters' signatures were collected and the following referendum saw the 'nays' prevail largely (see note 20). The revision had been heavily criticised by most scholars and opinion makers and did not find many defenders, especially after the general elections had been won by the centre-left coalition.

---

[23] See Constitutional Act 6 August 1993, n 1 and Constitutional Act 24 January 1997, n 1.
[24] Because in ad hoc breach of ordinary procedure of Art 138.
[25] See S Bartole, *Interpretazioni e trasformazioni della Costituzione repubblicana* (Bologna: Mulino, 2004) 432.

FROM THEORY TO PRACTICE: HOW ITALIAN CONSTITUTIONAL
ARRANGEMENTS HAVE CHANGED SHORT OF FORMAL AMENDMENTS TO THE
TEXT OF THE 1948 CONSTITUTION

Italian constitutional arrangements have also changed in these 60 years in a variety of ways short of the formal amendments which have been outlined in the previous part of this chapter.

I mentioned previously that the founding fathers themselves expected the Constitution to be implemented step by step in the years to come. However they could not imagine that this might take so long. In fact four months after the entry into force of the Constitution (on 1 January 1948), the Christian Democrats (DC) and their allies won a resounding victory over the Communist and Socialist parties' alliance, which was to shape the Italian party system for the next 45 years. As a consequence, the Socialists were ousted from all coalitions until the 1960s and the Communists until after the fall of the Berlin Wall. The DC and the other centre parties adopted a strategy of slow-moving implementation of the Constitution: the most convenient way to run the country with fewer checks and balances.[26] In short, the Constitutional Court was not established and convened until June 1956; the Superior Council of the Judiciary was not elected and convened until the end of 1958; the Referendum Act was passed only in 1970, and in the same year the first regional elections were called. The same can be said about other constitutional provisions: for instance article 95.3 It Const, which refers to a later law to establish the regulations concerning the functioning of the Presidency of the Council and fix the numbers, responsibilities and organisation of the ministries was only implemented in 1988 and 1999. It can therefore be said that this long process of implementation of the 1948 provisions of the Italian Constitution has indirectly given rise to the continuous transformation of the de facto Constitution, bound to change significantly as each major step has been taken towards its application.

In other cases constitutional provisions have simply been set aside and seem to have fallen into obsolescence: a most striking example is article 39 It Const which would allow registered trade unions to sign contracts binding on all workers and companies in a specific sector. It was never implemented and no one even mentions it any more. Another example is found in article 102.2 and 103 It Const which established that 'no extraordinary or special judge shall be established' aside from the administrative tribunals, the Court of Accounts and the military tribunals, and the Sixth 'Final Provision' which establishes that all other tribunals shall be dismantled within five years from the entry into force of the Constitution: these provisions have also never been implemented and they have been

---

[26] An author defined the 1948 elections as the 'authentic interpretation' of the Constitution, see A Di Giovine, 'Democrazia e diritto' in *Dall'approvazione all'attuazione della carta costituzionale: l'ineluttabile dilazione*, no 4, vol 26, 43.

interpreted in a way that even today, special Fiscal Commissions (*commissioni tributarie*), not truly independent, judge fiscal disputes between citizens and tax authorities.

Apart from the laws and constitutional laws implementing the original provisions of the Constitution, there have been several statutes which have significantly enhanced and articulated one or another constitutional provision: they can be regarded as substantive additions to the Constitution. They would deserve the name of 'landmark statutes' given by Bruce Ackerman to similarly influential Acts in the United States.[27]

In the case of Italy I would mention: (i) the 1970 law designed to enforce factory workers' rights (*Statuto dei lavoratori*), which protected both individual workers and the trade unions, changing labour relations forever;[28] (ii) the numerous Acts which, starting with the antitrust legislation of 1990, have introduced an entire set of independent regulatory commissions (or authorities) with a spectacular shift of powers from the ordinary central administration under the control of the Cabinet to relatively autonomous bodies in possession of significant powers, in the absence of any constitutional provision;[29] (iii) electoral laws, including those that regulate political campaigns and the private and public financing of the activities of political parties, along with the reimbursement of election year costs; in particular the Chamber Electoral Law which since 2005 includes a kind of de facto election of the President of the Council;[30] the same law grants 55 per cent of the seats to the winning party or coalition;[31] (iv) the 1988 law which regulates the internal activity of the Cabinet;[32] (v) the laws that have introduced the direct election of mayors, presidents of the provinces, and presidents of the Regions, setting a model which could be adopted at the national level as well;[33] (vi) the law on fiscal federalism which implements the 2001 reform of Title V mentioned previously and potentially provides for a veritable revolution in State-Regions-Municipalities relations.[34]

---

[27] B Ackerman, 'The Living Constitution', (2007) 120 *Harvard Law Review*, 7, 1738–1812.

[28] Act 20 May 1970, n 300.

[29] A set of Acts passed between 1974 and 1997 established independent regulatory commissions in charge of the stock market, antitrust laws, the regulation of strikes within the public services, the surveillance and regulation of the energy market, the surveillance and regulation of communications, and the protection of personal data.

[30] According to Law 21 December 2005, n 270, each list of candidates must designate a leader. Although Art 14-bis of the Electoral Law states that the powers conferred to the President of the Republic by Art 92 It Const. are confirmed (which is obvious), in relation to the power to appoint the President of the Council of Ministers, it is hard to believe that the President could appoint any other than the leader of the winning party or coalition. Some scholars regard this provision as unconstitutional, see A Pizzorusso, *Postfazione* note 8 above, 515.

[31] This provision makes it easier to reach the special majorities requested by the Constitution. It is regarded as illegitimate by some, see A Cerri, *Osservazioni sulla revisione della norma sulla revisione* (Rome: Astrid, 2006).

[32] Law 23 August 1988, n 400 (it is the functional equivalent of the British Ministerial Code).

[33] Law 25 March 1993, n 81; Law 23 February 1995, n 43; Constitutional Act 22 November 1999, n 1.

[34] Law 5 May 2009, n 42.

What has just been said applies also to other sources of rules which are not 'law' in the usual sense, but which directly implement the Constitution: most relevant of all is the case of the Standing Orders of the two Chambers. They regulate important constitutional matters such as, for instance, Cabinet-Parliament relations; in fact the evolution of the Standing Orders of the Senate and of the Chamber of Deputies directly reflects major political changes which influence the application of many constitutional articles; it would simply not be possible to evaluate the roles of the Cabinet and of Parliament within the Italian constitutional order without studying those Standing Orders. For instance, both the legal right of the Cabinet to ask for a confidence vote on any issue from each of the two Chambers and the right of each Chamber to pass a no confidence vote against a single member of the Cabinet (but not against the Cabinet) are regulated by the Standing Orders of the Chambers and not by the Constitution (which provides for a vote of no confidence against the whole Cabinet only).[35]

The Italian Constitution has also been changed by the European integration process: in Italy this has happened without a single formal amendment to the 1948 text. Italy is the only European nation with a textual Constitution which has never been amended in order to allow the ratification of any European Treaty, Maastricht included. Therefore the entire system of sources of law as well as Title III of Part I of the Constitution (on economic relations) have been very heavily affected by the simple ratification by ordinary law of these treaties (with the consent of the Constitutional Court, see decision 170/1984).

The most relevant single instrument of change, however, has been the jurisprudence of the Constitutional Court, along with the jurisprudence of other courts. Even though the Constitutional Court applies the Constitution and is not supposed to change it, no one would deny the creative function of any interpretation exercise; starting from its first decisions, the Italian Constitutional Court affirmed that the object of its ruling would not merely be the textual provisions of a particular piece of legislation, but the rules derived from them by the referring courts through their interpretation; the Court has applied the very same criterion in developing its own reasoning. Here are some examples.

---

[35] Until 1971 both Chambers adopted the 1920 Standing Orders of the Chamber. Thereafter the new Standing Orders reflected the consociational basis of the Italian political system of the time. When the political context changed the Standing Orders were also amended (in 1983, 1986, 1988 and 1997). According to art 64 para 1 It Const the Standing Orders are adopted by a special majority; therefore they share the rigidity of the Constitution. As far back as the 1950s some authors studied the impact of parliamentary regulations on the Constitutional order: see S Tosi, *Modificazioni tacite della Costituzione attraverso il diritto parlamentare* (Milano: Giuffrè, 1959), who applied to the Italian case concepts elaborated by German authors like G Jellinek, *Verfassungsänderung und Verfassungswandlung* (Berlin, 1906) and P Lerche, *Stiller Verfassungswandel als aktuelles Politikum*, Festgabe für Theodor Maunz (München: Beck, 1971). 'Modificazioni tacite' stands for 'tacit modifications'.

(i) Based upon Article 2 of the Constitution,[36] regarded as an *open textured provision* and based upon one of the other specific guarantees included in the Constitution, the Court has constantly expanded the list of rights protecting all human beings regardless of formal and explicit inclusion in the 1948 text. In this way the Court has asserted the right to sexual freedom, the right to have a home, the right to privacy, the right to emigrate, the right to one's own identity, the right to one's name, the right to marry, the right to one's reputation. The application of provisions deriving from international law, starting from the European Convention on Human Rights, has also been based on Article 2; by doing so the Court has somehow 'completed' the set of provisions to be found within the Constitution, reducing the need and the urgency for formal amendments.

(ii) Based upon article 3 of the Constitution[37] on 'the inviolable rights of man' the Court has addressed a range of disparate legal provisions involving unequal treatment, requiring that they should be based upon a reasonable case-by-case justification which pays full respect to the principles embedded in the Constitution and nurtured by the general values of Italian society; by doing so the Court has made 'unreasonable discrimination' illegal, although such a provision is not to be found in the Constitution.

(iii) More generally, the tendency to base decisions upon interpretation of very broad principles and values has enhanced the creative jurisprudence of the Court; an example is the rich jurisprudence concerning State–Region relations before and even more after the reform of Title V; to sum it up in few words, the Court has felt obliged to harmonise the amended text with the body of prior law to the point that some authors have spoken of a living regional constitutional law imposed by the Court,[38] while others have stressed the tendency of the Court to mitigate and even bypass some of the most striking innovations;[39] for instance (1) while the legislator deleted the very notion of 'national interest' from the text of the Constitution (it had been previously used to limit the autonomy of regions), the Court found several ways to reintroduce it; (2) the Court defined as 'transversal' some of the matters listed in article 117.2 It Const (that is 'protection of the environment'), thus making them implicitly cover additional objects not expressly listed therein; (3) the Court decided to apply the principle of

---

[36] 'The Republic recognises and guarantees the inviolable rights of man, both as an individual and as a member of the social groups in which one's personality affirms itself': 40 years ago a pioneering work predicted that Art 2 could become a gateway for the recognition of rights not already explicitly entrenched in the Constitution, see A Barbera, 'Commentario della Costituzione' in *Principi fondamentali. Art 2*, (Bologna-Roma: Zanichelli-Il foro italiano, 1975).

[37] 'All citizens possess an equal social status and are equal before the law ... It is the duty of the Republic to remove all economic and social obstacles which, by limiting the freedom and equality of citizens, prevent the full development of the individual'.

[38] A Barbera and C Fusaro, *Corso di diritto pubblico* (Bologna: Mulino, 2010), 346.

[39] M Cecchetti *Le riforme costituzionali del 1999–2001 sulla forma dello Stato dieci anni dopo*, in http://www.federalismi.it, n 6, 23 March 2010.

subsidiarity established by article 118 It Const in relation to administrative competences, extending it also to legislative competences and thus enlarging the legitimate attributions of Parliament vis-à-vis Regional Assemblies.

(iv) The Court claims that it has the duty and right to check the constitutional legitimacy of laws revising the Constitution, see paragraph 2 (a clear addition to article 134 It Const even where no such power of the Court is recognised in the text).

(v) According to the long series of decisions concerning the application of article 75 of the Constitution and Constitution Act 1/1953, article 2, it is for the Court to decide whether a request for a referendum can be admitted in respect of the provisions of article 75.2: the Court's jurisprudence on the matter has widely extended the list of issues on which a referendum is not admitted by the Constitution.[40]

(vi) The Constitutional Court has interpreted article 11 It Const[41] so that it allows the ratification of international agreements and treaties which not only limit the exercise of Italian sovereignty, but in fact bypass and in the end significantly change the Constitution itself, in particular legitimising the European integration process (see above).[42]

(vii) Resolving a conflict between the President of the Republic and the Minister of Justice on which of the two was entitled to grant individual pardons, the Constitutional Court stated that in spite of the general provision according to which all presidential acts must carry the countersignature by a member of the Cabinet, the power to grant pardon belongs to the President only, not to the Cabinet nor to both of them; the Court also stated that in article 89 It Const the words 'the proposing Minister' should be read as meaning 'the competent Minister':[43] by saying so the Court not only re-inforced its

---

[40] See decision 16/1978. This is one of the most controversial areas in 50 years of constitutional jurisprudence. The Court has felt the urge to add new limits to those listed in Art 75.2 (amnesty and pardon, budgetary laws, international treaties), stating that the following could not be submitted to a referendum (a) those Acts which regulate an object only along the lines dictated by the Constitution itself; (b) those Acts whose content is strictly dictated by European law; (c) those Acts which must be adopted according to a procedure which differs from the one which regulates the adoption of ordinary law; (d) those Acts which are strictly connected with those for which the Constitution expressly forbids referendum requests (eg laws which implement international treaties); (e) Acts which cannot be repealed, although the legislator may regulate the object in a variety of ways short of repeal. This principle has been applied to electoral laws, with the effect that all referendums meant to simply repeal one or the other electoral law have been rejected: this has prompted proponents to submit requests tailored in order to ensure that the electoral law may still function, a practice which originated the so-called 'manipulative referendums' (kind of bills in the shape of a referendum).

[41] 'Italy ... shall agree ... to such limitations of sovereignty as may be necessary to allow for a legal system that will ensure peace and justice between nations; it shall promote and encourage international organizations having such ends in view'. This provision was laid down to allow the participation of Italy in the United Nations. No one had envisaged the future European integration process as it would develop later.

[42] Starting from decision 14/1964.

[43] See decision 200/2006. Please note that in this chapter Council of Ministers and Cabinet are considered synonymous as they are in Italian legal language. Further, I refer to the President of the

decision on pardon, but potentially cleared the way for the recognition of additional powers in the President and reduced the powers of the Cabinet.[44]

(viii) Resolving another conflict (between the former minister of Justice and the Senate which had passed an individual no-confidence vote against him) the Court declared an individual no-confidence vote to be legitimate and consistent with the Italian parliamentary regime, indirectly diminishing the role of the President of the Council of Ministers and the very sense of cabinet collegiality.[45]

(ix) The Court has asserted that the right to decide whether an MP has expressed her/his opinion within or outside the exercise of her/his parliamentary functions does not pertain to the Chambers themselves as it had done hitherto, but it rather pertains to the Court itself (see article 68 paragraph 1 It Const states that MPs are not legally responsible for 'opinions expressed or votes cast in the exercise of their functions').[46]

(x) The Court has asserted its right to determine whether the adoption of a law decree by the Cabinet (article 77 It Const) is justified, even where Parliament has later approved it (therefore denying that the Cabinet is entitled to ask for a bill of indemnity and obtain it from its majority).[47]

It is telling by itself that not only both academics and the Court itself have been speaking of 'interpretative decisions' for years, but that even textbooks for students further classify the Constitutional Court's decisions as *additive* (they create new law), *integrative* (they complete existing law), *ablative* (they cancel wording of existing law), *sostitutive* (they introduce new provisions in place of pre-existing laws).[48]

The relevance of the role of the Constitutional court is confirmed by the increasing pressures on the Court from both opinion makers and politicians (in relation to the decisions it has to take) as well by the attention given to the selection of the 15 justices, especially the one-third elected by the two Chambers

---

Council (of ministers) and not to the Prime Minister, because according to the Constitution the President of the Council of Ministers is not hierarchically superior to the other members of the Council which is a collegial body (in fact the President of the Council formally is more than a Chairman but less than the word President would imply in English).

[44] The potential impact of this decision is relevant: the issue of presidential powers has often been raised and it influences the bulk of the political regime. There is little doubt that the Constituent Assembly by stating that 'no Act of the President shall be valid unless it is countersigned by the Ministers who have submitted it and who assume responsibility for it' (art 89.1 It Const) intended to affirm that all the powers listed in art 87 and by other constitutional provisions were meant to be either powers of the Cabinet or—in some instances—powers shared by both Cabinet and President (as is the case in all parliamentary regimes). No one thought the provision could be reversed and read as establishing an exclusive presidential power.

[45] See decision 7/1996.
[46] See decision 10/2000.
[47] See decision 126/2008.
[48] See eg, P Caretti and U De Siervo, *Istituzioni di diritto pubblico* (Torino: Giappichelli, 2008) 399.

and the one-third nominated by the President of the Republic (the last third is elected by magistrates among themselves, Article 135 It Const). That said, it must be added that the level of confidence in the party system has been (and still is) so low in Italy that apart from some news commentators and quite a few politicians (mostly right-wing, but also left-wing), scholars have hardly raised the issue of *le gouvernment des juges* (Lambert, the precursor in this line of thinking) or of the *judicialization of politics* (Shapiro and Sweet, Hirschl) or of *juristocracy* (Dworkin, Sunstein), nor complained against the risk of a *democratic dehabilitation* (Tushnet).[49]

Constitutional conventions and practices have also been influential in adding new provisions to the text of the Italian Constitution, without amending it, therefore playing a part in and contributing to the establishment of significant constitutional arrangements.[50] In particular this is the case where the Constitution is drafted in an imprecise way. A good example concerns the laconic provisions regulating a fundamental constitutional procedure such as the formation of the Cabinet. The drafting of article 92.2[51] could have been taken from the Statute of Carlo Alberto, although the general rule establishes that all acts of the President of the Republic must be countersigned by a member of the Cabinet: but the combined provisions of article 92.2 and article 89 raised the issue of who did what and who would finally be the decision-making body in the appointment of the Cabinet. What has happened is that a convention has been established according to which (a) the President meets formally with the leaders of all political parties represented in Parliament; (b) the President is entitled to select a politician in order to give him/her the mandate to form a government and report to him *before* formal appointment (which allows the President to remain in control of the entire process to the very end, and to change the nominee in case he/she does not offer solutions he supports or does not propose names of ministers he agrees upon); (c) the presidential decree which appoints the President of the Council of Ministers is signed a minute before the decrees which appoint the members of the Cabinet and they are all countersigned by the

---

[49] E Lambert, *Les gouvernment des juges et la lutte contre la legislation sociale en Etats-Unis* (Paris: M Giard & C, 1921); M Shapiro and AS Sweet, *On law, politics and judicialization* (Oxford: Oxford University Press, 2002); R Hirschl, 'The New Constitutionalism and the Judicialization of Pure Politics Worldwide', (2006) 721 *Fordham Law Review*; R Dworkin, *A Bill of Rights for Britain* (London: Chatto & Windus, 1990); CR Sunstein, *Designing Democracy: What Constitutions Do* (Oxford: Oxford University Press, 2002); M Tushnet, *Taking the Constitution Away from the Courts* (Princeton: Princeton University Press, 2000).

[50] Bartole, *Interpretazioni* note 25 above; L Paladin, *Per una storia costituzionale dell'Italia repubblicana* (Bologna: Mulino, 2004). See also GU Rescigno, *Le convenzioni costituzionali* (Padova: Cedam,1972); S Bartole, 'Le convenzioni della costituzione tra storia e scienza politica', (1983) *Il politico*, 151, and V Zangara, 'Costituzione materiale e costituzione convenzionale', in *Aspetti e tendenze del diritto costituzionale. Scritti in onore di C Mortati*, I, (Milano: Giuffrè, 1977) 359. Obviously the role of such conventions is more limited in a civil law system than in a common law system.

[51] Art 92.2 states only that 'The President of the Republic appoints the President of the Council and, on his advice, the ministers'.

incoming President of the Council.[52] As there are few constitutional proceedings as crucial as the formation of the Cabinet, here we can see how the effective functioning and therefore the specific role of constitutional bodies starting from the President of the Republic and the President of the Council of Ministers are determined by customary law (conventions of the Constitution we could say) and simple practice.

A variety of external influences impact on the way in which a system of government actually functions and affect the role of each organ, thereby influencing what the living Constitution becomes. This has certainly been the case in Italy. Here I will consider changes in political culture and in electoral behaviour, along with the outcomes of direct democratic decisions (referendums ex article 75, in particular). This is quite evident in connection with the main features of the political regime: as we have seen, the Constituent Assembly in 1948 opted to confirm the parliamentary regime as customarily developed in the previous hundred years after the Statute of King Carlo Alberto (Articles 92–94 It Const contain the relevant provisions).

Yet, although not a single word of these provisions has been amended, starting from the beginning of the1990s, the Italian parliamentary regime has undergone a set of major changes due to the combination of a new political culture (the trend towards competitive democracy supplanted the traditional consociational regime), a set of co-ordinated referendums concerning election laws and the public financing of political parties, the subsequent new local, regional and national electoral laws, and finally the establishment of an entirely renovated party system.[53] All this prompted a new interpretation of the parliamentary regime, featuring stronger Cabinets led by more influential Presidents of the Council (finally resembling Prime Ministers now), more stable Cabinets (some even able to remain in office for the full term of a legislature), less fragmented representation (fewer parliamentary groups: only five at the beginning of the twenty-sixth Parliament), decisive elections (in 1996, 2001, 2006 and 2008: with regular alternation), shortened procedures for the formation of the Cabinet, and a new role for the opposition: almost a *constitutional revolution*.[54]

Another example of how the political and cultural climate can impact on the interpretation of basic constitutional rules can be found in two strictly political conventions which have been in force for decades: (i) the convention among pro-Western political parties from the right, the centre and even the left according to which the Communist party could be involved in parliamentary business but never be included in the majority nor share governmental responsibilities;

---

[52] A true legal puzzle. This last practice was legalised by art 1 of the Act 23 August 1988, n 400, which regulates the functioning of the Cabinet.

[53] In 1994 none of the parties which had ruled Italy or led the opposition between 1946 and 1992 existed anymore.

[54] A revolution performed by constitutional means as it has been called with some emphasis, C Fusaro, *La rivoluzione costituzionale* (Soveria M: Rubbettino, 1993).

this convention was steadily applied until the Soviet Union ended (1993); it even received an academic name: *conventio ad excludendum*;[55] its sources can be traced back to the time of the Cold War when Italy was bound to take a firm pro-West stand; (ii) for decades (from the 1960s to the 1980s) all main political parties, including the Communist party and excluding the neo-Fascist Movimento sociale italiano, recognised each other as being entitled to an equal say on constitutional matters on the assumption that their parties or the parties they had derived from were the founding fathers and the 'substantive base' of the 1948 Constitution. This was an open application of Costantino Mortati's doctrine of the *substantial constitution* (see note 2).

Another example of how constitutional arrangements may be impacted on by the behaviour of both voters and political actors and even by demographics, is article 75 It Const. It regulates the referendum to repeal a law: it establishes that 'the proposal submitted to referendum shall be approved if a majority of those eligible have participated in the voting' (provided, of course, that the 'yes' prevails). This clause has recently prompted the opponents of referendum proposals to campaign for abstention rather than for a 'nay' vote: as a consequence *all* 24 referendums after 1995 have failed, not because nays prevailed but for low turn out. Nowadays it is very unlikely that a referendum will ever succeed again as the general trend is towards lower and lower turn out (regardless of the issue). Therefore article 75 risks falling into obsolescence. The impact on the constitutional system is heavy: it has lost a fundamental safety valve and deprived the voters of a significant power.

The role of the Cabinet in Parliament and in the law making process has also changed over time simply by a combination of its enhanced political power (due to the new electoral laws, the establishment of a new political system and the presidentialisation trend) and application of existing rules stretched to their very limit. A few examples are as follows: (a) After the Constitutional court in 1996 put an end to the practice of 'law decree chains' (a law decree if not approved within 60 days becomes null and void; in the 1980s it become customary for the Cabinet to adopt a new decree with the same content of a previous one the 59th day of its validity: in a record case this was done 23 times, allowing a specific regulation to remain in force for almost four years instead of 60 days[56]) the need for swift regulation induced Cabinets of all colours to resort to delegated legislation more and more:[57] now delegated legislation accounts for over 40 per cent of all Italian legislation. (b) Because the Italian Cabinet in Parliament is still deprived of powers that Cabinets have in most Parliaments, a practice has been developed according to which the Cabinet adopts a law decree, it negotiates some amendments in each Chamber, then it submits a 'jumbo amendment' possibly changing the whole text of the original decree while asking for a confidence vote

[55] L Elia, 'Governo (forme di)', *Enciclopedia del diritto* (Milano: Giuffrè, 1970).
[56] See art 77 It Const.
[57] See art 76 It Const.

on it: the effect is that each Chamber is forced to take it all or leave it (in which case the Cabinet would have to resign). *De facto* this is the functional equivalent of the French *vote bloqué* where the Cabinet can pass an entire law with a single vote. Laws including up to over one thousand articles have been passed in this way. This is in stark contrast to what article 72 paragraph 1 It Const states: 'every bill introduced to one of the Chambers shall be … examined … by the Chamber itself which shall approve it article by article, and with a final vote'.

Finally the international and European legal contexts have also combined to make the Italian living Constitution what it is today. For both the ordinary courts and the Constitutional Court, international treaties reflect and give effect to the textual Constitution in so far as they grant a higher level of protection in the area of human rights in particular. The provisions of the European Convention on Human Rights have become fundamental parameters adopted by the courts, and most recently by the Constitutional Court itself, in addition to what is established by the Constitution.[58] In relation to European law the case is different because it is directly enforced by all legal authorities, courts included: and it is enforced regardless of whether it infringes or bypasses existing ordinary or even constitutional provisions.[59] The only limit, according to a ruling by the Constitutional Court, very similar to the more famous one by the German *BundesVerfassungsGericht*,[60] is that European norms always prevail as long as they are not proven to infringe the 'supreme principles and inviolable human rights on which the Italian Constitutional order is based'. This is a limit that cannot be crossed, as we have seen, even in respect of the provisions of article 138, which regulates the revision of the Constitution, as the Constitutional Court has affirmed. In this sense one can say that technically the Italian juridical order is still dualist, but is monist in substance. What matters for our purposes is that both international treaty law and European law play a significant role among the sources of law within the Italian jurisdiction and they are capable of adding entire sets of new provisions and thereupon changing the living constitution, if not the textual one.

[58]   The Constitutional Court (see eg decisions 348/2007; 349/2007; 39/2008) regards the provisions of the ECHR as *norme interposte* (interposed norms), bound to be applied directly by the Italian courts as interpreted by the Strasbourg Court.
[59]   Recently, for the first time the Italian Constitutional Court agreed to apply directly art 267 TFEU (Treaty on the Functioning of the European Union), and requested the Court of Justice of the EU for a preliminary ruling before deciding a specific case (decisions 102, 103/2008).
[60]   I refer to the Maastricht Urteil (BVerfGE 89, 155 of 12 October 1993), recently re-inforced by the BVG's decision concerning the Lisbon Treaty (BVerfGE 123, 267 NJW 2009, 2267 of 30 June 2009).

CONCLUDING REMARKS

The purpose of the following remarks is to focus on what seems to emerge from Italian constitutional developments as they have been described above in the light of the assumptions and the framework of this book as presented in the introductory chapter.

Whatever definition we give to the notion of 'constitution', the Italian Constitution has changed greatly since it entered in force: the Constitution as a textual entrenched document has been amended, the constitution as a broader set of constitutional arrangements has changed, the living Constitution (made of written provisions both entrenched and not entrenched, of their interpretations by jurisprudence, academics and practitioners and so on) has been transformed. The Italian Constitution of 2010 is not the Constitution of 1948.

In fact the contrary would have been surprising and even unthinkable. But I will return to this later.

Let me list the major changes which have transformed the Italian Constitution, those which, according to generally accepted opinion, have impacted on it more and more directly:

(i) the Bill of Rights has been enlarged and extended (rights entrenched in the text of 1948 are guaranteed more than they used to be, new rights have been recognised although not listed);

(ii) the roles of both the judiciary and the Constitutional Court have been enhanced: both combined and as distinct authorities; a renowned author has written that it is up to the courts not Parliament, to make the Constitution effective: 'the Constitution is more and more the product of judicial interpretation and less and less the political outcome of the sovereign will of the people and of its representatives';[61]

(iii) the roles of the main executive and legislative bodies have evolved and their relations with one another have changed: the Cabinet and its leader (President of the Council of Ministers) are much stronger than they used to be; the President of the Republic, from being a mere notary if not a simple figurehead has turned into a very influential political figure; Parliament after 25 years of great influence as the arena where political parties would face each other and shape most relevant policies has evolved into a ratification body where the majority-opposition conflict is acted out in a more or less theatrical way, reflecting the diminished role of the parties since the reform of the electoral system; voters have been recognised as having a more significant role as at least occasional decision makers (a role they did not have when strictly proportional representation was the 'constitutional' rule

---

[61] See M Fioravanti, *Costituzione e popolo sovrano* (Bologna, il Mulino, 1998) 19; also A Spadaro, 'Prima la storia fa le Corti costituzionali e poi le Corti costituzionali fanno la storia', in C Salazar and A Spadaro (eds), *Riflessioni sulle sentt. 348–349 della Corte costituzionale* (Milano, Giuffrè, 2009) 5.

of Italian politics), while they are losing the real chance to resort to the referendum established by article 75 It Const (see above);

(iv) the hierarchy and system of sources of law have literally been subverted both in form and in substance: in substance most law enforced in Italy is produced by entities other than Parliament: EU institutions, Regions, Government, Independent Regulatory Commissions and even in the areas where primary sources of law—that is to say Parliamentary acts—are required, Parliament has become just one of the bodies involved in the legislative process (17 per cent of laws are law decrees adopted by the Cabinet and ratified by Parliament; 40 per cent of laws are delegated decrees adopted by the Cabinet after parliamentary authorisation); on the other hand, European law trumps internal law and it can even prevail over contrary constitutional provisions (subject to the 'fundamental principles' that have been recognised by the Constitutional Court);

(v) Italy, from being a highly centralised jurisdiction has become if not a federal, certainly a quasi-federal one, featuring a high level of devolution to regional authorities.

If we turn to the instruments, the processes and the primary actors of the changes summarised above we can observe the following. (i) Formal constitutional amendments (or revisions) have been significant but certainly not pivotal. A possible exception is devolution to the regions, but even then the revision of Part II It Const was anticipated by a set of ordinary laws.[62] (ii) New ways of interpreting the textual Constitution have proven of the utmost importance. One example for all: European integration with all its effects on the system of sources of law. (iii) The role of the Constitutional Court has been truly fundamental. (iv) Political and parliamentary actors have also been influential, at least at the beginning of the process: the ratification of the EC treaties and the ECHR treaty was authorised by Acts of Parliament. (v) The voters and pressure groups have become relevant actors: both with their ability to influence political decision makers and even more with the audacious use of the referendum in 1993: as a President of the Republic, Oscar Luigi Scalfaro said, this referendum 'dictated the content of the new electoral law'. (This was the same law which was bound to change the form of government.) (vi) Important reforms have been pursued by adopting sub-constitutional sources of law (ordinary laws and Standing Orders of the two Chambers).

Looked at over a 60 year time span, the changes in the basic constitutional arrangement of Italy reflect the transformation of Italy. It has changed from a centralised, impoverished, agricultural, almost isolated country featuring high illiteracy rates, nonexistent birth control, heavy emigration, and a country where fundamental rights were not systematically guaranteed, into a relatively rich,

---

[62] It is interesting to note that at the time the constitutional revision was motivated by the need to entrench changes already introduced in order to make them more stable and avoid steps back.

quasi-federal, post-industrial country, deeply embedded in the European Union and internationalised, among the top seven or eight world economies, where the guarantees of fundamental rights are not inferior to those of any other nation, and where an ageing population grows—when it grows—only due to heavy immigration.

The Italian case seem to show that in any given context, change tends to take place wherever it finds a weaker point of resistance and by whatever means. When formal constitutional change is not possible or is particularly difficult and burdensome those who pursue it try and eventually find other ways: partial, incremental, often badly coordinated and not always formally consistent change is much more within the reach of those who push for change, while global, transparent, well planned and elaborated change is much more difficult to pursue, and easier to resist, the more so in a modern poliarchical democracy like Italy (to use the words of a famous politologue, Robert Dahl[63]).

In Italy the legitimating theories of the Constitution have provided instruments and weapons in the struggle to change or not change constitutional arrangements. The Constitution has continuously been the object of 'political interpretations' of various kinds,[64] and as far back as the early 1980s the need for significant updating of the 1948 text seemed to be broadly accepted. However, an alliance of conservative vested interests has always been able to prevent a wide-ranging coordinated revision. In the last 10 years arguments to the effect that the only legitimate interpretation of the normative function of the Constitution is as a counter-majoritarian limitation of politics have been used instrumentally, causing many a misunderstanding. What is truly constitutional and what is simply a selection of discretionary political choices?

The idea that the Constitution is a sort of political programme, a manifesto imposed once and for all (a Constitution suited to accommodate progressive policies only, for instance) has been disseminated time and time again. But the notion of the 1948 Constitution as a sacred and virtually untouchable text dictating the only legitimate policies for today's Italy has contributed to delegitimising the Constitution itself. If the Constitution is a specific 'political' programme, all those who seek a different programme are bound to feel entitled to pursue changes to a set of arrangements they consider not only outdated, but designed to deny their legitimate political expectations.

The same effect has flowed from the 'invention' of more and more limits to formal constitutional amendments: no total or large revision is legally allowed,

---

[63] RA Dahl, *A Preface to Democratic Theory* (Chicago: Chicago University Press, 1956) and *Democracy and its Critics* (New Haven: Yale University Press, 1989).

[64] As Bartole shows convincingly in *Interpretazioni* note 25 above; he ends his book with these words: 'it is hard to deny that legislators, justices and governmental authorities have shown . . . a clear tendency to manipulate the Constitution . . . The events we have gone through seem to contradict the so frequent statements about the sacred nature of that text' 450.

only item revisions; more and more implied limits have been elaborated in more or less activist or radical interpretations of the Constitution.

But the Italian experience since 1948 seems to suggest that hyper-rigidity can produce attempts to change the constitutional arrangements other ways, through different, possibly less transparent and less participatory means. Nowadays a comprehensive updating of the Italian Constitutional arrangements (both textual and non textual), in spite of being generally regarded as necessary (bipartisan parliamentary resolutions have been approved by both Chambers as recently as December 2009), still seems far away, while in meantime the Constitution has already been surreptitiously changed in a variety ways we hope to have shown.

11

New Zealand

PAUL RISHWORTH*

INTRODUCTION

O
N THE SURFACE, New Zealand's constitution is beguilingly simple. New Zealand is a unitary state, and escapes the complications of federalism. It has a uni-cameral legislature, so is spared inter-house conflict and deadlocks. And with an 'unwritten' constitution—that is, no single supreme law setting out the structure of governance or rights of individuals— there is always scope for pragmatic constitutional tweaking without the difficulty of special amending formulas or high-stakes litigation. Simplicity may not always be a virtue, of course, but it does mean that constitutional matters keep a low national profile.

That New Zealand has opted, so far, to keep its constitution this way tells us something about the national character. Pragmatic and business-like, the archetypal New Zealander resists flourish and ornamentation. He is primarily concerned with whether things work. Any proposal for explicit constitutional reform brings the rejoinder 'if it ain't broke don't fix it', and possibly suspicion of the proposers' motives. But pragmatism is not the same as conservatism: while constitutional re-design may be unwelcome, our archetype is accepting of discrete constitutional changes if they are shown to be necessary or desirable, and able to be executed without fuss.

Most of all, our archetype dislikes conflict and 'navel-gazing'. A cast-iron excuse is needed before embarking on constitutional discussions, especially ones that might expose different and irreconcilable visions of the nation. So when, in 2004, the House of Representatives established a committee of its members to 'identify and describe ... the key elements in New Zealand's constitutional structure' and the 'processes it would be appropriate to follow if significant

---

* Thanks are due to Max Harris, LLB(Hons) 2011, research assistant.

reforms were considered in the future', the committee reached a very clear conclusion. There was, it said:[1]

> little merit in debate in isolation by experts commissioned to come up with a grand overall design. ... New Zealand's strong tradition has been to deal with them piece by piece, through a process of pragmatic evolution over time.

These notions of 'pragmatism' and 'piece-meal evolution' are a recurring theme in New Zealand constitutional scholarship.[2] Yet they beg numerous questions. How, exactly, does one distinguish 'pragmatic evolution' from other types of change? Who gets to say what is pragmatic? (Come to that, who presses for change that is *not*, at least as they see it, pragmatic?) How and by whom are the evolutionary forces—the ones that produce change—discerned? Whence comes the initiative for change? How should any change be accomplished? What degree of consultation and consensus is required? And, to foreshadow the chosen theme of this chapter, where do New Zealand's indigenous people, the Māori, fit in the constitutional scheme? In particular, what is the role of the Treaty of Waitangi, made between Māori chiefs and the United Kingdom sovereign in 1840, which led to the founding of New Zealand? Should the power of the state be redistributed or constrained to recognise the rights of the original occupants? Is embedded pragmatism really a defence against unsettling claims?

And so we find that, beneath the sapphire waters of New Zealand's Pacific constitution, there lurks a fair measure of complexity. Here one finds 'the structures, processes, principles, rules, conventions and even culture that *constitute* the generic ways in which public power is exercised'.[3] It is these that will define, perhaps imprecisely, what is regarded as possible within the constitutional order and what processes are required to change it.[4] In a country with an unwritten constitution, there is perhaps more 'constitutional law' of this type than in states with formal written documents. Much in this realm of constitutional law may be reasonably well settled, but it is here that new practices and understandings are evolving. These can lead to explicit constitutional change,

---

[1] Report of the Constitutional Arrangements Committee, 'Inquiry to Review New Zealand's Existing Constitutional Arrangements' (2005) *Appendix to the Journal of the House of Representatives* 1.24A.

[2] See M Palmer, 'New Zealand Constitutional Culture' (2007) 22 *New Zealand Universities Law Review* 565 especially at 571 ff; see also P Joseph, *Constitutional and Administrative Law in New Zealand*, (Thomson Brookers, 2007), ch 5.5.4. Palmer's work draws on the realist tradition to locate New Zealand's constitutional foundations in the embedded culture of those who operate it and who subscribe to a national culture. This culture 'forms a landscape that influences the likely success or failure, or at least the relative ease or difficulty of acceptance, of any constitutional reform'. (Palmer, 'New Zealand Constitutional Culture', 567). See further, B Harris, 'The Constitutional Future of New Zealand' [2004] *New Zealand Law Review* 269, arguing for a more structured approach to constitutional development, albeit still emphasising the need for this to be 'incremental in response to recognised need' (at 310) rather than 'dramatic' (at 283).

[3] M Palmer, 'Using Constitutional Realism to Identify the Complete Constitution: Lessons from an Unwritten Constitution' (2006) *American Journal of Comparative Law* 587, at 589.

[4] Ernest Young. 'The Constitution Outside the Constitution' (2007) 117 *Yale Law Journal* 408.

yet—to the extent that they play out in the working of the constitutional order—new practices and understandings might also *be* that change.

A major theme of this chapter is that, by virtue of the role played by the Treaty of Waitangi in its founding, New Zealand is now reckoning with the fact that it has a 'Treaty-based' constitution. In this regard, Hannah Pitkin usefully reminds us that 'constitution' is both a noun and a noun-verb—denoting not just the set of principles and rules by which a state is constituted,[5] but also the phenomenon of constituting, the 'shaping [of] something anew'.[6] That second sense is pertinent to New Zealand as it adjusts to its place in the world. Founded as a British colony on the basis of a treaty with its indigenous occupants, New Zealand in the twenty-first century now wrestles with being a considerable distance from world markets and living in the shadow of a larger and more prosperous sibling, Australia. These realities and many others manifest themselves in New Zealand's modern law and practice, including those parts of law and practice that are important enough to warrant the label 'constitutional'. They are reflected, for example, in New Zealand's embracement of international law (by the judicial branch in litigation but also in accession by the executive to treaties that promote New Zealand's engagement with the world), in its regard for fundamental human rights (an aspect of the last point), and in its steps toward harmonisation with Australia in matters affecting business and trade. And, especially, in reckoning with its own unique history and the implications of its own unique treaty, the Treaty of Waitangi.

The Treaty of Waitangi and the Māori dimension of New Zealand has become the elephant in the room of New Zealand's constitutionalism. The Treaty has never been a formal part of the constitution. But over the last three decades successive governments, and courts on such occasions as the Treaty comes before them, have accepted that the Treaty is a 'foundation' to the constitution, that it creates a 'relationship' between Māori and the Crown, and that it has constitutional implications.[7] It is now taken to speak, in particular, to the government's duties to protect the interests of Māori and to the need for consultation and good faith between the 'Treaty partners'. It has not always been seen this way, and certainly the actual text of the Treaty is not readily susceptible to these modern interpretations. But much has happened over the last 30 years. Salient factors include a renaissance in Māori tribal culture; general recognition of historic injustices to Māori; Māori political influence in New Zealand's mixed-member proportional Parliament since 1996; the convergence of international human rights imperatives with Māori aspirations for autonomy; a measure of litigation success by Māori in relation to fishing rights and rights to the seabed and

---

[5] Not all of these, as Ernest Young reminds us, need be found in the canonical text. There are other sources, and these can be termed 'the constitution outside the constitution'.

[6] H Pitkin, 'The Idea of a Constitution' (1987) 37 *Journal of Legal Education* 167, 168.

[7] See, in particular, *New Zealand Māori Council v Attorney-General* [1987] 1 NZLR 641 [the *Lands* case]: the Treaty of Waitangi was called a 'the foundation for the future relationship between the Crown and the Māori race' by Casey J at 714.

foreshore; burgeoning Māori economic power derived from settlements of historic claims; and changing demographics that see a steadily growing proportion of the population identifying as Māori.

Together these factors generate a view, certainly amongst elites who express opinions on constitutional matters, that any constitutional change in New Zealand will need to reckon with the Māori dimension—both substantively (what changes might be like) and procedurally (the need for consulting Māori when making them). This has implications for how the state is conceived, and how Māori institutions are conceived (the very idea of consultation with Māori implies the existence of such institutions with internal rules of membership and governance). Reckoning with the Treaty of Waitangi is far from the only challenge for New Zealand constitutionalism, but it is a pervasive one because the Treaty relationship will have some bearing on any proposal for constitutional change. To foreshadow one example, any future move to a New Zealand republic would sever the Treaty link—much valued by Māori—between the United Kingdom's sovereign and the Māori chiefs. Māori sentiment on the republican issue would need to be tested. New Zealand's most eminent judge, Lord Cooke of Thorndon, speculated in 1990 that a separate referendum amongst Māori would be required to demonstrate (to judges, were the legality of the instruments establishing republicanism put in issue) that there had been 'reasonably substantial Māori concurrence' in a republic.[8]

These, then, are the issues that arise when considering constitutional change in New Zealand. To explore them, it assists to conceive the New Zealand constitution as one that began as a transplanted British constitution, now slowly being rebuilt from the inside as New Zealand reinvents itself.

In broad terms, New Zealand's formal constitution is indeed a simplified version of the United Kingdom's. As a British colony, the legal instruments that brought New Zealand into being were instruments of the United Kingdom Parliament and executive. New Zealand's constitution therefore depended upon and shares with the United Kingdom an unbroken chain of legal validity extending back to the Glorious Revolution of 1688. But New Zealand's constitution remains relatively unexamined. It excites no popular veneration, such as swirls around the famous Constitution of the United States of America. This is partly because there is no single document—certainly no home-grown document—from which all things proceed. The constitution was imposed from the top down, albeit on a generally willing citizenry. The replication of a British constitution in New Zealand was, for the original settler community at least, precisely what they sought. It brought representative democracy and then responsible government (that is, an executive branch formed from members of,

---

[8] Sir Robin Cooke, 'The Suggested Revolution Against the Crown' in P Joseph (ed), *Essays on the Constitution* (Brookers, 1995), 28 at 38. The learned author also cites similar views by Professor FM Brookfield in an unpublished paper 'Republican New Zealand: Legal Aspects and Consequences' (1994).

and answerable to, the elected legislature). These were seen, in the nineteenth century, as the hallmark of independence from the mother country and the very essence of freedom.

In the early twentieth century New Zealand emerged to be an independent and autonomous state, but only minimal formal constitutional change was needed to mark this. A power to amend the constitution was conferred by the United Kingdom upon New Zealand's Parliament in 1947,[9] but independence and autonomy were already in place by then. In fact there has been little formal amendment since 1947. That said, the accumulation of law, principle and convention that makes up the total package of the 'unwritten constitution' is different compared to, say, 60 years ago. There has been much de facto evolution of the constitution—of the 'constitution outside the constitution'. When the time comes, as it assuredly will, to formulate a more comprehensive written document as New Zealand's 'Constitution', some of this evolved practice will likely be embraced with it. New institutions may be judged to better reflect what New Zealand has become or wishes to be: perhaps an upper house with formal Māori representation; certainly a republic; a clearer place for Māori institutions with some devolved power; along with a constitutional guarantee of equality and rights for all. Astute constitutional observers and political activists recognise that a tide is running in the 'beneath the surface-constitution', especially as it relates to Māori. But they also recognise that any attempt to press explicit constitutional reform at this point in time risks divisive debate and possible failure. Because the status quo works tolerably well, key players are for the moment content to let these underlying changes take their course rather than seek to crystallise them prematurely.

What follows, then, is a fuller account of New Zealand's developing constitutional arrangements, how and why they are in their current state, and how the process of change is expected to continue.

CONSTITUTIONAL BEGINNINGS: REPLICATING A BRITISH CONSTITUTION IN
THE PACIFIC

New Zealand was populated from around 1300 AD by successive waves of Polynesian migration from elsewhere in the Pacific. The Māori—the indigenous people of New Zealand—were unknown to the rest of the world until a fleeting visit paid by Dutch explorer Abel Tasman in 1642. More than a century passed before English explorer Captain James Cook arrived in 1769 and put New Zealand, quite literally, on the map. There followed whalers, sealers and adventurers, seeking to profit from the land's abundant resources.

Māori society was organised in a fluid way, around family (*whanau*), groups of families (*hapu*) and larger groupings (*iwi*, or tribes). Alliances were made or

---

[9] See the New Zealand Constitution Amendment Act 1947 (UK).

unmade, according to the exigencies of politics and trade. Europeans, when they arrived, were welcomed for their merchandise and new possibilities. Missionaries from the London Missionary Society followed in 1814, learning the Māori language and reducing it to writing. The Bible and other texts were translated.

By 1839, the Colonial Office in London faced a difficult choice. Many Europeans were settling in New Zealand. A frontier society of renegade sailors and traders had emerged, and it was literally lawless. France was also known to have designs on New Zealand. The Colonial Office in London resolved, reluctantly it is said, to make New Zealand part of the realm, ostensibly for the protection of Māori. A naval captain, William Hobson, was sent to negotiate a treaty of cession with the Māori chiefs. Arriving in late January 1840, Hobson had within a week prepared a treaty, had it translated into Māori by the local missionary, and procured signatures from many key chiefs in the populous north.[10] Over coming months it was taken around the country for more signatures. Eventually more than 500 were obtained, although not from all chiefs. In May 1840, a proclamation of the Crown's sovereignty over all the territory of New Zealand had been made, based upon the Treaty of Waitangi and (as to the South Island, in a 'belt and braces' approach) upon Captain Cook's discovery the previous century.

This treaty—the Treaty of Waitangi (1840)—now occupies a prominent place in the New Zealand constitutional landscape. It has never been formally a part of the constitution. But it made the constitution possible, and for that reason is often called its foundation. Surprisingly short, the Treaty's three articles traverse—from a United Kingdom perspective—what the occasion demanded. By article 1 Māori chiefs ceded 'sovereignty' to the Queen; article 2 affirmed that Māori property rights would be protected, with the Crown having the right of first refusal of land; and article 3 promised that Māori would thenceforth have the rights of British subjects.

For the contemporary British constitutional lawyer, this was a treaty for the archives rather than for constant recourse. It was a self-imposed condition precedent to establishing an English-style constitution, but not itself the constitution. The sovereignty obtained under article 1 would thereafter become the *grundnorm* for New Zealand, while the promises of continuing Māori property ownership and equality could be fulfilled by the ordinary operation of English common law. For these reasons, the Treaty of Waitangi never entered the realm of law. English common law was taken to apply in New Zealand, and the common law's 'dualist' conception of the relationship between international and domestic law meant that the Treaty of Waitangi was not cognisable in domestic courts unless incorporated into legislation. That remains the position to this day.

In the international realm, the Treaty of Waitangi had a similarly peculiar consequence for Māori. As Treaty parties, Māori tribes lost both their sovereignty

---

[10] The leading account of these events is by C Orange, *The Treaty of Waitangi*, (Allen & Unwin, 1987), 28–29.

and their 'international personality' through the act of signing—gone in a 'puff of logic', as respected commentator Matthew Palmer has recently put it.[11] That precluded access to international fora by Māori seeking to complain that the Treaty was not honoured. Such complaints were to come soon enough.

Once the Treaty of Waitangi was signed and British sovereignty asserted, the constituting of New Zealand proceeded apace. More settlers arrived. In the end, of course, it was force of numbers as much as words on paper that perfected New Zealand's acquisition by Britain. So far as the constitution was concerned, there seems never to have been the slightest thought that the Treaty required anything other than United Kingdom-style institutions. There was an initial 'Crown Colony' period, when a London-appointed Governor ruled together with an appointed Legislative Council. This period was emphatically not seen as one for democratic institutions: the very point of the United Kingdom's intervention had been to interpose the Crown between the rapacious settlers and Māori. But by 1852 pressure for settler representation in the legislature resulted in the United Kingdom Parliament enacting the New Zealand Constitution Act 1852 (UK), establishing a representative General Assembly with full power 'to make laws for the peace order and good government of New Zealand', albeit subject to various subject matter restrictions and to potential annulment by the Colonial Office in London. Soon after, responsible government was progressively established—the New Zealand Governor being instructed by his London superiors to appoint, and to act on the advice of, Ministers from amongst those elected to the House of Representatives.

So institutions on the British model were created, and Māori became subjects, but professedly equal ones. By this time Māori were outnumbered. The transfer of effective political power and law-making authority to the New Zealand community—effectively the settler community—exposed Māori to the ravaging effect of policy and legislation. The Treaty promises could not be appealed to by Māori in the courts, only in the political realm. One commentator has called this the 'fundamental breach' of the Treaty: that the Crown's solemn obligations of protection were effectively transferred to the New Zealand government and thus to settlers.[12] Over the years, Māori approaches to the Queen in the United Kingdom were batted back to New Zealand by her advisers. The poachers had become the gamekeepers, and although it might be said that the Treaty deemed Māori to be *equal* with the gamekeepers, they could never amount to a majority of them.

It is not that the settlers were anything other than egalitarian. In those earliest days of the franchise, four 'Māori seats' in the legislature were established to ensure representation of Māori at a time when individual property ownership

[11] M Palmer, *The Treaty of Waitangi in New Zealand's Law and Constitution*, (Victoria University Press, 2008), 160.
[12] H Wilberg, 'Facing Up to the Original Breach of the Treaty' [2007] *NZ Law Review* 527 and 'Judicial Remedies for the Original Breach?' [2007] *NZ Law Review* 713.

was an electoral qualification (and a difficult criterion for Māori to satisfy).[13] That was the beginning of a (modest) recognition of a Māori dimension in New Zealand's written constitution. As we shall see, it took root: the Māori seats remain to this day in the Electoral Act 1993, increased in number, with some extension of the idea into local government as well.

CONSTITUTIONAL DEVELOPMENT: PATRIATION OF THE AMENDING POWER

Imperial restraints on the legislative power of the New Zealand General Assembly (as the legislature was known) were all removed by 1947, most well before. New Zealand was thereafter able to amend its own constitution—principally the New Zealand Constitution Act 1852 (UK) —in every respect. The catalyst for requesting the United Kingdom to confer this power (which it was very willing to confer) was the desire in New Zealand's Parliament to abolish the then upper house of the bicameral legislature. The Legislative Council, by then judged by politicians to be ineffective and pointless, was duly abolished.[14] With new councillors appointed, it was compliant in its abolition. The House of Representatives remains as a unicameral legislature to this day.

In the 1950s there was talk of further constitutional reform, in recognition that a unicameral legislature might be thought a thin protection against despotism. There was even talk of a written constitution and a Bill of Rights. But nothing eventuated. In 1963 a New Zealand Bill of Rights Bill was introduced into Parliament, modelled on the then recent Canadian Bill of Rights 1960. But it lapsed at the next election, apparently popular with nobody. The idea of a written constitution was pursued in 1957 by a group styled the Constitutional Society for the Promotion of Economic Freedom and Justice, but, like a few other suggested constitutions essayed over later years, the Society's draft gained no traction with Parliament or the citizenry.[15]

Formal constitutional amendments since 1950 have, with the exception of the move to proportional representation, been quite technical, triggered by specific

---

[13] Māori Representation Act 1867.

[14] The Statute of Westminster 1931 (UK) had provided that United Kingdom enactments would not be taken to extend to the named colonies unless a colony requested and consented. It also allowed for colonial legislation to be repugnant to United Kingdom enactments operating in the colonies. New Zealand had asked, like Australia, to be exempted from the powers conferred in ss 2– 6 of the Statute of Westminster until such time as it adopted them, which it did by the Statute of Westminster Adoption Act 1947 (NZ). And then, because s 8 of the Statute of Westminster provided that nothing in it empowered the New Zealand legislature to amend the New Zealand Constitution Act 1852, it was necessary for New Zealand to pass the New Zealand Constitution Amendment Act (Request and Consent) Act 1947, seeking the enactment by the United Kingdom of the New Zealand Constitution Amendment Act 1947 (UK). That then enabled constitutional amendment and the abolition of the Legislative Council. See KJ Scott, *The New Zealand Constitution* (Oxford University Press, 1962), 20–22.

[15] Another proposal is that of Sir Geoffrey Palmer and M Palmer, annexed in their book *Bridled Power: New Zealand's Constitution and Government,* (Oxford University Press, 2004), appendix.

events. A court case in 1968 raised a legal question whether the General Assembly could validly enact a law with effect outside New Zealand's territorial waters.[16] It was common ground that the Statute of Westminster 1931 (UK) conferred power on the former colonies to legislate extraterritorially, but there remained a residual requirement in the 1852 Constitution that any New Zealand law must be for 'peace order and good government *of New Zealand*'. Could that always be claimed of legislation designed to operate elsewhere, such as in New Zealand's Antarctic territory or for the armed forces abroad? Officials perceived a need to remove this remaining subject-matter limitation on legislative power. A 1973 amendment dealt with the problem. This reform was seen as 'lawyers' law': no referendum or public consultation was undertaken nor even contemplated. It was non-contentious, particularly because it could be seen as elevating the status of New Zealand to match that of other independent former colonies. Only academics asked the question: could a limited law-making power be invoked to remove the limits?! Shades of that conundrum arose again in the next constitutional development.

That was in 1984 when a minor crisis occurred in the handover between governments at election time. For technical reasons, new Ministers could not lawfully be sworn into office immediately. Reform of electoral law was judged necessary. But the opportunity was taken also for a constitutional 'clean up' and restatement of the essentials. This explains the Constitution Act 1986, now the centrepiece of the formal Constitution for New Zealand. The Constitution Act is brief, describing what exists rather than being truly constitutive. Again, as technical lawyers' law, there was no talk of public consultation or referendum; nor was it politically partisan.

The Constitution Act 1986 usefully collects key ideas in New Zealand's constitution. It first defines the Head of State: 'the Sovereign in right of New Zealand'. The expression 'in right of New Zealand' denotes the fact that in her capacity as New Zealand's Head of State, Queen Elizabeth II acts on the advice of her New Zealand Ministers, and that her role is independent of the similar role played by her in relation to the United Kingdom. In New Zealand she is, by legislation, styled the 'Queen of New Zealand and her other realms'.[17] In practice the Queen is represented in New Zealand by her Governor-General, and the Constitution Act records that fact as well.

Part 3 deals with the legislative branch, providing that 'there shall continue to be a House of Representatives for New Zealand',[18] whose members are elected from time to time in accordance with the Electoral Act 1993. The General Assembly is renamed the Parliament of New Zealand—defined formally as 'the Sovereign in right of New Zealand and the House of Representatives'. Parliament

---

[16] *R v Fineberg* [1968] NZLR 119.
[17] Section 2 of the Royal Titles Act 1974 (NZ).
[18] Section 14(1).

'continues to have full power to make laws'.[19] The Constitution Act fixes the parliamentary term at three years, this being the only provision in the Constitution Act that is 'entrenched' against ordinary repeal or amendment. A special majority of 75 per cent of members, or a majority of voters at a referendum, is required to amend it. More will be said about 'entrenchment' shortly.

Part 4 of the Constitution Act deals briefly with the judiciary. Because the New Zealand courts were long constituted by other enactments, little needed to be said in the Constitution Act. It simply makes the usual provision for judicial independence (no salary reductions, superior judges removable only by the House of Representatives for misbehaviour or incapacity).

The Constitution Act 1986 therefore describes, even if it does not constitute, the three branches of the New Zealand Government. But it is the closest New Zealand has to a written constitution. It is in the small group of statutes that the consensus of commentators describes as the 'canon' of New Zealand's constitutional law. (The others are the Electoral Act 1993, and the New Zealand Bill of Rights Act 1990, to which reference is made shortly. The Treaty of Waitangi is routinely included as well, for reasons to come, though it is not, of course, a statute.)

The most intriguing feature of the Constitution Act 1986 is its provision that all the United Kingdom enactments of the nineteenth and twentieth century—the ones that originally constituted the New Zealand legislature and amended it from time to time—would immediately cease to be of further force or effect.[20] This could be interpreted as a revolutionary break in legal continuity—cutting off the branch of the tree upon which one sits. If so, it was a revolution so quiet and technical as to be unnoticed by the citizenry in 1986. It signified that the legitimacy of New Zealand's political institutions now rested on their acceptance by New Zealanders rather than their initial creation by the mother country.

As things stand, then, there are no subject matter limitations on Parliament's law-making power; no fetters imposed by constitutional rights for individuals or by federalism. Parliament is legally supreme, as in the United Kingdom. That said, the political process and the need to operate in the real world (observing requirements of international treaties, for example) supply copious practical constraints on the law that may or may not be enacted. Parliament's power is understood to include a power to amend the Constitution Act in the same way as any other Act.

Five key provisions of the Electoral Act 1993 and one in the Constitution Act are 'entrenched' against ordinary repeal, requiring for repeal a special majority of 75 per cent in Parliament or 50 per cent of voters at a referendum.[21] These concern the qualifications of voters, the mechanics of voting, the division of the country into electorates, the make-up of the Representation Commission, and

---

[19] Section 15.
[20] Section 26.
[21] Section 268 of the Electoral Act 1993.

the parliamentary term. These 'manner and form' requirements were imposed by Parliament itself. Parliament stopped short of entrenching the entrenching provision, meaning it is technically possible to repeal by simple majority the requirement for a 75 per cent majority or referendum. Successive Parliaments have never sought to do this, and it would be considered 'unconstitutional' if they did, even if technically legal. Interestingly, the idea of 'double entrenchment' (that is, entrenching the entrenching provision itself) was never attempted, it being believed that Parliament's supremacy precluded any true restraint on the power of a later Parliament. The modern consensus, however, is different. It is now thought that a New Zealand court would uphold a manner and form provision, and declare invalid a purported enactment not made in the required manner, so long as it was satisfied that there was a democratic pedigree to the double entrenchment. For example, such a view was a premise of the 1985 proposal for a supreme law Bill of Rights—although it was never tested because the proposal did not proceed. It is also a premise of a 1995 reform to Parliament's Standing Orders, which requires that any law imposing a manner and form requirement on future parliaments must itself be enacted using that manner and form. That embodies the assumption that a court would likely deem the entrenchment legally effective (subject, of course, to various other considerations including whether the protected subject matter was appropriate for entrenchment; that is, applying to matters of procedure and not substance).[22]

To complete the outline of New Zealand's constitution, reference should now be made to several post-1986 developments. First, there was the proposal, just mentioned, for a 'constitutional Bill of Rights', to be a supreme law empowering judicial review of legislation on the American model. The proposal did not proceed, being judged to be unwelcomed by the citizenry and by Māori. The New Zealand Bill of Rights Act 1990 was enacted instead. It is a statutory bill of rights, affirming rights and freedoms, requiring the Attorney-General to signify to the House if a parliamentary bill would be inconsistent with any rights, and requiring courts, when it can be done, to prefer statutory meanings that are consistent with affirmed rights over those that are not.[23]

Secondly, there was the move to Mixed-Member Proportional Representation (MMP) in 1993, with effect from the 1996 election. This was assuredly the most important constitutional change in the twentieth century, and the process employed to make it is explored further below. And thirdly, there was the abolition, from 2004, of appeals to the Judicial Committee of the Privy Council

---

[22] There is a discussion of these matters in Joseph, *Constitutional and Administrative Law* note 2 above, 560–81.

[23] See s 6 of the New Zealand Bill of Rights Act 1990. Section 4 provides that an enactment shall not be held to be invalid or ineffective, or to be impliedly repealed, by reason only of its inconsistency with the Bill of Rights. See, generally, P Rishworth, G Huscroft, S Optican and Mahoney R, *The New Zealand Bill of Rights*, (Oxford University Press, 2003).

and the creation of a new Supreme Court of New Zealand with a discretionary power to hear appeals from the New Zealand Court of Appeal. Again, the process behind that change will be examined.

The picture of New Zealand's Constitution just painted has been an essentially British one. But if there is anything that characterises the last three decades of New Zealand law and politics, it is the need to reckon with the Māori perspective of the Treaty of Waitangi and what this ought to mean for New Zealand. We explore this next. That will enable us to consider the process for change in light of New Zealand's Māori dimension.

REBUILDING THE CONSTITUTION? THE MĀORI DIMENSION OF NEW ZEALAND

The Treaty signed at Waitangi had been drafted in English but was translated by a missionary into the Māori language. The debates at signing ceremonies were largely in Māori, and it was the Māori version that was signed. So the Māori version has a certain claim to superiority over the English when deciding its meaning. It transpires that the Māori version (*Te Tiriti o Waitangi*) is subtly different in its import from the English version. That in itself might not have been significant, but serendipitously the linguistic differences capture exactly the pressure points of modern indigenous relations—not only in New Zealand, but in Australia and North America as well. Can the constitution reckon with a degree of sovereignty or autonomy for non-Crown institutions; can there be a space in the constitution for indigenous people?

Article 1 in English reads as a transfer of sovereignty but is, in Māori, a cession only of 'governorship'. This, it is now said, is less than complete sovereignty.[24] There are grounds for such a view. The Māori word chosen to translate 'sovereignty' was *kawanatanga*, formed by *kawana*—a transliteration of the English 'governor'—with the suffix *tanga* denoting the action of governing. The Māori New Testament, available before 1840, had described Pontius Pilate as *kawana* over Judea, while *kawana* was used also to describe Governor Macquarie across the Tasman Sea in New South Wales.[25] Since both these 'governors' answered to a higher power, Māori could be forgiven for thinking that their grant to the Crown of governorship was something less than cession of their sovereignty. The more so when the professed reason for British annexation was the need to control lawless immigrants and protect Māori. The power to govern—it might be said—was a power granted by Māori to govern *settlers*, not the Māori themselves.

---

[24] This has been the consistent view of the Waitangi Tribunal, discussed further below, almost since its inception. See, for a very helpful analysis, J Ruru, 'The Waitangi Tribunal', ch 6 in M Mulholland and V Tawhai, *Weeping Waters: The Treaty of Waitangi and Constitutional Change*, (Huia Publishers, 2010).

[25] This point was first made by RM Ross. 'Te Tiriti o Waitangi: Texts and Translations' (1972) *New Zealand Journal of History* 129, 140; cited in Palmer, above note 11, 63 and fn 164.

Article 2 contains a related translation issue. In Māori, article 2 affirms not just continuing ownership by Māori of their possessions, but *rangatiratanga*, or chiefly authority, over those possessions. (*Rangatira* is a chief; *rangatiratanga* chieftainship.) Further, in *te Tiriti* this relates not just to tangible possessions such as land and forests, but over *taonga katoa* ('all other sacred treasures')—a phrase now taken to include intangibles such as Māori culture and language. This affirmation of continuing political authority by Māori over matters sacred to them resonates with contemporary movements in indigenous societies for some form of tribal sovereignty or control. This, of course, is hard to reconcile with the strict legal sovereignty known to the law of the United Kingdom, in which individual Māori were subjects and there could be no other sovereign.

Standing back, and putting argument about word meanings aside, Māori in 1840 were confronted by a small group of British sailors and officials, and a settler population numbering hundreds rather than thousands. The idea that the signing of the Treaty would bring about the end of their own internal autonomy and way of life could not easily have been contemplated. That said, Māori had had over two decades of significant interaction with Europeans, and the surviving accounts of the speeches at Waitangi and elsewhere attest to their awareness of the huge shifts in power that were occurring in their country. It was clear enough that the signing chiefs recognised their own powers would be limited by the new arrangements.

Suffice to say that, once the United Kingdom claimed sovereignty, the influx of settlers was to result in the massive alienation of Māori land. And, as we have seen, United Kingdom institutions were created which, by necessity, supplied the rules for their own validity, backed by force when necessary. In a masterly account of Pacific colonisation, American legal historian Stuart Banner chooses two very appropriate titles for his chapters on New Zealand: 'conquest by treaty' (an allusion to the way in which the Treaty of Waitangi facilitated peaceful annexation of New Zealand by Britain) and 'conquest by land reform' (alluding to the fragmentation of communally owned Māori land over subsequent decades through legislation, and the speedy transfer of most of it to European settlers).[26]

But now, in the twenty-first century, the resilience of Māori society is, as already noted, the elephant in the room when the constitution is debated. Whatever is done by way of major constitutional change must reckon with Māori concerns for their place in the affairs of the country. Māori concerns loom large in almost all of the developments we are about to discuss concerning the process of constitutional change in New Zealand. How has this come about? Essentially through Māori political pressure and activism, the electoral success of Māori politicians, a growing sense of New Zealand history, Māori litigation successes, all allied with the imperatives of human rights law and corrective justice that give

---

[26] S Banner, *Possessing the Pacific: Land, Settlers and Indigenous People from Australia to Alaska*, (Harvard University Press, 2007).

Māori grievances a significant purchase on the conscience of (enough) New Zealand politicians and members of the citizenry.

Much of the wind in the sails of this Māori renaissance has been supplied by the Waitangi Tribunal, a body with undoubted constitutional significance—and protection—in that its abolition would be difficult to accomplish without Māori assent even though it is not legally protected in any way. The Waitangi Tribunal was created by legislation in 1975 in response to Māori political pressure on their favoured party, the Labour Party, which formed the Government from 1972 to 1975. The Tribunal was empowered to hear Māori complaints that the Crown had acted inconsistently with the principles of the Treaty of Waitangi.[27] Complaints could be made against legislation, as well as the Crown's policies and practices. Initially, a complaint could relate only to post-1975 matters, but when Labour was next returned to power, in 1984, a further amendment empowered complaints dating back to 1840 and the birth of the nation.

The Waitangi Tribunal soon became a significant contributor to the position of Māori and to constitutional debate. In the harsh particularity of specific Māori histories, or legislative proposals and policies, the Tribunal has conducted exegesis of the Treaty texts, in Māori and English, and stated the deep principles that underpin them. The Tribunal's statutory mandate to consider the 'principles' of the Treaty (and not just its text) allows for a certain reconstitution of the Treaty bargain to reflect the times. The Tribunal has blended the two versions, using modern language and concepts. While never going so far as to advocate a true Māori sovereignty at the expense of Parliament's ultimate supremacy, the Tribunal consistently speaks of Parliament's supremacy being qualified by its the need to recognise, protect and advance Māori interests. *Kawanatanga*, in short, is subject to *rangatiratanga*. Only in the clearest cases can the right to govern in the national interest, conferred by article 1, override the obligations owed to Māori under article 2. In putting it this way, the Tribunal observes that Parliament's supremacy is limited in practice by considerations such as international obligations. The limits imposed by the nation's founding Treaty ought, it says, to be no different. In a series of Tribunal Reports into past transactions and current policies, the generally measured and scholarly approach of the Tribunal has brought the injustices of the past and Māori aspirations for the present to a wider audience.

Save for a small category of case where it may make binding determinations, the Tribunal can only recommend. It depends for its influence on the cogency of its arguments. In historic cases its reports become a basis for settlement negotiations between tribe and Crown. In other types of claims—say claims about proposed policy or legislation—the reports will have such influence as governments allow. The Tribunal routinely speaks of the Treaty of Waitangi as being

---

[27] See the Treaty of Waitangi Act 1975.

constitutional in its import, as the foundation document for the New Zealand constitution. But it is not alone in doing so; the courts have used that language too, as has Government.

As to the courts, in 1987 the New Zealand Court of Appeal was required to reckon, for the first time, with the Treaty of Waitangi as a legal restraint on the powers of the Crown. The resulting case, *New Zealand Māori Council v Attorney-General*,[28] is arguably New Zealand's most important judicial decision. It was the heyday of privatisation and reconfiguring the state, and the Labour Government had introduced the State-Owned Enterprises Act 1986 to facilitate the transfer of state assets to new trading enterprises (forestry, post, rail, broadcasting and so on). Māori had lobbied successfully for a clause in the Act that read 'Nothing in this Act shall permit the Crown to act inconsistently with the principles of the Treaty of Waitangi'. Then, in the face of the proposed asset transfers which were going to involve nearly 52 per cent of the land mass of the country, Māori sought a restraining injunction on the grounds that the Crown would be acting inconsistently with the Treaty were it to divest itself of land that Māori tribes were known to be claiming or may well claim.[29] This brought the Court of Appeal into the arena in which, to that point, only the Waitangi Tribunal had been operating: declaring the principles of the Treaty of Waitangi and judging Crown action against them.

Granting the injunction, the Court of Appeal identified the salient principles of the Treaty of Waitangi (essentially, 'utmost good faith' between Crown and Māori, akin to a partnership). It offended the principle of 'redress', said the Court, for the Crown to seek to transfer land out of Crown ownership without establishing a mechanism to secure its return if needed to satisfy a Tribunal recommendation. Subsequently, Crown and Māori negotiated a set of protocols and a law change to satisfy both sides.

Cases over the next decade followed a similar pattern, as different parts of the state asset register were privatised or corporatised. So, for example, when the off-shore fisheries resource was commodified into ITQs (individual transferable quota), Māori successfully obtained injunctions on the basis that this was a breach of their customary fishing rights affirmed by the Treaty of Waitangi.[30] When the state's broadcasting assets were transferred to a corporatised Television New Zealand Ltd, Māori claimed that any transfer without assurance that TVNZ would promote Māori language programming would be inconsistent with Treaty

---

[28] The *Lands* case, above, note 7.

[29] Ibid, at 653 (per Cooke P).

[30] No final determination was required as the Government entered into a major settlement with all Māori in relation to commercial fishing, known as the 'Sealord Deal' because a part of the settlement was the provision of $150 million to be used by the Treaty of Waitangi Fisheries Commission to purchase a 50% share in Sealord Ltd, New Zealand's largest fishing company. Together with further fishing quota conferred on Māori, this resulted in an opportunity for Māori to gain a significant stake in New Zealand's commercial fishing sector.

principles.[31] When the FM radio spectrum was auctioned off, Māori claimed an entitlement to an allocation of frequencies to enable advancement of Māori language amongst young persons, and so on.[32] Not all cases were won, but it became plain that the new focus on the 'principles of the Treaty' meant that there was a Treaty-dimension to almost everything, so that the Treaty of Waitangi set some sort of standard for governments and the legislature.

All these developments put Māori and Māori claims firmly on the map, and the process was recognised to have a significant constitutional dimension. It was true that most of these cases turned on the fact that Parliament had specifically imposed the 'principles of the Treaty of Waitangi' as a fetter on the Crown's power. But it was significant that no politician suggested for a moment that the court's involvement could be circumvented by the simple expedient of amending the legislation and freeing the Crown from legislated restraints. The 'Treaty clause' in the State-Owned Enterprises Act 1986 had a practical sanctity— although it applied only in the realm of action under that Act, which has now effectively been spent.

Over the years since 1987 it has become a feature of legislation on major topics (environment, biosecurity, health, conservation, heritage, biotechnology, education, and so on) that it reckons with the Māori dimension of the legislation's subject matter. Treaty references of some sort are now common in legislation.[33] Successive parliaments, however, have been less willing to enact them in quite the robust form used in the State-Owned Enterprises Act 1986, where the Treaty was a positive limit on executive action. It became more normal to require that decision-makers 'have regard to' Treaty principles, or some other weaker formulation.[34] In some cases government makes a specific determination of what the Treaty principles ought to mean in the relevant context, and enacts that specific determination into law (thereby avoiding judicial review by courts armed with a broad 'Treaty clause'). These techniques were designed to curtail the ability of courts to rule on Treaty matters; politicians were very keen to keep the final judgment on Treaty-consistency to themselves and some were heard to lament the 'activism' that they perceived in the courts.

In retrospect the period from 1987 through to the mid 1990s was one in which litigation successes fuelled the Treaty of Waitangi as a significant constitutional document. It is no surprise, then, that publications emanating from Government itself routinely describe the Treaty of Waitangi as a source of the New Zealand constitution even though it is not technically a part of the law at all.[35]

---

[31] *New Zealand Māori Council v Attorney-General* [1994] 1 NZLR 513 (PC) (*Broadcasting Assets Case*).

[32] *New Zealand Māori Council v Attorney-General* [1991] 2 NZLR 129 (CA).

[33] See, for instance, the Resource Management Act 1991, s 8; the State-Owned Enterprises Act 1986, s 9; the Conservation Act 1987, s 4.

[34] The Crown Minerals Act 1991 is one statute that uses this formulation.

[35] Examples include the Cabinet Office Manual 2008, published by the Department of the Prime Minister and Cabinet, Parliament Buildings, Wellington, which lists the Treaty of Waitangi as a 'major

Throughout this period something similar was happening in relation to judges' conception of the Treaty. An infamous judgment of 1872 had said in passing of the Treaty of Waitangi that it was a 'simple nullity', because Māori society was claimed to be without rules and customs.[36] That period has long gone, and by the late 1980s the courts, while recognising that the Treaty was not in force as law, were taking it into account in matters of statutory interpretation and on occasion through the mechanisms of administrative law. At the same time, Māori began to win cases in relation to fishing rights on the basis that their customary rights existed after annexation by the United Kingdom unless removed by statute, and that they had not been removed.[37] This was the case-law development that drove the major fisheries settlement with Māori in 1992.

But the most far-reaching case was to come in 2003 when the New Zealand Court of Appeal ruled, contrary to the expectation of Government, that no New Zealand legislation precluded Māori tribes from claiming customary title in the foreshore and seabed surrounding New Zealand.[38] Since the foreshore is the land covered by the incoming tides, and the seabed extends 300 kilometres from the coast, this case was of enormous import—raising the spectre (tirelessly pointed out by politicians and others) that non-Māori New Zealand might have their free access to the New Zealand coastline curtailed by successful Māori claims.

The Labour Government's response was to reverse the Court of Appeal decision by legislation. This—the Seabed and Foreshore Act 2003—led to the defection of one of the Party's Māori members, Tariana Turia, to form a new Māori Party devoted to its repeal. The legislation never really gained any moral suasion—it therefore seemed inevitable that it would be repealed, as (at the time of writing) seems inevitable (interestingly, *with* the votes of Labour now in opposition). This Seabed and Foreshore Act saga exemplifies a number of points about the New Zealand constitution as well as its Māori dimension. The original Act with its ousting of Māori claims of customary title to the seabed and foreshore could readily be cast as discriminatory against Māori. No one but Māori was precluded from bringing a claim to ownership of the seabed and foreshore. Of course, the reality was that few, if any, would have grounds to do so, but an effective race-based distinction nonetheless jarred with the more egalitarian New Zealander who values everyone having a 'fair go'. It also elicited adverse comment from the visiting UN Special Rapporteur on the Rights of Indigenous

source of the constitution' (2). So too, the Governor-General's website says: 'Increasingly, New Zealand's constitution reflects the Treaty of Waitangi as a founding document of government in New Zealand.' See http://www.gg.govt.nz/role/constofnz.htm.

[36] *Wi Parata v Bishop of Wellington* (1877) 3 NZ Jur 72.
[37] *Te Weehi v Regional Fisheries Officer* [1986] 1 NZLR 680.
[38] *Attorney-General v Ngati Apa* [2003] 3 NZLR 643 (CA).

Peoples, Rodolfo Stavenhagen.[39] The replacement legislation looks to be the subject of much more comprehensive consultation and is gaining a reasonable degree of Māori assent, even though its stipulation that Māori prove unbroken historical connections with claimed land may mean that there will in practice be few successful claims.[40] But Māori value consultation and process, and relationships, and it was important that the new deal was worked out by Government and Māori together. That exemplifies the Treaty partnership: it may not always be easy, but conflict can ultimately be resolved by talking. Without a resolution, the issue was not going to go away.

THE PROCESS OF CONSTITUTIONAL CHANGE

How then, does change happen in New Zealand? With the exception of the entrenched provisions in the Constitution and Electoral Acts, we have seen that there are no laws that specify how the constitution must be changed. The historical record reveals several processes at work, differing according to context.

First, there are those changes that mark evolution to independence from Britain. In the main these changes were accomplished by Parliamentary legislation involving no significant public consultation. There was the extension of law-making powers in 1973, and the constitutional 'spring clean' wrought in 1986 that terminated the effect of the old United Kingdom enactments in New Zealand and asserted a home-grown legislative power. These were essentially technical changes, bringing the written constitution into line with the practical reality of New Zealand's situation. Although no special amending formulas were needed, there was in fact virtual unanimity in the legislature. When the Constitution Act 1986 went through its various stages in a bipartisan spirit, one Opposition member remarked that 'there can be few countries that in this way, in the course of an evening, more or less by agreement, and certainly without division by way of votes, change their constitution ...'.[41] This, of course, is because no one thought anything very significant was happening.

This can, perhaps, breed a certain casualness. In 2005 two changes to the Constitution Act 1986 were made: one to allow the resumption of Parliamentary business after a dissolution or prorogation of the House, the second to repeal the requirement that appropriation bills be recommended to the House by the Crown. The procedure to make these changes was quite unorthodox: amendments to the Constitution Act 1986 were introduced into an omnibus Statutes

---

[39] Rodolfo Stavenhagen (United Nations Economic and Social Council—Commission on Human Rights), *Report of the Special Rapporteur on the situation of human rights and fundamental freedoms of indigenous people*, E/CN.4/2006/78/Add.3, 13 March 2006, available online at http://www.converge.org.nz/pma/srnzmarch06.pdf.

[40] The new Bill is renamed the Marine and Coastal Area (Takutai Moana) Bill.

[41] Palmer, 'New Zealand Constitutional Culture', note 3 above, 594.

Amendment Bill then before the House, submissions were heard by a Parliamentary Committee for 20 minutes, and upon the Committee's report back to the House a still further amendment (to one of the two proposed amendments) was introduced. The amendments were then passed into law. This saga is described by respected constitutional commentator Matthew Palmer as constitutionally outrageous, even to the realist who (like him) recognised that in their substance the amendments were pragmatic and sensible.[42]

A second category of constitutional change is seen from the start as requiring more extensive public consultation, beyond the consultation that ordinary parliamentary legislation typically gets. The 1985 proposal for a supreme Bill of Rights is an example. The genesis of the Bill of Rights idea was a widespread public sentiment that the National Government of 1975 to 1984 had used the law-making power of Parliament, and the regulation-making power of the executive, to make some significant inroads into civil rights. Labour came to power in 1984 with the promise of constitutional reform and a Bill of Rights. By April 1985 it had produced a White Paper with a suggested bill of rights, announcing its intention to proceed only if there were widespread public support *and* specific support from Māori (the Bill would recognise and affirm the rights in the Treaty of Waitangi, so giving it constitutional effect). After public hearings conducted over many months by a Parliamentary Committee, the Government discerned there was little public or Māori support. The supreme law proposal was quietly abandoned. The Bill of Rights was subsequently enacted in 1990 as an 'ordinary' statute, by the votes of Government members over the National Party in Opposition, who decried it (perhaps inconsistently) as being both pointless and a Trojan Horse.

The Bill of Rights debate from 1985 to 1990 exemplifies two interesting points about how the New Zealand constitution works. First the subject matter of the New Zealand Bill of Rights Act—fundamental human rights for individuals sourced from the International Covenant on Civil and Political Rights—was plainly of constitutional significance. It *was* a Trojan Horse. The Bill of Rights is now firmly in the canon of New Zealand's significant statutes, even if it (like the Treaty) cannot be wielded to invalidate legislation. This also explains why the National Party, who became the Government a mere nine weeks after voting against it in the House, never contemplated repealing it. It is in the category of 'super-statutes'.[43] The second salient point about the Bill of Rights debate concerns its Māori dimension: Māori opposed the White Paper proposal for a Bill of Rights *because* it referred to the Treaty of Waitangi, and would render the Treaty a part of the legal system and hence susceptible to potentially restrictive judicial interpretation. Māori preferred then, as many would still do, to preserve the Treaty in the sphere where it serves as a reference point for whatever may

---

[42] Ibid, 596.
[43] See W Eskridge and J Ferejohn, 'Super-Statutes' (2001) 50 *Duke Law Review* 1215.

happen in courts and governments, but is not surrendered to those courts and governments for 'authoritative' interpretation.

Another major constitutional change, seen to require more-than-ordinary consultation, was MMP. Indeed, in MMP's case there was a legal requirement for a special majority or referendum to introduce it. MMP was in many respects the real solution to the sorts of concerns that had initially spawned the Bill of Rights idea—the phenomenon of hasty legislation interfering with civil rights, by a Parliament effectively dominated by the Executive. Also, a significant public sentiment had developed that the first past the post voting system delivered parliaments (and hence governments) that did not fairly reflect the votes cast. National and Labour were the two main parties who competed for power; minor parties had on occasion gained 21 per cent of the vote for only 2 per cent of the seats, or 15 per cent for none. In 1985 Labour established a Royal Commission on the Electoral System which recommended a move to MMP. But in truth neither major party was enthusiastic; the likelihood was that minority or coalition governments would become the norm. Labour took no further steps until, in the 1990 election, each party promised a referendum on the Commission's recommendation. In the result, National held an indicative referendum in 1992 in which the citizenry voted by a considerable margin for a change to MMP. A binding referendum in 1994 adopted MMP in time for the 1996 election.

MMP has been in place since then. It has indeed delivered coalition or minority government, often depending significantly on Māori members or (since 2008) the newly formed Māori Party. The current National Government is to honour a 2008 election promise to hold a further referendum on MMP at the 2011 election, at which voters will be asked whether they wish to retain MMP or would prefer an alternative.

The abolition in 2004 of appeals to the Privy Council, and the establishment of the Supreme Court of New Zealand, is an interesting case study of constitutional change in an unwritten constitution.[44] No referendum was required or held, although there were suggestions that one was appropriate for such an important change. The Labour Government of the day took the view that this was a necessary change, implicit in evolving independence, and one on which there had been a recommendation by the New Zealand Law Commission in 1989, research and discussion papers by the Solicitor-General since 1992, and consultation with the legal profession, Māori and business community. In the end, such opposition as there was came from the business community which saw the Privy Council judges as delivering a more 'certain' interpretation of business law, and Privy Council Law Lords as somehow more detached and independent than their New Zealand counterparts. The National, ACT, and New Zealand First political parties

---

[44] 'A significant milestone in New Zealand's constitutional journey' is how it is described by Joseph in his text (note 3 at p 799).

said that 'substantial constitutional change should not be made by a bare majority vote of a coalition of minorities in Parliament'.[45] But that is an accurate description of what did, in fact, occur.

This truth is that the Privy Council appeal abolition debate failed to ignite any popular concern. Nor was there Māori opposition. Removal of a connection to the Queen's Law Lords might have been seen as an undermining of the historic Treaty connection between Crown and Māori. But Māori leaders of 2004 were pragmatic, recognising that New Zealand judges could be expected to deliver robust Treaty judgments if called upon to do so. Indeed, in 2003, around the height of the abolition debate, the New Zealand Court of Appeal had delivered the seminal *Foreshore and Seabed* judgment discussed above.

There is a different arena of constitutional development in which proposals for change are not explicitly promoted. This is the arena in which certain statutes and values, or practices, simply evolve to have a certain importance and sanctity that earns the label 'constitutional'. Some of these can be briefly listed:

— The New Zealand Bill of Rights Act 1990, though only statutory, is widely regarded as constitutionally important because of its subject matter and because of its implications for law-making (the statutory role of the Attorney-General to bring to the attention of the House any provision in a bill that would be inconsistent with the Bill of Rights). As applied to statutory interpretation, it can generally accomplish the severing of 'unconstitutional applications' from broad powers or words,[46] and the courts have reserved a power to declare or indicate if an enactment is inconsistent and cannot be given a consistent interpretation.[47] Much of the ground of a constitutional bill of rights is covered by these developments, although obviously not all.

— The Treaty of Waitangi Act 1975 is similarly sacrosanct. Other enactments with a constitutional dimension are the Official Information Act 1982 (affirming freedom of information), the State Sector Act 1986 (public sector independence and control) and the Public Finance Act 1989.

[45] As supported by New Zealand Business Roundtable in its Press Release, 'Initiative on Privy Council Welcomed', 3 July 2003, online at: http://www.nzbr.org.nz/site/nzbr/files/releases/releases-2003/initiative_welcomed.htm.

[46] See *Drew v Attorney-General* [2002] 2 NZLR 58 (NZCA), *Brooker v Police* [2007] 3 NZLR 791 (NZSC).

[47] See *Moonen v Board of Film and Literature Review* [2000] 2 NZLR 9 (NZCA); R Hansen [2007] 3 NZLR 1 (NZSC). The idea of judicial declarations of inconsistency was expressly adopted by an amendment to the Human Rights Act 1993 that was enacted in 2001, which empowers the Human Rights Review Tribunal and courts on appeal to declare an enactment inconsistent with the rights against discrimination in s 19 of the Bill of Rights. The Human Rights Act is essentially an anti-discrimination statute, with the added dimension that complaints against legislation and not just public or private sector conduct are possible.

— The innovation in executive practice that allows parliamentary input into proposals for ratification of treaties (so as to remedy the so-called democratic deficit otherwise involved when treaty-making is exclusively the province of the executive).[48]
— The trend to harmonisation of laws with Australia, in recognition that many businesses are operating in both markets, and the use of common regulatory bodies. The Supreme Court of New Zealand has recently said in relation to competition law, for example, that 'it is important that the approach ... be broadly the same on both sides of the Tasman'.[49]

Then there are the contested areas, where some advocate changes of constitutional import that are simply too much for others. A current example concerns whether there should be an equivalent of Māori parliamentary seats at local government level. Although a previous government procured Parliamentary legislation to make this possible in relation to a regional municipality,[50] the current National-led Government vigorously rejected Māori representation on the new 'super-city' reforms of Auckland's local government.

A   WRITTEN CONSTITUTION?

There are recurring, if infrequent, calls for a formal written constitution, emanating from those with an interest in constitutional matters and, on occasions, from politicians. Some advocate the minimalist solution of bringing together the Constitution Act 1986 and Bill of Rights Act 1990 into a single document that would be higher law. If that were done, only the Bill of Rights component would likely generate controversy, with calls being made for a review of the substance of the rights and inclusion of further rights, perhaps social and economic ones and perhaps some sort of Treaty reference (for example, that limits on rights must not only be reasonable but consistent with the Treaty of Waitangi).

Others contend for more comprehensive reforms (republicanism, bicameralism and so on). As already noted, these calls gain no real traction amongst the citizenry who tend to regard constitutional debate as a preoccupation of pointy-headed academics. A major invitation-only conference in 2000 entitled 'Building the Constitution' was staged by a University research institute—portentously held in the old Legislative Council chamber in Parliament Buildings. The organisers

---

[48] See Joseph, above, note 3, at 331–33.

[49] *Commerce Commission v Telecom Corp of New Zealand* [2010] NZSC 111 at [31]. A think tank representing business interests has recently gone further in favour of harmonisation, proposing that the High Court of Australia be made New Zealand's final court of appeal: see New Zealand Business Roundtable *Submission on Questions Arising from the Regulatory Responsibility Bill Prepared by the Regulatory Responsibility Taskforce*, August 2010, online at: http://www.nzbr.org.nz/site/nzbr/files/ NZBR%200827%20Sub%20on%20Regulatory%20Responsibility%20Bill%20Questions.pdf. See also the Trans-Tasman Mutual Recognition Act 1997 (NZ).

[50] See Bay of Plenty Regional Council (Māori Constituency Empowerment) Act 2001, ss 5 and 6.

had striven to include poets, authors and historians to explore 'what constitutes our nation?' but by the end of the first day and thereafter most speakers were, as might be expected, lawyers and political scientists. Despite the best intentions of its promoters, the conference did not succeed in establishing a working group to carry the debate further.[51]

In 2004 a Parliamentary Committee was set up with the title 'Constitutional Arrangements Committee' and a mandate to conduct an 'Inquiry to Review New Zealand's Existing Constitutional Arrangements'. But this Committee was boy-cotted by the National Party, and its very creation was the result of inter-party deal-making that involved Labour's garnering minority party support for its then-proposed Privy Council abolition bill. The Constitutional Arrangements Committee focused on chronicling the timeline of New Zealand's constitutional development, considering the processes of change used in the past, and express-ing a view on how changes might, from a technical perspective, be made in the future. Its conclusions were that the constitution was not 'in crisis', that citizens needed better education about the constitution, including in schools, and that 'New Zealand may be better served if it developed a capacity for paying systematic attention to constitutional issues as they arise'.[52] Nothing ensued from this Commission's effort by way of further initiatives from the House of Representatives.

It is the Māori dimension of New Zealand politics that keeps the flame of what passes for constitutional debate flickering. There are several strains to that Māori dimension. One concerns Māori claims, based on common law doctrine, to customary title in the foreshore and seabed of New Zealand. We have encoun-tered the consequence of that doctrine already: a potentially far-reaching court judgment in 2003, legislation to reverse the judgment, and continuing disquiet that saw the legislation repealed and replaced. Because the criticised legislation was said to both discriminate and wrongly interfere with property rights, it fuels the debate about a more robust system for rights-protection. But these events also bolster Māori enthusiasm for a reformed constitution—and particularly one that protects Māori participation.

In this regard, the Māori seats in Parliament are a well-established feature of New Zealand politics. There are presently seven, and it is routine for there to be up to a dozen more Māori MPs elected in general seats or as list members. Before the 2008 election there had been calls in some quarters and amongst some political parties to abolish the Māori seats, which are not protected by any special manner and form provision. The Royal Commission on the Electoral System, which had recommended MMP, had also recommended the eventual abolition of Māori seats given that the MMP system would be expected to secure Māori their

---

[51] The record of the conference is in C James (ed) *Building the Constitution*, (Institute of Policy Studies, Victoria University of Wellington, 2000).
[52] See above note 2, at 9.

representation. So it was, then, that when the National Party sought a 'Confidence and Supply Agreement' with the Māori Party after winning the largest share of Parliamentary seats (though not a majority), the Māori Party exacted a promise from National in return:[53]

Status of the Māori Seats

Both parties agree to the establishment (including its composition and terms of reference) by no later than early 2010 of a group to consider constitutional issues including Māori representation. The Māori Party will be consulted on membership and the choice of Chairperson, and will be represented on the group. The National Party agrees it will not seek to remove the Māori seats without the consent of the Māori people. Accordingly, the Māori Party and the National Party will not be pursuing the entrenchment of the Māori seats in the current parliamentary term. Both parties agree that there will not be a question about the future of the Māori seats in the referendum on MMP planned by the National Party.

The proposed further inquiry into constitutional issues is, at the time of writing, only just getting started; it was delayed while the repeal and replacement of the Foreshore and Seabed Act 2003 was worked out. But it is practical reasons such as these—the need for governance arrangements—that will continue to keep constitutional change on the agenda. Of course, this can produce just more committee reports, and no actual change.

Actual change will be forced by outside events—that is, events outside political parties and outside the churn of political debate. It will come when something *has* to be done, and matters cannot simply be shelved as too difficult. What might be in this category? The most likely, already foreshadowed, is the move to a republic. While Queen Elizabeth II is greatly admired in New Zealand, and while her grandchildren have a minor celebrity status in magazines, the fact is that the accession of Prince Charles is, for all the prince's many qualities, likely to prompt renewed republican debate on both sides of the Tasman. Eventually such a question will assuredly go to a referendum, if not two (a separate one for Māori in view of the Treaty relationship with the United Kingdom sovereign). There is a fair prospect of success, depending on what is suggested as an alternative. At that point Māori may aspire for a reform that is more fundamental than crossing out Crown' and adding 'President'. Devolution to Māori institutions of some type will be on the agenda, as will the idea of a senate or similar with Māori representation—to represent the 'Treaty partnership'.

The restructuring of the Anglican Church of Aotearoa New Zealand in 1992 is sometimes heralded as a forerunner of what a national constitution might look like, the Church's General Synod now comprising three houses, Tikanga Māori, Tikanga Pakeha, and Tikanga Pasifika. The third, Pacific, stream is likely to be controversial if mooted for the nation: many Pacific peoples have made New

---

[53] Relationship and Confidence and Supply Agreement between the National Party and the Māori Party, 16 November 2008, 2.

Zealand their home but Māori may perceive that making a place for them in the system of New Zealand government devalues the Māori status as one of two Treaty partners, along with the Crown.

A bellwether in the embryonic republican debate is the New Zealand 'flag debate', which newspapers and sufficiently-motivated others seek to ignite from time to time. It may well be time for something more distinctive and meaningful than the Union Jack in the top corner alongside the four red stars of the Southern Cross constellation. Insofar as debates about flags can be a portent of future constitutional change (like Canada's in the 1970s) another interesting debate has been one over whether the 'Māori sovereignty flag' can be flown from the Auckland Harbour Bridge alongside the New Zealand flag on Waitangi Day, the national holiday that recognises the day the Treaty was signed. After several years of refusal by the appropriate authority, that was allowed for the first time in 2010.[54]

CONCLUSION

In the end, constitutional change is made and agreed by the people of New Zealand. It is in the national consciousness and culture that we must search for the drivers of that change. The account just given has emphasised pragmatism, and this is the national trait that New Zealand observers routinely agree upon. Matthew Palmer identifies 'authoritarianism' as well—a desire for effective and decisive government; a 'get on with it' attitude that is impatient with abstraction and symbolism. One early book of social commentary on New Zealanders was entitled 'The Passionless People', and perhaps that succinctly expresses these two traits.[55] And then there is egalitarianism, long associated with New Zealand settlers who were said to have created, in contrast to the mother land, a 'classless society'.

The small size of New Zealand is relevant to its constitutional order as well. The expression 'six degrees of separation' can in New Zealand be adjusted to two or three degrees. Politicians and prime ministers are not so far removed from ordinary people, and are held to account accordingly. If a law is passed that seems to fail some sort of 'sniff test', a mood can develop for its change—two recent examples being the Foreshore and Seabed Act, already mentioned, and the Electoral Finance Act 2007 (which imposed draconian limits on freedom of expression in conjunction with electioneering). The latter was repealed after a change of government, the former is almost certainly to be.

These examples, and others, suggest a political culture that is more engaged than New Zealanders are often given credit for, and one in which matters of

[54] See New Zealand Herald 'Flags Side by Side on Harbour Bridge', 6 February 2010, online at: http://www.nzherald.co.nz/waitangi-day/news/article.cfm?c_id=1500878&objectid=10624512.
[55] G McLauchlan, *The Passionless People*, (Cassell, 1976).

'constitutional' rights and process are at work, even if not enshrined in higher law. Indeed, the fact is that on matters of individual rights, there is little difference between the outcomes obtained politically in New Zealand and those obtained through litigation in North America and elsewhere (abortion rights, anti-discrimination law, civil unions, gay rights, separation of church and state, and so on).

When events force a reckoning with New Zealand's written constitution, as they may when the call for a republic comes, these national characteristics may well manifest themselves in calls for constitutional revision to express New Zealand's Māori dimension more formally, to give a more prominent place to individual rights, and to express New Zealand values. In looking for its place in the world, modern New Zealand may well be inclined to adopt a constitution that, by incorporating a Māori dimension in some form, is unique and home-grown. But this will not be easy, or inevitable: the egalitarian dimension to the settler consciousness may bridle at any explicit race consciousness linked to perceived advantage. At that stage a constitutional bill of rights affirming equality for all may seem, at the least, a necessary assurance. There will certainly be a difficult debate. Perhaps this is why constitutional matters are, for the moment, left to percolate and evolve in pragmatic and piece-meal ways.

12

The Republic of South Africa

HUGH CORDER*

INTRODUCTION

This Constitution provides a historic bridge between the past of a deeply divided society characterised by strife, conflict, untold suffering and injustice, and a future founded on the recognition of human rights, democracy and peaceful co-existence and development opportunities for all South Africans, irrespective of colour, race, class, belief or sex.[1]

SOUTH AFRICANS TEND to think of their country as exceptional. For the period from the end of World War II till 1990, this was for all the wrong reasons, in the eyes of most people across the world, as the apartheid regime pursued its racist policies in defiance of the tenets of basic justice, the rapidly developing 'human rights culture' on the international plane, and the speedy decolonisation of most of sub-Saharan Africa from the late 1950s. Since 1990, the country has been almost universally regarded as an emblem of 'miraculous transformation', proudly forging a path of justice and reconciliation, and staging international spectacles[2] which give the lie to the worst prejudices of Afro-pessimists to be found chiefly in the developed world.

Part of the national chauvinism is a pride in the Constitution, in terms of which the relationships of the almost 50 million inhabitants of South Africa are organised and regulated under law, and which is often described in glowing terms as the most progressive or sophisticated or just plain 'best' constitution in the world! Whatever the merits and shortcomings of constitutional governance in South Africa (and there are many, although at the level of theory the former

---

* I am indebted to Metumo Shilongo, Khiyara Krige and Marethe Herfurth for research assistance; to Mervyn Bennun for technical assistance; and to Pierre De Vos for constructive comment, in the preparation of this article. The usual disclaimer applies.

[1] Postamble or epilogue, headed 'National Unity and Reconciliation', inserted at the end of the 'transitional constitution', Constitution of the Republic of South Africa Act, 200 of 1993.

[2] Such as the Rugby Union World Cup of 1995, the Durban Conference on Racism, Racial Discrimination, Xenophobia and Related Intolerance of 2001, the Earth Summit on Sustainable Development of 2002 in Johannesburg, the Cricket World Cup of 2003, and the FIFA Football World Cup of 2010.

certainly outnumber the latter), the Constitution represents an astonishing change in methods of government through the law. The object of this chapter is to situate the current constitutional dispensation within its historical context, to describe critically the fundamental changes of the early 1990s and subsequent amendments to the Constitution, and to speculate (for that is what it must be at this stage of our development) on the forces which are likely to induce further constitutional change in the coming decades. Through this account, points of useful comparison with similar jurisdictions will be identified.

THE PAST

South Africa's legal system has been variously described as Roman Dutch or as common law in character, due to the colonial origins of the nation state which assumed its current boundaries just on 100 years ago.[3] Indeed, the origins of much of its private law and criminal law are civilian,[4] while the judicial process and most of its constitutional and administrative law, adjectival law and commercial law are based in the law and practice of the subsequent European imperial power, Britain. Inevitably, however, the influence of comparative borrowing which has characterised judge-made law in South Africa so much in the last half-century has lent its law a pluralistic character, so that it is best described and widely recognised today as a 'mixed legal system'.[5] For present purposes, however, due to the overwhelmingly British character of the practice of the judicial branch of government and the formal adherence to the Westminster system until 1983, South Africa falls within the Common Law family of legal systems.

South Africa's first constitution[6] which came into effect in 1910 mirrored its British parent in most respects, establishing the principle of legislative sovereignty in Parliament, an executive headed by a Prime Minister and Cabinet who were Members of Parliament, a superior court judiciary headed by a Chief Justice in the only court with national appellate jurisdiction, an electoral system based on first past the post constituency representation, and so on. However, it differed from its imperial parent in critical respects, none more so than that the franchise

---

[3]   Through the British Act of Parliament which established the Union of South Africa from the four colonies (Cape, Natal, Orange River and Transvaal) a mere eight years after the end of the Anglo-Boer War of 1899–1902, the South Africa Act, 1909.

[4]   Both through the national origin of the first European settlers at the Cape in 1652, and through a concerted effort by Afrikaner nationalists after 1948 to 'purify' the law, by taking it back to its roots in the 'old authorities' in the Europe of the enlightenment and thus purging it of any English influence. For a critical analysis of the latter process, see Hugh Corder and Dennis Davis, 'Law and Social Practice: An Introduction,' in Hugh Corder, *Essays on Law and Social Practice in South Africa* (Cape Town: Juta & Co, 1988), 6–15.

[5]   See the leading role played by South Africans in the World Society of Mixed Jurisdiction Jurists, and the comfortable comparison between aspects of Scottish and South African private law in Reinhard Zimmermann, Daniel Visser, and Kenneth Reid (eds), *Mixed Legal Systems in Comparative Perspective: Property and Obligations in Scotland and South Africa* (Cape Town: Juta & Co, 2004).

[6]   South Africa Act, 1909.

262

was reserved for those classified as 'European' (later 'white') in three of the four provinces into which the country was divided,[7] as well as the fact that Parliament was bound by the constitution to follow a special process[8] when amending its terms in two important respects: when altering in any way the status of English and Dutch (later Afrikaans) as official languages, and when amending the non-racial character of the franchise in the Cape. The special process required both Houses of Parliament (House of Assembly and Senate) to approve any amendment bill by at least a two-thirds majority in a unicameral sitting, as opposed to the normal simple majority being achieved bicamerally. These arrangements were an effective curb on the sovereignty of the Parliament.

The basic structure of constitutional government remained broadly modelled on Westminster until 1983, even to the extent of adopting the conventional underpinnings so essential to the smooth functioning of that approach to the organisation of government. But this formal adherence to the constitutional pattern set in the British colonies which eventually became the members of the Commonwealth was not matched in substance. Crucially, the 'sense of fair play' and the innate belief in the 'rule of law', essential to the informal limitations imposed on the exercise of their power by both the legislative and executive authorities in the Westminster system, were from the start in South Africa only applied to members of the electorate. Even in this respect, they were increasingly eroded when the apartheid regime unleashed its massive programme of race-based social engineering in the early 1950s and enacted increasingly invasive measures in the name of the preservation of 'state security' later that decade,[9] reaching a crescendo of 'state lawlessness' in the second half of the 1980s, when emergency powers were invoked by the executive, in what turned out to be the death-throes of apartheid.[10]

Constitutional amendments were generally not needed to implement the measures needed to lay the foundations in law of the apartheid policy.[11] It is important to note that the apartheid regime followed a formally legalistic course in order to achieve its ends, save for the last five years of its rule. In other words, race classification and all the injustice which flowed from that scheme were

---

[7] The exceptional province being the Cape, and to a minimal extent Natal, which preserved its non-racial but means-tested franchise arrangements when it entered the Union. Of course, the franchise was limited only to men throughout the country, until the Women's Enfranchise Act, 18 of 1930, extended the vote but only to 'European' women, while simultaneously removing the need to qualify by virtue of either education or income from all 'European' voters.

[8] Contained in ss 35, 137 and 152 of the South Africa Act, 1909.

[9] For a good survey of this process as it affected human rights and the courts, see John Dugard, *Human Rights and the South African Legal Order* (Princeton: Princeton University Press, 1978) *passim*.

[10] See Stephen Ellmann, *In a Time of Trouble: Law and Liberty in South Africa's State of Emergency* (Oxford: Clarendon Press, 1992) for a detailed treatment of the effects of emergency rule on the judiciary, and Geoff Budlender, 'Law and Lawlessness in South Africa', (1988) 4 *South African Journal on Human Rights* 139.

[11] The constitutions authorised Parliament to make law for the 'peace, order and good government' of the country (see the South Africa Act, 1909, s 59.

contemplated in advance in Acts of Parliament, subordinate legislation, and the formal allocation of discretion to government officials, many of which were challenged before the at least nominally independent superior courts. Some argue that this provides part of the explanation for the fact that those negotiating the post-apartheid constitution resorted to an entrenched constitution and judicial review as the cornerstones of that system of governance.[12]

However, constitutional amendments were needed to remove the franchise from those not classified 'white', and these attempts led to a celebrated series of court cases which turned the attention of scholars internationally to South Africa. This occurred in two stages. The first National Party government in the 1920s legislated to change the status of title to land held by black South Africans in the Cape Province,[13] then to remove all 'native'[14] voters from the common electoral roll and to provide that this part of the electorate be represented by two representatives (who had to be 'white') in each House of Parliament.[15] On this latter occasion, despite the passage of the Statute of Westminster by the British Parliament, which had limited the effects of the Colonial Laws Validity Act on the legislative capacity of dominions such as South Africa, Parliament duly observed the procedural strictures of the entrenched clauses. This was challenged in court by a voter affected by the change in his status, claiming that Parliament had erred in following the special procedure, but the Appellate Division was not prepared to entertain such an attack on the authority of a sovereign Parliament.[16]

The second attempt to change the franchise qualifications drew much greater controversy; indeed it is commonly described as the 'coloured vote constitutional crisis'. In seeking to implement apartheid after its election to office in 1948, the National Party passed legislation which placed 'coloured' male voters on a separate roll and provided for their representation in the same manner as had applied to black voters since the 1930s. The political climate had changed, however, and there was widespread mobilisation of opposition to this step, both within and outside the electorate. Part of the protest consisted in a series of legal challenges[17] to the failure by the government to follow the entrenched proce-dures, both initially and in subsequent attempts to manipulate the institutions of

---

[12] For a comprehensive recent discussion, see Jens Meierhenrich, *The Legacies of Law: Long-Run Consequences of Legal Development in South Africa, 1652–2000* (Cambridge: Cambridge University Press, 2008).

[13] Thus potentially affecting the non-racial franchise in that province. This was challenged on the basis that the legislation was not adopted according to the special process provided for in the 'entrenched clauses', but this did not succeed. See *R v Ndobe* 1930 AD 484.

[14] No account of the history, or indeed current situation, of South Africa can avoid the use of racial typology. These have changed over the decades. In this piece, 'black' refers to black Africans, 'coloured' refers to people of mixed race, 'Indian' refers to those who originated in Asia, while 'white' refers to those of European extraction.

[15] Through the passage of the Representation of Natives Act, 12 of 1936.

[16] See *Ndlwana v Hofmeyr NO*, 1937 AD 229.

[17] See *Minister of the Interior v Harris* 1952(4) SA 769 (AD): *Harris v Minister of the Interior 1952* (2) SA 428 (AD); and *Collins v Minister of the Interior*, 1957 (1) SA 552 (AD).

government to achieve an outcome favourable to the majority party.[18] After six years and an election in which the National Party was returned with a greater majority (but still not large enough to reach the two-thirds threshold), the highest court eventually succumbed to the cumulative effects of political pressure. The appellate judges were also affected by the almost doubling of its complement and the elevation to its ranks of those who were unlikely to resist a legislative package which included the doubling of the size of the Senate and the nomination to its ranks of sufficient political sympathisers to achieve the requisite majority.[19]

This cynical abuse of constitutional guarantees marks out South Africa's constitutional history before the advent of democracy in 1994, and sets a highly damaging potential precedent for the popular will (at least as expressed in electoral terms) trumping the rule of law. While the initial decisions of the Appellate Division of the Supreme Court established important 'manner and form' standards to be complied with by all legislatures, its subsequent submission to legislative injustice was both an acknowledgment of the limits of judicial authority under the separation of powers in Common Law systems, as well as a telling blow to its independence and stature.

South Africa adopted two further constitutions before the end of apartheid. The first was enacted consequent on the country's expulsion from the British Commonwealth, and amounted to a 'domestication' of the South Africa Act, with the replacement of the British monarch as head of state by the State President, but little else of substance.[20] The last remaining constitutional change was, in retrospect, a desperate throw of the dice to attempt to stave off the inevitable arrival of majority rule, although at the time it was touted by the government as a progressive step. This was the 'tricameral' constitution, which brought adult 'coloured' and Indian South Africans into the national Parliament as the result of race-based elections, but in separate Houses. The 'grand plan' was that each House would legislate and act as the executive for the 'own affairs' of its race group (such as housing, health, education and so on), while those issues involving all South Africans ('general affairs') would be dealt with in combined sessions of all three Houses. Unsurprisingly, the proportions of Members of Parliament from the three race groups were 4:2:1, which approximated the size of their respective electorates, but meant that the House representing whites would

[18] Which had insufficient support to achieve the special majority, while it relied on the Ndlwana decision to argue vigorously that it did not need to do so.
[19] For a detailed treatment of this troubling episode in the history of the courts, see Christopher Forsyth, *In Danger for Their Talents: A Study of the Record of the Appellate Division of the Supreme Court of South Africa 1950–80* (Cape Town: Juta & Co, 1985).
[20] This was the Republic of South Africa Constitution Act, 32 of 1961. It retained the entrenched procedure in regard to the status of the official languages, but by 1960 the non-racial franchise was in law a thing of the past.

always be able to trump even the combined forces of the other two Houses.[21] The further key consequence of this constitutional arrangement was that fully 80 per cent of the population was effectively excluded from participation in the government of their country, the theory being that black South Africans should give expression to their political views through the governing bodies set up in the rural 'homelands' to which they were allocated on 'ethnic' grounds, and through the equally discredited urban local authorities set up to administer the segregated black townships in the major cities.

The fundamental illegitimacy of this monstrous experiment in multi-sectoral governance predictably provoked a storm of protest throughout the country, which culminated in the government losing effective control over many areas of the country, and in turn necessitated the proclamation of rule by emergency powers from mid 1985. Taken together with the concerted efforts of exile groupings and the anti-apartheid movement in the developed world to force governmental authorities to implement trade, financial, cultural and sporting sanctions against South Africa, and finally with the demise of Soviet hegemony in central and eastern Europe and the disappearance of the 'communist threat' in southern Africa, the apartheid regime relinquished control over Namibia in 1989. State President De Klerk initiated the next major phase in South African constitutional change by freeing political prisoners and 'normalising' political activity at the opening of Parliament in February 1990.

In sum, therefore, constitutional change in this first stage of South Africa's history was characterised by the decolonising pull away from the imperial power until 1960, and by the increasingly devious and ultimately desperate attempts by successive white minority governments to justify the exclusion from participation in government and access to basic rights of the vast majority of its citizens. The last two decades have been dedicated to attempts to deal with the damage caused by this traumatic history, and to build a governing culture worthy of the values set out in the Constitution.

THE REVOLUTION 1990–1996

Constitutional change was foremost on the political agenda throughout the period under review, and it amounted to a thorough going revolution of the institutions and manner of public governance at all levels and in all parts of the country. Several authoritative and detailed accounts have been written about this

---

[21] All of this complexity was contained in the Republic of South Africa Constitution Act, 110 of 1983. See too Laurence Boulle, Bede Harris and Cora Hoexter, *Constitutional and Administrative Law: Basic Principles* (Cape Town: Juta & Co, 1989), chs 7– 10.

process,[22] and the current task is to reflect critically on the most influential pressures for adopting, as well as the main features of, the model which is currently in place.

There is no doubt that South Africa benefited from the happy congruence of substantial shifts in the balance of world political power around about 1990. The fall of the Berlin Wall in 1989 led to a burst of constitution-making activity in most constituent parts of the former Soviet Union, and the heightened emphasis on limited government under law and the protection of basic rights under the guardianship of an independent judicial authority which came to characterise this group of constitutions coincided with trends in the thinking of most constitutional scholars in South Africa. It is important to note that such views were shared, although not necessarily in the same form or substance, by lawyers influential both within government and among the exiled groupings in the late 1980s. For example, there can be little doubt that the work of the South African Law Commission on 'Group and Human Rights',[23] under the leadership of Judge Pierre Olivier from 1986 to 1993, made the protection of individual human rights acceptable in government circles, especially as it rejected the notion that 'group rights' could be an adequate substitute for such protection. Again, the main exiled group, the African National Congress (ANC), had a long history of adherence to the idea of charters of rights, chief among them the African Claims of 1943, the Freedom Charter of 1955, and the Constitutional Guidelines of 1988. Several meetings which took place outside South Africa in the period 1987 to 1989 served to strengthen common understanding between such people. In the nature of the intense negotiating process which ensued from 1990 to 1993, such individuals were able to bring considerable persuasive influence to bear on the groups which they were advising, and this explains some of the structure and content of the South African Constitution.

Most commentators agree that the essential steps in constitutional change from apartheid to democracy were as set out below. This list is drawn from many of the accounts of this period in history, and it is influenced also by my own observations as a member of the Technical Committee on Fundamental Rights during the Transition, as part of the Multi-Party Negotiating Process (MPNP) in Johannesburg from May to November 1989. The work of this committee was

---

[22] See, eg, Lourens Du Plessis and Hugh Corder, *Understanding South Africa's Transitional Bill of Rights* (Cape Town: Juta & Co, 1994); Richard Spitz with Matthew Chaskalson, *The Politics of Transition: A Hidden History of South Africa's Negotiated Settlement* (Johannesburg: Witwatersrand University Press, 2000); Hassen Ebrahim, *The Soul of a Nation: Constitution-Making in South Africa* (Cape Town: Oxford University Press, 1998). For a less detailed but contemporary account of the making of the transitional constitution, see Hugh Corder, 'Towards a South African Constitution,' *Modern Law Review* 57, no 4 (July 1994): 491–533.

[23] See its *Working Paper* of 1989 and *Interim Report* of 1991.

essentially the drafting of the chapter on fundamental rights in the interim Constitution, which forms the basis of the current Bill of Rights.[24]

The critical elements of the transition were that the process was as inclusive as possible[25] and agreement was reached on certain fundamental principles of constitutional governance which would be mandatory elements in any final constitution,[26] and also that there should be a phased transfer of power and process of drafting a lasting constitution.

There were essentially three phases: the first (January to May 1994) in the run-up to the first elections, when various 'transitional' governmental bodies consisting of elements drawn from the apartheid regime and the opposition groups took executive charge of certain institutions key to a free and fair electoral process; what came to be called the 'interim' phase (from May 1994 to June 1999), during which the final constitution was drafted (within two years) and executive government was in the hands of a Transitional Government of National Unity, in which each party which garnered more than 10 per cent of the vote was entitled to representation in Cabinet; and the full implementation of constitutional democratic government, after June 1999.

Important points were as follows:

— the process of negotiating the first constitutional framework was largely 'closed', which allowed deals to be brokered outside the glare of media attention;
— a spirit of compromise and a willingness to acknowledge and accommodate the views of others, even if strongly divergent from one's own, prevailed;
— there was immensely strong leadership from the two main political groupings, assisted by astute strategic thinking and action by hard-working and dedicated negotiators on the ground;
— disputes which threatened to derail the negotiations were frequently referred to 'technical committees', staffed mainly by lawyers, many of whom were close to one or more of the negotiating parties, where often fierce discussions took place but which usually resulted in a face-saving compromise which the negotiators were relieved to accept as the advice of 'experts';
— the drafters and negotiating parties learned from and incorporated many lessons from the constitutional experience of other countries, although attempts at prescriptive advice from foreign sources were fiercely resisted. For example, the structure and content of the transitional bill of rights was

[24] Further detail on each of the points which follow can be gained from the sources mentioned in note 22 above.
[25] Twenty-six political groups were represented around the table in the Negotiating Council, although they tended to associate together in informal alliances.
[26] There were 34 such Principles in total. Most of these were agreed on before the negotiations of 1993, during the Convention for a Democratic South Africa (CODESA), from December 1991 to May 1992, while some were added during the course of the MPNP, and one on the eve of the first elections in April 1994, in an endeavour to persuade certain political players to submit to the electoral test.

heavily influenced by the Canadian experience (which in itself was influenced by the German and European models), as well as the very recent constitution-making process in neighbouring Namibia; and

— the notion of 'sufficient consensus' was used as the basis for determining progress where unanimity could not be achieved. This amounted in fact to agreement between the National Party and the ANC, which so angered Chief Buthelezi of the Inkatha Freedom Party that he withdrew from the MPNP along with some like-minded parties in June 1993, only returning to the process when the general election was imminent in April 1994.

The first constitutional product of these tense years of negotiation was the 'interim' Constitution of 1993. At the time it was referred to frequently as the 'transitional' Constitution, a name which I prefer, as it emphasises a continuing process of constitutional change. However, the adjective 'interim' came to be almost universally used and accepted in later years. While formally a law passed by the tricameral Parliament in Cape Town,[27] thus preserving legislative continuity, this Constitution amounted to the legislative rubber-stamp of what had been agreed on at the MPNP. It was amended twice before the first election of April 1994 to appease parties who were holding out on participation in the elections, and on several occasions during its life, but no such changes are material to the current discussion. Much could be written about this Constitution, but for present purposes it is perhaps sufficient to note that in many respects it provided the framework for and a considerable proportion of the substance of the 'final' (and current) Constitution; that, while constitutional government was conducted in the country according to its provisions from mid May 1994 until early February 1997, the newly-elected Parliament doubled as a 'Constitutional Assembly' to draft the final Constitution; and that the first text produced by Parliament within the two-year deadline provided for in the interim Constitution and submitted to the Constitutional Court was returned to the Constitutional Assembly on the basis that it failed in seven important respects to comply with the Constitutional Principles.[28] The amended text was finally certified[29] as sufficiently compliant with the Constitutional Principles contained in the interim Constitution to allow President Mandela to sign it into law on 10 December 1996.[30]

---

[27] Its formal title is the Constitution of the Republic of South Africa, Act 200 of 1993.

[28] See *Re Certification of the Constitution of the Republic of South Africa,1996*, 1996(4) SA 744 (CC).

[29] See *Re Certification of the Amended Text of the Constitution of the Republic of South Africa*, 1997(2) SA 97 (CC).

[30] International Human Rights Day. Added symbolism was lent to the occasion by the venue of the signing ceremony being the site of the Sharpeville killings of 1960.

THE CURRENT CONSTITUTION

The current Constitution[31] has the following significant features. It starts with a chapter containing 'Founding Provisions', which includes the values immanent in the text as a whole[32] and various symbolic elements, including the status as 'official' of 11 languages.[33] The 'values' section encapsulates many of the values which underlay the Constitutional Principles in the interim Constitution, and which have now ceased formally to exist in law. So we see reference to the pre-eminence of human dignity, equality, freedom, non-racialism and non-sexism, the supremacy of the Constitution and the rule of law, free fair elections and a multi-party system of democratic government, 'to ensure accountability, responsiveness and openness'.[34] There are some who argue, however, that despite the formal disappearance of the Principles, their spirit lives on as an informal *Grundnorm* which would render any constitutional amendment which undermined them unconstitutional.[35] The importance of this section is emphasised by the fact that any proposed amendment of its terms requires a 75 per cent majority of all the members of the National Assembly, as well as the approval of six of the nine provincial legislatures, whereas any other provision of the Constitution requires the support of only two-thirds of the members of the Assembly plus six provincial legislatures.[36]

The Bill of Rights which follows[37] is modelled generally on the approach of the Canadian Charter of Fundamental Rights and Freedoms of 1982, but significantly includes a brace of protected socio-economic rights. So we see protection being given to basic levels of housing, health care, food, water and social security, although their grant is qualified by references to their 'progressive realisation' within available resources.[38] Not so, such rights for children, which are given directly and without formal qualification.[39] A further relative novelty in the Bill of Rights from the outset of the interim Constitution has been protection of the rights of access to information[40] and to court[41] as well as the right to administrative justice.[42] The inclusion of such rights was justified by the desire not to allow a resurgence of the gross abuse of discretionary authority by government under apartheid. The right to 'just administrative action' has been frequently invoked to

[31] Constitution of the Republic of South Africa, Act 108 of 1996, hereafter the Constitution.
[32] Ibid, s 1.
[33] See s 6.
[34] Section 1(d).
[35] See, eg, Johan D van der Vyver 'Book review: Democracy and Deliberation: Transformation and the South African Legal Order' (2006)16 *International Criminal Justice Review*, 215.
[36] See s 74.
[37] See generally the Constitution, Ch 2.
[38] Ibid, Ch 2, especially ss 26 and 27.
[39] See s 28.
[40] See s 32.
[41] See s 34.
[42] See s 33.

curb the procedurally unfair, unlawful, or unreasonable actions of public authorities,[43] both through the codified grounds of review in the Promotion of Administrative Justice Act which gives expression to the right,[44] as well as through the court's use of the 'principle of legality' which is a requirement of the rule of law.[45]

A final noteworthy aspect of the Bill of Rights is the set of instructions given to judges who interpret its provisions.[46] Not only must they 'promote the values that underlie an open and democratic society based on human dignity, equality and freedom' when doing so, but they 'must consider international law', and 'may consider foreign law'. The final word of encouragement was not strictly necessary, as counsel and judges have long since engaged in comparative research, but the richness of comparative jurisprudence has rapidly been established as one of the most remarkable features of the CC's jurisprudence to date.

Returning to the Constitution, provision is made for a bicameral national legislature[47] with the directly-elected National Assembly and the indirectly-elected National Council of Provinces, and a strong emphasis on public consultation and participation in the law-making activities of Parliament,[48] as well as on the obligation of Parliament to hold the executive accountable for its actions.[49] As regards executive government, there is a President who is indirectly elected by Parliament and who combines the functions of head of state and head of government and a Cabinet.[50] There is throughout a strong emphasis on both individual and collective ministerial responsibility[51] and the subjection of all aspects of executive action to scrutiny according to the provisions of the Constitution, including those presidential powers formerly regarded as part of the 'prerogative'.[52] Furthermore, there is a system of both legislative and executive government at provincial level, matching the provisions at national level in the

---

[43]   See, eg, *Zondi v MEC for Traditional and Local Government Affairs*, 2006 (3) SA 1 (CC); *Grey's Marine Hout Bay and Others v Minister of Public Works and Others*, 2005 (6) SA 313 (SCA); and *Joseph and Others v City of Johannesburg and Others*, [2009] ZACC 30.

[44]   Act 3 of 2000, on the complexities of which, see Cora Hoexter, 'The Future of Judicial Review in South African Administrative Law,' (2000) 117 *South African Law Journal*, 484–519 and Cora Hoexter, ''Administrative Action' in the Courts,' (2006) *Acta Juridica*, 303–24.

[45]   Which is one of the fundamental values of the Constitution, see s 1(c), and which is used as the basis to review and require adherence to standards of lawfulness, rationality and good faith in the exercise of all power by the executive branch of government. See, eg, *Pharmaceutical Manufacturers Association of SA: Re ex parte the President of the Republic of South Africa* 2000(2) SA 674 (CC) and *Masetlha v President of the Republic of South Africa* 2008(1) SA 566 (CC). For the best treatment of this subject, see Cora Hoexter ' The Rule of Law and the Principle of Legality in Administrative Law Today', 2010 (not yet published).

[46]   See s 39(1).

[47]   See the Constitution, Chapter 4.

[48]   Ibid, at s 59.

[49]   Ibid, at s 55(2).

[50]   For the executive, see the Constitution, ch 5.

[51]   See the Constitution, s 92(2).

[52]   Now codified in s 84(2), and reviewable by the courts: see *President of the RSA v Hugo* 1997(4) SA 1 (CC).

nine provinces into which the country is divided, and a system of local government through the division of the country into both metropolitan and municipal areas.[53]

A national court system at both superior and magistrate levels is provided for,[54] with the Constitutional Court (headed by the Chief Justice) as the final authority on constitutional matters, while the Supreme Court of Appeal has the final say on non-constitutional questions of law. It and all the High Courts in the country have constitutional as well as 'common-law' jurisdiction. Superior court judges are appointed formally by the President, but effectively (after an open process) by the Judicial Service Commission (JSC), consisting of both elected politicians and representatives of all parts of the legal profession, while the President has the final say in the appointment of justices to the Constitutional Court, from a shortlist provided to him by the JSC. There is also a set of 'state institutions supporting constitutional democracy', such as the Public Protector (ombudsman), Auditor General, Electoral Commission, Human Rights Commission, Commission for Gender Equality, and so on, whose task it is to develop the type of public conduct of government officials which is consistent with the values of the Constitution.[55] These bodies were established in recognition of the democratic deficit which existed in the country after decades of unjust government, and their record of achievement is mixed, with the Electoral Commission having done a very good job, the Commission on Gender Equality being a dismal failure, and the rest falling in between, with patchy rates of success in the discharge of their mandates.

Finally, there are chapters relating to the public and financial administration,[56] the security services[57] (with the emphasis on civilian control), traditional leadership,[58] and sundry other matters,[59] including express authorisation for the authority of customary international law as part of South African law, unless 'inconsistent with the Constitution or an Act of Parliament'.[60]

This Constitution is largely self-executing, although there are portions which are clearly more exhortatory than binding in nature. Thus Chapter 3[61] encourages the various levels and spheres of government to work with each other, setting out 'principles of co-operative government and intergovernmental relations'. Likewise, section 195 lists an extensive set of 'Basic values and principles governing public administration', towards which public servants are expected to strive. There are other such examples, but it would be wrong to view the

[53] See the Constitution, Chs 6 and 7.
[54] See the Constitution, Ch 8.
[55] See generally the Constitution, Ch 9.
[56] Ibid, Chs 10 and 13.
[57] Ibid, Ch 11.
[58] Ibid, Ch 12.
[59] Ibid, Ch 14.
[60] Ibid, s 232.
[61] Which contains only ss 40 and 41.

socio-economic 'rights' as such even though they are so formulated as to be closer to aspirational ideals tempered by practical and financial considerations than to 'rights' in the trumping, Dworkinian sense. While the authoritative determination of their scope is left to the interpretation of the courts, they undoubtedly remain enforceable at law.[62]

The *Grootboom* case[63] provides perhaps the most prominent example of the implementation of such rights. Here 900 women and children who were living in temporary shacks on a sports ground sought a court ruling imposing on the government the duty to provide some form of shelter and services against the cold and rain of a Cape winter. The Cape High Court relied on the rights of the children, as well as the necessity to keep them with their parents, as the basis for making its order against the government; while the Constitutional Court, after reviewing the housing strategy of the government, held that its rationality was impugned by the absence of any proper plan to deal with the temporary plight of those on the formal waiting list for state housing.[64] This was a sensible and nuanced approach which carefully navigated the separation of powers doctrine, and met with wide acclaim. Regrettably, enforcement of such judgments has been inconsistent.[65]

This Constitution has been in place for almost 14 years, and most observers agree that it has largely succeeded in turning around a 'culture of authority' into a 'culture of justification'[66] for every exercise of public power by both government and the private sector.[67] Indeed, one of the remarkable features of this Constitution is the extent to which non-state actors are expected to conduct their affairs according to the basic principles expected of government. This is a revolutionary undertaking and, although the word 'transformation' does not appear in it, the Constitution as a whole is all about the transformation of social and legal relationships in South Africa. Every constitution must be capable of amendment, and the recent adoption of the South African Constitution has not shielded it from demands for its alteration, for a range of reasons, to which I now turn.

[62] See, eg, *Khosa v Minister of Social Development*, 2004(6) SA 505 (CC) and *Minister of Health v Treatment Action Campaign (2)*, 2002(2) SA 721 (CC). For a comprehensive and authoritative recent treatment of this area of the Bill of Rights, see Sandra Liebenberg, *Socio-Economic Rights: Adjudication Under a Transformative Constitution* (Cape Town: Juta & Co, 2010).
[63] *Government of the Republic of South Africa v Grootboom*, 2001(1) SA 46 (CC).
[64] See Liebenberg, above note 62, *passim*, for an analysis of the importance of *Grootboom* in the jurisprudence of socio-economic rights in South Africa.
[65] For a detailed discussion about remedies in this area of the law, see Liebenberg, above note 62, at ch 8.
[66] A phrase coined by Etienne Mureinik in 'A Bridge to Where? Introducing the interim Bill of Rights' (1994) 10 *South African Journal on Human Rights* 31.
[67] See, eg, the generally 'horizontal' application of the Bill of Rights in s 8(2).

CONTINUING TRANSFORMATION

The Constitution had been amended on 16 occasions by the end of 2009, with two further amendments pending at mid 2010 and a further one in the offing. Those amendments already in place fall arguably into three categories: those of a formal nature, those necessitated by practical necessity, and those of substantial effect on the terms originally adopted in 1996. Some of the amending Acts contain elements of more than one of these categories.

The formal amendments[68] provided largely uncontroversially for name changes for places and officers, for an oath of office for an Acting President, and for technical matters. The amendments dictated by practical necessity[69] concerned common-sense matters such as classifying cross-provincial border municipalities, the timing of the announcement of elections, and how to allocate undistributed delegates in a proportional representation system such as applies in South Africa. None of these amendments gives much indication of the significant causes or motivation for constitutional change; it is the third category which sheds some light on this issue.

Let us start with a set of five constitutional amendments which stirred much political emotion over several years, dealing with the constitutionality of 'floor-crossing' at all three levels of government, national, provincial and local. In an electoral system based on proportional representation, the question arises whether a member of the legislature elected under the banner of one party, or the entire party itself, can lawfully join another party between elections, while retaining their status as such member. Political circumstances in 2002 made it acceptable for the ruling party and several other parties in Parliament to countenance such floor-crossing as acceptable, and three acts amending the Constitution[70] duly provided for this at all three levels of government. The majority party, the ANC, gained most from these arrangements, but the practice and some cynical use of it continued to create unease and in 2008 the Constitution was amended again twice[71] in order to abolish the right to retain membership of someone who resigns from the party under whose aegis they were elected. So the process has come full circle, but not without damage being done to the integrity and legitimacy of the representative branch of government.

A second and deeply controversial pair of amendments[72] was the result of the determination of the national leadership of the ANC, ostensibly in order to

---

[68] In which I include the First Amendment (Act 35 of 1997), Second Amendment (Act 65 of 1998), Sixth Amendment (Act 34 of 2001), Eleventh Amendment (Act 3 of 2003), and the Twelfth Amendment (of 2005—it appears inexplicably that amendment Acts after the Eleventh Act do not carry numbers).

[69] In which I include the Third Amendment (Act 87 of 1998), Fourth Amendment (Act 2 of 1999), and Fifth Amendment (Act 3 of 1999).

[70] The Eighth, Ninth and Tenth Amendments, Acts 18 and 21 of 2002, and Act 2 of 2003.

[71] Through the Fourteenth and Fifteenth Amendment Acts of that year.

[72] See the Thirteenth and Sixteenth Amendment Acts, of 2007 and 2009 respectively.

eliminate cross-border municipalities, to change the provincial boundaries of four of the provinces so as to move a local authority in one case, and part of one in the other case, from one province to an other. Both such shifts had the consequence of effectively moving tens of thousands of people from a better-run and wealthier province to a more inefficient and poorer one, and in each case a substantial majority of such residents fiercely and determinedly resisted such changes. Their efforts were, however, to no avail and several court battles at the highest level were not ultimately able to resist executive will,[73] with the result that the Constitution was amended to reflect these shifts. Like the floor-crossing saga however, but for reasons of a change in national leadership of the ANC in late 2007, there is now a political commitment to undo these changes; however this has yet to be translated into a constitutional amendment.

Other substantial matters which have been changed in the Constitution are to be found in the Sixth, Seventh and Eleventh Amendments.[74] These concerned essentially three matters: the manner of enacting financial legislation in Parliament; the authority vested in a higher level of government to intervene in the affairs of a dysfunctional governmental authority beneath it; and the lengthening of the terms of office of the justices of the Constitutional Court. The most controversial among these was the last, for the following reasons.[75] When it was decided that a Constitutional Court with final say over the interpretation of constitutional power should be part of the future constitutional democracy in South Africa, it was accepted that political independence and accountability would be best served by appointing its judges for a limited, fixed term of office. The interim Constitution determined this at seven years,[76] and the extension of the period to 12 years in the final Constitution was uncontroversial.[77]

Regrettably, the government waited until almost the last moment to attempt to change the terms of office of constitutional justices to that of all other judges in order mainly to allow the then Chief Justice, the much-respected Arthur Chaskalson, to remain on the Bench for a year or two longer. The apparently 'personal' nature of this proposed amendment proved deeply embarrassing to many, including the Chief Justice, and the amendment also drew substantial opposition from those who believed it completely inappropriate in principle that constitutional justices should stay on the Court for such long periods. In the end, a compromise was reached at a term of 15 years, with some qualifications, but as of autumn 2010 the matter has been raised again. While not yet finalised, the

---

[73] See *Matatiele Municipality and Others v President of the RSA and Others*, 2006(5) SA 47 (CC) and *Merafong Demarcation Forum v President of the RSA and Others*, 2008(5) SA 171 (CC), for example. In the case of *Matatiele*, the initial rebuff from the Court was remedied by Parliament; in the case of *Merafong*, the majority of the Constitutional Court found for the legislature.

[74] See Act 34 of 2001, Act 61 of 2001, and Act 3 of 2003, respectively.

[75] An excellent contemporary account of these events is to be found in Francois Du Bois, 'Tenure on the Constitutional Court,' (2002) 119(1) *South African Law Journal*, 1–17.

[76] See the Constitution, s 99(1).

[77] Ibid, s 176(1).

proposal is to put constitutional justices in the same position as all other superior court judges, that is that they serve till retirement at the age of 70, no matter when appointed. This is part of the package of reforms contained in the 'Superior Courts Bill' and it provokes suspicions of meddling with judicial independence, for a number of reasons described in the final part of this chapter.

Some constitutional amendments have been triggered by decisions of the Constitutional Court: for example, one of the amending Bills[78] pending attempts to remedy the difficulties in holding the state liable for its debts, which were pointed out by the Court.[79] In fact, the state proved tardy in meeting the deadline for amendment set by the Court in this case, so that the appellant had to return to court to obtain a further order of relief,[80] and the pending amendment Bill is the result of that order. However, now that the 'technical problems' have been ironed out of the Constitution and accepting that subsequent judgments of the Court will necessitate constitutional amendments infrequently, we must ask what the most likely causes of constitutional change will be in future and whether conventional practices to give expression to constitutional values are being established. It is to these questions that the final part of this chapter is devoted.

PRESSURES FOR CHANGE

Tensions between the three arms of government according to the doctrine of the separation of powers are bound to arise, even in stable democracies of long standing. If one considers the tortured and divisive history of South Africa I would surmise that most observers would be frankly astonished or at least surprised at the degree of comity which has existed between the judiciary on the one hand and the executive and legislature on the other. I have argued[81] that this is a tribute both to the leadership displayed by President Mandela during the critical first five years of democracy, as well as the political sensitivity of the judicial leadership, particularly in the Constitutional Court.[82] It is important to note that several of the justices appointed to the first Bench of this Court had

---

[78] See the Eighteenth Constitution Amendment Bill of 2009, published in June 2009. The Seventeenth Amendment Bill, also of 2009, like the Eleventh Amendment Act, would further authorise national government intervention in the executive affairs of local government, in the interest of 'regional efficiencies and economies of scale'.

[79] See *Nyathi v MEC for Department of Health, Gauteng and Another*, 2008(5) SA 94 (CC).

[80] See *Minister for Justice and Constitutional Development v Nyathi, Law Society of South Africa Intervening, and Legal Resources Centre and Others as Amici Curiae Re Nyathi v MEC for Health, Gauteng, and Another*, Case CCT 53/09 [2009] ZACC 29, reasons for decision handed down on 9 October 2009.

[81] See Hugh Corder, 'On Stormy Waters: South Africa's Judges (and Politicians) Test the Limits of Their Authority', Geoffrey Sawer Memorial Lecture (Australian National University, 2009) (unpublished) available at http://law.anu.edu.au/CIPL/Conferences&SawerLecture/2009/Corder_Paper.pdf.

[82] This has been characterised as a blend of 'principle and pragmatism', in a particularly incisive analysis: see Theunis Roux, 'Principle and Pragmatism on the Constitutional Court of South Africa', *International Journal of Constitutional Law* 7 (2009): 106–38.

long records of resistance to the tyranny of apartheid, as well as close personal links to the ANC leadership. This inevitably created a sense of trust which assisted in relations between the executive and the judiciary from 1994 till at least 1999. However, this does not mean that this Court has shied away from political issues. Indeed, the first judgment handed down by the Court declared the death penalty to be unconstitutional, a highly controversial step;[83] and one of the first decisions which went against the executive found fault with President Mandela and Parliament, and effectively in favour of the party of government under apartheid, which still commanded a majority in the Western Cape Province.[84] Nor has the Court been afraid to confront other instances of executive and legislative unlawfulness when it has reached it, but it has generally expressed its views in a nuanced and non-offensive manner which has allowed those who needed to remedy their actions to do so without losing face politically.

With the passage of time, however, and as political and judicial leadership has changed, it was perhaps inevitable that tensions would arise and that the executive would be tempted to seek a judiciary more compliant to their will, even while maintaining the essential foundations of judicial independence and impartiality. This area of political life provides a good case study of the pressures which are most likely to lead to constitutional changes in the immediate future, so are worth noting. The pretext for legislative (as well as constitutional) intervention in matters concerning the judiciary was an acknowledged need for various reforms to the administration of justice to equip it better to fulfil its role in the Constitution. Thus issues concerned with access to justice, court structure and services, judicial appointments, discipline short of dismissal, and the ethical and financial accountability of judges presented themselves for legislative intervention, along with the need for renaming the divisions of the courts and rationalising the remnants of apartheid in the administration of justice. It took 10 years for informal agreement to be reached in largely amicable discussions between the Minister for Justice and the judiciary, but no formal legislative steps were taken before the third general election of mid 2004 after which a new ministerial team took office. This led to the publication in early 2005 of a package of proposed legislation, much of it laudable and inoffensive, but elements of which were deeply threatening to judicial independence especially in the context of resolutions adopted by the ANC which called for the changing of judicial 'mindsets' to be in closer sympathy with the poor and powerless in society.

These 'judiciary bills' provoked a storm of protest from the ranks of lawyers and judges and equally angry responses from the ANC until President Mbeki removed them from consideration, pending further negotiations. In the end, nothing material happened for four years, as the leadership of the ANC became embroiled in internal battles for power and as the party itself fought proxy battles

---

[83] See *S v Makwanyane*, 1995(3) SA 391 (CC).
[84] See *Executive Council of the Western Cape Legislature v President of the RSA*, 1995 (4) SA 877 (CC).

with the courts on behalf of its new leader, Jacob Zuma, who was facing charges of corruption.[85] After the election of mid-2009 and the dropping of charges against Zuma, the new leadership at both ministerial and judicial levels seem to have reached agreement on a new regime. This is to be seen in the yet to be finalised Superior Courts Bill, read together with a proposed (nineteenth?) amendment to the Constitution, aimed at reintroducing the notion that constitutional justices should serve under the same conditions of tenure as all other judges. This arrangement meets most of the objections raised by the judiciary in 2005, and will effectively vest substantial authority and responsibility for judicial administration in the office of the Chief Justice.

I have given this account at some length, because in my view it exemplifies the pressures and circumstances which are most likely to lead to constitutional change in South Africa in the short and medium term. Frustration at the inability quickly to reverse the appalling effects of apartheid exploitation is often manifest in 'service delivery protests' which are mostly the product of the continuing levels of class inequality which exist throughout the country, of a desperate call to provide the most basic needs of the population as regards shelter, health care, education and nutrition, and of anger at gross inefficiencies and often corrupt practices at local government level. Political tensions arising from these frustrations often translate into impatience with the 'counter-majoritarian' and participative nature of the democracy[86] which is at the heart of the constitutional compromise of the early 1990s. The growth in prominence and indeed power of populist demagogues within the ranks of the ANC[87] adds substantially to this pressure, and the courts are increasingly the target of their attacks because they often provide the obstacles to unlawful (and sometimes unconstitutional) conduct, and probably also because there is a greater proportion of 'whites' in the judiciary than there is in the executive and legislative branches of government so it is easy to 'play the race card'. Sixteen years after the advent of freedom, much of the leadership in government (except at the most senior level) was not involved in the struggles for democracy of the period 1960 to 1990, and even President Zuma admitted that he did not understand why the courts had the power to overrule the will of the supreme legislature in Parliament.[88]

Thus concern about the meaning and viability of the Constitution is very much present despite frequent assurances from the ANC that it is as committed

[85] The effects of this period of sharp disagreement and public dispute have drawn sustained commentary, such as Murray Wesson and Max Du Plessis, 'Fifteen Years on: Central Issues Relating to the Transformation of the South African Judiciary,' (2008) 24 *South African Journal on Human Rights*, 187–213, and David Dyzenhaus, 'The Pasts and Future of the Rule of Law in South Africa,' (2007) 124 *South African Law* 734–61.
[86] Seen in the Constitution, s 1.
[87] To be seen particularly (but not only) in the leadership of the ANC Youth League.
[88] Likening the Constitutional Court as 'close to God', he made this statement in an interview not long before coming to power in 2009: see 'Zuma takes aim at top judges', published in *The Star* (Johannesburg) on 9 April 2009, at 1. available at http://www.iol.co.za/news/politics/zuma-takes-aim-at-top-judges-1.439557.

to the Constitution as anyone else, for it accords with much in their tradition and it was the majority party when the Constitution was drafted and adopted. How will these concerns be countered? If the disputes about the 'judiciary bills' are anything to go by, such potential amendments to the Constitution will be intensely contested both within[89] and outside[90] the ranks of government over perhaps a considerable period, while all parties become accustomed to the proposed change and compromises are reached. Such a process is likely to involve many diverse constituencies, thus easing acceptance of the change when it happens.

This is as much of a developing 'convention' of constitutional change as is evident to an interested observer at this stage of the development of the post-apartheid state. The Constitution is certainly alive and being applied daily in the courts and in government practice, but there is also considerable distance to be travelled. Some would argue that the proposed extension of the terms of the constitutional justices[91] and the appointment of apparently more compliant judges will undermine judicial independence, that the legitimacy of the courts is lowered by sustained and intemperate attacks on court judgments by leading politicians, and that the ANC, as the dominant ruling party, is working hard to narrow the gap between the interests of the state and those of the party itself. At the heart of this problem is the electoral system, which places undue influence in the hands of the leaders of political parties. Although it may be argued that party leaders exercise substantial power in any electoral system, the use of proportional representation together with a party list nationally, while persuasively justified by fears of race-based factionalism immediately after the end of apartheid, has allowed political parties to exploit the loyalty of its public representatives. Many have argued that a better quality of representation would be achieved by mixing constituency representation with proportional representation, perhaps on a 50:50 basis, as is the system used at local government level, thus encouraging a degree of accountability to the electorate directly, and diluting the hold of the party leadership. It seems, however, that the ANC is unlikely to accept such a change, given the strength of its position under the current system.

Constitutional change, in the form of adapting it to emerging political practices, is certain; the survival of the particular compromise reached in 1996 is not.

---

[89] The ANC is the dominant partner in a governing alliance, but both its partners and differing views within its ranks make for often heated and sometimes constructive debate.

[90] The views of political opponents and even the international community, while frequently vehemently dismissed as 'racist', 'unpatriotic' or 'imperialist meddling' are not unimportant, provided that they are constructively expressed.

[91] The reasons for this view are canvassed in F Du Bois, (2002) 119(1) 'Tenure on the Constitutional Court', *South African Law Journal*, 1–17.

13

Spain

ASCENSIÓN ELVIRA

INTRODUCTION

THE SPANISH CONSTITUTION of 1978 was approved—first by the Cortes Generales (Parliament) and later by referendum- after a transitional period following the end of Franco's dictatorship (1939–75), which he had imposed after the civil war (1936–39) that ended with the Second Republic (1931–39). Thus the 1978 Constitution is the outcome of a representative process, characterised by the 'consensus' reached among the majority political parties.

The Spanish Constitution follows the examples of other European Constitutions in the post-World War II era, basically Italy and Germany: it has an extensive Bill of Rights, which offers specific guarantees: an accelerated, summary procedure for its enforcement in the ordinary courts (thus it is self-executing), a constitutional appeal to the Constitutional Court, constitutional development through Acts of parliament, and an Ombudsman. Government is carried on in a parliamentary system, with two parliamentary chambers—*Congreso de los Diputados* and *Senado*; and the President (Head of Government) needs the support of the *Congreso*. The Head of State is the King, who has only symbolic functions. From a territorial point of view, the Autonomous Communities (Regions) have a high degree of autonomy which in practice almost results in a Federal State.[1]

The Spanish legal system may be classified as a civil law jurisdiction. The Constitution is the primary source of law and is enforced by the Constitutional Court, either on a direct application to the Court (*recurso de inconstitucionalidad*)

---

[1] For an introduction to the political transitional period and the characteristics of the system implemented by the 1978 Constitution, see Luis María Díez-Picazo and Ascensión Elvira, *La Constitución española de 1978.* (Madrid: Iustel, 2008); Ascensión Elvira, 'Implementing the Spanish Constitution', in *Policy and Change in Europe*, (Oxford: Oxford University Press, 1995), 214–40.

or on a preliminary reference from the ordinary courts (*cuestión de inconstitu-cionalidad*); constitutional provisions may be interpreted through a constitutional appeal (*recurso de amparo*) or in 'conflict of jurisdiction' proceedings (*conflicto de competencias*) between the State and Autonomous Communities.

The Constitution establishes a complex system of legal sources, ordered according to a hierarchy of laws—acts of Parliament (or sources with the same status, that is decree-laws, and governmental regulations)—and of the competences of the central State and Autonomous Communities. Here there is a Spanish peculiarity, in that the 'fundamental law of an Autonomous Community' is first enacted by the Autonomous Community's parliament and later passed by the State Parliament (*Cortes Generales*), whereupon it becomes an 'organic' law (*ley orgánica* of Spain[2]).

THE CONSTITUTIONAL REFORM PROCESS

The term 'reform' will be widely interpreted here, to include implicit reforms and changes, constitutional conventions and Constitutional Court interpretations that depart from a literal interpretation of the Constitutional text or from an initial Constitutional Court interpretation. Explanation of the differences between these kinds of change would exceed the scope of this article.

The present Spanish Constitution has only been subject to one formal, textual reform during its 30 years of existence. The reason for its permanence may be found in the difficulties imposed by the reform process in the Constitution, and in the difficulty in achieving, and the significance of, the consensus on which it was based. However, this lack of formal reform has not prevented the Constitution from being in effect amended for various reasons, due to a large extent to interpretation by the Constitutional Court.

Before explaining the various changes that have occurred, there follows a description of the reform processes which are set out in the Spanish Constitution:

(A) For an ordinary reform or amendment, Article 167 of the Spanish Constitution requires the approval of a majority of three-fifths of the members of each Chamber; if no such majority is reached, a joint committee is set up to put the new wording to the vote of both Chambers, in which case the proposal may be approved if the Upper Chamber (*Senado*) produces an absolute majority and the Lower Chamber (*Congreso de los Diputados*) a two thirds majority. The reform may be subject to a referendum if so requested by a tenth of the members of either Chamber.

(B) In the event of a total or partial update affecting Chapter Two, section one, of Title I (Basic human rights, enjoying maximum jurisdictional protection),

---

[2] This kind of law requires an absolute majority in the lower Chamber (*Congreso*).

or Title II (The Crown), pursuant to the provisions established in Article 168 Spanish Constitution, it is necessary to gain the approval of two-thirds of each Chamber and to call for an immediate dissolution of Parliament (*Cortes Generales*). The new Chambers must then ratify the decision and approve the new wording by a two-thirds majority in both Chambers, after which the text will need to be ratified in a referendum.

As will be seen, the procedures are so complex and demanding that unless there is consensus amongst the most representative political parties reforms are almost impossible. Moreover and because of the terms in which category B is drafted, any change, no matter how insignificant, in any of these parts will require this elaborate procedure. Because of these difficulties and the reluctance amongst political parties to face up to the problems, over the last few years there have been more and more requests for a formal, full-scale review of the Constitution, so that its wording can be adjusted to current reality.[3]

Another reason for the lack of formal constitutional reform in Spain is the absence of political consensus in this regard; the opposition of political parties and the absence of limits on possible reforms make it difficult to reach an agreement.[4] But the problem is not new: if we examine Spanish constitutional history, a salient fact is that all changes have ended with the drafting of a new Constitution rather than amendment of the old one.

The only reform approved so far was due to Spain's ratification of the European Union Treaty. Until then, the Constitution provided only for foreigners to exercise a right to vote (*sufragio activo*) in municipal elections[5] and excluded their right to stand as candidates. Therefore, in order to give effect to the right of European citizens to stand as candidates (*sufragio pasivo*) in municipal elections, the Constitutional Court, in a preliminary report requested by the Executive,[6] established the need to amend the relevant part of the Constitution if the Treaty was ratified, which entailed use of the amendment procedure in Article 167 Spanish Constitution and its final approval on 27 August 1992. In this case, given that the issue was strictly defined and all political forces were in agreement, no difficulties arose and the processes were rapidly completed.

As already mentioned, the lack of formal reviews of the Constitution has not prevented other types of reform, some of which took place even before the Constitution was approved. This paradox may be explained by the fact that, whilst the Constitution was being drawn up and in particular whilst discussions

---

[3] This was argued for in several newspaper articles, amongst others, written by renowned University professors: Francisco Rubio Llorente, 'Los retos de los hijos de la Constitución', *El País*, 2 December 2008; Francisco Caamaño, 'Treinta años … y ni uno más', *El País*, 5 December 2008; Francisco J Laporta, 'La rigidez constitucional y otras perversiones', *El País*, 18 December 2008.

[4] Francisco Rubio Llorente, 'Rigidez y apertura de la Constitución', in *La reforma Constitucional: ¿Hacia un nuevo pacto constituyente? Atlas de las XIV Jornadas de la asociación de Letrados del Tribunal Constitucional.* (Madrid: CEPC-TC, 2009), 19–40.

[5] If so foreseen in treaties or laws, under reciprocity conditions.

[6] Statement issued by the Plenary Meeting of the Constitutional Court 1/1992, 1 July.

were being held on the territorial or regional boundaries within the State, and the necessary commitments were sought in this regard, the government, political parties and citizens acted in anticipation of the constitutional proposals and eventually approved the 'preliminary autonomous systems' (*regímenes preautonómicos*) before the Constitution was approved, that is they approved the provisional self-government rules for the various territorial bodies that were eventually referred to as Autonomous Communities in the Constitution. This resulted in the firm configuration of a territorial map which, however, the Constitution left open-ended. First of all, the legal bases of the systems in Catalonia (Royal Decree-Law 41/1997, of 24 September) and in the Basque Country (Royal Decree-Law 1/1978, of 4 January) were approved. Both Autonomous Communities had traditionally indicated a wish for greater autonomy, which they have enjoyed in the past. After the Constitution came into effect, the legal bases for practically all the remaining regions in Spain were approved.[7] As is often the case, reality was a step ahead of the law.

This said, it is the Constitutional Court which, to a large extent, has been adjusting its interpretation of the Constitution in response to particular political and social scenarios. Many of these changes have been made in relation to the regional map of the State, but other subject areas have also been affected, such as rights. Furthermore, as has been the case in other European countries, some significant changes were responses to Spain's accession to the European Community. It could of course be disputed whether these developments may be classified as 'changes' or as mere constitutional interpretation. In any case, apart from the issue of terminology, it is clear that the current Constitution or system of government has changed since it was approved; furthermore, the lack of formal amendments in the constitutional text has encouraged interpretations that enable the Constitution to adjust to the passing of time.

---

[7] Galicia (Royal Decree-Law 7/1978, of 16 March), Aragón (Royal Decree-Law 8/1978, of 17 March), Canary Islands (Royal Decree-Law 9/1978, of 17 March), Valencia (Royal Decree-Law 10/1978, of 17 March), Andalusia (Royal Decree-Law 11/1978, of 27 April), Balearic Islands (Royal Decree-Law 18/1978, of 13 June), Extremadura (Royal Decree-Law 19/1978, of 13 June), Castilla y León (Royal Decree-Law 20/1978, of 13 June), Asturias (Royal Decree-Law 29/1978, of 27 September), Murcia (Royal Decree-Law 30/1978, of 27 September) and Castilla la Mancha (Royal Decree-Law 32/1978, of 3 October). A study of the constituent process and characteristics of the Spanish Constitution may be found in Luis María Díez-Picazo and Ascensión Elvira, *La Constitución de 1978*. (Madrid: Iustel, 2008).

CONSTITUTIONAL CHANGES

Basic Human Rights

Interpretation in matters related to rights is closely linked to the provisions of Article 10.2 Spanish Constitution.[8] This article has often been relied upon by the courts, together with universal instruments (UN Charters, general declarations of rights) and regional laws (the European Convention on Human Rights (ECHR) in particular), as well as European law. Of particular significance has been the case law laid down by the European Court of Human Rights (ECtHR),[9] which has not only backed up the Constitutional Court's interpretations but has also triggered certain changes. In this regard, of particular importance are matters in which the ECtHR has found breaches by Spain including, amongst others, the *López Ostra* and *Gómez Moreno* cases,[10] which added a right to an adequate environment to the rights included in Article 8 of the Treaty. This case law has led the way to similar interpretations in relation to the right to one's personal and family privacy (Article 18.1 Spanish Constitution). ECHR case law has also had an important impact on matters related to the right to privacy in communications and effective court protection.

In terms of Community law, matters related to equal treatment and non-discrimination are the most affected.

Nevertheless, to a large extent the Spanish Constitutional Court has itself determined the content of these rights (albeit backed up by the European Courts, see above). In this respect, the application for the protection of fundamental human rights (*recurso de amparo*[11]) has been the ideal procedure through which the Court has pronounced on the content, scope and limits of these rights, particularly before they were implemented by formal legislation. It should be noted that there had been a period in Spanish history during which there was no true recognition of rights and that the Spanish Constitution of 1978 practically started the development of rights from square one. Before the Constitution came

---

[8] Art 10.2: 'Provisions relating to the fundamental rights and liberties recognized by the Constitution shall be construed in conformity with the Universal Declaration of Human Rights and international treaties and agreements thereon ratified by Spain'. Spain is a monist country according articles'. We have to be present Art 96.1: 'Validly concluded international treaties, once officially published in Spain, shall be part of the internal legal system'

[9] See Argelia Queralt, *La interpretación de los derechos: del Tribunal de Estrasburgo al Tribunal Constitucional*, (Madrid: CEPC, 2008); Ascensión Elvira, 'Tribunal Constitucional y Tribunal Europeo de Derechos Humanos', *La reforma del Tribunal Constitucional*, (Valencia: Tirant lo Blanch, 2007), 511–24.

[10] *López Ostra* case, Decision of 9 December 1994; *Gómez Moreno* case, Decision of 16 February 2005.

[11] The *recurso de amparo* is a procedure used to protect basic human rights where infringements are alleged on the part of any public power.

into effect even academics, to a large extent, had merely drawn on the interpretations given by the Constitutional Court in their arguments in support of the significance of rights.[12]

Interpretations of the content of the rights set out in the Constitution is broader in the case of 'legally configured' rights, that is rights which the Constitution only declares but the full scope of which is subject to implementing acts. Examples are the right to participate in politics (Article 23 Spanish Constitution), and rights to effective court protection (Article 24) or trade union freedom (Article 28.1). Of interest in this regard is how constitutional interpretation has affected the right to participate in politics. In relation to Article 23.1, the Constitutional Court's interpretation had been that the right to participate in politics only referred to the citizens' direct or representative participation through the various provisions in the Spanish Constitution: participation in a referendum, in elections to the Lower and Upper Chambers, to the Legislative Assemblies of Autonomous Communities, town councils and, indirectly, to provincial Councils. Consequently, this first section is to a large extent related to the right to vote.

As regards Article 23.2, however, the Constitutional Court's interpretation grants the right to stand as candidates for election, and the right to security in one's job or office, this being understood as the right to exercise the duties inherent in the office. As a result, the specific definition of the right in Article 23.2 is provided by the Standing Orders issued by both chambers of Parliament. The Constitutional Court's interpretation of Article 23.2 included a right of citizens to access to posts in the Public Administration as civil servants, pursuant to Article 103.3 Spanish Constitution, which refers to the principles of merit and capability.

Institutions

The three traditional institutions of the State have been to some extent reinterpreted in constitutional terms.

The President or Head of Government is a separate figure from the Government, notwithstanding their collegiate status. The role of President has been strengthened by the party system, resulting in a practically two-party system at a national level (though certain regional parties exist in some Autonomous Communities). The President's primacy means not only that he controls the Government (he appoints and removes all ministers and adopts all important decisions on his own responsibility) but also that he leads his political party and

---

[12] An analysis of how Constitutional Court case law has affected constitutional rights would greatly exceed the scope of this study. Any comments would be a mere indication of their true scope. For a solid approach to the issue of rights in Spain see Luis María Díez-Picazo, *Sistema de derechos fundamentales*, (Madrid: Thomson-Civitas, 2008).

parliamentary group, whilst also reaching and implementing possible agreements with other political groups if the governing party does not hold an absolute majority in the Lower Chamber, which is necessary to implement its proposals.

The Upper Chamber of the legislature has undergone the greatest change since 1978. Although the Spanish Constitution defines the *Senado* as the chamber for territorial representation, its composition and operation suggest that it is more of a traditional second chamber. There is therefore an unbalanced two-chamber situation in which the predominant role is played by the *Congreso*. Attempts were made from the very start to convert the *Senado* into a chamber for the representation of the Autonomous Communities. However, as no such change occurred the Autonomous Communities Commission was created to fill the gap between theory and reality, acting as a forum for Spanish Autonomous Communities. However, the Commission's role has decreased and, as will be seen below, reform of the *Senado* is still outstanding.[13] A gap remains.

Amongst the attempts to boost the *Senado*'s territorial role, the Organic Act of the Constitutional Court was amended through Organic Act 6/2007. This changed the *Senado*'s participation in the election of a third of the Constitutional Court judges. Since this amendment, the *Senado* is obliged to elect four judges from amongst those proposed by Autonomous Community parliaments,[14] as a way of ensuring 'autonomous awareness' within the Constitutional Court. The passing of the act was controversial as it was deemed contrary to the Constitution, which imposes no limit whatsoever on alternative elections by the *Senado*. The leading Partido Popular (the main party in the opposition) challenged the issue before the Constitutional Court, which upheld the legality of the change.[15] The Court also issued an opinion on the constitutionality of reforming the *Senado* Standing Orders which implemented the Organic Act[16] as regards the means by which the proposal was to be implemented, indicating that the *Senado* need not necessarily approve the candidacies proposed by Autonomous Communities for the post of judges in the Constitutional Court if such proposals are politically inappropriate.

Nor has the Judiciary been exempt from amendments to its position. The Spanish Constitution provides that the State shall have exclusive competence over the Administration of Justice (Article 149.1.5 Spanish Constitution). However, in the *Estatutos de Autonomía* [Statutes governing regional independence or 'Statutes of Autonomy'] issued by Catalonia and the Basque Country, approved in

---

[13] Reform of the *Senado* has been the subject of many studies, a large number of which have proposed the creation of a body somewhat similar to the German '*Bundesrat*'.

[14] The general qualifications are held in Art 159.2 Constitution: 'Members of the Constitutional Court shall be appointed among magistrates and prosecutors, university professors, public officials and lawyers, all of whom must have a recognized standing with at least fifteen years' practice in their profession'

[15] Constitutional Court Decision 49/2008, of 9 April.

[16] Constitutional Court Decision 101/2008, of 24 July.

1979 and subsequently reproduced in other Statutes, the autonomous communities will 'exercise all those duties which the Organic Act of the Judiciary and General Council of the Judiciary acknowledge or entrust to the State (that is Spanish) Government'. This led to the interpretation that all Autonomous Communities could assume competences in matters covered by the 'administration of the Administration of Justice' (sic), that is matters affecting 'judicial office' or setting of the material and human resources for the service of the Administration of Justice but not incorporated therein in strict terms.[17] This development culminated in the reform of the Organic Act of the Judiciary, triggered by Organic Act 19/2003, of 23 December, which establishes the matters relating to 'judicial office' under the Autonomous Communities.

Subsequently, a reform of the Courts' Statutes opened the door to greater participation in the judicial system by the Autonomous Communities. The tendency now is for the High Courts of Justice (jurisdictional bodies at the top of the judicial system in each Autonomous Community, notwithstanding the jurisdiction entrusted to the Supreme Court of Spain) to act as courts of last instance, as long as autonomous community law is the applicable law, regardless of the jurisdictional order in question.[18] Some Courts' Statutes provide that the High Court of Justice will act as the final jurisdictional instance in all proceedings brought within the Autonomous Community, including any appeals that are brought within its territorial scope, regardless of the law that is relied upon.[19]

On the other hand, Autonomous Statutes have created the Councils of Justice of each Autonomous Community and defined them as bodies for the 'government of the judiciary' in each region. Each Council 'acts as a body with power delegated from the General Council of the Judiciary, without prejudice to the latter's competences, according to the provisions established in the Organic Act of the Judiciary'.[20] The Council's duties relate to participation in the organisation and operation of each Autonomous Community's judicial bodies. Nevertheless, Constitutional Court Decision 31/2010, of 28 June declares some of the innovations introduced by the *Estatuto de Autonomía* of Catalonia as regards the High Court of Justice and Senior Autonomous Council of Justice to be

---

[17] Constitutional Court Decisions 56/1990 and 62/1990, later reiterated in other Constitutional Court Decisions 105/2000, 253/2005, 270/2006 or 194/2006. Nevertheless, the transfer of competences to the various Autonomous Communities has been carried out gradually.

[18] Until then it was understood that this power was reserved to 'regional law', ie the civil law applicable in some Autonomous Communities, as opposed to the ordinary law applicable in other areas.

[19] See, for instance, Art 95 of the Statute of Autonomy of Catalonia or Art 140 of the Statute of Autonomy of Andalusia.

[20] Art 97 of the Statute of Autonomy of Catalonia. This *Estatuto* was subject to an appeal based on alleged unconstitutionality, resolved by Decision 31/2010, 28 June 2010. As regards the Council of Justice, its constitutionality was disputed due to the matter being covered by the *Estatuto*, rather than remaining within the competence of the State. Nevertheless, the other Statutes of Autonomy subject to reform that include similar references have not been the object of an appeal before the Constitutional Court, eg amongst others, Art 144 of the Statute of Autonomy of Andalusia or Art 33 of the Statute of Autonomy of Valencia (albeit with a much more generic reference).

unconstitutional. Not only does it identify certain insurmountable barriers imposed by the Constitution (the principle of jurisdictional unity), but it also shows that the amendments made to the composition and operation of the High Courts of Justice and the creation of Councils of Justice in each Autonomous Community, consolidated in the recently reformed *Estatutos de Autonomía*, cannot come into effect pending the necessary reform to the Spanish Organic Act of the Judiciary,[21] which is the rule that must decide the exact composition and duties of the High Courts of Justice and any judicial organ.

The Territorial Distribution of Power

As indicated above, the constitutional provisions about Autonomous Communities were overtaken by events, and once the Constitution was approved a competition to achieve autonomy began between some regions; some Autonomous Communities copied others, so that the differences between them are only those contemplated in the Constitution itself as to the method or process to be used to achieve autonomy—Articles 143 (ordinary procedure) and 151 (special procedure) in the Spanish Constitution.[22] However, this voluntary principle regarding the method by which to apply for autonomy was partly thwarted when, in relation to the 'historical' Autonomous Communities (Catalonia, the Basque Country and Galicia)[23] political agreements ('Autonomous Agreements' of 1981) rather than the law, closed access to the special procedure envisaged in Article 151 Spanish Constitution to other regions and only allowed Andalusia to benefit from it. All other Autonomous Communities had to follow the ordinary procedure. Nevertheless, this also entailed a requirement that the Constitution

[21] During the 2004–2008 sessions two bills were presented to reform the Organic Act of the Judiciary, which consolidated the innovations previously announced in the *Estatutos de Autonomía*. The end (dissolution) of the legislature meant that both bills failed, and they were never again presented. On the reform and problems of the judicial system existing in Autonomous Communities, see Luis Aguiar de Luque, 'Poder Judicial y reformas estatutarias', *Revista General de Derecho Constitucional*, no 1, 2006, 55–95; Ignacio Torres Muro, 'Las competencias autonómicas en materia de justicia', *El Poder Judicial. VI Congreso de la Asociación de Constitucionalistas de España*, (Valencia: Tirant lo Blanch, 2009), 385–411.

[22] Art 151 Spanish Constitution opened up the possibility of applying for maximum autonomy at an initial stage, if certain requirements were met: the initiative had to achieve a favourable vote of the provincial council and of three-quarters of the municipalities in the provinces affected, as well as the favourable vote of the absolute majority of voters in each province. The ordinary procedure foreseen in Art 143 Spanish Constitution limited the competences that could be assumed for at least a five-year period and required that the initiative be approved by the provincial councils and two-thirds of the municipalities. Nevertheless, any areas that already enjoyed a provisional autonomous system were exempt from these requirements, pursuant to the First Transitional Provision. The first two Transitional Provisions to a large extent enable the autonomous situation to adjust to the constitutional wording.

[23] These three Autonomous Communities benefited from the Second Transitional Provision of the Constitution. As they had previously subjected their *Estatutos de Autonomía* to a plebiscite and had provisional autonomy systems, they in fact did not have to follow the complex proceedings provided for in Art151 Spanish Constitution.

should be applied according to the circumstances, with the result that two Autonomous Communities (Valencia and the Canary Islands) were able to extend their competences through organic transfer acts (*leyes orgánicas de transferencia*)[24], thereby assuming similar competences to those of historic Communities or Andalusia. In this way a legislative instrument (Article 150.2 Spanish Constitution), which seemed to exist for the assignment of specific State competences, became just another device for the assignment of competences. Thus, as suggested by certain authors, 'the 1981 Autonomous Agreements merely approved an interpretation of Article 150.2 Spanish Constitution that would help evade the influence of the autonomous process foreseen in the Constitution.'[25]

This device for the assumption of competences was used again under the Autonomous Agreements of February 1992, with the same purpose of increasing the competences of Autonomous Communities before the relevant statutory reform was passed.[26] Thus the organic transfer Acts that ensued were no longer complementary to the Statutes and became another device (prior to the Statutes) for acquiring additional competences. This interpretation is hardly what was initially foreseen in the Spanish Constitution.[27]

On the other hand, the open-ended nature of Title VIII of the Constitution is of importance: according to the voluntary principle, not only were regions free to establish themselves as Autonomous Communities, but they were also entitled to decide which competences they would assume further to the distribution foreseen in the Constitution in Articles 148 and 149. However although Article 149.1 Spanish Constitution determines the matters to be entrusted to the 'exclusive' competence of the State, in fact it leaves a lot of room for Autonomous Communities to exercise some of these competences.

A certain amount of convergence has been taking place between the various regions, so that the enjoyment of more competences in one area inevitably leads to a greater demand for those competences in other regions, that is given the open-ended nature of the Spanish Constitution, greater demands from the regions seem never-ending.

The *Estatutos de Autonomía* are the first legislative instruments available to establish, amongst other issues, the scope of competences that are assumed by the Autonomous Communities. These rules have a unique status in the hierarchy of legal sources, due to their role in implementing constitutional provisions, with the formal status of combining both the will of the State, manifested through

---

[24] Organic Acts 11 and 12/1982, of 10 August.

[25] Manuel Medina Guerrero: 'La ampliación competencial de 1992. La inversión del proceso: la ley orgánica de transferencia como antesala de la reforma estatutaria', *Revista Española de Derecho Constitucional*, no 78, 2006, 83. This same author also mentions how this change has been occasionally defined as a true 'constitutional convention'.

[26] Organic Act 9/1992, of 23 December, on the transfer of competences to Autonomous Communities that assumed their autonomy by means of Art 143 Spanish Constitution; Organic Act 16/1995, of 27 December, on the transfer of competences to the Autonomous Community of Galicia.

[27] Medina Guerrero, note 25 above, 95, collects together the similar opinion of various authors.

approval by Parliament, and the will of the Assembly of each Autonomous Community, with the possibility of consulting the local population by referendum in certain cases. The Constitutional Court has highlighted that:

> *Estatutos de Autonomía*, further to the procedures established in Title VIII of the Constitution, are the foundation of each Autonomous Community; they endow it with the necessary political power and allow this power to evolve naturally through the passing of Acts within their scopes of competence, which are implemented in the regulations and applied, respectively, through the Governing Councils and Public Administrations. This confirms the constitutional definition of these Statutes as a 'basic institutional rule' in each Autonomous Community (Article 147.1 Spanish Constitution).

The Statutes are defined as 'an essential component in the territorial distribution of the State's political power'.[28] The *Estatutos de Autonomía* outline the generic provisions of the Constitution; Albertí even affirms that 'Spain has also undergone many changes in its basic autonomous order, although the Constitution has not been amended in this regard.'[29]

The distinction between State and Autonomous Community competences has been much disputed. Appeals on the grounds of unconstitutionality and conflicts of competence (depending on whether or not the rule in question enjoys status as an act) have allowed the Constitutional Court to build up its case law on the distribution of competences and their limits as between the State and Autonomous Communities.[30] This role of the Constitutional Court is why reference has recently been made to it as a 'constituent doctrine'.[31]

According to the Constitution there are other types of legislative provision that affect or may affect the distribution of competences between the levels of the State. However, the possibility of approving harmonization rules, foreseen in Article 150.3 Spanish Constitution, was apparently removed after Constitutional Court Decision 76/1983, of 5 August, in which the Constitutional Court upheld an appeal on the grounds of unconstitutionality brought against the Organic Act for Harmonization of the Autonomous Process (*Ley Orgánica de Armonización del Proceso Autonómico*) The Court rejected the idea of the legislator being competent to put an end to possible judicial interpretations by imposing a single interpretation on all public powers. The Constitutional Court affirmed that the legislator cannot 'issue rules that affect the constitutional system for the distribution of competences in order to deal with hypothetical vacuums arising from the Constitution', and

---

[28] Constitutional Court Decision 247/2007, of 12 December.
[29] Enoch Albertí Rovira, 'Las reformas territoriales en Alemania y en España y la sostenibilidad del paradigma autonómico español', (2006) 78, *Revista Española de Derecho Constitucional*, 11.
[30] Germán Fernández Farreres, *La contribución del Tribunal Constitucional al Estado Autonómico.* (Madrid: Tirant lo Blanch, 2005).
[31] José Antonio Montilla Martos, 'La inclusión de los nombres de las comunidades Autónomas', in Ángel J Gómez Montoro, *La reforma del Estado autonómico. Jornadas de estudio sobre el informe del Consejo de Estado.* (Madrid: CEPC-Universidad de Navarra, 2007), 44.

the state legislator cannot indirectly determine the definition of competences by interpretation of its foundational criteria. It is true that any process for legal implementation of the Constitution always entails an interpretation of the relevant constitutional provisions, carried out by whoever issues the implementing rule. But the ordinary legislator cannot issue rules for mere interpretation purposes that are exclusively aimed at fixing a single meaning, from amongst several possible ones, that should be attributed to a certain provision in the Constitution; by reducing the various possibilities or alternatives of the constitutional text to one, it in fact limits the role of the constituent power and usurps its position, thereby crossing the dividing line between the constituent power and constituted powers.

Given the failure of the Organic Act for Harmonization of the Autonomous Process, the legislator never again used this device and there is a general belief that this possibility no longer exists, at least in the current state of affairs.

Another provision that has played an important role in matters regarding autonomous competences is Article 149.3 Spanish Constitution. Its interpretation has been left to the Constitutional Court. This paragraph suggests that there are co-existing competences, that is competences that may be exercised by the Autonomous Communities if not assumed by the State. However, this interpretation was rejected by the Constitutional Court, which instead held that if these potential competences were assumed by the Autonomous Communities they would be excluded from State competences. As a result co-existing competences disappeared[32] and all competences became exclusive, though occasionally shared, to the State or Autonomous Communities. This interpretation of competences, has increased the level of conflict between the State and Autonomous Communities.

In relation to Article 149.3 Spanish Constitution, the Constitutional Court has introduced a new interpretation of the clause dealing with 'ancillary' (that is supplementary) provisions. This clause states that 'State law will in any case be ancillary to Autonomous Community law'. This took account of the fact that not all Autonomous Communities had to (or initially could) assume the same competences and, furthermore, even if they all assumed certain competences, these would not be used identically or with the same scope. The clause was assumed to enable the State legislature to exercise competences which it also possessed, in parallel with the Autonomous Communities. This was the opinion of legal scholars,[33] and was also upheld for a long time by the Constitutional Court, thus supporting the idea that the ancillary role of the State was designed

---

[32] Please note that some authors define 'co-existing competences' as those for which the State establishes the grounds and which are then implemented by the Autonomous Communities. See, in this regard, Eliseo Aja, *El Estado autonómico. Federalismo y hechos diferenciales.* (Madrid: Alianza Ed, 1999).

[33] One of the first studies on the matter was issued by Ignacio de Otto, 'La prevalencia del Derecho estatal sobre el derecho regional', (1981) 2 *Revista Española de Derecho Constitucional.*

to fill in any vacuums and to enable the legal order to be coherent and to cover all eventualities. This was the interpretation applied in Constitutional Court Decision 5/1981.

This understanding was later challenged, first in Constitutional Court Decision 118/1996, which dealt with an appeal on the grounds of unconstitutionality, challenging Act 16/1987 on the organisation of land transport, and subsequently, and more radically, with Constitutional Court Decision 61/1997, on an appeal challenging the revised text of the Act on land regulations and urban development. The Court departed from its previous interpretation and now held that the State legislature may only legislate on matters where it has been granted its own specific competence, and may not do so merely in an ancillary manner in cases where Autonomous Communities have assumed the relevant competences, regardless of whether they have exercised them.

In the first of these Decisions the Constitutional Court held that 'The State cannot issue rules of a merely ancillary nature in matters where it lacks competence; the State legislature cannot justify doing so on the basis of its power in relation to ancillary provisions, as this does not grant the State a power of general competence' (Sixth Paragraph of Decision). Nevertheless, this Decision analysed each provision to determine whether or not the State was granted the competence it claimed. In Decision 61/1997 the Constitutional Court went further and declared the unconstitutionality of all provisions classified as ancillary by the State legislature, without analysing the scope of the specific provisions in question. The Court also annulled the Repealing Provision. As a result, not only were former laws rendered effective once again, but the State legislature was deprived of the capacity to decide on the repeal of its own rules. Furthermore, legal uncertainty arose from the declaration of the validity of a set of scattered laws, some of which dated from before the Constitution of 1978.

Amongst the practical consequences of these decisions not only is the State prevented from passing ancillary legislation but also, if one or several Autonomous Communities have not implemented their competences (as was the case in matters covered by the Decisions noted above), the only possibility is to resort to former, sometimes pre-constitutional State laws, which, naturally, hardly fill in the legal vacuum or gaps in the law of the Autonomous Communities. Whilst it is true that the State's inability to create ancillary rules obliged Autonomous Communities to legislate in the areas in which they has assumed competences and, consequently, boosted their autonomous law, this did not resolve the issue of how to cover the vacuums accidentally left by the autonomous legislatures and undermined the coherence and comprehensiveness of the State legal order. Furthermore, in addition to the 17 Autonomous Communities that have legislative competences, full or shared depending on the subject matter, there are two autonomous cities, Ceuta and Melilla, without any legislative competences which, therefore, are subject to State laws and, according to the constitutional case law derived from Constitutional Court Decisions 118/1996 and 61/1997, the State legislature is deprived of its right to issue new laws for them.

Apart from any short-term difficulties caused by these decisions, the interpretation of the clause on ancillary provisions seems to treat the clause as a transitional provision only.[34] However many legal scholars[35] dispute this interpretation and consider it to be a permanent clause that acts as a general rule on the application of the law,[36] even if this rule is merely marginal in those cases where all Autonomous Communities have assumed the competences found in the Statutes or by law.

Another dispute surrounding the definition of competences is related to the definition of 'legal basis' or 'state grounds' (where the State defines the core of legislation which will be developed by the Autonomous Communities). Here also the Constitutional Court has defined their scope, without however laying down any clear rule; depending on the subject matter it has granted a smaller or wider scope to these grounds, consequently allowing greater or lesser autonomous intervention in the matter. Furthermore, there is a lack of formal guarantees, given that the requirement to pass an Act by the State legislature as a formal requisite foreseen in Constitutional Court Decision 69/1988 has subsequently not always applied. Both issues have not only decreased the scope of autonomous competences but have also determined its uncertainty.[37]

The most recent amendments with constitutional implications of the law relating to Autonomous Community matters have arisen from the reform to which the Statutes of Autonomy of the Communities have been subject over the last few years. This reform was carried out, in theory, to update the Statutes in relation to the competences assumed by the Autonomous Communities and in order for the Statutes to consolidate the institutional and organic changes that had taken place.[38] However, this reform has sometimes[39] led to a deep rift

---

[34] This interpretation was supported by Iñaki Lasagabaster, *Los principios de supletoriedad y prevalencia del Derecho estatal respecto del Derecho Autonómico*, (Madrid: Civitas, 1991).

[35] Amongst others, Juan Luis Requejo, 'El Estado Autonómico: ¿Un modelo transitorio?', (1997) 1 *Cuadernos de Derecho Público*; Paloma Biglino, 'La cláusula de supletoriedad: una cuestión en perspectiva', (1997) 50 *Revista Española de Derecho Constitucional*; R Gómez Ferrer, 'La cláusula de supletoriedad', *Informe Comunidades Autónomas 1997*, Instituto de Derecho (Barcelona: Público, 1998), 607 ff; Javier Tajadura, 'La redefinición del modelo autonómico a partir de la STC 61/1997 y el nuevo concepto de supletoriedad', (2006) 78 *Revista Española de Derecho Constitucional*.

[36] Please note that Constitutional Court Decision 61/1997 included a dissenting opinion issued by the magistrate Manuel Jiménez de Parga against the majority opinion, which upheld that ancillary provisions 'were a result of the State's exercise of its powers to include its provisions within a legal order which, in relation to the autonomous order, act as the ancillary provisions foreseen in Art 149.3 Spanish Constitution, given that it is the legal order of the State or of Spain'.

[37] On these issues, see José Antonio Montilla Martos, 'La legislación básica tras las reformas estatutarias', in (2006) 78 *Revista Española de Derecho Constitucional*, 105–50.

[38] The Statutes of Autonomy originally consolidated the institutions stated in the Constitution, ie Legislative Assembly and Government Council. Bit by bit, through autonomous laws, other bodies were created such as advisory councils or ombudsmen. For changes in relation to the judiciary, see above.

[39] Particularly with the reform of the Statute of Catalonia, later used as a template for the rest. On the Statutes reforms, Enrique Álvarez Conde, *Reforma constitucional y reformas estatutarias*, (Madrid: Civitas, 2007).

between the main political parties and has also introduced innovations that were not foreseen in, and may even be contrary to, the Spanish Constitution; this is why some legal scholars suggest that these statutory reforms are in reality constitutional reforms in disguise.[40]

A change has taken place in the way competences are acquired, establishing a wider and clearer definition of State competences and seeking a comprehensive and accurate list of the various sub-divisions within competences on the basis of which Autonomous Communities may seek to increase their competences.[41]

Another innovation was the introduction of a list of rights in some Autonomous Community Statutes. This led to huge controversy, given that some commentators considered, first, that powers to legislate for these rights are not included in the statutory enabling provisions because the only rights available are those referred to by the Constitution in relation to the Autonomous Community Statutes and, secondly, that these rights should be equal for all Spanish citizens. In the light of arguments that support the case for recognition of rights in the Autonomous Community Statutes, these commentators' opinion is that legislation for non-fundamental rights is open to the Autonomous Community legislature and, second, that the reference in the Constitution does not amount to a closed list of matters for Autonomous Community Statutes but merely a definition of minimum content, which may later be extended, as long as State responsibilities are not affected.[42] As a result of Constitutional Court Decision 247/2007 on the Statute of Valencia, it would seem that Statutes may refer to constitutional rights and duties. Decision 31/2010 upholds this, albeit reaffirming that *basic* human rights will only be those that the Constitution acknowledges as such.

The enactment by the Autonomous Communities and the State of *Estatutos de Autonomía*, therefore, is used as a means of remodelling the Spanish State of Autonomous Communities without changing the Constitution. However, the latest Decision (31/2010) has highlighted how this possibility of change is

[40] Francesc de Carreras, 'Reformar la Constitución para estabilizar el modelo territorial', en *La reforma Constitucional: ¿Hacia un nuevo pacto constituyente? Atlas de las XIV Jornadas de la asociación de Letrados del Tribunal Constitucional*, (Madrid: CEPC-TC, 2009), 59.

[41] Term used by Carles Viver, eg in 'La reforma de los Estatutos de Autonomía' in Viver, Balaguer and Tajadura, *La reforma de los Estatutos de Autonomía*, (Madrid: CEPC-TC, 2005).

[42] Amongst the authors against having a closed list of rights in the *Estatutos*, albeit with different arguments see: Luis María Díez-Picazo, '¿Pueden los Estatutos de Autonomía declarar derechos, deberes y principios?, in (2006) 78 *Revista Española de Derecho Constitucional*, 63–75; Víctor Ferreres Comella, 'Derechos, deberes y principios en el nuevo Estatuto de autonomía de Cataluña', in the book of the same title (Madrid: CEPC, 2006). In favour, amongst others: Francisco Caamaño, 'Sí, pueden (Declaraciones de derechos y Estatutos de Autonomía), 79 *Revista Española de Derecho Constitucional*, 33–46; Luis Ortega Álvarez, 'Los derechos de los ciudadanos en los nuevos estatutos de autonomía', *Estado compuesto y derechos de los ciudadanos*, (Barcelona: Institut d'Estudis Autonòmics, 2007), 55–81.

restricted by the constitutional framework, particularly the need to uphold the principles foreseen in the Constitution and exclusive State competences.[43]

CHANGES INTRODUCED BY SPAIN'S ACCESSION TO THE EUROPEAN
COMMUNITY AND AS A RESULT OF SUBSEQUENT EVENTS IN THE EUROPEAN
UNION

Spain's accession to the European Community entailed a change that was not subsequently reflected in the Constitution. Article 93 of the Constitution foresees the possibility of ratifying treaties entitling an international organisation to exercise constitutional competences through the passing by the Spanish Parliament of 'organic' acts;[44] this provision was specially introduced to facilitate Spain's future accession to the EC.[45]

As a result, the distribution of competences within Spain, which at the time of accession was still undergoing development, had to be adjusted. At the time there was discussion about whether accession meant that Community competences needed to be provided for at all, given that the State possessed competence in foreign relations.[46] However, the logical response (upheld by the Constitutional Court) was that competences would not be altered insofar as they were not affected by European competences, that is within Spain the responsibility for implementation and/or execution of European competences would fall to the State or to Autonomous Communities depending on who held the competence.[47]

Nor did the Constitution reflect the new competences granted to the European Union by the European Union Treaty, or the Treaties of Amsterdam, Nice or Lisbon, unlike the constitutions of most European States. Hardly any discussion arose in Spain and it was believed that Article 93 of the Constitution allowed successive Treaties to be ratified. However, Article 93 only refers to the *assignment* to an international organisation of 'the exercise of competences derived from the Constitution.' In European Union terms, this would seem to go beyond a mere 'exercise of competences'. At present there are many matters which have been entrusted to or are shared with the Union, and fewer remain exclusively in the hands of the States. The relevance of these matters has also changed: they are no

[43] For example, the Decision states that the term 'nation' may only apply to the entire State and not to an Autonomous Community, as indicated in the Preamble of the reformed *Estatuto de Autonomía* of Catalonia.
[44] Organic acts need an absolute majority in the Lower Chamber (*Congreso*), further to Art 81 Spanish Constitution.
[45] The Treaty of Accession was signed in 1985 and came into force in January 1986.
[46] This alternative, amongst other issues, would have deprived the Autonomous Communities of content, given that a large part of the statutory competences now envisaged would be transferred to the EC.
[47] See, in this regard, Constitution Court Decisions 252/1988, of 20 December and 79/1992, of 28 May.

longer matters necessary to construct a 'common market' but also affect other fields traditionally linked to State sovereignty, such as penal law, foreign relations and fundamental rights.

Many such matters are affected, including (amongst others) the extremely important 'Economic Constitution' relating to the Spanish State's ability to intervene in economic matters. References to 'public initiative in the economy' reserving to the public sector certain resources or essential services (Article 128.2 Spanish Constitution), or economic planning (Article 131 Spanish Constitution), make no sense in light of Community requirements. Furthermore, budgetary measures or policies in other sectors are conditioned by European Union decisions, apart from the single-currency and monetary policy.

Membership of the Union also affects the legislatures and executives (at State or Autonomous Community level), who must now exercise their functions in compliance with Community law. The executive and the administration (in any field) are responsible for implementing not only internal law but also European Union law. Finally, the judiciary must also act according to whatever rule is applicable to the case, which may be domestic or Community law, and are also obliged to uphold the principle of primacy of European Union law. The hierarchy of legal sources, therefore, is no longer the one foreseen in the Spanish Constitution.

Given the absence of constitutional provisions on these matters, relations between Parliament and the Government in relation to the European Union, and the former's control over the latter in this field, have meant that the use of ordinary checks and balances has not been sufficient. This has given rise to the formation of a Joint Lower-Upper Chamber Committee for the European Community. This was created by Act 47/1985 of 27 December (it was subsequently redefined and specified as a Joint Lower-Upper Chamber Committee for the European Union according to Act 8/1994, of 19 May[48]).

Nor is there any constitutional provision regarding cooperation between the State and Autonomous Communities in relation to the European Union. This had led to a series of lacunae or cases where solutions are found incrementally as issues arise, sometimes, once again, through the intervention of the Constitutional Court. Solutions have been adjusting to practical needs, leading to the creation of the *Conferencia para Asuntos Relacionados con las Comunidades Europeas* (CARCE) [Conference for European Community-Related Matters],[49] as a channel of communication between the State and Autonomous Communities in matters of common concern related to the European Union.

---

[48] As opposed to traditional parliamentary commissions created by Chamber Regulations, this Commission was created in an Act, precisely because of its particular and mixed nature, given the absence of joint regulations for the '*Cortes Generales*' (foreseen in Art 72.2 Spanish Constitution).

[49] Act 2/1997, of 13 March. This Conference consists of State and Autonomous Community representatives. As a result of the successful operation of this Conference, conferences have been created in other sectors in order to encourage cooperation between the State and Autonomous Communities.

The lack of any constitutional provision on these matters also means that the Autonomous Communities cannot easily participate in Community institutions, unlike the position in other countries such as Germany or Belgium with territorial structures similar to Spain's. Similar problems have arisen when the State has to intervene in the event of a breach of European law on the part of an Autonomous Community.

All State bodies are subject to Community law and consequently there is no longer a single decision-making institution and the entire internal structure has been altered.[50]

At the time, not even the Treaty that established a European Constitution, which was subject to the Constitutional Court's opinion, was considered contrary to the Spanish Constitution,[51] despite a few legal scholars arguing the need for the Constitution to deal with the matter expressly. As a result, the Constitution still does not include any reference to the European Union, to its significance with respect to internal law, or to any future limits.

ATTEMPTS AT CONSTITUTIONAL REFORM: THE COUNCIL OF STATE REPORT

After the March 2004 elections, the new Government proposed an initial reform of the Constitution. This proposal was the subject of a report from the State Council (the Government's top advisory body). There were four issues:

— the removal of a preference in favour of male successors to the throne;
— the Constitution's reflection of provisions for dealing with European developments in Spain's constitutional system;
— incorporation of the names of the Autonomous Communities; and
— a reform of the Upper Chamber (*Senado*).

The first point did not raise any significant problems because there is general consensus on the issue. The proposed reform provides that the succession rights of the current heir to the throne, the youngest of the King's three children, will subsist, that is the measure will only affect his own successors.

On the second point, it has already been pointed out that since 1985, when the Treaty of Accession of Spain to the European Community was signed, no reference has been made to the Union in the Spanish Constitution, unlike the case of most other European States, since there is no contradiction between the Constitution and European Treaties (except for the one indicated above). A

---

[50] A solid summary of how the European Union has affected constitutional mandates is available in Enoch Albertí, 'La cláusula europea en la reforma de la Constitución española', Rubio Llorente and Álvarez Junco (eds): *El informe del Consejo de Estado sobre la reforma constitucional* (Madrid: Consejo de Estado-Centro de Estudios políticos y constitucionales, 2006) 461 ff. A study is made of those issues that the Constitution should reflect in order to allow an adequate implementation of European law. Wording is also proposed for the relevant articles, sometimes confirming the existing situation and other times perfecting it.

[51] Statement issued by the Plenary Meeting of the Constitutional Court 1/2004, of 13 December.

reference to the European construction process would only reflect what has been happening in other constitutions of member states. Apart from subscribing to the Union, this would encourage the ratification of the treaties related to European integration and the role of European law in the hierarchy of legal sources. It would also lay down any potential limits on integration, in a similar way to other European countries.

Furthermore, the possibility was suggested of referring to relations between the *Cortes Generales* (national parliament) and the Government in the European construction process (allowing a greater participation of citizen representatives and greater control over the Government's actions), and to the relationship between the State and Autonomous Communities, likewise defining the role of each party both upwards and downwards.

Points three and four are inevitably linked. On the one hand, the Constitution needs to finalise the arrangements for the Autonomous Communities, partly closing off Title VIII. A reform of the Upper Chamber (*Senado*) would transform it into a real chamber for regional representation, as stated in the text of the Constitution, incorporating specific provisions as to its functions and the election of the majority of its members. The State Council suggests various alternatives for the election of Members, all based on the representation of Autonomous Communities, as opposed to the uniform provincial constituencies that currently exist which, to a large extent, merely duplicate the representation of the other Chamber.

The reform affecting the Crown requires the special procedure foreseen in Article 168 Spanish Constitution (discussed earlier in this chapter), whilst remaining matters are subject to the less demanding procedure of Article 167. However, the State Council considered that since the reform covered both kinds of matter, they should all be achieved through the special Article 168 procedure. Therefore, from a practical point of view, a change in the provisions governing succession to the Crown, the least disputed issue and one which, in fact, entailed a minor amendment, required the Article 168 procedure because the Constitution refers to it in Title II, instead of treating it as a change in the Head of State which, in fact, was what was really being protected. However, not all authors agreed with the single reform procedure proposed by the State Council, and some believed it preferable to follow two different procedures depending on the subject matter, that is except for succession to the Crown, all other matters would follow the procedure foreseen in Article 167 Spanish Constitution.[52] That Article would apply unless it were decided to include the reform, not (or not only) in the Titles actually affected, but in the Preliminary Title, which also requires the special

---

[52] Ramón Punset Blanco, 'El Consejo de Estado y el procedimiento de reforma constitucional. Un inventario de certidumbres y perplejidades', in Ángel J Gómez Montoro, *La reforma del Estado autonómico. Jornadas de estudio sobre el informe del Consejo de Estado*, (Madrid: CEPC-Universidad de Navarra, 2007), 3–12.

reform procedure of Article 168. As a result, and except for this latter case, the decision as to whether or not to follow a single procedure would rest with the proposer.[53]

The other matters covered by the reform proposal were more controversial. A reference to a European process was disputed as regards its specific wording; the other two matters were discussed as regards their scope: the incorporation of all Autonomous Community names entailed the risk of affecting the distribution of competences, leading to serious debate. As regards a reform of the Upper Chamber (*Senado*), there is broad consensus on the need for reform but not on how to implement it.

In relation to changing the *Senado* into a real chamber for territorial representation, the State Council suggests that members be elected for each Autonomous Community, increasing their number according to the population and provinces in each Community's region. Various election formulae have been discussed by the legislative assemblies of Autonomous Communities, namely direct election by the population,[54] or mixed formulae.

It should be noted that a reform of the *Senado* would not affect its status as a parliamentary Chamber or the unusual two-Chamber system established by the Constitution, even if new functions are attributed to it or existing ones are strengthened. Of importance, as highlighted in the Report, is the fact that the territorial nature of representation in the *Senado* would be apparent from where the members were elected and their functions, and it would affect their political behaviour. But there would be no legal requirements or mandatory law as to their territorial functions.[55]

An incorporation into the Constitution of Autonomous Community names would have greater consequences than meet the reader's eye. First of all, this would mean closing off the autonomous region map, which was left open by the Constitution (although, as stated above, this closure actually took place soon after the Constitution was approved). It would also, prima facie, seem to end the voluntary principle, at least to this extent. However, some commentators claim that this formula need not close off the system but that, at least in theory, the map may be changed as required by the regions involved from time to time. For this reason some authors do not want the articles referring to the means by which to acquire autonomy to be removed, even though they may be considered obsolete. Thus not only would the door be left open to a union between Navarre

---

[53] This was upheld by Piedad García Escudero in the debate that arose after Professor Punset's speech (cited in the preceding footnote),15 ff.

[54] Considered preferable by the State Council.

[55] Report issued by the State Council on Constitutional Reform, Rubio Llorente and Álvarez Junco (eds) note 50 above 232.

and the Basque Country, as foreseen in the Fourth Transitional Provision of the Constitution, but also to other possibilities, such as the union of other regions or a severance of part of a territory.[56]

Beyond the issue of incorporating Autonomous Community names into the Constitution, the State Council considers that it would be appropriate for the Constitution to include or define various principles that affect relations between the State and Autonomous Communities and relations between the latter: principles of solidarity, equal treatment, collaboration and cooperation.[57] Given the limited constitutional provisions at present, as on other occasions, the Constitutional Court has defined the scope of these principles and their consequence for the various parties.

Article 145 Spanish Constitution provides for cooperation agreements and the need for their authorisation by Parliament. However, very few agreements have been formalised in accordance with the Constitutional requirements, and other more flexible alternatives have been used to deal with the need for cooperation between Autonomous Communities.

The State Council Report also refers to the procedure for reform of the Statutes of Autonomy, and looks for solutions to possible disagreements between each Autonomous Community parliament and the State Parliament and a simplification of this procedure in certain cases. It also finds it appropriate to reintroduce a prior application on the grounds of unconstitutionality (*recurso previo de inconstitucionalidad*).[58]

Finally, a reference is made to the limits imposed on competences[59] in order to end discussions derived from the vague wording of the Constitution.

CONCLUSIONS

At the time of the thirtieth anniversary of the Spanish Constitution[60] there was a lot of support for reform which would enable the Constitution to remain a living instrument; it was argued that the praiseworthy consensus behind the Constitution should not be an obstacle to reform. As mentioned by some authors, a whole generation has grown up since it was passed, and it is time to allow this new generation to incorporate its ideas into this Magna Carta.[61] However, the political

---

[56] See in this regard the speech made by Eduardo Vírgala Foruría in *La reforma del Estado autonómico. Jornadas de estudio sobre el informe del Consejo de Estado, cit.*, 40–41, and some participants in subsequent discussions.

[57] Report, note 50 above, 158 ff.

[58] A prior appeal on the grounds of unconstitutionality is only currently available for international treaties. The Organic Act on the Constitutional Court originally established this possibility in other cases, but it was repealed in an Organic Act.

[59] Report note 50 above, 175 ff.

[60] December 2008.

[61] Francisco Rubio Llorente, 'Los retos de los hijos de la Constitución', in *El País*, 2 December 2008.

scenario seems to have rendered this reform unfeasible. It should be noted here that, notwithstanding the difficulties that inevitably arise from the Constitutional reform processes, an amendment would be possible if the main political forces were to reach an agreement.

Furthermore, it may be argued that some of the changes in legislative or interpretative terms affect the legal status of the Constitution, which has nevertheless remained theoretically the same since the date it was passed and which is still undisputed in formal terms. However, some legal reforms (for example, reforms of the *Estatutos de Autonomía*) seem to suggest (at least) a strained or 'forced' interpretation of the Constitution, as evidenced by Constitutional Court Decision of 28 June 2010. The risk of losing this legal status should be a solid argument in favour of a formal amendment.

Thus formal reform according to the processes provided for in the Constitution remains outstanding, unfinished business;[62] execution of this task would mean that the purpose of the 1978 Constitution has been accomplished. Although consensus prevailed at the time the Constitution was passed and resolved former disputes, reform (rather than stasis or adoption of a new Constitution) would mean that this consensus as to the procedure for reform was not an exceptional situation at a certain moment in history, but a new way of shaping Spain's constitutional future.

[62] In Spanish constitutional history, each constitutional innovation has ended with a new Constitution. A reform of the current Constitution would mean that, finally, a modern Constitution exists.

14

Switzerland

GIOVANNI BIAGGINI*

INTRODUCTION: DEVELOPMENT OF A SWISS CONSTITUTION

T HE BASIC STRUCTURES of the constitutional framework of the Swiss
Confederation date back to the establishment of the Federal State in 1848.
The first Federal Constitution (of 12 September 1848), which basically
created the foundations—which are still in place—of the Swiss federal state, was
replaced by the Federal Constitution of 29 May 1874. Around 125 years later, on
1 January 2000, the third Constitution, which had been approved ('adopted' in
Swiss terminology) in the referendum of 18 April 1999, came into force. For an
understanding of the development of Swiss constitutional law, it is important to
outline the formation and the basic content of these three Federal Constitutions
of 1848, 1874, and 1999.

One of the characteristic features of Switzerland is its diversity, in particular its
four national languages (German, French, Italian, and Romansh).[1] However, it is
not the language regions which function as basic political units, but the 26
cantons which differ in many respects from each other.[2] With the exception of
the Canton of Jura (established in 1979), they all existed as independent entities
before the establishment of the Federal State. The linguistic boundaries do not
always coincide with the boundaries of the cantons.[3] Besides the three bilingual

---

* The author would like to thank his research fellow Alexander Misic, Dr iur, LLM (Cornell) for
support and critical remarks and Joanna Niederer for translating the text. This paper refers to the
results of various earlier published works of the author: Giovanni Biaggini, 'Grundlagen und
Grundzüge staatlichen Verfassungsrechts: Schweiz' in Armin von Bogdandy et al (eds), *Handbuch Ius
Publicum Europaeum (IPE)*, Vol. I (Heidelberg, 2007) 565–623; 'Lo sviluppo del costituzionalismo e il
ruolo della dottrina: il caso svizzero' (2008) 4 *Quaderni costituzionali* 917–35; 'Entwicklungen und
Spannungen im Verfassungsrecht' (2010) 1 *Schweizerisches Zentralblatt für Staats- und Verwaltungsrecht (ZBl)* 1–41.
    [1] Romansh is only an official language of the Confederation when communicating with people
who speak Romansh (Article 70 of the Federal Constitution).
    [2] Today (2010), the total population of Appenzell Innerrhodes is around 15.600, and of Zurich
1.35 million.
    [3] See Thomas Fleiner, Alexander Misic and Nicole Töpperwien, *Swiss Constitutional Law* (Berne
and The Hague, 2005), 38.

cantons, there is a trilingual canton.[4] Switzerland is also not homogeneous in a confessional or religious sense. Many Swiss people belong to a linguistic, cultural or confessional/religious majority, but also to one or more local, regional or national minorities.

The Swiss tradition of compromise and proportional representation is connected to this diversity.[5] Since 1959, the Federal Council (Federal Government) has consisted practically uninterrupted of representatives from all the big political parties. Despite very comfortable (on paper) majorities in both chambers of the Federal Assembly (Parliament), the Federal Council must almost act as if it were a minority government, that is it must expect permanent opposition and forge cross-party majorities in intensive negotiation processes. An important role is accorded to the citizens, who, besides voting rights, also have many additional direct-democratic participation rights at their command at the federal level. Referendums on constitutional changes and popular initiatives (mandatory referendums) as well as on federal statutes and important international treaties (optional referendums) characterise political life in Switzerland, especially because the results of a referendum are always binding. Of the worldwide 728 referenda which were carried out between 1900 and 1993 at a national level, Switzerland accounted for around half (357).[6]

The Foundation of the Federal State: the Federal Constitution of 1848

The beginnings of the Swiss Confederation date back to 1291. The establishment of the Federal State in 1848 was preceded by a serious domestic crisis, through which the Swiss Confederation—at that time held together as a confederacy through the Confederate Treaty (Bundesvertrag) of 1815—was on the verge of breaking up. After the short 'Sonderbund' Civil War (3–29 November 1847)—in which the troops of seven conservative Catholic cantons and those of other, reform-minded, cantons fought each other—a Reform Commission began drafting a Federal Constitution on 17 February 1848. The draft Constitution was presented on 8 April 1848. On 27 June 1848, the Diet (the main body of the Confederation of States) passed the constitutional text on a majority vote. The Diet then submitted it to the cantons, which had to make a decision according to the various constitutional requirements on the adoption of the new Constitution. Between 5 August and 3 September 1848, referenda or 'Landsgemeinde' votes

---

[4] Bern/Berne, Fribourg/Freiburg and Valais/Wallis are bilingual cantons. Graubünden/Grischun/Grigoni is a trilingual canton.
[5] On Swiss concordance democracy, see (from a political science viewpoint) Wolf Linder, *Schweizerische Demokratie* 2nd edn (Bern, 2005) 301.
[6] See David Butler and Austin Ranney, *Referendums around the World*, (London, 1994). For a general overview, see Etienne Grisel, *Initiative et référendum populaires* 3rd edn (Bern, 2004).

took place in nearly all the cantons.[7] On 12 September 1848, the Diet declared (on a majority vote) that the new Federal Constitution was adopted and put it into force for the *whole* Confederation—although it had been rejected in eight cantons.[8] This decision clearly represented a break with the former confederative-contractual legal bases. Nevertheless, the outvoted cantons finally sent representatives into both chambers of the Federal Assembly. The history of this constitutional process is, according to today's democratic standards, not a shining example of the way it should articulate the constituent power of a people. However, over the course of time, the opinion has prevailed in Switzerland that at least some 'birth defects' cannot affect the validity of a constitution.

The fathers of the Constitution of 1848 had a pioneering task to perform. As a replacement for a rather loose union of (sovereign) states, they envisaged an efficient structure which should, however, not restrict the independence of the individual cantons too greatly. A structure was created that was unprecedented on the old continent: the first federal state in Europe. However, the constitutional text was not entirely free of remnants of the past confederacy, which have in part survived until now, that is the state designation in the Latin national languages (*Confédération suisse, Confederazione svizzera, Confederaziun svizra,*—a Confederation not a Federal State). Despite such imprecision, Switzerland was, unlike the United States of America, spared a debate on the legal nature of the new Confederation.

One of the most important organisational decisions was the creation of two new political authorities: the Federal Assembly as a two chamber federal parliament (on the US model) and the separate Federal Council as a collegial government made up of seven members, without a superior head of state or government[9] and each enjoying equal status, elected by the Federal Assembly for a fixed four-year term of office.[10] After the election has taken place, the Federal Council is not reliant on the confidence of the Federal Assembly. Neither the Federal Council nor individual government ministers can be forced to resign early.

These basic organisational structures have essentially survived until today. Down to the present day, the 1848 federal order is still largely based on three main pillars. The allocation of responsibilities and powers between the Confederation and the cantons follows the principle of conferral of competences. The

---

[7] As a prototype of direct democracy, the Landsgemeinde is a meeting of the voters 'in the open air' (in the truest sense of the word). Nowadays, there are still cantonal Landsgemeinde in the Cantons of Appenzell Innerrhodes and Glarus.

[8] Six of these eight cantons later rejected the Constitutions of 1874 and 1999, ie never approved a Federal Constitution.

[9] The annually changing federal president, who chairs the Federal Council, is just *primus inter pares* (first among equals).

[10] Note that the circle of eligible members for the Federal Council is very inclusive and not restricted to the members of the Federal Assembly (Article 175(3) of the Federal Constitution: *all Swiss citizens* who are eligible for election to the House of Representatives).

Confederation is only responsible if and as far as the Federal Constitution allocates it responsibility. Transfers of responsibility require a constitutional amendment. Under the Federal Constitution of 1848, the Confederation was responsible for foreign policy, customs, the postal sector, part of the military sector, and coinage (the right to mint coins). The cantons retained police, education and fiscal sovereignty, still continued to have their own troops, and remained responsible for key areas such as private and criminal law, the judiciary and health care, work, commerce and banking. A second federal state pillar is the participation of the cantons in the formation of the *volonté fédérale*. Since 1848, an important element has been the requirement of a double majority for constitutional amendments: the majority of voting Swiss citizens, and the majority of the cantons (the so-called *Ständemehr*).[11] A third pillar includes obligations between the Confederation and the cantons with regard to cooperation, mutual support and respect.

The Federal Constitution of 1848 is deemed to have been a successful *combinaison* of the national principle with respect for the cantons.[12] In the eyes of the fathers of the constitution, however, the work of 1848 remained in some respects unfinished (for instance on the unity of law and a national army). Measured against today's standards, the first Constitution contained notable deficiencies, above all in the area of *Rechtstaat* (the Rule of Law—see discussion below). A federal judiciary which deserved that name was still lacking. Basic guarantees such as freedom of speech, freedom of assembly or the guarantee of property were non-existent at the federal level.[13] However, from a comparative perspective, it does not seem entirely unusual that fundamental rights and liberties only received limited attention at the beginning of an integration process (compare US constitution in the 1787 version, and European Community/Union until 2009).

---

[11] Since 1874, it has been constitutionally required that the result of a popular vote in a canton determines the vote of the canton (*cf* today Article 142(3) of the Federal Constitution). This means: the vote of the canton (*Standesstimme*) is determined neither by the cantonal executive nor by the cantonal legislature.

[12] Jean-François Aubert, 'Geschichtliche Einführung' in Aubert et al. (eds), *Kommentar zur Bundesverfassung der Schweizerischen Eidgenossenschaft vom 29. Mai 1874* (Basel/Berne/Zurich, 1987–96), No 110.

[13] The following fundamental rights and liberties were granted: equality before the law, a limited freedom of establishment for Swiss citizens, freedom of trade between the cantons, freedom of religion and conscience (though at that time, only for members of Christian denominations), freedom of the press, and freedom of association (Articles 4, 29, 41, 44, 45 and 46). The selection of rights made at that time gives the impression that the constitutional fathers wanted to implement minimum standards on the whole territory of Switzerland in areas lacking federal power. Certain fundamental rights and liberties still play a role as an instrument of federal integration.

Expansion of the Federal Constitutional System: The Federal Constitution of 1874

In the 1860s, the supporters of an expansion of the democratic rights of the people and also the supporters of unification of the law gained in strength. However, in the referendum of 14 January 1866, eight out of the nine planned amendments of the Constitution were rejected. As a result, the Federal Council compiled proposals for several constitutional changes (1870). In the Parliament, a replacement of the Federal Constitution (*Totalrevision*) emerged out of the government bill. The main theme of the reformers was the strengthening of federal power. To compensate for the substantial expansion of federal powers, it was decided to introduce an optional referendum on federal statutes: henceforth, eight cantons or 30,000 persons eligible to vote (today 50,000) would be able to request that a federal statute passed by the Federal Assembly be submitted to a vote of the People. The replacement of the Federal Constitution failed in the referendum of 12 May 1872, although not by much,[14] as a result of the combined opposition of the conservative Catholic camp and the Federalists from the French-speaking part of Switzerland.

A second attempt at reform was promptly carried out and was successful. Through concessions in areas such as private law, military affairs, and educational affairs, the liberal-radical camp was able to win the support of the Federalists of the French-speaking part of Switzerland. It was not thought necessary to take the conservative-Catholic camp into consideration. The anti-Catholic constitutional articles contained in the failed constitutional draft version of 1872 were even strengthened.[15] The new Federal Constitution was approved relatively clearly in the referendum of 19 April, 1874.[16] It came into force on 29 May, 1874. Unlike the Federal Constitution of 1848, it did not involve an original constitutionally created act, but rather a derived constitutional process according to the procedure established in Article 111–114 of the Federal Constitution of 1848.

The new Federal Constitution mainly brought about a strengthening of the Confederation's position vis-à-vis the cantons (unification of a significant part of the area of private law, various new federal powers), and an expansion of democratic or political rights as well as of fundamental civil rights (free trade and industry, right to marry, extension of the right of establishment, and extension of the freedom of belief and conscience to members of all religions).

[14] With around 255,000 votes in favour and 260,000 votes against, as well as nine out of 13 cantonal votes.

[15] The Jesuit ban already contained in the Constitution of 1848 was strengthened and extended to a ban on the establishment of new monasteries and orders. In view of Switzerland becoming a party to the ECHR (1974), the two discriminatory constitutional provisions (Articles 51 and 52) were abolished in a referendum held in 1973.

[16] With around 340,000 votes in favour and 200,000 votes against, as well as 14.5 to 7.5 cantonal votes.

In the institutional area the basic structures of the political federal authorities (Federal Assembly, Federal Council) remained unchanged. With the Constitution of 1874, the Federal Supreme Court which had been created in 1848 was upgraded to a permanent supreme court. It was entrusted with the function of guaranteeing uniform interpretation of federal law as well as preserving certain constitutional judicial functions (Articles 113 and 114). Many years before the first modern constitutional courts (in Austria and the Czech Republic) were established, a specific legal remedy of constitutional jurisdiction emerged in Switzerland: the constitutional appeal ('Public Law Action'). However, this legal remedy was only available against acts of cantonal state institutions, not against acts of the federal authorities.[17] From a practical point of view, an important restriction of the constitutional jurisdiction arose, however, out of a constitutional clause newly created in 1874 (Article 113 (3)). In 1848, the constitutional fathers had still not seen any reason to regulate the delicate issue of the Federal Supreme Court's judicial review responsibilities in relation to federal powers. In the US, this question, also left open by the founding fathers, was as we know decided by the Supreme Court (1803)—in favour of the Supreme Court.[18] In Switzerland, politics decided—in favour of politics (1874). The constitutional clause stated that federal statutes as well as those international treaties approved by the Federal Assembly were binding on the Federal Supreme Court and thus on other courts and law-applying authorities (Article 113 (3)). This means, in other words, that norms contained in federal statutes had to be applied even if they proved to be unconstitutional.[19] This far-reaching limitation of the Federal Supreme Court's judicial review responsibilities is still in existence today (Article 190 of the Federal Constitution) though in a textually lightly modified form.

From the perspective of the third—judicial—branch, the results of the *Total-revision* of 1874 can be summarised as follows: First, the 'immunisation' of federal statutes (see above) and, secondly, a split constitutional jurisdiction: a constitutional judiciary was established at the federal level in order to curb the cantonal authorities. With regard to acts of federal authorities, there was neither constitutional nor real administrative law jurisdiction.

The introduction of the optional referendum against federal statutes is deemed to have been a 'masterpiece' of the reform (Aubert). This reform—in a sense the price for the proposed substantial expansion of federal powers—should allow a particular number of cantons or voters to force a referendum on one of the Federal Assembly's passed statutes and stop it in this way. Thus the disciplining of the federal legislature is not entrusted to the judiciary, but rather to the voters.

---

[17] For more details see Walter Kälin, *Verfassungsrichtbarkeit in der Demokratie* (Bern, 1987).

[18] US Supreme Court, *Marbury v Madison*, 5 US (1 Cranch) 137 (1803).

[19] This, of course, does not give the federal legislature—the Council—carte blanche to breach the provisions of the Constitution. In the case of cantonal statutes as well as ordinances of the Federal Council (Government), judicial review of norms is not subject to limitations, unless an unconstitutionality is authorised by a federal statute. See the Decision of the Federal Supreme Court, BGE 129 II 249 (263), 17 January 2003.

With the optional referendum, a touch of *Rousseau* entered the constitutional system of the Confederation, even though the solution of 1874 fell somewhat short of the firm demand of the *Social Contract*: '*Toute loi que le peuple en personne n'a pas ratifiée est nulle; ce n'est point une loi.*' (Contrat Social, 1762, III.15). The new direct-democratic instrument was to bring very deep, long-term consequences for the political system and, in particular, pave the way for today's system of concordance (*Konkordanzsystem*). The system of concordance—as opposed to the 'winner-takes-all'-system (the Westminster model)—is characterised by two ideas. (1) Since the Legislator and the Executive could be 'paralysed' by the permanent submission to referenda, the system of concordance is aiming at a far-reaching consensus among all political actors (consensus-driven democracy). (2) The system of concordance is also an arithmetic formula determining the composition of the Federal Council.

The advance towards centralisation triggered by the *Totalrevision* of 1874 was considerable; however, in retrospect, its effect seems rather modest in comparison to developments in the twentieth century. In that century the risky method of *Totalrevision* of the Federal Constitution was no longer used. Instead, a step-by-step procedure in the form of amendments to the Constitution itself was adopted. One hundred and twenty-five years were to elapse before the next *Totalrevision* of the Federal Constitution.

Towards Renewal of the Federal Constitution: the Federal Constitution of 1999

What led the Federal Council to produce a draft for a new Federal Constitution in November 1996? The necessity of constitutional renewal was explained in official communiqués in the 1990s as being primarily due to substantive and formal imperfections in the constitutional charter. Over the years, this had resulted in a confusing, incomplete, and in part barely understandable patchwork. A closer look shows that initially there was not really a list of deficiencies as such, but rather a hazy uneasiness which began to spread in Switzerland in the 1960s. Max Imboden (1915–69), a professor of constitutional law and a politician teaching in Basel, spoke of a 'helvetic malaise' (1964) and argued in favour of 'constitutional reform as a way into the future' (1965).[20] The idea became established in parliamentary circles. After a good two and a half years of work, a 46-person expert commission (set up by the Federal Council) submitted an expert draft proposal for a new Federal Constitution together with an accompanying report.[21] The constitutional draft was well received; however, it proved to be too ambitious. In a report on the *Totalrevision* of the Federal

---

[20] The title of two writings from Max Imboden, both in *Staat und Recht* (Basel, 1971) 279 and 309.
[21] Report of the expert commission for the preparation of a *Totalrevision* of the Federal Constitution, Bern 1977.

Constitution presented on 6 November 1985, the Federal Council outlined several possibilities for further steps, but without tying itself down. In Parliament there was wide scepticism. The 'saviour' of the reform was Kurt Eichenberger (1922–2005), a professor of constitutional law teaching, like Imboden, in Basel. In May 1986, in a newspaper article with the title 'Reality tied constitutional reform', Eichenberger came out in favour of reform of the constitution which should concentrate on 'getting the Federal Constitution in order, reducing its list of deficiencies [. . .], that is on updating it'.[22] The idea of an 'update' *(mise à jour)* of the Federal Constitution received positive feedback in Parliament. With the Federal Decree of 3 June 1987, the Federal Assembly set as a guideline that the constitutional draft to be worked out by the Federal Council 'should update the applicable written and unwritten constitutional law, present it comprehensibly, order it systematically, and standardise the density of the constitutional text and its language'.[23] The plan was soon brought to a halt, however. The main reasons for this were negotiations on the involvement of the European Free Trade Association (EFTA) States in the Common Market (European Economic Area, EEA) which were initiated in 1989.

After EEA Accession was narrowly rejected in the referendum of 6 December 1992,[24] the conviction among the reform-minded forces was that Switzerland first needed to strengthen both her capacity to act and her institutions before taking any bigger political integration steps. Therefore the *Totalrevision* project was re-launched. What was now needed was no longer just a 'constitutional update', but rather a reform which also included institutional questions. In the years 1993–94, the Federal Council developed the concept of Federal Reform 'in stages'. Based on an 'updated' constitutional draft, but in formally separated procedures, continual reforms should gradually come to fruition. Accordingly, along with the draft for a new Federal Constitution (20 November 1996), the Federal Council placed two further 'reform packets' on the agenda for later implementation—one on the subject of people's rights (instruments of direct democracy), a second concerning reforms of the judiciary.[25] Further reform packets were promised: one regarding the so-called '*Staatsleitung*' (reform of the organisational structures of Government and its relationship to Parliament), another one concerning Federalism (especially the reform of the system of equalisation of financial resources and burdens within the Confederation). Thanks to brisk deliberations, the Federal Assembly passed the new Federal Constitution, as planned, in December of the anniversary year (1998)—150 years

[22] Appeared in the *Neue Zürcher Zeitung* (NZZ) on 12 May 1986.
[23] Article 3 of the Federal Decree of 3 June 1987 on the *Totalrevision* of the Federal Constitution, BBl 1987 II 963.
[24] The weighting of votes amounted to 49.7%–50.3% (Difference: around 24,000 votes). Seven cantons voted in favour, 16 voted against. The voter turnout of 78.7% was quite high for Switzerland.
[25] See Federal Council, Message on a new Federal Constitution (from 20 November 1996), BBl 1997 I 1 ff, 436 ff, 487 ff, 589 ff. (available at http://www.admin.ch/ch/e/rs/c101.html.

after the establishment of the Federal State. The mandatory referendum scheduled for 18 April 1999 brought a positive result in favour of the new Federal Constitution.[26]

Features and Innovations in the New Constitution

The new Federal Constitution, in force since 1 January 2000, is shorter than its predecessors and more strongly structured, despite the slightly increased number of articles.[27] Beginning with some general provisions, which comprise the First Title (Articles 1–6), a more extensive catalogue of fundamental rights and liberties follows as the main part of the Second Title ('fundamental rights and liberties, citizenship and social goals'; Articles 7–41). The Third Title ('Confederation, Cantons and Municipalities'; Articles 42–135), governs the relationship of the state and federal levels with each other and defines the responsibilities and duties of the Confederation. The Fourth Title ('People and Cantons'; Articles 136–142) deals above all with the instruments of direct democracy. The Fifth Title ('Federal Authorities'; Articles 143–191) lays down the fundamental structures of the highest federal organs (Federal Assembly, Federal Council, Federal Supreme Court). The concluding Sixth Title (Articles 192–196, today Articles 192–197) summarises regulations concerning the 'amendment of the Federal Constitution and transitional provisions'. Usually, the provisions of the Federal Constitution are self-executing (for example, the fundamental rights and liberties) unless the constitutional provision delegates further implementation powers to the Legislator.

The concept of 'the consolidation of the achieved' prevailed. Textual traditions were consciously followed, exemplarily in Article 3 (Sovereignty of the Cantons).[28] Nevertheless, numerous reforms should be pointed out which might at first sight seem less spectacular but should however not be underestimated. The detailed catalogue of fundamental rights and liberties (Articles 7–36) is particularly noteworthy; it contains, inter alia, a general provision regarding the prohibition of discrimination (Article 8(2)), a provision concerning the 'protection of children and young people' (Article 11), and an express guarantee of

---

[26] Around 970,000 votes for (59.2%) to 670,000 votes against (40.8%), as well as 13 to ten cantonal votes. The voter turnout of 35.9% was low even for Swiss standards.

[27] See René Rhinow, *Die Bundesverfassung 2000* (Basel etc, 2000); Jean François Aubert and Pascal Mahon, *Petit commentaire de la Constitution fédérale de la Confédération suisse du 18 avril 1999* (Zurich, 2003); Andreas Auer, Giorgio Malinverni and Michel Hottelier, *Droit constitutionnel*, 2nd edn (Berne, 2006); Walter Haller, *The Swiss Constitution in a Comparative Context* (Zurich and St Gallen, 2009).

[28] See the first phrase in Article 3: 'The Cantons are sovereign insofar as the Federal Constitution does not limit their sovereignty.'

freedom of the media (Article 17).[29] Some of the central maxims of Swiss Federalism are mentioned in the constitutional text for the first time and are newly summarised in a general constitutional chapter on the 'Relationship of the Confederation and the Cantons' (Articles 42–53; see especially Article 44: duty of consideration, respect and cooperation). The constitutionalisation of some basic principles of environmental law continues to be part of the reforms (for example, the principle of sustainability, Article 73). In the area of federal powers, some specific extensions can be observed. No major alterations are recorded within the highest federal authorities. However, the Federal Assembly did not let the opportunity pass to resolve several quite lengthily discussed reforms on their (the Assembly's) own behalf.[30]

As in 1848 and 1874, the 'art of exclusion' was also practiced in the framework of the *Totalrevision* of the Federal Constitution of the 1990s. The independent reform packages mentioned above stood ready for institutional reforms. The fates of these reform packages differed in many ways. The parliamentary deliberations on the reform of the judiciary were concluded in 1999, but with several compromises over the original draft that was produced by the Federal Council. The expansion of constitutional jurisdiction over federal statutes (judicial review in case of their application) which was supported by the Federal Council was rejected in Parliament. In a modified form, the federal draft was approved in the referendum of 12 March, 2000. The draft of the Federal Council on the people's rights did not find the necessary support in Parliament. As a result, the Federal Assembly worked out its own reduced draft, which was passed on 4 October 2002, and was then approved in the referendum of 9 February 2003. In late autumn 2001, the Federal Council forwarded two rather large reform packages to the Parliament: one was a reform concerning the equalisation of financial resources and burdens within the Confederation and concerning the distribution of functions between the Confederation and the Cantons (in short: New Financial Equalisation; in German: *Neuer Finanzausgleich*, NFA) which impacted on around two dozen provisions of the Federal Constitution; the other package was a draft concerning the so-called *Staatsleitungsreform*. In March 2004, the *Staatsleitungsreform* was stopped in the House of Representatives (*Nationalrat*) temporarily; one further attempt was announced in the summer of 2010. In the vote of 28 November 2004, the Swiss People and the Cantons accepted the reform of Federalism (NFA) which had been passed by the Federal Assembly on 3 October 2003.[31]

The story of the *Totalrevision* of the Federal Constitution can, depending on one's point of view, be told as a short 1993–94 initial success story (which ended

---

[29] The influence of comparative constitutional and international law, particularly the ECHR, is noticeable in the area of fundamental rights and liberties. See particularly Article 13 (Protection of privacy) and Articles 29–32 (general and special procedural guarantees).

[30] In particular, the strengthening of Parliament's role in the areas of foreign policy (Article 166) and supervision of the Federal Council (Article 169).

[31] Note that these reforms are now found in the Federal Constitution (and not in separate documents).

with the coming into force of the new Federal Constitution on 1 January 2000) or as a long tale of woe with its beginnings in the 1960s and which is not yet finished for as long as the necessary reform of the *Staatsleitung* is ongoing.

Interpreting the Constitution

The special features of the history of the formation of the new Federal Constitution are not insignificant for the interpretation of the constitutional texts. According to the Federal Supreme Court (and to constitutional law scholars), the interpretation of constitutional provisions, in principle, follows 'the same methodological rules [. . .] as those developed for the interpretation of statutes at the sub-constitutional level'.[32] Using the wording as a starting point,[33] the Federal Supreme Court ascertains the meaning of a provision following all the recognised methods of interpretation. The Federal Supreme Court allows itself to be led by a, as it says itself, 'pragmatic pluralism of methods' and refuses to 'subordinate the different elements of interpretation under a hierarchy of importance'.[34] The weighting of the individual elements can vary enormously, depending on whether it has to do with an organisational or institutional provision or a constitutional right.[35] According to the Federal Supreme Court, the latter requires *concretisation* rather than interpretation. Case law and legal scholars generally lean towards an intermittent, teleological-shaped interpretation. When interpreting the new Federal Constitution, the rich history of its creation should, however, play a central role. In addition, according to the 'update idea', the practice and materials on the previous provisions of the Federal Constitution of 1874 still constitute a valuable source of information. However, there is no reason to fear a 'fossilisation' of constitutional law and its interpretation as of the end of 1999. The parliamentary debates clearly show that the Federal Supreme Court should also have the opportunity in the future to update the Federal Constitution, namely the fundamental rights and liberties catalogue, in accordance with the principles of the earlier case law.

---

[32] Decision of the Federal Supreme Court, BGE 116 Ia 359 (367), 27 November 1990. On constitutional interpretation and its particulars, see Giovanni Biaggini, *Bundesverfassung der Schweizerischen Eidgenossenschaft. Kommentar* (Zurich 2007) Introduction, No 18 ff; René Rhinow and Markus Schefer, *Schweizerisches Verfassungsrecht*, 2nd edn (Basel etc, 2009) 100; Pierre Tschannen, *Staatsrecht der Schweizerischen Eidgenossenschaft*, 2nd edn (Berne, 2007) 55.

[33] Note that the German, French and Italian versions of the text are of equal value (from a normative point of view).

[34] Expressly, Decision of the Federal Supreme Court, BGE 128 I 34 (41), 12 September 2001.

[35] See Decision of the Federal Supreme Court, BGE 116 Ia 359 (367), 27 November 1990.

Giovanni Biaggini

CONSTITUTIONAL DEVELOPMENT OUTSIDE THE *TOTALREVISION* OF THE
CONSTITUTION

Looking back over the sequence of constitutional charters, the development of
Swiss constitutional law presents itself as a three-stage process: Foundation
(1848), Expansion (1874), and Renewal (1999). For a better understanding of the
Swiss constitutional framework, it is important to take into account the uncount-
able smaller and bigger developmental steps which took place between the total
two replacements (that is between 1874 and 1999) and have taken place since
2000. Of course, most of the changes were made in the procedure of amendment,
but some of them took place partly also outside the formal amendment procedure, especially through the (evolutionary) interpretation of the Constitution in
the practice of the courts and among the political institutions of the
Confederation.[36]

While the Federal Constitution of 1848 underwent just one amendment in 26
years (1866), there were over 140 amendments made to the Constitution of 1874
during the 125 years of its validity.[37] Since the coming into force of the new
Federal Constitution of 1999 on the symbolic date of 1 January 2000, 15 drafts
have been approved at the constitutional level, among them five popular
initiatives. In this process, more than 50 (or according to some calculations 60)
constitutional provisions were newly inserted, changed or deleted as of May
2010); this is a high figure, whether from an international perspective or in
comparison with earlier decades (even when one takes into account that a part of
these changes date back to several bigger reform packages; see above). After a
short explanation of the main features of the amendment procedure in the
following paragraphs, the most important developments will be traced.

The Major Constitutional Amendment Procedures

The Federal Constitution can, according to Article 192 of the Federal Constitution, be fully or partly amended at any time. The amendment process shall follow
the ordinary legislative procedure for amendment unless the Federal Constitution and legislation deriving from it provide otherwise (Article 192(2)). A
distinction is drawn between the procedure of replacement (*Totalrevision*) (Article 193) and that of amendment (*Teilrevision*) (Article 194). There are two main
types of *Teilrevision*: the ordinary procedure, in which the Federal Assembly plays
a central role (so-called *Behördenvorlage*), and the procedure of the popular
initiative on the amendment of the Federal Constitution.

We shall consider first the amendment of the Federal Constitution (*Teilrevision*) by the ordinary procedure. The ordinary procedure (Article 194) is

---

[36] See Elisabeth Chiariello, *Der Richter als Verfassungsgeber?* (Zurich etc, 2009); Walter Haller,
'Verfassungsfortbildung durch Richterrecht' (2005) *Zeitschrift für schweizerisches Recht (ZSR)* I, 5.
[37] Note that amendments are always direct amendments to *the text* of the Constitution.

arranged in two stages: The constitutional change is advised and decided on by the Federal Assembly (usually on the initiative of the Federal Council or the Parliament or, rarely, on the initiative of a canton). Several months later, a referendum follows. It is mandatory that this be carried out (mandatory popular referendum according to Article 140). The constitutional amendment can only come into force if it is accepted by the People and by the Cantons in a referendum (Article 195). The ordinary constitutional amendment procedure is characterised by low hurdles in the parliamentary procedure—a qualified majority is not necessary—as well as by relatively high hurdles in the post-parliamentary process (mandatory binding referendum: majorities both among the voters and among the cantons), which are, however, not insurmountable.

The popular initiative (amendment of the Federal Constitution) allows 100,000 voters—that is only slightly more than 2 per cent of today's electorate—to demand an amendment of the Federal Constitution. Every matter that falls within a constitutional norm can in principle be the subject of a popular initiative. A popular initiative with the required number of signatures must be brought to a referendum. The exact wording of the initiative text may not be changed by Parliament; it must be approved or rejected 'as such' by the voters. The requirement of a double majority applies here too (that is, a majority of the People voting in the referendum and a majority of the Cantons; Article 142 of the Federal Constitution). The result of the referendum is binding.

The main type of popular initiative created in 1891—the initiative on the amendment of the Federal Constitution in the form of a prepared draft (Articles 139 (2) and (5)) —has the following special characteristics.[38] The text of the suggested constitutional law is formulated by the initiative committee. The Federal Assembly has limited freedom to respond (it has no influence over the text of the initiative[39]). The Federal Assembly can prevent a referendum resulting from a popular initiative by declaring the initiative invalid (wholly or partially). This (very rare) step is, however, only possible in the case of qualified reasons (see below). Thus, the Swiss version of a popular initiative allows a constitutional process which bypasses Parliament. The fate of an initiative is decided in the scope of a referendum, not in Parliament. The popular initiative is thus not only a 'request from the people', but 'also [a request] to the people', as Fritz Fleiner (1867–1937) so succinctly put it.[40] The Federal Assembly still has the right (and the duty) to state its opinion on the content of the initiative and to recommend that the voters approve or—as is generally the case—reject it (Article 139(5)). In

---

[38] Furthermore, the Federal Constitution names the popular initiative in the—rather seldom employed—form of the general proposal. On 9 February 2003, the People and the Cantons approved the replacement of this initiative through the so-called general popular initiative. Prior to the implementation of the reform, this step was however (for reasons which will not be discussed in this paper) again reversed in the referendum of 27 September 2009.

[39] See Article 99 of the federal statute of 13 December 2002 on the Federal Assembly (Parlamentsgesetz, SR 171. 10).

[40] Fritz Fleiner, *Schweizerisches Bundesstaatsrecht* (Tübingen, 1923) 398 (emphasis added).

addition, the Federal Assembly can, on the request of the Federal Council or on its own initiative, propose a so-called alternative draft or counter-proposal and submit its own constitutional draft on the same subject (Article 139(5)). It is often the case that the creators withdraw their popular initiative in favour of such an alternative draft, which meets their political demands, so that only the alternative draft is voted on.

The popular initiative is much favoured and is actively used, despite a rather limited chance of success in the referendum. So far, since 1891, 17 popular initiatives have been approved by the People and the Cantons. These represent rather more than 10 per cent of the initiatives brought to a referendum.[41] This unbroken popularity is closely connected with the important indirect effects of a popular initiative (such as the influence on the Parliament's and the Federal Council's agendas, change in the legislation, or in the practice of administrative agencies under pressure from popular initiatives, and so on).

The Limits of Constitutional Amendments

The Federal Constitution can be fully or partly amended at any time. However, certain limits must be observed. Three limits are mentioned explicitly in the Federal Constitution (Article 139; see also Articles 193 and 194). Popular initiatives and the *Behördenvorlage* (see above) may, in the interests of clear decision-making, only contain factually related questions on the item (respect for the principle of unity of subject matter). Furthermore, popular initiatives which mix initiative forms (respect for the principle of the unity of form) are impermissible. Popular initiatives and *Behördenvorlagen* must thus respect the mandatory rules of international law (*ius cogens*). The scope of this initially unwritten but now constitutionally fixed limit, which was first applied in 1996, is not yet completely clear.[42] 'Eternity clauses' following the pattern of the Italian Constitution of 1947 (Article 139) or the German basic law (Article 79(3)) do not exist in the Swiss Constitution.

When a popular initiative does not respect the principle of unity of form, the principle of unity of matter, or is against the mandatory rules of international

---

[41] The 17 adopted popular initiatives are unevenly distributed time wise: 1893 (1), 1908–28 (5), 1949 (1), 1982–94 (5), 2002– 2009 (5). Successful popular initiatives resulted—inter alia—in: change to proportional representation in the House of Representatives (*Nationalrat*) (1918); the protection of the alpine regions from the negative effects of transit traffic (1994); Switzerland's membership of United Nations Organization (2002); the ban on the building of minarets (2009).

[42] As an example of mandatory rules of international law, the following are often mentioned: the prohibition of torture, the core of humanitarian law in armed conflicts, human rights guarantees from which derogation even in time of emergency is prohibited (see Art 15 ECHR). Certain questions concerning the relationship between the (constitutional) term of mandatory rules of international law and the (international) term of *ius cogens* are still controversial. For the opposing positions, see Giovanni Biaggini, note 32 above, Art 139, No 13; Yvo Hangartner in Bernhard Ehrenzeller et al. (eds), *Die Schweizerische Bundesverfassung*, 2nd edn (Zurich etc, 2008) Art 139 (neu), No 29, 34.

law, the Federal Assembly has no choice but to declare it (wholly or partially) invalid (Article 139). This declaration is final and no legal remedy is available to annul it. In practice, the political institutions of the Confederation as well as constitutional law scholars acknowledge an unwritten fourth case for invalidating an initiative: the unfeasibility of a popular initiative.[43] Constitutional law scholars have repeatedly called for the recognition of further limits.[44] So far the Federal Assembly has not followed up on these demands. It also generally handles the recognised limits generously (according to the motto *in dubio pro populo*), especially (and not surprisingly) when the unity of subject matter is in question regarding its own drafts. Only four popular initiatives have been declared invalid so far.[45]

Milestones in Constitutional Development between 1874 and 1999

In the period between the replacements (*Totalrevision*) of 1874 and 1999, the constitutional law of the Confederation underwent large and small changes. Even though constitutional development is not based on a blueprint or plan, several main features can still be identified: expansion of the instruments of direct democracy, progressive centralisation—still with considerable cantonal autonomy, and the strengthening of *Rechstaatlichkeit* (Rule of Law).

One extremely important development in the Swiss constitutional order is the step-by-step establishment and expansion of today's characteristic citizens' rights (instruments of direct democracy). An important source of inspiration was (and is) developments in the cantons, which can indeed be called an experimental laboratory of direct democracy. The first Federal Constitution had created an essentially representative system at the federal level. With the Federal Constitution of 1874, the optional referendum against federal statutes was introduced (see above). Other important upgrading steps followed in the form of amendments:

— Introduction of the popular initiative concerning the *Teilrevision* of the Federal Constitution (1891) in the form of a prepared draft (today Article 139; see above): this innovation, requested by opposition groups (Catholic-conservative, social democratic) found, thanks to the support of the reform-minded wing of the majority, the necessary majority in the Federal Assembly and in the popular vote.

---

[43] The only precedent dates from 1955. The argument that the implementation of an initiative will be difficult in practice cannot be brought forward.

[44] 'Fundamental norms' of the Federal Constitution; invalidity of popular initiatives with retro-active effect etc. See Yvo Hangartner and Andreas Kley, *Die demokratischen Rechte in Bund und Kantonen der Schweizerischen Eidgenossenschaft* (Zurich, 2000) 200.

[45] The four cases date from 1996 (initiative 'for a reasonable asylum policy': violation of the principle of non-refoulement), 1995 (initiative 'for less military expenditure and more peace policy': unity of matter), 1977 (initiative 'against price increases and inflation': unity of matter) and 1955 (initiative 'temporary reduction in military expenditure (halt on armament)': unfeasibility).

— Introduction of the optional referendum concerning international treaties (1921): The catalyst for this newly created citizens' right (today Article 141) was the conclusion of an irrevocable international treaty between Switzerland, Germany and Italy on the Gotthard railway tunnel (1909) with strongly contested clauses (maximum tariffs).

— Democratisation of so-called emergency legislation (*Dringlichkeitsrecht*) (1949): According to the original version of the Federal Constitution of 1874, the Federal Assembly was competent to declare a legislative statute to be urgent in order to avoid a referendum. This option was frequently used by the Federal Assembly during World Wars I and II and the crisis years in the 1930s. It was abolished by popular initiative. Nowadays, emergency legislation is constitutionally limited in duration and, in principle, subject to an *ex post*-referendum (Article 165).

— Expansion of the optional referendum concerning international treaties and introduction of the mandatory referendum concerning the accession to supranational communities and organisations for collective security (1977; today Articles 140 and 141). Within the frame of the already mentioned reform of citizens' rights (2003), the treaty referendum was further refined.

However, the introduction of citizens' elections of the members of the Federal Council (Government), which has been repeatedly demanded, has not found majority support so far. The general (male only) right to vote and to stand for election, which existed from 1848, was expanded through constitutional change to encompass Swiss nationals living abroad in 1966, women (finally) in 1971,[46] and 18 and 19-year-olds in 1991. The road from representative to half-direct democracy, which characterises the Swiss model, has been a 'one way street' so far. Citizens' rights have been introduced, further developed, and adjusted as to number of signatures required for a referendum or a popular initiative.[47] Until now this has not led to the abolition of any of the citizens' rights mentioned above. In contrast, the People and the Cantons have rejected the expansion of their own rights on several occasions.[48]

It must be pointed out that action is only taken in respect of a small fraction of all Acts of Parliament subject to an optional referendum and that the success rate in the case of popular initiatives is low (see above). Nevertheless, the direct

---

[46] Before 1971, several cantons had already introduced women's suffrage in cantonal and communal matters; the remaining cantons soon followed—with the exception of the Canton Appenzell Innerhodes, which the Federal Supreme Court finally had to pressurise into action in a judgement that attracted a lot of attention (BGE 116 Ia 359, Theresa Rohner, 27 November 1990).

[47] Population growth and the introduction of female suffrage were reasons for the increase in the signature number for referenda (50,000 instead of 30,000) and popular initiatives (100,000 instead of 50,000) in 1977.

[48] For example, a popular initiative concerning the introduction of the so-called constructive referendum against statutes (a mixed form of a referendum and an initiative known in certain cantons) was rejected (24 September 2000).

democratic participation rights of the people—due to their many-sided indirect effects—have an enormous impact on the functioning of institutions and the political system.

The referendum, which works as a 'brake' in the political process, and the popular initiative, which usually acts as the 'motor' of legal development, have played major parts in the gradual development of the Swiss consensus-oriented democracy which seeks broadbased compromise solutions (see above). Equally important for this development was the introduction of the system of proportional representation for elections to the House of Representatives (approved by popular initiative in 1918).

Since the first days of the establishment of the Confederation, the development of federal policy has been characterised by the expansion of the competences of the Confederation. In this process of centralisation, the problematic US-American method of creative-extensive interpretation of the constitution has not usually been applied. Instead, the more difficult course of formal constitutional amendment has been taken. As a result, the various text layers of the Federal Constitution of 1874 reflected almost all of the economic and social state developments of the twentieth century. This is not the place to recap on the transfer of every single competency. Instead the focus will be on the 'big picture', the creation of a Swiss economic area. This project was of utmost importance after the establishment of the Confederation. With this development, desiderata in the area of infrastructure as well as in social and environmental policy gradually followed. Development did not follow a fixed plan, but rather responded to specific needs and political feasibility. A striking feature is that both of the Confederation's most important sources of income (direct federal tax and value added tax) are now based on a time-limited constitutional provision (see Article 196 Clauses 13 and 14 of the Federal Constitution: currently until the end of 2020), which may be extended from time to time by a popular referendum.

Despite these centralising developments, the Swiss cantons still possess a great deal of autonomy (Article 47 of the Federal Constitution) as compared to the sub-entities of other European federal states. In the late 1990s, there were increased efforts to buttress Federalism. The catalyst was on the one hand Switzerland's envisaged move towards European integration, and on the other hand the increasingly obvious need to reform the federal system for the equalisation of financial resources and burdens. Some of the reforms were tackled in the frame of *Totalrevision* of the Federal Constitution. For further reforms concerning the equalisation of financial resources and burdens and the allocation of powers between the Confederation and the cantons (NFA), a joint project between the Confederation and the cantons was set up, which prepared proposals for the relevant constitutional changes. The goal of NFA reform was fourfold: the simplification of the system of equalisation of financial resources and burdens through the reduction of financial compensation mechanisms; the unbundling of powers and financing in numerous areas; the improvement of the cooperation between the Confederation and the cantons in the 'not unbundled' areas;

the promotion of horizontal collaboration between the cantons as well as the intercantonal equalisation of burdens. The Federal Decree which summarised the approximately two dozen changes in the Federal Constitution was approved in the referendum of 28 November 2004.

A unique process has been the establishment of the Canton of Jura with effect from 1 January 1979. The twenty-sixth canton owes its existence to a series of referenda, which finally allowed—after long and not always peaceful disputes— the separation of three historically Catholic, French-speaking administrative districts from the predominantly German-speaking and protestant Canton of Berne. On 24 September 1978, the People and the Cantons gave their approval to the canton's establishment. In two later votes, they approved minor changes concerning modifications of territory between the cantons (1993 and 1996).

The Development of the Rule of Law (*Rechtstaat*)

Due to the circumstances at the time, the founding fathers of 1848 fixed their attention more on the federal and democratic foundations of the state than on promotion of the Rule of Law, which—compared to today's standards— remained initially underdeveloped at the federal level. The *Totalrevision* of the Constitution from 1874 brought further fundamental rights and liberty guarantees into the system and a rather effective constitutional jurisdiction by means of the Federal Supreme Court (see above). However, at the federal level, the emphasis was more on direct democratic control than on control by the courts. Some constitutional peculiarities—not to say constitutional anomalies—have survived until recently. This applies in particular to the system of legal remedies. Its modernisation took a considerable amount of time. One reason for this is that Switzerland has a long-standing tradition of settling disputes arising under the Constitution or administrative (statutory) laws through political authority. Access to 'judicial' protection against administrative acts was typically granted by the Executive. Following the administrative hierarchy, the procedure was initiated before the legal department of the superior administrative unit of the agency that issued the order and then went on to the Federal Council (Federal Government) in the role of an appellate body (with a possible appeal before Parliament).

In view of the changing framework—such as the extension of federal power and of federal legislation, and the increase in importance of federal administration—the solution found in 1874 could not be permanently satisfactory. At the forefront of the introduction and expansion of administrative law jurisdiction were constitutional law scholars, including Fritz Fleiner (1867– 1937).[49] Fleiner was a key figure in the drafting of a constitutional provision which would lay the foundation for an (initially limited) administrative law

---

[49] See Alfred Kölz, 2 *Neuere schweizerische Verfassungsgeschichte* (Bern, 2004) 851.

jurisdiction at the federal level. In 1914, the constitutional provision was approved by the People and the Cantons. However, the federal statute of implementation did not come into force until 1928. Furthermore, one had to wait until the end of the 1960s when the so-called 'general clause' was introduced, which granted the administrative courts general jurisdiction. However, the long list of exceptions of subject areas which could not be reviewed by the Judiciary was only slowly reduced in size. Since 1 January 2007, access to justice has been guaranteed through a newly created, self-executing fundamental right to access to a court (Article 29a of the Federal Constitution). However, even today, based on an opt-out clause (Article 29a Sentence 2), the Federal Council is still ultimately responsible for some legal disputes (for example, issues regarding domestic or external security of the country, neutrality or foreign affairs as long as international public law does not grant a right to judicial review).

In the area of constitutional jurisdiction, there were several attempts to eliminate or tone down the 'immunisation' of federal statutes from judicial control (Article 113(3) of the Federal Constitution of 1874, today Article 190; see above). In the referendum of 22 January 1939, the popular initiative 'protection of the constitutional rights of the citizens (expansion of the constitutional jurisdiction)' was clearly rejected. Further attempts at reform were also unsuccessful, most recently in the context of the reform of the judiciary (1999/2000) and in the context of the reform of the system for equalisation of financial resources and burdens within the Confederation (NFA; 2002/3). The government drafts on each of these issues were all defeated by Parliament. Thus federal statutes remain 'binding' for the time being.

However, over the course of time, the Federal Supreme Court and constitutional law scholars have developed a range of strategies which make it possible to mitigate certain consequences of the unsatisfactory (from the point of view of the Rule of Law) 'immunisation' of federal statutes from judicial control.[50] This 'hidden' correction of norms is based upon methodological devices such as contemporary interpretation, interpretation (or filling of lacunae) in conformity with the constitution, deviation from the statute on the grounds of general principles of law (such as protection of good faith, prohibition of the abuse of rights) in individual cases and so on. The fact that legal methodology in Switzerland is generally open to new, even unorthodox, approaches is partly rooted in the 'immunity' of federal statutes. The problem is also further alleviated by the fact that the Federal Supreme Court has over the last few years not been willing to apply federal statutes if these conflict with a norm of international law which supports the protection of human rights.[51] The European Convention on Human Rights and Fundamental Freedoms (ECHR) which Switzerland joined

---

[50]   In detail, Andreas Auer, *Die schweizerische Verfassungsgerichtsbarkeit* (Basel/Frankfurt aM, 1984) 85; Giovanni Biaggini, *Verfassung und Richterrecht* (Basel/Frankfurt aM, 1991) 426.

[51]   In this sense Decision of the Federal Supreme Court, BGE 125 II 417 (424 ff), 26 July 1999, concerning the collection of propaganda material of the Kurdish Worker party (so-called PKK case).

in 1974 after a long period of hesitation, played and continues to play an important role in the elimination of deficiencies in the Rule of Law. At the earliest opportunity, the Federal Supreme Court emphasised the constitutional nature of the ECHR guarantees and placed them (from a procedural perspective) on the same level as the constitutional rights of the Federal Constitution.[52] With help from the ECHR, the 'immune system' protecting federal statutes can be slightly 'sidestepped', especially because the Constitution declares not only federal statutes to be applicable, but also international treaties (Article 113(3) of the Federal Constitution of 1874) and international law as such (in the actual wording of the Federal Constitution; see Article 190). In Switzerland, according to a well established, albeit not always undisputed principle (see Article 5(4) of the Federal Constitution), international law has—in general—priority over domestic law in situations where they conflict.[53] As the guarantees of the ECHR and the fundamental rights and liberties of the Federal Constitution run parallel in many areas, there is a type of de facto constitutional control with respect to federal statutes in case of their application. The situation remains unsatisfactory, above all, in the case of constitutionally guaranteed fundamental rights and liberties which are not (or not fully) covered by the ECHR and the additional protocols ratified by Switzerland (for example, equality before the law, the right to property, and economic freedom).[54] The expansion of constitutional jurisdiction remains an important desideratum of the *Rechtsstaat*.

For the development of the Swiss *Rechtstaat*, developments outside the Constitution, in particular in the case law of the Federal Supreme Court, are also important. Encouraged by scholarly research in the field of constitutional law,[55] the Federal Supreme Court has gradually approved several so-called *unwritten* fundamental rights and liberties which could be invoked by every individual against federal and cantonal institutions: firstly, the right to property (1959– 1960), shortly afterwards, in an *obiter dictum*, freedom of speech (1961), afterwards personal freedom (1963), the freedom of language (1965), the freedom of assembly (1970), and finally the right to a secure existence (1995), which gives individuals who are in a situation of distress an enforceable right to those essential means necessary to live in dignity (today Article 12 of the Federal Constitution).[56] After initial vacillation, the Federal Supreme Court developed a

---

[52] Decision of the Federal Supreme Court, BGE 101 Ia 67, 19 March 1975.

[53] See Daniel Thürer, 'Verfassungsrecht und Völkerrecht' in Daniel Thürer, Jean-François Aubert and Jörg Paul Müller (eds), *Verfassungsrecht der Schweiz* (Zurich, 2001) 179; Helen Keller, *Rezeption des Völkerrechts*, (Berlin etc, 2003) 341 and 723.

[54] Switzerland has not ratified the 1st, the 4th and the 12th additional protocol to the ECHR.

[55] Especially by Zaccaria Giacometti (1893–1970), public law teacher in Zurich with roots in the Italian-speaking part of Graubünden, related to the artist Alberto Giacometti. See in particular, Zaccaria Giacometti, 'Die Freiheitsrechtskataloge als Kodifikation der Freiheit' (1955) in Zaccaria Giacometti, *Ausgewählte Schriften* (Zurich, 1994) 23.

[56] See the Decisions of the Federal Supreme Court of 11 May 1960 (reproduced in extracts in *Schweizerisches Zentralblatt für Staats- und Gemeindeverwaltung* (ZBl) 1961, 69 ff); BGE 87 I 114 (117), 3 May 1961; BGE 89 I 92 (98), 20 March 1963; BGE 91 I 480 (486), Association de l'Ecole

formula whereby those individual rights not named in the Constitution could be recognised as *unwritten* fundamental rights and liberties of the Confederation if they form a 'prerequisite for the exercise of other rights and liberties named in the Constitution or otherwise appear as essential components of the democratic federal *Rechtstaat*'; with a glance at 'the limits placed upon the constitutional judge's competencies', the Federal Supreme Court examines whether the guarantee in question already constitutes a widespread constitutional reality in the cantons and is supported by a general consensus.[57] This formula is still applied under the new Federal Constitution.

Even before the recognition of unwritten fundamental rights and liberties (and without the slightest textual basis in the Constitution), the Federal Supreme Court started to 'derive' certain guarantees and principles from the general principle of equality (Article 4 of the Federal Constitution of 1874, today Article 8(1)).[58] These derivative rights include amongst others protection from arbitrariness, various procedural guarantees (such as the right to a fair hearing in court, the right to free legal assistance when in need, and the prohibition of imposing excessive and formalistic requirements in order to block the individual's access to justice), the protection of good faith, the principle of legality, and the prohibition of *ex post facto* (retrospective) laws. The majority of these guarantees were codified within the framework of the *Totalrevision* of the Federal Constitution (see Articles 5, 9, 29–32 and 127).

In retrospect, the fact that constitutional law scholars and the Federal Supreme Court interacted in a committed and creative manner (particularly in the neglected area of fundamental rights and liberties), is not very surprising. It is noteworthy that in a legal system where direct democracy is stressed so emphatically in constitutional questions (and where each minor change in the Constitution requires a referendum) a significant amount of 'undemocratic' law created by constitutional judges could emerge. And it is even more astonishing that the criticism from the political side remained limited.[59] At the next opportunity, which however took until the end of the twentieth century (the *Totalrevision* of the Federal Constitution), the unwritten fundamental rights and liberties recognised by the Federal Supreme Court were codified, together with the 'derivatives' from Article 4 of the Federal Constitution of 1874.

Through specific changes to the constitutional text and above all thanks to innovative constitutional interpretation and constitutional evolution, which was

---

française, 31 March 1965; BGE 96 I 219 (224), 24 June 1970; BGE 121 I 367 (371), 27 October 1995. For a detailed analysis Peter Saladin, *Grundrechte im Wandel* (1970), 3rd edn (Berne, 1982).

[57] Decision of the Federal Supreme Court, BGE 121 I 367 (370–371), 27 October 1995.

[58] In detail, Arthur Haefliger, *Alle Schweizer sind vor dem Gesetze gleich* (Bern, 1985).

[59] To some extent, the Federal Supreme Court had to face strong criticism for some decisions in which it just fulfilled its function as a guardian of the constitution. Examples of this are the so-called crucifix decision (BGE 116 Ia 252, Comune di Cadro, 26 September 1990) and the decision concerning the inadmissibility of naturalisation decisions by popular vote (BGE 129 I 232, Schweizerische Volkspartei der Stadt Zürich, 9 July 2003).

also marked by the practice of political bodies, Switzerland has evolved step by step into a well-developed state under the Rule of Law. The *Totalrevision* of the Federal Constitution brought an important consolidation in this sense.

CONSTITUTIONAL DEVELOPMENT SINCE 2000

The first amendments to the text of the new Federal Constitution of 1999 were not long in coming. Besides the changes mentioned above, which were more or less directly linked to the *Totalrevision* of the Federal Constitution, various specific constitutional changes in a wide range of areas have been effected. The following examples are especially notable:

— The adoption of the popular initiative demanding Switzerland's accession to the United Nations (Article 197 Clause 1) in the referendum of 3 March 2002.
— The adoption of the popular initiative 'for foods from GM-free farming' (Article 197 Clause 7) in the referendum of 27 November 2005.
— The approval of the Federal Decree on the reform of the Third Title, Chapter 2, Section 3 regarding education (Article 61a ff.) in the referendum of 21 May 2006.
— The adoption of the popular initiative for 'no time limit for the right to prosecute or for penalties for sexual or pornography offences involving prepubescent children' (Article 123b) in the referendum of 30 November 2008.
— The—surprising—adoption of the popular initiative '*against the construction of minarets*' (Article 72(3)) in the referendum of 29 November 2009.[60]

A large number of proposed amendments have been rejected (at least for the time being).[61] In comparison to constitutional development under the Federal Constitution of 1874, two distinctive features are particularly striking under the new one: first, the approval of a total of *five popular initiatives* in a very short time (March 2002 to November 2009), and secondly, the repeated use of the already mentioned 'reform packets' procedure in the case of constitutional drafts (recently in the area of education). On the question of subject matter, it is remarkable that, apart from questions regarding competencies, institutional questions attract considerable attention. A closer look reveals less encouraging developments. Owing to popular initiatives, an increase in conflicts between

---

[60] See Ralph Zimmermann, 'Zur Minarettverbotsinitiative in der Schweiz' in (2009) *Heidelberg Journal of International Law* (*HJIL*) 829; Giovanni Biaggini, 'Die schweizerische direkte Demokratie und das Völkerrecht' in (2010) *Zeitschrift für öffentliches Recht/Journal of Public Law* (*ZöR*) 325. The approval of the Minaret ban initiative brought Switzerland not only wide international attention, but also further problems in the guarantees of international human rights (in particular Arts 9 and 14 ECHR).

[61] Over 30 popular initiatives with very diverse content, as well as Behördenvorlagen (see above) were rejected.

constitutional law and international human rights guarantees can be observed (Article 123a: life imprisonment; Article 72(3): minaret ban). Generally, the legal quality of the Constitution has suffered in the recent past.[62]

In Switzerland, new problems and areas of conflict, above all in the context of *Federalism*, are looming. With the reform of the system of equalisation of financial resources and burdens within the Confederation (see above), well-established cooperative federalism was 'enriched' with new principles and instruments. Thus, thanks to Article 48a of the Federal Constitution (as of the beginning of 2008), the Federal Assembly acquired the power to declare (upon the request of interested cantons) inter*cantonal* treaties to be *generally binding*, that is to oblige opposing cantons to join or be parties to such treaties in nine constitutionally-determined fields. This instrument of forced cooperation, which is in conflict with the idea of autonomy and democracy, will probably be very rarely implemented in practice; however, it is likely that (as a threat) it will cause some repercussions for the course of politics and the federal balance. In the framework of the new constitutional provisions on education, Article 63a of the Federal Constitution requires that the Confederation and the cantons conclude treaties in the area of higher education and transfer specific powers to joint institutions, which means that a kind of non-parliamentary, federalist *secondary law* will emerge. The constitutional and political problems of treaty-based 'pan-Swiss' solutions and of an increasingly institutionalised Cooperative Federalism (which tends to result in a strengthening of the executive branch) should not be underestimated.

Furthermore, a creeping 'inflation' of constitutional principles can be observed. The *Totalrevision* of the Federal Constitution led to the codification of several previously unwritten constitutional principles (for example, the principles of legality, proportionality, and good faith; see Article 5). With the coming into force of the new system of equalisation of financial resources and burdens within the Confederation (2008), the number of constitutional principles has again markedly increased. They include the principle of fiscal equivalence (meaning: the collective body that *benefits* from a public service shall bear the costs thereof, and the collective body that *bears* the costs of a public service may decide on the nature of that service) as well as the principle that basic services must be made available to everyone in a comparable manner (Article 43a). Such principles would not be out of place in an economics textbook. However, they will create rather than solve problems when they are incorporated in the constitutional charter and equipped with normative power.

Another issue is the debate about an overlapping federal principle, the so-called *Bundestreue* (federal loyalty, federal allegiance). Despite occasional

---

[62] For a detailed analysis, see Biaggini, 'Entwicklungen und Spannungen im Verfassungsrecht' (2010) 1 *Schweizerisches Zentralblatt für Staats- und Verwaltungsrecht (ZBl)* 1–41.

references in the case law of the courts and in scholarly research, the *Bundestreue* (a legal term which is used in Germany) has never really found a home in Switzerland.[63]

Actors and 'Neglected Issues' of Constitutional Development

A distinctive feature of Swiss constitutional development is the great number of participants and processes. Besides political bodies (the Federal Assembly, the Federal Council), the Federal Supreme Court plays an important and creative role, particularly in questions of the Rule of Law. In the framework of direct democracy, voting citizens also participate directly in the constitutional process. The instrument of popular initiative in particular ensures that the 'political establishment' (Federal Assembly, Federal Council, and political parties) is susceptible to pressures from 'outside'.

Regarding the evolution of the Constitution, one should not underestimate the input from constitutional law scholars, be it in the form of opinions *de constitutione ferenda* (in commentaries, monographs or essays), or political advice (participation in expert commissions, or advisory opinions on behalf of the Federal Council or the Parliament). An essential feature is engagement with neglected issues, that is with concerns which risk being overlooked by constitutional development shaped by the people's rights. For historical reasons, these neglected issues mostly deal with questions concerning the Rule of Law, but also sometimes with direct democracy or federalism. Swiss constitutional scholars see themselves as being rather problem-orientated and pragmatic in their approach (therefore more Anglo-Saxon than German).[64]

Despite their constitutionally guaranteed participation rights (see Articles 45, 142 and 160 of the Federal Constitution), the cantons have played a subordinate role in constitutional development over many years. This perhaps surprising finding can be mainly explained by the fact that the cantons (or the governments negotiating for them) have few active mechanisms at their disposal at federal level and do not have an actual veto power. Nevertheless, the cantonal governments have recently succeeded in intervening in the important early phase of significant reform processes, for example, in the elaboration of the draft of a new Federal Constitution, and even more intensively in the reform of the system of equalisation of financial resources and burdens within the Confederation. Apart from

---

[63] See for example, Decision of the Federal Supreme Court, BGE 118 Ia 195 (196), Canton de Berne contre Canton du Jura, 17 June 1992. For more details, see Patricia Egli, *Die Bundestreue Eine rechtsvergleichende Untersuchung,* (Zürich/St Gallen, 2010). Particularly sceptical Alfred Kölz, 'Bundestreue als Verfassungsprinzip?' (1980) *Schweizerisches Zentralblatt für Staats- und Gemeindeverwaltung (ZBI),* 145.

[64] See Giovanni Biaggini, 'Die Staatsrechtswissenschaft und ihr Gegenstand', and Oliver Lepsius, 'Was kann die deutsche Staatsrechtslehre von der amerikanischen Rechtswissenschaft lernen?', both in Helmut Schulze-Fielitz (ed), *Staatsrechtslehre als Wissenschaft, Die Verwaltung, Beiheft* 7 (Berlin, 2007) 267–91 esp 319–66.

that, the indirect influence of the cantons should not be underestimated: constitutional development in the Confederation is traditionally subject to many influences from cantonal legislative development, especially in the field of the rights of the people.

Other 'neglected issues' in constitutional development pertain to certain questions of a general nature. Sometimes, isolated problems and specific (point-by-point) reforms have blocked the ability to see the Constitution as a whole. Fundamental rights and liberties and the principles of the Rule of Law could not count on a sufficiently strong 'codification lobby'. It is of little surprise that the Federal Supreme Court was so creative in precisely this neglected area.

One can infer the emergence of specific constitutional understandings from the development of the Swiss Constitution. The Federal Constitution does not only establish and limit the 'fundamental order of the state'.[65] It not only constitutes a framework, but also formulates goals and binding guidelines at different levels of abstraction for politics and the process of the implementation of the law. In the course of the twentieth century, it became established that the allocation of a new power to the Confederation should be made in two steps: first, important substantive cornerstones are constitutionally anchored (mainly in the third title of the Federal Constitution) before being regulated in detail in a second step at legislative level.[66] The Federal Constitution not only lays down substantive guidelines for politics; in fact, it is the subject of day-to-day politics, too. The consequence is that the politics pursued by the Confederation are democratically legitimised to a high degree in a wide range of regulated areas. The flip side of the coin are constitutional norms with a rather high level of detail, which can sometimes strongly restrict the elbow-room of the legislator.

Switzerland is often termed a *Willensnation* (nation by will) because cohesion is not based upon a common language or culture, but on a long cooperative history based on the constant desire of all political actors to shape a nation.[67] At the time of the establishment of the Federal State (1848), there was no Swiss 'folk' or people in a traditional ethno-linguistic sense, and this is still the case today. Constitutional institutions such as the Federal Assembly, the Federal Council, the referendum, the popular initiative as well as the popular votes resulting from them ensure cohesion at the very least. This is why Switzerland can also be termed a 'constitutional nation'.

---

[65] Werner Kägi, *Die Verfassung als rechtliche Grundordnung des Staates* (Zurich, 1945).

[66] Example: the constitutional norm concerning reproductive medicine (Art 24 of the Federal Constitution of 1874, today Art 119) was adopted in the referendum of 17 May 1992; the implementing federal statute (reproductive medicine statute; SR 810.11) was passed in Parliament on 18 December 1998 and came into force on 1 January 2001.

[67] See Jonathan Steinberg, *Why Switzerland?* 2nd edn (Cambridge, 1996) 235, 249.

15

The United Kingdom

DAWN OLIVER

INTRODUCTION

T HE UNITED KINGDOM is unique among the members of the European Union in that it does not have an entrenched written constitution. It shares that characteristic only with Israel and New Zealand. And yet the UK is a fairly well-functioning liberal democracy. That is not to say the system is perfect—indeed the avalanche of constitutional changes in the last 20 years or so indicates that successive governments have felt it necessary to reform the system in a whole range of ways. And yet the basics remain in place: a constitutional monarchy which enjoys broad public support, especially in England; a sovereign bi-cameral Parliament, the lower chamber of which is elected at about four yearly intervals by universal suffrage on the first-past-the-post or relative majority system; a parliamentary executive; and an independent judiciary. To those basics have been added over the last decade or so a layer of devolved government—asymmetrical since, of the four nations of the United Kingdom, England (except for London) does not have devolved assemblies or executives, and the bodies in Scotland, Wales and Northern Ireland each enjoy different powers. The system is nowhere near being legally federal. The unentrenched Human Rights Act 1998 came into effect in 2001. And further measures of a constitutional kind, some of which will be noted below, have come into force covering matters such as the regulation of elections, changes in the operation of local government, reform of the judicial system, freedom of information and reform of the internal organisation of the House of Commons. Others are on the agenda of the coalition government that came to power in May 2010.

Our concern is not with the substance, but the processes, of change. In discussing constitutional change in the UK a difficulty is in knowing where to draw the line between constitutional and other matters. If, like most other countries, we had a Constitution, a document having special legal status in which at least the most important rules of the system of government were set out, then we could assume that most of the rules in that document were 'constitutional', at least in the eyes of that nation. That would not of course help us to identify the many other rules in the system that are of 'constitutional' importance.

We can look instead to scholarly commentators on constitutional law for definitions of, or at least criteria for determining whether a rule is, 'constitutional'. According to Bradley and Ewing '[C]onstitutional law concerns the relationship between the individual and the state, seen from a particular viewpoint, namely the notion of law... Law also concerns the structure and powers of the state'.[1] and Tomkins[2] refer to 'a body of rules that govern the political system, the exercise of public authority, the relations between the citizen and the state'.[3] These definitions are descriptive and purport to refer only to the UK. And they do not distinguish between what in other countries might be regarded as 'fundamental' rules and others. 'Fundamental' is in any event a difficult concept in UK law given that in principle all provisions in Acts of Parliament are of equal legal status, save only that a more recently passed law impliedly repeals any inconsistent previous law.[4] However, as we shall see the British courts have recently been elaborating principles which they consider to be 'fundamental' in the sense that very clear words in an Act of Parliament are required to displace them.

A further complication for the UK is that 'constitutional' carries normative as well as descriptive meanings. If we say that something is 'non-constitutional' we mean that it has nothing to do with the constitution. If we say that something is 'unconstitutional' we may of course mean that it is contrary to constitutional law. But we could mean that it is contrary to the values and principles of the constitution, even though it is legally valid. This point was made well in the case of *Madzimbamuto v Lardner Burke* by Lord Reid:

> It is often said that it would be unconstitutional for the United Kingdom Parliament to do certain things, meaning that the moral, political and other reasons against doing them are so strong that most people would regard it as highly improper if Parliament did these things. But that does not mean that it is beyond the power of Parliament to do such things. If Parliament chose to do any of them the courts could not hold the Act of Parliament invalid.[5]

While it is difficult to find criteria for determining what rules are 'constitutional' in the descriptive sense, some attempts have been made to identify the principal substantive rules or principles of the system. A useful source is the reports of the Constitution Committee of the House of Lords. In their first report the Committee set out 'five basic tenets' of the UK Constitution, namely: Sovereignty of the Crown in Parliament; the Rule of Law, encompassing the rights of the individual;

---

[1] Anthony Bradley and Keith Ewing, *Constitutional and Administrative Law*, 15th edn (2011), at 3.
[2] *British Government and the Constitution* (2007), 6th edn, at 3.
[3] See also discussion by G Marshall in *Constitutional Theory* (1971), ch 1.
[4] But note the discussion of the *Thoburn* case, below.
[5] *Madzimbamuto v Lardner Burke* [1969] 1 AC 645 (PC).

that the UK is a Union State; Representative Government; and Membership of the Commonwealth, the EU, and other international organisations.[6] A survey of the reports of that Committee in the 2001–2005 Parliament identified a number of more detailed substantive and normative principles. These included:[7]

(i) Procedural requirements

— Wide public consultation and debate of proposed legislation should take place.[8]
— Sufficient time should be allowed for parliamentary scrutiny.[9]
— The exercise of delegated powers, especially where individuals' rights are affected, should be subject to parliamentary scrutiny.[10]
— The grant of delegated sub-delegated powers should be clear, justified, and provision should be made for parliamentary scrutiny.[11]
— Provision should be made for Parliament to be informed promptly of all ministerial exercises of legislative power.[12]

(ii) The rule of law

— Clarity is required in order to protect the public purse against inappropriate payments being made out of public funds without clear parliamentary authorisation.[13]
— Laws should not have retrospective effect.[14]
— Laws should comply with principles of good regulation and regulatory impact assessments.[15]
— Provision should be made for prompt access to a court or tribunal for the resolution of disputes between individuals and the state and disputes between individuals.[16]

---

[6] First Report of the Select Committee on the Constitution, 2001–02, HL Paper 11, para 51.

[7] See D Oliver 'Improving the scrutiny of bills: the case for standards and checklists' [2006] *Public Law* 219, at 241–42.

[8] 14th Report, *Parliament and the Legislative Process*, 2003–04, HL Paper 173- I, paras 208, 213, 217.

[9] First Report, Inquiries Bill, 2004–05, HL Paper 21, para 5 and Appendix 3; Second Report, 2004–05, *Prevention of Terrorism Bill*, HL Paper 66, para 14; Third Report, 2004–05, *Serious Organised Crime and Police Bill*, HL Paper 65, para 24.

[10] Eighth Report, 2003–04, *Civil Contingencies Bill*, HL Paper 114, paras 9, 12.

[11] Fifth Report, 2002–03, *European Parliament (Representation) Bill*, HL Paper 65, Appendix I.

[12] Eighth Report, 2003–04, *Civil Contingencies Bill*, HL Paper 114, para 12.

[13] Tenth Report, 2004–04, *Age-Related Payments Bill*, HL Paper 124, para 8.

[14] Seventh Report, 2001–02, *Nationality, Immigration and Asylum Bill, Further Report*, HL Paper 173, paras 6–8.

[15] Sixth Report 2003–04, *The Regulatory State: Ensuring its Accountability*, HL Paper 68, para 130, 146.

[16] This principle is invoked in many of the committee's reports. For instance, Second Report, 2001–02, *Anti-terrorism, Crime and Security Bill*, HL Paper 41, Appendix; Sixth Report, 2003–04, *The Regulatory State: Ensuring its Accountability*, HL Paper 68, paras 230, 231, 232.

— Security of tenure of judges should be preserved.[17]

(iii)   Protection of individuals

— Individuals should be protected from excessive intrusion by the state or other bodies.[18]
— Law enforcement agencies, including the police, should be immune from ministerial control or politicisation.[19]

(iv)   Democratic system

— Appropriate oversight arrangements should be in place to secure the integrity of elections.[20]
— There should be separation between party political and other public interest functions and bodies.[21]

Of course the fact that these principles exist—none of them is surprising to constitutional commentators in the UK—does not prevent the UK Parliament from passing laws or the government from proposing laws that are inconsistent with those principles or acting inconsistently with those principles. In other words these principles are not legally binding.

The 'Political' Constitution

Despite the fact that the UK Parliament enjoys, in principle, legislative supremacy, and that in practice government controls Parliament's legislative activity, both the government and Parliament are constrained in the exercise of power by strong political forces. This brings us to one of the most brilliant insights into the UK system in recent years: in Griffith's words, it is a political constitution.[22] This will be a theme of this chapter. That is not to say that the UK constitution is not regulated by law at all, only that the exercise of many legal powers is legitimated or constrained by politics, that extensive areas of the system

---

[17] Fifth Report, 2001–02, *Justice (Northern Ireland) Bill*, HL Paper 95, page 4, para 9; Fourth Report, 2003–04, *Justice (Northern Ireland) Bill*, HL Paper 40, Appendix I.

[18] Eighth Report, 2003–04, *Civil Contingencies Bill*, HL Paper 114, para 2;Second Report, 2004–05, *Prevention of Terrorism Bill*, HL Paper 66, para 15; Fifth Report, 2004–05, *Identity Cards Bill*, HL Paper 82, para 4.

[19] Third Report, 2004–05, *Serious Organised Crime and Police Bill*, HL Paper 65, para 9.

[20] Eighth Report, 2002–03, *Health and Social Care (Community Health and Standards) Bill*, HL Paper 156, para 7.

[21] Fifth Report, 2003–04, Companies *(Audit, Investigations and Community Enterprises) Bill*, HL Paper 53, Appendix I.

[22] JAG Griffith 'The political constitution' (1979) 42 *Modern Law Review* 1. For academic discussion of Griffith's approach see G Gee and G Webber 'What is a political constitution?' (2010) 30 *Oxford Journal of Legal Studies* 273–99; G Gee 'The political constitutionalism of JAG Griffith' (2008) 28 *Legal Studies* 20–45; R Bellamy *Political Constitutionalism* (2007); T Poole 'Tilting at Windmills: Truth and illusion in the political constitution' (2007) 70 *Modern Law Review* 250–77; A Tomkins *Our Republican Constitution* (2005); G Gee 'The political constitutionalism of JAG Griffith' (2008) 28 *Legal Studies* 20–45.

are not governed by law in the positivist sense at all, but by politics, its processes, its values, its conventions and the de facto relationships between politicians, political parties and the people. In Griffith's view the political constraints in the system operated positively: they deterred governments from abusing their powers and they excluded the judiciary from exercising what Griffith considered to be essentially political powers, for instance in relation to human rights protection.

Since Griffith published his article many of the parts of the UK constitution which were not governed by law but fell within the 'political' sphere remain outside the sphere of legal in the sense of judicial control, but have become increasingly normativised. Politics and public opinion generate codes,[23] formulae,[24] concordats,[25] parliamentary resolutions,[26] memorandums of understanding,[27] conventions,[28] statements of principle,[29] Cabinet Office guides,[30] and most recently a 'Coalition Agreement'[31]—what we call 'soft law' or 'quasi-legislation'.[32] These norms, though not enforceable by the courts, in practice regulate and often 'depoliticise' much of the political process.[33] They regulate much activity of a constitutional kind. The relevance of all this to how constitutions change, the theme of this book, is that there are no formal requirements for their change. A government or the other authors of such sets of soft law rules may amend or abolish them at any time. Indeed it is customary for the Ministerial Code and other documents[34] to be revised by each new Prime Minister, and without any requirement for parliamentary or other consultation. Politically the authors of

---

[23] For example, *The Ministerial Code*, latest version 2010, published by the Cabinet Office.

[24] For example, the Barnett Formula which determines how much money goes to the devolved bodies from the Treasury. See D Bell and A Christie 'Finance—The Barnett Formula: Nobody's Child' in A Trench, (ed) *The State of the Nations* (2001).

[25] For example, Concordat on Co-ordination of European Union Policy Issues: Scotland (this was agreed between Scottish Ministers and the UK Government.

[26] For example, the House of Commons resolution on Ministerial Responsibility, HC Deb, 19 March 1997, cols 1046–47.

[27] For example, *Memorandum of Understanding*, 2001, Cm 5420, providing for a Joint Ministerial Committee for Ministers from Scotland, Wales, Northern Ireland and the UK. See R Rawlings 'Concordats of the constitution' (2000) 116 *Law Quarterly Review* 257; J Poirier 'The functions of intergovernmental agreements' [2001] *Public Law* 134.

[28] For example, the convention articulated in the House of Commons resolution on individual ministerial responsibility to Parliament, supra.

[29] For example, The Seven Principles of Public Life, Committee on Standards in Public Life, first report, 1995, Cm 2850.

[30] For instance *Guide to Making Legislation*, 2009; *Machinery of Government Changes—Best Practice*, 2010 and the draft *Cabinet Manual*, 2011.

[31] http://www.Cabinetoffice.gov.uk/media/409088/pfg_coalition.pdf.

[32] R Megarry 'Administrative quasi-legislation' (1940) 60 *LQR* 125.

[33] For discussion see D Oliver (2009) 'The UK Constitution in Transition: from where to where?' in Duncan Fairgrieve and Mads Andenas (eds) *Tom Bingham and the Transformation of the Law: A Liber Amicorum*, (2009), 147–62 and D Oliver, *Constitutional Reform in the UK*, (2003) 16–18 and 367–81.

[34] Available at http://www.cabinetoffice.gov.uk.

such documents may find that this attracts criticism and they may feel compelled to consult before doing so. But all this takes place in the realm of politics and not of law.

Theories of the Constitution?

Lastly in these introductory comments, we need to consider what legitimating theories, ideologies or values underlie the constitutional arrangements in the UK. Wade and Allison have both suggested that the system is largely legitimated, in the sense of being generally accepted by the people, by its history—the history of continuous evolution over many centuries—rather than by ideology or political theories.[35] The British constitution is, as Allison has shown, a historical constitution.[36] As he puts it

> what is constituted at the centre of the historical constitution is not a principle but an overarching mode of change that respects continuity, at least in form, and the reassurance it affords. That mode is not derived from normative theory but has evolved in legal and political practices of conservation and innovation by which the institutions of government are controlled and facilitated as they evolve, and stability is secured or re-established.[37]

The political and popular cultures in the UK, or at least in Great Britain, are by and large very pragmatic and not ideological. Constitutional arrangements having evolved over time,[38] there has not for over four centuries been a moment when a new legitimating theory, ideology or set of values has replaced a former one. In practice, then, a number of overlapping, interlinked and sometimes inconsistent theories find expression in the system of government and in the attitudes of Parliament, the government, the courts, and others involved in it. Two examples will illustrate the point. Birch, in 1964, discussed two parallel theories, those of representative and responsible government.[39] He concluded that the commitment to responsible, in the sense of prudent, government prevailed in the UK over the commitment to representative government. More recently McCrudden, discussing the problems over governmental legitimacy in Northern Ireland, identified 'pragmatic empiricism' as the tradition that has prevailed, and seems to do so successfully, in Great Britain;[40] that tradition however has not been apt to deal with the challenges to the legitimacy of

---

[35] HWR Wade 'The Crown, ministers and officials: legal status and liability' in M Sunkin and S Payne (eds), *The Nature of the Crown. A Legal and Political Analysis*, (1999), 23–32; and JWF Allison, *The English Historical Constitution*, (2007), 70–73.

[36] Allison ibid, 2007.

[37] Ibid, 235.

[38] See for instance E Wicks, *The Evolution of a Constitution*, (2006) and J Allison *The English Historical Constitution: Continuity, Change and European Effects*, (2007).

[39] AH Birch *Representative and Responsible Government*, (1964).

[40] C McCrudden in J Jowell and D Oliver (eds), *The Changing Constitution*, 6th edn, (2007).

government and the state in the divided communities of Northern Ireland; McCrudden suggests that a more ideological (in the sense of less party political or partisan) constitutionalism has been adopted in relation to Northern Ireland, focusing on explicitly normative principles, and institutional arrangements to mesh them with local needs. Hence the elaborate power-sharing devices in that province. There may, he has suggested, also be a trend towards a more ideological approach in Great Britain, but the mainland approach tends to be individualist whereas the Northern Ireland approach is more communitarian.

THE POLITICS OF CONSTITUTIONAL REFORM

Let us turn now to the issues connected with *how* the UK constitution changes or is changed. Proposals for principled reform are often made initially by non-politicians—at least in the sense of 'non-elected' persons or bodies. For instance Sir Leslie Scarman, an eminent judge at that time, proposed in his Hamlyn lectures of 1974, *English Law: The New Dimension*, that a number of reforms including a Bill of Rights should be introduced. Academics too, are frequently major contributors to debates about possible and desirable reforms long before such matters rise up the political agenda.[41] So there may be many good ideas for reform in the air at a given time—and some bad ones—but the question is why some reach the top of the political agenda and are implemented, and others do not.

Unless it is the courts which bring about reform by interpretation of development of the existing law (a matter discussed below), formal, legislated constitutional reform cannot in practice take place without government support, and this will depend upon the political background to and implications of each reform proposal. The Human Rights Act 1998 was passed partly because the Labour party, in opposition from 1979 to 1997, had been concerned at the ease with which the Thatcher government had been able to legislate to interfere with freedom to demonstrate during the miners' strike of 1989.[42] And all parties were embarrassed by the flow of cases in which the European Court of Human Rights had found UK law to be incompatible with the Convention. This led to a political argument that it would be better for our reputation if we were to do our dirty washing at home rather than send it abroad.[43] Significantly however the Human

---

[41] See, for instance, on the Bill of Rights debate, M Zander, *A Bill of Rights?* (1985); R Dworkin, *A Bill of Rights for Britain* (1990). And see generally, R Brazier *Constitutional Reform. Reshaping the British Political System*, 2nd edn (2008).
[42] See for instance K Ewing and C Gearty *Freedom under Thatcher*, (1990).
[43] Zander, note 41 above.

Rights Act preserves parliamentary sovereignty: the courts may not set aside a provision in an Act of Parliament that is incompatible with the Convention rights.[44]

As for devolution, the party political reasons why Labour—which is instinctively a centralising movement—committed itself to legislate for devolution to Scotland in its election manifesto in the 1997 general election was that it risked losing Scottish votes, and therefore seats in the Westminster Parliament, to the Scottish National Party unless it did so. It also committed itself to devolution to Wales for fear of losing votes and seats there, though the case for devolution to Wales was less developed than that for Scotland. And of course devolution to Northern Ireland was an essential part of the resolution of the troubles in that province.[45] As far as Scotland is concerned, the reasons for the growth in support for the Scottish National Party or for devolution were complex. There has for many years been lower support for the Conservative party in Scotland than in England; during the period of Conservative government from 1979 to 1997 the Scots resented the fact that they were subjected to Conservative policies which were not widely supported in Scotland; when North Sea oil was discovered and began to be exploited in the 1980s the Scots resented the fact that the revenue it generated went to the UK Treasury, although the wells were in what would be Scottish territorial waters if Scotland were independent; there is a strong sense of Scottish identity in Scotland and an awareness of a different English identity (of which the English are not very conscious): the English were considered in some quarters to be arrogantly disregarding of Scotland's identity and needs. So the reasons for the pressures for devolution to Scotland were a mixture of culture, politics, identity and economics.

Politicians may of course be driven by idealism and principle when proposing constitutional reforms. There is no doubt that the Human Rights Act was passed in part because of the conversion of John Smith, the leader of the Labour party in opposition (who died in 1994, whereupon Tony Blair became leader) to a human rights act on principle, and the fact that this commitment was taken up by Lord Irvine of Lairg, who became Lord Chancellor on the election of Labour and took a leading role in the programme of constitutional reform that followed the 1997 election. Personality and personal networks matter in British politics. Freedom of Information, too, was a policy commitment made in opposition—opposition parties commonly adopt a hostile attitude to the powers of the executive. But the

---

[44] An allegation that a court decision was in breach of fundamental rights may only be challenged by exercising a right of appeal or applying for judicial review: the challenged court may not be sued for compensation. HRA ss 6(1), 7(1)(a), and 9(1). If a case goes to the European Court of Human Rights on the basis that the Act in question was incompatible with the Convention the Strasbourg Court may find the British government to be in breach of its Convention obligations. In the dualist system as it operates in the UK this will not create any liability on the part of the UK court which decided the case in a way that turns out to have been incompatible with the Convention. Liability rests on the UK government.
[45] See C McCrudden in Jowell and Oliver, note 40 above.

details of such proposals for reform may be tinged with politics as well: the Human Rights Act 1998, in preserving the legislative supremacy of Parliament, reflects traditional Labour distrust of judges; the original proposals for a very liberal Freedom of Information Act that were published by the Labour government soon after its election[46] were strongly criticised, especially in the civil service. The passage of the Act was thus delayed until 2000 and its implementation was phased in from 2005. The provisions were greatly watered down from what had been intended by the architects of the system.[47] Hence changes to the system of government in the UK—as no doubt in all countries—tend to reflect changing social norms and culture, demographic influences, economic pressures, political culture, electoral behaviour, internationalisation and Europeanisation—and political expediency.

PROCESSES OF CONSTITUTIONAL REFORM

The process of constitutional reform may commence in informal ways—for instance by the inclusion of a reform proposal in a political party's election manifesto. This may be followed by processes of greater or lesser formality once a party (or coalition) is in government. Reform, or change, may involve the passing of an Act of Parliament. But some changes—for example to the functioning of the two Houses of Parliament and their relationship with the executive may be achieved by parliamentary resolutions and changes to Standing Orders, which though counting as part of 'the law and practice of Parliament' are not 'law' in the sense of rules over which the courts have jurisdiction, or Acts passed through the formal legislative procedures of the two Houses of Parliament. Yet other changes, for example to processes of policy implementation and accountability mechanisms, may be achievable by changes in practice or the adoption of codes and other forms of executive guidance. The Coalition Agreement of May 2010, which set out the agreements between the Conservative and Liberal Democrat members of the new coalition, provides an example. Court cases too may well have important constitutional implications, for instance as to judicial review of executive decision making.

Manifestos

Major constitutional changes will, and should, normally be foreshadowed in the election manifesto of the governing party. Manifesto commitments were made in relation to much of New Labour's constitutional reform legislation before the election of 1997—for instance a Human Rights Act, devolution to Scotland and

---

[46] *Your Right to Know: The Government's Proposals for a Freedom of Information Act*, Cm 3818 (1997).
[47] See R Austin in Jowell and Oliver, note 40 above.

Wales, and freedom of information. It would be a mistake to assume that the point of including commitments in a manifesto is to secure the support of a majority of voters for the commitments or for the party whose manifesto it is. Given the workings of the first past the post or plurality electoral system, the candidate who wins most votes, even if not a majority of votes, in each constituency wins the seat. The party (or, in the current coalition, the parties) with a majority of the seats in the House of Commons will have only rarely won 50 per cent plus one of the votes cast by the electors. This is the result of the fact that most seats are fought by candidates from more than two parties. In other words, it is many years since a government has won the support of a majority of the voters for itself, for its manifesto or for any of its policies.

The point of the manifesto is to make it more difficult for opposition parties to oppose such changes on principle. Inclusion of a policy in a manifesto also engages the Salisbury Convention in the House of Lords: the Upper House should not reject a 'manifesto bill' and should not insist on an amendment to such a bill if the Commons remains firm. This convention was formulated in 1945, at a time when the House of Lords' membership consisted (apart from 24 Bishops and Archbishops of the Church of England, and the Law Lords) entirely of hereditary peers. Since 1958 under the Life Peerages Act of that year many life peers have been appointed. The Salisbury Convention has weakened since the House of Lords Act 1999 excluded most hereditary peers from the House and by implication legitimated the rest of the members. It has no application where a coalition government is formed. It is by no means certain that the Lords would feel bound to give way to the Commons over controversial legislation, especially of a constitutional nature, in future.

Discussion of manifestos has normally taken place in a situation where one party wins a majority in the House of Commons, forms a government, and relies on its manifesto to secure the passage of bills based on manifesto promises. The situation after the general election of 2010 raised different questions. There being no party with a majority or able to rely on other parties not to bring it down, a coalition was formed between the Conservatives and the Liberal Democrats, and a Coalition Agreement was published. This agreement contained policies which had not been in the manifestos of the two parties, or which were in fact contrary to some of the coalition partners' manifesto commitments. This is inevitable where coalitions are formed unexpectedly. Some of the policies announced thereafter but not foreshadowed in the Coalition Agreement were also controversial within one or other or both of the coalition parties. This factor provided ammunition against government policies for the Opposition Labour party and for some members of the coalition parties. However, significantly David Cameron, Prime Minister, on announcing the coalition, emphasised the importance of national rather than party interests:

> Today we are not just announcing a new government and new ministers. We are announcing a new politics. A new politics *where the national interest is more important*

than party interest, where co-operation wins out over confrontation, where compromise, give and take, reasonable, civilised, grown-up behaviour is not a sign of weakness but of strength.[48]

The coalition agreement also sets the rules according to which and the constraints in respect of which their MPs will be allowed to dissent from one another and even from the Cabinet.

Consultation

It is normal for important constitutional rules to be changed by Act of Parliament—this will be discussed in the next section. There are however informal soft law rules and expectations about the pre-parliamentary process and procedures that should be followed before a measure reaches Parliament as a bill or draft bill. There was, for instance, extensive public consultation—conducted by the Campaign for a Scottish Assembly—before the general election of 1997 in which the Labour party promised devolution of powers to Scotland. The government's proposals followed very closely the recommendations of that body: the Scotland Act 1998 therefore has strong legitimacy in Scotland. In Northern Ireland prolonged attempts to win consensus between two communities through consultation, negotiation and collaboration between the United Kingdom and Republic of Ireland governments culminated in a peace agreement—the Belfast Agreement—followed by referendums in both the Republic and Northern Ireland, and legislation (the Northern Ireland Act 1998). And yet the implementation of that Act has depended upon the building up of trust between the communities and the parties. The fact of prior consultation does not always guarantee successful implementation of law and the policy which informs it.

In Wales there was extensive consultation before the passing of the Government of Wales Act 2006, which extends the powers of the Assembly for Wales and meets many of the demands from Wales.[49] But there had been relatively little consultation before the Government of Wales Act 1998 was passed.

Commonly, before a bill is introduced into Parliament, the government will have published a Green Paper for consultation followed by a White Paper setting out the government's conclusions in the light of responses to the Green Paper. This may be followed by a draft bill which is subjected to pre-legislative scrutiny in Parliament, and then by a bill. This procedure was followed in the Gordon Brown administration's proposals for constitutional renewal which were launched by a Green Paper in July 2007 and followed by a White Paper and a

---

[48] Reported in *The Guardian*, 12 May 2010, available at http://www.guardian.co.uk/politics/2010/may/12/coalition-government-seven-page-pact (my italics). It is usual for newly appointed Prime Ministers to assert their commitment to the service of the whole country: see the discussion above about the public interest principle.

[49] Report of the Richard Commission, 2004.

draft Constitutional Renewal Bill 2007–2008. The Constitutional Reform and Governance Act, which included some but by no means all of the proposals in the draft bill, was passed shortly before the dissolution of Parliament in April 2010 before the general election of that year.

This process of consultation conforms to general expectations as to how legislation, particularly important legislation, should be processed. But a consultation process, alone, may not suffice to legitimate a constitutional measure.

By contrast, the important changes to the system of justice eventually put into effect in the Constitutional Reform Act 2005—the new Supreme Court, alteration to the roles of the Lord Chancellor and the Lord Chief Justice, and a new Judicial Appointments Commission—were not preceded by Green or White Papers or a draft bill. They started their life as a press release (see discussion below). The lesson to be learned from that experience was that such a procedure may generate a lack of trust on the part of those affected—the judiciary in that case—even if the measures are actually wise, constitutional in a normative sense, and reforming.

The Coalition Agreement of 2010 contained a number of commitments to constitutional reform by legislation, and these commitments were followed up by a series of Bills at the start of the new Parliament which will be noted below. These had not been preceded by Green or White Papers, and not all were published in draft for pre-legislative scrutiny. It would therefore be impossible to say that there is even a convention that extensive consultation takes place before constitutional laws are changed. The fact of the matter is that there are no settled procedures for dealing with constitutional reform in the UK. Brazier has suggested that a Standing Constitutional Commission should be established which would strive for a consensual approach to constitutional reform,[50] but no measures have been taken to implement such an approach.

Referendums

Referendums are relatively recent phenomena in the UK. The first was held in 1975 on whether the UK should remain a member of the European Communities, as they were then known. A referendum was held in London in 2001 on whether there should be a Mayor for London: the answer was 'Yes' and the Greater London Act was passed to create the office of Mayor. A referendum was held in North East England in 2004 on whether an elected Regional Assembly should be established: the result was 'No'—and that put an end to the government's policy in favour of regional devolution within England.

In relation to Northern Ireland, the Belfast Agreement 1998[51] required referendums to be held in Northern Ireland and in the Republic of Ireland on whether

[50] R Brazier *Constitutional Reform: Reshaping the British Political System*, 2nd edn (2008), ch 2.
[51] Cm 3833.

the terms of that agreement should be implemented. Those referendums were held in 1998, majorities were in favour of the devolution provisions both sides of the border, and the devolution arrangements came into effect. Referendums were also held in Scotland and Wales before bills were introduced into Parliament for devolution to Scotland and Wales; though the majority in Wales was narrow, both achieved a majority of the votes cast. And so the Scotland Act and the Government of Wales Act 1998 both came into force. There was a referendum under the Government of Wales Act 2006 in March 2011 on the transfer of legislative powers to the Welsh Assembly: the answer was yes, but the conventions, if any exist, as to the holding of referendums, are rather fluid.

The arguments about referendums are complex. In a country where the people are considered to be sovereign a referendum may be taken to be an expression of that sovereignty. No such doctrine exists in the UK's constitutional arrangements. A referendum may legitimate a policy that the government wishes to implement by obtaining the consent of at least a proportion of the public. But as Bogdanor has pointed out, 'a referendum can articulate a submerged consensus, but it cannot create one'.[52] Some legislation will depend for its effectiveness on the affected population regarding it as legitimate and thus being willing to cooperate with new arrangements. This was essential to the resolution of problems between the two communities in Northern Ireland. But the fact that a majority, large or small, of the population votes in favour of or against a measure does not mean that the measure on which the referendum is held is wise or unwise. It only means that people voted for or against it. It relieves government of responsibility, and this may not always be appropriate. Votes in referendums may be cast to express general approval or disapproval of the government rather than to endorse or veto the referendum question.

Intra-governmental Procedures

The Cabinet's document *Guide to Making Legislation*[53] contains important advice to ministers, civil servants, government lawyers and others involved in the legislative process about the pre-parliamentary processing of proposed legislation, some of it dealing with constitutional matters. Broadly what happens at this stage of the process is that concerns about constitutionality may be referred to the Attorney General; parliamentary draftsmen may raise such issues with departmental lawyers; account needs to be taken of the fact that particular select committees will scrutinise the bill or draft bill (the House of Commons Justice Committee, the House of Lords Constitution Committee, and the Joint Committee on Human Rights) and that those committees may raise concerns of a constitutional nature; it is known that the House of Lords itself may raise issues

[52] V Bogdanor *The People and the Party System* (1981) at 91.
[53] Available at http://www.cabinetoffice.gov.uk/resource-library/guide-making-legislation-guide.

of a constitutional nature; thus either such measures should be carefully considered, or a specific strategy for dealing with matters in the House of Lords should be devised.[54]

REFORM BY ACTS OF PARLIAMENT

The most significant constitutional reform in recent years has been the accession of the UK to the European Economic Community (EEC). This was achieved by the passing of an Act of Parliament, the European Communities Act 1972, which came into effect on 1 January 1973. The UK is a dualist system so that the incorporation into domestic law of international obligations must be done by statute. The principal provision of the 1972 Act is section 2(1), which provides (inter alia):

> All such rights, powers, liabilities, obligations and restrictions from time to time created or arising by or under the [European] Treaties, and all such remedies and procedures from time to time provided for by or under the Treaties, as in accordance with the Treaties are without further enactment to be given legal effect or used in the United Kingdom shall be recognised and available in law, and be enforced, allowed and followed, accordingly; and the expression 'enforceable Community right' and similar expressions shall be read as referring to one to which this subsection applies.

Thus was European law incorporated into UK law. There was no requirement for a referendum[55] or special majorities in the two Houses for the passage of this Act. A number of Acts have been passed since then to incorporate treaty revisions.[56] And it is clear that the European Communities Act has altered the nature of the legislative supremacy of Parliament, since the courts will give effect to European law even if it is incompatible with a later Act of Parliament[57]—thus altering the former doctrine of implied repeal.[58]

There has been a flurry, even an avalanche, of legislation of a constitutional nature in the last 30 years or so. Griffith's political constitution has been substantially 'legalised'. For example, under the Conservative governments of Mrs Thatcher and John Major from 1979 to 1997, the National Audit Act 1979 strengthened the role of Parliament in the scrutiny of government expenditure by establishing the Comptroller and Auditor General as an officer of the House of

---

[54] See for instance D Oliver 'Constitutional scrutiny of executive bills' (2004) 4 *Macquarie Law Journal*, 33–55; and 'Improving the scrutiny of bills: the case for standards and checklists' [2006] *Public Law*, 219–46.

[55] A referendum was held in 1975 on whether the UK should remain a member of the EEC. There was a majority in favour.

[56] The European Community (Amendment) Acts of 1986, 1993, 1998, 2001, 2002; European Parliament (Representation) Act 2003; European Parliamentary Elections Acts 1978, 1999; the European Union (Accessions) Act 2003; and Treaty of Lisbon (2007/C 306). See http://eur-lex.europa.eu/LexUriServ/LexUriServ.do?uri=OJ:C:2007:306:0010:0010:EN:PDF.

[57] *R v Secretary of State for Transport, ex parte Factortame* [1990] 2 AC 85.

[58] *Ellen Street Estates v Minister of Health* [1954] 1KB 590.

Commons and no longer as a servant of the government, and requiring that he or she and his or her office, the National Audit Office, report to Parliament; the Greater London Council was abolished[59] and there was much further legislation on local government, the effect of which was generally to deprive local authorities of powers and to submit them to central control;[60] many publicly owned utilities and industries were privatised in the 1980s and 1990s and statutory regulators were put in place to regulate them in the public interest.[61]

The UK went through a phase of even more intense formal statutory constitutional reform after 1997, when 'New Labour' came to power.[62] The measures include the Human Rights Act, the Scotland Act, the Northern Ireland Act, the Government of Wales Act, all of 1998, the House of Lords Act and the Greater London Act, both of 1999, the Freedom of Information Act and the Political Parties Elections and Referendums Act of 2000, the Constitutional Reform Act 2005, the Government of Wales Act 2006, the Constitutional Reform and Governance Act 2010, and many Acts reforming local government. We do not have the space to consider these measures in detail here, but briefly the Human Rights Act incorporated most of the substantive rights articles in the European Convention on Human Rights into domestic law; the Scotland Act established a Parliament with extensive, residual legislative power for Scotland and a Scottish executive; the Northern Ireland Act established an Assembly for Northern Ireland with legislative power rather less extensive that the Scottish Parliament's and a power-sharing Northern Ireland executive; the Government of Wales Acts 1998 and 2006 between them established a Welsh Assembly with secondary legislative powers and the prospect of acquiring primary legislative powers, and a Welsh executive; the House of Lords Act 1999 removed most of the hereditary peers from the second chamber; The Greater London Act established a London Assembly and an elected Mayor; the Political Parties, Elections and Referendums Act established an Electoral Commission with responsibilities in relation to election law, election expenditure by the parties and referendums; the Constitutional Reform Act moved the top court for the UK, the Appellate Committee of the House of Lords, out of the chamber and established it as a Supreme Court—but without new powers. That Act also substitutes the Lord Chief Justice for England and Wales for the Lord Chancellor as head of the English and Welsh judiciary, and introduces new formal independent processes for the appointment of judges.

The coalition government that was formed in May 2010 committed itself to further constitutional reform—indeed it was part of the deal between the two

---

[59] Local Government Act 1985.
[60] See I Leigh 'The New Local Government' in Jowell and Oliver, (note 40 above).
[61] See generally C Veljanowski *Selling the State* (1987); C Graham *Regulating Public Utilities: A Constitutional Approach* (2000); T Prosser 'Regulation, Markets and Legitimacy' in Jowell and Oliver, note 40 above.
[62] See generally D Oliver *Constitutional Reform in the United Kingdom*, 2003.

parties that some of the reforms to which the Liberal Democrats were committed should be implemented or put to a referendum. Thus in the first session of the new Parliament a Fixed Term Parliaments Bill, a Parliamentary Voting Systems and Constituencies Bill (which was passed in March 2011), and a European Union Bill were introduced.[63]

All of the Acts listed above preserve the legislative supremacy of the UK Parliament, which retains the power to amend or suspend the operation of or repeal this legislation. This is made explicit in the Human Rights Act (under section 4 of which courts may make a 'declaration of incompatibility' but may not set aside a provision in an Act) and in the devolution legislation. Thus the Scotland Act provides by section 28(7): 'This section does not affect the power of the Parliament of the United Kingdom to make laws for Scotland'. And the Northern Ireland Act contains a similar section. But such provisions are included only for the avoidance of doubt, for as we have seen the doctrine of the legislative supremacy of Parliament includes a principle of implied repeal (save in relation to EU law): a provision in a more recent Act that is incompatible with a provision in an earlier Act will impliedly repeal the earlier provision to the extent of the incompatibility.[64] (We shall consider whether the doctrine of implied repeal still applies to all legislation and in particular to certain 'constitutional statutes' below.) Thus the Northern Ireland Assembly was suspended by Acts of Parliament, and direct rule from Westminster was restored, for a number of periods between 2000 and 2006 when relations between the parties broke down.

The Parliamentary Legislative Process[65]

In general bills having constitutional impacts go through the same legislative process as other bills. There are however permanent select committees—for instance the Joint Committee on Human Rights, and the House of Lords Constitution Committee and Delegated Powers and Regulatory Reform Committee, which engage in scrutiny and report to their House on constitutional issues. The constitutionality of new laws is essentially protected by intra-parliamentary rather than extra-parliamentary means. Special select committees are sometimes established ad hoc to scrutinise particular draft bills. Thus in 2008 a Joint

---

[63] Although in principle such Acts have direct effect, it is frequently not practicable for Acts to take effect as soon as royal assent is given (this being the final stage in the creation of Acts). Administrative arrangements have to be made, regulations have to be drawn up to deal with details, and so on. So Acts commonly provide for a date when particular provisions are to come into effect; or they grant a power to the relevant Secretary of State to bring provisions into effect by statutory instrument. This involves the Secretary of State laying a draft order bringing the provisions into effect before Parliament which will either come into effect automatically on the date provided for in the instrument unless it is vetoed by either House, or not come into effect unless each House passes an affirmative resolution.

[64] *Ellen Street Estates v Minister of Health* note 58 above.

[65] See R Rogers and R Walters *How Parliament Works*, 6th edn, (2006), ch 7 for a succinct account.

Committee on the draft Constitutional Reform Bill reported.[66] The Committee Stage of a measure of 'first class constitutional importance'[67] is, by the Standing Orders of the House of Commons, taken on the floor of the House and not in committee, thus enabling all MPs to participate in that stage of the legislative process. (In the House of Lords the Committee Stage of all bills is taken by a Committee of the Whole House or a Grand Committee.) A bill may receive royal assent without the consent of the House of Lords a year after it was introduced in the Commons.[68] The only exception is a bill to extend the life of Parliament beyond five years. Such a bill requires the consent of both Houses. It is rare for a bill to receive royal assent without the consent of the Lords.[69]

REFORMING PARLIAMENT

The two Houses of Parliament have themselves introduced significant changes in their modus operandi and their relations with the executive over many years. Each House has 'exclusive cognisance' of its proceedings and procedures, neither is regulated by statute, and each can act by resolution by a majority of those present and voting.[70] Most changes to their procedures are preceded by inquiries and reports by select committees of the relevant House. Although the governing party (or currently the two coalition parties between them) will have a majority on all House of Commons committees, the whip system does not operate in them and they are relatively independent. However, most changes to internal parliamentary rules are achieved by amendments to standing orders, which requires a majority of those present and voting in the House of Commons in plenary session; an obstacle to reforms of that House has been that single party governments, having a majority, may in effect prevent the implementation of reforms proposed by these committees if they would increase the accountability of government to the House.

Among the major reforms to House of Commons procedures in the last 30 years or so were the establishment in 1979, when the Conservatives came to power after a period in opposition, of a system of departmental select committees to monitor each government department. These reforms had been thought through before the election of 1979 and their implementation was included in

---

[66] This draft bill proposed, inter alia, reforming the procedure for the ratification of treaties, putting the civil service on a statutory footing and strengthening parliamentary involvement in the exercise by the government of its war powers. The Report is HL Paper 166, HC Paper 551 (2007–08).

[67] R Hazell 'Time for a new convention: Parliamentary scrutiny of constitutional bills 1997–2005' [2006] *Public Law* 247.

[68] Parliament Acts 1911 and 1949.

[69] Acts which received royal assent under the Parliament Acts (ie without the consent of the Lords) include the Parliament Act 1949 (which reduced the delaying power of the Lords from two years to one), the War Crimes Act 1991, the European Parliamentary Elections Act 1999, the Sexual Offences (Amendment) Act 2000 and the Hunting Act 2004.

[70] See generally Erskine May *Parliamentary Practice*, 22nd edn, (1997); *Griffith & Ryle Parliament: Functions, Practice and Procedures*, 2nd edn, (2003); Rodgers and Walters note 65 above.

that party's election manifesto; they were introduced very rapidly after the election, steered through the House by Norman St John Stevas, MP, who was strongly committed to them. It is common for a party in opposition to seek to secure greater influence of backbench members over the government. Some further tinkering was done with House of Commons procedures between 1979 and 1997. There was concern about standards of conduct of MPs in the 1990s which resulted in the appointment of the Committee on Standards in Public Life and the appointment by the House of a Commissioner for Standards, an officer of the House, to assist the House and its Standards Committee in dealing with complaints about conduct of MPs.

An important landmark in the period 1979 to 1997 was the House of Commons resolution on ministerial responsibility in 1997. The House resolved:[71]

> That in the opinion of this House, the following principles should govern the conduct of Ministers of the Crown in relation to Parliament:
>
> (1) Ministers have a duty to Parliament to account, and be held to account, for the policies, decisions and actions of their Departments and Next Steps Agencies;
>
> (2) It is of paramount importance that Ministers give accurate and truthful information to Parliament, correcting any inadvertent error at the earliest opportunity. Ministers who knowingly mislead Parliament will be expected to offer their resignation to the Prime Minister;
>
> (3) Ministers should be as open as possible with Parliament, refusing to provide information only when disclosure would not be in the public interest, which should be decided in accordance with relevant statute and the government's Code of Practice on Access to Government Information (second edition, January 1997);
>
> (4) Similarly, Ministers should require civil servants who give evidence before Parliamentary Committees on their behalf and under their directions to be as helpful as possibly in providing accurate, truthful and full information in accordance with the duties and responsibilities of civil servants as set out in the Civil Service Code (January 1996).[72]

The House of Lords passed a resolution in similar terms. Thus the two Houses asserted that the duty of ministerial responsibility was imposed by and owed to Parliament and was not solely a 'voluntary' obligation accepted or not at will by the executive. The Ministerial Code, revised in 1997—and again in 2001, 2005, 2007 and 2010—incorporates the resolution, thus acknowledging the obligation of individual ministerial responsibility.

The New Labour government-in-waiting committed itself, before the election in 1997, to 'renewing' Parliament.[73] In fact progress was slow. It was the responsibility of a new House of Commons Modernisation Select Committee. This committee was chaired by the Leader of the House, a strange character in the theatre that is British politics, being a member of the Cabinet as well as

---

[71] HC Deb, 19 March 1997, cols 1046–47.
[72] The Codes referred to in this resolution have since been updated.
[73] See the *Joint [Labour and Liberal Democrat] Report*, 1997, para 64.

Leader of the House. The first Leader of the House, Anne Taylor, was not very interested in modernisation. It was only when Robin Cook MP was Leader of the House from 2001 to 2003 that progress was made. After 2003 progress has again been slow until the scandals about MPs' expenses claims erupted in 2009. The public anger about MPs' false or extravagant claims for reimbursement of their expenses stimulated some members to take steps to enhance their reputation—or deflect attention from expenses—by recommending reforms to the business of the House, including independent election of chairs of select committees, election by the parties and not by the whips of select committee members and the establishment of a Backbench Business Committee which would deprive the government of control of the agenda for non-government business. These reforms were duly introduced before and after the election of May 2010.

The other 'modernising' changes to House of Commons practice and procedure since 1997 include the following:

— the articulation of a set of core tasks for select committees;
— the payment of additional salaries to select committee chairs;
— agreement by the Prime Minister to meet the members of the Liaison Committee (consisting of the chairs of select committees) to discuss public policy twice a year;
— the introduction of pre-legislative scrutiny of bills (at the government's option);
— the possibility of the carry over of bills from one session to the next;
— the timetabling or programming of bills; and
— the holding of debates in a parallel debating chamber off Westminster Hall in the Palace of Westminster.

'The other place' as it is referred to in the Commons, the House of Lords, is less constrained by politics in its operation. Indeed it is far less political. It too has introduced changes in its *modus operandi* of a constitutional nature, in particular in its select committees. The Delegated Powers and Regulatory Reform select committee was established in 1992; in 2000 The House established a Constitution Committee; and in 2004 a Merits Committee was established which reports on the substance of statutory instruments.

EXECUTIVE REFORM

In the period since 1979 many significant constitutional reforms or changes have been put in place by the government without Acts of Parliament, or with only relatively minor such provision, and with no prior debate in Parliament—indeed without even prior public consultation. The changes include public service reforms dating from 1982 including the agencification of much government activity,[74] the outsourcing of certain public services such as rubbish collection to private companies, and the introduction of choice—for instance allowing parents to choose what school a child should attend or patients to choose what hospital would treat them. Reforms also included the establishment of the Committee on Standards in Public Life (1995), of the Commissioner for Public Appointments (1995) and the House of Lords Appointments Commission (1999). None of these is statutory or permanent.

As with parliamentary reform, the drivers for these reforms varied. Agencification reflected New Public Management theory. The government was frustrated by the cost of the civil service and the fact that planned reforms proved difficult to implement. Agencification involved the professionalisation of management, the articulation of agency aims and objectives, and a contractual approach to relations between government and the chief executives of the agencies. The 'empowerment' of consumers of public services undermined the power of public sector trade unions, and the introduction of competition between providers was designed to reduce the cost and improve the quality and the efficiency of services. (Some of these reforms were reversed or modified from 1997 under New Labour in the light of experience.)

The Committee on Standards in Public Life was established in response to a whole series of disclosures of 'sleazy' conduct by Members of Parliament—the subordination by them of the public service ethos to selfishness—and aimed to put in place mechanisms for shaming such offenders in future and for making more open the standards required and the mechanisms for punishing breaches of them. The Commissioner for Public Appointments' appointment was a response to allegations and suspicions that the Thatcher government had been making public appointments on the basis of the commitment of appointees to government policy rather than on merit and commitment to the public service ethos. And the Appointments Commission for the House of Lords was set up as a gesture—misleading—that might deflect public opinion from election of members of the House, which the Prime Minister considered would result in undermining of the pre-eminence of the Commons. In other words although each of these appointments had genuine public interest justifications they were also influenced by political expediency—a further example of the operation of the political constitution.

THE COURTS AND CONSTITUTIONAL DEVELOPMENT

Lastly in our consideration of the processes by which the UK constitution is changed or changes, we consider the role of the courts. The judges have for centuries exercised an important role in the development of constitutional law.

---

[74] See D Oliver and G Drewry *Public Service Reform: Issues of Accountability and Public Law,* (1996).

Theoretically common law judges merely declare the law as it has always been: if this is the case there have often been widespread misunderstandings as to what the law is![75] In practice, it is clear that judges make the common law, though in doing so they may well be reflecting changes in the economy, politics and public opinion.

'The rule of law enforced by the courts is the ultimate controlling factor on which our constitution is based.'[76] The judges have played a big role in the development of the rule of law. In doing so they have reflected and responded to Parliamentary legislation and political developments. Although there is a range of views about the extent and content of the principle,[77] it includes, inter alia, a principle of government under law (legality) and a principle that discretionary power should be exercised reasonably and fairly. The development of the rule of law has been a joint project by Parliament and the courts.[78]

The doctrine of the legislative supremacy of Parliament has also been constructed partly by the courts.[79] Like the principles of legality and the rule of law,

---

[75] See RC Van Caenegem, *The Birth of the English Common Law*, 2nd edn (1988); FW Maitland, *The Constitutional History of England* (1974) 22–23.; SFC Milsom, *Historical Foundations of the Common Law*, 2nd edn, (1981), 1–8.

[76] Lord Hope in *Jackson v HM Attorney General* [2005] UKHL 56, at [107].

[77] For discussion see PP Craig 'Formal and substantive conceptions of the rule of law: An analytical framework' [1997] *Public Law* 467; J Jowell 'The rule of law and its underlying values' in Jowell and Oliver, note 40 above; Lord Bingham 'The rule of law' (2007) 66 *Cambridge Law Journal* 67–85, and *The Rule of Law* (2010).

[78] Cases and statutes in chronological order in which the principles of legality and the rule of law have been developed include: Magna Carta 1215 (access to justice, no punishment without a breach of the law); *Prohibitions del Roy* (1607) 12 Co Rep 6 (separation of courts from executive); *Case of Proclamations* (1611) 12 Co Rep 74 (law to be changed only by Act of Parliament); Bill of Rights 1689 (no executive power to suspend or dispense with law, no taxation without representation, no standing army without the consent of Parliament); Act of Settlement 1700, s 3 (independence of the judiciary); *Entick v Carrington* (1765) 19 St Tr 1029 (public interest claim does not justify interference with individual liberties, no interference without positive legal authority); *Bowles v Bank of England* [1913] 1 Ch. 57 (tax rates and other laws cannot be changed by mere resolution in Parliament without statutory authority); Supreme Court Act 1981 s 11 (formerly Act of Settlement s 3); *Congreve v Home Office* [1976] QB 629 (all ministerial discretions must be exercised in accordance with principles such as no taxation without the explicit consent of Parliament, private activity can only be criminalised by clear statutory provisions); *Council for Civil Service Unions v Minister for the Civil Service* [1985] AC 374 (executive powers are subject to judicial review regardless of their source unless they are not justiciable); *M v Home Office* [1994] 1 AC 377 (ministers of the Crown may be subject to injunctions); *R v Somerset CC ex parte Fewings* [1995] 3 All ER 20 (public decision makers do not have the same freedom of action as private ones, and are not entitled to indulge their personal moral values unless these are part of their view of the public interest); Human Rights Act 1998 (incorporates ECHR rights into UK law); *R v Secretary of State for the Home Department, ex parte Simms* [2000] 2 AC 115; *R v Lord Chancellor, ex parte Witham*, [1997] 1 WLR 104 (fundamental rights of access to the courts); *R v Secretary of State for the Home Dept, ex parte Pierson* [1998] AC 539, Lord Steyn's speech; *R (Anufrieva) v Secretary of State for the Home Department* [2003] 3 WLR 252 (a person cannot be deprived of entitlements until informed of the decisions on which that deprivation depends).

[79] *Edinburgh and Dalkeith Rly v Wauchope* (1842) 8 Cl and F 710 (courts will not go behind the Act of Parliament to inquire into parliamentary procedures); *Ellen Street Estates v Minister of Health* [1934] 1 KB 590 (a more recent statutory provision impliedly repeals an earlier one); *Cheney v Conn* [1968] 1 All ER 779 (an Act is the highest form of law and cannot be illegal, even if it is contrary to

this doctrine is also underpinned by statutory provisions. The doctrine as it developed in the seventeenth century in effect transferred absolute power from the monarch to Parliament: for instance, the Bill of Rights 1689 deprived the monarch of powers to raise taxation without the consent of Parliament[80] and to suspend or dispense with law.[81] However, the doctrine is not necessarily immutable at common law: in *Dr Bonham's* case[82] Chief Justice Coke indicated that the courts would not give effect to an unreasonable statutory provision—though this has not occurred.[83] More recently the courts have given strained interpretations to statutory provisions which they consider to be contrary to the rule of law.[84] And in the *Factortame II* case[85] the House of Lords gave effect to European law and disapplied a UK statute, relying on section 2 of the European Communities Act 1972 (set out above).

Since about 1960 the courts have elaborated principles of judicial review, commonly regarded as principles of *administrative* law. However, over the last ten years or so the courts have been articulating what they refer to as *constitutional* principles. The change in rhetoric is important here. Thus in *R v Lord Chancellor, ex p Witham*[86] Laws LJ held that rules which imposed an obligation on litigants to pay court fees when initiating litigation which impecunious litigants could not afford denied 'a fundamental constitutional right of access to the courts'. In *R v Secretary of State for the Home Department, ex parte Pierson*, Lord Steyn enunciated a general principle that:

> Parliament does not legislate in a vacuum. ... Parliament legislates for a European liberal democracy based upon the principles and traditions of the common law ... and ... unless there the clearest provision to the contrary, Parliament must be presumed not to legislate contrary to the rule of law.[87]

In *R v Secretary of State for the Home Department, ex parte Simms*, Lord Hoffmann observed that:

international law). Compare, however, the view of Jeffrey Goldsworthy to the effect that the doctrine of sovereignty is not the product of the common law: *Parliamentary Sovereignty: Contemporary Debates* (2010).

[80] Bill of Rights 1689, art 4.
[81] Bill of Rights 1689, arts 1 and 2.
[82] *Dr Bonham's* case (1610) 8 Co Rep 13b.
[83] See discussion of this case in J Goldsworthy *The Sovereignty of Parliament: History and Philosophy* (1999), ch 5.
[84] *Anisminic v Foreign Compensation Commission* [1969] 2 AC 223 (court did not give effect to an ouster clause, depriving a complainant of access to the courts, purportedly interpreting the statutory provision strictly and in accordance with the rule of law).
[85] *Factortame II* [1991] AC 603.
[86] *R v Lord Chancellor, ex parte Witham* [1998] QB 575.
[87] *R v Secretary of State for the Home Department, ex parte Pierson* [1998]AC 539, at 575.

The courts of the United Kingdom, though acknowledging the sovereignty of Parliament [will] apply principles of constitutionality little different from those which exist in countries where the power of the legislature is expressly limited by a constitutional document.[88]

In *R v Secretary of State for the Home Department, ex parte Daly*[89] Lord Cooke held that the common law by itself is a sufficient source of the 'fundamental right to confidential communication with a legal adviser' and said that 'some rights are inherent and fundamental to democratic civilized society'.

For the most part these principles have been applied to determine whether subordinate legislation such as the Prison Rules (*Pierson*), or court rules (*Witham*) or other discretionary executive action, have been invalid as being outside the powers granted by the law or 'unreasonable'. But the implication of the elaboration of '*fundamental*' or '*constitutional*' '*principles*' is that if measures that are incompatible with such principles were included in an Act, they would be 'unconstitutional'. If that were the case the next question would be whether their legal validity would be affected. We have already noted the orthodox position, namely that it would not be affected.[90] To date the received wisdom is that legal validity would not be affected, but this is currently something of an open question.[91]

Another issue in relation to provisions of a constitutional nature in Acts of Parliament is how they may be repealed, and in particular whether the doctrine of implied repeal applies to them. As noted above, the general principle (subject to the primacy of European law) is that a later statute impliedly repeals provisions in earlier statutes which are incompatible with it. There is no requirement for the earlier provisions to be expressly repealed. However, Lord Justice Laws in the Court of Appeal controversially suggested in *Thoburn v Sunderland City Council* that there was a category of 'constitutional statutes' to which the doctrine of implied repeal did not apply. A 'constitutional statute' was defined by Laws LJ as follows:

> A constitutional statute is one which (a) conditions the legal relationship between citizen and State in some general, overarching manner, or (b) enlarges or diminishes the scope of what we would not regard as fundamental constitutional rights.[92]

Laws LJ went on to give as examples of constitutional statutes Magna Carta 1297, the Bill of Rights 1689, the devolution Acts of 1998, the Human Rights Act 1998, the European Communities Act 1972, and others. Of the European Communities Act 1972 he states that 'The 1972 Act is, *by force of the common law, a*

---

[88] *R v Secretary of State for the Home Department, ex parte Simms* [2000] 2 AC 115.

[89] *R v Secretary of State for the Home Department, ex parte Daly* [2001] 3 All ER 433.

[90] See the reference to *Madzimbamuto v Lardner Burke*, note 5 above.

[91] See Lord Woolf 'Droit public—English style' [1995] *Public Law* 57–71; Sir John Laws 'Law and democracy' [1995] *Public Law* 72–93. And see dicta by Lords Steyn and Hope in *Jackson v HM Attorney General* [2005] UKHL 56.

[92] *Thoburn v Sunderland City Council* [2003] QB 151.

constitutional statute' (my italics). The implications of this approach (which has not been followed by other judges) are many: (i) constitutional provisions in Acts can only be repealed or amended by Parliament explicitly; (ii) it is the common law which determines whether or to what extent an Act of Parliament has legal effect; (iii) it is the common law, not European law, which gives effect to European law in the United Kingdom; and (iv) the common law determines the extent of the legislative supremacy of Parliament.

THEMES IN CONSTITUTIONAL REFORM

Accountability and Good Governance

Several themes recur in the constitutional reforms that have been put in place in the UK over the last 30 years or so and in discussions about future reforms. First, the need for a whole range of accountability mechanisms to be in place in order to secure that government is carried on honestly, prudently, legally, conscientiously, with the consent of representatives in Parliament and in the public interest. Accountability is about requiring public bodies to explain and justify what they do to a range of bodies—the courts, ombudsmen, auditors, Parliament and so on—if found to have erred to admit it, and to take such steps as are available to rectify the error. Accountability in the UK is the mechanism or set of mechanisms for protecting the country and individuals against the fallibility of their rulers.[93]

Of the measures we have noted above, the strengthening of individual ministerial responsibility, reformed select committees in parliament, improvements in the legislative process and judicial review, freedom of information, ombudsmen and complaints mechanisms which individuals can pursue, have all been directed to imposing what has become a web of accountability. Accountability has become a substitute for ideology.

Relations between the Citizen and the State

Debates have developed around the notion of British citizenship. These debates have passed through a number of phases as the relationship between the individual and the state has developed and as new concerns, for instance about the integration of immigrant communities, have surfaced. In the 1960s and 1970s the emphasis was on individuals' productive roles; government adopted a corporatist approach to public policy, negotiating policy, for example on wages and employment protection, with trade unions (all affiliated to the Labour party) and

---

[93] See for instance D Oliver *Constitutional Reform in the UK* (2003), ch 3.

business organisations.[94] This placed the emphasis on the interests of public employees and other workers as opposed to the recipients of public or other services.

From the 1980s individuals began to be viewed as recipients of public services, and public employees' primary duties were to provide good services. The 'Citizen's Charter'[95] movement of the early 1990s involved the notion of the citizen as a consumer, operating in the market, exercising choice as to the public services he or she claimed, and not as a politically active person who should make their voice heard via the political process.[96] Indeed, individual consumers were given statements of their 'rights', including rights to complain. This approach served to counteract the self-interests of public employees which had previously prevented improvements in these services.

The idea of 'active citizenship'[97] became popular in political circles in the early to mid 1990s: it could imply that the state could not be expected to supply all needs of individuals, and that therefore caring should increasingly be undertaken by men or women — in practice normally women — with whom the person in need was connected.

The Human Rights Act 1998 focused on the individual as a rights bearer rather than a responsible member of the political community. And after Gordon Brown became Prime Minister in July 2007 there was renewed interest in the responsibilities of citizens, in developing a statement of British values, and in promoting a sense of British identity. The coalition government that came to power in May 2010 has not committed itself on the issue, though the Conservative party had earlier pressed for the Human Rights Act to be repealed and replaced by a British Bill of Rights. But part of Prime Minister Cameron's vision is of a 'big society' in which individual citizens should contribute to and take part in their communities, including in the provision of public services via charities and the voluntary sector.[98]

Democracy?

But what about democracy as a theme in constitutional reform in the UK? This is a very slippery term, and one about which UK politicians are rather coy. While many commentators are uncomfortable with the fact that the upper chamber is not elected, the word 'democracy' seldom occurs in their proposals for reform. 'Election' does occur in these debates, but its significance is not articulated. When we discuss the future of reform of the House of Lords and the support, at least in the House of Commons, for election to that House we should not lose sight of

---

[94] See K Middlemas *Politics in Industrial Society* (1979).
[95] Cm 1599, 1999.
[96] A Barron and C Scott 'The Citizen's Charter programme' (1992) 55 *Modern Law Review* 526.
[97] Speaker's Commission *Encouraging Citizenship*, 1990.
[98] See J Norman *The Big Society* (2010).

the fact that election would increase the powers and influence of the political parties in that House—there are self interested motives here.

There is then no discussion of 'the general will' as a basis for government in British political discourse: such a concept would be regarded sceptically. We have moved beyond the point at which the will of a majority of the voters or of members of either House of Parliament is regarded as of itself 'democratic'— respect for minorities is an important part of the concept of good government or a good constitution.[99] While in the field of pure party politics majoritarianism dominates, and its domination is reflected in the doctrine of parliamentary sovereignty, the actual culture among politicians or the public in relation to constitutional matters is not by any means majoritarian: appeal is always made to independent non-partisan principles when constitutional reform is discussed— fairness, respect for individuals and minorities, tolerance and so on. This may be because every government is an opposition in waiting and vice versa: if a government were to rely solely on its majority and not on any more stable principles when in power it would expect the opposition when in power to do the same, and would object. The rhetoric is of preference for a non-partisan approach, neutrality as between parties, and consensus.

REFLECTIONS AND CONCLUSIONS

Despite the fact that a lot of legislation of a constitutional nature has been passed by the British Parliament over the last 30 years or so, the British constitution remains highly political. Where changes are instituted they are normally presented as being based on principle, but the reality commonly is that there are political benefits to the government to be reaped from any change it sponsors. While participatory theory is supposed to dictate the process for constitutional change, in reality the predispositions of governments favour ad hoc, opportunistic changes. If it suits government to follow participatory or consensual procedures, they will do so. If it does not they may seek to get away with unilateral changes. Only the prospect of protest from opposition parties and the press, or the real prospect of proposed changes turning out to be mistakes deters government from taking steps to change the system if it can do so. Lip service is paid to consultation and participation, but the evidence suggests that this is by no means entrenched in the culture of government or of politicians generally. Overall, then, *how* change comes about is pretty unregulated. As Professor Sir John Baker stated in his Maccabaean lecture in 2009: 'We have no proper mechanism for constitutional change.'[100]

---

[99] I hope I may be forgiven for noting here that men are in a minority in most populations.
[100] Lecture delivered at the British Academy on 24 November 24 2009, entitled 'Our Unwritten Constitution' in (2010) 167 *Proceedings of the British Academy*.

But not all constitutional change is initiated by government or by politicians. The British system of government changes organically—it evolves—and it is changed in a range of ways. Law in the usual, positivist sense, gives only a very partial picture of how the system actually works and what the rules really are. Its workability therefore depends in very large measure on the culture of its actors, especially parliamentarians, government members, judges, and civil servants, and on their observation of non-legal rules.

16

The United States of America

STEPHEN M GRIFFIN

INTRODUCTION

IT MAY BE that each country had a formative period for its present constitution, the historical era in which fundamental matters of political order were decided and the form of government took the essential shape that it has today. For many European countries, that period followed the end of the Second World War, although another demarcation line was reached with the end of the Cold War. For the United States, no one doubts that the 1787–89 period continues to be formative of the contemporary constitutional order. This is when the original US Constitution was adopted by the Federal Convention sitting in Philadelphia, it was ratified by special conventions of the people in the states, the first elections were held for national office pursuant to the Constitution, and the government began operating under the leadership of George Washington, the first president. There is thus a meaningful link, although not an identity, between the political order ratified by the people in the early republic and the US government as it exists today.

The Constitution was ratified in 1787–88 according to procedures specified in the document itself,[1] by special conventions in nine of the 13 original states of the American Union. It replaced an earlier constitution, the Articles of Confederation, that had proven ineffective, both in the opinion of many in the eighteenth century founding generation, as well as in the judgment of history.[2] The political and legal authority of the Constitution was understood to be founded on the idea of popular sovereignty, wherein in some sense the people themselves had adopted the Constitution as the 'supreme law of the land.'[3] Thus, in the United States, the people were and are the constituent power of the state.[4] Their approval was sufficient to make the Constitution self-executing. Further,

---

[1] See US Constitution, Art VII.
[2] For an accessible account of the adoption of the Constitution, see Richard Beeman, *Plain, Honest Men: The Making of the American Constitution* (Random House, 2009).
[3] US Constitution, Art VI.
[4] See RR Palmer, *The Age of Democratic Revolution: The Challenge* (Princeton, 1959), 215.

the Constitution's status as supreme law meant that it was both entrenched and in some sense prior to all other forms of law.

While there were some guarantees of individual rights in the original 1787–88 Constitution, the lack of a Bill of Rights was raised as an objection in the ratification process and so ten amendments guaranteeing various important rights against action by the federal (national) government were approved by the First Congress in 1789 and ratified by 1791. Because of the close link between the ratification of the original Constitution and the approval of the Bill of Rights, they are considered part of the same historical process. While some scholars might still prefer the word 'republic,' it is widely acknowledged that the form of government created by the Constitution was a representative democracy in a federal state, accompanied by limits on governmental power, expressed by enumerated powers and fundamental rights.

After a few months of sustained effort, the 1787 Federal Convention produced a document that most judge relatively brief. There was enough variation between the various elements of the original Constitution, however, so as to make judgments about length or brevity unhelpful. So, for example, the provisions in Article I specifying the conditions under which legislators shall be elected are specific and the powers of Congress are given by a lengthy list (although using general terms that have provoked controversy). By contrast, the bureaucratic structure of the executive branch is not further specified beyond the creation of the office of the president and a reference to executive departments.[5] While the Constitution created a Supreme Court and specified its jurisdiction by a relatively detailed list, the structure of the national court system was left for Congress to determine.[6] And again, while the separate state governments were prohibited from undertaking a list of specific actions solely under the jurisdiction of the national government,[7] other matters relating to the relationship of the states and federal government were left unclear. So far as the level of detail, the Constitution remains something of a mix. This had implications for constitutional change that will be explored below.

The US legal system belongs to the family of common law jurisdictions, including the United Kingdom and Commonwealth countries, although the common law is subordinate to both the Constitution and the doctrines of constitutional law developed by the courts. There is no specialised constitutional court independent of other national courts whose sole task is deciding on the constitutionality of statutes and regulations. Rather, the federal courts are courts of 'ordinary' jurisdiction and consider cases involving statutory and regulatory interpretation routinely along with constitutional cases. Further, constitutional cases must have a common law form in the sense that there must be actual parties in controversy over a concrete injury.

---

[5] See US Constitution, Art II.
[6] See US Constitution, Art III.
[7] See US Constitution, Art I, sec 10.

As for formal constitutional change, the means for amendment were provided by the founding generation in Article V. Most scholars judge that amendment to the Constitution has been infrequent since the approval of the Bill of Rights. Occasionally, significant amendments have been approved, most notably after the Civil War of 1861–65. Under Article V, amendments can be made when two-thirds of both houses of Congress agree and legislatures or special conventions in three-quarters of the 50 states concur, or when two-thirds of the legislatures of the states call for a convention to propose amendments and three-quarters of the legislatures or special conventions in the states agree to the proposed amendments. Because there has never been a constitutional convention called under Article V, all 27 amendments to the Constitution have been adopted through the former procedure.[8] There is evidence that the founding generation believed that the Constitution should be permanent and unchanging over the decades if not centuries to come, given that it contained the lasting principles by which government should be conducted. They anticipated that few amendments would be necessary, and this argued in favour of a multi-level process designed to make the process of amendment relatively difficult to preserve the permanent character of the Constitution.[9]

There were two provisions of the Constitution that were made immune to amendment—the equal representation of states in the Senate (the upper house of the bicameral legislature), and the restriction on banning the importation of slaves until 1808.[10] Although scholars have sometimes argued to the contrary, there is no doctrine prohibiting the amendment of any other provision of the Constitution. While in theory even the most cherished protections of the Bill of Rights could be altered, in practice there has never been a serious move to alter the provisions the founding generation thought essential to the constitutional scheme. On the other hand, the provision for amendment did allow later generations to rethink certain elements of the Constitution or, most famously in what are called the Civil War or Reconstruction amendments, to add new rights guarantees.

Beginning with the Thirteenth Amendment, approved by Congress in 1865, a number of alterations were made to the constitutional order. That amendment abolished slavery and the Fourteenth Amendment extended the protection of the Constitution to persons whose fundamental rights were violated by state and local governments. This altered the system of federalism and is only one example of the key significance of federalism to constitutional development as a whole. In addition, the Fourteenth Amendment gave the Constitution its first definition of

[8] Issues raised by the amendment process are usefully surveyed in Sanford Levinson (ed), *Responding to Imperfection: The Theory and Practice of Constitutional Amendment* (Princeton University Press, 1995).

[9] See Philip A Hamburger, 'The Constitution's Accommodation of Social Change', (1989) 88 *Michigan Law Review*, 239.

[10] See US Constitution, Art V.

citizenship (often known as 'birthright citizenship'), an antidiscrimination guarantee ('equal protection of the laws') was included that was to be of great importance in the twentieth century, and Congress acquired the power to enforce these new rights. The Fifteenth Amendment provided some protection to the right to vote.

The next group of amendments, numbered 16 to 19, approved during the first decades of the twentieth century, also deserve mention. In some ways, these amendments embodied the adjustment of the constitutional order to the new power of the national state. An income tax was allowed after the Supreme Court said it was not, senators were subject to being directly elected by the people rather than by state legislatures, prohibition of alcohol on a national level was made possible (although repealed 14 years later by another amendment), and women were granted the vote. However, here the story of change through formal enacted amendment ends. While there have been a total of 27 amendments to the Constitution, few lawyers or scholars in the US could account for the significance of or even name all of the last eight amendments. Certainly they have played no role in the evolution of constitutional doctrine by the federal courts. Any inquiry into constitutional change in the US must therefore look beyond the process of formal amendment.

THE ROLE OF JUDICIAL DOCTRINE IN CONSTITUTIONAL CHANGE

I will consider the course of constitutional change in the US over roughly the last 75 years. Why such a lengthy period? Unlike Europe, the Second World War is not a natural point of departure for the discussion of formal or informal amendments in the US, except perhaps in relation to foreign affairs. Instead, there was a widely noticed moment of constitutional change associated with the Great Depression and the 'New Deal' administration of President Franklin D Roosevelt.[11] This moment of change was not marked by formal amendments, but by revisions to the constitutional order sponsored by the Supreme Court and the political system itself. With respect to the former, it is not an overstatement to say that nearly the entire corpus of constitutional law studied by students in American law schools was a creation of the Court over the past three-quarters of a century under the leadership of Chief Justices Charles Evans Hughes (1930–41), Harlan Stone (1941–46), Fred Vinson (1946–53), Earl Warren (1953–69), Warren Burger (1969–86), and William Rehnquist (1986–2005).[12] While the personal influence of chief justices can be overstated by referring to the 'Warren Court' or the 'Rehnquist Court,' no scholar doubts the impact of the Court as a collective body on constitutional law understood as judicially created doctrine.

---

[11] President Roosevelt was the only president to be elected four times, serving from 1933 until his death in office in 1945.
[12] Since 2005, John G Roberts, Jr has been Chief Justice of the United States.

In a discussion of constitutional *change*, we reach a conceptual fork in the road once the importance of the Supreme Court's role in developing constitutional doctrine is recognised. Perhaps every shift in judicial doctrine that commentators would regard as significant should be described as an example of constitutional change. On this account, the study of constitutional change would be no different than studying the evolution of constitutional law. Such an approach would appropriately emphasise the central position of the Supreme Court within American jurisprudence. But it is deeply problematic if there is a sense in which the study of constitutional change is useful apart from the consideration of doctrine. So we have a choice between two paths—one leads to a focus solely on what the Court has done while the other seeks a context for judicial doctrine within the larger framework of the study of the evolution of American constitutionalism as a whole.

Why would such a study be useful if all concede the importance and centrality of judicial doctrine? Consider two initial problems. First, American lawyers tend to understate the significance of some judicial decisions for the constitutional order due to normative considerations that ultimately relate to the maintenance of an effective system of justice. According to a widely received understanding, federal court decisions are supposed to *interpret* the Constitution, not *change* it. Interpretation of prior law is often distinguished from amendment for this reason. Along this line, constitutional interpretation has never been conceived in the US as being separate in a strong sense from other sorts of legal interpretation. It is closely related both to the interpretation of statutes (given the Constitution's status as supreme law) and to common law reasoning (given the Supreme Court's reliance on precedent to decide cases). This cuts against the idea that in making decisions, the Court can not only change prior doctrine (which is acceptable), but change the Constitution itself (which is not). In addition, it is accepted that the Court's interpretations are subordinate to the Constitution in the sense that they can be rendered invalid through amendment.[13]

At the same time, American lawyers accept a doctrine of 'judicial supremacy' in which the Court's decisions as a matter of ordinary practice have the same status as the Constitution itself.[14] Many of them are also inclined to believe in the 'living Constitution.' This is a complex set of views about how the US constitutional system works and should work rather than a single accepted theory. However, a crucial element concerns the relative lack of formal amendments to the US Constitution, especially in the recent past. Most commentators see this as a positive good in that it improves the stability of the political system not to have fundamental points of the constitutional order continually at issue. Perhaps more important, they see the lack of amendment as confirming the inevitability of the Court's role in adapting an eighteenth century Constitution to new

---

[13] This has occurred several times. For example, the Fourteenth Amendment had the effect of rendering invalid the Court's ruling in the infamous case of *Dred Scott v Sandford*, 60 US 393 (1856).
[14] See *Cooper v Aaron*, 358 US 1 (1958).

circumstances. So while part of the living Constitution view is certainly normative in that it celebrates this role, there is a realistic descriptive element as well.[15]

These common views work against viewing any Court decision as tantamount to an amendment, a truly fundamental alteration of the existing constitutional order. Each decision usually has its supporters who work to harmonise it with the body of prior law. Further, these views downplay the importance of amendments generally. The Court becomes the centre of the constitutional universe and its doctrines are supreme. But these views have never been fully persuasive. Should not the Supreme Court's decisions be evaluated according to the standards set forth in the Constitution? The common law heritage of the US legal system encourages the belief that the judge-made precedents must be stable and non-political in order to be authoritative. Certain decisions have been plausibly likened to amendments in that they so fundamentally changed prior expectations about what the Constitution meant. At several points in its history, the Court has been likened to a continuous constitutional convention and there is a measure of truth in this.

The second problem is that the Supreme Court is indeed not a specialised court that can somehow decide every important constitutional issue. The Court has never attempted to develop substantial doctrine with respect to every constitutional provision. There are areas of constitutional power, most notably having to do with foreign affairs and war, where there is little relevant judicial doctrine on which lawyers can draw.[16] The executive and legislative branches of government must not only interpret the Constitution to do their business, they must do so without any assurance that the Court will underwrite their interpretations. This opens the door to the possibility of constitutional change without the judiciary.

There are other troubling issues with focusing solely on judicial doctrine as the measure of constitutional change that should be briefly noted. In particular, we lose the ability to ask interesting questions about the constitutional order. In the standard account of constitutional change highlighted in the introduction, it was noted that significant amendments were made following the Civil War. But why did the war occur? Were its causes related to felt constitutional principles and ideas? If so, did they flow in some sense from the original Constitution?[17] Isn't it important to understand the sources of the failure of the constitutional order as well as its success?[18] Or suppose we want to know what effect the Cold War had

---

[15] For an excellent exposition of this point of view, see David A Strauss, *The Living Constitution* (Oxford University Press, 2010).

[16] See generally Louis Henkin, *Foreign Affairs and the US Constitution*, 2nd edn (Oxford University Press, 1996).

[17] A case made in the important and thought-provoking book by Mark Graber, *Dred Scott and the Problem of Constitutional Evil* (Cambridge University Press, 2008).

[18] See, eg, Mark E Brandon, *Free in the World: American Slavery and Constitutional Failure* (Princeton University Press, 1998).

on presidential power. Finally, focusing solely on judicial doctrine is also inadequate on normative grounds. If presidential administrations take actions that are constitutionally questionable, it becomes difficult to assess their significance unless there is a Supreme Court decision on point. More generally, we lose the sense, crucial to our ability to analyse politics, of the Constitution as a working governing order that is immediately relevant to contemporary policy, an order that while it always imposes constraints, also offers to political agents creative opportunities for change.

I do not suggest that these considerations justify ignoring judicial doctrine as a source of constitutional change. We must select our targets carefully rather than regarding each new Supreme Court decision as if it heralded a significant moment of change. We can make progress by asking which decisions of the Court in the last 75 years made a permanent and structural difference to the constitutional order—the larger set of institutions, practices and expectations that structure the government. This sort of inquiry directs us to groups of decisions that reverberated throughout the national government and the federal structure of the country. We can then move to a discussion of contemporary constitutional change beyond judicial doctrine.

There were arguably two instances in the last 75 years where the Court's change in doctrine made a fundamental 'amendment-like' difference to the constitutional order.[19] The first are the New Deal cases regarding the power of the national government to regulate the economy and spend money to advance the general welfare.[20] These decisions opened the way for both the national government and the states to regulate conditions of labour and social relations generally.[21] They provided a secure constitutional foundation for the regulation of the national economy by the executive and legislative branches and the establishment of a limited welfare state.[22] These cases also created a possibility for

---

[19]   On this topic, the essential work of Bruce Ackerman should be consulted. See Bruce Ackerman, *We The People: Foundations* (Harvard University Press, 1991); *We The People: Transformations* (Harvard University Press, 1998) (Ackerman, *Transformations*); Oliver Wendell Holmes 'Lectures: The Living Constitution', (2007) 120 *Harvard Law Review* 1737 (2007) (Ackerman, 'The Living Constitution').

[20]   On spending power, see *United States v Butler*, 297 US 1 (1936). For a more recent case, see *South Dakota v Dole*, 483 US 203 (1987). With respect to the power of Congress to regulate interstate commerce, see *NLRB v Jones & Laughlin Steel Corp*, 301 US 1 (1937); *United States v Darby*, 312 US 100 (1941); *Wickard v Filburn*, 317 US 111 (1942). For more recent cases, see *United States v Lopez*, 514 US 549 (1995); *United States v Morrison*, 529 US 598 (2000); *Gonzales v Raich*, 545 US 1 (2005).

[21]   With respect to state power to enact social and economic regulations, see *West Coast Hotel Co v Parrish*, 300 US 379 (1937); *Williamson v Lee Optical Co*, 348 US 483 (1955).

[22]   One way in which the US system is a limited welfare state is that there was no system of universal health care. The 2010 approval of President Obama's health care initiative went some distance toward remedying this problem, but without a true guarantee of universal coverage.

further changes in the powers of the legislative and executive branches by announcing a doctrine of deference to their 'rational' decisions, at least ones that did not transgress fundamental rights.[23]

The second group of cases constituted dual but related developments affecting individual rights and the principles of federalism. These were cases ensuring that state and local governments would have to comply with most of the provisions of the Bill of Rights, especially the rights of freedom of speech and religion embodied in the First Amendment, as well as various rights attending the criminal process. These rights were 'incorporated' on state and local governments through the due process clause of the Fourteenth Amendment.[24] Further, the federal courts initially led the way, beginning with the epochal case of *Brown v Board of Education*,[25] in dismantling the system of segregation which oppressed black citizens in the South. The Supreme Court developed a body of jurisprudence enforcing the Fourteenth Amendment's guarantee of 'equal protection of the laws' as embodying an antidiscrimination principle, as well as voting rights.[26] Over time, all three branches of the national government cooperated in establishing a constitutional order that created new rights in such epochal statutes as the Civil Rights Act of 1964[27] and the Voting Rights Act of 1965.[28] These and other similar later measures fashioned what I have called a 'democracy of rights,' a system of governance concerned with creating, maintaining and enforcing a diverse set of rights for all citizens.[29]

In saying these changes were 'amendment-like,' I am not making a normative point with respect to debates over the legitimacy of these decisions as a matter of constitutional interpretation. Rather, these decisions illustrate how the Supreme Court participates in changing the larger constitutional order. It has been persuasively argued that the era of the Rehnquist Court saw the advent of a less aspirational or 'chastened' role for the Court.[30] There are no recent examples of Court decisions that have made the kind of difference to the constitutional order

---

[23] Here I refer to the doctrine announced in a footnote in the Carolene Products case that the Court would not defer to legislative judgment in cases involving (1) a denial of a specific constitutional right; (2) exclusion of groups from the democratic political process; (3) prejudice against 'discrete and insular minorities'. *United States v Carolene Products*, 304 US 144, 152 n 4 (1938).

[24] This development can be traced through *Palko v Connecticut*, 302 US 319 (1937); *Adamson v California*, 332 US 46 (1947); *Duncan v Louisiana*, 391 US 145 (1968). Most recently, the right to 'keep and bear arms' in the Second Amendment was incorporated into the set of rights state and local governments must respect. *McDonald v Chicago*, 561 US ____ (2010).

[25] *Brown v Board of Education* 347 US 483 (1954). The best comprehensive analysis of the Warren Court era in which these cases occurred is Lucas A Powe, Jr, *The Warren Court and American Politics* (Harvard University Press, 2000).

[26] The cases referred to here and in the preceding paragraph are discussed in a recent survey that is especially useful for non-US lawyers: Richard H Fallon, Jr, *The Dynamic Constitution: An Introduction to American Constitutional Law* (Cambridge University Press, 2004).

[27] Pub L No 88–352, 78 Stat 241.

[28] Pub L No 89–110, 79 Stat 437.

[29] Stephen M Griffin, 'The Age of Marbury: Judicial Review in a Democracy of Rights' in Mark Tushnet (ed) *Arguing* Marbury v Madison (Stanford University Press, 2005).

[30] Mark Tushnet, *The New Constitutional Order* (Princeton University Press, 2003).

that was the product of the New Deal or the Warren Court. That still leaves us with the question of how to account for the notion of a constitutional order. For that, we have to look beyond judicial doctrine.

CONSTITUTIONAL CHANGE BEYOND JUDICIAL DOCTRINE

Why has constitutional change other than through formal amendment or judicial doctrine played such a substantial role in the evolution of American constitutionalism?[31] One reason is that the 1787 Constitution was implemented through *multiple* independent and distinctive institutions, all of which mediated constitutional meaning. At the same time it established a textual template for these institutions, the Constitution created an agenda for future change by leaving important questions of constitutional power and structure unanswered.[32] Further, an internal logic of constitutional stability discouraged change through formal amendment that might have answered these questions.[33] Officials found themselves in a constitutional order in which they could use the existing text and institutions to implement their preferred visions of constitutional power outside Article V.[34] As the national state developed over time, this led to persistent use of informal means, including creative interpretation, institutional restructuring, and the constituent power of the people in democratic elections to initiate change and obtain constitutional settlements.

The process of implementing the Constitution led to the formation of constitutional orders. These are relatively stable patterns of institutional interaction with respect to basic aspects of the Constitution such as powers and rights. As patterns of interaction, constitutional orders must be constructed from the actions and norms put into operation by multiple institutions.[35] The working elements of a constitutional order are several and independent. The first is the text of the Constitution, an ineluctable source of authoritative rules of law nonetheless sometimes passed over in accounts that stress the importance of the 'living Constitution.' A second element is the political and policy interests of the

---

[31] In this section, I provide a summary of a theory of constitutional change that I have presented in greater detail in previous work. See Stephen M Griffin, *American Constitutionalism: From Theory to Politics* (Princeton University Press, 1996) (Griffin, American Constitutionalism); Stephen M Griffin, 'Constitutional Theory Transformed', (1999) 108 *Yale Law Journal* 2115 (Griffin, Transformed); Stephen M Griffin, 'Constituent Power and Constitutional Change in American Constitutionalism', in Martin Loughlin and Neil Walker (eds) 'The Paradox of Constitutionalism', (Oxford University Press, 2007) 49 (Griffin, 'Constituent Power'); Stephen M Griffin, 'Rebooting Originalism', 2008 *University of Illinois Law Review* 1185, 1209–23 (Griffin, 'Rebooting').

[32] Griffin, 'Constituent Power', ibid, at 53–56.

[33] Griffin, 'Rebooting', note 31 above, at 1211.

[34] Griffin, 'Constituent Power', note 31 above at 53–56.

[35] See the important book by Keith E Whittington, *Constitutional Construction: Divided Powers and Constitutional Meaning* (Harvard University Press, 1999).

public, elites, and state officials. A third is the structure and capacity for action of state institutions, whether constituted by statutes, regulations, judicial decisions or other means.

There is a reciprocal relationship between the authoritative text of the Constitution and the other two elements that make up constitutional orders. This allows for the possibility that the text could play a paradoxical role in enabling constitutional orders to change. While 'living constitution' theorists are correct to say that change does not happen solely through amendment, this does not make the text irrelevant.[36] The text can provide authority essential to those seeking to change the constitutional order outside Article V. Political actors can use powers given by the text to leverage constitutional change by exploiting their positional advantages. We should therefore avoid an approach which subsumes the written Constitution to the unwritten or 'living' Constitution. Powers granted by the text are central to understanding how informal constitutional change can happen. There is thus a creative (or possibly destructive, depending on the circumstances) tension between the 'written' and the 'unwritten' Constitution.

To make further progress in understanding informal constitutional change, we should distinguish and reject two alternative views. Call the first the idea of the pervasive 'small c' constitution, while the other is the less defended position that the US system has implicit constitutional conventions. The first idea can be explored through the account offered by realist theorist Karl Llewellyn.[37] Llewellyn was concerned to explain the role in the constitutional order of fundamental elements not mentioned in the original Constitution, such as the Senate filibuster and political parties. He proposed the notion of the 'working constitution'[38] as a 'living institution'.[39] The working constitution consists of practices that are fundamental and essential to the operation of the government.[40] He asserted that the working constitution controls the meaning of the paper document in all but a few cases,[41] stating that practice can negate the text.[42]

Llewellyn based his theory of the working constitution on the behaviour of political actors.[43] He stated: 'The argument is, that there is only one way of knowing whether, and how far, any portion of the Document is still alive; and that is to watch what men are doing and how men feel, in the connection.'[44] He

---

[36] See, eg, Karl N Llewellyn, 'The Constitution as an Institution', 34 *Columbia Law Review* 1 (1934).
[37] See ibid.
[38] Ibid, at 3.
[39] Ibid.
[40] Ibid, at 28–31.
[41] Ibid, at 12.
[42] Ibid, at 15–16.
[43] See ibid, at 15.
[44] Ibid.

proposed that the real Constitution is an institution[45] arising from the interaction of three key groups: specialists in government, private interest groups, and the public.[46] Whenever these groups decide to change the fundamental rules of government, government institutions change and so the constitution changes. As he insisted '*the working Constitution is amended whenever the basic ways of government are changed*'.[47]

Scholars might agree that Llewellyn's theory was provocative.[48] He challenged them to explain the constitutional status of the rules that structure fundamental institutions (such as congressional procedures) and key institutions not mentioned in the text such as political parties. It is less clear that he provided a feasible approach to understanding what he called the 'working Constitution'. In Llewellyn's theory, the working or unwritten constitution virtually swallowed the 'big C' Constitution whole.[49] The unwritten constitution replaced the written and the Constitution became a set of practices without a clear relationship to supreme law. The posited near-total transformation of the US constitutional system, based as it is on an authoritative text, into an 'unwritten' British-style system was not very plausible.

While we might agree that institutions are crucial to the determination of constitutional meaning, they cannot be understood solely as patterns of behaviour, as Llewellyn proposed. As much as Llewellyn wanted to avoid them,[50] rules are indispensable. In the US political regime that values law, rules are essential to guiding action. If we understand institutions as rule-based, then it is hard to avoid the relevance of the text, something Llewellyn was eager to do. In the end, while Llewellyn offered a plausible *definition* of the 'working Constitution,' he did not provide an *explanation* of how informal constitutional change occurs. In particular, the historical development of the institutions created by the Constitution was ignored. The fundamental practices Llewellyn highlighted, such as political parties, simply appeared out of nowhere, rather than being related to the historical development of the constitutional system. His theory went in the wrong direction by overemphasizing the pervasive character of the unwritten or 'small c' constitution. In fact, the institutions and powers created by the text are essential to a satisfactory explanation of how informal constitutional change occurs. What we require is a theory that usefully confronts the tension between the obvious relevance of the text and the historical developments that have informally changed text-based institutions.

---

[45] Llewellyn defined an institution as a pattern of behaviour. See ibid, at 17.
[46] See ibid, at 19, 21.
[47] See ibid, at 22 (emphasis in original).
[48] For a recent example of the use of Llewellyn's theory, see Ernest Young, 'The Constitution Outside the Constitution', (2007) 117 *Yale Law Journal* 408, 454 n 235 (Young, 'The Constitution').
[49] For a relevant discussion see Dennis J Goldford, *The American Constitution and the Debate over Originalism* (Cambridge University Press, 2005), 245–50.
[50] See Llewellyn, note 36 above, at 17.

It is therefore important to recognise that having a Constitution that is legally enforceable is dependent, at least in the US, on the existence of a hard barrier between constitutional law as judicial doctrine and norms in the document that the judiciary typically does not enforce. No doubt some norms with a clear meaning can be enforced as enacted in the Constitution without any need for judicial intervention. They are followed because everyone understands them and there are no disputes. But as to other unenforced norms, the judiciary and clear meaning are no help. This has the further consequence that American constitutionalism can have no meaningful *legal* doctrine of extra-constitutional norms or constitutional conventions. For if such norms existed, the question would be whether they are legally valid and, if so, how did they obtain that status without the use of amendment or judicial decision. After all, if they were validated through an institution other than the judiciary, then that institution would have an independent legal power of constitutional change. This would introduce the possibility of a conflict between two opposing sets of norms that had the same constitutional status. This explains why there is no *doctrine* (as opposed to occasional remarks) of extraconstitutional norms or constitutional conventions accepted by US courts.[51]

If we reject these alternative views, how should we proceed in understanding informal constitutional change? I suggest that we track informal change through the historical development of state institutions.[52] Based on the foregoing analysis of US constitutionalism, we can distinguish meaningfully between the sphere of the *legalised* Constitution and the informal or non-legalised Constitution. In the sphere of the legalised Constitution, the judiciary, guided by forms of legal argument influenced by the common law, holds sway.[53] Judicial doctrine as to the meaning of the Constitution *is* constitutional law. Indeed, the idea of a form of 'law' within this sphere that does not proceed from the Constitution itself, some other enactment recognised by the judiciary, or judicial doctrine developed in a common law framework literally does not make sense. The legalised sphere is effective in enforcing the Constitution partly because it is limited in scope. The judiciary does not attempt to take on all possible issues that exist with respect to the meaning of the Constitution or enforcing all norms in the Constitution on the other branches of government.

To understand how informal change works in the non-legalised sphere, Keith Whittington has advanced the concept of 'constitutional construction,' a political process distinct from legal interpretation.[54] Because Whittington concentrates on how political actors seek to structure constitutional meaning, especially at

---

[51] Of course, no harm is done if people speak of, say, political parties as extraconstitutional in the sense that they were not created by the Constitution, yet are not opposed to it. But this does not give political parties the same constitutional status as the three branches of government.

[52] On developmental theory, see Griffin, 'Rebooting', note 31 above, at 1209–23.

[53] See, eg, Philip Bobbitt, *Constitutional Fate* (Oxford University Press, 1982); Philip Bobbitt, *Constitutional Interpretation* (Blackwell, 1991).

[54] See Whittington, note 35 above.

'moments of unsettled understanding,'[55] his theory is complementary to my own. According to Whittington, constitutional constructions 'resolve textual indeterminacies'[56] within 'the context of political debate, but to the degree that they are successful they constrain future political debate.'[57] Whittington contends that construction allows for the introduction of 'an element of creativity'[58] into the interpretive process. This helps determine textual meaning in situations 'where the text is so broad or so underdetermined as to be incapable of faithful but exhaustive reduction to legal rules.'[59]

Given the case histories that Whittington discusses, such as the nullification crisis of 1832–33 and the impeachment of President Andrew Johnson,[60] it is clear that he is thinking of controversies involving structural issues such as federalism and separation of powers where there has been little judicial guidance on constitutional meaning.[61] Whittington describes such constitutional constructions as 'often highly partisan, messy, bitter disputes, in which the losers are driven from the public stage'.[62]

Whittington's work illustrates that theories of constitutional change have received increasing attention from US scholars. Ackerman's path-breaking theory of transformative constitutional moments is a signal example.[63] In place of Article V, Ackerman substitutes a complex, multi-stage process driven forward by social movements and election cycles that at a few epochal moments in American history has added something new to the Constitution—the functional equivalent of a constitutional amendment.[64] It would be more accurate to describe Ackerman's theory as one of *unconventional* change, because he argues that even formal amendments such as those ratified after the Civil War were adopted outside the strict provisions of Article V.[65] However, once we move to the twentieth century and more contemporary times, his account is best regarded as a theory of informal change to the extent that he concentrates on periods, such as the New Deal, in which there were no constitutional amendments under Article V to ratify apparently new governmental powers. Whatever the appropriate description, it is important to grasp that Ackerman is searching for a way to *legalise* changes of constitutional dimension that did not occur, at least not entirely, through legal enactment.

---

[55] Ibid, at 4.
[56] See ibid, at 9.
[57] Ibid, at 6.
[58] Ibid, at 5.
[59] Ibid.
[60] Ibid, at 17–18.
[61] Whittington's detailed case histories of constructions include the impeachments of Judge Chase and President Andrew Johnson, the nullification crisis of 1832–33, and President Nixon's impoundments. See ibid.
[62] Ibid, at 19.
[63] See Ackerman, above note 19.
[64] Ackerman, 'The Living Constitution', note 19 above at 1761.
[65] Ackerman, *Transformations*, note 19 above.

My alternative approach rejects an understanding of informal change that involves an effort to identify 'extracanonical norms'[66] that are asserted to have an entrenched status equivalent to the norms in the text.[67] Consistent with the conventional understanding of the US legal community, I contend that only norms that are part of the legalised Constitution are entrenched. So I do not argue, as does Ackerman, that the norms that result from informal change are the functional equivalent of Article V amendments.

Informal change to a constitutional order cannot be understood in the same way as change within the legalised Constitution. While we can study change in the legalised Constitution by examining amendments and judicial interpretations, there are no true analogues to these markers of change outside the legalised sphere. Without legal markers, the way to track informal change is by studying the succession of constitutional orders or, put another way, the relationship of constitutional powers and rights to the historical development of state institutions. These institutions may imitate the judiciary and use the forms of legal argument to justify constitutional change, but they are not obliged to do so. The legislative and executive branches swim in a sea of policy and politics. To be sure they make law, but not *entrenched* constitutional law. This power is reserved to the judiciary and the amendment process specified in Article V.

This has the further consequence that the norms of the non-legalised Constitution do not, as a practical matter, have the same status as those in the legalised Constitution. Given that they are not (or not typically) enforced by the judiciary, they lack the certainty, predictability and authority of legal norms. This can create ambiguity and tension within the constitutional system.[68] For these norms are still part of the Constitution and have the formal appearance of legal obligations. That they are not enforced by the judiciary can be a source of frustration for those who take them to be legally binding. There is often a belief that they *should* be legally binding. Practical experience, however, has shown that only some of the norms in the Constitution can be judicially enforced.

Although there are distinctions between Ackerman's theory and my own, there is one basic point on which we agree. Accounts of constitutional orders must be historicist. That is, we must take seriously the reality of historical change and institutional development over time. We should not 'flatten' history by treating events as if they were strings of legal precedents without a context. The ratification of the Constitution and the beginning of government operations in 1789 provide a meaningful historical baseline against which subsequent changes in the institutional/constitutional order can be assessed. But not all of them occurred through amendments or judicial decisions. In some instances, the constitutional

---

[66] Young, 'The Constitution', above note 48, at 449.

[67] Ibid, at 449–50.

[68] Compare constitutional scholar Edward Corwin's dictum that the Constitution 'is an invitation to struggle for the privilege of directing American foreign policy'. Edward S Corwin, *The President: Offices and Powers, 1787–1984* 5th rev edn (New York University Press, 1984), 201.

order was changed through determined efforts to alter institutional structures. The evolution of presidential power in foreign affairs is an important example.

PRESIDENTIAL POWER IN FOREIGN AFFAIRS

I will focus on the exercise of presidential power in foreign affairs since 1945 as an example of informal constitutional change, with specific reference to the post-9/11 presidency of George W Bush (Bush II). We can begin with Justice Robert Jackson's famous concurring opinion in the *Steel Seizure* case,[69] decided during the Korean War. The circumstances of the case led Justice Jackson, in a passage largely overlooked, to focus on recent changes to the presidency:

> [I]t is relevant to note the gap that exists between the President's paper powers and his real powers. The Constitution does not disclose the measure of the actual controls wielded by the modern presidential office. That instrument must be understood as an Eighteenth-Century sketch of a government hoped for, not as a blueprint of the Government that is. Vast accretions of federal power, eroded from that reserved by the States, have magnified the scope of presidential activity. Subtle shifts take place in the centers of real power that do not show on the face of the Constitution.[70]

Here Justice Jackson used the perspective afforded by a developmental approach to constitutional change to better understand the presidency and the Constitution itself. He focused on the difference between the institution described in the text ('paper powers') and the actual constitutional power the presidency had acquired over time. Jackson might have had in mind the changes that occurred during the New Deal administration of President Roosevelt (in which he served as Solicitor General and Attorney General) and those that followed entry of the US into the Second World War.

As Jackson suggested, it is impossible to track such constitutional changes by examining the text of the Constitution (there are no relevant amendments) or through judicial precedent. Most actions of the president are never subjected to judicial review. A theory that understands constitutional change in institutional terms offers a more promising approach. Of all the institutions established by the Constitution, the presidency is the most protean. The accumulation of power in the presidency during the twentieth century, to which Jackson referred, would not have been possible had it not been supported by the constituent power of the people expressed in democratic elections. The changes that have occurred in the presidency are part of a larger story in which a more democratised American polity informally changed the constitutional system in many respects.[71]

---

[69] *Youngstown Sheet & Tube Co v Sawyer*, 343 US 579 (1952).
[70] Ibid, at 653.
[71] Griffin, *American Constitutionalism*, note 31 above, at 195–96.

President Roosevelt's New Deal was a paradigmatic example of informal constitutional change through constituent power.[72] An older constitutional order based on ideas about the proper role and function of the national government collapsed under repeated legislative hammer blows, backed by FDR's enormous electoral majorities.[73] In national crises such as the Great Depression and world wars, the American people came to expect presidential action.[74] This is significant because the increased power of the presidency is often portrayed as something that presidents have done by themselves. In part, this reflects a mode of thinking inherited from the eighteenth century and expressed in the contemporary critique of the 'imperial presidency'—presidents seek to increase their power because that is what ambitious men in office tend to do. But it is at least equally the case that increased power has been something given to the presidency by a concerned public.

Increased presidential power was also a consequence of the perceived weaknesses of Congress in new circumstances. In the years prior to the Second World War, Congress discredited itself by adhering to a policy of isolationism and stridently refusing to follow presidential leadership in foreign affairs. After the outbreak of war, it seemed to many that Congress's feckless attitude had placed the US in greater peril.[75] If Congress was the danger, increased presidential power and authority appeared to be the solution.

Increased presidential power arguably led to a new series of constitutional dangers. Presidents assumed they had the unilateral power to lead the US into war, a problem many thought exemplified by the Vietnam War. The indefinite nature of the Cold War led presidents to apply tactics suited to foreign affairs to the domestic sphere, a phenomenon which contributed to the great scandal and constitutional crisis of Watergate.[76] Informal constitutional change appeared to offer flexibility at the price of unanticipated and unwelcome side effects.

The party system played an important role in shaping how the constitutional lessons of Vietnam and Watergate were perceived by political actors. Those lessons were absorbed principally by elites associated with the Democratic party. They believed that the presidency had become 'imperial' and had to be reined in by an assertive Congress cognizant of its role as the true repository of constituent power.[77] By contrast, the Republican party remained relatively unaffected by these supposed insights. For Republican elites, the lesson of the 1970s was that Watergate led to an overreaction against presidential power.[78] They continued to see the president as the natural leader of government, especially in foreign affairs,

---

[72]   Ibid, at 33–46.
[73]   See Griffin, 'Transformed', see note 31 above, at 2129–38.
[74]   Ibid, at 2133–34.
[75]   See Arthur M Schlesinger, Jr, *The Imperial Presidency* (Houghton Mifflin, 1973), 97–99, 122–26.
[76]   Griffin, *American Constitutionalism*, above note 31, at 196–99.
[77]   Schlesinger, above note 75.
[78]   Barton Gellman, *Angler: The Cheney Vice Presidency* (Penguin, 2008), 100–01.

and set forth the theory of the 'unitary executive' during President Reagan's administration in the 1980s. Many of these Republicans would later play key roles in the 9/11 administration of President Bush.[79]

Thus the Bush II administration's expansion of presidential power can be understood against the background of developments in the post-1945 constitutional order. While it is beyond the scope of this chapter to fully set the Bush presidency in a historical context, it is possible to see it as part of a pattern in which the aggressive exercise of power, especially in foreign affairs, suggests both the flexibility and deeply problematic character of informal constitutional change. After the 9/11 attacks, President Bush cleared the ground for informal change by using his Commander in Chief power to aggressively define the reality in which all branches of government would henceforth operate—a state of war equivalent to the Second World War. The changes were often secret in that the public (and indeed other administration officials) did not know they were taking place. They were further enabled by the Office of the Vice President (OVP) going operational in the manner of a cabinet department. Lawyers in the White House, OVP, and the Department of Justice (DOJ) used their positional advantages to immunise executive officials from legal liability by adopting the theory of 'preclusive' Commander in Chief powers.[80] Finally, as a related point, I suggest executive officials were driven primarily by a fear of accountability generated by the internal logic of the constitutional system rather than from the more commonly posited desire to aggrandise their own power. The discussion that follows develops these points.

An institutional approach to informal constitutional change highlights the latent power contained within roles created by the text. History suggested that after a Pearl Harbor-like attack, vast power to shape the nation's response would flow to President Bush given his textually-rooted power as Commander in Chief. Arguably the single most important constitutional action in the aftermath of the shocking and disorienting events of 9/11 was Bush's assertion that the United States was at war. The president had the option of encouraging public debate on the nature of the response. Instead, President Bush immediately categorised the attacks as a military operation, akin to an invasion by a foreign state. The President told his advisers 'we're at war'[81] just hours after the attacks occurred and made a global war on terror the official policy of the executive branch.[82] Two days after 9/11 the President told the press, '[N]ow that war has been declared on us, we will lead the world to victory'.[83]

---

[79] James Mann, *Rise of the Vulcans: The History of Bush's War Cabinet* (Penguin, 2004).

[80] See David J Barron and Martin S Lederman, 'The Commander in Chief at the Lowest Ebb—Framing the Problem, Doctrine, and Original Understanding', (2008) 121 *Harvard Law Review* 689.

[81] See National Commission on Terrorist Attacks upon the United States, The 9/11 Commission Report (2004) 326, available at http://govinfo.library.unt.edu/911/report/.

[82] Ibid, at 330–38.

[83] Robert Draper, *Dead Certain: The Presidency of George W Bush* 148 (Free Press, 2007).

Bush's definition of reality so thoroughly pervaded the public sphere that the press and the public were still having trouble escaping the 9/11 frame as the Iraq War began in early 2003.[84] This suggests that a theory that is not dependent on specifying a particular normative path for legitimate change and is more attuned to the disruptive potential of the exercise of textual power is more useful in understanding the presidency after 9/11.

By describing 9/11 as a war, the president short-circuited any meaningful debate over the nature of the attacks and the appropriate response. But his constitutional claims were as significant. While the president participated in the process that led to the September 2001 Authorization to Use Military Force (AUMF),[85] the legislative measure that authorised the war against terrorism, he reserved the argument that he did not need it to prosecute the war.[86] In two subsequent letters to Congress,[87] the president ignored the AUMF and apparently invoked his traditionally recognised power to respond to sudden attacks by stating that he had ordered military action 'pursuant to my constitutional authority to conduct US foreign relations and as Commander in Chief and Chief Executive.'[88] This meant that the president was not bound even by the broad terms of the AUMF.[89]

At the same time he bypassed Congress, the President was treating the war as a precedent-shattering world struggle against evil.[90] Taken cumulatively, these statements described a presidency at the zenith of its constitutional power—a Commander in Chief responding to a surprise attack with the backing of Congress. This put the war on terror on a legal and normative plane with the Second World War and suggested President Bush could exercise the same authority possessed by President Roosevelt. Executive branch attorneys lost no time suggesting that because Roosevelt had used military commissions to try Nazi saboteurs as 'unlawful combatants,'[91] Bush could do the same thing with respect to captured terrorists.

Bush's definition of reality after 9/11 was thus a remarkable example of the creative tension between the text and informal change. Bush and his administration used his power as Commander in Chief to leverage informal constitutional

---

[84] See W Lance Bennett, Regina G Lawrence and Steven Livingston, *When the Press Fails: Political Power and the News Media from Iraq to Katrina* (University of Chicago Press, 2007).

[85] See SJ Res 23 (18 September 2001); Pub L No 107–40, 115 Stat 224.

[86] See 'President Signs Authorization for Use of Military Force bill,' September 18, 2001, at http://georgewbush-whitehouse.archives.gov/news/releases/2001/09/20010918–10.html.

[87] See President's Letter to Congress on American Campaign Against Terrorism (24 September 2001) available at http://z22.whitehouse.gov/news/releases/2001/09/20010924–17.html; President's Letter to Congress on American Response to Terrorism (9 October 2001) available at http://georgewbush-whitehouse.archives.gov/news/releases/2001/09/20010924–17.html.

[88] See President's Letter to Congress, 24 September 2001, note 87 above.

[89] See Curtis A Bradley and Jack L Goldsmith, 'Congressional Authorization and the War on Terrorism', (2005) 118 *Harvard Law Review* 2047.

[90] President George W Bush, The President's State of the Union Address (29 January 2002) available at http://georgewbush-whitehouse.archives.gov/news/releases/2002/01/20020129–11.html.

[91] See *Ex p Quirin*, 317 US 1 (1942).

change that transformed the constitutional order. Empowered by these presidential claims of authority, the executive branch set into motion all of the questionable policies that would later come to light: indefinite detentions, military commissions, NSA surveillance, and extreme interrogation techniques.[92] Secrecy was essential to the creation of this new constitutional order.[93] The war on terror featured secret decisions,[94] secret executive orders,[95] and secret programs,[96] all not unusual in wartime. However, these initiatives also had *secret constitutional rationales*,[97] something that was critical to getting them off the ground by shielding them from the normal processes of interagency review.[98] Jack Goldsmith, head of the Office of Legal Counsel (OLC) in 2003–04 provides an example in his account of the secret NSA program. He states that Cheney and his counsel David Addington

> had abhorred FISA's [Foreign Intelligence Surveillance Act] intrusion on presidential power ever since its enactment in 1978. After 9/11 they and other top officials in the administration dealt with FISA the way they dealt with other laws they didn't like: they blew through them in secret based on flimsy legal opinions that they guarded closely so no one could question the legal basis for the operations.[99]

Among the Bush administration's most important institutional innovations was the change to the OVP. Vice President Cheney has been described as '[t]he most powerful vice president in American history.'[100] The positions advocated by Cheney and Addington were often decisive in the administration's councils.[101] Cheney had strong views about restoring presidential power prior to becoming vice president.[102] He believed that the presidency had sunk into a trough of weakness in the wake of mid 1970s congressional reform efforts and had never recovered.[103] Cheney 'told Bush, who later repeated the line, that if nothing else they must leave the office stronger than they found it.'[104]

---

[92]   Jane Mayer, *The Dark Side* (Doubleday, 2008) 33.

[93]   Ibid, at 268–69.

[94]   The meetings held by the President with his top advisers in 2003 to approve 'enhanced' interrogation methods are an example. See Anthony Lewis, 'Official American Sadism,' *New York Review of Books*, 25 September 2008, at 45, 45.

[95]   See Eric Schmitt and Mark Mazzetti, 'Secret Order Lets US Raid Al Qaeda In Many Countries', *New York Times*, 10 November 2008, at A1.

[96]   On the use of the CIA to conduct a secret war, see Mayer, note 92 above, at 39–43.

[97]   See Harold H Bruff, *Bad Advice: Bush's Lawyers in the War on Terror* (University Press of Kansas, 2009), 285.

[98]   Jack Goldsmith, *The Terror Presidency* (Norton, 2007), 166–67.

[99]   Ibid, at 106.

[100] Charlie Savage, *Takeover: The Return of the Imperial Presidency and the Subversion of American Democracy* (Back Bay, 2007), 7.

[101] Mayer, note 92 above, at 51–54, 63–64, 265, 308–11, 321–24.

[102] See Savage, note 100 above, at 9, 43.

[103] See Gellman, note 78 above, at 99–102.

[104] Mayer, note 92 above, at 7.

Cheney's institutional role, unique among vice presidents,[105] flowed in part from his unusual political status. He had no ambitions for the presidency[106] and could function as a sort of policy overlord,[107] his influence flowing both from his position as constitutional officer[108] and uber-staffer.[109] The practical consequence of Cheney's lack of a political future was that he was accountable only to Bush.[110] Indeed, Cheney seemed to loathe the standard forms of political accountability. After the 2006 elections in which Republicans lost control of Congress, Cheney compared the election results to a lone poll of public opinion.[111]

Cheney's role enabled the OVP to go operational in the manner of a cabinet department with statutory authority.[112] In this respect, what happened in the Bush administration had a noteworthy resemblance to Watergate in the Nixon administration and the Iran-contra scandal in the Reagan administration.[113] These episodes all involved the White House acting independently of executive branch agencies. Nixon used the 'Special Investigative Unit' to investigate intelligence leaks outside the FBI and CIA.[114] The Iran-contra scandal resulted when the National Security Council under Admiral Poindexter and Lt Col Oliver North assumed operational responsibilities for saving American hostages held in Lebanon.[115] While conducting operations from the White House allows for greater secrecy and flexibility, it can obviously lead to grave constitutional difficulties.

The consequences of OVP going operational played out in a variety of barely believable ways. OVP began running the legal side of the war against terror.[116] Cheney bypassed a pre-existing interagency review in obtaining an executive order to establish military commissions as the administration's way of handling detainees.[117] The OVP was intimately involved with running the NSA's arguably illegal domestic surveillance program.[118] An internal administration controversy over its legality nearly caused a constitutional crisis when Bush and Cheney decided, temporarily as it turned out, to go forward with the program in the face of the uniform opposition of the DOJ.[119]

---

[105] See Gellman, note 78 above, at 51.
[106] Ibid, at 16, 49.
[107] Ibid, at 51–53.
[108] Ibid, at 87.
[109] Ibid, at 44.
[110] See ibid, at 50.
[111] Ibid, at 390.
[112] Ibid, at 50–55, 127–28, 131–54.
[113] See Bruff, note 97 above, at 116–17.
[114] Stanley I Kutler, *The Wars of Watergate* (Norton, 1990), 101.
[115] Theodore Draper, A Very Thin Line: The Iran-Contra Affairs 3–6, 558–79 (Farrar,1991).
[116] Gellman, note 78 above, at 134–39, 350–52, 377–78.
[117] Ibid, at 162–68.
[118] Ibid, at 139–54, 277–93.
[119] Ibid, at 299–326.

An especially dangerous consequence of OVP's operational authority was the subordination of OLC to the White House.[120] As many commentators have pointed out, OLC, an office of the Department of Justice, functions as a sort of Supreme Court for the executive branch.[121] OLC opinions could be used to immunise executive branch officials for violations of federal law.[122] In addition, because OLC had the last word in disputes over constitutional interpretation, whoever controlled it had a decisive positional advantage in any legal debate within the executive branch.[123] Lawyers in OVP and the White House Counsel's office sought to reduce the historically independent role of OLC in their effort to control interrogation policy.[124]

Lawyers in OLC responded with a series of opinions that took the executive branch out of the system of checks and balances during wartime.[125] The 2001–02 OLC opinions were critical to the creation of an lax interrogation policy in which abuses were all but inevitable. After an extensive investigation, the Senate Armed Services Committee concluded:

> Legal opinions subsequently issued by the Department of Justice's Office of Legal Counsel (OLC) interpreted legal obligations under US anti-torture laws and determined the legality of CIA interrogation techniques. Those OLC opinions distorted the meaning and intent of anti-torture laws, rationalized the abuse of detainees in US custody and influenced Department of Defense determinations as to what interrogation techniques were legal for use during interrogations conducted by US military personnel.[126]

Here we can see the practical import, not only of questionable constitutional interpretation, but the key role of positional advantage within the executive branch. With OLC opinions behind them, those pushing for a forceful approach to interrogations within the Department of Defense were occupying the high ground.[127] We may infer that constitutional change in the Bush II administration thus had just as much to do with the complexities of institutional structure as it was a product of overly aggressive lawyering.

CONCLUSION

Understanding constitutional change through a theory rooted in an institutional perspective allows us to give concrete meaning to the concept of 'informal'

---

[120] See Goldsmith, note 98 above, at 24.
[121] Gellman, note 78 above, at 177.
[122] Ibid.
[123] Goldsmith, note 98 above, at 23.
[124] Gellman, note 78 above, at 133–39, 174–84.
[125] See Goldsmith, note 98 above, at 97–98.
[126] Inquiry Into The Treatment of Detainees in US Custody, Senate Armed Services Committee xxvi–xxvii (December 2008).
[127] See ibid, at xxviii.

constitutional change. I place the word in quotes because we are now in a position to appreciate that while the significant changes after 9/11 did not involve amendments or judicial interpretation, they did have a 'formal' element in terms of the role of governmental structures, public invocations of constitutional power and secret executive interpretations of the text, however strained.

The Bush presidency highlights the need for a different approach to the study of constitutional change. Bush's framing of 9/11 as a war and the transformation of OVP point away from theories founded on legal analogies or public deliberation. Change after 9/11 was fostered by an executive clique, not by an aroused citizenry deliberating over their options. Indeed, 9/11 and the Iraq War powerfully demonstrate how the constituent power of the people can be mobilised in support of extraordinary presidential action largely in the absence of deliberation. In light of these developments, whether there is still a meaningful connection between the original Constitution of the early republic and the contemporary US constitutional order is an important issue. It is one freighted with implications for the future of American constitutionalism.

Part III

17

Changing Constitutions:
Comparative Analysis

DAWN OLIVER AND CARLO FUSARO

INTRODUCTION

I N THIS FINAL Part of the book we review the ways in which constitutions
change, as illustrated in the country based chapters and the chapter on the
European Union in this study. We shall try to draw some lessons and
conclusions about constitutional change in liberal democracies from our analysis
in chapter 18.

It will be convenient to start with a number of recurring features of change in
the constitutions in our study: first, how and why new constitutions come into
being—and why they may not do so; secondly, the ways in which constitutions
and how they change are shaped by ideas as to sovereignty—whether of institutions or of principles; thirdly, the ways in which the rule of law is conceptualised,
and the extent to which constitutional documents are directly or indirectly
effective (we prefer this terminology to self-executing); fourthly, the very wide
range of procedural requirements, both formal and cultural, that are followed
when constitutional change is under consideration; fifthly the role of the courts
in constitutional change, whether in preventing 'unconstitutional' constitutional
change or in actually bringing about change by development of their jurisprudence; sixthly, how changes can take place without formal changes in the law, for
instance by praxis or changing constitutional conventions; and lastly in this
comparative analysis we shall compare the ways in which the countries in our
study which are members of the European Union have adjusted in different ways
to the implications of their membership.

THE BIRTH OF CONSTITUTIONS

The constitutional texts in our study were all new at some time. Here we consider
how they came into being, and why it is that the situations of their birth have
been so varied. When focusing on 'constitutional texts' we bear in mind that

while in most of the countries with which we are concerned there is a document called a Constitution in which are to be found most of the important rules of the system, there also exist in many of those countries further norms in the form of constitutional acts or even of ordinary acts, non-legal treaties, codes and other documents which regulate the system of government.

But not all of the countries in our study have a constitutional text in this sense. Israel, for instance, is building its constitution 'chapter by chapter' and has, instead of a single document known as a Constitution, a number of Basic Laws. The same can be said of New Zealand. The United Kingdom, as is well known, does not have a single document known as a Constitution, but that does not mean that its system is without a constitution: the rules are to be found in a series of important Acts of Parliament, in the jurisprudence of the courts, and in constitutional conventions and practice.

Let us consider in this section of the chapter, then, the different ways in which constitutions come into existence.

Granted and Patriated Constitutions

Some of the countries in our study were granted their constitutions by another state. New Zealand's constitution was originally granted by Act of the British Parliament. It was and is still based in part upon the terms Treaty of Waitangi of 1840 between the British Crown and the indigenous people, the Maori. New Zealand is a dualist country, but the Treaty of Waitangi is nonetheless regarded as fundamental to the constitution: an exceptional ingredient of a constitution for an ex-colony. India and Canada too, were granted their constitutions by the UK when they achieved independence. Legal continuity is ensured in this way. However, after independence under a granted constitution 'patriation' is likely to be required. New Zealand's patriation first took the form of the granting by the Westminster Parliament in 1947 of the right to amend the 1852 New Zealand Constitution Act (UK). The New Zealand Constitution Act of 1986 completed the patriation of the Constitution by providing that the constitutional legislation that had been passed by the Westminster Parliament should cease to have effect in New Zealand. Canada patriated its constitution in 1982 when it requested and consented to the passing by the British Parliament of the Canada Act 1982. While much of the Canadian legal system and the law continued as it had been, patriation represented an important step towards an autochthonous constitution.

Independence Constitutions

Many countries adopt their own first or new constitutions at the time when, or shortly after, they obtain independence by force from a colonial power: the USA is the obvious example. Unlike Canada, the USA formulated and adopted its own, unique Constitution of 1789. Thus while the USA retained the laws in existence at the time of independence, including English common law (as did Canada much later), in other respects it broke very deliberately from the UK: it embodied popular rather than parliamentary sovereignty, a separate, presidential executive in place of the monarchy and the British parliamentary system, and a charter of rights. And it was of course federal. India too adopted its own constitution on independence in 1948, based on the Constituent Assembly formed for that purpose.

Regime Change Constitutions

Other countries adopt their own new constitutions at a time of internal regime change: when Czechoslovakia adopted a new Constitution with effect from 1993 after the fall of the Communist regime in 1989, its constitution-makers looked back to the democratic period in Czechoslovakia from 1920 to 1948 and the Constitutional Charter of the then Czechoslovak Republic as a model. The Czech Republic in turn adopted a new Constitution, again based upon the 1920 Czechoslovak Constitution, on the dissolution of the federation with Slovakia in 1992.

Not all countries adopting a new constitution after internal regime change will have a model to look to: South Africa (RSA) is a case in point. There being no model for a developing country emerging from apartheid, the constitution makers borrowed ideas from a number of countries, particularly Germany, and produced their own unique model. Spain too adopted a new, unique Constitution on the fall of the Franco regime. It reinstated the monarchy, established a parliamentary system, and facilitated without naming them the establishment of autonomous communities in an asymmetrical, quasi-federal system. Like the RSA, Spain also borrowed ideas from a number of different constitutional arrangements (France, Germany and Italy in particular) and from its own previous constitutional experience.

Post-war Constitutions

The aftermath of war may also lead to a new constitution. Germany after the Second World War adopted a new Constitution, drafted following guidelines dictated by the allies, which strongly reflects the desire to avoid repetition of the mistakes of the Weimar Republic and of the Nazi regime. Italy's post-war Constitution of 1948 was adopted by a representative directly elected constituent assembly, and it seeks to prevent a repetition of the pre-war Fascist takeover of the country by including a bill of rights, entrenchment provisions, and a strong and independent judiciary.

The Quest for a Perfect Constitution?

France is perhaps unique in this study: the Constitution of the Fifth Republic is the latest in a long line of Constitutions each of which has replaced its predecessor in what could appear to be a bicentennial search for a perfect constitution. Since 1958 however, the Constitution of the Fifth Republic has remained in place, amended frequently in a pragmatic way.

Problems may arise if a constitution is designed to provide a long term 'perfect' entrenched political programme or manifesto and is not easily amendable. The Italian Constitution of 1948 was conceived as a sacred and virtually untouchable text which was later interpreted by many as setting out the only legitimate policies for the country. This inflexibility has contributed to delegitimising the Constitution itself: if a Constitution contains a specific 'political' programme, those who seek a different programme may pursue changes to the Constitution itself rather than to the policies of government, believing that the Constitution denies their legitimate political expectations. The same effect has flowed from the invention of more and more implied limits on possible amendments that have been elaborated in activist or radical interpretations of the Italian Constitution: the Constitution itself thus becomes a target of criticism.

CONTINUITY AND CLARIFICATORY CONSTITUTIONS

Some countries experience long periods of constitutional continuity: when a new constitutional text is adopted, the procedural and other rules in operation at the time of the adoption of the new Constitution are followed. New Zealand is an example: its Constitution Act of 1986 was passed as an ordinary Act of Parliament; it is descriptive not constitutive of the country's constitutional arrangements. Finland's Constitution of 2000 was passed as one step in what was to be a programme of reform, one that should not undermine the stability of the system; it is largely clarificatory. In such instances the existing constitution and its institutions provide the *pouvoir constitué* for the new one, and the constitutional arrangements in the country evolve in a continuous way. The same can be said about the Swiss Constitution of 1999 which stems from the necessity to re-draft the Constitution in a more simple, more consistent and updated text after the 1874 Constitution had been amended hundreds of times over 120 years.

In the case of such clarificatory constitutions the written text of the Constitution has been updated or even entirely re-drafted and in this sense it has been changed: however the substantive constitutional arrangements may or may not have been altered.

Evolutionary Constitutions

In some cases countries' constitutions evolve without a break over centuries and without formal constitutional amendments or the adoption of 'new' Constitutions. It has not been necessary—since the restoration of the monarchy in 1660—for the UK to adopt a new or even a descriptive written Constitution. Although the rules of the UK constitution are written down in a range of sources—Acts of Parliament, judicial decisions, soft law documents, academic commentary—the UK does not have a written constitution in the normal sense of a single document containing the principal rules of the system, probably having specially protected legal status.

New Zealand's system resembles that of the UK in many ways: its roots lie in continuous evolution since 1688. We have already noted that the Constitution Act 1986 is for the most part merely descriptive of the system. Provisions as to the term of the Parliament and elections are protected by 75 per cent parliamentary majority requirements, but the terms of the New Zealand Constitution enjoy no other special legal protection. Israel is the other country in our study which lacks a single written constitutional document. It is of course a much younger country than the UK or New Zealand. The Supreme Court of Israel has decided that the terms of their Basic Laws may only be overridden by Acts bearing the title 'Basic Law': hence these Laws have a degree of 'supra-legal' constitutional status. Each of these countries illustrates continual constitutional evolution without formal constitutional amendment or a 'new start'.

Other countries' constitutions of course evolve, as where constitutional amendments are passed or important changes are made that do not require amendment of the text: most of the countries in this study are evolutionary in this sense, though as we shall see some are so rigid that evolution by constitutional amendment is in practice nearly impossible and other ways have to be found to adapt to new political requirements: Spain is an example.

SOVEREIGNTY

The countries in this study vary as to whether 'sovereignty' is an essential ingredient in their constitutions, and if so whether it is taken to reside in the People, the Parliament, or both. There appears to be a trend in most, perhaps all, countries away from the need to identify an institutional sovereign—People or Parliament—and instead to develop fundamental principles of limited rather than sovereign government—for instance principles of constitutionalism and the rule of law. These issues affect the processes and legitimation of constitutional change in a range of ways. It may be that the will of the People or the sovereignty of their Parliament is considered to be subject to a set of 'super-constitutional provisions', 'constitutional constraints' or 'fundamental principles' and the rule of law; in the absence of such limitations the will of the People or the sovereignty of the Parliament, if exercised independently of the government, may serve to remove responsibility from governments—as where a referendum authorises and legitimates legislation that may be inconsistent with what would otherwise be 'fundamental principles': the referendum against the building of mosques in Switzerland provides an example.

Popular Sovereignty

'The People' are expressed, in various ways, to be sovereign in many countries. However, the concept has a range of meanings, and the legal implications of the principle that sovereignty rests with the People vary—from the most direct form of democracy—a popular veto or binding referendums on constitutional change—to little more than rhetoric, with possibly one significant exception: Switzerland is the country where the principle of popular sovereignty linked to direct democracy is strongest in our study. There popular initiative on constitutional change—and indeed of some other changes in the law—followed by binding referendums is the norm: this is the purest form that the sovereignty of the People can take. The Czech Republic purports to be a representative democracy in which the people are sovereign and may exercise power directly in referendums: however, only one national referendum has been held there—on accession to the EU. A general Act providing for national referendums has not yet been passed in the Czech Republic, in spite of the requirements in the text of the Constitution.

In France 'the will of the people' is considered sovereign. But in France too, it is rare for a referendum to be held on constitutional amendments. Whether a referendum is held is a matter for the President, who normally opts for the alternative procedure whereby amendments that have been passed by two-thirds majorities in both Houses go to a Congress of the two Houses sitting together for approval. It is not obvious how this procedure enables the people to exercise their sovereignty in relation to constitutional reform. However, referendums are held in France from time to time on other matters, and laws that implement the referendum result, being regarded as an expression of the will of the sovereign people, will not then be reviewed by the *Conseil constitutionnel*. Thus the theory of popular sovereignty in France affects, though only rarely, the legal status of reforming legislation if the People have been given the opportunity to vote on the matter in a referendum. But it still is a top down process: contrary to what occurs in Switzerland and in Italy, where voters have the initiative, in France the referendum can only be called by the executive.

The Constitution of the USA was produced by a Constituent Assembly: 'the People' were assumed and expressed to be sovereign, and an assumption of the approval of the People was in due course regarded as sufficient to make the constitution directly effective. However, amendment of the USA Constitution does not involve referendums but special majorities in Congress and the consent of three-quarters of the States. (The involvement of sub-national entities has since become commonplace in federal or quasi-federal jurisdictions.)

In Germany, Israel and India, too, the People are regarded as sovereign: and yet these countries are representative democracies with Parliaments enjoying powers limited by the Constitution, and with very little recourse to referendums. In practice, in the light of the jurisprudence of the German Constitutional Court, and the Israeli and Indian Supreme Courts, nowadays the constitutional arrange-ments in these countries are at least as much the product of judicial interpreta-tion of constitutional texts (including Israel's Basic Laws) as the political outcome of expressions of the sovereign will of the People and of its representatives.

The *legitimating* implications of the principle of popular sovereignty are, of course, as important as the legal ones. However, as with the legal implications, much of the legitimating effect of the principle may derive from rhetoric and appeal to the history of the constitution. Not all constitutions were in fact, originally, approved by the People—for instance via a referendum or a popularly appointed constituent assembly. Germany is an obvious example.

Parliamentary, Shared, and Mixed Sovereignty

In some countries sovereignty is stated to be shared between the People and the Parliament. The Finnish Constitution provides that 'the powers of the state in Finland are vested in the people, who are represented by the Parliament'. While there is provision for referendums—direct democracy—in the Finnish Constitu-tion only one has been held in recent years, on membership of the EU. However, when constitutional reform is proposed in Finland, special procedures need to be followed—normally a simple majority in Parliament, an intervening election, and then a two-thirds majority for the change in the new Parliament. Thus the Finnish people have an active role in the process for constitutional change through an election. Similar provisions are to be found in Spain when a 'total revision' of the Constitution is to take place.

Israel provides a different example of a mixed theory system. The Knesset is regarded both as the constituent power in the Constitution and as the legislative power. When elaborating the Constitution it exercises its constituent power, and those laws are supreme over laws passed by the Knesset as the legislature. In this doctrine, formulated by the Supreme Court in the *United Mizrahi Bank* ruling in 1995 and based on the terms of Basic Laws, Israel moved away from a system based on parliamentary sovereignty on British lines and became 'a constitutional state', a democracy in which the People's will as expressed by Parliament is no longer sovereign in absolute terms.

In the UK and New Zealand, almost uniquely, the Parliament is considered to be sovereign. The UK Parliament thus has the power to change constitutional laws by passing ordinary legislation without the requirement for a referendum, intervening election, or special majorities in Parliament. This doctrine of parlia-mentary sovereignty is however weakening even in the UK in two rather different ways. First, it has recently been suggested that the rule of law and constitutional-ism rather than parliamentary sovereignty, are the controlling principles of the British constitution: this is similar to the development of constitutionalism in Israel. At the very least this means that if the UK Parliament wishes to overturn established constitutional principles or common law doctrines it must use very clear language. In an important case, *Jackson v Attorney General* (2005), members of the top court reserved their position as to whether the court might exercise a power to refuse to give effect to an Act of Parliament which was contrary to important constitutional or fundamental principles. Secondly, there is currently speculation as to whether a new constitutional convention is evolving to the effect that major constitutional changes should be subject to referendums. Referendums were held in Scotland, Wales and Northern Ireland prior to the passing of legislation on the devolution of power to Scotland, Wales and Northern Ireland: all endorsed the government's proposals. A referendum was held in the North East region of England in 2004 on whether an elected regional assembly should be formed: the answer was 'No'. A referendum was held across the UK in 2011 on whether to switch from the first past the post electoral system to the alternative vote for elections to the House of Commons. A European Union Bill was introduced into the UK Parliament in late 2010 which, if passed, would require a referendum before any further powers were devolved to the EU. On the other hand there has not been pressure for a referendum on whether the UK should move to fixed term Parliaments, as is proposed by the Fixed Term Parliaments Bill, 2010. If a convention on the use of referendums is developing, the UK may be in the course of a transition to a mixed system of parliamentary, popular and constitutional sovereignty—as indeed are many countries, especially EU member states.

CONCEPTS OF THE RULE OF LAW

Understandings of the concept and the strength of the rule of law vary in the countries in our study. In Germany the *Rechtsstaatprinzip* is particularly important, stemming from the German legal positivist tradition and reinforced in the aftermath of the Second World War. In the UK at least one judge, Lord Hope of Craighead, has recently expressed the view that 'The rule of law enforced by the courts is the ultimate controlling factor on which our constitution is based' though what is to be understood by the phrase and whether it implies a right on the part of the courts to refuse to give effect to a statutory provision that was inconsistent with the rule of law is not completely clear.

De facto, day to day compliance with the law and the principle of legality does not always depend upon whether a Supreme or Constitutional Court has the power to compel observance of the law and the constitution. Finland does not have a Supreme or Constitutional court with power to enforce the Constitution. However, the ordinary courts may find a provision in an Act to be in conflict with the Constitution and, unless the Constitutional Committee of Parliament cleared the provision in relation to the situation in the case in question, that court may disapply the provision and apply the Constitution directly. Finland relies heavily upon intra-parliamentary scrutiny of bills for constitutionality by its Constitutional Committee. The constitutional culture in that country makes this an effective mechanism for protecting the constitution even without a Constitutional or Supreme Court on the American or German model: culture is an important influence in constitutionalism and constitutional change. But this does not mean that there is no concept of 'constitutional' law in Finland or in other countries lacking judicial review for constitutionality. In Finland the concept of 'constitutional law' goes back to 1766 when the new Freedom of the Press law included recognition of its constitutional nature. And even in the UK both Parliament and the courts recognise that certain laws are 'constitutional' in nature, even if they are not strongly protected against change. In Switzerland constitutional amendments require approval in referendums, and there has until recently been no recourse to the courts if an 'unconstitutional' amendment is approved in a referendum. Thus direct democracy has substituted for the rule of law in that country. On the other hand the Swiss Parliament may stop a popular initiative in some circumstances, declaring it wholly or partially invalid. This has happened only four times: but the fact that such a power exists (as well as the power to submit an alternative proposal) is telling about the checks and balances of a system based on a very peculiar mix of direct and representative democracy.

The legal effect of constitutions, and thus the legal implications of constitutional amendments, depend in part upon the extent to which the courts have a role in enforcing the terms of the constitution. The power of the ordinary courts or of a Constitutional or Supreme Court to review the legality or constitutionality of laws, either pre- or post-legislatively, may be plain in the text of the constitution. Where it is not plain the courts may be in a position to develop their own jurisprudence so as to review such laws. As we shall see later in this chapter, most of the top courts in the countries in our study have taken upon themselves from time to time a function in constitutional scrutiny.

Directly and Indirectly Effective Constitutions

If we associate the rule of law with the idea that independent courts have the power to uphold and give effect to constitutional provisions, the question whether or to what extent a Constitution is directly effective becomes of central importance. Of course there will be provisions in many Constitutions which are not suited to direct application, or which envisage that detailed implementing legislation will be passed before the Constitution can take effect. But provisions, for example, as to the protection of human rights, are treated in some countries as directly effective and in others as dependent upon the passing of implementing legislation.

Let us start with those constitutions in our study which are most strongly directly effective, those of the USA, RSA, India, and Germany. It was the US Supreme Court decision in *Marbury v Madison* which made clear that this was a

directly effective constitution (though even in the US there are 'political questions' which are not justiciable). The South African Constitution is largely
directly or indirectly effective, although there too, portions of the Constitution
are more exhortatory than binding in nature, for instance principles of cooperative government and intergovernmental relations and the lists of basic values and
principles governing public administration to which public servants are expected
to strive.

The directly effective characteristic of constitutions in common law countries
may reflect the fact that for historical reasons the authority of the courts in those
countries is less feared than in countries in which until relatively recent times it
was not accepted that judges would oppose the executive (in fear of the
'*gouvernement des juges*', as in France) and countries which subscribe to strict
separation of powers theories. Implicit in these differences are the different
understandings of the role of judges. In France they are supposed to be the
'bouche de la loi' and are essentially public functionaries, whereas in common
law traditions they were originally the instruments through which the monarch
discharged the role of fountain of justice which included articulating the law; as
representatives of the monarch (they are still 'Her Majesty's judges') they had and
still have a high legal and social status.

It was argued for Congress in *Marbury v Madison* that the separation of powers
in the US Constitution precluded judicial review of legislation: the Supreme
Court rejected the argument. Here we have different understandings of 'separation of powers' as between politicians and common lawyers. However, the
constitutions of some non-common law countries are also substantially directly
effective. In the Czech Republic the exception to direct effect is the Charter's
protections of social, cultural and economic rights (which would not be regarded
as directly effective in many constitutions). The German Constitution is also
directly effective with strong emphasis on the rule of law and Germany as a
Rechtsstaat. The Federal Constitutional Court (*BundesVerfassungsGericht*) has a
central role in upholding the Basic Law. The same can be said about Italy.

The Constitutions of many countries provide for the Parliament to pass
legislation before constitutional provisions can be implemented and enforced by
the courts. Italy has been an example. Major provisions in the 1948 Constitution
were not implemented by legislation for many years: the Constitutional Court
was not established and convened until June 1956; the Superior Council of the
Judiciary was not elected and convened until the end of 1958; the Referendum
Act was passed only in 1970, and in the same year the first regional elections were
called. On the other hand in Italy the constitutional provisions protecting human
rights were immediately treated as directly effective by the courts.

Finland too relies upon Parliament to pass legislation to give justiciable,
enforceable effect to many constitutional provisions. Thus constitutional provisions as to the enforceable rights and obligations of the individual are not to be
found in the constitution but in implementing legislation passed by the Parliament of Finland. Much of the Spanish Constitution is not directly effective.

However, the *recurso de amparo* permits human rights provisions to be protected in the Constitutional Court even before implementing legislation has been passed.

PROCEDURAL AND OTHER REQUIREMENTS FOR CHANGING CONSTITUTIONS

Commonly special procedures need to be followed where new laws are to be passed which either amend the constitutional text or alter important constitutional arrangements. In this section we are concerned with the range of approaches to the adoption of new constitutions and constitutional amendments.

Distinctions are made in some systems between amendment, revision and total revision. In Italy, for instance, academic commentary argues that, the Constitution having been established by the Constituent Assembly (the constituent power), it would be unconstitutional for a total or transforming revision to take place unless a new Constituent Assembly were to propose and adopt it. The Indian Parliament is regarded as a normal legislature when passing ordinary laws, but as exercising a constituent power when passing constitutional amendments.

Unamendable Provisions

Most Constitutions contain provisions which cannot be amended—we could call them 'superconstitutional provisions'. The German Basic Law's 'eternity clause' states that certain articles in the Basic Law may not be amended. The German Federal Constitutional Court, though enjoying a power to set aside unconstitutional Acts, in practice interprets the eternity clause of the Basic Law in a restricted way in order not to limit the room for amendment too much: a too strict interpretation of the substantive limits to constitutional amendment would make the amendment procedure impractical and lead to immobility. These eternity clauses protect the federal structure, the rights of Länder to participate in government, fundamental principles including human dignity and fundamental rights, the rule of law and separation of powers. In Finland too, the position of the Åland Island and possibly some other 'core' constitutional provisions are regarded as unamendable. In the USA provisions for the equal representation of the States in the Senate may not be amended. And in New Zealand no laws may be passed that contravene the provisions of the Treaty of Waitangi. In Italy and France the republican form of the state may not be changed by amendment. In India the Supreme Court has stated that the *basic structures* of the Constitution may not be changed even via constitutional amendment.

Consent and Consultation

The procedures and processes by which new constitutions are adopted or existing constitutional provisions are reformed may be laid down by law, or they may reflect the expectations of those affected by them. Cross-party consensus or the consent of particular interests may be thought appropriate. In Italy, for instance. the general understanding is that 'constitutional reforms must be worked out and approved by all'. However this has not prevented some very significant amendments being passed by the majority in power alone and without cross-party agreement.

The need for the consent of particular interests before constitutional arrangements are made or changed may be due to international requirements such as Treaty obligations. New Zealand illustrates the point strongly: the Treaty of Waitangi is taken to oblige the government to consult with the Maori over constitutional, and other, changes. Indeed it has been suggested by an eminent New Zealand judge in an academic article that for the courts to uphold legislation to replace the monarch as Head of State by a President would require evidence of consent from the Maori in a referendum, given the importance to them of their Treaty with the Crown. In Finland too, treaty obligations affect constitutional change: property rights in the Åland Islands are protected by a decision of the Council of the League of Nations—not a treaty—so that changes are only permitted with the consent of two-thirds of the members of the Åland Islands Legislative Assembly. Canada is a party to the North Atlantic Free Trade Agreement which is regarded by some commentators to have affected the constitutional division of powers as well as rights in Canada.

A range of consultation requirements may need to be satisfied before the amendment or revision of the text of a Constitution can take place, all designed to protect the constitution from rash or partisan or ill-thought-out change and to secure that reforms are broadly consensual. This reflects awareness of the importance of legitimacy in liberal democratic countries. Consultation may be required with expert public bodies such as the French Conseil d'État and its equivalents in Italy, Spain and other countries which came under Napoleonic rule. The Conseil d'État is consulted on constitutional bills before their adoption by the Government in the Council of Ministers. It reports to the Government. The Conseil's advice may undermine the bill as in the case of its opinion on a constitutional bill on decentralisation in 2002.

The RSA provides a particularly strong example of very wide consultation in the process of drafting and adopting first the interim constitution of 1993 and then the final constitution of 1996. Much thought had been given to the project by the main parties in the years running up to the new constitution—much groundwork had been done, especially by lawyers. First a provisional constitution was brought into effect by the tricameral parliament of the time in 1993 after a Multi-Party Negotiating Process, thus ensuring both legal continuity and 'sufficient consensus'—one of the parties, the Inkhatha Freedom Party having left the

MPNP and only rejoining the process at the time of the general elections of 1994; and then, three years later, the present Constitution of 1996 was adopted by the newly elected Parliament sitting as a Constitutional Assembly and was signed into law by the newly elected President Mandela.

In the RSA constitutional reform was urgent, given the fall of the apartheid regime. Spain provides another example of the effects of urgency of constitutional change on consultation, after the fall of the Franco regime when the 1978 Constitution was put in place. Urgency may then provide the oil for the wheels of change without which change is impossible.

In the absence of urgency, failure to find sufficient consensus on constitutional change may mean—and has meant since 1978 in Spain, for instance—that formal constitutional reform is impossible so that other ways of allowing the system to develop have to be found: in Spain this has been done by Constitutional Court decisions (for example, in response to European Court of Human Rights decisions and European law), by agreements reached between the Autonomous Communities (ACs) and the Centre, and by changes in constitutional practice.

Not all legislation of a constitutional kind requires consultation beyond that involved in the normal legislative process. When the New Zealand Parliament passed the Constitution Act 1986, which was not politically partisan and merely described and did not constitute the system, wide consultation was not considered necessary. The same has been true of other constitutional statutes in New Zealand, including the NZ Bill of Rights Act of 1990.

In the UK a custom of consultation before constitutional change has developed, for instance in relation to devolution, the Human Rights Act and freedom of information: consultation papers were published before the legislation was passed. Further, before the Scotland Act 1998, which established a Scottish Parliament and Executive, was passed, a referendum was held in Scotland in which there was a clear majority for devolution. The Scottish Constitutional Convention—an organisation of civil society in which many Scottish organisations had participated (but not the Scottish National Party or the Conservative Party in Scotland)—had reached agreement as to the terms on which devolution should be granted: the Government accepted most of these proposals and incorporated them into the Scotland Act. Devolution to Scotland was thus 'gold-plated' with support both from civil society and the referendum after wide consultation and opportunities to participate in it.

However, the UK coalition government that was formed in the summer of 2010 introduced legislation on important matters such as fixed term parliaments and a referendum on a change to the election system without prior consultation outside the two coalition parties: a sense of urgency in the coalition explains this short-circuiting of normal expectations, but it was met with protests from parliamentarians and others. There was no suggestion that the opposition parties should support these proposals before they were implemented: cross-party consensus about constitutional change is not considered necessary in the UK. But changes which would give institutionalised advantages to the party or parties in government are considered abusive. Hence proposals for the reduction in the number of seats in the House of Commons and the consequent redistribution by boundary changes, coupled with a possible move to the alternative vote electoral system, were objected to by Labour, the largest opposition party, partly for self-interested political reasons since they would lose most of the reduced seats, but partly because it was seen as party-politically partisan and had not been preceded by wide consultation.

Entrenchment and Constitutional Change

Many constitutions require special majorities for constitutional change in the legislature (and perhaps additional processes such as a referendum). In Germany a two-thirds majority in favour of amendment of the Basic Law is needed in each chamber: this is regarded in Germany as an example of rigidity, simplicity and parity (between the Länder as represented in the Bundesrat and the people as represented in the Bundestag). In practice, though 'rigid', the Basic Law has been amended several times. The constitution of the Czech Republic requires three-fifths of all deputies and three-fifths of senators present at the session to vote in favour of the amendment and, unlike the position with ordinary legislation where laws can be made without the consent of the Senate, the senators' votes are essential. The Italian Constitution requires the support of at least 50 per cent of the members of each chamber on two occasions separated by at least three months. There is provision for the holding of a referendum if the request for one is supported by either one-fifth of the members of the legislature, or a certain number of voters or regional assemblies, unless the Act received the support of two-thirds of the members of both chambers. The Spanish Constitution requires the approval of three-fifths of the members of each Chamber in principle for an ordinary constitutional amendment; if no such majority is reached, a joint committee is set up to put the new wording to the vote of both Chambers, in which case the proposal may be approved if the Upper Chamber (*Senado*) produces an absolute majority and the Lower Chamber (*Congreso de los Diputados*) a two-thirds majority.

Intra-parliamentary Protections of Constitutions against Change

Intra-parliamentary checks on constitutional changes may take other forms than special majorities. The powerful Constitutional Committee of the Finnish Parliament conducts pre-legislation, *ex ante*, inquiries into constitutional bills and other matters and reports to the Parliament on them. The Israeli Knesset recognises its special responsibility to secure that legislation is correctly and constitutionally passed, even though no special majorities are required for alterations to the Basic Laws. And the UK House of Lords Constitution Committee and the Joint Parliamentary Committee on Human Rights act in fairly non-political ways to scrutinise bills for constitutional and human rights implications, and advise each House of any concerns about constitutionality—and are taken seriously by the government and the two Chambers.

Extra-parliamentary Participation in Constitutional Change: Referendums and Intervening Elections

In a number of countries extra-parliamentary approval in a referendum may be required before a constitutional amendment can be implemented. Switzerland relies most strongly on direct democracy to legitimate constitutional amendments. The Parliament passes the amendments in the ordinary way— without the need for a qualified majority—and thereafter referendums (always binding) are held, and the approval of a majority of the voters both in the confederation and in a majority of the cantons is required, before the constitutional text can be amended. Unlike the position in Spain, noted below, these rather elaborate requirements have not prevented a number of constitutional reforms. Switzerland is exceptional in not requiring a special majority in Parliament for constitutional amendments. In most countries the referendum is additional to special majorities in the Parliament.

We have already noted the referendum requirement in Italy. In Spain certain reforms may be subject to a referendum if so requested by a tenth of the members of either Chamber. For more extensive and deep changes (*revisión total*) in Spain a two-thirds majority in each chamber is required, followed by an immediate dissolution of Parliament and a general election, and subsequent two-thirds majorities in each of the newly elected chambers. (We have already noted that in Finland too, amendment of the constitutional text requires a simple majority in Parliament, an election, and a two-thirds majority in the new Parliament: these requirements have not prevented constitutional amendments in Finland.) The stringent provisions in Spain have meant that constitutional amendment is almost impossible: only one (uncontroversial) amendment, on voting rights on accession to the EU, has been passed since the constitution came into effect in 1978. Cumulatively, then, requirements which make constitutional amendment too difficult may push a country to find alternative ways of changing the system, whether by adoption of a new Constitution or by less formal means that legislation.

In Germany special provision is made for territorial change to be subject to a referendum. For instance under the German Basic Law the accession of Länder to the Federal Republic, or provisions as to new boundaries for Länder are governed by a special procedure requiring a referendum. However, such changes may be—and on the reunification of Germany in 1990 were—achieved by special provisions. By contrast the Constitution of Spain does not lay down territorial boundaries for the Autonomous Communities, only a mechanism for their establishment, thus avoiding the need for amendment of the Constitution—a near impossibility in that country.

Terminological Requirement

Israel, unusually, imposes a terminological requirement on constitutional change. Basic Laws so-called can only be amended by Basic Laws, recognised as such by the Knesset. Certain specified Basic Laws may only be amended by laws passed by a majority of all Knesset members (that is not by a majority of those present and voting): the mildest form of entrenchment.

Acts of Exception

So far in this section of the chapter we have been mainly concerned with provisions for amendment of the main Constitutional text. However some constitutions allow for constitutional reform by legislation other than amendment to the constitutional text. In our study two countries, Finland and the Czech Republic, allow for the passing of Acts which, though inconsistent with the Constitutional text, will nevertheless be valid laws. Acts of Exception may be passed by the Finnish Parliament following constitutional-like procedures (simple majority, election, two-thirds majority) and these Acts effectively derogate from the constitutional text without actually amending it. In the Czech Republic Constitutional Acts may be passed which amend the constitution or, exceptionally, are valid though inconsistent with it. Generally however Acts of Exception are not permitted in written constitutions. In the German Basic Law it is expressly provided that no Acts may take effect that are inconsistent with the Basic Law—textual amendment is required; the same is the case in France where Bills deemed by the *Conseil constitutionnel* to be contrary to the Constitution can only be approved after amending the Constitution.

Rigid and Flexible Constitutions

The Indian Constitution has been amended 95 times since 1950; other Constitutions have been hardly amended at all: the Spanish Constitution only once since 1978. It could be inferred from this that the Indian Constitution is flexible, the Spanish Constitution rigid. Constitutions may however contain a combination of rigid and flexible procedural requirements—to have flexible rigidity: in India some constitutional amendments require special majorities in Parliament, and some require ratification by half of the states in addition: in practice this Constitution can be flexible or rigid, depending on the subject matter of change.

Quite apart from rigid, flexible or mixed procedural requirements, in some countries the culture and politics are such that formal constitutional amendment or change are achievable even if strict procedural requirements have to be complied with: this is the case in Germany, the Czech Republic, India and the Republic of South Africa in our study, in all of which there have been several constitutional amendments despite rigid looking procedural requirements. In other countries tradition, culture, politics and procedures combine to make formal change difficult or impossible, as in Italy and Spain: in such cases, as we have noted, alternative methods of change for example, by informal agreements between institutions or by practice, may be found. And lastly even where constitutional change is procedurally easy, pressures for change may be resisted by the political establishment and sections of the public. This culture may however change over time. From the 1940s until 1979 proposals to change constitutional arrangements in the UK (except in respect of local government) were strongly resisted for largely political, but also cultural reasons: since 1979 the politics have changed and the UK has experienced an avalanche of formal—and informal—constitutional change, including the Human Rights Act and devolution to Scotland, Wales and Northern Ireland in 1998 and since then a Freedom of Information Act, the establishment of the Supreme Court and many other provisions.

THE ROLE OF THE COURTS IN THE INTERPRETATION AND PROTECTION OF CONSTITUTIONS AND CONSTITUTIONAL PRINCIPLES

Most of the Constitutions in our study expressly grant to their Constitutional or Supreme Courts the power to check the constitutionality of laws, whether pre- or post-legislatively. In France the power of the *Conseil constitutionnel* has recently been enlarged. Until 2010 the jurisdiction of the *Conseil constitutionnel* was limited to pre-promulgation determination as to whether a new law would be compatible with the constitution. Since March 2010, after a constitutional amendment passed in 2008, the Conseil has the power to determine post legislatively, in a concrete case in front of a court, whether a law that has been promulgated is compatible with the constitution, and if not, to invalidate it.

In other countries, however, no express provision in a Constitution or a Basic Law confers on any of the courts the power to decide that a law is invalid as being contrary to the constitution. This is the position in Finland, for instance: the Supreme Court there, though exercising important constitutional jurisdiction from time to time, does not have or claim the power to invalidate unconstitutional legislation, though the Courts can disapply an ordinary Act and implement the Constitution directly in a particular case if there is an evident conflict between the Act and the Constitution.

In some countries by contrast, the courts or Supreme Courts have claimed jurisdiction to invalidate laws on their own initiative and have built up a significant jurisprudence on what is often termed 'constitutionalism'. The USA is the prime example: the decision in *Marbury v Madison*, in which the Supreme Court held a particular Act to be invalid as contrary to the Constitution, represents a high watermark in judicial creativity and development of concepts of the rule of law and constitutionalism. The Canadian Supreme Court has held that unwritten constitutional principles underlie constitutionalism, and that it is legitimate for the Court to use them to fill gaps in the Constitution. The Israeli

Supreme Court has also taken upon itself the power to determine matters of constitutionality in what has been called a 'constitutional revolution' (see the *United Mizrachi Bank Ltd v Migdal Cooperative Village* case). In India all courts may hear constitutional issues in ordinary cases and the higher courts and Supreme Court may strike down unconstitutional laws. And even in the UK, in the absence of a Constitution or Basic Law, the courts have developed principles of constitutionality, protected by requirements as to the use of very clear express terms in legislation that might override them, which effectively protect constitutional principles from inadvertent change.

Centralised and Decentralised Systems

Before we summarise the ways in which the courts in our study have developed constitutional principles, we need to note which courts have the power to do so. A distinction is to be made between centralised and decentralised arrangements for judicial review as to constitutionality. In most common law countries—and in Finland—the norm is for all courts to have the power to deal with constitutionality points as and when they arise—a decentralised system. However in the USA only the Supreme Court has the power to set aside a Federal law that is unconstitutional; and in the UK no court has the power to set aside an 'unconstitutional' statute, unless European law is at issue; if a statutory provision is incompatible with the rights in the European Convention on Human Rights then the higher courts may declare it to be incompatible, but may not set it aside.

In most civil law countries in our study the system is centralised—only the Supreme or Constitutional Court has the power to set aside unconstitutional laws: this is broadly the position in Italy, France (since the reforms of 2008) and Germany.

In Spain, by contrast, all courts may deal with issues of human rights as they arise, but not with other constitutional issues. In addition the Spanish Constitutional Court has a special jurisdiction under the *recurso de amparo* to deal with constitutional cases on the application of a citizen. The position is similar in Germany thanks to the so called *Bundesverfassungsbeschwerde.*

Constitutional and Human Rights Jurisprudence

Courts in many countries have developed a number of techniques for determining the constitutionality of laws. In the UK, for instance, there is a duty to interpret legislation so far as possible compatibly with constitutional principles that have developed in the common law, and with what have been termed 'Constitutional Acts'. In addition the Human Rights Act 1998 imposes a statutory duty on the courts to interpret legislation so far as possible compatibly with Convention rights.

Interpretation is a flexible concept, and many courts have 'interpreted' constitutional provisions as implying fundamental rights and liberties. As is well known the US Supreme Court has been very influential in the field of human rights and interpretation of the Constitution, for example, in desegregation of education, abortion, and via the Fourteenth Amendment (due process) extending much of the Bill of Rights to state and local government, especially in relation to freedom of speech and religion, and the criminal process.

The Swiss Federal Supreme Court has articulated a number of unwritten fundamental rights and liberties that are enforceable against federal and cantonal institutions, which are 'prerequisite for the exercise of other rights and liberties named in the Constitution or otherwise appear as essential components of the democratic federal *Rechtsstaat*'. That court has also derived certain rights (derivative rights) from the constitutional right to equality—many of them now codified in the latest constitution. Thus there has been an 'inflation of constitutional principles' in Switzerland since the revision of the constitution in 2000, though judicial development by the Federal Constitutional Court had been taking place over many years before then.

The French *Conseil constitutionnel* has changed its role since 1971 from being a defender of the Executive's powers against a potentially invasive Parliament to guarantor of rights and freedoms and promoter of French constitutionalism. The *Conseil constitutionnel* and the *Conseil d'État* interpret the French Constitution, the Declaration of the Rights of Man, and the Preamble to the 1946 Constitution in ways that now provide full human rights protection for citizens. The *Conseil constitutionnel* has also recognised the existence of 'general principles recognized in the legislation of the Republic'. Thus in 1971 for the first time the *Conseil constitutionnel* held a new bill that would interfere with freedom of association to be contrary to principles in the legislation of the Third Republic. The proposed legislation was therefore dropped. As a result of this decision, the Constitution of 1958 is no longer regarded as an exhaustive statement of all constitutional principles. Instead the expression 'block of constitutionality' is used to designate all constitutional rules and principles, including those extracted by the *Conseil* from sources other than the Constitution

The Italian Constitutional Court has developed a large jurisprudence of human rights based on references in the Constitution to the inviolable rights of man. It has also developed, among other things, a theory of implied limits in the constitution, a doctrine of 'the supreme principles of the constitution' which reflect the importance of human rights and democracy and a framework for regionalism in which the powers of Parliament and the national interest are upheld. Thus the Italian Constitution is more and more the product of judicial interpretation and less and less the political outcome of the sovereign will of the people and of its representatives.

In India, where all courts may hear constitutional issues in ordinary cases and the higher courts and the Supreme Court may strike down unconstitutional laws, the Supreme Court has developed a large jurisprudence on human rights and other issues, including some decisions having only prospective operation: the Court can examine whether an amendment changes the *basic structure* of the

Constitution and invalidate such an amendment if so. On the contents of this *basic structure* the judges have enumerated among other features the republican form of government, democratic polity, federal structure, judicial review and separation of powers.

The South African Constitutional Court has had to deal with resource allocation problems in relation to the social and economic rights that are included in the Constitution. It has developed a subtle case law on the subject. In the *Grootboom* case (2001) 900 women and children who were living in temporary shacks on a sports ground sought a court ruling imposing on government the duty to provide some form of shelter and services against the weather. The Constitutional Court held that the rationality of the government's housing strategy was defective because of the absence of any proper plan to deal with the temporary plight of those on the formal waiting list for state housing.

In other countries the jurisdiction of courts to adjudicate on constitutional issues is not based on interpretation of constitutional texts, but is inherent or else has been assumed by the courts. The Israeli Supreme Court has been particularly creative in developing constitutional principles. In the *United Mizrachi Bank Ltd v Migdal Cooperative Village* case the Court held that Basic Laws, once passed by the Knesset, have 'supra-legal' constitutional status which limits the powers of the Knesset, and that the Supreme Court had power to judicially review acts that were inconsistent with them. We have already noted that this case was regarded as a constitutional revolution. This 'revolution' was followed by a period of 'judicialisation' of government in the 1990s by the Supreme Court, which resulted from the inability of the Knesset to gather support for the enactment of a basic law on human rights—a judicial response to political stasis.

A strong example of judicial inventiveness is provided by the decision of the Czech Constitutional Court to treat human rights treaties as part of the 'constitutional order', despite the fact that only Acts are supposed to form part of that order according to the text of the Constitution. That Court has also set aside a constitutional act providing for an early election to the Chamber of Deputies as unconstitutional. By doing so it added the Czech Republic to the list of countries where the Supreme Court reserves the power to adjudicate on the legitimacy not only of ordinary acts but of *constitutional* acts.

CONSTITUTIONAL CHANGE AND EU MEMBERSHIP

A particular point for countries that have joined the European Union (formerly the European Communities) has been the effects of membership on their constitutional arrangements, in particular on their sovereignty, the powers of their Parliaments and protections of human rights provided in their Constitutions. While the case law of the European Court of Justice, notably *Costa v Enel* claims that EU law has primacy over the law of member states, including their constitutions, the courts and governing institutions of the member states do not all take the same view. The senior court in the UK (in the *Factortame* case) decided that the primacy of European law in the UK derived from the UK European Communities Act 1972—an ordinary Act of the UK Parliament—and thus from the law of the UK rather than, directly, from the EU. And the German Federal Constitutional Court (in the *Solange I* and *Solange II* cases of 1974 and 1986) recognised European law only on the basis that and as long as (*solange*) it ensures protection to basic rights comparable to that afforded by the German Basic Law. That court has also reserved to itself (in the Maastricht Treaty and Lisbon Treaty cases) the right to determine whether European law is ultra vires European institutions and whether it violates the constitutional identity of the state. Such difficulties have normally be resolved by amendments to the German Basic Law.

For some member states the act of joining the European Communities or Union required constitutional amendments; for others the process was much simpler. No constitutional amendment to the Italian Constitution was made when Italy joined the EC: the Italian Parliament approved ratification of the European Treaties by passing an ordinary, not a Constitutional, Act: when this was brought to the Constitutional court, the court upheld its consistency with Article 11 Italian Constitution; European norms always prevail in Italy (even if inconsistent with the Constitution or any other constitutional act), provided that they are not proven to infringe the 'supreme principles and inviolable human rights on which the Italian Constitutional order is based', the Court said. This is similar to the position reached in Germany in the *Solange* jurisprudence of the Federal Constitutional Court.

Some constitutional problems arose after countries joined the European Union. For instance the Constitution of Finland had to be amended to make clear that the Prime Minister for the Council of State (the name of the government) should represent Finland in the European Council, not the President. When the Treaty of European Union was found to compromise French national sovereignty a constitutional amendment was made and a new title on European Union was inserted; parliamentary control over European affairs was strengthened and further transfers of sovereignty need to be authorised individually if the *Conseil constitutionnel* identifies them.

The Spanish Constitution of 1978 anticipated Spanish membership of the European Communities. No constitutional amendment was required on accession. An uncontroversial amendment was later made to the Spanish Constitution to allow EU citizens to exercise voting rights in certain elections. Ordinary checks and balances in the Spanish system have not been sufficient to enable the Parliament to check the Executive in relations with Europe, and hence a Joint Lower-Upper Chamber Committee for the European Community has been established. Informal rather than statutory arrangements have been made for cooperation between the Spanish government and the Autonomous Communities, who do not have the power to represent Spain in the EU, unlike the position of the Länder in Germany. Issues to do with the participation of sub-national governments in EU affairs have also arisen in the UK: there the solution has been to agree Memorandums of Understanding between the UK and devolved executives which provide for inputs from devolved bodies in EU matters. The UK Parliament has also established a system of committees to scrutinise European laws, and a 'scrutiny reserve' which prevents British ministers from committing to EU laws before Parliament has completed its scrutiny procedures.

OTHER WAYS IN WHICH CONSTITUTIONS CHANGE

In many countries 'ordinary' laws are passed which, while not inconsistent with the Constitution and not passed in accordance with special procedures for constitutional amendment or change, nevertheless have important constitutional implications. This is true of course in the UK, New Zealand (save in relation to the term of Parliament and elections) and Israel where special procedures for constitutional change are not laid down. But in other countries too—Italy for example—important changes of a constitutional nature have been achieved without the need for compliance with special legislative procedures. Landmark statutes (for instance electoral laws) often prove to be acts of these kind.

Constitutional Conventions and Practice

The development of conventions and practice are the favoured methods for much change of a constitutional nature in the UK: examples include the passing of resolutions on ministerial responsibility to Parliament by the two Houses in 1996, and the development of concordats and memorandums of understanding between the UK and devolved levels of government. In Spain too, relations between the state and the Autonomous Communities and between those communities are negotiated and agreed. Other countries in which conventions are recognised as constitutional phenomena which affect the operation and change of constitutions include Canada (in relation to the roles of the Governor General and the Prime Minister, and the role of the Senate), the Czech Republic (where convention regulates whom the President should invite to be prime minister), India (on the exercise of presidential powers for example, of appointment of the Prime Minister and of state governors, on collective ministerial responsibility, and on judicial appointments), and the RSA (on the resolution of disagreements between the executive and the judiciary on bills the judiciary consider to be unconstitutional by compromise).

Constitutional practice plays a big role in Italy: for instance there has been a long-standing opinion that constitutional matters should be regulated by bipartisan initiatives and through consensual decision making processes only. This practice has however recently been contradicted by both main coalitions. Further, appointments to the Cabinet are in large part regulated by convention and not by the Constitution's textual provisions: and it is by effect of a consolidated early

402

practice that the Italian President has been able to retain control of the process of government formation starting from the consultations with the parliamentary groups until it is completed.

In Finland there are no constitutional conventions as such, but there are customary mechanisms or praxis such as respect for the autonomy of the Åland Islands, the use of advisory referendums and representation of Finland in the European Council.

In lieu of the Courts and Parliaments: Cultural, Political and Democratic Influences in Constitutional Change

We have already noted at a number of points the effect of political culture on the operation of a constitution. In some countries cultural changes, for instance as to the operation of the party system or of the style of politics—have important effects. Thus in Italy a new political culture—competitive rather than consociational—has transformed the system in recent years, leading to stronger and more stable Cabinets and a stronger premiership (but also to a more influential President, in dubious accordance with the constitution). This has been brought about by reform of the electoral system to a more majoritarian one, changes in party funding and other reforms such as those which introduced the direct election of mayors and Regions' presidents.

In some countries heavy reliance is placed on political and democratic processes as checks on constitutional change, and the courts have no power to regulate these processes. The paradigm example is the UK in which there are no externally imposed special procedural requirements for constitutional change, the courts will not intervene (save as to interpretation of constitutional laws) and reliance is placed on politicians and the political culture to secure the quality of Constitutional reforms. In New Zealand too, there is little by way of legal restriction on the passing of laws that alter the constitutional system, save that certain changes to the electoral system require the support of 75 per cent of the vote in the single party parliament. In Switzerland all federal statutes are by the Constitution binding on the federal courts including the Supreme Court: no court, not even the Supreme Court, has power to judicially review or set aside federal legislation. The role of control is instead given to the voters if the optional and binding referendum is invoked. In Finland too, no court has the power to set aside statutes for unconstitutionality. And yet in each of these countries the political system and the cultures of the population are driving forces which operate so as to influence constitutional innovation; they can inhibit if not prevent governments from proposing and parliaments from passing legislation that would be contrary to basic constitutional or democratic principles, although in other instances they might exert the opposite effect.

18

Towards a Theory of Constitutional Change

CARLO FUSARO AND DAWN OLIVER

I N THIS FINAL chapter we attempt to formulate some hypotheses based on our comparative analysis and the chapters before them, which might contribute to a theory of constitutional change. We shall formulate a set of general statements that *describe* how constitutions change (the title of this book, of course) in relation to certain characteristics, most of which were analysed in the previous section of this Part. We suggest that it should then be possible to *predict* how a given constitution can be expected to change, taking into consideration its specific traits. From the combination of description and prediction it may be possible to draw potentially useful lessons concerning one or other of the features which characterise a given constitution or concerning the procedures regulating (or not regulating) constitutional change.

At this point we need to clarify some terminology. The notion of 'constitution' which will be used in this section is substantive rather than formal. We shall not limit our discussion to the more or less comprehensive texts which most contemporary jurisdictions nowadays have, nor to the set of entrenched provisions which most jurisdictions also have. We shall be concerned with what we could more broadly call 'constitutional arrangements', that is to say the entire set of written or unwritten rules which regulate the functioning of the structures and powers of the state including national, sub-national and local relations, as well as the relations between society (individuals and groups, citizens and non-citizens) and public authorities.

The reason for this approach is that not all jurisdictions have a written constitution, not all jurisdictions which have written constitutional provisions have a single comprehensive text, and not all have entrenched provisions or entrenched provisions only. There is only one jurisdiction in our study which claims to have a single all-inclusive systematic constitutional text: this is positivist Germany. But even in this case one could doubt whether that text truly includes *all* the constitutional arrangements in the country (what about electoral laws, for instance?). In fact, in several jurisdictions (Israel, Italy, New Zealand, UK and the USA), electoral laws are regarded as of substantive constitutional importance and this could apply to Germany as well. But it is not only electoral law that, even if not contained in a constitution, is of substantive constitutional importance. Practically everywhere case law (at least the established interpretation of the constitutional provisions by the courts) can be and generally is regarded as an essential part of those constitutional arrangements.

In other words nowhere (with the partial exception of Germany) is constitutional law entirely codified, nor could it be.

This has to do with the fact that law in general is a product of societies which live and develop—as societies do. Constitutional law does so even more, whatever effort is made to crystallise or freeze it. For a positivist the basic rules of the constitutional arrangements of a polity are founded on a political basis, the Kelsenian *Grundnorm* at the top of the hierarchical sources of law. But that system itself, being different in detail in every country, can only be the explicit or evolutionary product of politics and power. To this extent constitutional law is structurally at the borderline between law and politics. This can be seen most clearly in those jurisdictions which have never had entrenched constitutional provisions (the UK, for example): but in all jurisdictions which have been presented in this book—with no exception—at least part of the constitution is 'political' in the sense of the concept of 'political constitution' applied in the UK chapter and introduced by Griffith: if all constitutions are 'political', what differentiates them is the ways in which and the extent to which they are political.

Based upon this we can more easily understand the reason why the notion of the 'living constitution' has been developed in the UK, in the USA, in Italy and indeed by scholars practically everywhere. There are different definitions of the concept: according to some the living constitution is nothing else than the constitution as it is effectively applied and interpreted in a given jurisdiction; according to others it is a summation of written and unwritten constitutional provisions, of how they have been interpreted and elaborated upon, of the practice of the authorities, and of the jurisprudence of the courts. This definition is very similar to the one proposed by Ackerman, according to whom in the USA the living constitution is made up of 'landmark statutes'—alias 'framework legislation' in the words of Griffin in this book—passed by the Congress, and of 'super-precedents' established by the courts.[1]

In other words the concept of 'living constitution' stems from recognition that any written legal text and any set of constitutional provisions, however introduced, at the end of the day produces different normative outcomes when the context in which they are embedded and to which they are to be applied significantly changes.

[1] B Ackerman, 'The Living Constitution', *Harvard Law Review*, 7, vol 120, May 2007, 1738–1812.

This does not mean that we support the idea that a written constitution (where it exists) can be subsumed in the unwritten or living constitution: the living constitution is not a constitution entirely *other* than the written one (it is not a *different* constitution); the living constitution is normally based upon the written one and builds upon it, although, under ordinary circumstances, it cannot be in conflict with it (unless it is not entrenched, like the New Zealand Constitution Act, or a conflict is authorised, for instance by Acts of Exception regulated by the constitution itself, as some jurisdictions provide for: see Finland and the Czech Republic). In this sense 'transformative constitutional moments' in the words of Ackermann should not be considered the functional equivalents of constitutional amendments: they are not necessarily legalised nor entrenched. However, as the US Supreme Court wrote almost 100 years ago

> 'provisions of the Constitution of the United States are not mathematical formulas having their essence in their form, but are living institutions transplanted from English soil. Their significance is not to be gathered simply from the words and a dictionary, but by considering their origin and the line of their growth'.[2]

Some kind of tension between the relevance of the text and the historical developments which have informally changed text-based institutions, as Griffin states in the US chapter, will always exist and a theory of constitutional change should be able to take it into account and possibly explain it.

When we refer to *how constitutions are changed* we primarily refer to changes which affect textual constitutional provisions, which mostly follow specific pre-established rules and are structurally 'political' in the sense that they are the product of the will of the legitimate authorities in the pursuit of a relatively transparent institutional strategy: in this sense they are formal.

However, when we refer to *how constitutions change* we refer to changes which *do not* affect textual constitutional provisions (whether any exist or not): such changes tend to be evolutionary or contextual; they have to do with the living constitution or living constitutional arrangements, they can be informal and political as well as the product of the decisions by the courts. They do not deny the relevance of the text but are the effect of the historical developments mentioned above.

Starting from this elementary conceptual framework, what set of hypotheses can we formulate as to how constitutions change and are changed, based upon the 15 jurisdiction-based chapters of this book?

TYPOLOGIES OF CONSTITUTIONS AND CONSTITUTIONAL CHANGE

There is a wide range of constitutions in this study: it includes common law and civil law systems; systems that are directly effective and systems that are indirectly

---

[2] *Gompers v US*, 233 US 604 [1914].

effective; evolutionary, unwritten, written codified; federal, semi-federal, unitary; autonomous, forming part of a supranational legal order, mono- or pluri-textual; evolutionary or entrenched; short or long; rigid or flexible. Some of these distinctions turn out to be less important than is commonly supposed. Others have significant effects on constitutions and how they change or are changed. We draw a number of propositions from comparison of the different natures of these constitutions.

Common law, Civil Law and Nordic Systems

Unlike civil law systems, some common law and Nordic systems tend to have in common that the courts may not hold Acts of the Parliament to be legally invalid. They rely on the political system to avoid unconstitutionality, and they protect the courts from the controversy that would be caused if judges had the power to refuse to give effect to Acts of the Parliament. It appears from the jurisdiction-based chapters in this book that the main difference between common law and civil law systems, the role of the judiciary and the relevance of judicial decisions as sources of law, has in part faded away, particularly in the area of constitutional change: nearly unanimously the chapters emphasise that the impact of Supreme Courts or Constitutional Courts everywhere extends beyond bare interpretation of constitutional texts or other laws (Canada, Czech Republic, EU, France, India, Israel, Italy, the Republic of South Africa, Spain, Switzerland, UK and the USA).

Directly and Indirectly Effective Constitutional Provisions

The distinction between directly and indirectly effective provisions applies to written and entrenched constitutional arrangements only; un-entrenched and in particular evolutionary constitutional legal provisions tend to be directly effective: if they are not directly effective they are not law. Entrenched constitutional arrangements may be directly effective only in part; this applies especially to newly established constitutional arrangements which may require some kind of subsequent implementing legislation to be passed. For instance it is not sufficient that the constitution purports to establish or require the establishment of bodies or authorities which did not exist before. They need to be established and able to exercise their powers by Act of Parliament, and if Parliament does not pass the statutory provisions which will regulate in detail how those bodies will be formed (elected in many cases) and how they might exercise their powers, they cannot exist. When this is the case, the Constitution may not give an accurate picture of reality. The case of the referendums provided for by the 1948 Italian Constitution and by the 1992 Czech Republic Constitution are clear examples of that: the referendum requirement was introduced by the 1948 Italian Constitution but was regulated only 22 years thereafter and the first referendum took place in 1974; in the Czech Republic after 18 years there still is no law regulating the referendum introduced by the Constitution. Another example is the set of constitutional amendments introduced in France in 2008, some of which the amending act itself stated would enter into force 'according to the provisions established by the laws necessary to their implementation'.

The impossibility of most written and entrenched constitution being entirely directly effective can influence the balance between *pouvoir constituant* and *pouvoir constitué*, in practice assigning to the various parliamentary majorities the power to decide whether to implement parts of the constitution or not; this might imply a more or less extensive gap between the written text of the constitution and effectively enacted constitutional arrangements and leaves very little if any room for the courts to fill the gap with their decisions even when they can be accessed.

The less a constitution is directly effective the broader is going to be the gap between the constitution on paper (more a project or a programme than a set of actual constitutional provisions) and the living constitution, the more its implementation will be at the disposal of the alternating political majorities which end up somehow endowed with a de facto constituent power.

Federal and Non-federal Constitutions

Whether a jurisdiction is 'federal' (in the loose sense that it includes sub-national entities with significant powers) or not influences constitutional changes both in content and in procedure. Some federal jurisdictions may prohibit constitutional changes which might seriously limit the role of sub-national entities (Germany); most establish procedures for amending the constitution which require the assent of a qualified majority of those sub-national entities. Both of these kinds of provisions affect the degree of rigidity of the constitution. This is the case in the European Union more than any other jurisdiction, but see also Canada, Germany and the USA.

Membership of a Supranational Legal Order

Membership of another 'constitutional' (supranational) order certainly is an additional major agent of constitutional change, impacting on parliamentary sovereignty, on the role of the judiciary and in general on the sources of law in a legal system. This is very clearly shown by all European states which are members of the EU as well as by signatories to the European Convention on Human Rights.

Pluri- and Mono-textual Constitutional Arrangements

The question whether constitutional arrangements are pluri- or mono-textual does not seem to influence the way those arrangements change significantly. The only jurisdiction which can effectively claim to be based upon a single textual constitution is Germany. Other constitutional arrangements which seem particularly 'compact' are Finland, India, RSA and the USA. But it would be hard to determine whether the extent and depth of change is any different in those countries than in the other jurisdictions which we have taken into consideration.

Evolutionary and Unentrenched Constitutions

Evolutionary and unentrenched constitutions can be, paradoxically, both the most difficult and the easiest to change (see the case of the UK). They are politically difficult to change because the constitution is made up of values and principles which are deeply embedded in society and the political and institutional culture which are their direct and immediate historical expression; while in theory they are easy to change because any political majority can change the constitution, the existence of and widespread acceptance of some 'fundamental principles' can make it practically impossible to legislate for change that challenges those principles (as is the case in the UK).

Short or Long, Framework or Details

Textual constitutions are long or short in the sense that they include a Bill of Rights or not (nowadays they mostly do, but Israel is an exception); further, constitutional arrangements in general may regulate the functioning of public authorities in detail or lay down framework provision only; framework provisions may be very detailed or general.

Some constitutions, for instance, deliberately leave Government–Parliament relations (or the form of government, which determines who runs the country) indeterminate and not regulated in detail: see Czech Republic, France, India and Italy, not to mention the UK. Germany, Israel, RSA and Spain could be regarded as intermediate cases as the formation of a new government and the substitution of a new government for another within a legislative term are now regulated in various ways. The USA and Switzerland are completely different cases, neither of the two being a parliamentary democracy.

In general there is an issue concerning the amount of indeterminacy which a set of constitutional arrangements can feature: indeterminacy allows room for variable and potentially changeable interpretations, but this is an outcome which might be desired or not and which strongly affects the normative capacity of the constitution and the modes of change. Some elasticity is needed and sought after; an excess of elasticity can be dangerous (see the case of the USA): the issue concerns what is to be left to politics and what to law, how much you are willing to trust politicians and how much you are willing to trust courts, and the delicate balance between the two.

Levels of Rigidity and Eternity Clauses

On paper the most rigidly entrenched set of constitutional arrangements is the EU treaties. Although the Lisbon Treaty may have slightly softened the procedure for matters included in Part III of the Treaty on the Functioning of the EU, as far as truly constitutional matters are concerned amending the treaties is an extraordinarily complex *integrated* procedure. This includes requirements for a unanimous decision by a conference of all the member states' governments as well as ratification by each state. In many if not most cases member states will have to amend their constitutions, which in some instances require that the final decision be submitted to a referendum: the cases of Ireland and, in the future, possibly of the UK are examples. Similar requirements are not limited to EU member states: another very rigid entrenchment system is that established by Article V of the US constitution.

Does comparative constitutional practice indicate that there is a connection between the level of *formal* rigidity and the quantity and quality of formal constitutional changes in a given jurisdiction (which determine its *substantive* rigidity)? Although the EU case seems to indicate the opposite (in spite of all the procedural obstacles the Treaties have been changed often and it seems that they will be again even in the near future), constitutional rigidity does impact on the quantity and quality of formal constitutional changes. It should be emphasised, however, that the rigidity of a constitution is not a function of the established procedures only, but of a much broader context (external, internal, related to the political system and to the culture—political, constitutional, general—of society): this explains why the very same procedural restraints might make a constitution rigid here and (relatively) flexible there. The degree of substantive rigidity of a constitution is important because it affects other, informal, ways of pursuing change.

Many constitutions exclude some basic principles or arrangements (central-sub-national relations, the republican nature of the jurisdiction, a chosen set of human rights, the amendment clause itself, for instance) from even the possibility of change. These provisions may be 'eternity clauses'. The German constitution is a prime example. By doing so they enhance the distinction between *pouvoir constituant* and *pouvoir constitué* (and accordingly impose limits on parliamentary sovereignty, majoritarianism and politics).

THE REGIONAL, INTERNATIONAL AND CULTURAL CONTEXTS OF CONSTITUTIONAL CHANGE

The participation of states in regional and other international organisations may affect constitutional change. (European membership is considered in the next section of this chapter.) These organisations constitute an external impetus for change, although international treaties on human rights are often recognised as having a special status within the sources of law of the various jurisdictions as well, at least in the sense that national courts tend to be influenced by the ways in which the main international tribunals (that is the ECtHR court, but one could also mention the Inter-American Court of Human Rights) interpret human rights protection in these international instruments.

Another kind of contextual change which can directly or indirectly impact on the constitutional arrangements of a country and have a transformative effect on them can be major changes in its international borders: its division into more than one single jurisdiction (as in the case of the Czech and Slovak Republics) or its unification into one jurisdiction (as in the case of Germany after reunification, or of Italy in the nineteenth century).

In several instances the effective pursuit of significant and problematic constitutional changes has become possible because of a shift in the balance of international relations and of the world's political power structure: certainly this has twice been the case for entire classes of states, first in the 1970s (following the so called *detente*) which paved the way to new constitutional arrangements in the Mediterranean (Greece, Portugal and Spain); and second in an even more spectacular way when the fall of the Berlin Wall and the end of the Soviet Union paved the way to a democratisation wave which was followed by a generation of new constitutional arrangements from Namibia to Russia, from Finland to the RSA. For the countries with which this book is concerned, it impacted on the constitutional arrangements of the Czech Republic, Finland, Germany and the RSA and on some of what had previously been established interpretations of the Italian constitution.

Constitutional developments around the world and the constitutional courts' jurisprudence of some more influential jurisdictions can be regarded as triggers of domestic constitutional changes as well: several authors signal the growth of the references to comparative law and data by courts, although in only one constitution is there a specific provision which allows the courts to take into consideration the jurisprudence of foreign supreme courts (RSA) and although the risk of instrumentalism also exists (especially through selective picking of cases).

Foreign influence (in the sense of influence by one or more other States) has been more blatant in the past (see after World War II the cases of Italy, Germany and Japan); but it has still been relevant in more recent times, although exerted in softer forms and mostly through international organisations, in a sort of pluralist way (see, in Europe, the role of the Venice Commission of the Council of Europe in coaching new democracies after the fall of the Berlin Wall, for instance). This is also the case for nearly all post-conflictual constitutionalisation processes as part of nation building and peace consolidation strategies in the last 15 years all over the world (from Timor Leste to Burundi to Iraq).

Cultural factors in constitutional change should not be under-estimated: the search for what one of our authors has defined as 'constitutional perfection' (Boyron, referring to France) is nothing else than a tendency to over-estimate the normative effects of legal provisions. This is a rather frequent tendency within divided societies experiencing some difficulty in running their public affairs, as in the French situation until the fifth Republic and the Italian situation after World War II.

THE EU CONTEXTS OF CONSTITUTIONAL CHANGE

We have already emphasised that participation in supranational organisations and in particular membership of the EU affects constitutional change—except where the most fundamental and unamendable principles which each national constitutional arrangement features are at stake. In reality even this exception applies more often in theory than in practice as the EU's own 'constitutional' provisions basically protect the same principles and values as do those of the constitutions of member states. Membership of the EU affects constitutional change because in matters devolved in the EU treaties EU law, according to the European Court of Justice, trumps not only statutory and (where it exists) common law but also entrenched domestic provisions. Thus EU law can and does effectively claim to change each member state's constitutional arrangements and—save for the right to secede from the Union which each state is entitled to—establishes what could be considered a kind of integrated *monist* jurisdiction. This is the case in spite of the fact that most constitutional arrangements seem to pay lip service to a dualist conception of the relations between internal and international law.

In practice the jurisdictions of 'dualist' EU member states are still truly dualist in relation to international law other than European law, which is in reality constitutional rather than international in nature, or 'supranational' if one is looking for an adjective other than 'constitutional'.

In this respect the constitutional arrangements of each EU member state belong to a different category as far as EU law is concerned, as compared to those of non-members. The constitutional arrangements of member states are at least in part subject to a substantially higher set of constitution-like arrangements, in the establishing of which each state takes part on an equal footing. These European arrangements are protected by a special court according to a centralised model of judicial control; this court pays attention to the goal of integration rather than to the 'original intent' of the first treaties. There remains however the lack of a so-called *Kompetenze-kompetenz* in EU 'constitution-like' arrangements. This refers to the fact that it is not the Union which decides which competences it shall enjoy: its competences must all be granted or devolved to it by member states. However, the ECJ does claim the sole right to determine whether a particular competence has been granted to the EU: it is not, according to the ECJ, for the member states' courts to do so. Is this consideration enough to substantiate the assertion that member states keep both legal and de facto sovereignty despite their membership of the EU? It is reasonable to entertain serious doubts about that.

THE DRIVERS OF CONSTITUTIONAL CHANGE

Constitutional change can be influenced and/or determined by both domestic and external actors and factors. In quite a few cases comparative research shows that change has been brought about not by one only but by a combination of the actors considered below: for instance, formal constitutional amendments have followed more or less creative interpretations by governmental bodies and/or the courts; in other cases landmarks statutes have followed referendums on constitutional issues.

The People

The people may influence constitutional change directly via referendums. Examples of countries where this is or has been provided for are France, Italy, New Zealand, RSA and, occasionally, the UK. Switzerland is the strongest case, providing as it does for compulsory and binding referendums. The people also influence constitutional change via elections. This is particularly the case if and when the voters elect a strong majority or a presidential leader for such an extended period of time that they may enforce a new interpretation of constitutional provisions or establish firm conventions, thus paving the way for 'transformative constitutional moments' in the words of Ackerman noted above. The USA case during the *New Deal* is an example: then constitutional change came about through the President and the Congress during Franklin D Roosevelt four terms, a form of what Griffin calls 'the constituent power of the people expressed in democratic elections'. But that power can also be mobilised in support of presidential actions in the absence of appropriate deliberation (as in the post 9/11 developments in the US form of government).

The People and the Courts

The people and the courts within those jurisdictions which allow individuals direct access to the courts to claim judicial review of legislation and constitutional amendments clearly influence constitutional change. Examples include Germany with its *Bundesverfassungsbeschwerde* and Spain with its *recurso de amparo*, but another excellent one is the ECJ in the EU system.

Legislative Assemblies

Legislative assemblies effect or influence constitutional change by passing landmark statutes—whether by special majorities or not—and in some cases by passing 'Acts of Exception' as in Finland, or Constitutional Acts as in the Czech Republic. In both countries such Acts will be valid despite any inconsistency with the terms of the Constitution. Legislative assemblies may also undertake forms of pre-legislative constitutional review as in Finland whose Constitutional Committee has a formal role in relation to constitutional bills, and in the UK where the

House of Lords Constitution Committee and the Joint Committee on Human Rights scrutinise bills for constitutional or human rights implications and report to Parliament on their findings.

Legislative assemblies can also significantly alter the working of the constitution by their Standing Orders if relations between the government and Parliament are not regulated by the Constitution or by other ordinary law in detail. This is the case in Italy, New Zealand and the UK, for example.

The Courts

Almost everywhere the courts have the power to alter the operation of the constitution by their jurisprudence: the most striking case, apart from the US Supreme Court of John Marshall (in *Marbury v Madison*[3]), is probably the Israeli Supreme Court's decision in *United Mizrachi Bank Ltd*[4] with which it established its own power to review legislation (including Basic Laws); in that case the Court filled a legislative vacuum showing that weak parliaments tend to pave the way to strong courts. By contrast, courts tend to restrain themselves when the doctrine of parliamentary sovereignty and majority rule are supported by effective and prompt legislation.

Spain (only one constitutional amendment in 32 years: 1978–2010) provides a striking example of change by judicial interpretation of the Constitution so as to strengthen the protection of rights. But Canada, the Czech Republic, India, Italy, Switzerland and the USA have also experienced judicial constitutional creativity, often providing examples of how necessary change can take place in other ways when textual changes to written constitutions appear hardly possible.

In both Italy and Spain the constitutional courts have been decisive in determining the respective legislative powers of the central State and the Regions or *Comunidades Autonomas*.

Governments and their Leaders

Governments and especially their leaders can also influence constitutional change by virtue of the practices they adopt, in particular in relation to the indeterminacies in written constitutional arrangements concerning top governmental relations and powers. A strong example is provided by the USA during the period of office of George Bush II when the modus operandi of the Presidency was changed unilaterally by the President as well as the role of the Vice-President.

---

[3] *Marbury v Madison* (1803) 1 Cranch 137.
[4] *United Mizrachi Bank Ltd v Migdal Cooperative Village*, 49 (4) PD 221, 272 (1995) (see English translation at http://elyon1.court.gov.il/files_eng/93/210/068/z01/93068210.z01.pdf.

Supra-national Institutions

European integration is the most influential ongoing constitutional transformative force which affects member states. It does so in a variety of ways. On the one hand European law trumps domestic law thus subverting the previous hierarchies of sources of law in all member states. On the other hand the decisions of the ECJ (in indirect coordination with the decisions of the ECtHR Court) have step by step raised the standards of protection of human rights in each member state jurisdiction to the level of the highest in each area. Further, executive–legislature relations within most member states have been affected by membership of the EU: the matters devolved to the Union have been transferred from the competences of the national Parliaments to the primary competence of the Council (on proposals of the Commission and with the consent of the European Parliament) where the national governments are the decision makers who thus de facto gain power indirectly within the domestic system from their parliaments. On the other hand, the Lisbon Treaty acknowledges a new and potentially more effective role for the 27 national parliaments in relation to the application of the principles of subsidiarity and proportionality (see Protocol 1 'On the role of National Parliaments in the EU'). This provision may in fact allow future changes in the constitutional arrangements of each member state in favour of the domestic parliaments. Of course the different ways European integration has affected and affects the domestic constitutions of the member states has a lot to do with the different traditions, cultures and legitimising doctrines prevailing in each jurisdiction. Similarly, participation in NAFTA (North American Free Trade Agreement) may have brought about changes to Canada in the magnitude of order of a change to its constitutional arrangements.

CONSTITUTIONAL CHANGE AND LEGITIMISING THEORIES

The roles of internal and external actors in constitutional change which we have just discussed are related to the most influential legitimising theories. Here we consider those theories.

The General Concept of Sovereignty

Based upon contemporary constitutionalism, 'sovereignty' seems to have become a partially outdated principle. It is only in theory that an ultimate truly sovereign authority may be recognised in the jurisdictions studied in this book. In practice all constitutional arrangements are built in such a way as to ensure some sharing of sovereignty. This is not just a matter of checks and balances and of separation of powers: the fact is that no internal authority has a final say and exercises ultimate authority by itself. This is particularly clear if one thinks about the role of parliaments and the role of the courts. Further, no domestic jurisdiction is truly free from external influences or even from the penetration of legally binding provisions within the domestic field which come from a (supposedly) different legal order. This is particularly evident in the case of the EU, but also in the case of treaty obligations in New Zealand relating to the Maori, and international obligations in Finland relating to the Åland Island Settlement or international obligations in Canada stemming from the NAFTA Treaty. In fact, many constitutional arrangements include provisions which formally open the internal order to international law, both customary and treaty based.

It is also true that very recently a tendency has developed in some EU member states, Germany in particular, to counterbalance their openness to integration with a re-affirmation of so called 'counter-limits' or 'structural guarantees' that is meant to ensure that the essence or core of national sovereignty is somehow protected, for instance by the recognition of the participatory rights of their parliaments as the only truly legitimate representatives of the people's sovereignty. It is early to determine how the new involvement of all member states' Parliaments in the evaluation of subsidiarity as established by the Lisbon Treaty will impact on this matter. The recent trend in the decisions of the Supreme Court of the USA to reject comparative law also suggests concern about 'integration' of legal systems.

Parliamentary Sovereignty

One can register some ups and downs of parliamentary sovereignty, which is majoritarian by definition in the countries in this study. Parliamentary sovereignty generally tends to be restrained either legally or politically more and more as international law, European law, and rigidly entrenched constitutional law increase in influence. This is the case even in countries where parliamentary sovereignty has been a fundamental doctrine, as in Israel and the UK, and to a lesser extent in New Zealand. In fact, parliamentary sovereignty seems to be intrinsic to a majoritarian rather than a counter-majoritarian approach to constitutional change. But as we have seen it has been called in question, not only in the UK but also in the jurisprudence of the German *Bundesverfassungsgericht* (BVG) by membership of the EU. (The position in Denmark is similar.) The supremacy of Parliament has been affected and the application of the doctrine of implied repeal has been altered in the UK thanks to the cumulative jurisprudence of the ECJ.

In some jurisdictions the constitutional legitimacy of new legislation is challenged through pre- rather than post-legislative processes; in France, until 2008–2010, the *Conseil constitutionnel* would decide on the constitutional consistency of new legislation *only before* it entered into force. Once promulgated such laws could not be challenged. (Now they can, although with some limitations: another example of the trend away from traditional parliamentary supremacy.) In other countries intra-parliamentary challenges on grounds of unconstitutionality may be possible (but no extra-parliamentary challenge is available). The Constitutional Committee of the Finnish Parliament and some of the select committees of the UK Parliament have roles in intra-parliamentary, pre-legislative scrutiny. These are all cases in which parliamentary sovereignty as opposed to constitutional review of legislation by the judiciary is the legitimating theory of the constitution.

Sovereignty of the People versus the Last Word to the Courts or ... Pouvoir Constituant versus Pouvoir Constitué

Along with the waning of parliamentary sovereignty, the last 50 years have also witnessed less and less scope for the exercise of *pouvoir constituant* (conceived as unrestrained by definition, as the 'will of the people'), even in cases of regime change or the establishment of substantially and formally new constitutional arrangements. The cases of the RSA and of the Czech Republic seem to confirm this. The *pouvoir constituant* may have not disappeared, but it tends to be exercised so as to respect pre-existing procedures in making formal constitutional changes. It is as if the *pouvoir constituant* tries to hide itself behind established rules in search of a screen of legality: a substantive *pouvoir constituant* in the shape of *pouvoir constitué*, one could say, conceived and interpreted as a useful tool for achieving smoother and more peaceful regime changes, the expression of a more consensual way to pursue even the most radical changes. To this extent the case of the RSA is a paradigm.

In a striking Spanish case the Constitutional Court stated that Parliament cannot pass rules which purport to impose on the courts one of several possible interpretations of the Constitution: by doing so it would exercise a *pouvoir constituant* instead of a legitimate *pouvoir constitué*. Also in India and Italy the Supreme Courts accurately differentiate *pouvoir constituant* from *pouvoir constitué*: an effective way to reassert their roles, for instance when they assert their power to test the constitutional legitimacy of constitutional amendments. By doing so these courts rather than being instruments of change, adopt a conservative approach to interpretation and act as the ultimate guarantors of the constitutional arrangements then in force.

By contrast, the US Supreme Court decisions concerning what it recognises to be a 'political question' can be regarded as a form of respect for the role of Congress: the recognition that not everything to do with the management of collective decisions and policies can be regulated by the law and made justiciable. It is not always possible, nor wise nor legitimate, to test such decisions against a previously defined standard which a court might enforce: the implicit admission is that all constitutional arrangements include a 'political' element, in the absence of which the clash between electorally legitimised (political) and nominated, only indirectly legitimised (judicial), authorities may become difficult to avoid.

Representative versus Direct Democracy

A number of theories deal with voters' participation in the process of amending or revising the constitution as well as in the initial procedure by which a new constitution is adopted. The debates are between the claims to sovereignty of the People directly, of Parliament or of the People as the electors of Parliament. The French tradition after World War II, for instance, is for giving the final say to the People in a referendum (as was the case in 1946 and 1958 and even before). The Irish Constitution of 1937 can be amended only if approved in a referendum. Under the Swiss constitution voters can actually initiate and decide on constitutional amendments. Other countries have different traditions which may or may not include direct voter involvement. Italy's Constitution of 1948 was approved by a Constituent Assembly, although directly elected; the German *Grundgesetz* of 1949 was approved by a similar body the members of which had been nominated by the assemblies of the Länder; voters have had no direct say in changing constitutional arrangements in Finland, Israel, RSA and the USA and they may not in Italy either, depending on the level of parliamentary consensus granted to the amendment.

The Spanish procedure according to which a 'total' revision of the constitution requires the dissolution of Parliament and a second vote by the new Parliament is another way of involving semi-direct voters' participation in constitutional change decisions. A similar procedure is followed in Finland unless, as in Italy, the amending constitutional act is approved by a large majority of the members of Parliament (two-thirds) after five-sixths have declared it urgent.

Let us return to the Swiss case: the Swiss approach to amending the constitution foresees a bottom-up procedure which establishes a peculiar and distinct balance between the role of voters and the role of Parliament. In particular, what has happened in Switzerland seems to show that where voters have a particularly significant say in legislative decisions including constitutional provisions the role of Parliament can be protected only through a consensual approach designed to involve a large majority of political parties. By contrast, according to the interpretation of the 1958 French Constitution, the President, on the proposal of the government, may call a referendum on constitutional projects affecting the organisation of 'public powers': in this way voters have a final say, but only if the executive decides so. The voters may only participate at the end of a top-down process which is conceptually the opposite of what happens in the Swiss Confederation. In fact there have been only two such referendums in France. However, in general it is up to the President in France to decide *not* to submit a constitutional amending Act to the voters and to submit it to a joint session of the two Chambers instead: in this case the Act is approved when two-thirds of the members vote in favour.

All this raises the fundamental constitutional issue of the relationship between direct and representative democracy (and their respective sources and procedures): this is an issue that has also frequently been raised in relation to the selection of the top governmental bodies, which has de facto become a power that is exercised by voters rather than by Parliaments, enhancing a more or less strong populist trend in many established parliamentary democracies: this could be the case of Italy after the 1993 electoral reforms which have paved the way to local, regional and national populist leaders (starting with Mr Berlusconi).

Grundnorm Setting

In some instances the legitimating force for the establishment of a new set of constitutional arrangements has been the previous setting of one or more *Grundnorms* bestowed by some external or internal force. This could be the case of some constitutional arrangements which have been historically founded upon a basic decision other than the approval of a new constitution: for instance in the RSA (the so-called *interim* Constitution), but also in the cases of Germany, Italy and Japan after World War II, and France in 1958 (the de Gaulle cabinet drafted its project on the basis of a set of basic principles and directives approved by Parliament). Similarly there are constitutional arrangements based upon international treaties (treaty based constitutions): first of all the EU, but also New Zealand because of the constitutional relevance of the Waitangi Treaty.

Majoritarian and Counter-majoritarian Theories

There is currently a debate about the relative merits and legitimacy of majoritarian and counter-majoritarian theories. According to majoritarian theory what the majority of elected representatives or of voters desires should be implemented because it is democratic to do so. These theorists object to restrictions on the powers of the majority as being 'counter-majoritarian' and therefore anti-democratic.

On another approach if what the majority desires is, for instance, discrimination against sections of society, then to give effect to such a desire would not respect human rights: modern democracy is not only about the will of the majority of 'the people', but requires equal respect for all individuals within the jurisdiction; therefore it would not be compatible with the principles of democracy to enact discriminatory legislation. This means that even in a democracy based upon majority rule there are some restraints on its application.

The issue raises questions in relation to constitutional change and consensus. Should formal constitutional change be based upon a bipartisan approach? Acceptance of this idea is widespread and many pay lip service to it: after all it makes sense not only because it is in the nature of constitutional arrangements to regulate the very basic political and civil relations within a community no matter which political majority runs it at any given time, but also because it can hardly be justifiable to operate on the basis that each alternating majority may customise the constitution to implement its strategies of the moment. However, even if there is a general trend towards bipartisanship in constitutional change, in fact there are as many examples of majoritarian as of bipartisan constitutional changes, in some instances led by the governmental authorities: France is the most striking case, the UK is another. The bipartisan or majoritarian nature of changes is determined by who supports the projected change and who does not.

But it is also possible for constitutional changes to be non-partisan in relation not to who proposed and voted them, but to their intrinsic content: this was the case with the UK Human Rights Act and the Freedom of Information Act. Both were in many senses 'altruistic' changes, neither was particularly popular with the public, but the Labour Party had committed to them in opposition because they were convinced, or at least their leaders were convinced, that this was the right thing to do. Their legitimacy flowed from the fact that they were introduced by a government with a majority of the seats in Parliament though far less than a majority of the votes cast in the election, from the fact that they were altruistic policies and from the fact that they had been promised in the election manifesto of the Labour Party. So one could say that these constitutional changes were at the same time majoritarian because proposed and voted by the majority, but also non-partisan as they were not in the sole interests of the party in power. (However, the legitimacy of the UK Human Rights Act is not embedded in the British culture and there are many calls for its repeal, particularly where the Act leads the courts to uphold the rights of unlawful immigrants and failed asylum seekers who have been convicted of serious criminal offences, or suspected foreign terrorists not to be deported where this would interfere with their family lives or expose them to torture in the country to which they are deported.)

CONSTITUTIONAL CHANGE AND CONFLICTING LEGAL DOCTRINES

Positivism

Apart from legitimising theories, legal doctrine, notably positivism, has been influential in determining how to deal with the issue of constitutional change. As we have seen in some jurisdictions a strictly positivist approach has been adopted: in particular the example of the German constitutional arrangements could be regarded as a case of *constitutional codification* and of *extreme legal positivism*. All constitutional law is expected to be codified within the comprehensive text of the *Grundgesetz*. Clarity and transparency are some of the advantages of this approach.

In other jurisdictions positivism is reflected in the idea that as long as the established procedures for constitutional change, are respected (whether the change is to be by amendment or a broader revision of the constitution) any constitutional change is feasible. In this case legitimation and legality tend to coincide. It is, however, very difficult to find jurisdictions where this kind of positivism is wholly applied: everywhere there is a sense that there is a set of principles and values which do in fact go beyond what a strictly positivist approach would allow and which ought to be respected.

Contemporary positivism in fact tends to be more subtle and less strict: it takes into account both the main features of constitutionalism and the wisdom of going beyond legalism and taking a holistic approach to institutional arrangements. This is particularly true in constitutional matters. *Legal institutionalism* originated as a reaction against the excesses of formalism: this is true of the institutionalism associated with Santi Romano[5] and Maurice Hauriou,[6] but also of the more recent neo-institutionalist theorists.[7] As an anti-formalist stance, institutionalism is an attempt at overcoming a too narrow conception of law and of legal science, the one essentially equated with the command of the 'political superior,' or state, the other understood as a purely logical and systematic exercise in norms and institutions. Legal positivism is such a conception: it forestalls any recourse to strong normative (moral, political) arguments and dismisses as pointless any taking into account of the social context in which legal norms are set. Opposition to this view asserts the normative, and hence the legal value of social facts. Institutionalism proves particularly helpful in explaining constitutional practice, the more so in relation to constitutional arrangements which are not regulated in detail (for instance the form of government and the relations between Parliament and Government).

Neo-constitutionalism

In recent years a *neo-constitutionalist* approach has developed which falls between natural law and positivism approaches: it implies that constitutional arrangements inevitably feature provisions with a specific value-oriented content. Neo-constitutionalism can be defined as a series of principles and values that are meant to shape the constitutional arrangements of a specific jurisdiction. Constitutionalism is an influential and demanding normative theory about the content of constitutional arrangements and therefore, in most instances, about the content of constitutional texts. This content (in terms of principles, values and basic solutions instrumental to pursue them) does change over time as any product of society does; in the case of constitutionalism the content has changed incrementally.

Among the contents of modern constitutionalism one could list: the protection of human rights; the sovereignty of the people along with significant limits to majority rule; the autonomy of the political from the religious sphere (in order not to discriminate against anyone because of their religious belief); some degree of separation of powers; and openness towards international law. Further,

---

[5] S Romano, *L'ordinamento giuridico* (Firenze, Sansoni, 1946).

[6] M Hauriou, *Aux sources du droit: le pouvoir, l'ordre et la liberté* (Paris, Blout & Gay, 1933).

[7] N MacCormick and O Weinberger, *An institutional theory of law: new approaches to legal positivism* (Dordrecht, Reidel, 1986).

modern constitutionalism seems to require that the main features listed above shall be entrenched or protected in some way, for instance by principles of statutory interpretation and legal presumptions in favour of principles of constitutionalism; that procedural entrenchment processes shall be all inclusive and negotiated; and that permanent maintenance of the constitutional arrangements shall be ensured as a necessary function. Our research seems to emphasise the advances made by 'constitutionalism' as a true 'ideology of the constitution' according to which constitutional arrangements should operate so as to ensure a certain limitation of power and the basic protection of individual and collective rights.

CONSTITUTIONAL HYPOTHESES

As promised, here we attempt to sum up the outcome of our research in a coherent set of hypotheses which refer to the set of assumptions we started with in our introductory chapter and which we hope might contribute to the future development of a theory of constitutional change.

(1)   No constitution, no contemporary set of constitutional arrangements, is solely written, nor solely unwritten nor solely evolutionary.

(2)   All constitutions are pluri-textual.

Although only some constitutions openly identify themselves as pluri- or multi-textual (the Czech Republic) or are considered as such because they have never had a (relatively comprehensive) constitutional text (Canada, New Zealand, Finland until 1999), all constitutions are pluri-textual in the sense that their constitutional arrangements are based upon the constitution *plus* other entrenched Acts (Czech Republic, Italy) or in the sense that, apart from the constitution and other entrenched Acts, they also feature landmark statutes dealing with constitutional matters; even Germany is not an exception to this proposition.

(3)   Constitutional continuity is valued more than ever.

After World War II an era of constitutional continuity in place of constitutional breaches began worldwide. This is manifested most strikingly in regime changes (in some cases even revolutionary changes). Thus Czechoslovakia looked back to its 1919 Constitution when the Communist regime collapsed, and the Czech Republic did so again when the formerly unified states separated into the Czech and Slovak Republics. Continuity has formed part of the effort to avoid violent political change: it suggests contemporary constitutionalism requires that even regime change should be regulated and take place in a legal way; constitutional breaches are less and less frequent, and they are regarded as something to refrain from whenever possible as they are often accompanied by potentially costly if not violent conflicts.

(4)   Constitutional breaches can be avoided where incremental constitutional change is possible.

The experience of the 1958 French fifth Republic confirms that adjustment and adaptation through relatively frequent incremental changes is possible: in other words, when constitutional maintenance is ensured, there is then less ground for either breaching the current constitutional arrangements or for 'interpretation twisting'. If constitutional arrangements are allowed to evolve through incremental adaptation both rupture and forced interpretation are less likely. The French case is particularly telling because of its previous constitutional traditions (more than a dozen constitutions after the Revolution until 1958).

(5)   No constitution is totally rigid nor totally flexible.

The rigidity or flexibility of constitutions does not depend solely upon the provisions regulating the amendment or revision process, nor whether their provisions are entrenched or not. In fact no constitution is totally rigid nor totally flexible. All constitutions allow for margins of interpretative adaptation, however detailed their textual provisions might be. But the more the provisions of a constitution are open-ended the more room there will be for diverse and even opposing interpretations by both political bodies and the courts. (The powers of the President of the Republic in Italy are a good example.)

(6)   All constitutions are 'political' to some extent.

While the UK constitution is said to be 'political' and this is commonly regarded as an exception, in practice arrangements in all constitutions include parts which are less regulated than others, leaving room for the elected and representative bodies in particular to exercise their powers and interpret their role with some degree of relative freedom, according to their political strategies (see the indeterminate definition of Government–Parliament relations in many constitutions of parliamentary democracies, for example, Italy or the Czech Republic).

(7)   All constitutions change continuously.

However much the 'sanctity' of a constitution may be recognised, constitutions are subject to change; they have always been and this is even more true in recent times. A constitution which may not change or adapt–one could claim—does not effectively serve its purpose and the values and principles it is based upon. Formal changes to a constitutional law or text are normally regulated by requirements for special majorities in the Parliament, intervening elections, referendum or other means. If change is regulated so strictly that it is impossible to achieve, those pressing for it will always seek and often find, different, informal ways. This has been the situation in Spain, for instance. The level of substantive constitutional rigidity, in the sense of de facto inability to permit formal change, determines to what extent resort is had to creative interpretation by both representative bodies and the courts, or to informal negotiation between constitutional institutions. Any set of constitutional arrangements tends to evolve continuously either formally or informally (the American and the UK examples are among the most striking).

(8)   One of the most influential constituent choices is how to balance rigidity and flexibility.

One of the most delicate decisions in constitution making is to find the appropriate balance for the country in question between rigidity and flexibility. This balance will depend upon matters such as the relationships between the state and regions in a federation, the party balance, the political culture. Although the 1793 French Constitution (Article 28) stated that every generation should have the right to revise or change its constitution, all constitutional arrangements strive for a certain level of stability and continuity: stability and continuity are recognised and sought-after values almost embedded in the concept of 'constitution'. The more rigid a constitution the less it is supposed to be subject to political and majoritarian changes. However it is not necessarily the case that rigidity is a better guarantee for minorities, for instance. It depends on its content. What is certain is that a more rigid constitution is more difficult to change for the worse, but also for the better. Therefore, in many jurisdictions the need is felt to mitigate real or perceived excesses of rigidity: the Finnish technique of Acts of Exception falls into this category. It may be regarded as a way of giving to Parliament the power to decide in what circumstance the Constitution might be not applied. This is a highly political decision, although subjected to strict procedural requirements (the same as those for constitutional amendments). This is a way also to afford some primacy to politics. However, since 2000 the use of Acts of Exception has been frowned upon in Finland and they are genuinely exceptional. Similar points could be made about the 'notwithstanding clauses' or 'limitation clauses' which are to be found in Canada, Israel and New Zealand in the human rights legislation. They too are tools intended to ensure some constitutional flexibility. India's Constitution is probably the most sophisticated one in establishing a great variety of procedures to adapt and change its arrangements based upon the careful selection of different matters (almost a model of *variable rigidity* or even *flexible rigidity*, if an oxymoron is tolerated here). Another example of an attempt to mitigate a possibly excessive rigidity is Article 48.6 of the TEU which after the Lisbon Treaty has established 'simplified revision procedures' for changing the Treaties.

(9)   Entrenchment is a way to promote checks and balances, transparency, caution and stability.

The purposes of entrenchment seem evident: (a) to make change possible only if based upon a larger than simply majoritarian consensus; (b) to involve a multiplicity of bodies which might exert a certain amount of reciprocal checks and balances; (c) to ensure a higher level of transparency and offer the opportunity for second thoughts or reflection; (d) to favour conservation and stability, regarded as values in themselves.

(10)   Formal constitutional change promotes transparency, contestability and stability.

One of the most relevant advantages of formal (not necessarily entrenched) constitutional changes (like any other formal change) is that they are more transparent compared to informal ones. For the same reason formal changes are more exposed (and therefore subject) to strong opposition: this explains why in most cases they prove more difficult to achieve. Therefore, formal constitutional changes (changes via legal enactment) once introduced can be expected better to resist successive attempts to change them in the opposite direction.

(11)   Incremental and limited constitutional changes are easier to achieve than comprehensive revisions.

Change by degrees—gradual change—provokes less opposition and its reasons are easily communicated. Such a strategy for change is often practised: in the case of Israel the deliberate piecemeal but progressive entrenchment of constitutional provisions has been expressly explained as the only way to reach consensus in a deeply divided community. Another reason why extensive and comprehensive constitutional amendments are difficult to enact is that the more provisions are to be changed the more opposition on specific different points they are going to stir up so that the whole project becomes impossible: the experiences of Canada, Italy and Spain illustrate the point.

(12)   Formal constitutional change is usually a relatively long process.

The cases of Switzerland (in relation to the recent re-writing of the entire Constitution) and of Finland, as well as German and Italian experiences of constitutional change, support the proposition that large and comprehensive constitutional changes are generally very lengthy processes. This length tends to be a function of the depth and the width of the expected amendments even when the Constitution does not establish a particularly complex procedure. These long drawn out processes of constitutional change may be perceived as signs of failure (for instance this is the case nowadays in Italy) but prove in the end necessary. In fact a long deliberation process can be a precious tool to foster the cultural transformation which might facilitate the acceptance of projected changes, thereby ensuring the required level of consensus. This has been the case in the countries mentioned above. In some instances a lengthy discourse on the necessity, object and means of constitutional change may also influence how the constitutional arrangements in force are interpreted and therefore applied for the time being (see Italy and New Zealand).

(13)   It is widely acknowledged that constitutional change should not serve the sole interests of the party in power.

The idea that constitutional matters ought to be decided on the basis of a consensus as broad as possible, and in all instances not limited to the contingent majority in power, is widespread and present nearly everywhere. With some emphasis it has been written that 'a partisan constitution is not a constitution'.[8] This acknowledged, in several instances constitutional change has been decided in a majoritarian way (France, Israel, Italy and the UK). It is difficult to say what link there is between constitutional change and a bipartisan approach: there are examples of strictly majoritarian, very significant constitutional changes which subsequently have been accepted by all (France, Italy) as well as bipartisan changes which have later been called into question. The search for consensus often blurs constitutional strategies and makes them less effective or even unsuited to achieve the desired effects; in other cases it simply makes change impossible (as veto power is recognised in too many actors).

(14)   Constitutional change is particularly difficult to achieve in federal systems.

There is a link between how easy or how difficult it is to pursue constitutional change (that is how rigid the constitution is) and the 'federal' nature of a jurisdiction: in most federations the sub-national entities are involved in constitutional change. As a consequence of the multiplicity of decision makers whose approval of amendments is required, change becomes difficult: Canada, Germany, Spain and the USA in our study all illustrate this point.

(15)   Constitutional change appears easier to achieve under the pressure of internal and external emergencies.

As in most human activities crisis is the ideal context for introducing innovations. The sense of urgency often helps to overcome resistance that in ordinary times would be sufficient to block change; it conveys the perception of a

---

[8]   A Ruggeri, *Riforme della Costituzione e riforme della politica* (Roma, http://www.federalismi.it, 27 June 2007).

truly constitutional moment so that influential actors and decision makers set aside at least some of their partisan concerns in the pursuit of the necessary consensus. Experience in Germany after World War II, in Spain after the death of Franco, and in the RSA after the end of apartheid, all illustrate the point. Partisan concerns often prevail when no sense of urgency is felt or when it is not felt by the required majority of decision makers.

(16) All constitutional arrangements include superconstitutional provisions or principles which are regarded as unamendable.

Whatever the formal provisions might be, every constitutional arrangement is based upon a set of core principles which cannot be changed and which can be regarded as intrinsic to its specific identity: this explains the tendency in many constitutional arrangements to identify a set of *superconstitutional* provisions which the constitution's text itself, or even more frequently the courts (by induction), state cannot be amended or suppressed. This is the case in the Czech Republic, Finland, Germany (see the so-called *eternity clause*, Article 79.3 *Grundgesetz*), India (the so-called *basic structures* doctrine, affirmed by the Supreme Court) and Italy (the so-called *principi supremi dell'ordinamento*). These superconstitutional provisions could be referred to as the genetic code of the constitutional arrangements, almost the admission that unrestricted *pouvoir constituant* hardly exists anymore: even in the UK the courts have elaborated principles they regard as fundamental to the UK's mostly unwritten constitutional arrangements and which may only be changed by very clear words in a statute; it has even been hinted in the *Jackson* case that a court might refuse to give effect to an 'unconstitutional' law. An even more striking case is South Africa: here the 1996 Constitution has been the faithful implementation of the 1993 *interim* Constitution, in full compliance (judicially ensured) of the procedure it established and of the 34 principles it laid down. Another example is the Waitangi Treaty in New Zealand: although some have considered its domestic legal validity as somewhat questionable, it contains provisions which have been recognised as an integrative interpretative tool and even as a limit to some constitutional changes (such as turning the country from a monarchy into a republic): the Waitangi Treaty's legal status resembles that of the preambles featured by many constitutions (the Czech Republic, EU Treaty, France, Germany, India, the RSA, Spain, Switzerland and the USA).

(17) Constitutional arrangements and changes are the product of a multiplicity of institutional and societal actors.

No constitution is the product of a single actor; how much each actor influences the establishment or the changing of constitutional arrangements varies from one jurisdiction to another as well as within each jurisdiction over time. It depends on historical developments and prevailing legitimising theories. Compared to the past, constitutional change, not to mention giving birth to a new set of constitutional arrangements, has become a more broadly participative process which involves Parliaments (or constituent assemblies), Governments (the cases of France and UK), the People (for example, the cases of France, Italy, Spain, Switzerland), and the Courts (the case of the RSA). These processes often include a variety of forms of consultation (through special committees, hearings and so on).

(18)   Constitutions also change in informal ways

Constitutional change can and generally does also come about informally, due to changes in state bodies' practice, evolution (for instance in decisions of the courts), significant contextual changes (such as the birth of new political parties, domination of Parliament and Government by a specific party, coalition or single leader) or external events (international pressures, economic crisis, indirect effects of membership of supranational entities). Each of these can permanently affect how the existing arrangements are implemented and interpreted, in some cases even generating conventions suppressing textual entrenched provisions (Canada) or major constitutional innovations (as in the case of Israel). Even more than formal change, informal constitutional change tends to have a pluralistic nature because of the number of actors who concur in it (for instance when new conventions are introduced which affect the relations between the Government, Parliament, political parties and, as in the case of Italy, the President of the Republic). On the other hand, informal constitutional changes because of their nature tend to escape any kind of regulation. They are also mostly less transparent in the sense that they occur in evolutionary ways outside any previously announced and therefore openly debated strategy (for instance when membership of the EU produces a shift in the balance of powers between executive and legislative assemblies).

A comprehensive *institutional* approach is the best suited to evaluate informal constitutional changes because more than a strictly positivist one it permits appreciation of the latent powers contained within the roles created by the textual provisions of the constitution; it also allows to take into consideration those societal factors which may be the legitimating base of informal changes.

(19)   Constitutional indeterminacy can facilitate anti- or un-constitutional
        activity

Indeterminacies and lack of precision in written (and even more so unwritten) constitutional arrangements may leave room for anti- or un-constitutional actions, or for interpretations that are so twisted that they may amount to a substantial breach of constitutional provisions. The recent case of the American Presidency is an example. Even when it is not a matter of anti-constitutional actions, the fact that a suitable constitutional parameter does not exist may foster an unwanted and potentially disruptive competition between political practice and judicial review. The dispute over the power to grant pardon between the President and the Cabinet in Italy, surprisingly and innovatively solved by the Constitutional Court in favour of the first, is a good example.

(20)   There is a trend away from parliamentary sovereignty and towards constitutionalism.

It is doubtful whether it still makes sense to speak of a difference between the constitutional state model and the model based on parliamentary sovereignty: all the established relatively stable democracies can nowadays fall within the category of constitutional states; in none is Parliament still truly sovereign for the simple reason that no single institution is sovereign (at least in the sense that its activities and its decisions are totally self-referential and free from any kind of review and in particular not justiciable under any circumstance). The cases of India, Israel, New Zealand and to a lesser extent the UK, seem to support this statement.

(21)   While legislative procedures for constitutional change tend to be regulated there is no general requirement for pre-legislative procedures

Legislative procedures for formal constitutional change are normally structured and regulated in detail by constitutional arrangements, whether in the formal constitution or in conventions and practice. There seems to be no settled requirement as to pre-legislative procedures where constitutional changes are under consideration. The actors involved in the pre-legislative period vary (they might be Parliaments and political parties, or Governments, central or sub-national authorities, and so on) as do the pre-legislative steps to be followed. These tend to be unregulated except by practice, and the practices are varied: in some cases ad hoc preparatory committees are summoned (in France in 1958, in Italy in 1983, 1993 and 1997 and in Finland), in other cases relatively independent bodies are consulted (the Councils of State in France and Spain), so-called *white papers* might be circulated or not (the UK case), but within each jurisdiction practice varies in time according to basically political circumstances.

(22)   Interpretation of constitutions by the courts is the most common form of constitutional maintenance and it often goes beyond maintenance.

The most effective and most frequently referred to alternative to formal constitutional innovation is adaptive (fitness promoting) interpretation of constitutional arrangements by the courts; in this way the courts ensure that the function of constitutional maintenance is discharged, and in some cases they are considered to go beyond that (the US case is probably the most striking, but see also

Canada). There are however structural (for instance textual) limits beyond which this alternative cannot be pursued in relation to written constitutional provisions, so that a modification of the constitutional arrangements becomes necessary (this could be the case of Italy where the Constitutional Court has stated that the wording of the Constitution as it is does not allow gay marriage). There can also be political limits if and when the courts' involvement and the justifications they offer for it clash with the prevailing legal and institutional culture (for instance in relation to how the democratic principle is interpreted): this can be the case in those jurisdictions where courts' progressive interpretations stir up controversies about *juristocracy*[9] or *the judicialisation of politics* or about a *democratic dehabilitation*,[10] with the consequent risk of turning the courts into institutions viewed as political.

CONCLUSIONS: SOME LESSONS ABOUT CONSTITUTIONAL CHANGE

We now move on to try to draw some lessons about constitutional change from the jurisdictions in this study in this concluding section of the chapter.

(A)   Constitutional maintenance through piecemeal innovation is a sound institutional strategy

Any constitutional arrangement should be organised in a way that allows for (relatively) easy incremental innovation; evolutionary unwritten constitutions are better suited to ensuring the implementation of such a continuously evolutionary strategy, even if at the cost of some degree of transparency. But the lack of transparency and the consequent potential lack of public deliberative debate explain why unwritten constitutions are a category seriously threatened with extinction.

(B)   A quantitative and qualitative excess of procedural requirements for constitutional change is to be avoided

In the long run excessive rigidity may hamper any kind of formal amendment. As a consequence all adjustments may depend on informal processes only, limiting the transparency of decision making process. The courts may become the only alternative channel for adjustment, which brings a risk of judicial activism and of an unforeseen, ultimately intolerable, shift in 'sovereignty' from the people (directly or indirectly involved) to the courts. Lack of legitimacy in the long run is a fatal danger for any set of constitutional arrangements. Loss of legitimacy

---

[9] R Dworkin, *A Bill of Rights for Britain* (London, Chatto and Windus, 1990); C R Sunstein, *Designing Democracy: What Constitutions Do* (Oxford, Oxford University Press, 2002).

[10] M Tushnet, *Taking the Constitution Away from the Courts* (Princeton, Princeton University Press, 2000).

may be the effect of either no or insufficient adaptation, or adaptation devolved to bodies that are independent but detached from the source of legitimacy.

(C)   To reconcile opposing demands (the protection of core principles and values as well as the necessary continuous constitutional maintenance) a constitution can ensure selectively differentiated levels of constitutional rigidity.

A constitution may be endangered by lack, excess or unsuitable forms of change: in order to avoid those risks, the most appropriate strategy can be to grant *variable rigidity* (or a *flexible rigidity*) as has been done in several jurisdictions, in particular, Canada and India.

(D)   It is up to each polity to decide which parts of its constitutional arrangements and to what extent might be left less regulated in order to allow room for elected bodies to make their strictly political choices without incurring judicial review

A fully regulated set of constitutional arrangements which do not leave the slightest room for the political interpretation and exercise of judgement by the elected bodies is not easy to conceive in practice and is inadvisable. Not all constitutional arrangements are, nor should they necessarily be, legalised, unless one is willing to risk the shift in 'sovereignty', and therefore in legitimacy, we mentioned previously.

(E)   The constitutional legislator should be aware of the fact that indeterminacies in written and even more so unwritten constitutional arrangements may allow for practices against the constitution.

Therefore a lack of precision should be avoided in those areas subject to constitutional provisions which are regarded as most sensitive in each given jurisdiction (and possibly in those areas only).

(F)   The balances between continuity and the need for maintenance and innovation, between the roles of representative bodies, and between voters and courts, are the most crucial aspects of constitution making, particularly in relation to the design of constitutional arrangements, so as to make future change possible.

The starting point should be a recognition that change will certainly be needed, even more so today than in the past given an increasingly fast evolving environment. If a constitution does not establish an effective way to transform itself, change will occur anyway: but it will happen in ways which will have been unforeseen and which might prove not easy to reconcile with the shared legitimising theories and therefore potentially inconsistent with the fundamental set of values which are at the base of any constitutional arrangement (even a purely organisational constitution implies a choice of values). On the other hand a constitution totally unsuited for change sooner or later is doomed to become an instrument incapable of serving its purpose, bound therefore to be superseded. In the end, constitutional patriotism is best served by ensuring that a given set of constitutional arrangements can be adapted and incrementally changed rather than making out of it a petrified object of devotion.

Jurisdiction-based Chart

CANADA

General

The Constitution is poly-textual, consisting of a number of statutes passed by the British Parliament from confederation until the 1982 patriation, effected by the Canada Act, 1982. This Act patriated the Constitution and rendered the statutes of which it was composed the supreme law of Canada. The Constitution contains special provisions in relation to Aboriginal peoples, a Charter of Rights, amendment procedures, the division of powers, and the separation of powers. The Supreme Court has power to strike down unconstitutional legislation if it is inconsistent with any provision of the Constitution. Nevertheless, the Constitution allows Parliament and provincial legislatures to override some constitutional rights. A number of unwritten constitutional principles are considered to be embedded in the constitutional statutes. Other unwritten principles derive from the UK system. These formal sources are justiciable. A number of conventions are informal, non-justiciable parts of the constitution.

Westminster style parliamentary executive. The Governor General and Lieutenant Governors act on behalf of the Queen, the Head of State. Federation. Canada has adopted the North American Free Trade Agreement which is regarded by some commentators to have affected the division of powers as well as rights in Canada.

Legal system/Family

Common law and civil law (Quebecs legal system is French/civil law).

435

Constitutional Amendments and Formal Constitutional Change

Amendment of the text of the Constitution may be made in seven ways, depending on the subject matter. Only ten such amendments have been made since 1982.

Reform without Constitutional Amendments

Conventions are an important source of constitutional rules and affect or change the operation of the system of government. Canada's adoption of the North American Free Trade Agreement is regarded by some commentators as a constitutional change. Parliament has legislated, without amendment of the constitution, to grant in effect a power of veto over future constitutional amendment to three provinces.

Constitutional and Human Rights Cases

Constitutional questions may be referred to the Supreme Court. That Court has held that unwritten constitutional principles underlie the Constitution, and that it is legitimate for the Court to use them to fill gaps in the Constitution. Therefore, even legislation that is consistent with the written Constitution may be ruled unconstitutional by a court if it is inconsistent with the unwritten principles. In *Quebec Secession Reference* the Supreme Court read a secession provision into the Constitution, the reliance on which would not amend the text of the Constitution. In that case, the Court prescribed a legally binding formula for the secession of a province, based on four principles: federalism, democracy, constitutionalism and the rule of law, and the protection of minorities.

Federal Arrangements

Canada is a federation made up of Provinces. Politically negotiated and non-justiciable secession, for example, by Quebec, is a legal possibility.

CZECH REPUBLIC

General

The current Czech Constitution 1993 together with a Charter of Fundamental Rights and Freedoms and other documents having constitutional force form a poly-textual constitution with a defined 'constitutional order'. Monist system—international treaties approved by the Parliament are considered to be part of the Czech legal system, but their supremacy only applies to statutory law and subordinate legislation. Human rights treaties are part of the constitutional order. Bi-cameral Parliament. Representative democracy in which the people are sovereign. Republic with a strong president. Parliamentary executive. Constitutional Court. Constitutional provisions are self-executing, except for the Charter's protections of social, cultural and economic rights.

Legal System/Family

Civil law in the German/Austrian tradition. Strong influence of Austrian-Hungarian law.

Constitutional Amendments and Formal Constitutional Changes

The text of the 1993 Constitution has been amended six times, and in all 14 constitutional Acts have been passed since 1993. Both amendments to the Constitution and constitutional Acts require special majorities in Parliament.

Reform without Constitutional Amendments or Constitutional Acts

Some conventions have developed, for instance as to whom the president should invite to be prime minister and to form a government.

Regional Arrangements

There is a system of higher territorial self-governing units/regions.

437

Constitutional and Human Rights Cases

Under the Communist Constitution the Constitutional Court was abolished. This meant there was no organ with power to declare laws that were incompatible with the Constitution to be invalid.

Under the Constitution of 1993 the Constitutional Court has taken upon itself the jurisdiction to determine on the constitutionality of constitutional Acts, even though the Constitution provides that it is bound by constitutional Acts. The Court treats human rights treaties as part of the constitutional order, despite the fact that only Acts are supposed to form part of that order. It has set aside a constitutional Act providing for an early election to the Chamber of Deputies as unconstitutional.

EU Membership

Accession was preceded by a referendum. European law is considered to be part of the Czech legal system having supremacy over domestic legislation except unamendable constitutional provisions.

EUROPEAN UNION

General

The EU legal order has evolved into a set of *supranational* constitutional arrangements which, however limited in scope, closely resemble what for States is a constitution: multi-textual, entrenched, rigid, enforced by effective judicial review, with partial but significant direct effect, and consisting of both States and citizens.

Legal System/Family

The system originated as international law, being treaty based. The EC was founded by civil law countries, but now includes common law and Nordic countries. The ECJ case law has moved towards a common law pattern.

Constitutional Amendments and Formal Constitutional Change

According to the Lisbon Treaty of 2009, the Treaties may be amended as follows: under the ordinary procedure proposals originate from States' Governments, from the European Parliament, or from the Commission; these are submitted to the Council which refers them to the European Council and informs the national Parliaments. The European Council can decide by a simple majority to convene a Convention made up of the representatives of the national Parliaments and Governments, of the European Parliament and of the Commission. The Convention gives its advice on each amendment and submits them to an intergovernmental conference. Alternatively the European Council can decide to convene the conference directly, in case of minor changes. The conference decides by unanimity the amendments to be made; these enter into force when ratified by all States. The simplified procedure—reserved to amendments concerning the internal policies and action of the Union—avoids both the Convention and the conference. It is the European Council which decides the amendments to be made by unanimity. (They must later be ratified by each State.)

Reform without Constitutional Amendments

The basic arrangements of the EU have evolved without treaty amendments due to the jurisprudence of the European Court of Justice (starting from the rulings on direct effect and supremacy of European law), to the practices of the European Parliament (in relation to the designation of the members of the Commission) and of the Council (in relation to its decision making process).

Human Rights and Constitutional Cases

The status of human rights in the EU legal order has been recognised by the Court of Justice, which has interpreted the treaties as a list of individual rights. The ECJ ensures that Union legislation is compatible with the fundamental rights guaranteed by national constitutions as well as with the international treaties for the protection of human rights.

439

Federal Arrangements

According to the case law of the ECJ, EU law is supreme. However its supremacy has been occasionally challenged by constitutional courts in member states.

FINLAND

General

Tradition of evolutionary development since early nineteenth century. The 1919 Constitution defined Finland as a language-liberal state based on the idea of 'one people, one state, two languages'. Current 2000 Constitution's text is a codification of certain practices and a re-writing of some provisions. Generally not self-executing in relation to individuals. Unicameral Parliament. Proportional representation. Parliamentary sovereignty. The formerly semi-presidential system is moving towards a parliamentary system with clear parliamentary accountability. No Constitutional Court.

Legal System/Family

Nordic system

Constitutional Amendments and Formal Constitutional Changes

Special parliamentary procedures—normally simple majority, election, two-thirds majority. The Parliament is the *pouvoir constitué* for constitutional amendments. Few amendments 1919 to 1985, since then several minor ones and two larger (fundamental rights in 1995 and the entire constitutional text in 2000), and one in process as of 2010. Acts of Exception may be passed. Intra-parliamentary, *ante legem*, scrutiny of bills for constitutionality is carried out by the Constitutional Committee of Parliament. If the committee has concerns about the constitutionality of a bill and cannot propose a reformulation on the bill, the special procedure that applies to Constitutional amendments must be followed for its passing. If the Constitutional Committee finds that a bill is not constitutionally objectionable, the courts cannot later in a concrete case find the Act based on the bill unconstitutional.

Reform without Constitutional Amendments

An Act of Exception is a limited derogation from the Constitution. It is regarded as an 'ordinary' Act of Parliament which violates the core meaning of a constitutional provision, but which has been passed by the Parliament in the manner prescribed on two occasions, separated by an election. The Constitutional Committee decides whether a Bill should follow the procedure for an Act of Exception, and that decision is binding on Parliament. Only one Act of Exception has been passed since 2000. Before then there were many. Since 2000 principles have developed to the effect that legislation by Act of Exception should be avoided.

Evolutionary changes take place from time to time, for example, in relation to the Åland Islands, and practices such as post legem/advisory referendums (now covered in the Constitution of 2000) and representation in the European Council, in which both the President and the Prime Minister have taken part which is now governed by the Lisbon Treaty which provides for the head of government, the Prime Minister, to do so.

Constitutional and Human Rights Cases

No American style 'judicial review' of constitutionality of laws. Ordinary courts exercise some judicial review in relation to the exercise of powers in concrete cases. Courts can set aside/disapply an ordinary act and implement the Constitution directly in a particular case if there is an evident conflict between the Act and the Constitution, and if the Constitutional Committee has not dealt with a situation such as that in which the problem with constitutionality has emerged. Courts have no power to strike down/nullify Acts of Parliament. Fundamental rights provisions are generally not self-executing but are implemented by separate legislation.

Regional Arrangements

The Åland Islands have a special, effectively entrenched, constitutional status as a result of a decision of the Council of the League of Nations.

EU Membership

An advisory referendum on accession was held. Since the Lisbon Treaty the Prime Minister represents Finland in European Council summits.

FRANCE

General

Constitution of the fifth Republic 1958 was amended most recently in 2008. President is directly elected. Bicameral legislature, the Senate being indirectly elected. Parliament's powers to legislate are enumerated and limited. Semi-presidential semi-parliamentary system. Ministers disqualified from membership of the legislature. Referendums permitted by the constitution on major institutional questions—reflects the fact that the will of the people, not the parliament, is considered sovereign. Mixed representative and direct democracy. The Declaration of the Rights of Man and the Citizen 1789 and the Preamble to the 1946 constitution have been interpreted by the Conseil d'État and the Conseil constitutionnel as giving rise to rights, and in 2005 a Charter for the Environment was annexed to the 1958 constitution. The Conseil constitutionnel has had the power to review the constitutionality of Acts prior to their coming into force since its inception; however, the constitutional reform of 2008 has allowed ordinary courts to refer for control an Act already in force. Thus constitutional provisions are now largely self-executing. A strong public administration and system of administrative law have compensated for past constitutional and political instability. Only recently have constitutional law and constitutionalism become central. Monist system. International rights treaties give rise to rights enforceable in the courts.

Legal System/Family

Civil law.

442

Constitutional Amendments and Formal Constitutional Change

Amendments require consent of the two chambers of the legislature plus consent of the two chambers sitting together in a 'Congress,' or a referendum. The 1958 constitution has been amended 24 times since coming into force, five times in the first three decades and 19 times in the last 20 years.

Human Rights and Constitutional Cases

The *Conseil constitutionnel* has changed its role since 1971 from being a defender of the Executive to guarantor of rights and freedoms and promoter of French constitutionalism. The *Conseil constitutionnel* and the *Conseil d'Etat* interpret the constitution, the Declaration of the Rights of Man and the Preamble to the 1946 Constitution in ways that provide human rights protection for citizens. The *Conseil constitutionnel* has also recognised the existence of 'general principles recognized in the legislation of the Republic'. Thus in 1971 the *Conseil constitutionnel* held a new bill that would interfere with freedom of association to be contrary to principles in the legislation of the Third Republic. The proposed legislation was then dropped. As a result of this decision, the Constitution of 1958 is no longer an exhaustive statement of all constitutional principles. The expression 'block of constitutionality' is used to designate all constitutional rules and principles.

The *Conseil constitutionnel* has been transformed into a body resembling a constitutional court by the reform of July 2008: a new article 61–1 has given claimants the right to apply for review of constitutionality of legislative provisions already in force.

Regional Arrangements

System of départements and régions. Not federal.

EU Membership

Constitutional amendment was required in 1992 to authorise the loss of French sovereignty under the Treaty of European Union and to increase Parliament's control over European affairs. Further amendments required with subsequent EU treaties.

443

GERMANY

General

Federal Republic formed after World War II. The Constitution is the 'Basic Law' of 1949. Parliament (*Bundestag*) and Federal Council (*Bundesrat*) representing the Länder governments participate in the legislative process. Parliamentary system, Chancellor as head of the federal government. The Basic Law contains explicit values (the protection of human dignity, the recognition of inviolable and inalienable human rights as the basis of every community, of peace and of justice in the world, and the subordination of legislative, executive and judicial powers to respect for fundamental rights) and a charter of rights. The Federal Constitutional Court (*Bundesverfassungsgericht*—BVerfG) has the power of constitutional review. Principle of popular sovereignty is exercisable through elections. Proportional representation—Additional Member System. Self-executing constitution. Strong rule of law. Dualist system. Re-unification in 1990 took place by accession of the re-established Eastern Länder (former German Democratic Republic) to the Federal Republic of Germany, without a new Constitution and in accordance with treaties negotiated with reunification in mind between the two countries and the four Allies of World War II. Only a few constitutional amendments were required.

Legal System/Family

Germanic civil law system.

Constitutional Amendments and Formal Constitutional Change

An eternity clause protects some essential constitutional principles against amendment. Thus, the republican, federal, social and democratic principles, as well as the principle of the rule of law, cannot be subject of constitutional amendments. Special procedure for constitutional amendments—two-thirds majorities in each house. Flexible in practice—many amendments have been made. No Acts of Exception allowed.

Reform without Constitutional Amendments

Important constitutional changes can take place without the need for formal textual constitutional amendment, for example, accession of the Länder of East Germany.

Human Rights and Constitutional Cases

The BVerfG has the power of abstract or concrete review of Acts and decisions (by administrative and judicial authorities) on grounds of unconstitutionality. Complaints against alleged violations of their fundamental rights may be brought by citizens. Unconstitutional laws may be nullified.

Federal Arrangements

The federal principle and the rights of the Länder, for example, to participate in the legislative process are given constitutional protection.

EU Membership

Acts of Ratification, for example, of EU treaties, are exempt from the normal requirement of a textual amendment to the Constitution. However, a specific integration clause (Article 23 Basic Law) provides for structural guarantees of essential principles as well as for procedural rules for Germany's participation in the EU.

The BVerfG's *Solange* decisions seek to protect Basic Law principles (that is protection of fundamental rights) from European undermining. In BVerfGE 55, 155 ff. the BVerfG explicitly reserved for itself the competence to decide whether Community acts were *ultra vires* or within the domain of Community competence. In 2005 BVerfGE 113, 273 (*Europäischer Haftbefehl*), 19 July 2005 the BVerfG declared the German act for implementation of the EU Arrest Warrant unconstitutional, mainly due to insufficient participation by Parliament; for similar reasons, in BVerfGE 123, 267 (*Lissabon*), 30 June 2009 it declared the act accompanying the ratification of the Lisbon Treaty unconstitutional. Although accepting '*de facto*-monism' in the relationship between the German and EU legal systems, the BVerfG considers the State to be the ultimate defence of the rights of citizens. Thus, the question of constitutional limits to integration is not yet definitively resolved.

445

INDIA

General

Very detailed independence Constitution of 1949 in the Euro-American tradition. Federal state. Provisions for Fundamental Rights (FRs) with limitations, Directive Principles of State Policy (DPs) and inclusion of Fundamental Duties (FDs). Special provision is made for Scheduled Castes and Scheduled Tribes. Parliamentary system, indirectly elected President as nominal Head of State. First past the post electoral systems. Dualist. No supremacy clause but self-executing in the common law tradition. No strict public law private law divide.

Legal System/Family

Common law.

Constitutional Amendments and Formal Constitutional Change

Constitution characterised by flexible rigidity. It has been amended at least 95 times since 1950. Some constitutional amendments require special majorities in Parliament, and some require ratification by half of the states in addition. Any amendments that are contrary to the basic structure will be held by the Supreme Court to be ineffective.

Reform without Constitutional Amendments

Conventions have developed around the office of Head of State to the effect that s/he must act on the aid and advice of the Council of Ministers and, when a new government is to be formed, should invite the leader of the largest party in the elected chamber to be Prime Minister or, in the case of a State, the Chief Minister; conventions have also developed around votes of confidence and in relation to collective responsibility, and around appointment of the Chief Justice, the appointment of State Governors. The Supreme Court has recognised some conventions as, in effect, law.

Constitutional and Human Rights Cases

Largely decentralised judicial review save for disputes between the States and between the Centre and the States, where the Supreme Court has exclusive jurisdiction. All courts may hear constitutional issues in ordinary cases. The higher courts and Supreme Court may strike down unconstitutional laws. The Supreme Court has developed a large, activist and important jurisprudence on human rights and other issues, including some decisions having only prospective operation: the Court can examine whether an amendment changes the basic structure of the Constitution and invalidate such an amendment if it comes to the conclusion that it does so. On the contents of the basic structure the judges have enumerated among other features the republican form of government, a democratic polity, the federal structure, judicial review, separation of powers,and so on. Many cases have raised issues as to the balance and need for harmony between FRs and DPs which are taken to be part of the basic structure of the constitution.

Regional/Federal Arrangements

Federal state—regional legislatures and executives follow the Westminster model.

447

ISRAEL

General

The first Knesset after independence in 1948 passed a compromise decision that became known as 'the Harrari Resolution', according to which, the constitution would be adopted 'chapter by chapter', in stages. Each chapter would bear the title of 'Basic Law'. No new Basic Laws enacted since 1992. Doctrine of parliamentary sovereignty has been replaced, as a result of Supreme Court decisions, by the doctrine of a 'limited Parliament' or a 'constitutional state', closer to the USA or German approach than to the British tradition. No Basic Law provision for referendums but referendums may be provided for in ordinary/regular legislation for example, as to the future of the Golan Heights. Parliamentary system with proportional representation and coalition government.

Legal System/Family

Mixed legal system, with English common law and civil law.

Constitutional Amendments and Formal Constitutional Change

Following a judicial decision, Basic Laws may only be amended by Basic Laws so-called, though most Basic Laws do not impose special procedures for amendment. Regular law may change constitutional arrangements as long as they are not inconsistent with Basic Laws, for example, regular law could provide for referendums (this issue, whether a regular law may provide for a referendum, is still pending).

Constitutional and Human Rights Cases

Supreme Court strikes down laws and decisions that are incompatible with the Basic Laws. In HCJ 6821/93 *United Mizrachi Bank Ltd v Migdal Cooperative Village*, 49 (4) PD 221 the Israeli Supreme Court, in a 'constitutional revolution' declared that basic laws had a 'supra-legal' constitutional status, by virtue of which they could limit the Knesset's legislative powers, and that the court was empowered to enforce these limitations by judicially reviewing Knesset legislation. It has taken on the role of pronouncing new rights that are not expressly mentioned in the basic laws. It has struck down about eight laws, or sections of laws, by reason of their violation of human rights anchored in the Basic Laws, and contrary to the provisions of the limitation clause prescribed therein.

Regional Arrangements

None. A unitary state.

ITALY

General

1948 Constitution, rigid/inflexible, containing lacunae which enable Parliament to legislate to 'integrate' or fill the gaps. Regional arrangements. Republic. Bi-cameral parliament. Parliamentary executive. Strictly proportional representation until 1993, later a combination of proportional with plurality. Constitution only partly self-executing; when the 1948 constitution was adopted it was expected that it would be implemented gradually by legislation. In fact this has taken a very long time. The only expressly unamendable provision in the Constitution is that the republican form of government cannot be changed. This entails a doctrine of implied limits to constitutional change and *supreme principles* which have been developed by the Constitutional Court and scholars. Frequent recourse to referendums but since 1995 low turnout has almost ended their utility. Dualist system.

Legal System/Family

Civil law. Strong hierarchy of laws.

Constitutional Amendments and Formal Constitutional Changes

By political convention constitutional reform is expected be consensual/non partisan: however in two instances the practice has been majoritarian. Special procedure required for amendment to the text of the Constitution. Laws that are inconsistent with the Constitution may be passed by the same procedure as is needed to amend the Constitution. Two votes three months apart needed for constitutional amendments and new constitutional acts, with 50 per cent plus one of members of each chamber in favour. If a two-thirds majority is in favour, the vote is final. If less than a two-thirds majority is in favour there is the possibility of a referendum. The 1948 Constitution has been directly amended 14 times as of 2010. Altogether 32 out of the original 139 articles have been modified, some of them more than once; five have been repealed.

Reform without Constitutional Amendments

Conventions and practices have been influential in the development of the constitution without textual amendment for example, on the appointment of the President/chair of the Council of Ministers (approximate equivalent of a Prime Minister). Informal changes have resulted from a trend towards competitive democracy from the previous consociational regime. The Constitutional Court has achieved substantial constitutional changes through its case law.

Constitutional and Human Rights and Cases

Mixed system of judicial review of legislation (any court can activate the Constitutional Court which alone can declare a law null and void). Constitutional Court has developed implied rights by interpretation, for instance sexual freedom, privacy, personal identity and so on, and has elaborated other fundamental principles which are regarded as implicit in the Constitution.

Regional Arrangements

Increasing devolution to the regions has reduced the scope of central government and Parliamentary power. The devolutionary process is still under way and is expected to last many more years.

EU Membership

No constitutional amendment required when Italy joined the EC nor when the Union was established (Maastricht) or reformed (Amsterdam, Nice, Lisbon). The Constitutional Court has elaborated a doctrine concerning the counter limits (in relation to EU law), similar to that of the German BVG, theoretically intended to ensure the final supremacy of the Italian Constitution (and of its *supreme principles*).

450

NEW ZEALAND

General

Constitution modelled on that of the UK. The Constitution Act 1986 describes but does not constitute the legislative and executive branches of government in NZ, which owe their origins to UK legislation and instruments. Provisions for a three year parliamentary term and relating to elections are procedurally entrenched by a requirement for a 75 per cent majority in the House of Representatives or a referendum. But the entrenching provisions are not entrenched. Unitary state, unicameral sovereign parliament. Indigenous Maori people protected by the Treaty of Waitangi 1840, negotiated between the British Crown and the Maori chiefs. This is regarded as constitutional, the foundation document of the NZ constitution: a treaty based constitution. Dualist system. Mixed member proportional representation electoral system. Parliamentary executive. NZ Bill of Rights Act 1990 is not entrenched. Courts must, when it 'can' be done, prefer statutory meanings that are consistent with affirmed rights over those that are not. Courts may not refuse to give effect to incompatible legislation.

Legal System/Family

Common law.

Constitutional Amendments and Formal Constitutional Change

Acts of a constitutional kind are passed from time to time, by the normal legislative procedure. Waitangi Tribunal formed in 1975 to deal with Maori complaints that the Crown had acted inconsistently with the principles of the Treaty of Waitangi.

Reform without Constitutional Amendments

A de facto 'constitution outside the constitution' has evolved.

Regional Arrangements

None.

Human Rights and Constitutional Cases

In *New Zealand Maori Council v Attorney-General* (1987) Maori challenged the proposed transfer of Crown land over which Maori had pending or likely future claims. The Court of Appeal identified the salient principles of the Treaty of Waitangi (essentially, 'utmost good faith' between Crown and Maori, akin to a partnership) and held that it offended the principle of 'redress' under the Treaty for the Crown to seek to transfer land out of Crown ownership without establishing a mechanism to secure its return if needed to satisfy a Tribunal recommendation in favour of Maori claims. Subsequently, Crown and Maori negotiated a set of protocols and a law change to satisfy both sides. Several other cases have upheld Maori claims against government action. By the late 1980s the courts, while recognising that the Treaty was not in force as law, were taking it into account in matters of statutory interpretation and on occasion through the mechanisms of administrative law.

Other constitutional cases include those where fundamental common law rights lead courts to 'read down' enactments.

REPUBLIC OF SOUTH AFRICA

General

Current post-apartheid Constitution adopted in 1997. It includes 'founding provisions' including statements of values. Processes for drafting the Constitution had been negotiated and agreed in the Multi-Party Negotiating Process. Parliament is the *pouvoir constituant*. Legislative continuity in adoption of the new Constitution. The Constitution is self-executing. Bicameral national legislature—directly-elected National Assembly and indirectly-elected National Council of Provinces. President, indirectly elected by Parliament, is both head of state and head of government. Cabinet government. System of legislative and executive government at provincial level. Proportional representation in Parliament using national party lists gives great power to party leaders. Human rights protected by a Canadian style charter which includes some socio-economic rights Constitutional Court has power to strike down unconstitutional laws.

Legal System/Family

Mixed Roman Dutch and common law.

Constitutional Amendments and Formal Constitutional Change

The present Constitution of 1996 was passed by the first democratically elected legislature; its basic principles had been agreed by the Multi-Party Negotiating Process: it has been amended over 16 times. Amendments have been either of a formal nature or necessitated by practical necessity (both kinds being uncontroversial), or, more controversially, amendments having substantial effect on the terms originally adopted in 1996, for instance on 'floor-crossing' by MPs, alterations of provincial boundaries and the length of terms of office of Justices of the Constitutional Court. Amendment of section 1 of the Constitution requires the support 75 per cent of the members of the National Assembly, the rest require the support of two-thirds of the members. In addition all amendments require the support of six out of the nine provincial legislatures.

Reform without Constitutional Amendments

Conventions are developing as to relations between the executive and the judiciary: when 'judiciary bills' designed to 'reform' the judiciary are proposed by the executive and the judiciary object to some of the provisions on constitutional grounds, these are hotly contested on both sides. Discussion takes place between the two, compromises are reached and objectionable proposals are normally dropped. A shift from a culture of authority to a culture of justification is taking place gradually.

Human Rights and Constitutional Cases

The Bill of Rights requires judges to promote the values that underlie an open and democratic society based on human dignity, equality and freedom The Constitutional Court found the death penalty to be unconstitutional, held that the principle of legality is a requirement of the rule of law. In the *Grootboom* case the Constitutional Court, after reviewing the housing strategy of the government, held that its rationality was impugned by the absence of any proper plan to deal with the temporary plight of those on the formal waiting list for state housing,

SPAIN

Regional Arrangements

Nine provinces with legislative and executive power.

General

Written Constitution 1978. Partly self-executing, but some rights require implementing legislation (for example, political participation). Constitutional Monarchy. Regions are Autonomous Communities (ACs). Proportional representation. Two chambers (*Congresso* and *Senado*—Autonomous Communities not formally represented in *Senado*). Human Rights protected. Constitutional Court. Complex hierarchy of laws, made yet more complex by EU membership.

Legal system/family

Civil law system.

Constitutional Amendments and Formal Constitutional Change

Rigid/inflexible—complex procedural requirements for reform of the Constitutional text. Only one amendment since 1978, to deal with voting rights on Spain's accession to the EU. After 2004 elections a report from the State Council recommended amendments of the Constitution on the male succession to the throne, EU membership, the names of the ACs and reform of the *Senado*. However, due to the complexity and difficulty of procedures for constitutional amendment and lack of consensus on all of these issues, this has stalled.

Reform without Constitutional Amendments

Reform is commonly achieved without textual amendments (i) by Constitutional Court decisions for example, in response to ECtHR decisions and European law and in relation to the competences of the ACs, (ii) by agreements for example, between the ACs and the Centre and (iii) by changes in practice. Constitutional reforms are not a usual practice in Spain. Historically, when changes were required, a new Constitution was eventually adopted.

Constitutional and Human Rights Cases

Breaches of rights and other constitutional issues (especially in relation to the ACs) may be raised by way of a preliminary reference procedure (*recurso de amparo*) or an appeal on grounds of unconstitutionality (*recurso de inconstitucionalidad*) in the Constitutional Court. A broad interpretation is applied particularly to unconfigured constitutional rights where implementing legislation is required.

Regional Arrangements

Spain is almost a federal state. The Constitution provides a framework within which regions can assume new powers as ACs via Statutes of Autonomy passed by the AC and by the Spanish Parliament. No constitutional amendments are required for this. The Constitutional Court has decided that ACs may adopt their own rights protection laws as long as they are not inconsistent with the basic rights in the Spanish Constitution. Constitutional Court decisions on the areas of competence of ACs and their relations with the State (for example, the State's co-existing and ancillary legislative powers) have given rise to legal uncertainty which only seems to be amenable to resolution through constitutional amendment.

EU Membership

Spain's accession to the EU did not require amendment of the Constitution; a minor, consensual, amendment was required after the Treaty of the European Union in order to allow European citizens to be candidates in local elections. There is a Joint Parliamentary Committee for the EU. It is not normally possible for the ACs to participate directly in Community institutions' decision making.

SWITZERLAND

General

First Constitution 1848 agreed to by all but eight of the cantons after referendums, and by the Diet, the main body of the Federation of States at the time. First federation in Europe. The People assumed to be the constituent power. Legal continuity since then has led to the current Constitution, 2000, passed by the Federal Assembly and approved by the people and the cantons in a referendum. Federal state, diversity of language, religion and culture. Two chamber Federal Assembly/Parliament. Separate executive is a seven member 'Federal Council' elected by the Federal Assembly for a four year term. Presidency rotates annually among the Federal Council members. Proportional representation means the government has to engage in minority-government type behaviour, negotiating with other parties. The frequent use of referendums is regarded as part of citizens' rights—direct democracy. The Confederation only has the responsibilities/competences assigned to it by the Constitution. The cantons have residual competences. Catalogue of fundamental rights and liberties included in the Constitution. Federal Supreme Court has jurisdiction over constitutional appeals from the cantons, but not over the constitutionality of federal laws: in Switzerland this is a matter for voters in referendums. A trend from representative to half-direct democracy characterises the Swiss model. Monist system. Influence of legal scholars in constitution.

Legal System/Family

Civil law.

Constitutional Amendments and Formal Constitutional Change

A full revision of the constitution resulted in the 2000 Constitution, passed by the Parliament and approved by a majority of the cantons and the People in a national referendum. Other constitutional amendments are passed from time to time by the Parliament and then submitted for double majority approval (cantons and people on a national referendum). Such amendments result in changes to the constitutional text.

Reform without Constitutional Amendments

The Federal Constitutional Court has developed fundamental rights in the absence of constitutional provisions.

Human Rights and Constitutional Cases

The Federal Supreme Court has held that rights in international treaties, including human rights, are binding. It will disapply federal and cantonal legislation and decisions that are incompatible with international treaties. The Federal Supreme Court has also 'derived' a number of rights and certain guarantees and principles from the general principle of equality (Article 4 of the Federal Constitution of 1874, today Article 8(1)), including protection from arbitrariness, various procedural guarantees (such as the right to a fair hearing in court, the right to free legal assistance when in need and protection against excessive procedural formalism), the requirement of good faith, the principle of legality, and the prohibition of *ex post facto* (retrospective) laws. The majority of these guarantees were codified within the framework of the total revision of the Federal Constitution (see Articles 5, 9, 29–32, 127).

Federal Arrangements

Cantons have strong autonomy thought the trend is towards centralisation. Cantons are subject to judicial review for constitutionality and legality of their laws and acts. The consent of a majority of cantons (in the form of the votes of a majority of voters in referendums) is required for constitutional amendments.

UNITED KINGDOM

General

Sources of constitutional rules include statutes, common law, conventions and the law and practice of Parliament. Parliamentary sovereignty. No codified or entrenched constitution. All Acts of Parliament are self-executing unless found by a court to be non justiciable. Constitutional monarchy. Parliamentary system. Two chambers (House of Commons, House of Lords, neither representing the nations of the UK). House of Commons elected by first past the post system. Human Rights Act 1998. Asymmetric devolution to some countries/regions. Dualist system. Decentralised constitutional and human rights jurisdiction.

Legal System/Family

Common law.

Formal Constitutional Reform by Act of Parliament

Constitutional change may be effected by ordinary Act of Parliament. Parliament the *pouvoir constituant* for Acts effecting constitutional change, though advisory referendums sometimes used. A largely 'political' constitution. Recent statutory changes include devolution Acts, Human Rights Act 1998, Constitutional Reform Act 2005.

Reform without Statutory Provisions

Executive has power under the royal prerogative (a source recognised at common law) to change departmental organisation by fiat, for example, establishing new departments, introducing agencification of government activities.

  Much executive activity is regulated by constitutional conventions, codes, resolutions of the two Houses of Parliament and so on rather than by law. Where these are in documentary form they may be changed unilaterally and often without formality by the government or Parliament.

Human Rights and Constitutional Cases

Human Rights Act 1998 incorporates most rights in the ECHR into domestic law. Higher courts may declare a provision in an Act to be incompatible with the Convention rights. The provision will be legally valid but the incompatibility may be removed by ministerial order.

  The courts have elaborated common law constitutional or fundamental principles, for example, rights of access to justice, duties to give a fair hearing to a person before an adverse decision is taken by a public body, duties on decision makers not be act arbitrarily or disproportionately. These principles affect the interpretation of Acts of Parliament and may provide common law grounds for quashing discretionary executive decisions.

Decisions of the courts may effect changes of a constitutional nature, for example, by subjecting the exercise of royal prerogative powers to judicial review, altering the principles for statutory interpretation, modifying the principle of parliamentary sovereignty in favour of the rule of law.

Regional Arrangements

Asymmetrical system. There are devolved legislatures and executives in Scotland and Northern Ireland, a devolved executive with potential legislative power in Wales, approved in separate referendums in each country. No devolution of legislative or executive power in England except to the Greater London Authority; the Mayor has executive power.

EU Membership

European Communities Act 1972 gave domestic effect to European law with effect from 1 January 1973. No referendum on joining. Referendum in 1975 on whether to remain in EC—Yes.

UNITED STATES OF AMERICA

General

Written Constitution 1789 starts 'We the people' and came into effect following special conventions of nine of the original 13 states according to the provisions in the constitution itself. Self-executing. Presidential system. Two chamber Congress, House of Representatives and Senate, states represented in the latter. First past the post electoral system. Human Rights protected by constitutional amendments in the Bill of Rights, 1791. Federal state. Supreme Court. Simple hierarchy of laws.

Legal System/Family

Common law, though Louisiana is a mixed jurisdiction, based partly on the French legal system—civil law.

Constitutional Amendments and Formal Constitutional Change

Twenty-seven amendments since 1789. Amendments normally require two-thirds majorities in the two Houses of Congress and the support of three-quarters of the states. Amendments include the Bill of Rights 1791, the abolition of slavery, equal protection of the law, legalisation of income tax, votes for women, direct election of senators.

Some Acts of constitutional importance are passed by normal procedures, for example, Civil Rights Act 1964 and Voting Rights Act 1965, partly in response to Supreme Court decisions.

Reform without Constitutional Amendments

Pattern of persistent use of informal means to change the system, including creative interpretation, institutional restructuring, and the use of the constituent power of the people in democratic elections to initiate change and obtain constitutional settlements. This has enabled Presidents to increase their de facto power in foreign affairs.

Supreme Court interpretation and reinterpretation of the Constitution has been very significant, for example, the New Deal, regulation of the national economy, limited welfare state, 'deference' to executive and legislature's decisions.

Constitutional and Human Rights Cases

Supreme Court asserted its right to review Acts for constitutional compliance. Very influential in field of human rights, for example, in desegregation of education, abortion, and via Fourteenth Amendment (due process) extending much of the Bill of Rights to state and local government, especially re freedom of speech and religion and the criminal process.

460

Federal Arrangements

Federal level—the bureaucratic structure of the executive branch is not specified beyond the creation of the office of the President and a reference to executive departments. Federal government has enumerated powers, some exclusive. Bound by fundamental rights.

States have powers in which federal government may not interfere. Supreme Court has held them to be bound by the (federal) Bill of Rights. Other matters relating to the relationship of the states and federal government are left unclear by the Constitution.

Index

Index

Index

Index